TimeOut

London

timeout.com/london

Penguin Books

PENGUIN BOOKS

Published by the Penguin Group
Penguin Books Ltd, 27 Wrights Lane, London W8 5TZ, England
Penguin Books USA Inc., 375 Hudson Street, New York, New York 10014, USA
Penguin Books Australia Ltd, Ringwood, Victoria, Australia
Penguin Books Canada Ltd, 10 Alcorn Avenue, Toronto, Ontario, Canada M4V 3B2
Penguin Books (NZ) Ltd, 182-190 Wairau Road, Auckland 10, New Zealand

Penguin Books Ltd, Registered Offices: Harmondsworth, Middlesex, England

First published 1989
First Penguin edition 1990
Second edition 1992
Third edition 1994
Fourth edition 1995
Fifth edition 1997
Sixth edition 1998
Seventh edition 1999
Eighth edition 2000
Ninth edition 2001
10 9 8 7 6 5 4 3 2 1

Copyright © Time Out Group Ltd, 1989, 1990, 1992, 1994, 1995, 1997, 1998, 1999, 2000, 2001
All rights reserved

Colour reprographics by Icon, Crown House, 56-58 Southwark Street, London SE1
and Precise Litho, 34-35 Great Sutton Street, London EC1
Printed and bound by Cayfosa-Quebecor, Ctra. de Caldes, Km 3 08 130 Sta, Perpètua de Mogoda, Barcelona, Spain

Edited and designed by
Time Out Guides Limited
Universal House
251 Tottenham Court Road
London W1T 7AB
Tel + 44 (0)20 7813 3000
Fax+ 44 (0)20 7813 6001
Email guides@timeout.com
www.timeout.com

Editorial

Editor Will Fulford-Jones
Deputy Editor Richard Lines
Listings Editor Zoë Sanders
Researcher Miranda Morton
Proofreader Rachel Sawyer
Indexer Marion Moisy

Editorial Director Peter Fiennes
Series Editor Ruth Jarvis
Deputy Series Editor Jonathan Cox
Editorial Assistant Jenny Noden

Design

Art Director John Oakey
Art Editor Mandy Martin
Senior Designer Scott Moore
Designers Benjamin de Lotz, Lucy Grant
Scanning/Imaging Dan Conway
Picture Editor Kerri Miles
Deputy Picture Editor Olivia Duncan-Jones
Ad Make-up Glen Impey

Advertising

Group Advertisement Director Lesley Gill
Sales Director/Sponsorship Mark Phillips
Sales Manager Alison Gray
Advertisement Sales James Coulbault, Jason Trotman
Copy Controller Angela Davis
Advertising Assistant Catherine Shepherd

Administration

Publisher Tony Elliott
Managing Director Mike Hardwick
Financial Director Kevin Ellis
Marketing Director Christine Cort
Marketing Manager Mandy Martinez
General Manager Nichola Coulthard
Production Manager Mark Lamond
Production Controller Samantha Furniss
Accountant Sarah Bostock

Features in this guide were written and researched by:

Introduction Will Fulford-Jones. **History** Jonathan Cox, Sarah McAlister (*Pearls of wisdom* Richard Lines; *Death becomes them, The name game* Catherine Arbuthnott; *Parliament of members* Andrew White). **London Today** Will Fulford-Jones. **Architecture** David Littlefield. **The River** Jack Leavis. **Fictional London** Nicholas Royle. **Accommodation** Hugh Graham, Richard Lines. **Sightseeing** *Central London* Jonathan Cox, Will Fulford-Jones, Lesley McCave; *North London* Will Fulford-Jones, Louise Gray; *East London* Ian Cunningham, Will Fulford-Jones, Angela Jameson; *South London* Ian Cunningham, Michael Ellis, Richard Lines; *West London* Victoria Cohen, Patrick Marmion; *Assorted museum & gallery reviews* Sophie Blacksell, Christi Daugherty, Michael Ellis, Richard Lines (*Bridges over troubled water* Craig Dixon & Will Fulford-Jones; *Step back in time, Almost famous, Crime time* Gwen Cheeseman; *An hour in...* Michael Ellis; *What the Dickens* Jack Leavis; *Rebirth, marriages and deaths, Opening the floodgates, Bathe in glory* Craig Dixon; *Triangles, circles and squares, Travel light* Zoë Sanders; *On the buses, A route mastered* Andrew Berry; *A brief history of sex* Will Fulford-Jones; *Dead and buried* Gene Friedman & Richard Lines; *Here's looking at you, Oh, deer* Victoria Cohen; *Go directly to jail* Catherine Arbuthnott; *Small but perfectly formed* Andrew White). **Restaurants** Richard Lines (*A lot of bottle* Gwen Cheeseman; *Let them entertain you* Craig Dixon; *Grease is the word* Isaac Davis). **Pubs & Bars** Will Fulford-Jones (*Strange but true* Catherine Arbuthnott; *Breaking the chains* Jack Leavis). **Shops & Services** Richard Lines (*You're booked* Zoë Sanders; *A taste of home* Craig Dixon). **London by Season** Richard Lines (*Ashes to ashes* Will Fulford-Jones). **Children** Nana Ocran. **Clubs** Dave Swindells. **Comedy** Isaac Davis. **Dance** Kevin Ebbutt. **Film** Will Fulford-Jones. **Galleries** Michael Ellis (*But is it art?* Richard Lines). **Gay & Lesbian** Dan Gould, Louise Tondeur. **Music** Will Fulford-Jones. **Sport & Fitness** Andrew Shields. **Theatre** Victoria Cohen (*tkts, please* Richard Lines). **Trips Out of Town** Ruth Jarvis, Richard Lines. **Directory** Zoë Sanders.

The Editor would like to thank:

Sophie Blacksell, Nyx Bradley, Jan Coothanx, Sally Davies, Kevin Ebbutt, Luz Echeverri, Sarah Guy, Kevin Hudson, Fritha Lindqvist, Lesley McCave, Rebekah McVitie, Kenny Merengue, Alex Poots, Leo Roberts, Adolpho Rollo, Nicholas Royle, Marc Werner.

Maps by JS Graphics, 17 Beadles Lane, Old Oxted, Surrey RH8 9JG.

Photography by Matt Carr except: pages 7, 9, 17 AKG; pages 10, 12, 20, 311 Hulton Getty; pages 15, 18, 87, 160 Mary Evans Picture Library; pages 21, 263 PA; pages 86, 260 Jon Perugia; page 104 (left) Phil Sayer; page 104 (right) Dennis Gilbert/View; page 118 Stuart Emmerson; page 132 Olivia Duncan-Jones; pages 188, 200 Sol Abajo; pages 192, 238, 242 Alys Tomlinson; page 195 Barry J Holmes; pages 197, 200 Paul Avis; page 213 Tony Gibson; pages 217, 219, 220 Frank Bauer; page 221 Georgie Scott; page 223 Luca Zampedri; pages 231, 242, 245 Victoria Gomez; pages 238, 257 James Winspear; page 250 Sarah Blee; page 262 All Sport; page 266 Neil Massey; page 286 Bill Cooper; page 303 Hadley Kincade; pages 324, 326 Empics; pages 340, 342, 343, 347, 354 Paul Avis; page 351 Trevor Ray Hart.

The following photographs were supplied by the featured establishments: pages 37, 38, 329, 332, 333, 353.

Contents

Introduction

The locals are rude; legendarily so, in fact. The traffic is horrific, choking the city daily in a fug of fumes, and the public transport is unreliable and cramped. More or less everything is wallet-bogglingly expensive. The complex, disorganised street layout means that getting from A to B may find you making unscheduled and unwanted stops at E, V and J. Its best natural feature – the river that runs through it – is filthy, underused and probably poisonous. The bars close at 11pm, after which time you'll have trouble finding a cab to take you home. Et bloody cetera.

And yet despite all this – gritty urban extremists and suckers for punishment would even switch the 'despite' for a 'because' – London is still a great city. Like New York, its main competitor for the unofficial designation of Best City On Earth, London somehow has the guts, wherewithal and pure bloody-minded arrogance to disregard its many and varied faults and problems and carry on as if nothing were wrong while residents and visitors alike tear their hair out in frustration.

But those who arrive here hirsute and leave bald are missing the point. London is not designed for those who expect things neatly presented on a plate and served by a waiter wearing a bow tie and an ingratiating rictus grin. Rather, it's a town that rewards the intrepid, that challenges all and sundry to beat it at its own game. Not for nothing do many locals choose to move out of central London and, in some cases, leave the city entirely in their mid- to late 30s. Exhausted by the daily grind, by the commute and the kids, and no longer blessed with the arrogant, youthful verve that saw them take on the town to begin with, they've no longer got the energy or desire to play London as it needs to be played. London has beaten them, and they know it.

Still, at least their departure makes more room for those still prepared to live by the maxim that pleasure is that much sweeter if it's been worked for. It's the only way to approach the town. Nothing's made easy; and, in many ways, the opposite is true. Those with high blood pressure, faint hearts or short tempers should probably just put this book back on the shelves and head somewhere more genteel, relaxed and altogether more forgiving. Their backyard, for example. But those with a spirit of adventure and a sense of fun should make reservations immediately.

There are tangible pleasures. Pubs, shops and restaurants; a spectacular array of museums; the strikingly complete, anything-goes cultural heritage. But London is a great deal more than just an I-Spy checklist of been-there-done-thats. It's the getting there as much as the 'there' itself. Walk whenever and wherever you can while in town; breathe in the air of the neighbourhoods outside the Circle line; and above all, don't be defeated by the many challenges laid in your path by the city itself. Fortune favours the brave, remember.

At around this point, journalistic cliché and tradition dictate that we should wrap up this introduction with what's become known as The Samuel Johnson Quote About London™. But, well, that would be too easy. Instead, we'll settle for another, less heralded remark casually dropped by Peter Ackroyd, author of the wonderful *London: The Biography*. It was while reviewing one of the finest books about the city, Iain Sinclair's *Lights Out for the Territory*, that Ackroyd wrote: 'It is a book about London; it is, in other words, a book about everything.' A more perfect summation of the city you couldn't hope to find. Whatever you're after, you're guaranteed to find it here. Just be prepared to look.

ABOUT THE TIME OUT CITY GUIDES

The *Time Out London Guide* is one of an expanding series of *Time Out* City Guides, now numbering over 30, produced by the people behind London and New York's successful listings magazines. Our guides are all written and updated by resident experts who have striven to provide you with all the most up-to-date information you'll need to explore the city or read up on its background, whether you're a local or a first-time visitor.

THE LOWDOWN ON THE LISTINGS

Above all, we've tried to make this book as useful as possible. Addresses, telephone numbers, websites, transport information, opening times, admission prices and credit card details have all been included in the listings.

There is an online version of this guide, as well as weekly events listings for over 30 international cities, at www.timeout.com.

venue in this guide (such as Soho, Covent Garden, Westminster, et cetera), along with map references that point to our street maps at the back of the book (starting on page 390). However, for the sake of comprehensivity, we recommend that you follow the example of the locals and invest in a standard *A-Z* map of the city the minute you arrive.

TELEPHONE NUMBERS

The area code for London is 020. All telephone numbers given in this guide take this code unless otherwise stated: add 020 to the numbers listed throughout the book if calling from outside London; otherwise, simply dial the number as written. Numbers priced at non-standard rates – for example, mobile phone numbers (starting 07), free numbers (which take an 0800 or 0808 code) and premium rate numbers (beginning 09) – have been designated as such in the listings. For more details of phone codes and charges, *see p376*. The international dialling code for the UK is 44.

ESSENTIAL INFORMATION

For all the practical information you might need for visiting London, including visa and customs information, advice on disabled facilities and access, emergency telephone numbers and local transport, turn to the **Directory** chapter at the back of the guide. It starts on page 356.

MAPS

The map section at the back of this book includes orientation and overview maps of the area and city, a large-scale locality map for planning trips out of town and street maps most of central London, with a comprehensive street index. The maps start on page 390.

LET US KNOW WHAT YOU THINK

We hope you enjoy the *Time Out London Guide*, and we'd like to know what you think of it. We welcome tips for places that you consider we should include in future editions and take note of your criticism of our choices. There's a reader's reply card at the back of this book for your feedback, or you can email us at londonguide@timeout.com.

And, as far as possible, we've given details of facilities, services and events, all checked and correct as we went to press. However, owners and managers can change their arrangements at any time. Before you go out of your way, we'd advise you to telephone and check opening times, ticket prices and other particulars. While every effort has been made to ensure the accuracy of the information contained in this guide, the publishers cannot accept responsibility for any errors it may contain.

PRICES AND PAYMENT

We have noted where venues such as shops, hotels and restaurants accept the following credit cards: American Express (**AmEx**), Diners Club (**DC**), MasterCard (**MC**) and Visa (**V**). Many businesses will also accept other cards, including Switch or Delta and JCB. Most shops, restaurants and attractions will accept sterling travellers' cheques issued by a major financial institution such as American Express.

THE LIE OF THE LAND

Thanks to the chaotic street plan – or, rather, the lack of one – London is one of the most complicated of all major world cities to find your way around. To make it a little easier, we've included an area designation for every

In Context

Feature boxes

slow slow quick quick slow

For a quick step to the airport, take
Gatwick Express
and
Heathrow Express

Traffic on the roads is at an all time high. Congestion, jams, road rage – why risk it? You can always rely on Gatwick Express and Heathrow Express to whisk you between the airports and central London in the fastest time possible – trains depart every 15 minutes*, 7 days a week.

Straightforward, comfortable and stress free.

Gatwick Express: telephone 08705 30 15 30 or visit us at www.gatwickexpress.co.uk
Heathrow Express: telephone +44 (0) 845 600 15 15 or visit us at www.heathrowexpress.co.uk

*Gatwick Express trains run hourly through the night.
Heathrow Express trains run between 0510 & 2340.

Afbeelding van de
STADT LONDON. Representation curieuse de l'embrasement de la
VILLE de LONDRES. Delineation of the
CITIE LONDON,

History

From Iceni doom to Millennium Dome in 2,000 years.

London was founded by the Trojan prince
Brutus and run by a race of heroic giants
descended from the Celtic King Lud. Or so, at
least, thought the 12th-century chronicler
Geoffrey of Monmouth. However, the truth is
rather more prosaic. Though Celtic tribes did
live in scattered communities along the banks
of the Thames prior to the arrival of the
Romans in Britain, there's no evidence to
suggest there was a settlement on the site of
the future metropolis before the invasion of the
Emperor Claudius' legions in AD 43. During the
Romans' conquest of the country, they forded
the Thames at its shallowest point and, later,
built a timber bridge here (near the site of
today's London Bridge). Over the following
decade, a settlement developed on the north
side of this strategically vital crossing.

During the first two centuries AD, the
Romans built roads, towns and forts in the
area, and trade flourished. The first mention of
London (Londinium), by the Roman historian
Tacitus, was in AD 60, when he described it
as being 'filled with traders… a celebrated
centre of commerce'. Progress was brought to a

halt in AD 61 when Boudicca, the fearsome
widow of an East Anglian chieftain, rebelled
against the Imperial forces who had seized
her land, flogged her and raped her daughters.
She led the Iceni in a savage revolt, destroying
the Roman colony at Colchester, and then
marching on London. The inhabitants were
massacred and the settlement was burned to
the ground.

After order was restored, the town was
rebuilt and, around AD 200, a two-mile
(three-kilometre) long, six-metre (18-foot)
high defensive wall was constructed around
it. Chunks of the wall survive today, and
the names of the original gates – Ludgate,
Newgate, Bishopsgate and Aldgate – are
preserved on the map of the city. The street
known as London Wall traces part of its
original course.

By the fourth century, racked by barbarian
invasions and internal strife, the Empire was in
decline. In 410, the last troops were withdrawn
and London became a ghost town. The Roman
way of life vanished, their only enduring
legacies being roads and early Christianity.

SAXON & VIKING LONDON

During the fifth and sixth centuries, history gives way to legend. The Saxons crossed the North Sea and settled in eastern and southern England, apparently avoiding the ruins of London; they built farmsteads and trading posts outside the walls.

In 596, Pope Gregory sent Augustine to convert the English to Christianity. Ethelbert, Saxon King of Kent, proved a willing convert, and Augustine was appointed the first Archbishop of Canterbury. Since then, Canterbury has remained the centre of the English Christian Church. London's first Bishop, though, was Mellitus: one of Augustine's missionaries, he converted the East Saxon King Sebert and, in 604, founded a wooden cathedral dedicated to St Paul inside the old city walls. On Sebert's death, his followers reverted to paganism, but later generations of Christians rebuilt what is now St Paul's Cathedral.

London, meanwhile, continued to expand. In 731, the Venerable Bede describes 'Lundenwic' as 'the mart of many nations resorting to it by land and sea'. This probably refers to a settlement west of the Roman city in the area of today's Aldwych (Old English for 'old settlement').

In the ninth century, the city faced a new danger from across the North Sea: the Vikings. The city was sacked in 841 and, in 851, the Danish raiders returned with 350 ships, leaving London in ruins. It was not until 886 that King Alfred of Wessex – aka Alfred the Great – regained the city, soon re-establishing London as a major trading centre with a merchant navy and new wharfs at Billingsgate and Queenhithe.

Throughout the tenth century, the Saxon city prospered. Churches were built, parishes established and markets set up. However, the 11th century brought more Viking harassment, and the English were even forced to accept a Danish king, Cnut (Canute, 1016-40), during whose reign London replaced Winchester as the capital of England.

In 1042, the throne reverted to an Englishman, Edward the Confessor, who devoted himself to building the grandest church in England two miles (three kilometres) west of the City at Thorney ('the isle of brambles'). He replaced the timber church of St Peter's with a huge abbey, 'the West Minster' (Westminster Abbey; consecrated in December 1065), and moved his court to the new Palace of Westminster. A week after the consecration, though, Edward died and was buried in his new church. Now, London grew around two hubs: Westminster as the centre for the royal court, government and law; and the City of London as the commercial centre.

THE NORMAN CONQUEST

On Edward's death, there was a succession dispute. William, Duke of Normandy, claimed that the Confessor (his cousin) had promised him the English crown. However, the English chose Edward's brother-in-law Harold. Piqued, William gathered an army and invaded, and, on 14 October 1066, defeated Harold at the Battle of Hastings and marched on London. City elders had little option but to offer William the throne, and the conqueror was crowned in Westminster Abbey on Christmas Day, 1066.

Recognising the need to win over the prosperous city merchants by negotiation rather than force, William granted the Bishop and burgesses of London a charter – still kept at Guildhall – that acknowledged their rights and independence in return for taxes. But, 'against the fickleness of the vast and fierce population', he also ordered strongholds to be built alongside the city wall, including the White Tower (the tallest building in the Tower of London) and the now-lost Baynard's Castle at Blackfriars. The earliest surviving written account of contemporary London was written 40 years later by a monk, William Fitz Stephen, who vividly conjured up the walled city and, outside, pastures and woods for hunting, youths wrestling and fencing in Moorfields, and skating on frozen ponds.

THE MIDDLE AGES

In the growing city of London, much of the politics of the Middle Ages – the late 12th to the late 15th centuries – revolved around a three-way struggle for power between the king and the aristocracy, the Church, and the Lord Mayor and city guilds.

> **'Rioting, persecution and the occasional lynching and pogrom were commonplace in medieval London.'**

In the early Middle Ages, the king and his court frequently travelled to other parts of the kingdom and abroad. However, in the 14th and 15th centuries, the Palace of Westminster became the seat of law and government. The noblemen and bishops who attended court built themselves palatial houses along the Strand from the City to Westminster, with gardens stretching to the river.

The Model Parliament, agreeing the principles of government, was held in Westminster Hall in 1295, presided over by Edward I and attended by barons, clergy and representatives of knights and burgesses. The first step towards establishing personal

Wat Tyler meets his death at Smithfield, ending the **Peasants' Revolt**. *See p10.*

rights and political liberty – not to mention curbing the power of the king – had already been taken in 1215 with the signing of the Magna Carta by King John. In the 14th century, subsequent assemblies gave rise to the House of Lords (which met at the Palace of Westminster) and the House of Commons (which met in the Chapter House at Westminster Abbey).

Relations between the monarch and the City were never easy; indeed, they were often outright hostile. Londoners guarded their privileges with self-righteous intransigence, and resisted all attempts by successive kings to squeeze money out of them to finance wars and building projects. Successive kings were forced to turn to Jewish and Lombard money-lenders, but the City merchants were as intolerant of foreigners as of the royals. Rioting, persecution and the occasional lynching and pogrom were all commonplace in medieval London.

CITY STATUS & COMMERCIAL CLOUT

The privileges granted to the City merchants under Norman kings, allowing independence and self-regulation, were extended by the monarchs who followed, in return for financial favours. In 1191, during the reign of Richard I,

the City of London was formally recognised as a commune – a self-governing community – and, in 1197, won control of the Thames that included lucrative fishing rights, which it retained until 1857. In 1215, King John confirmed the city's right 'to elect every year a mayor', a position of great authority with power over the Sheriff and the Bishop of London. A month later, the Mayor joined the rebel barons in signing the Magna Carta.

Over the next two centuries, the power and influence of the trade and craft guilds – later known as the City Livery Companies – increased as trade with Europe grew, and the wharfs by London Bridge were crowded with imports such as fine cloth, furs, wine, spices and precious metals. Port dues and taxes were paid to customs officials such as part-time poet Geoffrey Chaucer, whose *Canterbury Tales* became the first published work of English literature.

The city's markets, already established, drew produce from miles around: livestock at Smithfield, fish at Billingsgate and poultry at Leadenhall. The street markets, or 'cheaps', around Westcheap (now Cheapside) and Eastcheap were crammed with a variety of goods. As commerce increased, foreign traders and craftsmen settled around the port; the population within the city wall grew from about 18,000 in 1100 to well over 50,000 in the 1340s.

BLACK DEATH & REVOLTING PEASANTS

However, perhaps unsurprisingly, lack of hygiene became a serious problem in the city. Water was provided in cisterns at Cheapside and elsewhere, but the supply, which came more or less direct from the Thames, was limited and polluted. The street called Houndsditch was so named because Londoners threw their dead animals into the furrow that formed the city's eastern boundary. There was no proper sewerage system; in the streets around Smithfield (the Shambles), butchers dumped the entrails of slaughtered animals.

These conditions provided the breeding ground for the greatest catastrophe of the Middle Ages: the Black Death of 1348 and 1349. The plague came to London from Europe, carried by rats on ships. During this period, about 30 per cent of England's population died of the disease. Though the epidemic abated, it was to recur in London on several occasions during the next three centuries, each time devastating the city's population.

These outbreaks of disease left the labour market short-handed, causing unrest among the overworked peasants. The imposition of a poll tax – a shilling a head – proved the final straw, and led to the Peasants' Revolt. In 1381, thousands marched on London, led by Jack Straw from Essex and Wat Tyler from Kent. In the rioting and looting that followed, the Savoy Palace on the Strand was destroyed, the Archbishop of Canterbury was murdered and hundreds of prisoners were set free. When the 14-year-old Richard II rode out to Smithfield to face the rioters, Wat Tyler was fatally stabbed by Lord Mayor William Walworth. The other ringleaders were subsequently rounded up and hanged. But no more poll taxes were imposed.

CHURCHES & MONASTERIES

Like every other medieval city, London had a large number of parish and monastic churches, as well as the great Gothic cathedral of St Paul's. Although the majority of Londoners were allowed access to the major churches, the lives of most of them revolved around their own local parish places of worship, where they were baptised, married and buried. Many churches were linked with particular craft and trade guilds.

Monasteries and convents were also established, all owning valuable acres inside and outside the city walls. The crusading Knights Templars and Knights Hospitallers were two of the earliest religious orders to settle, though the increasingly unruly Templars were disbanded in 1312 by the Pope and their land eventually became occupied by the lawyers of Inner and Middle Temple. The surviving church of St Bartholomew-the-Great (founded 1123) and the names of St Helen's Bishopsgate, Spitalfields and St Martin's-le-Grand are all reminders of these early monasteries and convents. The friars, who were active social workers among the poor living outside the city walls, were known by the colour of their habits: the Blackfriars (Dominicans), the Whitefriars (Carmelites) and the Greyfriars (Franciscans). Their names are still in evidence around Fleet Street and the west of the City.

TUDORS, STUARTS & DIVORCE

Under the Tudor monarchs (who reigned from 1485 until 1603), spurred by the discovery of America and the ocean routes to Africa and the Orient, London became one of Europe's largest cities. Henry VII brought to an end the Wars of the Roses by defeating Richard III at the Battle of Bosworth and marrying Elizabeth of York.

He's **Henry VIII**, he is, he is, he's Henry VIII, he is. *See p11.*

Henry VII's other great achievements included the building of a merchant navy, and the Henry VII Chapel in Westminster Abbey, the eventual resting place for him and his queen.

> **'Deemed "a naughty place" by royal proclamation, Bankside was the Soho of its time.'**

Henry VII was succeeded in 1509 by arch wife-collector (and despatcher) Henry VIII. Henry's first marriage to Catherine of Aragon failed to produce an heir, so the king, in 1527, determined that the union should be annulled. As the Pope refused to co-operate, Henry defied the Catholic Church, demanding that he himself be recognised as Supreme Head of the Church in England and ordering the execution of anyone who refused to go along with the plan (including his chancellor Sir Thomas More). Thus, England began the transition to Protestantism. The subsequent dissolution of the monasteries transformed the face of the medieval city with the confiscation and redevelopment of all property owned by the Catholic Church.

On a more positive note, Henry did manage to develop a professional navy in between beheading his wives, founding the Royal Dockyards at Woolwich in 1512 and at Deptford the following year. He also established palaces at Hampton Court and Whitehall, and built a residence at St James's Palace. Much of the land he annexed for hunting became the Royal Parks, including Hyde, Regent's, Greenwich and Richmond Parks.

There was a brief Catholic revival under Queen Mary (1553-8), and her marriage to Philip II of Spain met with much opposition in London. She had 300 Protestants burned at the stake at Smithfield, earning her the nickname 'Bloody Mary'.

ELIZABETHAN LONDON

Elizabeth I's reign (1558-1603) saw a flowering of English commerce and arts. The founding of

Pearls of wisdom

Instantly recognisable by their outrageous suits, London's **Pearly Kings and Queens** have become capital clichés almost as hackneyed as bobbies and beefeaters. However, if you're lucky enough to spot one out and about, while you may feel faintly privileged, you may not have any idea what you're looking at. Because for all their costumes and Cockney values, you'll find that even most Londoners know very little about the Pearlies' past or present.

Pearly Kings and Queens have their origins in the 'aristocracy' of London's early Victorian costermongers, who would elect 'kings' and 'queens' as representatives to safeguard their interests from competitors and roughs. The costermongers were known for their 'flash boy outfits', worn to distinguish themselves from other traders and notable for rows of pearl buttons sewn along the seams of waistcoat and trousers. But that's only half the story.

Pearly Kings and Queens owe more to an enterprising Victorian orphan, Henry Croft. In 1875, while working as a roadsweeper and ratcatcher at Somers Town market, 13-year-old Henry took it upon himself to begin a series of charitable collections on behalf of the orphanage in which he was raised. In need of a gimmick, Croft decided to take the costermongers' flash-boy outfits a step further and totally covered a suit with pearl buttons.

So successful was his pearly suit that Croft became inundated with applications from hospitals and churches asking him to help with their fundraising. Willing but unable to cope with the workload, Croft turned to the Somers Town costermongers, who had a certain regard for the lad (and his natty outfit) and agreed to help. And with that, the pearly monarchy began.

In 1911, the Pearly Kings and Queens Association was formed, establishing a king and queen for every London borough by the time of Croft's death in 1930. Today, there are around 100 Pearlies, who continue the Association's charitable works. Anyone who wants to get a good look at some in their natural habitat should attend the Pearly Kings and Queens Harvest Festival, where the monarchs get together in full regalia for a harvest thanksgiving service (see p264).

Death becomes them

Next time you walk down Carnaby Street, listen for the whispers of the dead. Keep your ears peeled in Vincent Square, too, particularly beneath the school sports ground that was once known as Tothill Fields. And in Brompton, near Harrods, you may feel a ghostly presence either under the Ismaili Centre, the taxi rank opposite Brompton Oratory or on the corner by the Scotch House.

The Great Plague of 1665 seems to have caught officials unawares. Granted, victims were, at first, buried as normal in churches and churchyards. But while some churchyards were big enough to contain the vast numbers of dead (1665 saw 2,111 die in one parish alone), most were not. Funds were provided for labourers to dig comparatively shallow graves, which had to be covered periodically with soil and quicklime to lessen 'annoyance' from the corpses. These shallow graves are known as plague pits, and can be found in all the places mentioned above (historians are divided as to the exact location of the pit in Brompton, hence the bet-hedging).

Frequently, pits can be found under large grassy patches in built-up areas. They have remained green because, although the bodies contained in them were buried with speed and little ceremony, the ground was consecrated and cannot be used for building anything else.

However, in the City – where the disease claimed most of its victims – there are a great many plague pits on land that was never consecrated and that is now covered by buildings. Bishopsgate covers a pit; Charterhouse incorporated one in 1371 after the Black Death of 1348; St Bartholomew's Hospital, Clerkenwell Road and Goswell Road cover more. Many places in and around the City with the suffix 'fields' are plague pits: the 'great pit at Finsbury Fields' and Moorfields, for instance.

Half a million dead were supposed to have been buried at Smithfields during the Black Death, though historians have queried this huge figure. Where did they come from, they wonder, and who buried them? After all, London did not contain that many people until at least 1530. Perhaps they were tourists...

the Royal Exchange by Sir Thomas Gresham in 1566 gave London its first trading centre, allowing it to emerge as Europe's leading commercial centre. The merchant venturers and the first joint-stock companies (Russia Company and Levant Company) established new trading enterprises, and Drake, Raleigh and Hawkins sailed to the New World and beyond. In 1580, Elizabeth knighted Sir Francis Drake on his return from a three-year circumnavigation; eight years later, Drake and Howard defeated the Spanish Armada.

As trade grew, so did London. By 1600, it was home to some 200,000 people, many living in dirty, overcrowded conditions, with plague and fire constant hazards. The most complete picture of Tudor London is given in John Stow's *Survey of London* (1598), a fascinating first-hand account by a diligent Londoner whose monument stands in the City church of St Andrew Undershaft.

The glory of the Elizabethan era was the development of English drama, popular with all social classes but treated with disdain by the

Corporation of London, which went as far as to ban theatres from the City in 1575. Two theatres, the Rose (1587) and the Globe (1599), were erected on the south bank of the Thames at Bankside, and provided homes for the works of Marlowe and Shakespeare. Deemed 'a naughty place' by royal proclamation, Bankside was the Soho of its time: home not just to the theatre, but also to bear-baiting, cock-fighting, taverns and 'Stewes' (brothels).

The Tudor dynasty ended with Elizabeth's death in 1603. Her successor, the Stuart King James I, narrowly escaped assassination on 5 November 1605, when Guy Fawkes and his gunpowder were discovered underneath the Palace of Westminster. The Gunpowder Plot was a protest at the failure to improve conditions for the persecuted Catholics, but only resulted in several messy executions and an intensification of anti-papist feelings in ever-intolerant London. The date is commemorated – and, a little incongruously, celebrated with fireworks galore – as Bonfire Night to this day.

But aside from his unwitting part in the Gunpowder Plot, James I merits remembering for other, more important reasons. For it was he who hired Inigo Jones to design court masques and what ended up as the first examples of classical Renaissance style in London, the Queen's House in Greenwich (1616) and the Banqueting House in Westminster (1619).

CIVIL WAR

Charles I succeeded his father in 1625, but gradually fell out with the City of London (from whose citizens he tried to extort taxes) and an increasingly independent-minded and antagonistic Parliament. The last straw finally came in 1642 when he intruded on the Houses of Parliament in an attempt to arrest five MPs. The country soon slid into a civil war (1642-9) between the supporters of Parliament (led by Puritan Oliver Cromwell) and those of the King.

Both sides knew that control of the country's major city and port was vital for victory. London's sympathies were firmly with the Parliamentarians and, in 1642, 24,000 citizens assembled at Turnham Green, west of the city, to face Charles's army. Fatally, the King lost his nerve and withdrew, and was never to seriously threaten the capital again; eventually, the Royalists were defeated. Charles was tried for treason and, though he denied the legitimacy of the court, he was declared guilty. On 30 January 1649, he was beheaded outside the Banqueting House in Whitehall, declaring himself to be a 'martyr of the people'.

For the next 11 years the country was ruled as a Commonwealth by Cromwell. However, the closing of the theatres and the banning of the supposedly Catholic superstition of Christmas, along with other Puritan strictures on the wickedness of any sort of fun, meant that the restoration of the exiled Charles II in 1660 was greeted with considerable relief and rejoicing by the populace.

PLAGUE, FIRE & REVOLUTION

However, two major catastrophes marred the first decade of Charles's reign in the capital. In 1665, the most serious outbreak of bubonic plague since the Black Death devastated the capital's population. By the time the winter cold had put paid to the epidemic, nearly 100,000 Londoners had died.

But on 2 September 1666, just as the city was breathing a sigh of relief, a second disaster struck. The fire that spread from a carelessly tended oven in Farriner's Baking Shop on Pudding Lane was to rage for three days and consume four-fifths of the city, including 87 churches, 44 livery company halls and more than 13,000 houses.

Despite the obvious tragic element, though, the Great Fire at least allowed planners the chance to rebuild London as a spacious, rationally planned modern city. Many blueprints were drawn up and considered, but, in the end, Londoners were so impatient to get on with business as soon as possible that the city was reconstructed largely on its medieval street plan, albeit this time in brick and stone rather than wood. The towering figure of the period turned out to be the extraordinarily prolific Christopher Wren, who oversaw the work on 51 of the 54 churches that were rebuilt. Among them was his masterwork, the new St Paul's, completed in 1711 and, effectively, the world's first Protestant cathedral.

After the Great Fire, many well-to-do former City residents moved to new residential developments that were springing up in the West End. In the City, the Royal Exchange was rebuilt, but merchants increasingly used the new coffee houses in which to exchange news. With the expansion of the joint-stock companies and the chance to invest capital, the City was emerging as a centre not of manufacturing, but of finance.

Anti-Catholic feeling still ran high, however. The accession of Catholic James II in 1685 aroused fears of a return to Catholicism, and resulted in a Dutch Protestant, William of Orange, being invited to take the throne with his wife, Mary Stuart (James's daughter); James later fled to France in 1688 in what became known – by its beneficiaries – as the 'Glorious Revolution'. One of the most significant developments during William III's reign was the founding of the Bank of England in 1694, initially to finance the King's wars with France.

GEORGIAN LONDON

After the death of Queen Anne, and in accordance with the Act of Settlement (1701), the throne passed to George, great-grandson of James I, who had been born and brought up in Hanover, Germany. Thus, a German-speaking king – who never learned English – became the first of four long-reigning Georges in the Hanoverian line.

During his reign (1714-27), and for several years afterwards, the Whig party – led by Sir Robert Walpole – had the monopoly of power in Parliament. Their opponents, the Tories, supported the Stuarts and had opposed the exclusion of the Catholic James II. On the King's behalf, Walpole chaired a group of ministers (the forerunner of today's Cabinet), becoming, in effect, Britain's first prime minister. Walpole was presented with 10 Downing Street as a residence; it remains the official home of all serving prime ministers.

During the 18th century, London grew with astonishing speed, in terms of both population and built-up area. New squares and streets of terraced houses spread all over Soho, Bloomsbury, Mayfair and Marylebone, as wealthy landowners and speculative developers who didn't mind taking a risk given the size of the potential rewards cashed in on the demand for leasehold properties.

South London, too, became more accessible with the opening of the first new bridges for several centuries, Westminster Bridge (1750) and Blackfriars Bridge (1763). Until then, London Bridge had been the only bridge over the Thames. The old city gates, most of the Roman Wall and the remaining houses on Old London Bridge were demolished, allowing easier access to the City for traffic and people.

The name game

It's easy to convince yourself you've got the hang of London place names. After all, many are so descriptive as to remove all the mystery from their history. Yes, cows did cross the Fleet on their way to Smithfield Market at Cowcross Street. Silver Street was, indeed, where silversmiths operated. Chancery Lane was where information for the Rolls of Chancery was processed, not far from where the 'Clerken' of the Order of St John made merry at the Well. Anything with -gate at the end had a gate, and anything that ended -bury came with a group of houses attached.

But all is not so simple. While Saffron Hill was where saffron was grown, and Cloth Fair where traders sold cloth, no shoes were made in Shoe Lane: it's named for the shoe-shaped land upon which it sits. Gutter Lane, too, was not for rainwater, but was owned by Guthran. And then there's Pudding Lane, where the Great Fire of 1666 began. It wasn't caused by some hapless cook napping over the cakes: these 'puddings' were actually the discarded entrails of animals. Said animals did not end up in Mincing Lane, either: 'Mincing' comes from the Old English word 'mynecenu', meaning 'nuns'. Snow Hill, meanwhile, was not known for its snow, but 'sneu', old English brushwood.

You may also be disappointed to discover that Turnagain Lane does not refer to Dick Whittington, who 'turned again' to become Lord Mayor: it's named thus as it's a dead end. Were goods cheap at Cheapside? Possibly, but not definitely, as cheap actually meant 'market'. Some names were changed. Sherbourne Lane is a polite form of Shitebourne Lane. Monkwell Square was not home to a great many monasteries: it was once Muckwell. And Spital? Are you getting the idea? Well, no, you're wrong. It's a contraction of 'hospital'.

The more colourful the names, the better the story behind them. Paternoster Row, Ave Maria Lane and Amen Corner are thought to refer to Beating the Bounds, a service at Ascensiontide. Parts of the rosary were recited – among them the Our Father ('Pater noster' in Latin) and Hail Mary ('Ave Maria') – before the service ended at Amen Corner. Threadneedle Street, the home of the Bank of England, either derives from the three needles found in the Needlemakers' Company coat of arms, or from the ancient children's game of Threadneedle. Other places were named after inn signs, such as (disappointingly) Bleeding Heart Yard and (even more disappointingly) Elephant and Castle: it refers not to the mythic 'Infanta de Castille', but rather an inn sign representing the Cutler's Company. The 'castle' was the howdah on top of the elephant: the ivory for knife-handles.

But in any case, we hope you are enjoying your trip to the Londino's Settlement [London]. Perhaps you are staying in Bayard's Watering Place [Bayswater], near the road down which Queen Victoria once travelled [Queensway]. Please visit our seat of Government and the Abbey of the Western Monks [Westminster]. Shop where knights once fought each other to death on a bridge [Knightsbridge], then head west to the film set on a hill belonging to the family of Knotting [Notting Hill]. Don't miss the swinging '60s on the King's Road in Chalk Landing Place [Chelsea], and the bijou restaurants in the road belonging to Fulla's farm [Fulham Road].

Back in town, head to the British Museum in Bleymond's manor [Bloomsbury]. See the buskers in the garden belonging to a convent [Covent Garden]. At the weekend, more shopping in the market belonging to the Earl of Camden [Camden Market], and perhaps a trip to the Roundhouse at Chalcot's farm [Chalk Farm]. But keep enough energy for nightlife where, if you strain your ears above the crowds and music, you might hear an ancient hunting cry. 'Soho... '

POVERTY & CRIME

In the older districts, however, people were still living in terrible squalor and poverty, far worse than that of Victorian times. Some of the most notorious slums were around Fleet Street and St Giles's (north of Covent Garden), only a short distance from streets of fashionable residences maintained by large numbers of servants. To make matters worse, gin ('mother's ruin') was readily available at very low prices, and many poor Londoners drank excessive amounts in an attempt to escape from the horrors of daily life. The well-off seemed complacent, amusing themselves at the popular Ranelagh and Vauxhall Pleasure Gardens or with organised trips to Bedlam (Bethlehem or Bethlem Hospital) to mock the mental patients. On a similar level, public executions at Tyburn – near today's Marble Arch – were among the most popular events in the social calendar.

The outrageous imbalance in the distribution of wealth encouraged crime: robberies in the West End took place in daylight. Reformers were few, though there were exceptions. Henry Fielding, author of the picaresque novel *Tom Jones*, was also an enlightened magistrate at Bow Street Court. In 1751, he established, with his blind brother John, a volunteer force of 'thief-takers' to back up the often ineffective efforts of the parish constables and watchmen who were the only law-keepers in the city. This group of early cops, known as the Bow Street Runners, were the forerunners of today's Metropolitan Police (established in 1829).

Disaffection was also evident in the activities of the London mob during this period. Riots were a regular reaction to middlemen charging extortionate prices, or merchants adulterating their food. In June 1780, London was hit by the anti-Catholic Gordon Riots, named after ringleader George Gordon; the worst in the city's violent history, they left 300 people dead.

> **'Pick any street within five miles of central London, and the chances are its houses will be mostly Victorian.'**

Some attempts were made to alleviate the grosser ills of poverty with the establishment of five major new hospitals by private philanthropists. St Thomas's and St Bartholomew's were already long established as monastic institutions for the care of the sick, but Westminster (1720), Guy's (1725), St George's (1734), London (1740) and the Middlesex (1745) went on to become world-famous teaching hospitals. Thomas Coram's Foundling Hospital for abandoned children was another remarkable achievement of the time.

However, it was not only the indigenous population of London that was on the rise in the 18th century. Country people (who had lost their own land because of enclosures and were faced with starvation wages or unemployment) drifted into the towns in large numbers. The East End increasingly became the focus for poor immigrant labourers, especially with the buildings of the docks towards the end of the 18th century. By 1801, London's population had grown to almost a million, the largest in Europe. And by 1837, when Queen Victoria

An early ride on the **Metropolitan Railway**, London's first Underground train line. *See p16*.

Crystal Palace, site of the Great Exhibition of 1851.

came to the throne, five more bridges and the capital's first railway line (from London Bridge to Greenwich) gave off further hints that a major expansion might be around the corner.

THE VICTORIAN ERA

As well as being the administrative and financial capital of the British Empire, spanning a fifth of the globe, London was also its chief port and the world's largest manufacturing centre, with breweries, distilleries, tanneries, shipyards, engineering works and many other grimy industries lining the south bank of the Thames. On the one hand, London boasted splendid buildings, fine shops, theatres and museums; on the other, it was a city of poverty, disease and prostitution. The residential areas were becoming polarised into districts with fine terraces maintained by squads of servants, and overcrowded, insanitary, disease-ridden slums.

The growth of the metropolis in the century before Victoria came to the throne had been spectacular enough, but during her reign, which lasted until 1901, thousands more acres were covered with housing, roads and railway lines. Today, if you pick any street at random within five miles (eight kilometres) of central London, the chances are that its houses will be mostly Victorian. By the end of the 19th century, the city's population had swelled to over six million.

Despite the social problems – memorably depicted in the writings of Charles Dickens – major steps had been taken to improve conditions for the great majority of Londoners by the turn of the century. The Metropolitan Board of Works installed an efficient sewerage system, street lighting and better roads, while the worst slums were replaced by low-cost building schemes funded by philanthropists such as the American George Peabody and by the London County Council (created in 1888).

The Victorian expansion of London would not have been possible without an efficient public transport network with which to speed workers into and out of the city from the new suburbs. The horse-drawn bus appeared on London's streets for the first time in 1829, but it was the opening of the first passenger railway seven years later, running from Greenwich to London Bridge, that hailed the London of the future. In 1863, the first underground line – which ran between Paddington and Farringdon Road – proved an instant success, attracting more than 30,000 travellers on the first day. Soon thereafter, the world's first electric track in a deep tunnel (the 'tube') opened in 1890 between the City and Stockwell, later becoming part of the present-day Northern line.

THE GREAT EXHIBITION

The Great Exhibition of 1851 captured the spirit of the age: confidence and pride, discovery and invention. Prince Albert, the Queen's Consort, was involved in the organisation of this triumphant event, for which the Crystal Palace, a giant building in iron and glass – designed not by a professional architect but by the Duke of Devonshire's talented gardener, Joseph Paxton – was erected in Hyde Park. During the five months it was open, the Exhibition drew some six million visitors from Great Britain and abroad, and the profits inspired the Prince Consort to establish a permanent centre for the study of the applied arts and sciences: the result is the South Kensington museums and Imperial

College. After the Exhibition, the Palace was moved to Sydenham and used as an exhibition centre until it was destroyed by fire in 1936.

When the Victorians were not colonising the world by force, they had the foresight to combine their conquests with scientific developments. The Royal Geographical Society sent navigators to chart unknown waters, botanists to bring back new species, and geologists to study the earth. Many of the specimens that were brought back ended up at the Royal Botanic Gardens at Kew.

THE 20TH CENTURY

During the brief reign of Edward VII (1901-10), London regained some of the gaiety and glamour that it lacked in the dour last years of Victoria's reign. A touch of Parisian chic came to London with the opening of the Ritz Hotel in Piccadilly; the Café Royal hit the heights of its popularity as a meeting place for artists and writers; and 'luxury catering for the little man' was provided at the Lyons Tea Shops and new Lyons Corner Houses (the Coventry Street branch, which opened in 1907, could accommodate an incredible 4,500 people). Meanwhile, the first American-style department store, Selfridges, opened to an eager public on Oxford Street in 1909.

Road transport, too, was revolutionised. Motor cars put-putted around the city's streets, before the first motor bus was introduced in 1904. Double-decked electric trams had started running in 1901 (though not through the West End or the City), and continued doing so for 51 years. In fact, by 1911, the use of horse-drawn buses had been abandoned.

WORLD WAR I (1914-18)

London suffered its first air raids in World War I. The first bomb over the city was dropped from a Zeppelin near Guildhall in September 1915, and was followed by many nightly raids; bombing raids from planes began in July 1917. Cleopatra's Needle, on Victoria Embankment, was a minor casualty, receiving damage to the plinth and one of its sphinxes that can still be seen. In all, around 650 people lost their lives as a result of Zeppelin raids.

BETWEEN THE WARS

Political change happened quickly after World War I. Lloyd George's government averted revolution in 1918-19 by promising (but not delivering) 'homes for heroes' for the embittered returning soldiers. But the Liberal Party's days in power were numbered and, by 1924, the Labour Party, led by Ramsay MacDonald, had enough MPs to form its first government.

After the trauma of World War I, a 'live for today' attitude prevailed in the 'Roaring '20s' among the young upper classes, who flitted from parties in Mayfair to dances at the Ritz. But this meant little to the mass of Londoners, who were suffering greatly in the post-war slump. In 1921, Poplar Council in east London refused to levy the rates on its impoverished population. The entire council was sent to prison but was later released, having achieved an equilisation of the rates over all London boroughs that relieved the burden on the poorest ones.

Still, things didn't improve immediately. Civil disturbances brought on by an increased cost of living and rising unemployment resulted in the nationwide General Strike of 1926, when the working classes downed tools in support of the striking miners. Prime Minister Baldwin encouraged volunteers to take over the public services and the streets teemed with army-escorted food convoys, aristocrats running soup kitchens and students driving buses. After nine days of chaos, the strike was called off by the Trades Union Congress (TUC).

The economic situation only worsened in the early 1930s following the New York Stock Exchange crash of 1929; by 1931, more than three million people in Britain were jobless. During these years, the London County Council began to have a greater impact on the city's life, undertaking programmes of slum clearance and new housing, creating more parks and taking under its wing education, transport, hospitals, libraries and the fire service.

London's population increased dramatically between the wars, too, peaking at nearly 8.7 million in 1939. To accommodate the influx, the suburbs expanded at a tremendous rate, particularly to the north-west with the extension of the Metropolitan line to an area that became known as Metroland. Identical gabled, double-fronted houses sprang up in their hundreds of thousands, from Golders Green to Surbiton.

And all these new Londoners were entertained by the new media of film, radio and TV. London's first radio broadcast was beamed from the roof of Marconi House in the Strand in 1922, and families were soon gathering around their enormous Bakelite wireless sets to hear the latest sounds from the British Broadcasting Company (the BBC; from 1927 called the British Broadcasting Corporation). Television broadcasts started on 26 August 1936, when the first BBC telecast went out live from Alexandra Palace studios.

WORLD WAR II (1939-45)

Neville Chamberlain's policy of appeasement towards Hitler's increasingly aggressive Germany during the 1930s finally collapsed when the Germans invaded Poland, and on 3 September 1939, Britain declared war. The government implemented precautionary measures against the threat of air raids – including the digging of trench shelters in London parks, and the evacuation of 600,000 children and pregnant mothers – but the expected bombing raids did not happen during the autumn and winter of 1939-40, a period that became known as the 'Phoney War'. In July 1940, though, Germany began preparations for an invasion of Britain with three months of aerial attack that came to be known as the Battle of Britain.

> **'But for all the planned changes after the war, life for most people was drab, regimented and austere.'**

For Londoners, the Phoney War came to an abrupt end on 7 September 1940 when hundreds of German bombers dumped their loads of high explosives on east London and the docks. Entire streets were destroyed; the dead and injured numbered over 2,000. The Blitz had begun. The raids on London continued for 57 consecutive nights, then intermittently for a further six months. Londoners reacted with

tremendous bravery and stoicism, a period still nostalgically referred to as 'Britain's finest hour'. After a final massive raid on 10 May 1941, the Germans focused their attention elsewhere, but by the end of the war about a third of the City and the East End was in ruins.

From 1942, the tide of the war began to turn, but Londoners still had a new terror to face: the V1, or 'doodlebug'. In 1944, dozens of these explosives-packed pilotless planes descended on the city, causing widespread destruction. Later in the year, the more powerful V2 rocket was launched, and over the winter, 500 of them dropped on London, mostly in the East End. The last fell on 27 March 1945 in Orpington, Kent, around six weeks before Victory in Europe (VE Day) was declared on 8 May 1945. Thousands of people took to the streets of London to celebrate.

POST-WAR LONDON

World War II left Britain almost as shattered as Germany. Soon after VE Day, a general election was held and Churchill was heavily defeated by the Labour Party under Clement Attlee. The new government established the National Health Service in 1948, and began a massive nationalisation programme that included public transport, electricity, gas, postal and telephone services. But for all the planned changes, life for most people was drab, regimented and austere.

In London, the most immediate problem was a critical shortage of housing. Prefabricated bungalows provided a temporary solution (though many were still occupied 40 years later), but the huge new high-rise housing estates that the planners began to erect were often badly built and proved to be unpopular with residents.

However, there were bright spots during this otherwise rather dour time. London hosted the Olympics in 1948; three years later came the Festival of Britain (100 years after the Great Exhibition), a celebration of British technology and design. The exhibitions that took over derelict land on the south bank of the Thames for the Festival provided the incentive to build the South Bank Centre.

THE 1950S AND 1960S

As the 1950s progressed, life and prosperity gradually returned to London, leading Prime Minister Harold Macmillan in 1957 to proclaim that 'most of our people have never had it so good'. The coronation of Queen Elizabeth II in 1953 had been the biggest television broadcast in history, and there was the feeling of a new age dawning.

However, many Londoners were moving out of the city. The population dropped by half a million in the late 1950s, causing a labour

St Paul's survived the **Blitz**. But only just.

Parliament of members

The public appetite for scandal is insatiable. And, as true servants of the people, politicians more than satisfy the nation's hunger. All manner of sexual indiscretions and the occasional spy story litter past and current parliamentary affairs. Members of parliament have resigned from their ministerial jobs, governments have lost credibility and the media have had a field day.

Scandal-ridden lives have not always prevented a rise to the top. Gladstone and Disraeli almost alternated power for 20 years in the late 19th century, during which time

they both demonstrated an extravagant response to sexual temptation. Disraeli, also almost always in debt, had a succession of liaisons with (usually) married older women, and was cited as 'co-respondent' in a divorce case with a Mrs O'Kane. He was 79 years old at the time, hence the popular joke 'She was Kane but was he able?'. He also never resigned, using a combination of brazen openness and legal threats to disarm his critics.

William Gladstone, Prime Minister the small matter of four times, also lacked subtlety, bringing prostitutes back to 10 Downing Street and reading extracts from the Bible to these 'erring sisters' (as he called them). It is doubtful Gladstone ever succumbed to temptation – he was a high church moralist – but his diary entries suggest that he did indulge in self-flagellation on a regular basis, seemingly as penance for his charged meetings with prostitutes. He, too, never quit.

The media's influence, though, can't be understated. Conveniently confusing the public interest with the interests of the public, the 20th century has seen all manner of scandals plastered across the pages of the national papers. Jeremy Thorpe, while leader of the Liberal Party, was charged with conspiracy to murder ex-lover Norman Scott. His acquittal didn't prevent his political exile. Cecil Parkinson, darling of the Tory faithful, was outed as the father to a child out of marriage and had to observe the obligatory temporary resignation from office. David Mellor, Minister of Culture, went from 'Toe Job to No Job', as *The Sun* newspaper put it, when his romps in a Chelsea football shirt with an actress tickled the tabloids' taste for sex and power with a kink.

There are those, however, that will always be remembered because they brought a government down. In 1963, John Profumo, Minister of War, was forced to resign after it emerged he was dallying with call girl Christine Keeler. It was not enough alone to destroy a government, but Keeler was also sleeping with the Soviet naval attaché, and the fear was that national security had been compromised. The final blow was Profumo lying to the House.

Neil Hamilton's case, meanwhile, symbolised the sleaze that destroyed John Major's hopes in 1997. Hamilton strenuously denied *The Guardian*'s allegations that he received brown envelopes full of money from Mohammed Al Fayed, the owner of Harrods, in return for his influence in Parliament. He insisted on standing in the 1997 election, only to find himself up against a BBC war reporter, dressed in a white suit, presenting a manifesto of integrity and honesty. Hamilton's constituents, and the nation as a whole, went with the white knight.

Hamilton continues to protest his innocence. But the press and the people have moved on, eagerly anticipating the next member to succumb to temptation. And as night follows day, so it will happen.

shortage that prompted huge recruitment drives in Britain's former colonies. London Transport and the National Health Service were particularly active in encouraging West Indians to emigrate to Britain. Unfortunately, as the Notting Hill race riots of 1958 illustrated, the welcome these new emigrants received was rarely friendly. However, there were areas of tolerance, among them Soho, which, during the 1950s, became famed for its seedy, bohemian pubs, clubs and jazz joints, such as the still-jumping Ronnie Scott's.

By the mid-'60s, London had started to swing. The innovative fashions of Mary Quant and others broke the stranglehold of Paris on couture: boutiques blossomed along King's Road, while Biba set the pace in Kensington. Carnaby Street became a byword for hipness as the city basked in its new-found reputation as the music and fashion capital of the world.

The year of student unrest in Europe, 1968, saw the first issue of *Time Out* (a fold-up sheet for 5p) appear on the streets in August. The decade ended with the Beatles naming their final album *Abbey Road* after their recording studios in London, NW8, and the Rolling Stones playing a free gig in Hyde Park (July 1969) that drew around half a million people.

THATCHERISM

The bubble, though, had to burst, and burst it did. Many Londoners remember the 1970s as a decade of economic strife: inflation, the oil crisis and international debt caused chaos, and the IRA began its bombing campaign on mainland Britain. The explosion of punk in the second half of the decade, sartorially inspired by the idiosyncratic genius of Vivienne Westwood, provided some nihilistic colour.

History will regard the 1980s as the Thatcher era. When the Conservatives won the general election in 1979, Britain's first woman prime minister – the propagandist for 'market forces'

Yeah baby! London swung in the 1960s.

and Little Englander morality – set out to expunge socialism and the influence of the 1960s and 1970s. A monetarist policy and cuts in public services savagely widened the divide between rich and poor. While the professionals and 'yuppies' (Young Urban Professionals) profited from tax cuts and easy credit, unemployment soared. In London, riots erupted in Brixton (1981) and Tottenham (1985); mass unemployment and heavy-handed policing methods were seen as contributing factors.

The Greater London Council (GLC), led by Ken Livingstone, mounted spirited opposition to the Thatcher government with a series of populist measures, the most famous of which was a revolutionary fare-cutting policy on public transport. So effective was the GLC, in fact, that Thatcher decided to abolish it in 1986. There then followed a 14-year stretch where London was without an elected governing body, but in May 2000, the Greater London Assembly was created and a mayor elected. His name? Ken Livingstone. What goes around…

> **'Only a stubborn, short-sighted cretin could argue, with a straight face, that the Dome merited a cash outlay of close on £1 billion.'**

The spectacular rise in house prices at the end of the 1980s (peaking in August 1988) was followed by an equally alarming slump and the onset of a severe recession that only started to lift in the mid-1990s. The Docklands development – one of the Thatcher enterprise schemes, set up in 1981 in order to create a new business centre in the docklands to the east of the City – has faltered many times. Although it can now be counted as a qualified success in terms of attracting business to the Isle of Dogs, the bleakness of the surrounding area and lack of infrastructure make it unpopular with Docklands' office workers, while the locals in the area resent the intrusion of the yuppies.

The **Poll Tax Riots** helped see off Thatcher, but the Tories clung on for seven more years.

RECENT PAST AND NEAR FUTURE

The replacement of the by-now hated Thatcher by John Major as leader of the Conservative Party in October 1990 signalled an upsurge of hope in London. A riot in Trafalgar Square had helped to see off both Maggie and her inequitable Poll Tax.

Yet the early years of the decade were scarred by continuing recession and an all-too-visible problem of homelessness on the streets of the capital. Shortly after the Conservatives were elected for another term in office in 1992, the IRA detonated a massive bomb in the City, killing three people. This was followed by a second bomb a year later, which shattered buildings around Bishopsgate, and by another Docklands bomb in February 1996, which broke a fragile 18-month ceasefire. Yet now, with the Good Friday Agreement, there's a real chance of a permanent peace in the province, and the terrorist threat to the capital has been massively reduced.

In May 1997, the British people ousted the tired Tories, and Tony Blair's notably unsocialist Labour Party swept to victory on a wave of enthusiasm. What remained of that enthusiasm in 2000, though, was all but obliterated after a countrywide petrol crisis in which the capital was left without vehicle fuel for 48 hours thanks to protesters and blockaders at the country's oil refineries. With Blair expected to call a general election in early to mid-2001, the race for power more open than it's been at any point during Labour's reign, though they should still be returned to government thanks to the lack of a credible opposition.

The millennium celebrations went off with a bang – though not as much of a bang as hoped, given the mysterious non-appearance of a much-heralded 'wall of fire' that was to have illuminated the river as the clock struck midnight – but London's hugely hyped assortment of celebratory projects met a mixed reception. Both the London Eye, a massive observation wheel by the Palace of Westminster, and the new Tate Modern gallery have been unqualified successes.

However, in prototypical displays of British organisational ineptitude, the Millennium Bridge linking St Paul's and the Tate Modern opened late, and then had to be immediately closed when it was discovered that it wobbled when people walked across it. Meanwhile, the Millennium Dome... Well, we don't have room here to tell the whole sorry story, suffice to say that while the attraction had its admirers – around six million visited during the year it was open, making it the country's most popular attraction – it was mismanaged from the word go, and only a stubborn, short-sighted cretin could argue, with a straight face, that it merited a cash outlay of close on £1 billion.

Expensive and unreliable public transport, traffic-choked roads and environmental pollution remain major problems in London. However, while some of the proposed solutions to these problems seem a little ill-advised – the proposed pedestrianisation of Westminster and Trafalgar Square, for example, would likely cause more problems than it solves – there is hope in the capital. Tourism has never been stronger, the city is still building on the international renown for the excellence of its shops, restaurants, clubs and creative talent, and the new GLA has at last provided the city with a democratic voice for local issues. Bringing shades might be pushing it a little, but the future does, touch wood, look bright.

Key events

AD 43 The Romans invade; a bridge is built on the Thames; Londinium is founded.

61 Boudicca burns Londinium; the city is rebuilt and made the provincial capital.

200 A city wall is built; Londinium becomes capital of Britannia Superior.

410 Roman troops evacuate Britain.

c600 Saxon London is built to the west.

604 St Paul's is built by King Ethelbert; Mellitus is appointed Bishop of London.

841 The Norse raid for the first time.

c871 The Danes occupy London.

886 King Alfred of Wessex retakes London.

1013 The Danes take London back.

1042 Edward the Confessor builds a palace and 'West Minster' upstream.

1066 William I is crowned in Westminster Abbey; London is granted a charter.

1067 Work begins on the Tower of London.

1191 Henry Fitzalwin is made the first mayor.

1213 St Thomas's Hospital is founded.

1215 The Mayor of London signs the Magna Carta, strengthening the City's power.

1240 First Parliament sits at Westminster.

1290 Jews are expelled from London.

1327 The first Common Council of the City of London.

1348-9 The Black Death devastates London.

1381 Wat Tyler leads the Peasants' Revolt.

1397 Richard Whittington is Lord Mayor.

1476 The first ever printing press is set up by William Caxton at Westminster.

1513 The Royal Dockyard at Woolwich and Deptford is founded by Henry VIII.

1534 Henry VIII cuts off the Catholic Church.

1566 Gresham opens the Royal Exchange.

1599 The Globe Theatre is built on Bankside.

1605 Guy Fawkes fails to blow up James I.

1642 The start of the Civil War; Royalists are defeated at Turnham Green.

1649 Charles I is executed; Commonwealth is established under Cromwell.

1664-5 The Great Plague.

1666 The Great Fire.

1675 Building starts on the new St Paul's.

1692 Lloyd's first insurance market opens.

1694 The Bank of England is established.

1717 Hanover Square and Cavendish Square are laid out, signalling the start of the development of the West End.

1750 Westminster Bridge is built.

1766 The city wall is demolished.

1780 The anti-Catholic, anti-Irish Gordon Riots take place.

1802 The Stock Exchange is founded.

1803 The first public railway opens, horse-drawn from Croydon to Wandsworth.

1812 Prime Minister Spencer Perceval is assassinated at Parliament.

1824 The National Gallery is founded.

1827 Regent's Park Zoo opens.

1829 London's first horse-drawn bus runs from Paddington to the City; the Metropolitan Police Act is set up.

1833 The London Fire Brigade is established.

1835 Madame Tussaud's opens.

1836 The first passenger railway opens, from Greenwich to London Bridge; the University of London is founded.

1837 Parliament is rebuilt after a fire.

1843 Trafalgar Square is laid out.

1848-9 A cholera epidemic sweeps London.

1851 The Great Exhibition takes place.

1853 Harrods opens its doors.

1858 The Great Stink: pollution in the Thames reaches hideous levels.

1863 The Metropolitan line, the world's first underground railway, opens.

1864 The Peabody buildings, cheap housing for the poor, are built in Spitalfields.

1866 London's last major cholera outbreak; the Sanitation Act is passed.

1868 The last public execution is held at Newgate Prison.

1884 Greenwich Mean Time is established.

1888 Jack the Ripper prowls the East End.

1889 A London County Council is created.

1890 The Housing Act enables the LCC to clear the slums; the first electric underground railway opens.

1915-8 Zeppelins bomb London.

1940-4 The Blitz devastates much of London.

1948 The Olympic Games are held.

1951 The Festival of Britain takes place.

1953 Queen Elizabeth II is crowned.

1966 England win the World Cup at Wembley.

1982 The last of London's docks close.

1986 The GLC is abolished.

1990 Poll tax protesters riot.

1991 Riots in Brixton.

1992 Canary Wharf opens; the IRA bomb the Baltic Exchange in the City.

1997 Princess Diana dies and is buried at Westminster Abbey.

2000 Ken Livingstone is elected Mayor; new attractions include the Tate Modern, the London Eye and the Millennium Dome.

London Today

New century, new mayor, new attractions…
but has the city really changed?

It's been a momentous year. But then again,
how could it not have been a momentous year?
It kicked off with the biggest fireworks display
ever seen in this country, and ended with…
well, various politicians and public servants
squabbling so much over another fireworks
display that it had to be cancelled. In between,
London got a huge slew of new sights and
attractions, its first proper coating of snow
in seven winters, and, crucially, a new system
of local government and a mayor.

Given the year the capital had in 2000, then,
it's a surprise how little has changed. London
takes things in its stride more than almost any
other city, regarding both setbacks and steps
forward with the same withering, slightly
weary glance. The town may have plenty more
tangible attractions of which it can be proud,
but pride is rarely on the agenda in London,
at least not when it can maintain the sneering
arrogance it's held through bad times as well as
good. Although it only began work in May

2000, London's new Greater London Authority
and its mayor Ken Livingstone – who's usually
anything but publicity-shy – have been
conspicuous by their absence from the public
eye. This may change in 2001, but for now,
it's business as usual.

An essential listen when in the city is
Robert Elms's radio show on BBC London
Live (94.9 FM, 9am-noon Monday to Friday),
a treasure trove of anecdotal trivia and serious
discussion on a London theme. Each Monday
at around 9.20am is a slot called the 'Listed
Londoner', in which a famous resident of the
capital is asked 15 posers about their life in
the city. One question runs something along
the lines of 'What's the first thing you would
do to improve London?' Potentially intriguing
though this question sounds, it's usually the
least enlightening point of the interview,
because more or less everyone, regardless
of social background, age or politics, settles
for variations on the same answer.

TRAVEL SICKNESS

London's transport system is in a truly parlous state. The roads are clogged with cars; the tube is at breaking point (the service breaks down every 16 minutes); buses might as well be going backwards at many central London flashpoints; there are never enough cabs on the road… In almost every aspect imaginable, it's a mess.

It's a truth that was realised early on by the four London mayoral candidates: the Conservative Steven Norris, Labour's Frank Dobson and the Liberal Democrat Susan Kramer, plus Livingstone, who broke away from the Labour Party after a bitter battle for its official nomination, and went on to win May's election by a massive majority on an independent ticket. Transport became the key election issue, as the quartet struggled to convince both themselves and a travel-sick electorate that they could solve the puzzle of how to get London moving again.

> **'Chaos, noise and dirt are ingrained in the very fabric of the city.'**

The answer, though, is surely not Livingstone's attention-grabbing proposal to slap a £5 'congestion charge' – kind of road toll meets poll tax, in essence – on drivers entering central London during the day. Consultation on the controversial idea began in early 2001, with proposals to be finalised later in the year.

But while such a scheme will likely net Livingstone a considerable sum of money that's he's already promised to throw at public transport, it may not do much to solve the traffic problem. It's wishful thinking to assume that drivers are going to be priced out of their motors by a £5-a-day road toll, especially since the alternative, a day's pass to ride on a public transport system that verges on the laughable, costs nearly as much. The introduction of more red routes (stretches of road where pulling over for any length of time is prohibited) and bus and cycle lanes would be of far greater benefit to the traffic flow of public transport, while stiffer penalties for those who flout the law – and, for that matter, greater enforcement of said laws – would surely help even more.

Of course, London is not Amsterdam; but more to the point, it never will be, and it never should be. Chaos, noise and dirt are ingrained in the very fabric of the city, and no attempts at petty beautification will ever change that. This is why, although there's no doubt things could be improved, anyone seriously hoping that the city's traffic will ever run with a perfectly smooth serenity through the streets is missing

the point entirely, and why the multifarious pedestrianisation schemes mooted for London – from the grandiose and ill-conceived (Trafalgar Square) to the small-scale and merely irritating (Soho's Old Compton Street) – should have been ditched at planning stage. One Covent Garden is more than enough, thanks all the same.

It doesn't get any better underground, either, with Livingstone locked in battle with the government in early 2001 over its proposals to sell off part of the London Underground in a series of Public-Private Partnerships (PPPs). Having hired the highly respected former New York subway chief Bob Kiley as his Commissioner for Transport, Livingstone hopes to force a governmental climbdown on the plans, which Kiley is set against. Whatever is eventually decided upon in 2001, though, something needs to be done, a fact obvious to anyone who's ridden the tube at rush hour.

BUSINESS AS USUAL

The transport problem is a hardy perennial in London. But the city still faces the same other challenges it's faced for as long as anyone can remember. Only many of them have been amplified with the years, magnified with the passing of time. London's never been more expensive, for one thing, with the price of flats and houses in particular having reached unmanageable levels. Crime, too, is still a concern for many. Street crime is again on the increase, though it was two specific events – the two murders at 2000's Notting Hill Carnival, and the brutal, incomprehensible killing of 10-year-old Damilola Taylor on a Peckham housing estate at the close of the year – that shocked the usually unshockable locals.

In addition, the long-term problem of homelessness in the capital shows no signs of abating, while issues that afflict the country as a whole – a chronic shortage of teachers in schools, a beat-up and beleaguered National Health Service, an undermanned police force – reach their apogee in the capital. Whether the GLA – which is, in fairness, still just getting its feet wet – will be able to do much about any of these issues remains to be seen.

But it's not, of course, all bad news. The millennial year saw a rash of new attractions open in London, many to great acclaim. Best of all, though, many are aimed in equal measure at locals as at visitors. The resurrection of Somerset House has been, perhaps, the highlight: the conversions of the previously closed buildings into a series of excellent museums and a marvellous restaurant, and of the once car-strewn courtyard into one of the most stunning public spaces in town, have been an unqualified success.

Stop the pigeon

If ever there was an example of a city needing to pay more heed to its residents and less to its visitors, it's the issue of the pigeons in Trafalgar Square. There can be no greater indicator of this than the pathetic response to Mayor Ken Livingstone's recent proclamation that he wants to rid Trafalgar Square of the birds that have blighted it for decades.

Trafalgar Square is grand, expansive, pride-inducing; one of London's great public spaces. Or, at least, it would be were it not overrun with disease-spreading, shit-dropping, sky-clogging winged rats whose presence is tolerated only by the most clueless tourists and actively despised by everyone of sound mind and body who actually lives here. Livingstone's stated intention to clear the area of pigeons – which began in late 2000 with the eviction of Bernard Rayner, the last legal feed-seller in the square – should have been greeted by universal acclaim. Champagne was put on ice, street parties were organised, bunting was hung from lampposts in readiness.

But rather than join in, the media instead gave widespread coverage to the bleatings of writer and animal activist Carla Lane, who claimed the pigeons would starve to death. Leaving aside the obvious response – the only good pigeon is a dead pigeon – the truth

is that they wouldn't die at all. Rather, they'd just leave the square in search of food and leave us all alone.

Several years ago, a teenager named Jason Lidbury was discovered to be stealing the pigeons from Trafalgar Square in order to sell them on to restaurants. Dubious motives aside, his actions should have made him a London hero fêted from High Barnet to Morden, Epping to Ealing. Indeed, the 150-year conundrum as to what should fill the empty statue plinth in the square seemed to have found an answer: a huge bronze figure of Lidbury, carrying a cardboard box full of pigeons and grinning like he'd just won the Lottery, would have done the trick. So, what happened? Lidbury was dragged off to court and fined £475. And the pigeons, despite Ken's best efforts, are still there. Ugh.

Close behind was the Tate Modern, widely and rightly acclaimed by both press and public (who voted with their feet to the tune of 20,000 visitors a day during 2000). Like the breathtaking Great Court at the British Museum, which opened in November 2000, the British Airways London Eye has not been without its problems – it opened over a month late; it's been hampered by a dire ticket bookings system; and it had to close for a month in January 2001 for repair work – but it's proved a wonderful addition to the London skyline. The Wallace Collection, the Science Museum, the Dulwich Picture Gallery…

The list goes on, and on, and on. It's barely tempered by 2000's most vainglorious failure: the Millennium Dome, whose business plan appeared to have been written by a five-year-old with a suitably cursory grasp of mathematics. Brits are often stereotyped as moaners, but no wonder the locals spend so much time whingeing when the best part of £1 billion is tossed down the drain by a bunch of self-serving meritocrats who couldn't organise

an orgy in a brothel. (Which is more than can be said for those behind the Millennium Bridge, who, if the pants-peeingly amusing failure of the first-hyped, then-wobbly, now-closed construction is anything to go by, would have screwed up the building of the brothel in the first place.)

SAME OLD, SAME NEW

But ultimately, these are all mere garnishes, sprinklings of salt and dollops of ketchup tossed atop the bloody great big fried breakfast that is life in London. God may be in the detail, but London's long been a godless city, always far greater than the sum of its parts. The surface appearance may undergo the occasional makeover, and the machine that runs it may receive a full service from time to time, but it'll take a lot more than a handful of museums, a revamped public transport system and a new government to change London to any great degree. Assuming, that is, this stubborn, cocksure, irascible but oddly loveable town can ever find it in its heart to change at all.

Canary Wharf Station.
See p31.

Architecture

Built up from the ruins of a 17th-century fire, London is a showcase for over 300 years' worth of architectural trends.

Last year, BBC radio ran a programme asking whether cars should be banned from central London. One of the show's panelists, architect Piers Gough, flew in the face of popular fashion by declaring himself against the idea. London, he said, is a dirty, gritty, hard-working city and there's no point in pretending otherwise.

He's right. Unlike other major cities, it's never been beautified or planned. It is a hotch-potch, the product of a gradual accumulation of towns and villages, adapted, renewed and disfigured by the changing needs of its population. The tide of history has given London no distinctive architectural style, being at once imperial, industrial, medieval and experimental.

LONDON'S BURNING

There are any number of events that have left their imprint on the buildings of the city, but the Great Fire of 1666 is a useful historical marker: it signals the end of medieval London and the start of the city we know today. Commemorated by Christopher Wren's 202-foot-high **Monument** (*see p91*), the fire destroyed five-sixths of the city, burning 13,200 houses and 89 churches.

But the city was asking for it. London was a densely populated city built of wood, where rubbish would go uncollected and fire control was primitive. It was only after a three-day inferno that the authorities felt they could insist on a few basic building regulations. From now on, brick and stone would be the construction materials of choice, and key streets would be widened to act as the fire breaks of the future. Most of what can now be seen is a testament to the talents of Wren and his successors.

In a sense, though, the city of the Plague did not entirely disappear. In spite of grand proposals from architects hoping to remodel the city from scratch, London reshaped around the old street lines. And the buildings that had survived the fire stood as monuments to earlier ages. One building which did withstand the heat was the church of **St Ethelburga-the-Virgin** (68-70 Bishopsgate, The City, EC2), noteworthy as the city's smallest chapel as well as for its splendid name. Sadly, where the fire failed, the IRA succeeded, destroying two-thirds of this 13th-century building in a 1993 bomb attack.

The Norman **Tower of London** (*see p92*), begun soon after William's 1066 conquest and extended over the next 300 years, remains the country's most perfect example of a medieval fortress thanks to the Navy that cheated the advancing flames by clearing the surrounding houses before the fire could get to them six centuries later.

And then there is **Westminster Abbey** (*see p134*), begun in 1245 when the borough lay far outside London's walls and completed in 1745 when Nicholas Hawksmoor added the west towers. (That said, though, cathedrals are never really finished: the statues set over the main entrance, with Martin Luther King taking centre stage, were added just a couple of years ago.) Although the Abbey is the most French of England's gothic churches, deriving its geometry, flying buttresses and rose windows from across the Channel, the chapel, added by Henry VII and completed in 1512, is pure Tudor. 'Stone seems, by the winning labour of the chisel, to have been robbed of its weight and density, suspended aloft, as if by magic,' gushed American author Washington Irving centuries later.

'Nothing cheers a builder like a natural disaster.'

The Renaissance came late to Britain, making its London debut with Inigo Jones's 1622 **Banqueting House** (*see p133*). The addition of a sumptuously decorated ceiling by Rubens in 1635, celebrating the benefits of wise rule, made the building a must-see for the public who could watch from the balconies as Charles I dined. As it turned out, the king's wisdom was a trifle lacking: 14 years later, he provided the public with an even greater spectacle as he was led from the building and beheaded.

Tourists have Jones to thank for **Covent Garden** (*see p123*) and the **Queen's House** at Greenwich (*see p169*), but these are not his only legacies. By the 1600s, Italian architecture, rooted in the forms and geometries of the Roman era, was all the rage. So, as a dedicated follower of fashion, Inigo Jones became proficient in the art of piazzas, porticos and pillasters, changing British architecture forever. His work not only influenced the careers of succeeding generations of architects, but introduced an unhealthy habit of venerating the past that would take 300 years to kick. Even today, London has a knack for glueing fake classical extras over the doors of cheap kit buildings in the hope it will lend them a little dignity. **Devonshire House** (60 Goswell Road, EC1) is a good example of this pathetic practice.

RELIGIOUS ICONS

Nothing cheers a builder like a natural disaster, so one can only guess at the relish with which Christopher Wren and co began rebuilding in the aftermath of the Fire. Taking their cue from Jones, they brandished classicism like a new broom: the pointed arches of English Gothic were rounded off, Corinthian columns made an appearance and church spires became as multi-layered and complex as a Baroque wedding cake.

Wren blazed the trail with daring plans for **St Paul's Cathedral** (*see p84*), spending an astonishing £500 on the oak model of his proposal. But the scheme, incorporating a Catholic dome rather than a Protestant steeple, was too Roman for the reformist tastes of the establishment and the design was rejected. To his credit, the undaunted architect did what any wounded ego would do. He quickly produced a redesign and gained planning permission by incorporating the much-loved spire, only to set about a series of mischievous u-turns once work had commenced, giving us the building – domed and heavily suggestive of an ancient temple – that has survived to this day.

So prolific was the building of churches that Londoners managed to turn a blind eye to the odd synagogue. Allowed back into England by Oliver Cromwell in 1657, the city's Sephardic community from Spain and Portugal later commissioned a Quaker to build them a home in a square in a quiet enclave. **Bevis Marks Synagogue** (2 Heneage Lane, The City, EC3), the UK's oldest synagogue, was completed in 1701 and gives little of its semitic purpose away from the outside… and very little internally. The Rabbi even jokes that the once-trendy baroque cupboard (or ark) at one end of the building has more to do with an 18th-century trip to Ikea than Jewish iconography. It is a tribute to the pride lavished on the building that the extraordinary chandeliers that festoon the interior have yet to be electrified, leaving the staff to spend hours lighting and extinguishing hundreds of candles for each service.

Bevis Marks Synagogue.

Inigo Jones's **Banqueting House**. *See p27.*

Wren's architectural baton was to be picked up by Nicholas Hawksmoor and James Gibbs, who were to benefit from an anxiety that London's population was becoming ever more ungodly. The 1711 initiative to construct an extra 50 churches was, therefore, a significant career opportunity. Gibbs became busy in and around Trafalgar Square, building the steepled Roman temple hat is **St Martin-in-the-Fields** (*see p130*), the baroque **St Mary-le-Strand** (Strand, WC2; now set against the monstrous lump of **King's College**) and the tower of **St Clement Danes** (*see p97*).

Gibbs' work was well-received, but the more prolific and experimental Hawksmoor had a rougher ride. His imposing **St Anne's** (Commercial Road, Limehouse, E14) proved so costly that the parish was left with insufficient funds to pay for a vicar, and **St George's** in Bloomsbury (*see p105*) also broke the bank. Hawksmoor spent three times its £10,000 budget and took 15 years to build it, although recent cracking in the pale blue interior suggests the authorities again need to dig deep.

Later to be dismissed as the 'most pretentious and ugliest edifice in the metropolis' (in 1876; sadly, the quote's author remains anonymous), St George's tries hard to evoke the spirit of the ancients. Rather than a spire, there is a pyramid topped by a statue of George I decked out in a toga, while the interior boasts all the Corinthian columns, round arches and gilding you'd expect from a man steeped in Antiquity. Many of these features are repeated in Hawksmoor's rocket-like **Christ Church Spitalfields** (*see p155*), currently undergoing much-needed restoration.

THE ADAM FAMILY & BEYOND

One of a large family of Scottish architects, Robert Adam found himself at the forefront of a movement that came to see Italian Baroque as a corruption of the real thing. Architectural exuberance was eventually dropped in favour of a simpler interpetation of the ancient forms. In the interests of brevity, purists should look away now; the buildings became more Plain Jane than Big Hair.

The best surviving work of Adam and his brothers James, John and William can be found in London's great suburban houses **Osterley Park**, **Syon House** and the library of **Kenwood House**, but the project for which they are most famous no longer stands. In 1768, they embarked on the cripplingly expensive Adelphi housing estate (after the Greek for 'brothers') off the Strand. Built over vaults used to store goods off-loaded from river barges, most of the complex was pulled down in the 1930s and replaced by an office block of the same name, but part of the original development survives in what is now the **Royal Society for the Arts** (8 John Adam Street, Covent Garden, WC2), a good example of how the family relieved the simplicity of brick with elegant plasterwork.

Just as the first residents were moving into the Adelphi, a young unknown called John Soane was embarking on a tour of his own. In Rome, Soane met the wealthy Bishop of Derry who persuaded the 25-year-old to abandon his travels and accompany him to Ireland in order to build a house. But the project came to nothing and Soane dealt with the setback by working hard and marrying into money.

His loss is our gain, however, as he went on to build the **Bank of England** and the recently remodelled **Dulwich Picture Gallery** (*see p171*). Sadly, the Bank was demolished between the wars, leaving nothing but the perimeter walls and depriving London of what is said to have been Soane's masterpiece. But a hint of what these ignorant bankers might have enjoyed can be gleaned from a visit to Soane's house, now **Sir John Soane's Museum** (*see p99*) and a collection of exquisite architectural experiments with mirrors, coloured glass and folding walls. In the well-stocked gallery, listen through to the end of the warden's explanation: it ends with a display of architectural inventiveness that will make you gasp.

A committed Mason, Soane shared the fascination with death that seems to characterise the fraternity. The Dulwich Picture

Gallery incorporates a dimly lit mausoleum containing the earthly remains of the building's benefactors, a rehearsal for the design of his own resting place. This is worth the quick walk north of King's Cross to the churchyard of St Pancras Old Church: just look for the square tomb with the gently curving roof – one of only two Grade 1-listed tombs in the country, the other being that of Karl Marx – and you'll see where Sir Giles Gilbert Scott later got his inspiration for the traditional red phone box.

'Regent Street began as a device to separate the toffs and the riff-raff.'

A near-contemporary of Soane, John Nash was a less talented architect, but his contributions to the fabric of London have proved greater than any other individual. Among his buildings are **Buckingham Palace** (*see p130*), the **Haymarket Theatre** (Haymarket, St James's, W1) and **Regent Street** (W1). The latter began as a proposal to link the west end to the planned park further north, as well as a device to separate the toffs and the riff-raff. In Nash's words, the intention was 'complete separation between the streets and squares occupied by the nobility and gentry, and the narrow streets and meaner houses occupied by mechanics and the trading part of the community.'

THE 19TH CENTURY

By the 1830s, the classical form had been established for 200 years, and a handful of upstarts began pressing for change. In 1834, the **Houses of Parliament** burned down, leading to the construction of Charles Barry's gothic masterpiece (*see p133*). This was the beginning of the Gothic Revival, a move by the new romantics to replace what they considered to be foreign and pagan with a style that was not only native but Christian. The architectural profession was divided, but the argument was never resolved, merely made irrelevant by the advent of modernism a century later.

Barry would have preferred a classical design, but the brief was unambiguous and Gothic was to prevail. He needed help, and sought out a designer whose name alone makes him worthy of a mention, Augustus Welby Northmore Pugin. The result of Pugin's labours was a Victorian fantasy which, while a fine example of the perpendicular form, shows how the Middle Ages had become distorted in the minds of 19th-century architects. New buildings were constructed as a riot of turrets, towers and winding staircases that would today be condemned as the Disney-fication of history.

Even in renovating ancient buildings, architects would often decide that they weren't gothic enough; as with the 15th-century **Guildhall** (*see p86*), which gained its corner turrets and central spire in 1862. Bombed by the Luftwaffe, the Guildhall was rebuilt largely as the Victorians had left it, apart from the interior statues of Gog and Magog, the protagonists in a legendary battle between ancient Britain and Troy. In the post-war reconstruction of this stately building, these two ugly bastards got even uglier. There's also a good statue of Churchill, looking stereotypically grumpy.

The argument between the classicists and goths erupted in 1857, when the government commissioned Sir George Gilbert Scott, a leading light of the gothic movement, to design a new HQ for the **Foreign Office**. Scott's design incensed anti-goth Lord Palmerstone, then prime minister, whose diktats prevailed. But Scott exacted his revenge by building an office in which everyone hated working (*see p31* **Birth pangs**), and by going on to construct gothic edifices all over the capital, among them the **Albert Memorial** (*see p138*) and **St Pancras Station** (*see p105*).

St Pancras was completed in 1873, after the Midland Railway commissioned Scott to build a London terminus that would dwarf that of their rivals next door at King's Cross. Using the project as an opportunity to show his mastery of the gothic form, Scott built an asymmetrical castle that obliterated views of the train shed behind, itself an engineering marvel completed earlier by William Barlow. This 'incongruous medievalism' did not go unnoticed by critics, prompting one to write that company directors should go the whole hog and dress their staff in period costume. 'Their porters might be dressed as javelin men, their guards as beefeaters.'

Still, the gothic style was to dominate until the 20th century, leaving London littered with charming, imposing but anachronistic buildings such as the **Royal Courts of Justice** (*see p97*), the **Natural History Museum** (*see p139*), **Liberty** (*see p233*) and **Tower Bridge** (*see p92*). World War I and the coming of modernism led to a spirit of tentative renewal, and the **Royal Institute of British Architects** (aka RIBA; *see p297*) and the BBC's **Broadcasting House** (Portland Place, Marylebone, W1) are good examples of the pared-down style of the '20s and '30s.

THIS IS THE MODERN WORLD

It must be evidence of the British love of animals that perhaps the finest example of between-the-wars Modernism can be found at **London Zoo** (*see p109*). Built by Russian emigre Bethold Lubetkin and the Tecton group,

Charles Holden's hugely influential, still-stunning **Arnos Grove Station**.

the spiral ramps of the Penguin Pool were a showcase for the possibilities of concrete, which was also put to good use on the underground: it enabled the quick and cheap building of large, cavernous spaces with the sleek lines and curves associated with speed. The Piccadilly line was a particular beneficiary: its 1930s expansion yielded the likes of Charles Holden's **Arnos Grove Station**, the first of many circular station buildings and the model for the new **Canada Water Station**.

However, there was nothing quick or cheap about the **Daily Express** building (Fleet Street, The City, EC4). A black glass and chrome structure built in 1931, it was the first of its type in the capital, a 'curtain wall' construction where the façade is literally hung on to an internal frame. Recently refurbished and extended for a new occupant, the developers have, happily, not compromised the deco detailing of the original building, leaving the crazy flooring, snake handrails and funky lighting to dazzle passers-by. Being a corporate HQ, public access is not guaranteed, but it's worth sticking your head around the door of what *Architects' Journal* called a 'defining monument of 1930s London'.

WHAT IS IT GOOD FOR?

World War II left large areas of London ruined, providing another opportunity for builders to cash in. Lamentably, the city was little improved by the rebuild, and, in many cases, was left worse off. The destruction left the capital with a dire housing shortage, giving architects a chance to demonstrate the speed and efficiency with which they could house large numbers of families in tower blocks. Most were not a success and deserve to be pulled down. Some of them have gone already.

But the legacy of post-war architecture is viewed with horror by most Londoners, an experience that has both tempered the arrogance of the architectural profession and created a planning process that places so many hurdles in the way of developers that it's a wonder anything gets built at all. There are a few diamonds among the coal, however, including the **Royal Festival Hall** on the South Bank (*see p307*): the sole survivor of the 1951 Festival of Britain, it was built to celebrate the war's end and the centenary of the Great Exhibition. In spite of its size, it can be a crowded and awkward space, but refurbishment work is restoring what little grandeur the builders of post-war Britain managed to impart. It's now a much-loved piece of London's fabric.

> **'The edifices on architectural death row are reminders that when things get that bad, they can only get better.'**

The South Bank is currently the centre of the biggest planning question to face Londoners for a quarter of a century: a debate to settle the future of the **Hayward Gallery** (*see p73*) and **Queen Elizabeth Hall** (*see p307*), concrete, windowless structures and exemplars of the '60s Brutalist movement. In a sense, it's unfortunate they function perfectly well, a factor that has frustrated one architect after another when asked to rethink this botched neighbourhood. The latest scheme by Rick Mather is now mired in politics and his plans are unlikely to come to fruition for a couple of years, but the days of these stained bunkers are surely numbered.

It would take a peculiar brand of courage to say 'thank God for Brutalism', but the edifices now on architectural death row are, at least, reminders that when things get that bad they can only get better. Against that background, the glass and granite of American corporatism was a welcome relief. Cesar Pelli's enormous **Canary Wharf** tower (Isle of Dogs, E14) has become the archetypal expression of 1980s architecture and holds an ambiguous place in the city's affections. Its splendid isolation lent it an element of star quality, but the current building boom is providing this giant obelisk with a couple of equally large neighbours, opening up another part of the city's traditionally low-rise skyline to high-rise clutter. Richard Rogers' **Lloyd's Building** (Lime Street, The City, EC3) is the exception to the 1980s norm, combining office space with oil-refinery aesthetics and managing to make it look good. Mocked upon completion in 1986, the building still manages to outclass more recent projects, a fact not lost on Channel 4 when it commissioned Rogers to design its new HQ in Horseferry Road, SW1, in the early 1990s.

It is largely the doing of Rogers and close friend and rival Norman Foster that London is becoming a showcase for brave and innovative buildings. Future Systems' **NatWest Media Centre** at Lord's Cricket Ground (see p325), built from aluminium in a boatyard and perched high above the pitch like a giant bar of soap, is arguably London's most daring construction to date, especially given its traditional, old world setting. And Will Alsop's multi-coloured **Peckham Library** (171 Peckham Hill Street, Peckham, SE15) has redefined community architecture so comprehensively that it fully deserved the £20,000 Stirling Prize awarded it late last year. The annual award, bestowed by the Royal Institute of British Architects, fielded a particularly strong shortlist in 2000, including the **London Eye** (see p69), a 135-metre-high structure that has already become a globally recognised London icon, and Foster's **Canary Wharf Station** on the recently extended Jubilee line, a poem in concrete.

The problem with being innovative, though, is that things can go wrong. And there's no better example of this than Foster's daring

Birth pangs

Anyone planning on making their mark on London's skyline needs their head examined. No matter how talented the architect or how noble the plan, there'll always be somebody ready to sneer and drag reputations through the mud. This element of the capital's character has a long and distinguished history and begins with Sir Christopher Wren, who was put on half-pay 22 years into the construction of **St Paul's Cathedral** because it was taking so long to build. He eventually finished it 13 years later.

John Nash's **All Soul's Church** in Langham Place, W1, completed in 1824, was not then seen as the treasure it is today. In fact, a popular cartoon of the time illustrated the architect with the church's needle-like spire shoved up his arse. Similarly, Nash's **Buckingham Palace** took nearly 20 years to build and so exceeded the budget that he was summoned to Parliament to account for himself. He was sacked. And when the building was completed in 1837, the drains were faulty, the bells wouldn't ring and most of the 1,000 windows refused to open.

During the construction of the **Houses of Parliament**, the bell of Big Ben cracked on a test run. And when the hands were fitted to the clock face, they were so heavy the

mechanism refused to move. The heating and ventilation system was so poor inside the building that one member called for the architect to be hanged.

Sir George Gilbert Scott, builder of the **Foreign Office**, also found himself on the wrong end of the government's ire. Prime Minister Lord Palmerstone derided Scott's original gothic plans as a 'mongrel affair', prompting a redesign that kept no one happy. The rooms were dark, cold and airless, coal fumes filled the corridors, and the ceilings were so high that echo made conversations impossible. But the building still stands.

The stress of building the **Royal Courts of Justice**, dogged by design changes, budget cuts and strikes, caused architect Edmund Street to die an early death. He wasn't the only one: the builder of the court's clock, which overlooks Fleet Street, died from strangulation when his tie became caught in the mechanism.

And even the most heralded recent addition to the London skyline hasn't been immune from criticism. The concept of the **London Eye** was first mooted in 1992, as an entry in a competition sponsored by The Times for a structure to celebrate the millennium. It came second. Nobody can now recall what won.

The **Lloyd's Building**, Richard Rogers's eye-catching City masterpiece. *See p31.*

Millennium Bridge that links St Paul's with the new Tate Modern. Designed as an elegantly thin suspension structure, the bridge's opening was first delayed due to construction problems, and then descended into farce. The bridge began to sway noticeably as soon as the public were allowed to cross it in mid-2000, requiring the closure of the bridge just a few days later. After a long-running battle over who would pay for the repairs, the bridge is now slated to reopen in late summer 2001.

THE SHOCK OF THE OLD

London's architecture is also marked by the presence of a 'green belt', a slice of protected countryside which prevents the city from bursting its banks and spilling into the rest of south-east England. In consort with a small but vocal army of conservationists, the green belt forces architects to work with old buildings rather than pull them down. Done well, the new is grafted on to the old in a way that is often invisible from street level; visitors will be surprised by the way contemporary interiors have been inserted into elderly buildings.

Fortunately, the best examples of this can be found in the public museums and art galleries, many of which have undergone millennium make-overs and expansion programmes. The **National Portrait Gallery** (*see p130*), the **Royal Opera House** (*see p307*) and **Tate Britain** (*see p135*) are good examples of architects adding modern signatures to old buildings, while the **British Museum** (*see p101*), the **National Maritime Museum** (*see p169*) and the **Wallace Collection** (*see p108*) have all gone one better. With the help of large

lottery grants and glass roofs, these last three have considerably added to their facilities by invading what were once external courtyards. Foster's exercise in complexity at the British Museum, with its new £100 million Great Court, is without doubt the most impressive, not for creating the most spectacular and largest covered square in Europe, but because he has managed to get away with it.

It's this 'money for old rope' mentality that made the conversion of Sir Giles Gilbert Scott's power station into a premier league art venue, the **Tate Modern** (*see p77*), possible, making a mockery of the architectural mantra 'form follows function'. This imposing edifice was dragged from obscurity and thrust before an adoring public by Swiss architects Herzog and de Meuron, who managed to preserve much of the original building while installing seven new floors of exhibition space. The sheer immensity of the place is a guarantor of the 'wow' factor, but the architects have also managed to squeeze some cosy little spaces from its bulk.

But what of Piers Gough, the pro-car architect extolling the virtues of hard-working, gritty London? He's just finished building a funky yellow eco-bridge over the new **Mile End Park** in the East End. Reserved for pedestrians and cyclists, access is denied to traffic and the bridge is planted with trees and wild flowers.

> ▶ For more on cultural events at the **South Bank Centre**, *see p307*.
> ▶ For more on the new Great Court at the **British Museum**, *see p101*.

The River

Trade and transport route, lovely open space and crass cultural divide: the Thames is all things to all people.

The one constant in a city whose history stretches back over 2,000 years has been the River Thames. While neither the longest nor the most impressive waterway, it nonetheless stands as one of the most famous stretches of water in the world, synonymous in our minds with the great city that grew up around it, with Tower Bridge and Shakespeare's Globe, with Chaucer's pilgrims and fallen noblemen locked in the Tower of London. It's integral to England's cultural history, a leading player in the urban geography that has made London the focus of the UK and the premier capital in Western Europe.

It's unlikely that the Romans had such grand visions of the future in mind when they decided on a site around the highest parts of the river upon which to establish Londinium in AD43. Tamesis, as the Romans called the river, was a convenient alleyway into Roman Britain for men, supplies and goods. By utilising the rising tide, boats could be easily swept inland from the North Sea, reducing the need for over-exertion among the rowers. The growth of London has since been tied to the now-murky stretch of water that slices the capital in two, as successive generations of its inhabitants have used the river – locals never call it by its given name – as a centre for agriculture and trade, government and protection.

Although the organisational and building skills of the Romans based around the river fuelled the dramatic growth of London almost 2,000 years ago, the history of the river as a centre for survival stretches back further than the Roman Empire. Archaeological finds suggest the Thames Valley was probably first inhabited 400,000 years ago, with evidence of settlements in the Neolithic era at points further west than London. In keeping with the age – and pre-empting the river's future as an agricultural centre – farming and fishing were integral to river life. The Bronze Age saw an upturn in trade to ports on the continent and first established the Thames Valley as an area for trade and manufacture. The Romans finished the job by building the first crossing of the river, linking modern-day Southwark and the City: London Bridge. London was born around the Thames.

Rich though the industrial heritage of the river may be, the cultural and political lives and events that have played out close to its banks have contributed not merely to the city of London itself, but to Britain and Europe's development over the last 1,000 or so years. Festivals have long been a part of the river's life, not least for the recent millennium celebrations, which featured the grandest fireworks display London has ever seen set over the water. Back in the 17th and 18th centuries, Frost Fairs were the big draw: held on the iced-over river, they were great celebrative gatherings featuring the fairground amusements of the era. It was only after London Bridge was replaced in 1831 and the river could no longer freeze sufficiently to bear such extravagances that the fairs came to an end.

'Artists regard the water as the metaphorical blood giving life to the city.'

Slightly earlier in the 17th century, when London theatre was arguably at its most popular and the theatre district was based much closer to the river than it is now, river parades and processions were frequently held, many including dramas acted out on the waters. Until the recently reconstructed Globe Theatre at Bankside was completed, this aspect of the river's history had passed almost into folklore, but much of London's business and pleasure in the first half of the 17th century was still based entirely around the Thames. Indeed, poets and artists, composers and playwrights have long sought to capture something of the river's nature in their works, many regarding the water as both the metaphorical blood giving life to the city – an obvious but nonetheless correct theory – and a beauty unto itself.

As integral as the river has been to work and play, it has also been a regular threat to London and its inhabitants. Floods were relatively frequent, the first recorded instance in 1099. Throughout the ensuing centuries, and doubtless before this date, the river often burst its banks, often with disastrous consequences for those unable to escape. The river walls have regularly been heightened in an attempt to ward off disaster, and the river itself dramatically deepened. In 1953, 300 drowned as floods ravaged parts of the east coast, prompting authorities to consider the potentially devastating effects if one such

natural disaster were to reach the city itself. The Thames Barrier, finished in 1982, was the eventual solution to the problem.

The river today is, perhaps necessarily, less a trading mechanism than a cultural and residential centre with a tourist sideshow along its southern bank. The fruits of 2,000 years of organised expansion and some of the key elements of London and Britain's history – Parliament and the Tower of London, for example – mix with grandiose housing and office developments and cultural havens such as the South Bank Centre to form an overpowering mish-mash of architectural styles adorning its edges. The greater development of road and rail in the latter half of the 20th century lessened the need for industry's reliance on the river to do their business. Reflecting this, the Port of London moved eastwards to Tilbury in the 1960s, and, although the docks held on for a few years after that, the end was nigh for the trade on the river.

Rapid redevelopment of the Docklands area began in the late 1970s, and is still ongoing today. In 1981, the London Docklands Development Corporation was set up and became a huge landowner, literally transforming huge parts of the lower East End into residences and office blocks. The property boom that accompanied the Thatcher years saw the façade alter dramatically from bustling docks to a businesslike, corporate cityscape. But when the boom turned to bust, developers were left high and dry and the Docklands were left in limbo. Even now, a trip along the Docklands Light Railway past these former ports offers a view of an unfinished area, where old, tired structures yet to be reinvented rub shoulders with the likes of Canary Wharf.

When you consider its vast historical significance, it's odd how the river has taken a back seat, forced to retire from its centuries-old working life and take on new uses and meanings for contemporary consumers. It's fair to say that, in comparison with other cities of the world and with the river's rich history, today's generation of Londoners have found little use for their river. For such a central – both historically and geographically – element of the city, the river is underused as a mode of transport for commuters, as an area for festivities, and, of course, for industry. In the rush of a working day, Londoners perhaps miss the charms of their river, and attempts to produce a greater interaction between the water and the people haven't had the desired effect: despite a transport system that's crumbling around them, many commuters still won't leave the Underground in favour of a river service.

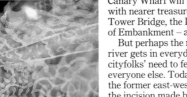

Scenes from the annual **Thames Festival**.

The metaphorical potency of a river running through the heart of a city translates itself into the river's features. In an era when trade has lessened along the waters and the once-frantic docks have been displaced, the formerly rumbustious river bizarrely lends an air of calm to the centre of town. While trains rush over it and traffic roars around it, and while Londoners go about their business oblivious, the river lies in the centre superfluous to everything. It's this that makes it such an impressive sight. Under London's almost ubiquitous grey skies, the deep grey river both sums up the city's mood and detracts from the madness around it. By night, it takes on a different resonance; the stringed lights along the South Bank and the glitter one expects from a city give off a magical glow from the water. To pause for a minute and take it all in is to breathe deeply on the essence of the city.

Waterloo Bridge, which stands on a central corner of the river, is perhaps the best vantage point from which to take in the varied sights of English history that nestle themselves around the banks of the river. Look westwards and Big Ben and the Houses of Parliament stand out grandly amid the chaos, neatly set off by the London Eye. Look east and the enormity of Canary Wharf will be blinking in the distance, with nearer treasures – the Tower of London, Tower Bridge, the Lloyd's Building, the length of Embankment – all on show.

But perhaps the most frequent exposure the river gets in everyday conversation comes from cityfolks' need to feel one step ahead of everyone else. Today, Londoners have replaced the former east-west divide with one based on the incision made by the river. Those north of it suggest, with cool snobbery, that there's nothing below the river worth visiting, and even if there were, it's impossible to get down there anyway since cabbies won't make the trip and tube stations are sparse. Those on the south feign indifference to their northern neighbours' posturing.

It's perhaps worth pointing out that the only Londoners who subscribe to the above theories, a self-perpetuating set of myths fuelling a rather nonexistent rivalry, are the ones born outside the city. But the river is caught in the middle, used as a weapon. It's the most obvious reminder that times have changed, that this river will never again have the vital industrial role to play that it held for, literally, millennia. So, then: which side are you on?

Recent cultural developments have addressed the negative attitudes somewhat, the magnificent London Eye at Waterloo being the biggest of all riverside successes. The Millennium Wheel, as it was originally dubbed by a Y2K-frenzied press, has been loved far more by Londoners than the Millennium Dome in Greenwich, offering, as it does, spectacular views of London and beyond, while bringing a futuristic looking element to the river's appearance. In particular, the sight of the snaking river and its hotch-potch array of buildings from many and varied eras are well worth the half-hour journey: the sometimes shambolic but ultimately glorious variety of the city and the river come across wonderfully from on high.

▶ For more on **river tours**, *see p67*.
▶ For more on the sights along the **South Bank**, *see p69*.

Fictional London

Exposure to London's modern fiction can only deepen one's appreciation for and, indeed, love of the city.

If the Londons of Dickens (*see p87* **What the Dickens**) and the Bloomsbury Group (*see p103* **Triangles, circles and squares**) strike you as lost in the peasoupers of the past, this is the chapter for you. The selection of references is meant to be neither comprehensive, nor random, but somewhat partial and more or less up to date. It is how today's London is seen through the eyes of its authors and filmmakers.

ARRIVALS & DEPARTURES

The narrator of **M John Harrison**'s story 'The New Rays' arrives in London to undertake treatment for a mysterious disease. 'Two nights in succession I had dreamed the name of a street, Agar Grove.' Agar Grove exists; it links Camden with Lower Holloway. But Harrison's narrator might well have dreamed up the address of Dr Alexandre. In *Junk Mail* (1995), **Will Self** recalls answering the door to a schizophrenic who asked Self to drive him to Leytonstone. Halfway there, Self challenged the man to pinpoint his destination in the *A–Z*. Replied the man: 'You and I know that the *A–Z* is a plan of what's going to be built.' In this

man's version of London, the Geographers' A–Z Map Co Ltd have dreamed up the entire city.

Harrison is drawn back to Camden in another story, 'The Incalling', from the same collection, *The Ice Monkey* (1983): 'The incalling was held somewhere in that warren of defeated streets which lies between Camden Road and St Pancras, where the old men cough and spit their way under the railway arches every evening to exercise their dogs among the discarded fish-and-chip wrappers.' It sounds grim, but it could be worse. It could be Albania.

Undergoing brainwashing in Sidney J Furie's 1965 film **The Ipcress File**, Harry Palmer (Michael Caine) learns from his captors that he is being held in a Stalinist country ('What's the matter with these zombies? Can't they speak?' 'You don't speak English in Albania.'). Imagine his surprise when, upon his escape, the first thing he sees is a Routemaster bus. Finding a phone box, he pinpoints his location as Austin's Wharf Lane. No such street exists, but in **Len Deighton**'s original novel, the unnamed agent – he would only be named in the films – discovers he's been held in Wood Green.

When shooting Cold War thrillers in the '60s, it was mandatory to include a shot of traffic flowing over Westminster Bridge. (Nowadays, the preferred shot is of the MI6 building by Vauxhall Bridge, though traffic hardly *flows* over any of the bridges any more.) Also made in the '60s, swinging London pictures would be incomplete without a montage of strip clubs and neon signs; Soho having since been sanitised, they now look somewhat dated. Recent cinema's most enchanting representation of the district must be Michael Winterbottom's exquisite **Wonderland** (1999), filmed *vérité*-style with hand-held 16mm cameras in venues such as Duke's Café on Old Compton Street.

Soho is the setting for much of **Robinson** (1994), the first novel by writer and filmmaker Chris Petit. Petit takes the 'shivering, naked heart of the city' and makes it his setting for a study of disintegrating personalities. The narrator is a film editor whose career has run aground when he meets Robinson, a shady but charismatic Soho character. The narrator's fascination with Robinson grows into obsession as the pair frequent Soho pubs and the narrator avoids going home to his wife. 'My horizons shrank until it became hard to leave the area. It felt as though I would be breaking a spell.' Soho becomes a special, idealised place, like **Alain-Fournier**'s lost domain or M John Harrison's Egnaro; indeed, it has its own 'border post', the archway at the western end of Manette Street where the narrator and Robinson first meet, at which 'all obligation could be left behind'.

WAY OUT WEST

Petit's first feature film, **Radio On** (1979) – an English road movie that found in the Westway a stretch of macadam worthy of the genre – created a fusion of electronic/new wave music and dreamlike monochrome cinematography to enhance the ambiguous qualities of its locations. The David Beames character parks his old Rover opposite the Plaza cinema in

Soho features heavily in **Wonderland**.

Camden (demolished in 2000). Later, he stops at Gillette Corner off the Great West Road, then heads west out of town on the M4 past the Agfa building at Brentford listening to David Bowie's 'Always Crashing in the Same Car'. One of the film's most haunting shots is of the car leaving the Westway to join the M41. The camera is way up above, on top of one of the tower blocks near Latimer Road, granting us an aerial view of Shepherd's Bush that encompasses the old Franco-British Exhibition Halls and White City's Central Line tube depot.

The White City Estate is fictionalised in *The Scholar* (1997), the first novel by **Courttia Newland**, himself born and raised in the Bush. It's the powerful story of teenage cousins raised on the Greenside Estate; one gets into petty crime and soft drugs, while the other studies. Both are seeking an escape route. 'Greenside – a term the police use for all of west London – is every estate I've ever been to, both in London and all over the country,' Newland explained in an interview. 'It's not just the White City Estate. Geographically it is, but it's not.'

It's further west, in Hammersmith, that the hapless Jack Vail, hero of **Trevor Hoyle**'s extraordinary novel *Vail* (1984), enjoys the hospitality of TV vamp Virgie Hance. 'Lord Napier Place, Upper Mall,' she tells him. 'Nine o'clock. Bring an erection.' Vail also wanders through Harrods after a bomb attack: 'The goods on display, despite being bomb-blasted and blackened by the smoke, were still of the usual first-rate quality, and amazingly varied. – Black Mamba snakeskin belts. Piano-shaped fudge in 3 kilo boxes. Platinum "His 'n' Hers" roller skates… Pearl-inlaid toilet roll holders.'

Down the road from Harrods, you'll find Hotel 167, at 167 Old Brompton Road. **Jane Solomon** was 20 when her debut novel, *Hotel 167*, was published by Picador in 1993. It tells the story of Maud, who sees a psychiatrist for psychotic depression. Her routine consists in obsessive observation, mental note-taking and cutting her arms with razor blades. The hotel of the title – 'Faintly Tunisian in style… Painted a medium mint green, with a black sign' – is both an aid to auto-erotic/suicidal fantasies and a prop that anchors her chaotic intellect in reality.

UNDERGROUND, OVERGROUND

From Jane Solomon to *King Solomon's Carpet*. **Barbara Vine**'s 1991 novel represents one of the most successful fictional engagements with the Underground. The main character lives in a house overlooking the Jubilee line, and rooms are let out to characters variously linked with the tube (one train-surfs, another busks). In **Emma Tennant**'s *Hotel de Dream* (1976), in which residents of the Westringham boarding

Dislocations

Some were never there, some were once there but have vanished, some have been transposed across town, but many locations in works of London fiction don't exist. Among those in the latter category is **Peter Ackroyd**'s *The House of Dr Dee*, which begins with a journey to a house on Cloak Lane in Clerkenwell. The real Cloak Lane runs parallel to Cannon Street. Other locations half-exist: the opening story of **Clive Barker**'s *Books of Blood* takes place at 65 Tollington Place, a mile south of Barker's then-home in Hillfield Avenue, Crouch End. In reality, the street doesn't go up to 65. Perhaps it's just as well, what with it being an 'intersection on the highway of the dead'.

Others you can imagine existing, fitting into the spaces described. The Scaramanga sisters in **Michael Moorcock**'s *Mother London* live in Bank Cottage on the south side of the Grand Union Canal, in the lee of the Kensal Green gasholders and facing the cemetery across the water. With their garden full of sweet-smelling flowers there is a hint of paradise about the place. In fact, the fences and brick walls that separate the towpath from Sainsbury's and the gasworks are unbroken and fringed only by nettles and weeds.

Fun can even be had with phone numbers. In Mike Hodges' superb London thriller **Croupier** (*pictured*; 1997), scripted by Paul Mayersberg, the phone number of Jack (Clive Owen), a would-be writer who works in a casino, is given as 0171 475 3275. A call to that number at the time of the film's pitiful release was met with a recorded message: 'This service is not compatible with this call.' In late 2000, the equivalent number offered: 'Sorry, there is a fault. Please try again.' In **Courttia Newland**'s story, 'Suicide Note', dialling 020 8932 2005 is how you reach the organisation of the title, which will arrange your death for a fee. No matter how many times you dial that number, it just rings and rings.

And there are streets that exist only in the author's head. The unnamed detective in **Derek Raymond**'s Factory novels lives at the invented Acacia Circus in Earlsfield; the unexplained deaths he investigates are at Thoroughgood Road, Albatross Road and Empire Gate, which you won't find in the *A–Z*. The Nine Foot Drop pub in Hammersmith prompted one disturbed borrower of *The Devil's Home on Leave* to scratch in the margin of his library copy, 'No such pub cunt head'.

---

house invade each other's dreams. Given that the space we inhabit influences our dreams, Tennant could be dreaming dreams once dreamed by another London writer, **Derek Marlowe** (1938-96), for she now lives in the same house in Blenheim Crescent, W11, where Marlowe lived in 1964.

Marlowe's first novel, **A Dandy in Aspic** (1966), made into a film scripted by the author himself, is a hot Cold War thriller that offers up some key London locations. Among them is Chesterfield Street in Mayfair, home to both Somerset Maugham (1874-1965, who lived at no.6) and Beau Brummell (1778-1840, a onetime resident of no.4). Brummell, the original dandy, was a hero of Marlowe's, whose own flamboyant dress sense was expressed in velvet suits, white jeans and fancy shirts. Eberlin, the protagonist of *A Dandy in Aspic*, could afford to dress in

bespoke suits thanks to his working for both the Russians and the British. Eberlin's British bosses were based at 4 Chesterfield Street, while his own rooms were at 24 South Street, W1.

If there is a current shortage of good London writing by women – the *Waterstone's Guide to London Writing*, edited by Nick Rennison, features 32 men in its 'London Since 1945' section, but only nine women – it may have something to do with the fad for 'chick lit' or 'chick fic'. Whatever you want to call these books, they are invariably execrable yet incredibly popular. A ray of light, though, is that good women writers are making repeat appearances in magazines and anthologies: **Kate Pemberton**, **Tamara Smith**, **Jacqueline Lucas**, **Rhonda Carrier** and **Hilaire** are all writing good London stories. Nor are they alone: **Gareth Evans**, **Conrad**

Williams, **Michael Marshall Smith** and **Christopher Kenworthy** are attacking London's fictional possibilities in the short story field away from the 'lad lit' fashion.

If there's one London film location to which we would like to consign all those responsible for 'chick lit' and 'lad lit' – as well as the makers of **Sliding Doors** (1997), for that matter – it's Russell Square tube station. In **Death Line** (1972), plague-ridden ghouls survive in the tunnels by feasting on human flesh. When one of the creatures loses his wife, he emerges into Russell Square station in search of fresh meat.

> **'Dogshit Park, in Amis's *The Information*, could be any London green space.'**

Geoff Ryman's *253*, set on the Bakerloo line between Embankment and Elephant & Castle, was published online in 1996 (www.ryman-novel.com), later appearing in a 'print remix'. The title refers to the number of passengers there would be on a Bakerloo line train if every seat were taken, plus the driver. Ryman uses 253 words to describe each character and tell us what they are thinking. Readers who enjoy *253* would also appreciate **Giles Gordon**'s experimental short story 'Fourteen Stations on the Northern Line', published in *The New SF* (1969, edited by Langdon Jones).

The Northern line calls at King's Cross, home to the UK's most photographed gasholders. The huge Victorian structures are used to good effect in Mike Leigh's **High Hopes** (1988): leading couple Cyril and Shirley live in the scruffy splendour of the Battle Bridge Road/ Stanley Buildings community. And up the Jubilee line, the interiors in Clive Barker's **Hellraiser** (1987) were shot in an empty house on a leafy Dollis Hill avenue. Despite the obvious London location, when Andy Robinson and family move in they're aided by removal men whose transatlantic overdubs are not even in synch. Come the climactic conflagration, we seem to be standing not on Dollis Hill, but on some desolate docklands plain ten miles away.

Docklands locations had been put to better use in **The Long Good Friday** (1979), in which Bob Hoskins played a gangster with a vision for developing the area. Hoskins also played a villain in Neil Jordan's **Mona Lisa** (1986), in which he's hired as Cathy Tyson's chauffeur. Jordan might have overdone King's Cross – the area hasn't seen quite that many tarts for years – but the film takes its locations seriously, from Tyson's assignations in the Park Lane Hotel to her flat in Trinity Court, an art deco block on Gray's Inn Road.

Overdoing it is something **Martin Amis** is fond of, for comic effect. Just as his characters come across more as caricatures, so his locations are exaggerated. The Black Cross in *London Fields* (1989) is so horrible it stands not just for any pub but for all pubs of that type; likewise, Dogshit Park, in *The Information* (1995), could be any London green space.

THE STREETS OF LONDON

It could even be the patch of green in the middle of Powis Square. In Nicolas Roeg and Donald Cammell's **Performance** (1970), on-the-run hood Chas (James Fox) seeks refuge *chez* rock star Turner (Mick Jagger), at the north-west corner of Powis Square, W11. Numbered 81 in the film, the house is, in fact, no.25. As Chas walks up the west side of the square, he passes nos.23-24 before arriving at no.81... and this is *before* trying Turner's hallucinogenic mushrooms. Disappointingly, the interiors were filmed in Belgravia, but the exteriors linger in the mind.

If you walk south down the west side of Powis Square – the direction taken by the white Rolls in the final shot of the film – and go right at the bottom, in a few blocks you hit Portobello Road. Turn right and across the street is the newly reopened Electric Cinema, where Stuart Cooper's **The Disappearance**, based on Derek Marlowe's novel *Echoes of Celandine* (some nice, melancholy South Kensington locations), played in 1977. We're now just yards away from the Travel Bookshop in Blenheim Crescent, as featured in **Notting Hill** (1999). If you want to visit the shop, you'll have to fight your way past fans of the Hugh Grant vehicle.

Walking the streets is the best way to spot the links between different locations. In **Geoff Nicholson**'s novel *Bleeding London* (1997), Mick Wilton falls in with Judy Tanaka, who used to conduct walking tours for a man named Stuart London, who conceives the idea of walking down every street in London, scoring through them in his *A–Z* as he goes. Odd, really, that he doesn't use a *Nicholson Streetfinder*.

Wilton Road, SW1, appears in the title of a story by one of the great English short story writers, **William Sansom** (1912-76). In World War II, Sansom served as a London fireman and he drew on the experience in his first collection, *Fireman Flower* (1944). 'Trouble in Wilton Road, Victoria' appeared in the 1954 collection of 'ballad-stories' *Lord Love Us*. Writing of the open window that 'echoed hopscotch cries and lovebleats from the traffic', he was telling it, in his own unique, lyrical way, how it was. The story evokes a time that's gone for good, much like the poor narrator's Addie, run off with a pilchardman. Used Penguin editions of *Among the Dahlias* and *South* are widely available.

Still in print is **Maxim Jakubowski**'s *London Noir* (1994), a crime anthology. The title of the editor's own contribution, '71-73 Charing Cross Road', is double-edged with irony: the address is that of his own Murder One bookshop. It's the saddest piece, and one hopes it draws only lightly from experience. Stories by **Derek Raymond** and **Mark Timlin** are shot through with the spirit of London. When **Christopher Fowler**'s Dutch filmmakers are casting a film in an old warehouse in 'Perfect Casting', actor Peter Tipping arrives in the Edgware Road 'skirting filthy puddles to locate a small turning between the kebab shops and falafel bars'.

'If the reality of London is the warp, Iain Sinclair's stories are its weft.'

Graham Greene was also familiar with the Edgware Road. He wrote the same haunted cinema story twice. In 'A Little Place Off the Edgware Road', Craven 'knew all the side streets round the Edgware Road only too well'. And well he might. The narrator of a shorter piece, 'All But Empty', passed 'out of the Edgware Road and found it [the same cinema] in a side street'.

Derek Raymond's real name was Robin Cook, but the years he spent out of the UK saw the rise of two other Robin Cooks: a medical thriller writer (remember *Coma*?) and a future foreign secretary. Back in London and propping up the bar at the French House on Soho's Dean Street or the Troy Club on Hanway Street, W1, Cookie became Derek Raymond, author of the Factory series of crime novels. The Factory, a cop shop, is 'in Poland Street bang opposite Marks & Sparks' (*see p38* **Dislocations**).

DIGGING DEEPER

If the last decades of the old millennium belong to any London writers above others, it's those who dig beneath the surface of our metropolitan existence and fiddle around in the interstices of history, those who conjure strange new tales out of the zone between myth and reality; the Mythical Realists, if you like. **Peter Ackroyd**, with his compelling popular blend of London past and present, is one (*see also p38* **Dislocations**). **JG Ballard**, with his unique, increasingly popular and now even respectable blend of science fiction, surrealism and fetishistic obsession, is another. *Crash* (1971), *Concrete Island* (1974) and *High-Rise* (1975) are classic London novels, although technically *Crash* is more a London Airport (as was) work. The concrete island where Robert Maitland is marooned after his Jaguar leaves the road is the one we see in the aerial shot of *Radio On*.

There are two more names that have been conspicuously absent from this chapter so far. The first is **Iain Sinclair**'s. Welsh-born, Dublin-educated, East End-naturalised, Sinclair worked as a book dealer and parks gardener, self-publishing his own darkly intuitive poetry. Goldmark Books of Uppingham put out his first novel, *White Chappell, Scarlet Tracings*, a compelling fusion of low-life book dealers and Ripper lore. *Downriver* and *Radon Daughters*, quintessential London novels, followed.

The most uncompromising writer around, Sinclair calls his work 'future memories'. Acknowledged by Ackroyd, he has become *the* London authority (at least before Ackroyd's *London: The Biography*), a *Newsnight* conscript, merciless iconoclast, his blistering attack on the Dome (*Sorry Meniscus*, 1999) as inevitable as the failure of the great blister itself. To extract locations from his output is pointless: they're present on every page. Speculations about the mythology of London run as deep in his fiction as the city's lost rivers. If the reality of London is the warp, his stories are its weft.

The films Sinclair has made with Chris Petit – *The Cardinal and the Corpse* (1993), *The Falconer* (1998), *Asylum* (2000) – explore the rich territory where fiction and documentary overlap. In *Asylum*, they visit the other so far absent name, **Michael Moorcock**, who is said to embody a thousand years of London's literary history. His *Mother London* (1988) is probably the best London novel of all time. If your tight schedule permits you to read only one title recommended in this chapter, then it should be *Mother London*; happily, the recent publication of a supposed sequel, *King of the City* (2000), means that it's back in print.

And if you have time to watch only one London film, it's got to be **London** (1994), directed by Patrick Keiller. It's both the oddest and most engaging film ever made about the capital, the sort of thing you might expect if a surrealist were to become head of a socio-geographic documentary film-making unit. There's no plot as such, and no characters apart from the voice of the narrator (Paul Scofield) and his friend, Robinson, whom we never see. A slyly humorous blend of satire, anecdote and myth-making, it is a unique triumph. Do see it.

Nicholas Royle is the author of London novels 'The Matter of the Heart' and 'The Director's Cut' (Abacus) and editor of 'The Time Out Book of London Short Stories Vol 2' (Penguin).

▶ For more on **spoken word**, *see p284.*
▶ For more **London books & films**, *see p380.*

Accommodation

Accommodation   **43**

Feature boxes

Good Value Accommodation
in Central London

WESTPOINT HOTEL

170–172 SUSSEX GARDENS, HYDE PARK, LONDON W2 1TP

- ☑ Pleasant central location
- ☑ Convenient for all major sights, museums & theatres
- ☑ Close to all shopping districts, Oxford Street, Piccadilly Circus
- ☑ Clean, comfortable, well decorated rooms
- ☑ All rooms with ensuite shower, toilet, colour TV & radio
- ☑ Lift to all floors
- ☑ Free luggage room facility
- ☑ 2 minutes from Paddington Station, Heathrow Express & Airbus

RATES PER PERSON PER NIGHT		
	LOW SEASON	HIGH SEASON
Singles	from £ 44	from £ 49
Doubles	from £ 29	from £ 34
Triples	from £ 24	from £ 28
Family room	from £ 21	from £ 23
includes continental breakfast, service charge and all taxes		

Tel: (020) 7402 0281
Fax: (020) 7224 9114
www.westpointhotel.com
e-mail info@westpointhotel.com

ABBEY COURT HOTEL

174 SUSSEX GARDENS, HYDE PARK, LONDON W2 1TP

- ☑ Convenient location 2 minutes from Paddington Station, Airbus & Heathrow Rail Express
- ☑ Easy access to all London's important tourist sights, shopping districts and theatres
- ☑ Ensuite shower and w.c. in all rooms
- ☑ Lift to all floors
- ☑ Each room with colour TV, radio & intercom
- ☑ Car parking by arrangement

RATES PER PERSON PER NIGHT		
	LOW SEASON	HIGH SEASON
Singles	from £ 44	from £ 49
Doubles	from £ 29	from £ 34
Triples	from £ 24	from £ 28
Family room	from £ 21	from £ 23
includes continental breakfast, service charge and all taxes		

Tel: (020) 7402 0704
Fax: (020) 7262 2055
www.abbeycourt.com
e-mail info@abbeycourt.com

SASS HOTEL

11 CRAVEN TERRACE, HYDE PARK, LONDON W2 3QD

Sass Hotel offers superb value for money accommodation in a convenient, quiet location, just 3 minutes walk from Hyde Park and Lancaster Gate tube station. Paddington station with Heathrow Rail Express and Airbus is just 5 minutes away. Easy access to all London's famous sights and entertainment.

- ☑ All rooms with ensuite shower, toilet & colour TV
- ☑ Friendly personal service
- ☑ Car parking by arrangement

RATES PER PERSON PER NIGHT		
	LOW SEASON	HIGH SEASON
Twins	from £ 24	from £ 29
Doubles	from £ 24	from £ 28
Triples	from £ 21	from £ 24
Family room	from £ 18	from £ 21.50
includes continental breakfast, service charge and all taxes		

Tel: (020) 7262 2325
Fax: (020) 7262 0889
www.sasshotel.com
e-mail info@sasshotel.com

Accommodation

London offers a fine choice of hotels, but it'll cost you dearly.

The year 2000 was a landmark one for London's hoteliers. The city reached its 1995 target of 10,000 new rooms, which means, if not cheaper prices – this is London, after all – at least greater choice. The most spectacular launch of the year was the Conran-designed **Great Eastern Hotel** (*see p44*), itself indicative of the burgeoning trends for designer hotels and East End locations. The **Sanderson** (*see p47*), the latest flamboyant creation by über-cool duo Ian Schrager and Philippe Starck, continued where **St Martin's Lane** (*see p47*) left off. And Tim and Kit Kemp, purveyors of modern Englishness and fast becoming the Schrager and Starck of trad hotels, opened the **Charlotte Street Hotel** (*see p49*), their most striking yet.

The popularity of the Kemps' 'classical modern' style (they're presently revamping 16 Sumner Place, too) hints at an imminent backlash against the trendier designer hotels. The typical aesthetic package – minimalist rooms, modernist furniture, Japanese garden/restaurant, fashion-model staff – is now verging on self-parody, and a growing chorus of critics have dismissed 'Hotel Cools' as tired, homogenised, style-over-substance joints. But despite the sniping, bookings remain healthy.

Speaking of bookings, it would be foolish to show up in London without one. The city's hotel sector may be rapidly expanding, but it can still barely keep up with the spiralling demand. There's also no getting away from the fact that London's hotels are Europe's second most expensive, behind only Paris. And while London is spoiled for choice in the luxury market, stylish, middle-range hotels are notoriously lacking. If you're not fussed about personality, a chain hotel is an easy option (*see p50* **Chain reaction**). However, half the fun is in avoiding the name-brand chains and looking for the kind of more personal, characterful options on which, with a couple of exceptions, we've tried to focus.

Information & booking

If you haven't booked ahead, visit a London Tourist Board centre (*see p377*). Staff will search for an appropriate booking, within your area and price range, for a £5 fee. If you book a few weeks in advance, a deposit may be required. The LTB also publishes *Where to Stay and What to Do* (£4.99).

Most hotels now have their own websites through which bookings can be made. You can also peruse what's available and make bookings at the LTB website.

London Tourist Board Hotel Booking Line

7604 2890/www.londontown.com. **Open** 9am-6pm Mon-Fri; 9am-1pm Sat; closed Sun.

Visitors with disabilities

While we've tried to indicate which hotels offer rooms adapted for the needs of disabled guests, check specifics with the hotel directly before booking. A useful organisation is **Holiday Care**, which has information on accessible hotels in the UK for the disabled and elderly.

Holiday Care

Information Unit, Second floor, Imperial Buildings, Victoria Road, Horley, Surrey RH6 7PZ (01293 774535/www.holidaycare.org.uk).

Complaints

To lodge a complaint about any hotel, inform the management in person, and then, if necessary, in writing. The LTB will, depending on the circumstances, look into complaints, regardless of whether you booked through them. *Time Out* always appreciates any feedback on any of the hotels listed here.

Hotels

London's highest concentration of big-name, starry hotels – your Hiltons and Four Seasons *et al* – are in Mayfair. However, we're pleased to see that a plethora of hotels are recognising the East End's potential – even the Hilton is getting in on the buzz, with a Petticoat Lane address in the works for 2003 – while the City and Canary Wharf are currently hubs of building activity.

Further down the ladder, Bloomsbury brims with mid-priced hotels. And for cheaper beds, try Ebury Street near Victoria (SW1), Gower Street in Bloomsbury (WC1), and Earl's Court (SW5). Other areas worth exploring for small budget hotels include Bayswater and Paddington (W2) and South Kensington (SW7). For gay and lesbian accommodation, *see p305*.

Prices & classification

British hotels are now classified according to a star system agreed upon by the English Tourism Council, the AA and the RAC. However, we haven't listed star ratings here; instead, we've classified hotels according to the price of the cheapest double room per night.

Note, too, that all the room rates listed here are inclusive of 17.5 per cent VAT (sales tax). Despite the fact that VAT is included in the quoted price of almost everything in the UK, most of the hotels listed under the Deluxe and Expensive brackets below sneakily quote room prices exclusive of the tax, presumably to soften the shock of the prices. Don't be taken in, and always ask whether the price you're being quoted includes tax or not. After adding the VAT, we've rounded the rates up or down to the nearest pound; to check the rates without VAT, simply divide the quoted price by 1.175.

Rates rarely fluctuate from season to season, but if there is an 'off-season', it's in January and February: many hotels do discounts and some deluxe hotels offer special weekend breaks. Always ask for a special rate when booking.

All deluxe and expensive hotels come with an en suite bath and/or shower and toilet. Most cheaper hotels involve sharing bathrooms. 'Including breakfast' often means continental – sometimes little more than tea and toast – whereas 'English breakfasts' are of the glorious, fried-everything variety.

Deluxe (over £250)

All hotels in this bracket offer air-conditioning, bar(s), concierge, laundry, limousine service and restaurant(s), and can arrange babysitting; in-room services for all include dataport, mini-bar, phone, turndown and 24-hour room service. Other services are listed by each hotel's review.

Blakes

33 Roland Gardens, South Kensington, SW7 3PF (7370 6701/fax 7373 0442/www.hempelhotel.com). Gloucester Road or South Kensington tube. **Rooms** 51. **Rates** £194 single; £282-£382 double; £605-£934 suite. **Credit** AmEx, DC, MC, V. **Map** p397 D11.

Opened in the early '80s and arguably the blueprint for many of today's boutique hotels, Blakes uses Far Eastern decor to evoke sumptuous Bangkok rather than the stark Muji aesthetic so popular of late. Designer Anouska Hempel eschews the minimalist white look in favour of dramatic blacks, browns and crimsons, accompanied by rich oriental exotica. The decadent boudoirs are the opposite of clinical cool, filled with antique treasures, silk embroidered cushions and exquisite marquetry chests. The basement restaurant has been described as 'an opium den managed by Coco Chanel', an apt summary of the

whole hotel. Celebs love its discreet air, so if ogling stars is your thing, try St Martin's Lane (*see p47*). For a boutique hotel that's been around forever, Blakes is a long way from passing its sell-by date. **Hotel services** *Business services. Cooking facilities. Garden. No-smoking rooms. Parking.* **Room services** *TV: satellite/VCR.*

Covent Garden Hotel

10 Monmouth Street, Covent Garden, WC2H 2HB (7806 1000/fax 7806 1100/www.firmdale.com). Covent Garden or Leicester Square tube. **Rooms** 58. **Rates** £223 single; £258-£329 double; £382-£699 suite. **Credit** AmEx, MC, V. **Map** p399 L6.

After Schrager and Starck, Tim and Kit Kemp are fast becoming London's most celebrated hotel design team – Charlotte Street, Dorset Square (for both, *see p49*), the Pelham (*see p50*), known for their high-gloss, modern-classical fusion of period elegance and contemporary luxury. The plush rooms here feature bold fabrics, four-poster beds, and mahogany and marble bathrooms. Quirky touches, such as upholstered mannequins and Jelly Bellies in the mini-bars, reflect the general showbiz ambience (there's a screening room in the basement). The loveliest spot in the hotel is by the fireside on the bright plaid sofas of the rather fetching lounge. **Hotel services** *Business services. Gym.* **Room services** *TV: pay movies/satellite/VCR.*

Dorchester

Park Lane, Mayfair, W1A 2HJ (7629 8888/fax 7409 0114/www.dorchesterhotel.com). Green Park or Hyde Park Corner tube. **Rooms** 248. **Rates** £323-£347 single; £358-£394 double; £646-£2,262 suite. **Credit** AmEx, DC, MC, V. **Map** p400 G7.

Sister to the Beverly Hills Hotel, the Dorchester epitomises old-school Hollywood glamour from a pre-Met Bar age when stars really were stars: Liberace's piano is in the bar, Prince Philip had his stag night here, and the OTT Oliver Messel Suite – where Liz Taylor and Richard Burton honeymooned – features gold leaf toilet seats, yellow silk walls, and, hilariously, fake bookshelves that hide a mini-bar. Other rooms are similarly dripping in slightly faded '30s glitz. But there's nothing faded about the lobby, an opulent yellow-gold marble space with Corinthian columns and Asprey & Garrard diamonds displayed in showcases. As for the fairytale ballroom, well, they don't do ballrooms at the Metropolitan, do they? **Hotel services** *Beauty salon. Business services. Disabled: adapted rooms. Garden. Gym. No-smoking floors.* **Room services** *TV: cable/pay movies/satellite/VCR.*

Great Eastern Hotel

Liverpool Street, The City, EC2M 7QN (7618 5000/fax 7618 5001/www.great-eastern-hotel.co.uk). Liverpool Street tube/rail. **Rooms** 267. **Rates** £229 single; £264-£300 double; £358-£605 suite. **Credit** AmEx, DC, MC, V. **Map** p405 Q6.

This once neglected Victorian railway hotel has been reborn as a mammoth urban style mecca, a City rival to St Martin's Lane (*see p47*). Close to corporate

The best Hotels

For style on a budget
The **Rushmore Hotel** (see p55).

For free bathroom toiletries
The Bulgari range at the **Ritz** (see p46).

For getting away from it all
The **Plough Inn** (see p55).

For butler service
The **Lanesborough** (see p45).

For the big museums
The **Gallery Hotel** (see p53).

For the cooler-than-thou
The **Sanderson** (see p47).

For a slice of Florida in Earl's Court
The **Amsterdam Hotel** (see p54).

For anyone with a backpack
The **Generator** (see p57).

For all-round great value
The **Vancouver Studios** (see p57).

For running into rent-a-celebs
The bar at the **Metropolitan** (see p46).

offices and to fashionable Hoxton, Shoreditch and Clerkenwell, the clientele is a mixture of suits and beautiful people: the lobby has modern art on loan from the Whitechapel Art Gallery (see p155) and copies of the *Financial Times* everywhere, as a Guggenheim-style rotunda and six-storey atrium overlook a Zen rock garden lounge. If you've read your style mags, you've seen the rooms: Eames chairs, Jacobsen lamps, chocolate shagpile rugs and crisp white bed linens. The three bars include a gorgeous, wood-panelled Jacobean pastiche, the George, while among the four restaurants are a mandatory Japanese joint and the heavily listed Aurora, which boasts a magnificent stained glass dome.
Hotel services *Beauty salon. Business services. Disabled: adapted rooms. Gym. No-smoking floor.* **Room services** *TV: cable/satellite.*

Halcyon Hotel
81 Holland Park, Kensington, W11 3RZ (7727 7288/fax 7729 8516/www.thehalcyon.com). Holland Park tube. **Rooms** 42. **Rates** £205-£258 single; £323 double; £370-£775 suite. **Credit** AmEx, DC, MC, V.
Amid the elegant white townhouses of leafy, residential Holland Park sits the equally elegant Halcyon, which brings the tranquil garden feel of its neighbourhood indoors with a quiet grace. While

London is saturated with by-the-numbers, antique-filled hotels, the charm here is in the subtle sense of exclusivity – this is a hush-hush celeb favourite – and the genuinely eccentric design touches: some rooms are decorated in Egyptian and Russian themes, while the summery Halcyon Suite has an oriental-style conservatory overlooking gardens. Some bathrooms have corner tubs or jacuzzis; the scent of fresh cut flowers wafts through the air. The pretty French restaurant Aix is headed up by Nigel Davis, former head chef at the Ivy.
Hotel services *Business services. Garden. Parking.* **Room services** *TV: cable/pay movies/satellite/ VCR/web TV.*

Hempel
31-5 Craven Hill Gardens, Bayswater, W2 3EA (7298 9000/fax 7402 4666/www.the-hempel.co.uk). Lancaster Gate or Queensway tube/Paddington tube/rail. **Rooms** 47, 6 apartments. **Rates** £300 single; £347 double; £517-£1,527 suite.
Credit AmEx, DC, MC, V. **Map** p394 C6.
The Hempel makes other hotels' attempts at minimalism and the Zen aesthetic seem laughable: this is feng shui at its most breathtaking. The trance-inducing, white-on-white lobby is part-chic gallery, part-Buddhist retreat: gazing skyward up the five-storey atrium must have a great deal in common with experiencing one of those near-death, white-light epiphanies. You don't so much as walk through this hotel, you float: one of the monochromatic bedrooms even has a bed that hangs from the ceiling. The stark Japanese-influenced rooms – too clinical for some tastes – feature Muji-ish storage compartments with which to banish clutter and mini-bars stocked with inhalable oxygen in a can. Translucent stairs lead down to the implausibly pricey I-Thai restaurant.
Hotel services *Disabled: adapted rooms. Garden. Parking.* **Room services** *TV: cable/pay movies/ satellite/VCR.*

Lanesborough
Hyde Park Corner, Belgravia, SW1X 7TA (7259 5599/fax 7259 5606/www.lanesborough.com). Hyde Park Corner tube. **Rooms** 95. **Rates** £311-£376 single; £435-£529 double; £670-£5,288 suite.
Credit AmEx, DC, MC, V. **Map** p400 G8.
Housed in what was once St George's Hospital, the Lanesborough combines Regency formality, unbridled luxury and mind-boggling technology. The Ritz (see p46), the Savoy (see p47) and the Dorchester (see p44) may have instant name recognition, but surely nothing matches the opulence here. The marble, butler-filled lobby positively gleams, while the stately Library bar features vintage cognac for up to £750 a swill; surely too much for even the most generous expense account. The Conservatory restaurant, with its palms and chinoiserie, is a swish remake of the Brighton Pavilion. But the real extravagance is reserved for the rich mahogany bedrooms, in which space-age entertainment centres bring you digital movies, music, the web, software and email in a

jaw-dropping demonstration of this information age we keep hearing about. Personal butlers are available at your beck and call, 24-7-365.

Hotel services *Business services. Disabled: adapted rooms. Gym. No-smoking rooms. Parking.* **Room services** *TV: cable/satellite/DVD/web TV.*

Metropolitan

Old Park Lane, Mayfair, W1Y 4LB (7447 1000/ fax 7447 1147/www.metropolitan.co.uk). Green Park or Hyde Park Corner tube. **Rooms** £300 single; £341-£382 double; £482-£1,645 suite. **Credit** AmEx, DC, MC, V. **Map** p400 G8.

Like a living, breathing *Wallpaper** magazine shoot, this legendary style haunt has launched numerous imitations, but nobody does modernist, '60s apartment chic better. Probably the highest concentration of black-clad young things in London congregate here, blending in with the staff's DKNY/ Issey Miyake garb. The rooms aren't as cold and clinical as you might expect: soft mauves, olives and natural woods add warmth to the requisite off-whites and technological gadgetry, a feeling enhanced by the lush park views. The Met Bar has become as hackneyed a showbiz hangout as exists in London, but while trendy Japanese eaterie Nobu can also operate a snobby door policy, there is a banquet-style, spillover room for plebeian diners.

Hotel services *Beauty salon. Business services. Gym. No-smoking floors. Parking.* **Room services** *TV: cable/pay movies/satellite/VCR.*

No.5 Maddox Street

5 Maddox Street, Mayfair, W1R 9LE (7647 0200/fax 7647 0300/www.living-rooms.co.uk). Oxford Circus tube. **Rooms** 12. **Rates** £265 double; £294-£370 suite; £470 2-bedroom; £646 3-bedroom. **Credit** AmEx, DC, MC, V. **Map** p398 J6.

Part ultra-hip metropolitan apartment, part tiny Japanese hotel, the aesthetic here is bamboo floors meet state-of-the-art technology. The amazing lobby aquarium fit is for a Bond villain's pad, while the rooms combine traditional Japanese flourishes with contemporary furnishings in chocolate, beige and white; faux sable throws adorn the beds and linen kimonos the closet. The kitchen and mini-bars are fully stocked with Planet Organic and Ben and Jerry's, and you get the feeling these apartments host cooler parties than you'd find in neighbouring Soho. Round-the-clock room service will arrange anything from grocery shopping to personal chefs.

Hotel services *Business services. Cooking facilities.* **Room services** *TV: satellite/VCR.*

One Aldwych

1 Aldwych, Holborn, WC2B 4BZ (7300 1000/fax 7300 1001/www.onealdwych.com). Covent Garden or Temple tube/Charing Cross tube/rail. **Rooms** 105. **Rates** £323 single; £347-£417 double; £523-£1,339 suite. **Credit** AmEx, DC, MC, V. **Map** p401 M7.

In a sea of sometimes painfully trendy hotels, One Aldwych stands out from the pack. Less showbiz and hyper-cool than some competitors, it's also more elegant and less intimidating. Housed in a restored

One Aldwych: one of London's finest.

Edwardian bank building, the simplicity of the lobby bar is offset by stunning modern art, dramatic floral sculptures and full-length arched windows. The rooms epitomise understated modern luxury, where God is in the details: bathrooms with miniature, bendable TVs, and inspired floral displays that manage to make fresh peppers look arty. The shimmering basement lap pool plays Bach underwater. But bells and whistles aside, the best feature of the hotel is the unpretentious, international staff.

Hotel services *Beauty salon. Cooking facilities. Disabled: adapted rooms. Gym. No-smoking floors. Parking. Swimming pool (indoor).* **Room services** *TV: cable/pay movies/satellite/VCR.*

Ritz

150 Piccadilly, St James's, W1V 9DG (7493 8181/fax 7493 2687/www.theritzhotel.co.uk). Green Park tube. **Rooms** 131. **Rates** £347 single; £405-£488 double; £570-£887 suite. **Credit** AmEx, MC, V. **Map** p400 J8.

The Ritz has just undergone a multi-million-pound refurbishment – haven't they all? – rescuing it from '80s unfashionability and returning it to its original Louis XVI splendour, which means heavy on the gold-leaf moulding, rococo mirrors and extravagant chandeliers. Prince Charles throws his staff Christmas parties here, and Barbara Cartland loved the place: if aristo-spotting is your hobby, you'll be in paradise. The luxurious rooms call to mind *Dynasty* as much as Versailles: largely done up in pinks and creams, with 24 carat-gold paint trim, damask silk bedspreads, and sumptuous floral carpets. You can almost justify the rates by stocking up on the bathroom's Bulgari toiletries.

The gym here is surprisingly small for a hotel of its size and stature, but then you don't come to the Ritz for Stairmasters.

Hotel services *Beauty salon. Business services. Garden. Gym. No-smoking floors.* **Room services** *TV: cable/satellite/VCR.*

St Martin's Lane

45 St Martin's Lane, Covent Garden, WC2N 4HX (0800 634 5500/7300 5500/fax 7300 5501). Covent Garden or Leicester Square tube. **Rooms** 204. **Rates** £288 single; £323-£411 double; £423-£529 suite. **Credit** AmEx, DC, MC, V. **Map** p401 L7.

Theatrical minimalism is the best way to describe this frighteningly fashionable Schrager-Starck collaboration. There's no sign outside – if you have to ask, you're not cool enough to stay here – but the luminescent yellow glass doors and designer-clad doormen are a giveaway. The lobby induces awe and giggles in equal measures. Oversized columns and a white/fluorescent yellow colour scheme play host to the usual quirky Starck creations: gold molar-teeth stools, giant chess pieces *et al*. In contrast to the vibrancy of the lobby, the serene rooms are textbook guides to minimalism: crisp and white, white and crisp, it's almost a shame to touch anything for fear of soiling it. The celeb-filled Light Bar is generally members and hotel guests only. Still, there's nothing stopping you checking out the lobby, as good an expression of the zeitgeist as you'll find in London.

Hotel services *Business services. Disabled: adapted rooms. Garden. Gym. No-smoking floors. Parking.* **Room services** *TV: satellite/VCR.*

Sanderson

50 Berners Street, Fitzrovia, W1T 3NG (7300 1400/fax 7300 1401/reservation@sanderson. schragerhotels.com). Oxford Circus or Tottenham Court Road tube. **Rooms** 150. **Rates** £229-£317 single; £258-£347 double; £441-£881 suite. **Credit** AmEx, DC, MC, V. **Map** p398 J5.

The latest playful style hotel from Schrager and Starck, the 'urban spa'-themed Sanderson is a dreamier version of St Martin's Lane (*see above*) with a Fitzrovia (sorry… ugh… *Noho*) address. The exterior of the building – originally the head office of Sanderson fabrics, hence the name – is ugly-chic, '50s office block style. Male models guard the entrance to the fantasy-land lobby, all billowy diaphanous curtains, avant-garde furniture you're afraid to sit in, and gilt-edged Louis XV touches. The minimalist, white and silver bedrooms feature sleigh-type beds, and more sheer flowing curtains which act as walls to the glass bathrooms. The cave-like Purple Bar, all dark Venetian glass and dim-lighting, is perfect for cocooning, while, off the lobby, the light, sophisticated Long Bar feels like part of the adjoining Japanese garden. Clean and serene.

Hotel services *Beauty salon. Business services. Disabled: adapted rooms. Garden. Gym. No-smoking floors. Parking.* **Room services** *TV: cable/satellite/DVD.*

Savoy

Strand, Covent Garden, WC2R OEU (7836 4343/fax 7240 6040/www.savoy-group.co.uk). Covent Garden or Embankment tube/Charing Cross tube/rail. **Rooms** 228. **Rates** £329-£347 single; £388-£435 double; £523-£1,739 suite. **Credit** AmEx, DC, MC, V. **Map** p401 L7.

While the Ritz (*see p46*) and the Dorchester (*see p44*) are ornate, the Savoy's grandeur is more dignified and gentlemen's club in feel. Built in 1889, there's a great deal of neo-classical elegance here, but there are also some deco touches in evidence from its 1920 expansion, seen especially in the wonderfully glam American Bar and the doorways to the relatively unspectacular – for these prices – rooms. Still, history emanates from these walls: Monet painted his Thames views from his window, Noel Coward played piano, and Elton John overflowed his bathtub. The rooftop indoor pool is tiny, but a jetstream system means you can swim in one spot for hours and still get a great workout. Oh, and the massive watering-can shower heads are the best in London.

Hotel services *Beauty salon. Business services. Gym. No-smoking rooms. Parking. Swimming pool (indoor).* **Room services** *TV: cable/pay movies/satellite/VCR.*

Expensive (£151-£250)

All Expensive hotels offer concierge, laundry and a limousine service, and can arrange babysitting; in-room services include a dataport and a phone. As before, other services are listed below each review.

Academy Hotel

21 Gower Street, Bloomsbury, WC1E 6HG (7631 4115/fax 7636 3442/www.etontownhouse.com). Goodge Street or Tottenham Court Road tube. **Rooms** 49. **Rates** £135 single; £170-£194 double; £217-£265 suite. **Credit** AmEx, DC, MC, V. **Map** p399 K5.

Recently refurbished, this elegant Laura Ashley-esque townhouse hotel is soft, fragrant and floral, with gleaming wood floors and a *House & Garden*-style, yellow and green colour scheme. The bar, by contrast, is bright, bold and urban. Designed to compete with Kit Kemp's Firmdale hotels, the prices are better but the antiques less stunning. The rooms, though, are subtle and polished, and there's a soothing air throughout. One of the five terraced houses (with eight bedrooms) can be sealed off and rented for £1,500 per day; perfect for wedding parties.

Hotel services *Air-conditioning. Bar. Business services. Garden. No-smoking rooms. Restaurant.* **Room services** *Mini-bar. Room service (7am-midnight). Turndown. TV.*

Blooms

7 Montague Street, Bloomsbury, WC1B 5BP (7323 1717/fax 7636 6498/www.bloomshotel.com). Holborn or Russell Square tube. **Rooms** 27. **Rates** £130 single; £195-£205 double. **Credit** AmEx, DC, MC, V. **Map** p399 L5.

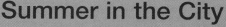

Another tasteful period townhouse hotel, Blooms is most notable for its clubby library bar with 35 malt whiskies, a secluded ivy-covered walled garden backing onto the British Museum, and a selection of themed rooms: the showy Theatre Royal room, the cricket-themed Lord's room, and a Dickens suite with various associated paraphernalia. It's always nice to find a period hotel with a lift, too.

Hotel services *Bar. Garden. Laundry. Restaurant.* **Room services** *Room service (24hrs). Turndown. TV: satellite.*

Charlotte Street Hotel

15 Charlotte Street, Fitzrovia, W1P 1HB (7806 2000/fax 7806 2002/www.firmdale.com). Goodge Street or Tottenham Court Road tube. **Rooms** 52. **Rates** £206 single; £229-£329 double; £347-£529 suite. **Credit** AmEx, MC, V. **Map** p399 J5.

The latest boutique hotel in Kit and Tim Kemp's mini-empire – the others being the Covent Garden (*see p43*), Dorset Square (*see below*) and the Pelham (*see p50*) – comes with the same winning formula: exquisite period decor and modern creature comforts, English understatement and American gloss. Kemp largely uses soft beiges, greys and greens here, mixing it up with the odd splash of colour, African print or brave plaid-floral combination. The lobby is a warm expanse of burnished pine, and the fireside lounge, a Kemp staple, features art from the Bloomsbury Group.

Hotel services *Air-conditioning. Bar. Business services. Disabled: adapted rooms. Gym. Parking. Restaurant.* **Room services** *Mini-bar. Room service (24hrs). Turndown. TV: DVD/satellite/VCR.*

Dorset Square Hotel

39 Dorset Square, Marylebone, NW1 6QN (7723 7874/fax 7724 3328/www.firmdale.com). Baker Street tube/Marylebone tube/rail. **Rooms** 38. **Rates** £135 single; £154-£247 double; £282 suite. **Credit** AmEx, MC, V. **Map** p384 F4.

Located opposite the original Lord's cricket ground, this restored Regency townhouse – the first Kit Kemp creation – brings an elegant country estate feel to central London. A grandfather clock, hunting prints, fireside library and classical music soundtrack give the place an autumnal, pastoral air. The Lord's connection explains the cricket touches, and the cellar restaurant, the Potting Shed, is a rustic, *Country Life* affair, with garden pots, dried flowers, and pretty baskets. Guests have access to the historic private garden out front, and the antique-laden, flower-filled rooms feature luxurious marble bathrooms.

Hotel services *Air-conditioning. Bar(s). Business services. Garden. Gym. No-smoking rooms. Restaurant(s).* **Room services** *Mini-bar. Room service (24hrs). Turndown. TV: satellite/VCR.*

The Gore

189 Queen's Gate, South Kensington, SW7 5EX (7584 6601/fax 7589 8127/www.gorehotel.com). Gloucester Road tube. **Rooms** 53. **Rates** £164-£182 single; £206-£311 double; £335 suite. **Credit** AmEx, DC, MC, V. **Map** p397 D9.

Like sister hotel Hazlitt's (*see below*), the Gore permeates lived-in, historic charm as opposed to ersatz period feel. Owner and antique collector Peter McKay scours reclamation yards and auctions to cram this comfortable, creaky Victorian townhouse with eclectic old art and furniture, including 5,000 paintings and prints and magnificent oversized mahogany headboards. For a treat, splash out on the Tudor Room, an Elizabethan suite featuring a 16th-century four-poster, a minstrels' gallery and a wooden Thomas Crapper throne. Drama queens might fancy splurging on the Venus Room for a chance to sleep in Judy Garland's old bed.

Hotel services *Bar. Business services. No-smoking floors. Restaurants.* **Room services** *Mini-bar. Room service (24hrs). TV: satellite/VCR.*

Hazlitt's

6 Frith Street, Soho, W1V 5TZ (7434 1771/fax 7439 1524/www.hazlittshotel.com). Tottenham Court Road tube. **Rooms** 23. **Rates** £164 single; £206 double; £241 triple; £352 suite. **Credit** AmEx, DC, MC, V. **Map** p399 K6.

Following its appearance in Bill Bryson's *Notes from a Small Island*, business is booming at this 18th-century townhouse hotel. Not that it needed the plug, mind: this one-time home to essayist William Hazlitt is a legendary literary haunt. Hazlitt's oozes historical charm: the floors are lopsided, the furniture is worn and everything feels slightly frayed, but this only adds to the authentic charm. The staff are young and good-humoured, and there are modem points in the comfy rooms. Literary guests from Ted Hughes to JK Rowling have left signed editions of their books in the library: chances are if they've made fiction prize shortlists, they've stayed here. There's no bar or restaurant, but just step outside into Soho or curl up in the library with a good book.

Hotel services *Air-conditioning. Business services.* **Room services** *Room service (24hrs). TV: satellite/VCR.*

Montague on the Gardens

15 Montague Street, Bloomsbury, WC1 5BJ (7637 1001/fax 7637 2516/www.redcarnationhotels.com). Holborn or Russell Square tube. **Rooms** 104. **Rates** £188 single; £211-£247 double; £247-£493 suite. **Credit** AmEx, DC, MC, V. **Map** p399 L5.

If trendy minimalist hotels are getting on your nerves, check out the exquisite gaudiness of the Montague, decked out like a Christmas tree with period glitz. Bordering on kitsch, the lounge's elaborate chandeliers, crimson walls, chintz and velvet drapes create a feeling of extravagant luxury from a bygone era. A flowery motif dominates throughout, from the fragrant conservatories and handsome garden to the busy bedspreads, curtains and wallpaper adorning the bedrooms. There's a gym and sauna and conference facilities galore.

Hotel services *Air-conditioning. Bar. Business services. Cooking facilities. Disabled: adapted room. Garden. Gym. No-smoking rooms. Restaurant.* **Room services** *Mini-bar. Room service (24hrs). Turndown. TV: pay movies/satellite.*

myhotel bloomsbury

11-13 Bayley Street, Fitzrovia, WC1B 3HD (7667 6000/fax 7667 6001/www.myhotels.co.uk). Goodge Street or Tottenham Court Road tube. **Rooms** 76. **Rates** £200 single; £247-£288 double; £417 suite. **Credit** AmEx, DC, MC, V. **Map** p399 K5.

Feng shui design principles and attentive, individualised service – hence the name, although pedants like us will point out that the hotel is actually in Fitzrovia, not Bloomsbury – are the niche of this sleek, chic hotel. The minimalist lobby and bar buzz with young groovers and shakers. Meticulously placed flowers and candles add a hint of colour to the lobby's off-white/grey tones; the pine library has internet access and coffee table design books; there's a jinja therapy room and modern fitness suite. Oriental-style corridors lead to airy Conran-designed rooms, decorated with pristine white sheets, laminated wood furniture and white orchids. **Hotel services** *Air-conditioning. Bar. Beauty salon. Business services. Gym. No-smoking floors.* **Room services** *Room service (24hrs). Turndown. TV: pay movies/satellite/VCR.*

Pelham

15 Cromwell Place, South Kensington, SW7 2LA (7589 8288/fax 7584 8444/www.firmdale.com). South Kensington tube. **Rooms** 51. **Rates** £170 single; £211-£276 double; £347-£699 suite. **Credit** AmEx, MC, V. **Map** p397 D10.

Another Kit Kemp hotel, this is virtually a carbon copy of the muted period luxury of the Dorset Square (*see p49*), only with bigger rooms and a trendy SW7 location. It gets packed with fashionistas during London Fashion Week – the wardrobes are huge – but it's also the place to stay during the Chelsea Flower Show. The rooms range from subtle greys and beiges to bright florals and plaids; all have portable phones and a turndown service, while room 104 has rather wonderful grey flannel pinstripe walls. There are get-to-know you sessions every Wednesday in the basement restaurant, Kemps. **Hotel services** *Air-conditioning. Bar. Business services. Parking. Restaurant.* **Room services** *Mini-bar. Room service (24hrs). Turndown. TV: cable/pay movies/satellite/VCR.*

A book at bedtime from **Hazlitt's**. *See p49.*

Chain reaction

For those who couldn't care less about authenticity and eccentric English charm, the chains have come to set you free. Below we've listed contacts for a number of major chains, along with the number of hotels they run in Greater London.

Best Western *0345 747474/ www.bestwestern.co.uk.* **Hotels** 21.

Choice Hotels (Quality Hotels, Comfort Inn) *0800 444444/ www.choicehotels.com.* **Hotels** 21.

Forte Hotels Reservations Line *0345 404040/www.forte-hotels.co.uk.* **Hotels** 16.

Hilton *0800 856 8000/www.hilton.com.* **Hotels** 12.

Holiday Inn *0800 897121/ www.holiday-inn.com.* **Hotels** 17.

Marriott *0800 221222/ www.marriotthotels.com.* **Hotels** 6.

Radisson Edwardian *0800 374411/ www.radisson.com.* **Hotels** 11.

Travel Inn *01582 414341/ www.travelinn.co.uk.* **Hotels** 4.

Thistle *0800 181716/ www.thistlehotels.com.* **Hotels** 23.

Pembridge Court Hotel

34 Pembridge Gardens, Notting Hill, W2 4DX (7229 9977/fax 7727 4982/www.pemct.co.uk). Notting Hill Gate tube. **Rooms** 20. **Rates** £125-£165 single; £155-£195 double. **Credit** AmEx, DC, MC, V. **Map** p394 A7.

General manager Valerie Gilliat, here since 1970, sure makes her dynamic presence felt. Where most townhouse hotels have the usual identikit period prints hung for that air of authenticity, the Pembridge has a dazzlingly original array of framed Victoriana: exotic fans, gloves, jewellery, and makeup cases, all worthy of a V&A exhibition. The warm brick walls of the lobby and cellar restau-bar make a refreshing change from flock wallpaper, and there are power showers, VCRs and CD players in the rooms. The back door of the hotel opens onto Portobello Road. **Hotel services** *Air-conditioning. Bar. Business services. No-smoking rooms. Parking (free).* **Room services** *Room service (24hrs). TV: satellite/VCR.*

Portobello Hotel

22 Stanley Gardens, Notting Hill, W11 2NG (7727 2777/fax 7792 9641/www.portobello-hotel.co.uk). Notting Hill tube. **Rooms** 24. **Rates** £140 single; £185-£350 double. **Credit** AmEx, DC, MC, V. **Map** p394 A6.

Take a seat at the **Westbourne Hotel**.

There are shades of Blakes (*see p44*) at the romantic Portobello, full of Victorian exotica from far-off climes: Oriental, Japanese, and Moroccan rooms, and a suite with a clawfoot bathtub and gauze curtain in the middle of the room. Decorated with Imperial art, palm trees and ornately carved furniture, there's a slight air of mystery about the place, and a Last Days of the Raj ambience. Some rooms are pokey, but not the highly sought-after 'Round Bed' room, which features, you guessed it, a circular bed, and a real Victorian bathing machine. It's a favourite with rock stars – Damon Albarn used to tend bar here – and only steps away from Portobello antiqueing and Hugh Grant fantasies.
Hotel services *Air-conditioning. Bar. Business services. Restaurant.* **Room services** *Mini-bar. Room service (24hrs). TV: cable/VCR.*

Rookery

12 Peter's Lane, Cowcross Street, Clerkenwell, EC1M 6DS (7336 0931/fax 7336 0932/ www.rookeryhotel.com). Farringdon tube/rail. **Rooms** 33. **Rates** £206 single; £241 double; £311-£558 suite. **Credit** AmEx, DC, MC, V. **Map** p402 O5.
Hidden down a brick lane in Smithfield – the 'Soho of the East', or something like that – the Rookery has a feel of Dickensian London about it. A refreshing alternative to the so-hip-it-hurts boutique hotels of the West End, the most striking characteristics here are the rich, dark panelling, elaborate gothic beds, and the gentlemen's club feel: rarely has decadence felt quite this masculine. Open fires, stone-flagged floors and astonishing Victorian bathrooms – with antique claw foot bath tubs, copper pipes and cast iron toilets – evoke a genuine historic atmosphere without sacrificing modern luxury at this fine establishment.
Hotel services *Bar. Business services. Garden. No-smoking rooms.* **Room services** *Mini-bar. Room service (7am-10pm). Turndown. TV: pay movies/satellite/VCR.*

Westbourne Hotel

163-5 Westbourne Grove, Notting Hill, W11 2RS (7243 6008/fax 7229 7201/ www.westbournehotel.com). Notting Hill Gate tube. **Rooms** 20. **Rates** £206-£300 double. **Credit** AmEx, MC, V. **Map** p394 A6.

Located in Notting Hill, the Westbourne is another new 'style hotel' that fuses a stark modernist aesthetic with oriental themes, aimed, of course, at international bright young things. There's the '60s-chic, airport-loungey lobby/bar, and the requisite Far Eastern touches throughout, including Japanese gardens front and rear. The niche here is that each simple room features art by young Brit artists – Bridget Riley, Gavin Turk, Dan Macmillan – coupled with DVD players and modem facilities. There's an iMac for Internet access at the bar, and, in early 2001, a Chinese tea room was in the works. More intimate and relaxing than others in the Hotel Cool school.
Hotel services *Air-conditioning. Bar. Business services. Disabled: adapted rooms. Garden. No-smoking rooms.* **Room services** *Room service (24hrs). TV: satellite/DVD.*

Moderate (£101-£150)

All these hotels offer a laundry, a limo service (unless stated) and an in-room phone over and above the services detailed beneath each review.

Abbey Court Hotel

20 Pembridge Gardens, Notting Hill, W2 4DU (7221 7518/fax 7792 0858/www.abbeycourthotel.co.uk). Notting Hill tube. **Rooms** 22. **Rates** £99-£135 single; £145-£165 double; £175-£195 suite. **Credit** AmEx, DC, MC, V. **Map** p394 A7.
Located smack-bang in the heart of Notting Hill, the rooms in this white stucco Victorian townhouse are thoughtfully decorated with period pastoral scenes, oil portraits and antique lamps. Bathrooms include heated towel rails, terrycloth robes, and, best of all, jacuzzi bathtubs. The pretty conservatory breakfast room/honesty bar features summery green banquettes and opens onto a tiny garden with fish pond.
Hotel services *Babysitting. Bar. Business services. Concierge. Garden. No-smoking rooms. Restaurant.* **Room services** *Dataport. Room service (24hrs). Turndown. TV: satellite.*

Colonnade Town House

2 Warrington Crescent, Little Venice, W9 1ER (7286 1052/fax 7286 1057/www.etontownhouse.com). Warwick Avenue tube. **Rooms** 43. **Rates** £141-£206 double; £258-£276 suite. **Credit** AmEx, DC, MC, V.
This sparkling townhouse has three distinguishing characteristics: it's in Little Venice, off the tourist path; it was the birthplace in 1912 of code-breaker Alan Turing; and it has a truly stunning, dark green JFK suite featuring a four-poster bed custom-made for the man himself. There's an old-fashioned turndown service, but there's also a modern breakfast room with Swedish-style smörgåsbord eats. Ask about romantic specials involving champagne, love poems and rose petals sprinkled on the beds.
Hotel services *Air-conditioning. Babysitting. Business services. Concierge. Garden. No-smoking rooms. Parking.* **Room services** *Dataport. Mini-bar. Room service (24hrs). Turndown. TV: satellite.*

LANCASTER COURT
HOTEL

- Centrally located and family run for the last 21 years.

- **Unbeatable prices -** Basic singles from **£35 per room** per night.

- Basic Doubles **from £55**

- All rooms individually and tastefully decorated - mostly en-suite, all with colour TV.

- *Special* Midweek/Weekend offers stay 4 nights pay for 3

- Recommended by all established and reputable guides.

- Convenient for Madame Tussaud's, Harrods, Oxford Street, Hyde Park, Buckingham Palace, Theatreland, Antique Markets and all the major sights.

- Limited Car Parking available.

- Free luggage room facility for guests.

Paddington Station - (3 mins walk) for Heathrow Express (Heathrow to Central London only 15 mins), Mainline Railway & Underground. Heathrow Express Coach Service is available to the hotel.

Lancaster Gate Underground Station - (3 mins Walk) for tube and Airbus.

Waterloo International Station - (20 mins by tube) for Eurostar.

2001/2002 TARIFF	prices are per room per night			
	Low Season		High Season	
Singles	from £35	to	£45	
Doubles	from £55	to	£75	
Triples	from £75	to	£85	
Quads	from £85	to	£99	

Including complimentary continental breakfast, service charge and VAT.

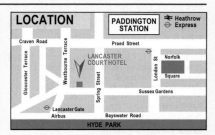

LOCATION

PADDINGTON STATION — Heathrow Express

Craven Road · Praed Street · Gloucester Terrace · Westbourne Terrace · LANCASTER COURT HOTEL · Spring Street · London St · Norfolk Square · Sussex Gardens · Lancaster Gate Airbus · Bayswater Road · HYDE PARK

202/204 Sussex Gardens, Lancaster Gate, London W2 3UA
Tel: 020 7402 8438 (4lines) Fax: 020 7706 3794

Email: lancohot@cs.com
www.lancaster-court-hotel.co.uk

LONDON

Cranley Gardens Hotel.

Cranley Gardens Hotel

*8 Cranley Gardens, South Kensington, SW7 3DB
(7373 3232/fax 7373 7944/cranleygarden@aol.com).
Gloucester Road tube.* **Rooms** 85. **Rates** £85-£95
single; £109-£115 double; £135 suite. **Credit** AmEx,
DC, MC, V. **Map** p397 D11.

A pleasant mid-range hotel occupying four listed
Victorian townhouses, minutes away from the museums and Harrods. The handsome lobby is entered
through an elegant portico, with the breakfast room
a cheery yellow and blue space. All the bedrooms
are reasonably sized if generic in decor, and the front
rooms – some with balconies – overlook a pretty
garden square. There's not much in the way of an
authentic atmosphere (and there's no limo service),
but it's pleasing and comfortable in a Holiday Inn
kind of way, with a great location and attentive staff.
Hotel services *Babysitting. Bar(s). Business
services. Concierge. Restaurant(s).* **Room services**
Room service (8am-midnight). TV: satellite.

Five Sumner Place

*5 Sumner Place, South Kensington, SW7 3EE (7584
7586/7823 9962/www.sumnerplace.com). South
Kensington tube.* **Rooms** 15. **Rates** £99 single;
£150 double. **Credit** AmEx, MC, V. **Map** p397 D11.

Three-time winner of the London Tourism Awards'
Bed & Breakfast gong, Five Sumner Place is located
in a row of pretty white Victorian terraced houses
handy for Knightsbridge, Chelsea and South
Kensington's museums. Rooms are pleasantly decorated in a faux-period style, the breakfast room is a
bright and airy conservatory, and the friendly

proprietor takes great pride in his high standards.
There's also a lift, always a Godsend in tall town-
houses such as this one.
Hotel services *Garden. No-smoking floors.
Parking.* **Room services** *Dataport. Mini-bar.
Room service (8am-8pm). TV.*

Gainsborough Hotel

*7-11 Queensberry Place, South Kensington, SW7
2DL (7957 0000/fax 7957 0001/www.eeh.co.uk).
South Kensington tube.* **Rooms** 15. **Rates** £79-£102
single; £141-£176 double; £223-£258 suite.
Credit AmEx, DC, MC, V. **Map** p397 D10.

Part of the Elegant English Hotels mini-chain, the
Gainsborough is a relaxed, mid-range hotel with
smarter period decor than others in its range, done
out in not-at-all tacky chintz, corona beds and subtly patterned wallpaper. The lobby is stately home
in feel, while the Picasso bar/breakfast room strikes
a glamorous chord with its yellow silk walls and
heavy, tasselled drapes. If you stay at this good-
value hotel three nights, you'll receive a free three-
day pass to several top museums and galleries.
Hotel services *Air-conditioning. Babysitting.
Bar. Business services. Concierge.* **Room
services** *Room service (24hrs). TV: satellite.*

Gallery Hotel

*8-10 Queensberry Place, South Kensington, SW7
2EA (7915 0000/fax 7915 4400/www.eeh.co.uk).
South Kensington tube.* **Rooms** 36. **Rates** £141-
£176 double; £258 suite. **Credit** AmEx, DC, MC, V.
Map p397 D10.

Across the road from its sister, the Gainsborough
(*see above*), this smart, mid-priced Victorian townhouse exudes relaxed gentlemen's club in the lobby
bar, where you can sink into red and green pin-
striped sofas and peruse the broadsheets. The air-
conditioned rooms are middle-class Ritz, with
tasteful floral bedspreads, heavy drapes, and
damask wallpaper. Three-night stays include free
passes to several London museums and galleries.
Overall, it's good value, almost approaching luxury.
Hotel services *Air-conditioning. Babysitting.
Bar. Business services. Concierge. No-smoking
floors.* **Room services** *Dataport. Room service
(24hrs). TV: satellite/VCR.*

London Elizabeth Hotel

*Lancaster Terrace, Bayswater, W2 3PF (7402
6641/fax 7224 8900/www.londonelizabeth.co.uk).
Lancaster Gate tube.* **Rooms** 49. **Rates** £110
single; £125-£160 double; £180-£250 suite.
Credit AmEx, DC, MC, V. **Map** p395 D6.

Situated on the north edge of Hyde Park, this traditional, glitzy hotel offers widely varying rooms, from
not-so-thrilling standards to almost Dorchester-
worthy suites. B-list celebs stay in the sumptuous
Hyde Park suite, a bargain at £250, though the split-
level Conservatory Suite (£180) is another stunner.
There's a rose garden terrace on which to take
drinks in the summer; at the girlish Rose Garden
restaurant, a wonderfully tacky, pink wall mural
plays backdrop to country classic cuisine.

Hotel services *Air-conditioning. Babysitting. Bar. Business services. Concierge. Garden. No-smoking floors. Parking. Restaurant.* **Room services** *Dataport. Room service (24hrs). TV.*

Mornington Lancaster Hotel

12 Lancaster Gate, Bayswater, W2 3LG (7262 7361/fax 7706 1028/www.mornington.com). Lancaster Gate tube. **Rooms** 66. **Rates** £115 single; £130-£140 double; £155 suite. **Credit** AmEx, DC, MC, V. **Map** p395 D7.

The regal Victorian exterior and library-like lobby belie the resolutely modern, IKEA-influenced bedrooms with their clean, laminated-wood aesthetic and contemporary plaid upholstery. Swedish-owned and run, 50% of the clients here are Swedes: there are Swedish papers in the bar (as well as English ones) and marinated herring is available with your English breakfast. Clean as a whistle, it's a chintz-free breath of fresh air. No limo service.
Hotel services *Bar. Business services. Concierge. No-smoking rooms.* **Room services** *Dataport. Room service (7-10am, 4-11pm). TV: cable/pay movies.*

Topham's Belgravia

28 Ebury Street, Belgravia, SW1W OLU (7730 8147/fax 7823 5966/www.tophams.co.uk). Victoria tube/rail. **Rates** £115 single; £130-£150 double; £170 triple. **Credit** AmEx, DC, MC, V. **Map** p400 H10.

In the hotel business, the phrase 'home from home' is an overused and often ridiculously inappropriate cliché (even the Dorchester uses it, for Chrissakes). But in the case of Topham's Belgravia, a cosy Georgian townhouse, it's definitely appropriate. This cute rabbit-warren of a hotel has been family-owned since 1937, and feels like visiting your gran's quirky old house: brimming with character, it's full of narrow low passages, creaky floors, china teacups and classic-lined bookshelves. There are quaint, nook-and-cranny-ish restaurant and bar areas, an all-in-the-family staff feel, and a clientele that returns repeatedly.
Hotel services *Babysitting. Bar. Disabled: adapted rooms. Restaurant.* **Room services** *Dataport. Room service (24hrs).Turndown. TV: satellite.*

Moderate to cheap (£75-£100)

All hotels here offer an in-room telephone in addition to the services detailed below.

Amsterdam Hotel

7 Trebovir Road, Earl's Court, SW5 9LS (7370 2814/fax 7244 7608/www.amsterdam-hotel.com). Earl's Court tube. **Rooms** 27. **Rates** £74-£82 single; £84-£98 double; £98-£160 suite. **Credit** AmEx, DC, MC, V. **Map** p396 B11.

Name and location aside, everything about this refreshing and contemporary Earl's Court hotel suggests smart and breezy Florida condo. A profusion of lush palms and ferns spill out of the cream and pink tiled lobby. The sunny holiday feel extends to

History lessons at the **Morgan Hotel**. See p55.

the bedrooms, with their flamboyant tropical upholstery and bold Caribbean prints; white wicker and bamboo in the breakfast room furthers this theme.
Hotel services *Business services. Concierge. Garden. Laundry. No-smoking rooms.* **Room services** *Kitchenette. TV.*

Crescent Hotel

49-50 Cartwright Gardens, Bloomsbury, WC1H 9EL (7387 1515/fax 7383 2054/ www.crescenthoteloflondon.com). Russell Square tube/Euston tube/rail. **Rooms** 27. **Rates** £43-£70 single; £82 double; £93 triple; £102 quad. **Credit** MC, V. **Map** p399 L3.

Family-run since 1956, this Georgian townhouse B&B sits in a pretty Bloomsbury crescent overlooking gardens and tennis courts, both of which are available to guests (racquet and balls on loan). Breakfast is served from an old-fashioned cooking range, enhancing the hotel's period decor. The proprietors have compiled handy binders full of tourist information.
Hotel services *TV room.* **Room services** *Dataport. Turndown.*

Harlingford Hotel

61-3 Cartwright Gardens, Bloomsbury, WC1H 9EL (7387 1551/fax 7387 4616/ www.harlingfordhotel.com). Russell Square tube/Euston tube/rail. **Rooms** 43. **Rates** £70 single; £88 double; £98 triple; £108 quad. **Credit** AmEx, DC, MC, V. **Map** p399 L3.

There's not much to choose between the string of hotels along this lovely Regency crescent, but the recently refurbished, varnished wood bathrooms here are a rarity in townhouse hotels of this ilk, and the staff are friendly. As with the Crescent (*see above*), there's access to the gardens and tennis courts behind.
Hotel services *TV room.* **Room services** *TV.*

Hotel 167

167 Old Brompton Road, South Kensington, SW5 0AN (7373 0672/fax 7373 3360/ www.hotel167.com). Gloucester Road tube. **Rooms** 19. **Rates** £72-£86 single; £90-£99 double. **Credit** AmEx, DC, MC, V. **Map** p397 D11.

Black and white tiled floors, potted palms and eccentrically decorated rooms give this Victorian hotel a funky, retro feel. The rooms, generally free of clichéd English fuss, are an eclectic mix, with art deco touches, Mexican bedspreads and kitsch

figurines. Don't expect obsequious service here, but it's atmospheric enough to have had both a novel (Jane Solomon's 1993 *Hotel 167*) and a song (an unreleased Manic Street Preachers track) written about it.
Room services *TV: satellite.*

Jenkins Hotel

45 Cartwright Gardens, Bloomsbury, WC1H 9EH (7387 2067/fax 7383 3139/ www.jenkinshotel.demon.co.uk). Russell Square tube/Euston tube/rail. **Rooms** 14 . **Rates** £52-£72 single; £85 double; £95 triple. **Credit** MC, V. **Map** p399 L3.
Located on a quiet, pretty Georgian crescent near the British Museum, the Jenkins offers 14 comfortable, impeccably clean rooms. A warm welcome is guaranteed from the proprietors and their friendly black labradors.
Hotel services *No-smoking throughout.* **Room services** *Mini-bar. TV.*

Kensington Gardens Hotel

9 Kensington Gardens Square, Bayswater, W2 4BH (7221 7790/fax 7792 8612). Bayswater or Queensway tube. **Rooms** 16. **Rates** £53-£58 single; £79 double; £100 triple. **Credit** AmEx, DC, MC, V. **Map** p394 B6.
Situated on the south side of a lovely square, the entrance hall to this restored Victorian townhouse is surprisingly gracious for a mid-priced hotel. The rooms have handsome high ceilings and mini-bars, though the decor is rather utilitarian. Still, both value and location are good: vibrant Bayswater is crammed full of shops, multicultural restaurants and pubs, and is close to Hyde Park and Notting Hill.
Hotel services *Concierge.* **Room services** *Mini-bar. TV: satellite.*

Mayflower Hotel

26-8 Trebovir Road, Earl's Court, SW5 9NJ (7370 0991/fax 7370 0994/mayfhotel@aol.com). Earl's Court tube. **Rooms** 48. **Rates** £59 single; £79 double; £89-£220 triple. **Credit** AmEx, MC, V. **Map** p396 B11.
The Mayflower makes an effort to get away from fussy English budget tack: the grey lobby with black leather couches suggests the designers have been reading style mags, while the rooms feature sponge-effect painted walls and contemporary upholstery. Enquire about the adjoining Court Apartments, where you can get a smart, stylish four-room suite for less than the price of a closet at the Metropolitan.
Hotel services *Business services. Concierge. Parking. Payphone.* **Room services** *TV: satellite.*

Morgan Hotel

24 Bloomsbury Street, Bloomsbury, WC1B 3QJ (7636 3735/fax 7636 3045). Tottenham Court Road tube. **Rooms** 20. **Rates** £57-£67 single; £83 double; £110 suite; £125 triple. **Credit** MC, V. **Map** p399 K5.
If *EastEnders* were set in a hotel, the family-run Morgan could easily fill in for the Queen Vic: its owners are jovial old-school Londoners, and London

memorabilia fills the caff-style breakfast room. The rooms are pretty basic, but most have air conditioning, and, in a separate townhouse, big apartment-style suites are available for £110, a real bargain. The Bloomsbury location is also a winner.
Hotel services *Air conditioning. Payphone.* **Room services** *TV.*

Plough Inn

42 Christchurch Road, East Sheen, SW14 7AF (8876 7833/fax 8392 8801). Richmond tube/rail, then 33,337 bus/Mortlake rail. **Rooms** 8. **Rates** £60 single; £80 double; £100 family. **Credit** AmEx, DC, MC, V.
This atmospheric 200-year-old pub located a half-hour train ride from Waterloo has eight cosy rooms tucked upstairs with half-timber flourishes and satellite TVs. Downstairs, the quaint, atmospheric pub is perfect for observing the locals and sampling trad pub grub. It's a bit off the beaten track, but this leafy, rural neighbourhood is steps away from Richmond Park.
Hotel services *Bar. Garden. Laundry. Parking (free). Payphone. Restaurant.* **Room services** *TV: cable.*

Riverside Hotel

23 Petersham Road, Richmond-upon-Thames, Surrey TW10 6UH (8940 1339/fax 8948 0967/ www.smoothhound.co.uk/hotels/riversid.html). Richmond tube/rail. **Rooms** 22. **Rates** £60 single; £80-£115 double. **Credit** AmEx, DC, MC, V.
For a rural respite from West End mayhem, the Riverside has a picturesque location overlooking the Thames and is conveniently located for Kew Gardens, Hampton Court and various stately homes, while only a 15-minute train trip to Waterloo. The rooms at the back of this family-run Victorian hotel have river views and pleasing retro English decor.
Hotel services *Laundry. No-smoking rooms. Parking (free). TV room: satellite.* **Room services** *Dataport. Room service (10am-11.30pm). TV: satellite.*

Rushmore Hotel

11 Trebovir Road, Earl's Court, SW5 9LS (7370 3839/fax 7370 0274). Earl's Court tube. **Rooms** 22. **Rates** £59 single; £79 double; £89 triple; £99 family. **Credit** AmEx, DC, MC, V. **Map** p396 B11.
This lovely little hotel has an Italianate breakfast room almost as chic as any of the big-name style hotels, complete with black granite counters, Tuscan wrought iron chairs and dainty glass tables. Many rooms also have an Italian feel, with ornate stencilling and fresco-ish rural scenes on the walls, and handsome beige marble bathrooms. Proof that, with a little imagination, budget hotels can be stylish.
Hotel services *Business services. Payphone.* **Room services** *TV: cable.*

Swiss House Hotel

171 Old Brompton Road, South Kensington, SW5 0AN (7373 2769/fax 7373 4983/ www.swiss-hh.demon.co.uk). Gloucester Road tube. **Rooms** 15. **Rates** £48-£68 single; £85-£99 double; £114-£128 quad. **Credit** AmEx, DC, MC, V. **Map** p397 D11.

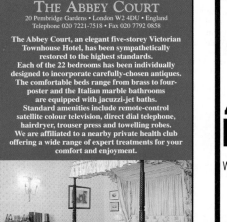

The rooms in this sweet South Kensington townhouse are most notable for their profusion of pine furniture and simple navy sheets where so many others throw on the chintz. Formerly a staff residence for SwissAir crews, the hotel is filled with greenery and art posters, yet the breakfast room is down-home country kitchen. All rooms have fans; back rooms have garden views.
Hotel services *Babysitting. Laundry. Limousine service. No-smoking rooms.* **Room services** *Dataport. Room service (12.30-9pm). TV: cable.*

30 King Henry's Road

30 King Henry's Road, Primrose Hill, NW3 3RP (7483 2871/fax 7483 4587/ www.30kinghenrysroad.co.uk). Chalk Farm tube/Primrose Hill rail. **Rooms** 3. **Rates** £90-£100 single; £100 double. **No credit cards.**
A real, old-fashioned, country-style English B&B in which you literally stay in someone else's home: the not-so-humble abode of Andrew and Carole Ingram, and their greyhounds Grace and Joe. Breakfast is served in a rustic-modern kitchen with a real Aga and splendidly detailed table setting. The personal, hospitable service comes with a pretty Primrose Hill address, which more than compensates for the rooms coming without telephones.
Hotel services *Air conditioning. No-smoking throughout.* **Room services** *TV.*

Vancouver Studios

30 Prince's Square, Bayswater, W2 4NJ (7243 1270/fax 7221 8678/www.vienna-group.co.uk). Bayswater or Queensway tube. **Rates** £75 single; £95-£110 double; £130 suite. **Credit** AmEx, DC, MC, V. **Map** p394 B6.
A real discovery, this: funkily decorated studio apartments with power showers, mini-kitchens and Kandinsky posters, all in a traditional Victorian townhouse in Bayswater. The public areas come dressed in warm, country-casual decor sprinkled with cactuses, pot pourri, and cat paraphernalia, including a real wandering feline. Off the comfy lounge, there's a lush ivy-covered walled garden. All in all, excellent value.
Hotel services *Business services. Concierge. Cooking facilities. Garden. Laundry.* **Room services** *Dataport. Kitchenette. TV.*

Cheap (under £75)

Abbey House

11 Vicarage Gate, Kensington, W8 4AG (7727 2594/ fax 7727 1873/www.abbeyhousekensington.com). High Street Kensington or Notting Hill Gate tube. **Rooms** 16. **Rates** £45 single; £74 double; £85 triple; £100 quad. **No credit cards. Map** p394 B8.
One of the best quality B&Bs in this price range, Kensington's Abbey House is an elegant Victorian house with many of its original fittings. The rooms are simply decorated but spacious and comfortable.
Hotel services *Babysitting. Payphone.* **Room services** *TV.*

Arosfa

83 Gower Street, Bloomsbury, WC1E 6HJ (tel/fax 7636 2115). Euston Square or Goodge Street tube. **Rooms** 16. **Rates** £37 single; £50 double; £68 triple. **Credit** MC, V. **Map** p399 K4.
Quaint and quiet, the Arosfa – it's Welsh for 'place to stay', in case you were wondering – is run by the friendly Mr and Mrs Dorta, who offer basic but pleasantly decorated rooms in the former home of the artist John Everett Millais. There's a 2% surcharge on credit cards.
Hotel services *Garden. Lounge. No-smoking floors. Payphone. TV room.* **Room services** *TV.*

Ashlee House

261-5 Gray's Inn Road, King's Cross, WC1X 8QT (7833 9400/fax 7833 9677/www.ashleehouse.co.uk). King's Cross tube/rail. **Rooms** 26 (175 beds). **Rates** (per person) £17-£19 4-6-bed room; £15-£17 8-10-bed room; £13-£15 16-bed room; £22-£24 twin; £34-£36 single. **No credit cards. Map** p399 M3.
This friendly, affordable hostel caters mainly to young backpackers and student groups. The rooms, all with bunks, sleep between one and 16 people; the price per person decreases the more people you share with. Facilities include a large kitchen/dining area downstairs and an Internet access room.
Hotel services *Cooking facilities. Laundry. No-smoking rooms. Payphone. TV room.*

Cartref House & James House

129 Ebury Street, Belgravia, SW1W 9QU & 108 Ebury Street, Belgravia, SW1W 9QD (Cartref 7730 6176/James 7730 7338/www.jamesandcartref.co.uk). Victoria tube/rail. **Rooms** *Cartref* 11. *James* 6 (3 en suite). **Rates** £50-£60 single; £68-£82 double; £90-£105 triple; £130 quad. **Credit** AmEx, MC, V. **Map** p400 H10.
Under the same ownership, these no-smoking B&Bs on a chic Georgian street in Belgravia provide bright, basic rooms and a cheery welcome.
Hotel services *No-smoking rooms. Payphone.* **Room services** *TV.*

Garden Court Hotel

30-31 Kensington Gardens Square, Bayswater, W2 4BG (7229 2553/fax 7727 2749/ www.gardencourthotel.co.uk). Bayswater or Queensway tube. **Rooms** 32 (16 en suite). **Rates** (incl English breakfast) £35-£52 single; £56-£84 double; £72-£92 triple; £82-£96 quad. **Credit** MC, V. **Map** p394 B6.
Built in 1870, this popular family-run B&B overlooks a quiet Victorian garden square. The rooms are comfortable and clean and the hotel also boasts an attractive paved garden and large lounge. Good quality and good value.
Hotel services *Garden.* **Room services** *Telephone. TV: satellite.*

Generator

Compton Place (off 37 Tavistock Place), Bloomsbury, WC1H 9SD (7388 7666/fax 7388 7644/ www.the-generator.co.uk). Russell Square tube. **Rooms** 217 (833 beds; none en suite). **Rates** (per

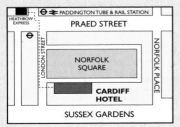

person, incl breakfast) £36.50-£38.50 single; £23-£26.50 twin; £20-£22.50 3-6-bed room; £19-£21.50 7-8-bed room; £15 dorm. **Credit** MC, V. **Map** p399 K4.

This industrial-sized, industrial-style (exposed ventilation, stenciled room numbers) hostel has room for over 800 guests. The rooms are basic, with just bunks and a washbasin in each, but what sets the Generator apart are its communal areas, which include a games room, an Internet access room, a vast self-service canteen and a lively bar (open until 2am). Ideal for backpackers, student groups and the more adventurous. **Hotel services** *Air-conditioning. Bar. No-smoking rooms. Payphone. Restaurant. TV room.*

Hampstead Village Guesthouse

2 Kemplay Road, Hampstead, NW3 1SY (7435 8679/ fax 7794 0254/www.hampsteadguesthouse.com). Hampstead tube/Hampstead Heath rail. **Rooms** 6. **Rates** £48-£66 single; £72-£84 double; £90-£150 studio. **Credit** AmEx, DC, MC, V.

Located in a rambling Victorian Hampstead townhouse, each of the six rooms here is filled with a fabulous array of books, antiques and clutter, accumulated and lovingly arranged by its exuberant owner, Annemarie van der Meer. There is a separate outhouse with a tiny corner kitchenette, available for use as a private suite (sleeps one to five people). Credit card payments are subject to a 5% surcharge. **Hotel services** *Babysitting. Cooking facilities. Garden. Laundry. No-smoking throughout. Parking.* **Room services** *Telephone. TV.*

Highfield Guesthouse

12 Downhill Road, Hither Green, SE6 1HJ (8698 8038/fax 8698 8039). Hither Green rail. **Rooms** 3 (1 en suite). **Rates** £30-£45 single; £45-£65 double/twin; £60-£65 triple. **Credit** AmEx, MC, V.

This immaculate guesthouse boasts excellent facilities and comfortable rooms decked out in well-chosen IKEA-style furnishings. Owner Michel Tournier goes to great lengths to accommodate his guests (he's happy to collect them from Hither Green station, which has frequent trains into town). Rooms like these would be twice the price further north. **Hotel services** *Garden. No-smoking throughout. Parking (free). Payphone.* **Room services** *TV: cable.*

London County Hall Travel Inn Capital

County Hall, Belvedere Road, South Bank, SE1 7PB (7902 1600/fax 7902 1619/www.travelinn.co.uk). Waterloo tube/rail. **Rooms** 313 (all en suite). **Rates** £69.95. **Credit** AmEx, DC, MC, V. **Map** p401 M9.

Travel Inns promise 'everything you want for a good night's sleep', and they deliver. The flat rate of £69.95 per room (with 1-2 adults sharing) is remarkably good value in such an area (next to the London Eye): while all the rooms look the same and aren't exactly luxurious, they are all comfortable and clean and, hell, no one here comes for the character. **Hotel services** *Bar. Disabled: adapted rooms. No-smoking rooms. Payphone. Restaurant. TV room.* **Room services** *Dataport. Telephone. TV.*

Mad Hatter Hotel

3-7 Stamford Street, South Bank, SE1 9NY (7401 9222/fax 7401 7111/www.fullers.co.uk). Blackfriars or Waterloo tube/rail. **Rooms** 29. **Rates** £69-£89. **Credit** AmEx, DC, MC, V. **Map** p404 N8.

A rash of Fuller's pubs with hotels attached has hit London, offering great value for money. Though the Mad Hatter is on a fairly busy road, the windows are double glazed so any noise from traffic is minimal. Rooms are large and pleasantly decorated in pastel hues. Three rooms are adapted for the disabled, and others have linked doors to the next rooms. **Hotel services** *Bar. Disabled: adapted rooms. Laundry. No-smoking floor. Payphone. Restaurant.* **Room services** *Telephone. TV.*

Oxford House Hotel

92-4 Cambridge Street, Pimlico, SW1V 4QG (7834 6467/fax 7834 0225). Victoria tube/rail. **Rooms** 15 (none en suite). **Rates** (incl English breakfast) £50-£52 double; £63-£66 triple; £84-£88 quad. **Credit** MC, V. **Map** p400 H11.

This hotel is a real find: bright, comfortable accommodation just around the corner from Victoria Station. The shared facilities are clean and well kept. **Hotel services** *TV room: cable.*

St Margaret Hotel

26 Bedford Place, Bloomsbury, WC1B 5JL (7636 4277/fax 7323 3066). Holborn or Russell Square tube. **Rooms** 64. **Rates** £48.50-£50.50 single; £60.50-£62.50 double; £88-£95 triple. **Credit** MC, V. **Map** p399 L5.

A friendly, characterful, family-run B&B with 64 spacious rooms. Those at the back of the hotel have views of the Duke of Bedford's private gardens. **Hotel services** *Concierge. Disabled: adapted rooms. Garden. No-smoking rooms. Payphone. TV room.* **Room services** *Telephone. TV: satellite.*

Vicarage Hotel

10 Vicarage Gate, Kensington, W8 4AG (7229 4030/fax 7792 5989). High Street Kensington or Notting Hill Gate tube. **Rooms** 18. **Rates** £45 single; £74-£98 double; £90-£98 family. **No credit cards. Map** p394 B8.

An ornate red and gold entrance hall is your first impression of this atmospheric if slightly worn Victorian townhouse. The rooms, for the price, are impressively decorated with period furniture and subtle floral decor, as is the comfy TV lounge. If you're willing to share a bathroom – only two rooms en suite – this is great value in a good location. **Hotel services** *Payphone. TV room.* **Room services** *TV (some rooms).*

Woodville House & Morgan House

107 Ebury Street, Belgravia, SW1W 9QU (7730 1048/fax 7730 2574/www.woodvillehouse.co.uk) & 120 Ebury Street, SW1W 9QQ (7730 2384/fax 7730 8442/www.morganhouse.co.uk). Victoria tube/rail. **Rooms** *Woodville* 12 (none en suite); *Morgan* 11 (3 en suite). **Rates** (incl English breakfast) £42 single; £62-£80 double; £110-£115 quad. **Credit** MC, V. **Map** p400 H10.

Hotels by area

The South Bank & Bankside

Butlers Wharf LSE Residence (University residences, *p64*); **London County Hall Travel Inn Capital** (Cheap, *p59*); **Mad Hatter Hotel** (Cheap, *p59*).

The City

Barbican YMCA (YMCAs, *p63*); **City of London Hostel** (Youth hostels, *p61*); **Great Eastern Hotel** (Deluxe, *p44*); **London City YMCA** (YMCAs, *p63*).

Holborn & Clerkenwell

High Holborn Residence (University residences, *p64*); **One Aldwych** (Deluxe, *p46*); **Rookery** (Expensive, *p51*).

Bloomsbury & Fitzrovia

Academy Hotel (Expensive, *p47*); **Arosfa** (Cheap, *p57*); **Blooms** (Expensive, *p47*); **Cartwright University Halls** (University residences, *p64*); **Charlotte Street Hotel** (Expensive, *p49*); **Crescent Hotel** (Moderate to cheap, *p54*); **Generator** (Cheap, *p57*); **Harlingford Hotel** (Moderate to cheap, *p54*); **Jenkins Hotel** (Cheap, *p55*); **Montague on the Gardens** (Expensive, *p49*); **Morgan Hotel** (Moderate to cheap, *p55*); **myhotel bloomsbury** (Expensive, *p50*); **Passfield Hall** (University residences, *p64*); **St Margaret Hotel** (Cheap, *p59*); **Sanderson** (Deluxe, *p47*).

Marylebone

Dorset Square Hotel (Expensive, *p49*); **International Students House** (University residences, *p64*).

Mayfair & St James's

Dorchester (Deluxe, *p44*); **Goldsmid House** (University residences, *p64*); **Metropolitan** (Deluxe, *p46*); **No.5 Maddox Street** (Deluxe, *p46*); **Ritz** (Deluxe, *p46*).

Soho

Hazlitt's (Expensive, *p49*); **Oxford Street Hostel** (Youth hostels, *p61*).

Covent Garden & St Giles's

Covent Garden Hotel (Deluxe, *p44*); **King's College Conference & Vacation Bureau** (University residences, *p64*); **St Martin's Lane** (Deluxe, *p47*); **Savoy** (Deluxe, *p47*).

Knightsbridge & South Kensington

Blakes (Deluxe, *p44*); **Cranley Gardens Hotel** (Moderate, *p53*); **Five Sumner Place** (Moderate, *p53*); **Gainsborough Hotel**

Blakes. *See p44.*

Located close to Victoria, these Georgian B&Bs are owned and operated by exuberant couple Rachel Joplin and Ian Berry. While the Woodville has traditional, flowery decor, the Morgan is more contemporary in flavour. Families are particularly well catered for.
Hotel services *Air-conditioning (selected rooms, Woodville). Babysitting. Garden. Payphone (Woodville).* **Room services** *Kitchenette (Woodville). TV.*

Women-only accommodation

Townsend House

126 Queen's Gate, South Kensington, SW7 5LQ (phone/fax 7225 3777). Gloucester Road tube.
Open *Phone enquiries* 9am-1pm, 4-7.30pm Mon-Fri; closed Sat, Sun. **Rates** *B&B* £18 twin. *Hostel* £68.27/wk double, twin; £62.80/wk triple.
No credit cards. Map p397 D10.

Run by the Girls' Friendly Society (look for the small 'GFS' sign on the front door), Townsend House is a clean, women-only B&B/hostel. Most of the rooms are given over to the long-stay hostel, open to women aged 18-30 with low support needs, for a minimum stay of one month. The hostel operates a waiting list. The B&B (14 days maximum) consists of just ten rooms on the top floor, but all guests can use the house's amenities, which include a large kitchen, two large lounges, laundry facilities and a chapel.

Youth hostels

Hostel beds are either in twin rooms or in dormitories. If you are not a member of the International Youth Hostel Federation (IYHF), you'll have to pay an extra £2 a night to stay at hostels (after six nights you automatically

(Moderate, *p53*); **Gallery Hotel** (Moderate, *p53*); **The Gore** (Expensive, *p49*); **Hotel 167** (Moderate to cheap, *p54*); **Pelham** (Expensive, *p50*); **Swiss House Hotel** (Moderate to cheap, *p55*); **Townsend House** (Women-only accommodation, *p59*).

Belgravia & Pimlico
Cartref House (Cheap, *p57*); **James House** (Cheap, *p57*); **Lanesborough** (Deluxe, *p45*); **Morgan House** (Cheap, *p59*); **Oxford House Hotel** (Cheap, *p59*); **Topham's Belgravia** (Moderate, *p54*); **Woodville House** (Cheap, *p59*).

North London
Arcade Halls (Holloway, University residences, *p63*); **Ashlee House** (King's Cross, Cheap, *p57*); **Hampstead Heath Hostel** (Golders Green, Youth hostels, *p61*); **Hampstead Village Guesthouse** (Hampstead, Cheap, *p59*); **St Pancras Hostel** (King's Cross, Youth hostels, *p61*); **30 King Henry's Road** (Primrose Hill, Moderate to cheap, *p57*); **Walter Sickert Hall** (Islington, University residences, *p64*).

East London
Lee Valley Campsite (Chingford, Camping & caravanning, *p64*); **Tent City Hackney** (Hackney, Camping & caravanning, *p64*).

South London
Crystal Palace Caravan Club Site (Crystal Palace, Camping & caravanning, *p64*); **Highfield Guesthouse** (Hither Green, Cheap, *p59*); **Lee Valley Leisure Centre Camping &**

Caravan Park (Edmonton, Camping & caravanning, *p64*); **Plough Inn** (East Sheen, Moderate to cheap, *p55*); **Riverside Hotel** (Richmond-upon-Thames, Moderate to cheap, *p55*); **Rotherhithe Hostel** (Rotherhithe, Youth hostels, *p61*); **Wimbledon YMCA** (Wimbledon, YMCAs, *p63*).

West London
Abbey Court Hotel (Notting Hill, Moderate, *p51*); **Abbey House** (Kensington, Cheap, *p57*); **Amsterdam Hotel** (Earl's Court, Moderate to cheap, *p54*); **Colonnade Town House** (Little Venice, Moderate, *p51*); **Earl's Court Hostel** (Earl's Court, Youth hostels, *p61*); **Garden Court Hotel** (Bayswater, Cheap, *p57*); **Halcyon Hotel** (Kensington, Deluxe, *p45*); **Hempel** (Bayswater, Deluxe, *p45*); **Holland House Hostel** (Kensington, Youth hostels, *p61*); **Kensington Gardens Hotel** (Bayswater, Moderate to cheap, *p55*); **London Elizabeth Hotel** (Bayswater, Moderate, *p53*); **Mayflower Hotel** (Earl's Court, Moderate to cheap, *p55*); **Mornington Lancaster Hotel** (Bayswater, Moderate, *p54*); **Pembridge Court Hotel** (Notting Hill, Expensive, *p50*); **Portobello Hotel** (Notting Hill, Expensive, *p50*); **Rushmore Hotel** (Moderate to cheap, *p55*); **Tent City Acton** (Acton, Camping & caravanning, *p64*); **Vancouver Studios** (Bayswater, Moderate to cheap, *p57*); **Vicarage Hotel** (Kensington, Moderate to cheap, *p59*); **Westbourne Hotel** (Notting Hill, Expensive, *p51*).

---

become a member). Alternatively, join the IYHF for £12 (£6 for under-18s) at any hostel. Always phone hostels first to check the availability of beds. All the following hostels take MasterCard, Visa and travellers' cheques. You can become a member or book rooms through the IYHF's website (www.yha.org.uk).

City of London *36-8 Carter Lane, The City, EC4V 5AB (7236 4965/fax 7236 7681). St Paul's tube.* Beds 193. Reception open 7am-11pm daily; 24hr access. Rates (incl breakfast) £23.50-£26; £19.90-£21.50 under-18s. Map p404 O6.
Earl's Court *38 Bolton Gardens, Earl's Court, SW5 0AQ (7373 7083/fax 7835 2034). Earl's Court tube.* Beds 154. Reception open 7am-11pm daily; 24hr access. Rates (incl breakfast) £18.95; £17.95 under-18s. Map p396 B11.
Hampstead Heath *4 Wellgarth Road, Golders Green, NW11 7HR (8458 9054/fax 8209 0546). Golders Green tube.* Beds 199. Reception open

6.45am-11pm daily; 24hr access. Rates (incl breakfast) £19.90; £17.70 under-18s.
Holland House *Holland House, Holland Walk, Kensington, W8 7QU (7937 0748/fax 7376 0667). High Street Kensington tube.* Beds 201. Reception open 7am-11pm daily; 24hr access. Rates (incl breakfast) £20.50; £18.50 under-18s. Map p394 A8.
Oxford Street *14 Noel Street, Soho, W1F 8GJ (7734 1618/fax 7734 1657). Oxford Circus tube.* Beds 75. Reception open 7am-11pm daily; 24hr access. Rates £21.50-£23.50; £16.85-£17.50 under-18s. Map p398 J6.
Rotherhithe *Island Yard, Salter Road, Rotherhithe, SE16 5PR (7232 2114/fax 7237 2919). Rotherhithe tube.* Beds 320. Reception open 7am-11pm; 24hr access. Rates £23.50; £19.90 under-18s.
St Pancras *79-81 Euston Road, King's Cross, NW1 2QS (7388 9998/fax 7388 6766). King's Cross tube/rail.* Beds 152. Reception open 7am-11pm daily; 24hr access. Rates £23.50; £19.90 under-18s. Map p399 L3.

Holland House Hostel. *See p61.*

YMCAs

You may need to book months ahead to stay at a Y: many specialise in long-term accommodation. A few of the larger hostels are listed below (all are unisex), but the National Council for YMCAs (8520 5599, www.ymca.org.uk) can supply a full list. Prices are around £25-£30 per night for a single room and £40-£45 for a double.

Barbican *2 Fann Street, The City, EC2Y 8BR (7628 0697/fax 7638 2420). Barbican tube.* **Beds** 240. **Map** p402 P5.
London City *8 Errol Street, The City, EC1Y 8SE (7628 8832/fax 7628 4080). Barbican tube/ Old Street tube/rail.* **Beds** 111. **Map** p402 F4.
Wimbledon *200 The Broadway, Wimbledon, SW19 1RY (8542 9055/fax 8540 2526). South Wimbledon tube/Wimbledon tube/rail/.* **Beds** 110.

Staying with the locals

Staying in a Londoner's home is often more fun than being in an impersonal hotel. The following organisations can arrange accommodation; rates include breakfast.

At Home in London *70 Black Lion Lane, Hammersmith, W6 9BE (8748 1943/fax 8748 2701/www.athomeinlondon.co.uk).* **Open** *Phone enquiries* 9.30am-5.30pm Mon-Fri; closed Sat, Sun. **Rates** *(per room incl breakfast)* £29-£65 single; £52-£90 double. **Credit** MC, V.
Bulldog Club *14 Dewhurst Road, Kensington, W14 OET (7371 3202/fax 7371 2015/ www.bulldogclub.com).* **Rates** from £85. *Membership* £25/3yrs. **Credit** AmEx, MC, V.
Host & Guest Service *103 Dawes Road, Fulham, SW6 7DU (7385 9922/fax 7386 7575/ www.host-guest.co.uk). Fulham Broadway tube.* **Open** 9am-5.30pm Mon-Fri; closed Sat, Sun. **Rates** from £16.50/person. *Students* from £85.90/wk. **Credit** MC, V. **Minimum stay** 2 nights.

London Bed & Breakfast Agency *71 Fellows Road, Swiss Cottage, NW3 3JY (7586 2768/fax 7586 6567/www.londonbb.com).* **Open** *Phone enquiries* 9am-6pm Mon-Fri; 10am-2pm Sat; closed Sun. **Rates** £20-£42. **Credit** MC, V. **Minimum stay** 2 nights.
London Homestead Services *Coombe Wood Road, Kingston-upon-Thames, Surrey KT2 7JY (8949 4455/fax 8549 5492).* **Open** *Phone enquiries* 9am-7pm daily. **Rates** from £18 single; from £35 double. **Credit** MC, V. **Minimum stay** 3 nights.

Self-catering apartments

It can be expensive to rent in London, but if you're in a group, you may save money by renting a flat from one of the following places: all specialise in holiday lettings. *See also p305* **Accommodation Outlet**.

Apartment Service *1st floor, 5-6 Francis Grove, Wimbledon, SW19 4DT (8944 1444/fax 8944 6744). Wimbledon tube/rail.* **Open** 9am-6.30pm Mon-Fri; closed Sat, Sun. **Rates** from £90 double studio. **Credit** AmEx, DC, MC, V.
Astons Apartments *31 Rosary Gardens, South Kensington, SW7 4NH (7590 6000/fax 7590 6060/www.astons-apartments.com). Gloucester Road tube.* **Open** 8am-9pm daily. **Rates** £70.50 single studio; £99.87 double studio. **Credit** AmEx, MC, V. **Map** p396 C11.
Holiday Serviced Apartments *273 Old Brompton Road, Earl's Court, SW5 9JA (7373 4477/fax 7373 4282/www.holidayapartments.co.uk). Earl's Court tube.* **Open** 9.30am-6pm Mon-Fri; closed Sat, Sun. **Rates** from £80 single/double studio. **Credit** AmEx, MC, V. **Map** p396 C11.
Independent Traveller *Thorverton, Exeter, Devon EX5 5NT (01392 860807/fax 01392 860552/www.gowithit.co.uk).* **Rates** *apartments* £250-£2,000/wk. **Credit** MC, V. **Minimum stay** 3 nights.
Palace Court Holiday Apartments *1 Palace Court, Bayswater Road, Bayswater, W2 4LP (7727 3467/fax 7221 7824/www.palacecourt.co.uk). Notting Hill Gate or Queensway tube.* **Open** 8.30am-11pm daily. **Rates** £60 single studio; £76 double studio; £84 triple studio. **Credit** AmEx, MC, V.
Perfect Places *53 Margravine Gardens, Hammersmith, W6 8RN (8748 6095/fax 8741 4213/www.perfectplaceslondon.co.uk). Barons Court tube.* **Open** *Phone enquiries* 9am-7pm daily. **Rates** from £550/wk. **Credit** AmEx, MC, V.

University residences

During university vacations much of London's student accommodation is opened to visitors, representing a basic but cheap place to stay.

Arcade Halls *The Arcade, 385-401 Holloway Road, Holloway, N7 ORN (7607 5415/fax 7609 0052/ www.unl.ac.uk/accommodation). Holloway Road tube.* **Rooms** *Self-contained flats for 4-6 people.* **Rates** £17/night; £80/wk. **Available** 2 July-3 Sept 2001.

Butlers Wharf LSE Residence *11 Gainsford Street, Bankside, SE1 2NE (7407 7164/fax 7403 0847/butlers.wharf@lse.ac.uk). Tower Hill tube/ London Bridge tube/rail.* **Rooms** *Self-contained flats (sleeping up to 7) 46.* **Rates** from £22.50/person; under-12s half-price. **Available** 1 July-23 Sept 2001. **Map** p405 R9.

Cartwright University Halls *36 Cartwright Gardens, Bloomsbury, WC1H 9BZ (7388 3757/ fax 7388 2552/www.cartwrighthall.com). Russell Square tube/Euston or King's Cross tube/rail.* **Rooms** *Single 153. Twin 40.* **Rates** £28-£33 single; £39-£47 twin. **Available** all year. **Map** p399 L3.

Goldsmid House *36 North Row, Mayfair, W1K 6DN (bookings 01273 207 481/7493 8911/fax 7491 0586). Bond Street or Marble Arch tube.* **Rooms** *Single 10. Twin 120.* **Rates** £22 single; £30 twin. **Available** 8th June-22nd Sept. **Map** p398 G6.

High Holborn Residence *178 High Holborn, Holborn, WC1V 7AA (7379 5589/fax 7379 5640/www.lse.ac.uk/vacations). Holborn tube.* **Rooms** *Single 400. Twin 48.* **Rates** £34 single; £57-£67 twin. **Available** 30 June-29 Sept 2001. **Map** p399 M5.

International Students House *229 Great Portland Street, Marylebone, W1N 5HD (7631 8300/8310/fax 7631 8315/www.ish.org.uk). Great Portland Street tube.* **Rooms** *Single 158. Twin 107.* **Rates** £31 single; £22.50 twin; £9.99-£17.50 dormitory. **Available** all year. **Map** p398 H5.

King's College Conference & Vacation Bureau *Strand Bridge House, 138-42 Strand, Covent Garden, WC2R 1HH (7848 1700/fax 7848 1717/www.kcl.ac.uk/services/vacbro/index.html). Temple tube.* **Rooms** *apx 2,000 beds in six halls.* **Rates** £18-£33 single; £42-£47 twin. **Available** 27 Mar-19 Apr, 14 June-15 Sept 2001. **Map** p404 N8.

Passfield Hall *1-7 Endsleigh Place, Bloomsbury, WC1H 0PW (7387 3584/fax 7387 0419/ www.lse.ac.uk/vacations). Euston tube/rail.* **Rooms** *Single 100. Twin 34. Triple 7.* **Rates** £22.50, £24 single; £44 twin; £57 triple. **Available** 17 Mar-21 Apr, 30 June-27 Sept 2001. **Map** p399 K4.

Walter Sickert Hall *29 Graham Street, Islington, N1 8LA (7477 8822/fax 7477 8825/ www.city.ac.uk/ems). Angel tube.* **Rooms** *Single 226. Twin 6.* **Rates** £30-£40 single; £55-£60 twin. **Available** 1 July-18 Sept 2001 (selected rooms available year round). **Map** p402 P3.

Camping & caravanning

None of these campsites are especially central, and transport into town isn't what it might be, but all are predictably, conveniently cheap. Both Tent City operations have large tented hostels as well as the usual pitches.

Crystal Palace Caravan Club Site *Crystal Palace Parade, SE19 1UF (8778 7155). Crystal Palace rail/3 bus.* **Open** *Office Mar-Oct 8.30am-8pm daily; Nov-Feb 9am-8pm daily.* **Rates** £13.80-£16 caravan pitch. **Credit** MC, V.

Lee Valley Campsite *Sewardstone Road, Chingford, E4 7RA (8529 5689/fax 8559 4070/scs@leevalleypark.org.uk). Walthamstow Central tube/rail then 215 bus.* **Open** *Apr-Oct* 8am-8pm daily. *Nov-Mar closed.* **Rates** £5.50; £2.40 under-16s. **Credit** MC, V.

Lee Valley Leisure Centre Camping & Caravan Park *Meridian Way, Edmonton, N9 0AS (8803 6900/fax 8884 4975/ leisurecentre@leevalleypark.org.uk). Edmonton Green rail/W8 bus/Tottenham Hale tube, then 363 bus.* **Open** 8am-10pm daily. **Rates** £5.65; £2.35 5-16s. **Credit** MC, V.

Tent City Acton *Old Oak Common Lane, Acton, W3 7DP (8376 3432/www.tentcity.co.uk). East Acton tube.* **Open** *June-Sept* 24hrs daily. *Oct-May closed.* **Rates** £6; £3 under-12s; free under-5s; 10% discounts for groups. **No credit cards.**

Tent City Hackney *Millfields Road, E5 0AR (8376 3432/www.tentcity.co.uk). Liverpool Street tube/rail/ Hackney Downs rail, then 242 bus/38 bus.* **Open** *June-Sept* 24hrs daily. *Oct-May closed.* **Rates** £5; £2.50 under-15s; free under-5s. **No credit cards.**

Emergency accommodation

Shelter is a national charity that provides advice on housing and homelessness. If you get stranded in London without anywhere to stay, call its 24-hour helpline on 0808 800 4444.

Longer stays

If you're planning on staying for months rather than weeks, it may work out cheaper to rent a place. Even so, accommodation is still highly expensive – plus you'll normally have to pay a month's rent in advance and a further month's rent as a deposit – and competition is fierce. The best source for places to rent is *Loot*, published daily. Capital Radio publishes a flatshare list, available from the foyer (30 Leicester Square, WC2H 7LA, Leicester Square tube) every Thursday around 4pm. Also try *Time Out* magazine (available from Tuesdays in central London and Wednesday further out), and *Midweek* (free from outside tube stations on Thursdays).

As a rough guide, you're unlikely to get a studio (no separate bedroom or, often, kitchen) or a one-bedroom flat for less than £500 per month without using up a lifetime's worth of luck or moving to one of outer London's less desirable suburbs. If you want to stay in a hip area such as Notting Hill, expect to fork out around double that, perhaps more. If, however, you can stomach a room in a shared flat/house, you can find accommodation for less than £300 a month in the further reaches of the East End and south London, rising to around £600 a month in the swankier likes of Fulham or Hampstead.

Sightseeing

Feature boxes

Introduction

London starts here.

After the storm, now the calm. With the opening of the British Airways London Eye, the (now-closed) Millennium Dome, Tate Modern, the assorted museums at Somerset House, the Great Court at the British Museum and the Wellcome Wing at the Science Museum, along with countless smaller projects, London's sights had a startlingly busy year in 2000.

It's no surprise, then, that 2001 will be quieter on the openings and revamps front. But there's nothing wrong with that: London's museums circuit is now better than ever, and a little bit of quiet (and proud) consolidation won't hurt a bit.

Find your way around with our pick of the best sights (*see p67*) and our chapter by chapter area guide, which contains comprehensive reviews of the city's attractions. You'll discover that the old cliché about the city holding something for everyone is actually grounded in fact.

London Pass

The **London Pass** offers free entry to more than 50 attractions and free travel on public transport, and is available for one, two, three and six days, priced at £22/£14 child,

Don't miss London's capital sights.

The best Sights

For views of London
British Airways London Eye (p69); the Monument (p83); St Paul's Cathedral (p91); Primrose Hill (p145); Waterloo Bridge (p71).

For being at one with nature
Chelsea Physic Garden (p143); WWT Wetland Centre (p176); swimming in Hampstead Ponds (p148).

For a romantic rendezvous
Albert Memorial (p138); National Gallery (p129); London Zoo (p109).

For ghouls, ghosts & spooks
Jack the Ripper Mystery Walk from London Walks (p68); London Dungeon (p78); Old Operating Theatre, Museum & Herb Garret (p78).

For leaving the tourist loop
Horniman Museum (p172); Lord's Tour & MCC Museum (p145); Dennis Severs' House (p154).

For culture vultures
Tate Modern (p77); British Museum (p101); Hayward Gallery (p73).

For summer in the city
Soho Square (p121); St James's Park (p130); Royal Botanic Gardens (Kew Gardens) (p176).

For winter in the city
Ice-skating at Somerset House (p96); candle-lit evening tours of Sir John Soane's Museum (p99); Christmas exhibition at the Geffrye Museum (p155).

For olde England
Tower of London (p92); Hampton Court Palace (p178); the Inns of Court (p96).

For millennial improvement
Wellcome Wing at the Science Museum (p139); Wallace Collection (p108); Dulwich Picture Gallery (p172).

£39/£24 child, £49/£30 child and £79/£42 child, respectively. However, before you rush in, remember that many of London's premier attractions – such as the British Museum, the Tate Modern and the National Gallery – are free anyway, and some of those that charge admission offer free entry in the late afternoon. You'll also have to do some pretty intensive sightseeing to make the card pay... but you do get a range of 'extras', such as £5 worth of free phone calls, a commission-free currency exchange, unlimited free Internet access, photo processing offers, deals at selected restaurants and a guidebook.

For more information, and to buy online, go to www.londonpass.com, or call 0870 242 9988 for credit card bookings (8.30am-8pm Mon-Fri; 10am-4pm Sat). The cards are also available from assorted tourist information centres.

Trips & tours

Balloon tours
Adventure Balloons *Winchfield Park, London Road, Hartley Wintney, Hampshire, RG27 8HY (01252 844222/www.adventureballoons.co.uk).* **Flights** *Apr-Oct* morning & evenings daily, weather permitting. **Fares** £130-£150. **Credit** MC, V.

Bicycle tours
See p361.

Bus tours
Big Bus Company *7233 9533/0800 169 1365/www.bigbus.co.uk.* **Open-top bus tours** two different routes, 2-3hrs; both with live commentary. **Departures** every 15mins from Green Park, Victoria and Marble Arch. *Summer* 8.30am-7pm daily. *Winter* 8.30am-4.30pm daily. **Pick-up** Green Park (near the Ritz); Marble Arch (Speaker's Corner); Victoria (outside Royal Westminster Hotel, 48 Buckingham Palace Road, SW1). **Fares** £15; £6 children; tickets are valid for 24hrs, and are interchangeable between routes, allowing you to hop on and off the bus at over 50 different locations.
London Pride *01708 631122/ www.londonpride.co.uk.* **Departures** *Apr-Sept* 8.30am-8pm daily. *Oct-Mar* 9am-6pm daily; grand tour 1hr 45mins. **Fares** from 50p; £12.50 (for all tours), £5.50 5-15s, £30 family, valid 24hrs. Also routes from Buckingham Palace, Russell Square to the South Kensington museums, Bayswater to Euston Station and Bloomsbury to Tate Gallery.
Original London Sightseeing Tour *8877 1722/ www.theoriginaltour.com.* **Departures** *Summer* 9am-7pm daily. *Winter* 9.30am-5pm daily. **Pick-up** Victoria Street; Grosvenor Gardens; Marble Arch (Speaker's Corner); Baker Street tube (forecourt); Haymarket (at bus stop L); Charing Cross Station (Strand); Charing Cross. **Fares** £14; £7.50 concessions.

Helicopter tours
Cabair Helicopters *Elstree Aerodrome, Boreham Wood, Hertfordshire WD6 3AW(8953 4411/ www.cabair.com). Elstree rail.* **Flights** from 10.30am Sun. **Fares** £125. **Credit** AmEx, DC, MC, V.

On the buses

As anyone who's ever stumbled off the back of one on the way home from the pub, or dashed out of the rain onto one on Oxford Street will testify, the **Routemaster** is the quintessential mode of London transport. These bright red, open-backed, double-decker buses have been patrolling London's streets since the mid-1950s and are now as closely associated with the city as Beefeaters or red phone boxes.

The beauty of catching the bus is that it gives you an impression of the city as a whole. On the bus, you can trace the route from one area to the next and get a feel for them in relation to each other. And the beauty of the Routemaster is that its

open back allows you to hop on or off when the bus comes to halt. So if something catches your eye, leap off and investigate there and then, rather than being driven another half-a-mile down the road and having to walk back.

There really is no better way to tour the city, and the cheapness of the fares (£1 within Zone 1, 70p everywhere else; free with a Travelcard) make them the best bargain in town. Head down to one of the busy stops at Trafalgar Square, Piccadilly Circus, Victoria Station, King's Cross or Oxford Street and spend an afternoon exploring. You may want to start with one of our featured routes (see p110, p151 and p159), or try buses 8, 10, 12 or 73.

Personal tours

Tour Guides *7495 5504.*
Tailor-made tours with Blue Badge guides for individuals, small or large groups, on foot, by car, coach or boat.

River tours

See p359.

Specialist tours

Architectural Dialogue *7267 7697.* **Departures** 10.15am Sat; 10.45am Sun. **Meeting point** outside gates of Royal Academy of Arts, Piccadilly, W1 (Piccadilly Circus tube). **Duration** 3hrs (and occasional one-day tours; phone for details). **Tickets** £18.50; £13 students; advance booking advisable.
Beatles Walks *7624 3978/www.walks.com.*
Beatles Magical Mystery Tour Departures 2pm Wed; 11am Thur, Sun. **Pick-up** Dominion Theatre, Tottenham Court Road, W1 (Tottenham Court Road tube). **Beatles In My Life Tour Departures** 11.20am Tue, Sat. **Meeting point** Marylebone tube. **Duration** *Both* 2hrs 30mins. **Tickets** *Both* £5; £3.50 concessions.
Garden Day Tours *01935 815924/from USA 1-800 873 7145/www.gentlejourneys.co.uk.*
Departures *May-Sept* 8.45am Tue-Fri, Sun (return 6.30pm). **Meeting point** Victoria Coach Station. **Tickets** £56 per day (lunch not included).
Jack the Ripper Mystery Walk *8558 9446/ mobile 07957 388280/www.mysterywalks.co.uk.*
Departures 8pm Wed, Sun; 7pm Fri.

Duration 2hrs. **Meeting point** Aldgate tube. **Tickets** £5; £3.50 concessions. Ghost walk also available; phone for details.

Taxi tours

Black Taxi Tours of London *7289 4371/ www.blacktaxitours.co.uk.* **Cost** £70.
A tailored two-hour tour for up to five people.

Walking tours

Ever-increasing numbers of companies and individuals are running (often themed) walks around London. Arguably the best is **Original London Walks** (7624 3978, www.walks.com), which encompasses walks on everything from Sherlock Holmes to riverside pubs. Also recommended is **ZigZag Audio Tours** (7435 3736, www.zigzagtours.com), which offers two anecdote-filled self-guided walks in various languages, one in the City and one around the royal sights of London; for £7.95, it will deliver a Walkman with a tour on cassette to your home or hotel. Other walk companies include **Citisights** (8806 4325), **Historical Tours** (8668 4019), **Capital Walks** (8650 7640), **Cityguide Walks** (01895 675389) and **Stepping Out** (8881 2933). If you want to do it yourself, the excellent **Green Chain** walks connect many of the green spaces of south-east London (8921 5028, www.greenchain.com).

Finally, the *Time Out Book of London Walks* (£9.99) details 30 walks by different writers around the capital.

The South Bank & Bankside

Revitalised by millennial projects, London's riverside is more attractive than ever.

Maps p403, p406 & p407

The south side of the Thames, between Lambeth and Tower Bridges, may seem an unorthodox place to start a tour of central London, but, in terms of history and culture and a wealth of millennium developments, there's no more absorbing and rewarding part of the city. Indeed, if you're returning to London after a few years away, the chances are you'll hardly recognise the area, such is its new image and atmosphere.

Quite aside from the myriad cultural delights found along it, the South Bank is defined by its pedestrian-friendly accessibility. While most of the north side of the river is dominated by fume-filled expressways, the entire length of the south side can be walked without coming into contact with a single car. The river is arguably London's greatest asset, and the South Bank is said river's focal point. Enjoy it.

The South Bank

Lambeth Bridge to Hungerford Bridge

Just north of Lambeth Bridge huddle the red-brick buildings of **Lambeth Palace**, official residence of the Archbishops of Canterbury since the 12th century and closed to the public. Next door is the **Museum of Garden History** (*see p70*) in the old church of St Mary-at-Lambeth. St Thomas's Hospital, containing the **Florence Nightingale Museum** (*see p70*), stands on one side of Westminster Bridge, but the dominant presence is the looming bulk of the revamped **County Hall**. Home of the Greater London Council until its abolition in 1986, it contains two hotels, restaurants, the two-floor arcade-game nirvana of **Namco Station**, the **London Aquarium** and the **Dali Universe** (for both, *see p70*). Next door, backing on to the pleasant Jubilee Gardens, is the stunning **British Airways London Eye** (*see below*). However, assuming Rick Mather's plans get the go-ahead, the stretch of river from the Eye to **Hungerford Bridge** (whose revamp has been delayed; *see p127*) will be dramatically redeveloped in the next few years; *see p71* for details.

See the town from the **London Eye**.

British Airways London Eye

Jubilee Gardens, next to County Hall, SE1 (0870 500 0600/www.ba-londoneye.com). Westminster tube/ Waterloo tube/rail. **Open** *Oct-Mar* 10am-7pm daily. *31 Mar-25 May, 10 Sept-30 Sept* 10am-8pm daily. *26 May-9 Sept* 10am-10pm daily. **Admission** *until 1 Apr* £8.50; £6.50 OAPs, disabled. *2 Apr-1 July, 1 Oct-31 Dec* £9; £7 OAPs, disabled. *2 July-30 Sept* £9.50; £7.50 OAPs, disabled. *All year* £5 5-15s; free under-5s (must have ticket). **Map** p401 M8.

For a long time, it didn't look good for the British Airways London Eye. After the initial controversy over the design of the mammoth big wheel came the comedy of errors that was the erection of the thing. The problems didn't end once it had been hoisted up onto its base opposite Jubilee Gardens: the grand Millennium Eve opening was delayed by safety concerns, and it was a good few weeks before the wheel started turning with passengers on board.

But since then, the public reaction has been almost uniformly positive, and London now loves its big wheel. The Eye is now an established part of the capital's skyline, visible from all over town, and locals and visitors have been completely won over by the stunning vistas afforded from one of the 32 capsules (which each hold 25 people) on the 30-minute journey: views of up to 25 miles (40km) can be enjoyed on clear days. With the public barred from London's three tallest buildings (Canary Wharf Tower, NatWest Tower and BT Tower), the London Eye, as the city's fourth tallest structure, offers an unparalleled picture of the capital. Were it not for the nightmarish bookings system – don't expect to just turn up and take a ride; advance booking is more or less mandatory – it'd be just about perfect.

Dali Universe

County Hall, Riverside Building, SE1 (7620 2420/ www.daliuniverse.com). Waterloo tube/rail. **Open** 10am-5.30pm daily. **Admission** £8.50; £6 concessions; £5 children, £22 family. **Map** p401 M8.
Dali Universe opened in June 2000, and, with dripping clocks aplenty, it's been packing them in ever since. Appropriately, in a surreal kind of way, it's located next door to the London Eye. Curated by longtime Dali friend and collector Benjamin Levi, the exhibit features more than 500 works by the famed Spanish artist, including *Spellbound*, the enormous oil painting he created for the set of the 1945 Alfred Hitchcock film of the same name. Along with dozens of sculptures (including *Persistence of Memory*), the show includes hundreds of graphics, watercolours and lithographs, as well as a few pieces of furniture such as his *Mae West Lips Sofa*. If you like your clocks runny and your elephants tall, this is your kind of place.

Florence Nightingale Museum

St Thomas's Hospital, 2 Lambeth Palace Road, SE1 (7620 0374/www.florence-nightingale.co.uk). Westminster tube/Waterloo tube/rail. **Open** 10am-5pm Mon-Fri (last entry 4pm); 11.30am-4.30pm Sat, Sun (last entry 3.30pm). **Admission** £4.80; £3.60 concessions; £10 family. **Credit** AmEx, MC, V. **Map** p401 M9.
Florence Nightingale's chief achievement in a long career of social campaigning was to establish nursing as a disciplined profession: 'her lady and the lamp' care in the Crimea was but a small part of her contribution to medicine. In 1859, she set up the first nursing school at St Thomas's, a fact celebrated in the well thought-out displays of this small museum.

London Aquarium

County Hall, Riverside Building, Westminster Bridge Road, SE1 (7967 8000/www.londonaquarium.co.uk). Westminster tube/Waterloo tube/rail. **Open** 10am-6pm daily (last entry 5pm). **Admission** £8.50; £5 3-14s, £6.50 concessions; £24 family; free under-3s, wheelchair-users. **Credit** MC, V. **Map** p401 M9.
When push comes to shove, an aquarium is basically an aquarium. But as bloody great big fish-tanks go, this one's a definite winner. The tanks are somewhat randomly divided by ocean (Atlantic, Pacific and Indian), animal type (Invertebrates) and, well, everything else (Freshwater, Rainforest, Mangrove, Coral Reef). Of these, the Pacific wins hands down. Huge menacing tiger sharks prowl through a strange setting of enormous, Easter Island style statues of human heads. Rays flutter gracefully by, moonfish gaze back ethereally, and even the big ugly fish act cute, scratching their backs on stones on the 'ocean' floor. Children will love trying to touch the rays in the hands-on room, and the adults will find it all just as interesting, making it one of those rare things you can do with the kids that won't bore you to death.

Museum of Garden History

St Mary-at-Lambeth, Lambeth Palace Road, SE1 (7633 9701). Waterloo tube/rail/C10, 507 bus. **Open** *Feb* 11am-2pm Mon-Fri; *5 Mar-Dec* 10.30am-4pm Mon-Fri; 10.30am-5pm Sun. **Admission** free; donations appreciated. **Map** p401 L10.
Inside St Mary-at-Lambeth Church, antique horticultural tools and photographic panels on famous garden designers and plant hunters illustrate the development of the English passion for gardening. The tireless John Tradescant, gardener to James I and Charles I, is given particular prominence. A replica of a 17th-century knot garden has been created in the tiny church courtyard. One of the sarcophagi here contains the remains of Captain Bligh, abandoned by his mutinous crew on the Pacific.

London Aquarium. Chips not pictured.

Bridges over troubled water

London Bridge

Original bridge: London's first bridge, it was built during the Roman occupation of the city, perhaps as early as 43 AD.

Current bridge: The most recent of several London Bridges opened in 1973, replacing John Rennie's 1831 model.

Best known for: Being sold to the US. The aforementioned Rennie model was bought by an eccentric American, Robert McCulloch, who paid $2.46 million for the bridge, flew it across the Atlantic brick by brick, and re-erected it in Lake Havasu City, Arizona. Legend has it he thought he was buying Tower Bridge. D'oh.

Betcha didn't know: The nursery rhyme *London Bridge Is Falling Down* has its origins in an 11th-century Norse poem.

Tower Bridge

Original bridge: Built between 1886 and 1894 to the designs of Horace Jones, who didn't live to see its completion.

Current bridge: The bridge that stands today is the original Tower Bridge. In fact, it was London's newest bridge for 106 years, until the construction of the Millennium Bridge in the years leading up to 2000.

Best known for: It's a bascule bridge, meaning that it can be raised to allow tall boats to pass. It was built with this feature after fears that it would disrupt river traffic, and is still raised around 500 times a year, much to the entertainment of visitors and the profound irritation of drivers trying to cross the river.

Betcha didn't know: The original pedestrian walkways, 112 feet above the water, had to be closed after they proved too popular with suicidal types looking to make a grand exit.

Waterloo Bridge

Original bridge: Built between 1811 and 1817 to designs by John Rennie, and opened on the second anniversary of the Battle of Waterloo, 18 June 1817.

Current bridge: Designed by Sir Giles Gilbert Scott, it was completed in 1942.

Best known for: Some stunning views of the city, the best from any of London's bridges. And for its starring role in the Kinks' *Waterloo Sunset*.

Betcha didn't know: When the original Waterloo Bridge was demolished in 1936, the 70,000 tons of stone from which it was built was turned into ornamental fireplaces.

Sightseeing

Hungerford Bridge to Blackfriars Bridge

The arts complex on the south bank, known, imaginatively, as the **South Bank Centre** (*see p307*), represents London at its most self-consciously modern. Denys Lasdun's **Royal Festival Hall** was built to mark the 1951 Festival of Britain. The new buildings were a showcase for contemporary architectural and building skills. It would be fair to say that it's not universally admired, although appreciation is not made easier by the raised concrete walkways that stranglingly swirl about it and the proximity of the true smack-in-the-face brutalism of the **Hayward Gallery** (*see p73*).

But at long last, this too-shabby stretch of prime London real estate – from County Hall down to Waterloo Bridge, to be precise – looks set to be revamped. After assorted ideas fell by the wayside, a plan put together by architect Rick Mather has been given the thumbs-up after public consultation. Part one of the plan, a £50-million, 50th-anniversary refurbishment of the Festival Hall that includes everything from the

staff offices to the hall's acoustics, has just begun. Assuming funding is secured and final planning permission is approved, then phase two, which could start in 2002, will see the extension of **Jubilee Gardens** from the London Eye to the Hungerford Bridge, a stretch that will also provide a home for the BFI's proposed **Film Centre** (a five-screen cinema, a library, education facilities and a museum). And phase three will see the extension – though not, sadly, demolition – of the Hayward Gallery, plus some kind of as-yet undecided redevelopment work on the vile building that houses the Queen Elizabeth Hall and Purcell Room, the other two components in the South Bank Centre. Should this go ahead – and assuming the ongoing modernisation of the nearby **Royal National Theatre** (*see p330*), London's leading repertory theatre, is finished on schedule in 2003 – then London's riverfront should at last make for a stunning sight. For now, though, make do with one of the richest cultural strips in the world, and some stunning views – especially after dark, or at the sunset so memorably eulogised by the Kinks – from Waterloo Bridge.

Money From Home In Minutes.

If you're stuck for cash on your travels, don't panic. Millions of people trust Western Union to transfer money in minutes to 176 countries and over 78,000 locations worldwide. Our record of safety and reliability is second to none. For more information, call Western Union: USA 1-800-325-6000, Canada 1-800-235-0000. Wherever you are, you're never far from home.

www.westernunion.com

WESTERN UNION | MONEY TRANSFER

The fastest way to send money worldwide.

Between Waterloo and Blackfriars bridges, the most distinctive building is the beautifully restored **Oxo Tower Wharf**. The cleverly conceived art deco tower incorporates the word 'OXO' into its design, thereby circumventing council rules against large-scale advertising. The building now contains flats and small retail crafts units, and is topped by a glitzy restaurant and bar (*see p207*), run by the people behind Harvey Nichols' Fifth Floor restaurant (*see p205*). Anyone can enjoy the views from the top from the eighth-floor public viewing gallery. The tower and much of the surrounding housing (plus the cutesy shops of **Gabriel's Wharf**) are maintained by the admirable, non-profit-making Coin Street Community Builders, who have done much to retain the integrity of this fast-developing area and ensure that the original inhabitants are not priced out.

Hayward Gallery

Belvedere Road, SE1 (box office 7960 4242/ recorded information 7261 0127/www.sbc.org.uk). Embankment tube/Waterloo tube/rail. **Open** *During exhibitions* 10am-6pm Mon, Thur-Sun; 10am-8pm Tue, Wed. **Admission** varies (phone for details). **Credit** AmEx, DC, MC, V. **Map** p401 M8.
The Hayward, part of the South Bank's thriving arts scene, is one of London's finest venues for contemporary and historical art, partly because of the flexibility of its space. The high admission charges of around £8 are usually justified, with retrospectives (Anish Kapoor, Bruce Nauman and Belgian artist Panamarenko in recent years) and themed shows –

such as last year's Sonic Boom (work involving sound) and Spectacular Bodies (the science and art of the human body) – featured on a regular basis. In 2001, there'll be a retrospective of photographer Brassaï alongside an exhibition of Goya's Drawings (until 13 May); a show given over to the work of photorealist American painter Malcolm Morley (14 June-27 Aug); and, in autumn (dates to be confirmed), a show of contemporary Japanese art.

The Museum of...

The Barge House, Oxo Tower Wharf, Barge House Street, SE1 (7401 2255/www.themuseumof.org). Southwark tube/Waterloo tube/rail. **Open** noon-6.30pm Wed-Sun (last entry 6pm); closed Mon, Tue. **Admission** free. **Map** p404 N7.
This unique and often captivating venture aims to 'ask questions about our relationship with material culture'. As the name suggests, the museum's subject matter varies: all the exhibits here are temporary, with the museum taking the name of its theme as and when it changes. If forthcoming shows such as the Museum of the River Thames (Mar 22 until late June 2001) are as entertaining as previous exhibitions such as the Museum of Me and 2000's Museum of the Unknown, they should be well worth a look.

Around Waterloo

A walkway links the Royal Festival Hall to **Waterloo station**, where Eurostar trains arrive and depart from under Nicholas Grimshaw's glass-roofed terminus. This short walk once involved negotiating a complicated,

The Millennium Bridge. See, it doesn't wobble at all. Honest. *See p74.*

unpleasant route across busy roads and down stinking alleys, but, again, great strides are being taken to make the experience easier and more pleasant. The roundabout outside Waterloo station was once home to legions of homeless people who camped out in 'cardboard city'. No longer. The £20-million **BFI London IMAX Cinema** (*see p292*) has been built on the site, featuring the biggest screen in Europe.

Behind the station on the other side, **Lower Marsh** has a lively market on weekdays and leads on to The Cut, home of the Young Vic (*see p336*) and the Old Vic theatres. The former contains the excellent Konditor & Cook café (*see p206* **Cafés, coffee and light lunches**).

Bankside

The original Blackfriars Bridge (1760-9) was the third to span the Thames. It was under here that Italian banker Roberto Calvi was found hanging in 1982. The area between here and London Bridge, known as **Bankside**, was, for many centuries, London's pleasure zone. As it was outside the puritanical jurisdiction of the City, theatres, bear-baiting pits, bawdy houses, inns and other dens of iniquity could freely prosper. There's no little irony that Bankside (officially deemed 'a naughty place' by royal proclamation in 1547) fell within the sway of the Bishops of Winchester. Far from condemning the depravity, the church made a tidy sum from its regulation – it controlled the local brothels, among other things – and if anyone got too unruly they could always be cast into the dank depths of the Clink Prison (now the **Clink Prison Museum**; *see below*). Next door are the remains of **Winchester Palace**, though little is left beyond the rose window of the Great Hall.

Like Battersea Power Station upriver, Bankside Power Station was designed by Sir Giles Gilbert Scott; it makes a magnificent home for the **Tate Modern**'s art collection (*see p77*). Tiny in comparison, and a reminder of the Bankside of old, is its neighbour, the reconstructed **Shakespeare's Globe** (*see p75*). Standing in its shadow is another old playhouse, the **Rose Theatre** (*see p75*), and next door is a curious little terrace, containing the house in which Wren is said to have lived during the construction of St Paul's Cathedral.

St Paul's is now linked to Bankside – and, specifically, the Tate Modern – by Norman Foster's **Millennium Bridge**. It's just a shame that this eye-catching structure, London's first new bridge in over a century, was closed to the public after a few days due to it being comically 'blessed' with a pronounced wobble when a number of people walked across it; expect it to reopen in autumn 2001 (*see p32*). Art-lovers

may find something of interest at the **Bankside Gallery** (48 Hopton Street), home to the Royal Watercolour Society and the Royal Society of Painter/Printmakers. Further east is the redeveloped **Southwark Cathedral** (*see p77*).

Information on all the sights in the Bankside and Borough areas can be gleaned from the **Southwark Information Centre** opposite London Bridge station (7403 8299, open 10am-6pm Mon-Sat, 10am-5.30pm Sun).

Clink Prison Museum

1 Clink Street, SE1 (7378 1558/www.clink.co.uk).
London Bridge tube/rail. **Open** 10am-6pm daily.
Admission £4; £3 concessions; £9 family.
No credit cards. Map p404 P8.
The Clink was the Bishop of Winchester's private prison, and housed all manner of raffish misbehavers – prostitutes (the locals brothels were controlled by the church), drunks, actors and more – back between the 12th and 16th centuries. It's also the origin of the phrase 'in the clink', meaning 'in jail'. Given this fascinating history, then, it's positively shameful that the exhibition devoted to it should be such a shoddy affair. The few recreations of prison scenes have seen better days, while the explanatory notes and displays are less than illuminating and shabbily maintained. Bankside's feeblest 'attraction' (and we use the word advisedly).

Golden Hinde

St Mary Overie Dock, Cathedral Street, SE1
(7403 0123/www.goldenhinde.co.uk). Monument
tube/London Bridge tube/rail. **Open** daily, times vary; phone for details. **Admission** £2.50;
£2.10 concessions; £1.75 4-13s; £6.50 family.
Credit MC, V. **Map** p404 P8.
This full-size reconstruction of Sir Francis Drake's 16th-century flagship looks impressively pristine considering the two decades it has spent circumnavigating the world as a seaborne museum. Years of research went into producing this authentic reproduction, now in a dry dock, and it shows: the interior has been recreated in minute detail and the diminutive proportions of the gun deck and hold feel painfully real. The kid-friendly atmosphere on board is fleshed out by 'crew' in Elizabethan costume. Tickets are sold from the card shop next to the ship.

HMS Belfast

Morgan's Lane, Tooley Street, SE1 (7940 6328/
www.hmsbelfast.org.uk). London Bridge tube/rail.
Open *Mar-Oct* 10am-6pm daily (last entry 5.15pm).
Nov-Feb 10am-5pm daily (last entry 4.15pm).
Admission £5; £3.90 concessions; free under-16s.
Credit MC, V. **Map** p405 R8.
One of the most spectacular sights on the Thames, this 11,500-ton battlecruiser, built in 1938, was instrumental in the sinking of the German battleship *Scharnhorst* during World War II and remained in active service until just after the Korean War. Exploring its seven decks, boiler and engine rooms and massive gun turrets is great fun, especially for

An hour in… The Tate Modern

The must-see exhibits for visitors in a rush

Kandinsky's *Cossacks* (Manifestos Room, History/Memory/Society, level 5): A great work from the noted Russian abstract artist

Duchamp's Fountain (Marcel Duchamp & Francis Picabia Room, Still Life/Object/Real Life, level 3): Thankfully, this is one urinal not open to the public

Richard Long & Claude Monet (Richard Long & Claude Monet Room, Landscape/Matter/Environment, level 3): Whose side are you on?

Mark Rothko's *The Seagram Murals* (Mark Rothko Room, Landscape/Matter/Environment, level 3): A stunning work from an undervalued American artist

Jackson Pollock's *No.23* (Automatism Room, Nude/Action/Body, level 5): Splish, splash, he was making a dash

Warhol's *Jackie* (Andy Warhol Room, History/Memory/Society, level 5): The cult of celebrity simultaneously revered and trashed

children. Oddly, the front two turrets are trained on the Scratchwood motorway services on the M1, 122 miles (20km) away to the north-west of London; more, one assumes, to demonstrate the guns' range than to comment on the quality of motorway food.

Rose Theatre

56 Park Street, SE1 (7593 0026/ www.rosetheatre.org.uk). Cannon Street or London Bridge tube/rail. **Open** 10am-5pm daily (last entry 4.30pm). **Admission** £3; £2 5-15s; £2.50 concessions. **Credit** DC, MC, V. **Map** p404 P8.

Everyone knows the Globe, but, until excavations carried out by Museum of London archaeologists in 1989, few knew of the 16th-century Rose Theatre. In fact, the Rose – built by Philip Henslowe and operational as a theatre from 1587 until 1606; what the Globe is to Shakespeare, the Rose is to Marlowe – was the first playhouse to be built at Bankside. Without it, the Globe would have ended up somewhere else, if it had been built at all. In the long term, the Rose Theatre Trust hopes to fully excavate the site. At the moment, funding is scarce, so for now, the space has been converted by William Audley into an engaging and occasionally fascinating sound, vision and light exhibition aimed at raising awareness of the Rose and funding for its continuing excavation.

Shakespeare's Globe

New Globe Walk, SE1 (7902 1500/ www.shakespeares-globe.org). Mansion House or Southwark tube/London Bridge tube/rail.

Open *May-Sept* 9am-12.30pm daily; *Oct-Apr* 10am-5pm daily. **Admission** £7.50; £5 5-15s; £6 concessions; £23 family. **Credit** AmEx, MC, V. **Map** p404 O7.

The original Globe, where many of Shakespeare's plays were first staged, burned down in 1613 during a performance of *Henry VIII*, when a cannon spark set fire to the thatched roof. Nearly 400 years later, it was rebuilt not far from its original site, using construction methods and materials as close to the originals as possible. You can't help but feel that Shakespeare would be pleased with the reconstruction of his beloved theatre, which offers an impressive exhibition of theatrical memorabilia related to famous performances of his works. The centrepiece is a guided tour of the theatre itself. However, it's a little self-congratulatory, and it's not beyond the realms of possibility that non-*aficionados* may consider it dull; surely only true disciples of the stage or devoted students of Bill are likely to find themselves caught up in the lingering discussion of every detail of the theatre's construction and operation.

That said, the Globe's theatrical repertory under Mark Rylance has confounded those critics who thought it would be nothing more than a period piece. Productions here are staged from May to September only, and are historically authentic, relying on natural light, a simple, unchanging set and audience participation. Note that there are no guided tours in the afternoon from May to September, when performances are held (though visitors still have access to the exhibition). For more on the theatre, *see p331*.

London has only one museum. The Museum of London.

Discover the fascinating history of London from prehistoric to modern times. With permanent galleries, special exhibitions and events for visitors of all ages, the Museum of London aims to inspire a passion for London in all our visitors.

London Wall, EC2
close to St Paul's
Information 020 7600 0807
www.museumoflondon.org.uk

MUSEUM OF LONDON

Southwark Cathedral

Montague Close, SE1 (7367 6700/www.dswark.org).
London Bridge tube/rail. **Open** 8am-6pm daily
(closing times vary on religious holidays). **Services**
8am, 8.15am, 12.30pm, 12.45pm, 5.30pm, Mon-Fri;
9am, 9.15am, 4pm, Sat; 9am, 9.15am, 11am, 3pm, Sun.
Admission suggested donation £2.50. **Map** p404 P8.
Originally the monastic church of St Mary Overie,
this splendid building became an Anglican cathedral in 1905. The first church on the site may date
from as early as the seventh century; the oldest parts
of the present building are still over 800 years old.
After the Reformation, the church fell into disrepair
and was partially used as a bakery and a pigsty.
Heavy-handed Victorian restoration added to the
fascinating mix of architectural styles, including a
fine Gothic choir. John Harvard, benefactor of
Harvard University, was born in Southwark in 1607
and baptised in the church; more recently, the John
Harvard Chapel was the setting for the film *The
Slipper and the Rose.*

Despite its charm and history, the cathedral is all
too often overlooked by visitors to the capital.
However, it's to be hoped that the addition in 2000
of a visitors' centre, a refectory, a theological library
and – simplest yet best of all – some stunning flood-
lighting that shows off the cathedral wonderfully
well at night will help to draw more interested parties to one of the most unsung treats in Bankside.

Tate Modern

25 Sumner Street, SE1 (7887 8000/
www.tate.org.uk). *Southwark tube.* **Open**
10am-6pm Mon-Thur, Sun; 10am-10pm Fri, Sat.
Admission free. **Map** p401 O7.
In May 2000, one of the most eagerly awaited of all
London's millennium projects opened to the public:
the new home of the Tate's collection of international
modern art from last century. And it's hard to imagine how it could have been any more successful,
attracting many times more visitors in its first year
than were ever expected.

Understandably, it's the building itself that has
received much of the attention. Sir Giles Gilbert
Scott's former Bankside Power Station was internally remodelled by Herzog and de Meuron to make
the most of a vast concourse in the heart of the building. This space, the **Turbine Hall**, creates a dramatic entrance to the museum if you go in via the
wide sloping path to the west. The galleries themselves run along a slice of the building on its northern face, and are arranged thematically rather than
by chronology or place of origin. This works well:
the themes are wide enough in scope for several
artists to break ranks and drift from one grouping
to another. The Still Life/Real Life/Object section
takes in the likes of Léger, Duchamp, Susan
Hiller and Bill Woodrow; Monet, Beuys and Rothko
inhabit the Landscape/Matter/Environment space;
Bruce Nauman, Sam Taylor-Wood and Louise
Bourgeois share the Nude/Action/Body zone; and
History/Memory/Society are tried and tested by the
likes of Mondrian, Warhol and Stanley Spencer.

Temporary exhibitions are given space on level
four. The first new show of 2001 will be Century
City: Art and Culture in the Modern Metropolis
(until 29 April), looking to certain cities at decisive
moments through the art produced there: Vienna
from 1910-20, for example, where psychological and
sexual introspection and analysis were reflected in
the work of Schiele and Kokoschka. Zero to Infinity:
Arte Povera 1962-1972 will follow (1 June-19 Aug),
overlapping with a show of Giorgio Morandi (22
May-12 Aug). The main show for autumn/winter is
Surrealism: Desire Unbound (20 Sept-16 Dec).

For six months of the year, the vast, breathtaking
Turbine Hall is also given over to temporary
exhibits in the shape of the Unilever Series of commissions. The next work in the series is by Juan
Muñoz, whose new installation kicks off in June and
will play with the scale of the hall and the dwarfed
visitors within it. Prior to that, the space will be
employed by the aforementioned Century City show,
and then left as an architectural space.

In addition to all the art, the Tate Modern has a fantastic shop, choc-a-bloc with books and posters, a
large café on the ground floor and a restaurant with
views across to the City on the top floor (if you can
ever get in). Shuttle buses and boats wend their way
between the Tate Modern and **Tate Britain** (*see
p134*) for those with an insatiable appetite for art and
its surroundings. *See also p75* **An hour in....**

Vinopolis, City of Wine

1 Bank End, SE1 (0870 444 4777/
www.vinopolis.co.uk). *London Bridge tube/rail.*
Open 11am-9pm Mon; 11am-6pm Tue-Fri, Sun;
11am-8pm Sat; (last entry 2 hrs before closing).
Admission £11.50; £5 5-18s; £10.50 OAPs;
£1 discount in advance. **Credit** AmEx, MC, V.
Map p404 P8.
As long as you realise that Vinopolis, set in a large
Bankside warehouse, is little more than an excuse
to wander around drinking under the pretence of
learning about wine-making around the world, you
won't be disappointed. Most country displays con-
sist of a few colour photos on the wall and a video,
although the fact that each visitor is given a head-
set to which they can listen as they wander the place
means the whole exhibit is eerily silent. The audio
dialogue discusses the types of wine produced in
each region. The problem is that it's all a bit silly –
'These grapes will be crushed like no other grape,'
the recording announces dramatically at one point;
irony is conspicuous by its absence – and there's
only so much to say.

Then there's the 'ride through a vineyard on a
Vespa,' which actually involves sitting like an idiot
on a non-moving motorcycle as a film shot in a vineyard is displayed on the windshield. You can listen
to the roar of the engine through headphones if you're
completely uncool. Though each admission ticket
entitles you to five wine tastings, the selection of
wines is not very creative. And sure, they might be
'tastings', but the equivalent of one glass of wine (for
that's approximately what the five will equal in total)

Sightseeing

doesn't represent a great return for the not inconsiderable financial outlay. All in all, you'd be better off spending your money in a wine bar and reading the back of the bottle.

Borough

If you like literature, you'll love Borough. One of the area's biggest draws is the magnificent pub the George, London's sole surviving galleried coaching inn. Before custom-built theatres were introduced, plays were performed in the courtyard while people watched from the galleries. The White Hart Inn, where Mr Pickwick first meets Sam Weller in *The Pickwick Papers*, stood in **White Hart Yard** (it was pulled down in 1889). **Talbot Yard** marks the site of the Tabard Inn, where Chaucer's pilgrims meet at the beginning of *The Canterbury Tales*. The church of **St George-the-Martyr** (on the corner of Borough High Street and Long Lane) is mentioned in Dickens' *Little Dorrit*: the heroine is born in Marshalsea Prison, which used to stand a few doors away. The author's father was jailed in Marshalsea for debt in 1824.

For years, Borough was a congested place, and a recent resurgence has meant that after being more or less forgotten by locals for years, it's getting that way again. Until 1750, **London Bridge** was the only crossing point into the City, and **Borough High Street** became a stagecoach terminus. The 17th-century poet Thomas Dekker described the street as 'a continued ale house with not a shop to be seen between'. The chaotic and raucous Southwark Fair was held here every September from 1462 to 1763, until it was suppressed by the spoilsport Corporation of London.

However, much of the area's heritage is under threat. Borough's unique streets, little touched this century and long popular for period film sets, are threatened by a rail improvement scheme (*see p79* **Step back in time**). The greatest tragedy would be the destruction of covered **Borough Market**, a fruit and vegetable market that has been on the site since the 13th century. The good news is that the area has been given a new lease of life by the weekly Saturday food markets held here, selling gourmet cheese, meat and bread (*see also p255*). The presence of other new interests, such as the acclaimed **fish!** restaurant and shop (*see p193*), have helped raise the profile of the area.

Several attractions are clustered around London Bridge station: the **Old Operating Theatre, Museum & Herb Garret**, the gory **London Dungeon** (for both, *see below*) **Winston Churchill's Britain At War Experience** (*see p79*) .

London Dungeon

28-34 Tooley Street, SE1 (7403 7221/ www.thedungeons.com). London Bridge tube/rail. **Open** *Oct-Mar* 10.30am-6pm (last entry 5pm) daily; *Apr-Sept* 10am-6.30pm (last entry 5.30pm) daily. **Admission** £10.95; £9.50 students; £6.95 5-14s, OAPs, disabled; free under-5s, wheelchair users. **Credit** AmEx, MC, V. **Map** p405 Q8.
Despite its undeniably high cheese 'n' corn quotient, the London Dungeon actually manages to pull off the creepy thing effectively enough. The low lighting adds to the atmosphere, of course, as does the constant soundtrack of screams and moans that never lets up as you stumble through one ghoulish exhibit after another on the Plague, medieval torture, execution and disease. The staff embrace their jobs with admirable enthusiasm: wearing costumes and theatrical makeup, they mutter, 'You're going to die,' as they stride by. It's not very nice, but it is quite pleasantly chilling.

It is, though, a relief when the gloom is balanced by interactive theatre in which you are led before a stern and often hilarious 'judge' for a mock trial. The punishment for all crimes is execution, which comes in the form of a weird boat ride that's supposed to be frightening, but that only scares even slightly when they shut the lights off and send you spinning about in the dark. The most effective part of the whole exhibit is the grim, disturbing and ultimately fascinating Jack the Ripper section, in which actors portraying prostitutes wander among tour groups and discuss the killings in a realistic and deadly serious manner. All in all, far more satisfying than the **Clink Prison Museum** (*see p74*) and the Chamber of Horrors at **Madame Tussaud's** (*see p110*) combined.

London Fire Brigade Museum

94A Southwark Bridge Road, SE1 (7587 2894/ www.london-fire.gov.uk). Borough tube. **Tours** 10.30am, 12.30pm, 2.30pm Mon-Fri by appointment only; closed Sat, Sun. **Admission** £3; £2 7-14s, concessions; free under-7s. **Credit** MC, V. **Map** p404 O9.
Book in advance for a two-hour guided tour of this small museum, which explains the history of firefighting in London since 1666, the year of the Great Fire. Old firefighting appliances are among the exhibits, and visitors might glimpse firefighting recruits training at the adjacent centre.

Old Operating Theatre, Museum & Herb Garret

9A St Thomas's Street, SE1 (7955 4791/ www.thegarret.org.uk). London Bridge tube/rail. **Open** 10.30am-5pm (last entry 4.45pm) daily. **Admission** £3.25; £2.25 concessions; £1.60 under-16s; £8 family. **Map** p405 Q8.
London's only surviving example of an early 19th-century operating theatre – now *there's* a claim to fame – is reached via a narrow flight of stairs to the belfry of an old church. Here, in an adjoining room, ancient banks of viewing stands rise in semicircles

Step back in time

Modernisation and preservation have always been sparring partners. In the case of the **Borough Market** area, they are really locking horns. Ongoing throughout 2000 was a public inquiry in order to decide whether or not Railtrack should receive the go-ahead for their Thameslink 2000 project. Its proposal is to allow trains to run straight through the capital between Kings Lynn and Brighton. Railtrack argue that their project would revolutionise train routes, easing congestion where travellers presently have to change trains and facilitate commuter journeys. But what of this pocket of London whose fate is presently being determined?

The area around Borough Market is one of the last surviving niches of Dickensian London. With the market itself, Southwark Cathedral, Victorian terraced houses and arches, you would be forgiven for thinking you had stepped back in time. Buildings such as the Wheatsheaf pub on Stoney Street date from the mid-18th century (remarkably, this lovely boozer has even resisted major structural modernisations inside as well as out), while a stroll along Park Street reveals rows of terraced houses built in 1831. And the increasingly popular Borough Market, with its excellent range of stalls selling all manner of tempting fresh produce, is

London's last operational wholesale and retail food market and was founded by Royal Charter in 1756.

The disruption of this unique slice of the capital would not only rob us of a thriving community but also one of London's greatest film locations. For besides offering a valuable source of revenue for the area, these streets have set the scene for some great moments in movie history. Since 1980, the area has been utilised in films as wide ranging as *An American Werewolf In London*, *Howards End*, *Lock, Stock and Two Smoking Barrels*, *Entrapment* and *Bridget Jones' Diary*. Christian McWilliams, a freelance location manager, comments that he brings film-makers to Borough 'because of the architecture, atmosphere and the streets. There's nothing like it in London.' Considering that London is used as a location in the making of 80 per cent of British films and television programmes, losing the area would be monumental to the industry.

Borough is a thriving community with unequalled architecture, atmosphere and history. For a taste of London unlike any other, it's a wonderful place to visit. Let's hope that it will remain untainted for the visitors of the future. The view from the window of a train somehow won't be the same.

around a crude wooden bed. Close your eyes and you can almost hear the screams from an unanaesthetised, blindfolded patient as a blood-stained surgeon saws through his leg. Exhibits in the garret illustrate the history of surgery and nursing at Guy's and St Thomas's hospitals.

Winston Churchill's Britain at War Experience

64-66 Tooley Street, SE1 (7403 3171/ www.britainatwar.co.uk). London Bridge tube/rail. **Open** *Apr-Sept* 10am-5.30pm (last entry 5pm) daily. *Oct-Mar* 10am-4.30pm (last entry 4pm) daily. **Admission** £5.95; £3.95 concessions; £2.95 5-16s; £14 family. **Credit** AmEx, MC, V. **Map** p405 Q8.
This 'real life' experience is, inevitably, nothing of the sort. Rather, this is a somewhat shabby attempt to evoke Blitz-time London, with rickety speakers blaring out '40s radio broadcasts and showtunes, and awkward-looking dummies dressed up in period costumes. There is a lot of fascinating memorabilia, though, if you care to look for it among the muddled wall displays, and children might enjoy the atmospheric reproductions of an air raid shelter, a dance hall and a huge darkened bombsite.

Tower Bridge & Bermondsey

The stretch of the river from London to Tower Bridges is dominated by the uncompromising bulk of **HMS Belfast** (*see p74*) and the massive, soaring, glass-roofed arcade of Hay's Galleria. Its centrepiece is David Kemp's splendidly silly *The Navigators* mechanical sculpture. This is the start of **Bermondsey**, an area that was long a focus for Christianity – **Tooley Street** was once home to no fewer than three abbots, a prior and the church of St Olave's. Its near-namesake, **St Olaf House**, a fabulous art deco 1930s warehouse, is worth a look. The area immediately west of Tower Bridge is set to be transformed by the building of the new Norman Foster-designed HQ for the **Greater London Authority** (GLA), due to be completed in 2003.

The capital's most spectacular bridge, **Tower Bridge** is a relatively recent addition to the London skyline, opening not much more than a century ago. If you want to find out more about it, undergo the **Tower Bridge**

Sightseeing

Experience (*see p92*). East of here, **Butler's Wharf** is the home of a trio of Sir Terence Conran restaurants and, just a little further on, the excellent **Design Museum** (*see below*), which Conran, the man who did much to bring good household design to the ordinary punter, helped establish. Around the corner is the more idiosyncratic charm of the **Bramah Tea & Coffee Museum** (*see below*).

Much of this area has a Dickensian feel to it. Check out **St Saviour's Dock**, a muddy creek between towering warehouses, visible over a low parapet in Jamaica Road. In Dickens's day, the streets around here formed a slum called Jacob's Island, where Bill Sikes gets his come-uppance in *Oliver Twist*. Bermondsey Square is home to a superb antiques market (*see p255*).

Bramah Museum of Tea & Coffee

corner of Gainsford Street & Maguire Street, SE1 (7378 0222/www.bramahmuseum.co.uk). Tower Hill tube/London Bridge tube/rail//P11, 15, 42, 47, 78 bus. **Open** 10am-6pm daily. **Admission** £4; £3 concessions. **Credit** AmEx, DC, MC, V. **Map** p405 S9.
Though he's been in the business for half a century, it was only in the early 1990s that Edward Bramah, a former tea taster, set up this unusual museum to chart the history of tea and coffee drinking. The new premises allow the two infusions to be studied separately, and their important role in British society to be documented. There's also an impressive collection of coffee makers and teapots (including the world's largest), and a café where you can try out the real thing.

Design Museum

28 Shad Thames, SE1 (7403 6933/ www.designmuseum.org). Bermondsey or Tower Hill tube/London Bridge tube/rail/15, 78, 100 bus. **Open** 11.30am-5.50pm Mon-Fri; 10.30am-5.50pm Sat, Sun (last entry 5.30pm). **Admission** £5.50; £4 concessions; free under-5s. **Credit** AmEx, MC, V. **Map** p405 S9.
This beautifully designed 1930s-style, sparkling white building is stark and spacious within, the perfect setting for a collection of innovative design. Incredibly user-friendly, the museum consists of two levels. The first floor holds the **Review Gallery** (state-of-the-art innovations from around the world) and the **Temporary Gallery**. Exhibitions for 2001 include shows devoted to the work of Mexican artist Luis Barragan (until 8 July) and to fashion designer John Galliano (30 Nov 2001-31 Mar 2002).

The **Collection Gallery**, devoted to the study of design for mass production, is housed on the second floor. Arranged thematically, it concentrates on different types of product. The car is one such focus: look for the wooden model made up from drawings by the architect and designer Le Corbusier dating from 1928. There are also early televisions, washing machines, telephones, chairs (including one designed by Rennie Mackintosh) and a collection of tableware. However, the museum is scheduled to undergo a revamp in late 2001 or early 2002, which will allow more space for temporary exhibitions.

The **Blue Print Café**, which shares the building and boasts a balcony overlooking the Thames, is a suitably stylish establishment. Note, though, that it's a restaurant rather than a café, with prices to match.

The **Design Museum**, one of the riverside's best attractions.

The City

Old crosses swords with new in London's fascinating financial district.

Maps p402-p405

Founded as a port, commerce has always been the *raison d'être* of the City: according to Tacitus, in AD60 Roman Londinium was already 'filled with traders and a celebrated centre of commerce'. And if the trading is now in virtual rather than actual commodities, it's still possible to trace a direct lineage from the chaotic, cacophonous stalls of medieval Cheapside to the chaotic, cacophonous dealing rooms of today's business district. For the City is one of the key financial centres on the planet: there are more foreign banks in London than in any other city and its foreign exchange market is the largest in the world. Yet the City is more than blokes in suits shouting into phones.

For most of the capital's history, the City of London *was* the city of London; hence that all-important, self-important capital letter. Apart from a brief Saxon excursion westward, it was only in the 17th century that there was significant, systematic building outside the boundaries of the old Roman wall.

Today's City – a square mile, or as near as damnit – subsumes the original site of Roman Londinium. Its boundaries are defined by Temple Bar to the west, Smithfield and Moorfields to the north, Tower Hill to the east and the Thames to the south. Flattened by the Great Fire of 1666, and again by the 1940-1 Blitz, the City has always been in such a hurry to rebuild, to get back to business, that no grand Haussmann-like scheme to rationalise the place has ever been able to get off the ground. But the City, though proud of its lack of sentimentality, hasn't entirely forgotten its past. Dull office blocks may line many of the streets today, but these streets still largely follow their medieval courses, their names speaking their history: Old Jewry, Ironmonger Row, Poultry, Bread Street. Several fine museums and a magnificent crop of 17th-century churches provide links to the City's colourful past.

But despite a working population of 250,000, only 6,000 live within the governance of the City's ruling body, the Corporation of London. Come on a Saturday or Sunday, or after 9pm on a weekday, and you'll be wandering a ghost town of deserted office buildings, shut-up shops and pubs, and empty streets. Yet visit on a weekday and you'll see what the fuss is about.

City Information Centre

St Paul's Churchyard (south side of the cathedral), EC4 (7332 1456/www.cityoflondon.gov.uk). St Paul's tube. **Open** *Apr-Sept* 9.30am-5pm daily. *Oct-Mar* 9.30am-5pm Mon-Fri; 9.30am-12.30pm Sat; closed Sun. **Map** p404 O6.

A source of information on sights, events, walks and talks within the Square Mile.

Along Fleet Street

Chancery Lane tube/Blackfriars tube/rail.

Fleet Street, once synonymous with Britain's national daily and Sunday newspapers, leads eastwards from the **Strand** towards **Ludgate Hill** and St Paul's. It still bustles, but the bitterly fought departure of the papers to Wapping and Docklands in the late 1980s has torn the heart out of Fleet Street. The grandiose, *Daily Telegraph* building (no.135) is occupied by finance houses; the ground-breaking *Daily Express* building at nos.121-128 (the first glass-curtain structure in Britain; *see p30*) is similarly hack-free, though at least it's now in use. In fact, only the Reuters/Press Association building (no.85) remains as a reminder of the 500-year association of Fleet Street with the printed word, which started when William Caxton's successor, Wynkyn de Worde, brought his presses here from Westminster in 1500 and set up shop at **St Bride's** (*see p94* **God is in the detail**), still affectionately thought of as the printers' and journalists' church.

Literary figures, too, were familiar with the hostelries of Fleet Street. A plaque on Child's bank (no.1) marks the site of the Devil's Tavern, where Ben Jonson, Samuel Pepys and Samuel Johnson all supped. Johnson was also a regular at the charmingly creaky Ye Olde Cheshire Cheese (*see p218*). The corpulent doctor's only surviving London home in Gough Square, restored and opened to the public as, logically enough, **Dr Johnson's House** (*see p82*), is a stagger away. Nearby is **Johnson's Court**, where Charles Dickens delivered what was to become his first published story, 'stealthily one evening in twilight, into a dark letterbox in a dark office up a dark corner of Fleet Street'.

As you head down into the Fleet valley – the river is now underground – towards Ludgate Circus, the view of St Paul's, particularly at night, floodlit and apparently floating over the City, is magical.

Sightseeing

Dr Johnson's House

*17 Gough Square, off Fleet Street, EC4 (7353 3745/
www.drjh.dircon.co.uk). Chancery Lane or Temple
tube (both closed Sun)/Blackfriars tube/rail.* **Open**
May-Sept 11am-5.30pm Mon-Sat; closed Sun. *Oct-Apr*
11am-5pm Mon-Sat; closed Sun. **Admission** £4; £3
concessions, £1 under 14s; free under 5s; £9 family.
No credit cards. Map p404 N6.

When a man is tired of London, he is probably tired
of all the interminable Samuel Johnson references.
This is the only surviving London residence – he had
17 – of the inimitable doctor. Johnson lived in this
late 17th-century house from 1748 to 1759, while
working on the first comprehensive English dictionary. Visitors can wander through his home, guided
by descriptions, anecdotes and quotes on laminated
sheets. There's not much in the way of furniture: it's
mainly engravings, paintings and curios. The top
room is the long garret, which was 'fitted out like a
counting-house' when Johnson and his six clerks did
their lexicographing here. A video provides insights
into aspects of Johnson's life and work.

Sam I am: **Dr Johnson's House**.

Around St Paul's

St Paul's tube.

Wren's masterwork may now be forced to jostle
for position with graceless office blocks, but St
Paul's Cathedral (*see p83*) still stands proud as a
symbol of British resilience thanks to wartime
photos of the flame-licked but apparently
untouched cathedral weathering the Blitz. It
suffered several direct hits, and in one night
alone a total of 28 incendiary bombs fell in the
immediate vicinity, but the image of brave St
Paul's keeping its head while all about it were
losing theirs was the tonic the nation needed.

Adjoining **Paternoster Square** fared less
well: all but flattened by the Luftwaffe, it was
rebuilt in the 1960s as a precinct of shops and
offices that almost immediately became a
byword for architectural ugliness. After a ten-
year wrangle, plans were finally agreed a few
years back to rebuild the square in a mixture of
classical and modern styles, which has resulted
in one of London's more dramatic building sites.

The old marketplace of medieval London,
Cheapside ('ceap' or 'chepe' being the Old
English word for market) runs down from the
cathedral to Bank. Shakespeare used to drink in
the raucous taverns here that once quenched the
thirsts of the hoarse street sellers, while the
surrounding area echoed to the work of
craftsmen (no prizes for guessing what was sold
and made in Milk Street and Bread Street).

Bow Lane, by the side of St Mary-le-Bow
(*see p95* **God is in the details**), is now an
appealing, narrow pedestrianised street, lined
with shops, sandwich bars and pubs. At its
southern end, St Mary Aldermary is one of
Wren's rare experiments with the Perpendicular

style, based on the pre-Fire church. Over Queen
Victoria Street is **Garlick Hill**, its medieval
name proving false the supposed antipathy
between the English and the pungent bulb. At
the bottom of the street is Wren's church of St
James Garlickhythe, which has the highest roof
in the City after St Paul's. Its light-filled interior
remains much as it was in the 17th century, and
has earned it the nickname of 'Wren's Lantern'.

Between here and **Cannon Street** is wine
and Whittington territory. The four-time Mayor
of London lived on half-cobbled **College Hill**
(a plaque on nos.19-20 marks the site), and was
buried in St Michael Paternoster Royal at the
foot of the hill. Inside, 1960s stained glass by
John Hayward depicts an anachronistically flat-
capped Dick, together with his apocryphal cat.
The name of this Wren church derives from two
ancient thoroughfares nearby: Paternoster Lane
(where rosaries were once made) and La Réole, a
wine-making region near Bordeaux, popular
with London's medieval wine importers. The
Vintners' Hall (*see p89* **London's guilds**) is
close by, across **Upper Thames Street**.

South of St Paul's lies a little explored but
delightful tangle of alleyways, concealing
shops, pubs and the dinky Wren church of St
Andrew by the Wardrobe. Built in 1685-95, the
church's curious name dates from 1361, when
the King's Wardrobe – the ceremonial clothes of
the royal family – were moved to the adjoining

building. Nearby, two other Wren creations, St Benet and St Nicholas Cole Abbey, are, unfortunately, usually closed. Facing the former across scruffy **Queen Victoria Street** is the unexpectedly neat red-brick, 17th-century mansion of the **College of Arms** (*see below*), which still industriously examines and records the pedigrees of those to whom such things matter. Just west of here, at traffic-swept **Blackfriars**, the Dominicans – the 'black friars' – once had a monastery (it was dissolved in 1538; all that remains is a chunk of wall in Ireland Yard), and the Normans built one of their defensive forts, Baynard's Castle, to keep the unruly Londoners in check. Just east of here is Foster's **Millennium Bridge** linking the City with Bankside, scheduled to reopen in late summer 2001 after an absurd, in-built wobble caused it to close after only three days of operation in 2000.

North of Blackfriars station is Apothecaries' Hall, one of the most charming of the livery halls (*see p89* **London's guilds**), and, close by on Ludgate Hill, stands the church of St Martin within Ludgate, its lead spire still visible over the surrounding buildings as Wren intended (which, alas, is more than can be said for those of most of his other churches). After reflecting on the works of God, ponder upon the sins of man around the corner in the most famous court in the land, the **Old Bailey** (*see below*), built on the site of the infamous Newgate Prison.

College of Arms

Queen Victoria Street, EC4 (7248 2762/ www.college-of-arms.gov.uk). Blackfriars tube/rail. **Open** 10am-4pm Mon-Fri; closed Sat, Sun. **Admission** free. **Map** p404 O7.

The College of Arms has been granting coats of arms and checking family pedigrees since 1484. Its 17th-century mini-mansion has been beautifully restored. Only the Earl Marshal's Court (the wood-panelled entrance room hung with paintings of various worthies) can be viewed without notice. Book a tour if you want to see the Record Room and the artists at work on the elaborate certificates. If you wish to trace your roots, ask to see the Officer in Waiting, though you may be charged a small fee for him to look up the information.

Old Bailey

corner of Newgate Street & Old Bailey, EC4 (7248 3277). St Paul's tube. **Open** 10.30am-1pm, 2-4pm, Mon-Fri; closed Sat, Sun. **Admission** free (no under-14s admitted, 14-16s accompanied by adults only). **Map** p404 O6.

The Old Bailey – or Central Criminal Court – has dealt with some of the most publicised criminal cases in London's history, including Oscar Wilde in 1895, Dr Crippen in 1910, William 'Lord Haw-Haw' Joyce in 1945, and Peter Sutcliffe in 1981). The court was built on the site of the notorious Newgate Prison –

demolished in 1902; *see p147* **Go directly to jail** – and the bronze figure of Justice on the copper-covered dome overlooks the area where convicts were once executed. Stones from the prison made up the façade with Pomeroy's sculpted group over the main entrance – representing the Recording Angel supported by Fortitude and Truth. The tradition of judges carrying a posy of flowers into court has its origin in the need to mask the foul stench and ward off germs emanating from the prison. The public are admitted to watch trials.

St Paul's Cathedral

Ludgate Hill, EC4 (7236 4128/www.stpauls.co.uk). St Paul's tube. **Open** 8.30am-4pm Mon-Sat; closed Sun (except for services). *Galleries, crypt & ambulatory* 10am-4pm Mon-Sat. Last entry 4pm. **Admission** *Cathedral, crypt & gallery* £5; £2.50 6-16s; £4 concessions. *Audio guide* £3; £7 family; £2.50 concessions. *Guided tour* £2.50; £1 6s-16s; £2 concessions; 11am, 11.30am, 1.30pm, 2pm Mon-Sat; closed Sun. **Credit** *Shop* MC, V. **Map** p404 O6.

Impressive enough today, the effect that Sir Christopher Wren's masterpiece must have had in the 17th century is impossible to comprehend. A Roman temple dedicated to Diana probably stood on the site where King Ethelbert built the first wooden church in AD604. Two more Saxon cathedrals followed (all three burned down), before the Normans constructed 'Old St Paul's' at the end of the 11th century. This colossal Gothic building, destroyed in the 1666 Great Fire, was, amazingly, even larger and taller than

The *good* dome: **St Paul's Cathedral**.

Wren's successor. Today's St Paul's is one of the few cathedrals ever to be designed by one architect, supervised by one master builder (Thomas Strong) and built within their lifetimes (construction lasted 35 years). Wren's epitaph, inscribed on the wall by his simple tomb in the crypt, could not be more apposite: 'If you seek his monument, look around.'

Rather like St Peter's in Rome, the scale of the thing means that any feeling of sanctity is sacrificed on the altar of grandeur, but there's a wonderful sense of proportion, space and harmony that even the endless stream of coach parties can't spoil. One of the biggest surprises is the dazzlingly rich, almost Byzantine-like mosaics of the Creation in the **Choir**; these, like Holman Hunt's incongruous *Light of the World* hanging in the south aisle, are late 19th-century additions. In the clock tower on the West Front hangs '**Great Paul**', the heaviest swinging bell in England, some 3m (5ft) in diameter. It is tolled daily at 1pm.

High up in the dome, frescoed with stories from the life of St Paul by James Thornhill, people in the **Whispering Gallery** strain to hear reverberating voices above the muffled din. Higher still are the viewing galleries: the **Stone Gallery** (at the base of the dome) and the **Golden Gallery** (at the top). It's a long, hard climb, involving 530 steps, but worth it for the unrivalled views over London. The bright, whitewashed **Crypt** (one of the largest in Europe) centres around grandiose monuments to the Duke of Wellington and Admiral Nelson; it raises a wry smile to see a modest monument to Florence Nightingale amid all the military bigwigs who did so much to keep her supplied with customers. **Painters' Corner** contains memorials to Reynolds, Lord Leighton, Alma-Tadema, Turner, Millais and Holman Hunt. The most interesting item in the **Treasury** is an extraordinary cope (a ceremonial cape), embroidered with the spires of 73 churches. Also down here are a decent café and restaurant.

It's worth doing one of the lively, anecdote-packed guided 'Supertours', which allow access to areas you're not normally allowed into, such as the magnificent choir area, with carving by Grinling Gibbons.

North to Smithfield

Barbican or St Paul's tube.

The two major presences north of St Paul's are **Smithfield Market** and St Bartholomew's Hospital. Both have ancient roots. Smithfield was originally 'smooth field': it had no blacksmithery connections, although there was an equine link. William Fitz Stephen, in 1173, wrote of 'a smooth field where every Friday there is a celebrated rendezvous of fine horses to be sold'.

As a large open space near the City, Smithfield was in demand for all manner of public events: jousts, sports, tournaments, executions and the most famous of all London's once-numerous annual fairs. Founded in 1123, **Bartholomew Fair** was renowned as a cloth fair before transmogrifying into the raucous entertainment fest that Ben Jonson captured so vividly in his 17th-century play of the same name. The spoilsport City authorities finally suppressed the fair in 1855, blaming it for encouraging public disorder, and built **Smithfield Market** on the site 13 years later. Livestock had been traded here for centuries, but now the slaughtering took place elsewhere and the area became – and remains – a meat market (or, rather, four linked markets). Now officially known as London Central Markets, a £70-million refit and refurbishment has left Horace Jones's immense Victorian East and West Markets looking splendid, repainted in their original colours of deep blues, reds and green with gold stars. If you want to see the working market, an early rise will be necessary – kicking off at around 3am, all the action is over by 8am – but you can reward your dedication with a fried breakfast and a pint with the meat porters in one of the nearby pubs (which have special early licences).

The instigation of Bartholomew Fair was only one of the actions of Rahere, court jester to Henry I, who almost died from malarial fever on a pilgrimage to Rome, and vowed to build a hospital on his return. He kept his promise, establishing **St Bartholomew's Hospital**, as well as a priory and the hugely atmospheric church of **St Bartholomew-the-Great** (*see p93* **God is in the detail**), London's oldest and best-loved hospital. It was to here that Wat Tyler was brought after being stabbed at Smithfield by the Lord Mayor in 1381, although he was immediately dragged out and beheaded by the King's men. A small museum of the hospital's history can be visited (*see below*).

St Bartholomew's Hospital Museum

West Smithfield, EC1 (7601 8152/guided tours 7837 0546). Barbican or St Paul's tube. **Open** 10am-4pm Tue-Fri; closed Mon, Sat, Sun. *Guided tours* 2pm Fri. **Admission** free. *Guided tours* £4; £3 concessions. **No credit cards. Map** p404 O5.

Meat the workers at **Smithfield Market**.

Inside the grounds of this hospital is an informative museum of its history and the only survivor of its original four chapels, **St Bartholomew-the-Less**. The **Great Hall** and the staircase, its walls decorated with epic biblical murals by William Hogarth, can also be viewed from the museum, but the seasonal weekly tours offer a better view, while also taking in Smithfield and the surrounding area.

Around Bank

Mansion House tube/Bank tube/DLR.

The City has no indisputable centre, but if any place can lay claim to being the heart of the Square Mile, it's the great convergence of streets at **Bank**, overlooked by the unshakeable, self-confident triumvirate of the **Bank of England**, the **Royal Exchange** and the Lord Mayor's official residence, **Mansion House** (*see p86*).

Britain's national bank was founded in 1694 to provide William III with the necessary finance to fight the French. It had its ups and downs, but eventually secured its position as the government's banker, with the authority to print and issue banknotes, and the responsibility of storing the country's gold reserves, managing the national debt and safeguarding the value of the British currency. The present building dates from 1925 to 1939, although the outer 'curtain' walls of Sir John Soane's 1788 structure have been retained. The admirably accessible exhibition of the bank's past and present in the **Bank of England Museum** (*see below*) is worth a look. Behind the bank is the modern **Stock Exchange**.

Overshadowing the bank is the massive neoclassical portico of the Royal Exchange, built by William Tite and opened by Queen Victoria in 1844. Sir Thomas Gresham created it in 1566 as a meeting and trading centre for merchants – he is honoured by a statue over the entrance in Exchange Buildings and his grasshopper emblem on the bell tower. The Royal Exchange is now HQ of the futures market, but trading no longer takes place on the premises.

Further west is the centre of the City's civic life, **Guildhall** (*see p86*), base of the Corporation of London, as well as an excellent library, the **Clockmakers' Company Museum** (*see below*), the church of **St Lawrence Jewry**, and the **Guildhall Art Gallery** (*see p86*), housing the Corporation of London's art collection, which opened in 1999.

Next to Mansion House stands one of the City's finest churches, **St Stephen Walbrook** (*see 95* **God is in the details**), Wren's trial run for St Paul's. Nearby is the heap of stones that was once the Roman **Temple of Mithras** (*see p89*). Other notable churches in the vicinity

include Nicholas Hawksmoor's idiosyncratic **St Mary Woolnoth** at the junction of King William Street and Lombard Street and Wren's exquisite **St Mary Abchurch** off Abchurch Lane (for both, *see p94-5* **God is in the detail**).

Around the corner from St Mary Abchurch, set into the wall of the Overseas-Chinese Banking Corporation at 111 Cannon Street, is one of the City's most esoteric and, frankly, unimpressive sights: **London Stone**. A rough-hewn chunk of Clipsham limestone, barely visible behind an iron grille and glass in the wall opposite Cannon Street Station, its origins are unmarked are murky. It probably dates from Roman times and may have been a milestone, but was already a landmark in 1198 when it was referred to as 'Lonenstane'. It was originally set in the ground on the opposite side of the road before being swapped to the north side of the street in 1742 and embedded in the wall of St Swithin's (now demolished) church on this site in 1798. No one has ever been sure about the purpose of the stone, but it was considered, in some vague unspecified way, to be the symbolic cornerstone of the City.

As is the case all over the City, wandering where the fancy takes you is the best way to get to know this enigmatic part of London. Further north, a brief foray off Cornhill down St Michael's Alley takes you to the **Jamaica Wine House**, a popular pub on the site of the Jamaica Coffee House. Opened in the 1670s, sea captains and traders would meet at the Jamaica to discuss business with the West Indies and buy the best rum to be found in London.

Bank of England Museum

entrance on Bartholomew Lane, EC2 (7601 5545/ www.bankofengland.co.uk). Bank tube/DLR. **Open** 10am-5pm Mon-Fri; closed Sat, Sun. **Admission** free. **Map** p405 Q6.
This unexpectedly interesting museum centres on a restoration of the bank's Stock Office, designed by Sir John Soane in 1793, complete with figures in period costume and a stuffed tabby cat. Well thought-out displays tell the bank's 300-year story, explaining its vital role in providing the stability and wherewithal for Britain to build up a global empire, and give an enlightening, informal course in national finance for beginners. Visitors come tantalisingly close to a stack of gold bars, learn via interactive screens about the complexities of banknote production and security, and budding City high-flyers can play at foreign exchange trading.

Clockmakers' Company Museum

The Clockroom, Guildhall Library, Aldermanbury, EC2 (7332 1868/1870). Mansion House or St Paul's tube/Bank tube/DLR/Moorgate tube/rail. **Open** call to check. **Admission** free. **Map** p404 P6.

This cramped but easily digestible collection of time-pieces is the world's oldest, and includes the watch that Sir Edmund Hillary wore on the first successful ascent of Everest in 1953 and John Harrison's 18th-century prizewinning chronometer, a remarkable invention that made it possible for ships at sea to chart their exact position, giving the edge to Britain's empire builders. The museum will be closed for restoration work for most if not all of 2001; be sure to phone before visiting.

Guildhall

Gresham Street, EC2 (7606 3030/guided tours ext 1460/www.corpoflondon.gov.uk). Bank tube/DLR. **Open** *Apr-Sep* 9.30am-5pm daily. *Oct-Mar* 9.30am-5pm Mon-Fri; 9.30am-12.30pm Sat; closed Sun. **Admission** free. **Map** p404 P6.

For more than 800 years, Guildhall has been the centre of the City's local government (as well as the site of major trials such as those of Lady Jane Grey and Archbishop Cranmer in 1553). The stunning 15th-century Great Hall was gutted during the Great Fire and again in the Blitz, but has been sensitively restored. It is decorated with the banners and shields of the 100 Livery Companies; the windows record the names of every Lord Mayor since 1189; and there are monuments to Wellington, Nelson, Churchill and the two Pitts. Look out for the almost oriental-looking statues of legendary giants Gog and Magog guarding the West Gallery. They are post-war replacements for originals destroyed in the Blitz; the phoenix on Magog's shield symbolises renewal after fire.

Royal Exchange. *See p85.*

Meetings of the Court of Common Council (governing body for the Corporation of London, presided over by the Lord Mayor) are held here once a month on a Thursday at 1pm, except during August (visitors welcome; phone for dates). The hall is also used for banquets and ceremonial events. Below the Guildhall is the largest medieval crypt in London.

The buildings alongside house Corporation offices, the **Guildhall Library** (partly financed by Mayor Dick Whittington's estate and the first local authority-funded public library), a shop with books on London and the **Clockmakers' Company Museum** (*see p85*). See also below.

Guildhall Art Gallery

Guildhall Yard, off Gresham Street, EC2 (7332 3700/www.guildhall-art-gallery.org.uk). Mansion House or St Paul's tube/Bank tube/DLR/Moorgate tube/rail. **Open** 10am-5pm Mon-Sat; noon-4pm Sun. **Admission** £2.50; £1 concessions; free under 16s; £5 family. Free to all after 3.30pm daily and Fri. **Map** p404 P6.

The Guildhall Art Gallery reopened its doors to the public in 1999, having been closed since World War II when the original building of 1885 was destroyed by fire. Of the Corporation of London's 4,000 paintings, only about 250 can be displayed at any one time; part of the space is given over to rolling exhibitions in order to air the more obscure elements of the collection. Generally, the paintings are more of historic than artistic interest: a group of London cityscapes stretching from the 17th century to the present; portraits of former mayors and the imperious judges appointed to assess property claims following the Great Fire; and battle paintings such as John Singleton Copley's massive opus *The Defeat of the Floating Batteries, September 1782*. Of more aesthetic, but equally sentimental appeal are the Victorian paintings, which include Millais' *The Woodman's Daughter* and Frederic Lord Leighton's *The Music Lesson*. A digital gallery accessible at terminals dotted throughout the building allows you to search on screen for the many paintings held in store.

Mansion House

Walbrook, EC4 (7626 2500/www.cityoflondon.gov.uk). Bank tube/DLR. **Open** for group visits by written application to Ms Sarah Jane Mayhew, at least two months in advance (min 15, max 40 people). **Admission** free. **Map** p404 P6.

Squaring up to the Bank of England and the Royal Exchange is another neo-classical portico – that of the Lord Mayor's official residence, Mansion House. Designed by George Dance, it was completed in 1753 and contains sumptuous state rooms, such as the Egyptian Hall, scene of many an official banquet. Mansion House is the only private residence in the UK with its own Court of Justice, complete with 11 cells.

Temple of Mithras

On the raised courtyard in front of Sumitomo Bank/Legal & General Building, Temple Court, 11 Queen Victoria Street, EC4. Mansion House tube. **Open** 24 hrs daily. **Admission** free. **Map** p404 P6.

What the Dickens

Ragged orphans, illiterate thieves, murderers waiting for the gallows and overcrowded workhouses. These are images with which **Charles Dickens**'s London has become synonymous, with the poverty stricken Oliver Twist leading the way. But it is only one part of the story of the Victorian novelist's relationship with the city that provided much of the inspiration for his life's work, for Dickens paid as much heed to the machinations of high society as he did to those scrabbling around under duress on or beneath the bottom rung of the ladder.

Following the early success of his comical and much-loved *Pickwick Papers* (depicted on a modern-day £10 note), Dickens quickly became a key figure on London's literary-political scene, being elected in 1837 to the prestigious Athenaeum Club (then, as now, at 107 Pall Mall, SW1). A childhood of struggle and frequent moves that took the youngster to a dozen or so addresses in as many years now seemed to be behind him as he mixed with and observed the leading lights of London's cultural and political scene and stayed abreast of the developments among the fashion conscious Victorian aristocracy. This networking would later furnish works such as *Bleak House*, but for now the writer was enjoying the freedom of his city and working hard to establish his talents.

Throughout his London novels – among them *David Copperfield*, from which Mr Micawber is pictured above – there is a strong grasp of a society pulling both ways. While it is fairly noted that Dickens' chief societal concerns were abject poverty and the heavy-handed punishments handed out to the afflicted, there also lies within his canon the flip side of the coin: the privileged living it up in a swinging London that, for the rich, was experiencing something of a heyday. These experiences were no doubt personal for the young and successful author.

And perhaps the reason for the dichotomy was the fact that the London of the mid-19th century was far from the perfectly segregated city many imagine it as today. There were areas where wealth was supreme, but largely the poor were situated a stone's throw from the rich. Lincoln's Inn Fields, the area situated between Holborn and the Strand and the setting for much of *Bleak House*, was a

social melting pot comprising the law courts and chambers, modest housing, slums and even the homeless. Similarly, areas such as that surrounding the British Museum in Bloomsbury – where Dickens lived for a time; *see p104* – were a mix of the fortunate and the less fortunate. In Victorian London, one was never far from either extreme, a truism of which its leading author was especially aware.

Although he spent more than half his life as a resident of the city, it wasn't until his move away to Rochester in Kent that Dickens really found himself at home. While the visions of his novels were anchored firmly in the social injustices that reached fruition most completely in the slums of the inner city, Dickens' heart was seemingly set on leaving the place that acted as something of muse for him. Today, the best loved author of his day is celebrated around London with no less than nine blue plaques, signifying a house lived in here, a book written there or, perhaps, a particular character's address. And while most of the concrete traces of Dickensian London are now long gone, the ghost of this remarkable writer and chronicler lives on.

KIDS GET IN FREE*

Kids these days. You let them in free, you give them a whole floor to themselves, and they still don't listen when you tell them for the hundredth time that it really is time to go. Come and discover why at the Science Museum. But please remember, we've all got homes to go to.

science museum | NEAREST TUBE: SOUTH KENSINGTON
www.sciencemuseum.org.uk

*HOW YOU GET THEM OUT AGAIN IS YOUR PROBLEM

AN AMAZING CINEMATIC EXPERIENCE
THEN THE FILM STARTS

THE ARTS COUNCIL OF ENGLAND

Your jaw drops. You have pinch yourself to make su it's real. All this, and the fi hasn't even started yet. Measuring staggering 20m x 26m the IMAX screen is the biggest in Britain. It's th height of five double-decker buses ar yes, you have to hang on tight. 3-D ar 2-D films take in your whole field vision, so that when they start to ro you feel you're in them, not watchir them. It's an experience not to b missed. You really must go there.

Nearest tube: Waterloo.
To book call 020 7902 1234.

bfi LONDON
IMAX
C I N E M A
GO THERE

During the third century AD, the rival cults of Mithraism and Christianity were battling for supremacy. The worship of the macho Persian god Mithras appealed particularly to Roman soldiers, and the troops on the British frontier built the small temple to their champion near this spot (cAD240-50). The reconstructed foundations (looking as they did when they were unearthed in 1954) aren't much to look at, but show the Roman influence on the later design of churches: rounded apse, central nave and side aisles.

Around the Tower of London

Tower Hill tube.

For over 900 years, the **Tower of London** (*see p92*) has acted as the eastern anchor of the City; there's no more potent symbol of the capital. Sometime palace, sometime prison, sometime place of execution, the Tower's associations, stories and legends are legion. Add to this the fact that it is Britain's most perfect medieval fortress, and it comes as no surprise that the Tower is one of London's top five attractions.

The entire Tower Hill area, unappealingly bisected by a busy road, is a major focus for visitors. Just outside Tower Hill tube station in Wakefield Gardens is one of the most impressive surviving chunks of London's **Roman wall**. Although medieval additions have increased the height of the wall from around six metres (20 foot) to 10 metres (35 foot), its scale still impresses. A 1.7-mile (2.8-kilometre) walk, punctuated by 21 explanatory plaques, follows the course of the old wall from the Tower to the **Museum of London** (*see p91*). The tourist-targeted **Tower Bridge Experience** (*see p91*) and St Katharine's Dock are nearby, but a far greater insight into London's past – and present – can be had by stepping a little off the tourist trail.

Samuel Pepys lived and worked on Seething Lane; there's a bust of the promiscuous diarist in the tiny green oasis of Seething Lane Gardens. Also here is the church of **St Olave Hart Street** (dubbed by Dickens 'St Ghastly Grim' after the grinning skulls around the entrance to the churchyard) where Pepys and his wife worshipped and are buried. Opposite the bottom of Seething Lane stands **All Hallows by the Tower** (*see p92* **God is in the detail**), from the tower of which Pepys surveyed the progress of the Great Fire.

Between here and London Bridge stand two reminders of London's great days as a port: the early 19th-century **Custom House**, with a façade by Robert Smirke, and, next door, the former **Billingsgate Market**. For many centuries, Billingsgate wharf was famed for two things: the landing of fish and the foul language of its porters. The market was moved to a

larger site on the Isle of Dogs in 1982, but Horace Jones's 1870s market building has been impressively restored (look for the fish on top of the weather vanes).

The lanes behind the waterfront are a rewarding hunting ground for church-spotters. **St Magnus the Martyr**, **St Mary at Hill**, **St Margaret Pattens** and **St Dunstan in the East** are all within a couple of minutes' walk of each other. The gardens of the latter are a wonderfully lush haven in which to relax after struggling to the top of **The Monument** (*see p91*). In nearby Pudding Lane, in the early hours of 2 September 1666, a fire started in a bakery that was to blaze for three days,

London's guilds

The City's **guilds**, or **livery companies**, are the old union headquarters of once-powerful trades that largely no longer exist. The Barber-Surgeons, Cordwainers and Periwig-Knitters may have lost their halls to the Great Fire or the Blitz, but they still vie in a medieval league table of self-importance. The livery companies do a lot of work for charity, dress up in ruffles and big-buckled shoes for the Lord Mayors' Show, pull strings Masons-style, and still own 15 per cent of the City.

With persistence and luck, access may be gained to view the architecture and treasures of the most interesting of the remaining halls. Top of the curiosities is at the 18th-century **Fishmongers' Hall** (London Bridge, EC4; 7626 3531) where, amid a jumble of precious loot, is preserved the 12-inch dagger used by fishmonger-Mayor William Walworth to stab Wat Tyler in the back and put down the Peasants' Revolt of 1381. There's even a life-size wooden statue of the murderous Walworth, dagger in hand. In comparison, the pride of the **Skinners' Hall** (Dowgate Hill, EC4; 7236 5629) – some exquisite panelling and an overblown 18th-century Russian glass chandelier – seem tame.

The **Vintners' Hall** (Upper Thames Street, EC4; 7236 1863) is the oldest surviving HQ, dating back as far as 1671; the **Apothecaries' Hall** (Blackfriars Lane, EC4; 7236 1180) boasts a Reynolds sketch and portraits of James I and Charles I; while the Renaissance-style **Goldsmiths' Hall** (Foster Lane, EC2; 7606 7010) is one of the easiest to visit, staging occasional exhibitions.

destroying four-fifths of medieval London. Although, remarkably, only nine people are thought to have died, more than 13,000 houses, 87 churches and 44 livery halls were reduced to ashes. The Lord Mayor, woken soon after the fire started, lived to regret his immediate dismissal of the danger with the words, 'Pish! A woman might piss it out.' Thankfully, the fire put paid to the City's brown rats, carriers of the Great Plague, which had wiped out 100,000 of the capital's population the previous year.

A little further north, around Bishopsgate, is the area with the greatest concentration of City tower blocks. Manhattan it ain't, and the lack of architectural imagination, daring and flair is depressing. The **NatWest Tower** on Bishopsgate is typically unexciting, although, with 52 storeys and at 373 metres (660 feet) high, it at least had the distinction of being the tallest office block in Europe when it was built in 1980.

The one outstanding exception is Richard Rogers' extraordinary **Lloyd's Building** (1986), on Lime Street. Its guts-on-the-outside design draws much from Paris's Pompidou Centre, also by Rogers, and is the sort of daring, uncompromising architectural vision that is so rarely seen in the conservative City. Part of the façade of the old 1928 building (on Leadenhall Street) has been left standing. Lloyd's of London, the largest insurance market in the world, is a remarkable and unique organisation; a society of underwriters ('Names') that accepts all insurance risks for personal loss or gain that traces its roots back to the 1680s. Traditionally, being a Name seemed to involve nothing but waiting for regular fat cheques to pop through your letterbox. That this was all too good to be true was made brutally clear in the early 1990s, when a series of disasters caused Lloyd's to suffer record losses of over a billion pounds. Many Names were personally ruined and the company came to the brink of collapse.

Next door is one of the City's most delightful surprises: **Leadenhall Market**. 'Foreigners' – meaning anyone from outside London – were allowed to sell poultry here (and, later, cheese and butter) from the 14th century. The current arcaded buildings, painted in green, maroon and cream with wonderful decorative detail, are the work of Horace Jones (architect also of Smithfield Market and Tower Bridge). One of the market's greatest characters was a gander from Ostend called Old Tom. Somehow he avoided the fate of 34,000 other geese who were slaughtered in the space of two days, and became a much-loved feature of Leadenhall, waddling around the local pubs to be fed tit-bits. He died in 1835 at the venerable age of 38 and was buried in the market. Today, Leadenhall remains a great place to wander, particularly around lunchtime. Reassuringly, the fresh produce stalls haven't actually been displaced – there are still fabulous cheesemongers, butchers and fishmongers.

Between Leadenhall and Liverpool Street rail station there are more churches to discover: **St Helen Bishopsgate**, off Bishopsgate (*see p94* **God is in the detail**), **St Andrew Undershaft** on St Mary Axe, **St Botolph Aldgate** (*see p93* **God is in the detail** and **St Katharine Cree** on Leadenhall Street. The latter, one of the few churches to be built in England during the years preceding the Civil War, is an extraordinary hybrid of classical and Gothic styles.

Near here is Britain's oldest synagogue, the superbly preserved **Bevis Marks Synagogue**, in a courtyard off Bevis Marks; it was built in 1701 by Sephardic Jews who'd escaped from the Inquisition in Portugal and Spain. This area suffered considerable damage from the IRA bombs of April 1992 and April 1993, although most have now been fully restored. The tiny pre-Fire church of **St Ethelburga** (built 1390) on Bishopsgate was devastated, but, appropriately, is to be rebuilt at a cost of £4.5 million as a 'Centre for Reconciliation and Peace' and a world research centre investigating the role of religion in ending conflict.

Old meets older at the wonderful **Tower of London**. *See p92.*

Fire, away... **The Monument**.

The Monument

Monument Street, EC3 (7626 2717). Monument tube. **Open** 10am-5.40pm daily. **Admission** £1.50; 50p 5-15s; free under-5s. **No credit cards**. **Map** p405 Q7.

Erected in 1671-7 by Christopher Wren and Robert Hooke, this simple Doric column, topped with a flaming urn of gilt bronze, commemorates the Great Fire of 1666. At 61m (202ft) – the distance from here to the site of the bakery on Pudding Lane where the Fire began – the Monument was the tallest isolated stone column in the world in its time. Anyone who labours up the 311 steps won't find that hard to believe (although you will at least get a certificate for your trouble on the way out). Unless you're terminally unfit, it's worth the effort for the wonderful views from the top. Although the gallery is entirely enclosed in an iron cage – it had been a notorious spot for suicides – those who suffer from vertigo may agree with James Boswell that it is 'horrid to be so monstrous a way up in the air'. Look for the gap at the bottom of the Latin inscription on the side of the Monument. After telling of how the Fire was finally extinguished, the words '(but Popish frenzy, which wrought such horrors, is not yet quenched)' were added in 1681. Not until 1830 were these bigoted (and foundationless) words erased.

Museum of London

150 London Wall, EC2 (7600 3699/24hr information 7600 0807/www.museumoflondon.org.uk). Barbican or St Paul's tube/Moorgate tube/rail. **Open** 10am-5.50pm Mon-Sat; noon-5.50pm Sun. **Admission** (tickets valid for one year) £5; £3 concessions; free under-16s, registered disabled. Free for all after 4.30pm. **Credit** AmEx, MC, V. **Map** p402 P5.

The concrete 'drawbridge' across a 'moat' of traffic makes an appropriate, if daunting, approach to this exploration of London's history. The museum opened in 1976, purpose-built in the middle of a busy City roundabout, on the site of the Roman fort. Inside, you'll find one of the most imaginatively designed museums in the capital. Visitors can trace the growth of London from prehistoric times up to the present day with an absorbing combination of models, artefacts and reconstructions. Plans for redevelopment in 2001 will increase gallery space to allow more coverage of post-1945 history.

In the meantime, it's well worth lingering over the impressive Roman interior, with its original mosaic pavement; the Cheapside hoard (a cache of fine jewels, dating from 1560 to 1640, found in a box under a shop); and the **Great Fire Experience**, an illuminated model with sound effects and commentary depicting the fire that destroyed four-fifths of London in 1666. Reconstructions of Newgate prison cells, and the Lord Mayor's ceremonial coach and shop/restaurant interiors from Victorian and Edwardian London all help to create an atmospheric and informative experience. On show during 2001 will be Creative Quarters (30 Mar-15 July), a show about the evolution of the London art world over the last 300 years that includes work by Bacon and Reynolds

Tower Bridge Experience

SE1 (7403 3761/www.towerbridge.org.uk). Tower Hill tube/London Bridge tube/rail. **Open** *Apr-Oct* 10am-6.30pm daily. *Nov-Mar* 9.30am-6pm daily. Last entry 1hr 15mins before closing). **Admission** £6.25; £4.25 5-15s, OAPs, students; £18.25 family. **Credit** AmEx, MC, V. **Map** p405 R8.

Despite its mock-Gothic appearance, Tower Bridge was actually a pioneering steel-framed structure. The 'Tower Bridge Experience' might sound a bit naff, but visitors do get a fact-packed insight into the history of London's famous bridge, which opened in 1894 and was once described as 'a colossal symbol of the British genius'. The tour is helped along by lively animatronics, interactive displays and the 'ghost' of Horace Jones, the original architect of the bridge, who died shortly after foundation work began. The views from the elevated walkways – which will likely be opening until 8.30pm in August, though call to check before visiting – are far-reaching, if a little obscured by the glass and metal of the corridors. The tour ends in the engine rooms, which house the steam pump engines used to raise the bridge until 1976 (it's all done by electrics now). To find out when the bridge will next be lifted (usually at least once a day), and the name and type of vessel passing beneath, phone 7378 7700.

Sightseeing

Tower of London

Tower Hill, EC3 (7709 0765/www.hrp.org.uk).
Tower Hill tube/Fenchurch Street rail.
Open *Mar-Oct* 9am-5pm Mon-Sat; 10am-5pm Sun;
Nov-Feb 10am-4pm Mon, Sun; 9am-4pm Tue-Sat.
Admission £11; £8.30 concessions; £7.30 children.
Credit AmEx, MC, V. **Map** p405 R7.

The Tower has been a castle, a palace and a prison during its long history and it remains one of the capital's most important sights. Be warned that 2.5 million people annually traipse around the Tower; arrive early if you want to avoid the worst of the crowds. A good introduction is provided by the free, hour-long guided tours that depart every half-hour, hosted by the snappable Beefeaters (more soberly known as Yeoman Warders).

The oldest part of the complex is William the Conqueror's **White Tower**, begun in 1076 (its name refers to the period during Henry III's reign when it was whitewashed). It now houses a portion of the extensive **Royal Armouries** and, on the second floor, the exquisite, austere **Chapel of St John**, which, dating from 1080, is the oldest church in London. Although popularly notorious as a site of aristo beheadings, only seven people were ever executed on **Tower Green**; a plaque in the centre of the green records their names. The proprietorial ravens that squawk about the green have been protected by royal decree for centuries and are a reminder of the extensive menagerie that was kept at the Tower from 1235 until it was transferred to London Zoo in 1831. The 19th-century Waterloo Barracks, north of the White Tower, contain the celebrated **Crown Jewels**, the centrepiece of which is the Imperial State Crown, set with a 317-carat diamond.

South of the White Tower is the gloriously named **Bloody Tower**. It was here in 1483 that the 12-year-old Edward V and his ten-year-old brother were incarcerated by their uncle, the future Richard III. Subsequent Tudor propaganda asserted that Richard had the boys murdered – and the skeletons of two children were discovered in the tower in 1674 – but the true fate of the young princes remains one of history's great mysteries. A hundred years later, Sir Walter Raleigh was imprisoned in the tower on three separate occasions, the last being for six weeks in 1618 before his execution at Westminster. On the waterfront, south of the Bloody Tower, is **Traitors' Gate**, by which prisoners used to enter the Tower, having been ferried down the Thames from the law courts at Westminster. The gate is part of **St Thomas's Tower**, which, with neighbouring **Wakefield Tower**, has been converted to resemble Edward I's medieval palace.

The Tower Environs Scheme, which began a couple of years ago, has already shown benefits in the area. The edge of the wharf has been tarted up, and, in late March 2001, refurbishment on the subway

God is in the detail

In 1665, nearly 100 churches stood within the City walls. The Great Fire of 1666, though, destroyed 87 of them, leaving the City with some serious rebuilding to do. In the end, 54 were rebuilt, all but three by Sir Christopher Wren. Thus, not only do the great majority of City churches date from a very narrow historical period – the late 17th century – but, uniquely, they are also almost all the work of one man. The fact that this has not resulted in a monotony of style is a testament to Wren's incomparable genius, particularly as he was forced to work only on the original cramped sites.

The churches exhibit an extraordinary diversity of design and decoration, although many do share certain features in common: light interiors, painted in white and gold, clear glass windows, fine wood carving, painted altarpieces and imaginative use of ironwork. The Victorian 'improvers', preferring the dim light and stained glass of the Gothic style, mangled many of Wren's churches, and bomb damage in World War II destroyed 11 more. Today, only 38 remain; St Ethelburga's in Bishopsgate – one of the few medieval churches to survive both the Great Fire and the Blitz – was almost completely destroyed by an IRA bomb in 1993 (*see p91*). Many City churches put on free lunchtime concerts (*see p310*).

All Hallows by the Tower

Byward Street, EC3 (7481 2928/
www.allhallowsbythetower.org.uk). Tower Hill tube. **Open** 9am-5.45pm Mon, Wed, Fri; 8am-5.45pm Tue; 9am-6.45pm Thur; 10am-5pm Sat, Sun. **Map** p405 R7.

Samuel Pepys surveyed the progress of the Great Fire from the tower of All Hallows. The church survived the disaster, only to be all but destroyed by Luftwaffe bombs in 1940. Only the walls and 17th-century brick tower were left standing, but the post-war rebuilding has created a pleasingly light interior. A Saxon arch testifies to the church's ancient roots (seventh century). Other interesting relics include Saxon crosses, a Roman tessellated pavement, Tudor monuments, sword-rests and brasses, a superb carved limewood font cover (1682) by Grinling Gibbons, and a collection of model ships.

linking Tower Hill tube and the North Moat walkway will be completed with the addition of 30 specially commissioned panels from artist Stephen B Whatley. Further on, a new coach station will open in 2002, around the time when long-overdue landscaping work should begin on Tower Hill itself.

Around Liverpool Street Station

Liverpool Street tube/rail.

The broad expanse of **Finsbury Circus** offers vital breathing room for local office workers: n rare commodity in the City, where open spaces are most often seen less as enhancements to the quality of life than wasted development opportunities. Tall sweeps of offices (none of the early 19th century originals survives) overlook an agreeable, almost provincial, scene.

However, metropolitan values unmistakably reassert themselves in the huge **Broadgate** office development along the west side of Liverpool Street Station. Spacious, if somewhat isolated, **Exchange Square**, with its view into Liverpool Street Station, is also worth a look, if only for a quick peek at the modern piece of sculpture there, the rather fancifully named, vaguely Beryl Cook-esque *Broadgate Venus*.

Liverpool Street station is one of London's busiest, daily pumping in the City's lifeblood – tens of thousands of commuters – and then returning them back to their East Anglian homes at the end of the day. An impressive redevelopment of the station in the late 1980s and early 1990s has made it fit for the 21st century. Within striking distance, to the east, are the endangered **Spitalfields Market** (*see p153 and p256*) and, further east, the curry houses of **Brick Lane** (*see p154*).

North of London Wall

Barbican or Moorgate tube/rail.

Running to close to Liverpool Street station, **London Wall** follows the northerly course of the old Roman fortifications. Part of the wall, and the remains of one of the gates into the Cripplegate Roman fort, can be seen in **St Alfage Gardens**. The area just to the north of here was levelled during the Blitz. Rather than encourage office developments, the City of London and London County Council purchased a 14-hectare (35-acre) site in 1958 to build 'a genuine residential neighbourhood, with schools, shops, open spaces and amenities'. Unfortunately, we ended up with the **Barbican**.

St Bartholomew-the-Great

West Smithfield, EC1 (7606 5171/ www.greatstbarts.com). Barbican tube/ Farringdon tube/rail. **Open** *Mid-Nov-mid-Feb* 8.30am-4pm Mon-Fri; 10.30am-1.30pm Sat; 2-6pm Sun. *Mid-Feb-mid-Nov* 8.30am-5pm Mon-Fri; 10.30am-1.30pm Sat; 2-6pm Sun. **Map** p402 O5.
The only surviving part of the Norman priory founded by Rahere in 1123, and London's

oldest and most atmospheric parish church (*pictured*). The nave once extended the length of the churchyard to the 13th-century gateway, now the entrance from Smithfield. Although the nave was torn down during Henry VIII's monastic purge, it's still a wonderfully evocative place; most of the Norman arches are original. Hogarth was baptised here, and Benjamin Franklin served a year as a journeyman printer in the Lady Chapel,.

St Botolph Aldgate

Aldgate, EC3 (7283 1670). Aldgate tube. **Open** 10am-4pm Mon-Fri; 9.30am-1pm Sun; closed Sat. **Map** p405 R6.
The original St Botolph, built by the City's east gate, may date back to the tenth century. The galleried interior of the current plain brick, stone-dressed structure (built by George Dance in 1744) is notable for John Francis Bentley's weird if highly original ceiling, lined with angels. Daniel Defoe was married here in 1683. St Botolph has a distinguished history of campaigning on social issues and it maintains the tradition today, with a crypt that's currently used as a day centre for the homeless.

▶

In the brave new post-war world, it must have looked great on paper. This was how we would all live in the future: 6,500 state-of-the-art flats, some in blocks of 40 storeys and more, rising higher than 135 metres (400 feet) – the tallest in Europe at the time – a huge arts centre with concert halls (home to the London Symphony Orchestra), a theatre (London base of the Royal Shakespeare Company), a cinema, art gallery, exhibition space, cafés and restaurants. The complex also incorporates one of the city's best museums, the **Museum of London** (*see p91*), the **Barbican Art Gallery**, with its wide-ranging exhibitions (*see p95*), the Guildhall School of Music and Drama and the City of London School for Girls.

Tragically – considering the immense cost of the Barbican (the arts centre alone accounted for over £150 million) – the ideas behind the development were already out of date by the time it was completed in the early 1980s. Granted, occupancy rates are high (there is little choice of residence if you want to live in the City; five-sixths of the inhabitants of the Square Mile live here) and the events programmes at

the arts centre are usually first rate. It's just that, try as hard as you can to like the place, it has no soul, no warmth, no sense of community.

Marooned amid the towering blocks is the only pre-war building in the vicinity – the heavily restored 16th-century church of **St Giles**, where Oliver Cromwell was married and John Milton buried. The Nonconformist connection continues further north-east. **Bunhill Fields** was set aside as a cemetery during the Great Plague, although seemingly not used at that time. Instead, because the ground was apparently never consecrated, it became popular for Nonconformist burials, gaining the name of 'the cemetery of Puritan England'. Much of the graveyard is now cordoned off, but it's still possible to walk through and see the monuments to John Bunyan, Daniel Defoe and that most unconformist of Nonconformists, the mighty William Blake.

Opposite Bunhill Fields on City Road is the **Museum of Methodism** and **John Wesley's House** (*see p95*). The founder of Methodism lived his last years in the Georgian

▶ God is in the detail (continued)

St Bride's

Fleet Street, EC4 (7427 0133). Blackfriars tube/rail. **Open** *8am-4.45pm Mon-Fri; 10am-4pm Sat; 9.30am-12.30pm, 5.30-7.30pm Sun.* **Map** *p404 N6.*
Completed by Wren in 1703, St Bride's is one of the finest examples of the Italian style in England. The spire, at 69m (226ft), is the architect's tallest; the four octagonal arcades of diminishing size are said to have been the inspiration for the first tiered wedding cake. The church was gutted in the Blitz, revealing Roman and Saxon remains, which are now displayed and labelled in the crypt, along with information on the connections between St Bride's and the printing and newspaper publishing businesses. The press may have deserted Fleet Street, but St Bride's, where Wynkyn de Worde set up the first printing press in the City, is still known as the journalists' or printers' church.

St Helen Bishopsgate

Great St Helen's, EC3 (7283 2231/ www.st-helens.org.uk). Bank tube/DLR/ Liverpool Street tube/rail. **Open** *9am-5pm Mon-Fri; closed Sat, Sun (except for services).* **Map** *p405 R6.*

Having survived the Great Fire and weathered the Blitz, St Helen's was badly damaged by the 1992 and 1993 IRA bombs in the City. Founded in the 13th century, the spacious building incorporates 15th-century Gothic arches and a 14th-century nuns' chapel. The unusual double nave shows that this was once two churches side by side, one belonging to a Benedictine nunnery. St Helen's is known as the 'Westminster Abbey of the City' because of its splendid collection of medieval and Tudor monuments to City dignitaries. **St Andrew Undershaft**, nearby, and **St Olave's**, on Hart Street, are also pre-Fire churches.

St Mary Abchurch

Abchurch Yard, Abchurch Lane, EC4 (7626 0306). Bank tube/DLR/Cannon Street tube/rail. **Open** *10.30am-2pm Mon-Fri; closed Sat, Sun.* **Map** *p405 Q7.*
The simple, Dutch-influenced red-brick exterior of this Wren church (1681-6) conceals a splendidly rich yet light interior, largely unaltered by subsequent 'improvers'. Below the shallow dome (painted by William Snow) is superb 17th-century woodwork. The highlight, however, has to be the limewood reredos (altar screen), the only one in the City that can be attributed with certainty to Grinling Gibbons. The original church on the

house and is buried by the unexpectedly ornate chapel. Upstairs, in 1951, Denis Thatcher married Margaret Hilda Roberts.

Barbican Art Gallery

Level 3, Barbican Centre, Silk Street, EC2 (box office 7638 8891/enquiries 7382 7105/ www.barbican.org.uk). Barbican tube/Moorgate tube/rail. **Open** 10am-6pm Mon, Tue, Thur-Sat; 10am-8pm Wed; noon-6pm Sun. **Admission** £7; £5 concessions. **Credit** AmEx, MC, V. **Map** p402 P5.
The main gallery of this notoriously disorienting City arts centre regularly mounts interesting exhibitions of modern and historical works, frequently showcasing major photographic shows alongside more populist ventures such as 2000's hugely popular show devoted to *Star Wars*.
Sure to be among the most popular of all the Barbican's exhibitions during 2001 is a show devoted to the work of photographer Helmut Newton, staged to coincide with his 80th birthday (8 May-8 July). At the same time, the awkwardly titled Jam #2.001: London–Tokyo offers a selection of art, design and fashion from both cities, all as part of the Japan Festival. Later on, The Americans (showing 18 Oct-6 Jan 2002) features contemporary art from 35 US artists.

Up on the Curve, the Barbican's other art gallery, is work from 20 Iranian contemporary artists (12 Apr-3 June), and noted piss-artist Andres Serrano (15 Nov-13 Jan 2002).

Museum of Methodism & John Wesley's House

Wesley's Chapel, 49 City Road, Finsbury, EC1 (7253 2262). Old Street or Moorgate tube/rail. **Open** 10am-4pm Tue-Sat; noon-2pm Sun; closed Mon. **Admission** £4; £2 concessions; additional visits free within same month. **Map** p403 Q4.
Appropriately enough, Bunhill Fields, just across the City Road, is the burial ground of many of London's religious dissenters. John Wesley's unorthodox assemblies resulted in the establishment of a church that now has a following of over 50 million around the world. In 1778, Wesley opened this chapel for worship, and in 1981 a museum of the man's work opened in the crypt. Highlights include the pulpit and a large oil portrait of the scene at his death bed. His house next door has been restored to its original Georgian interior design, right down to the paint it's thought that Wesley would have chosen. In the kitchen and study you can see his nightcap, preaching gown and, bizarrely, his personal experimental electric-shock machine.

site dates from the 12th century and may have been named 'up church' because it was upriver from its then-owner, the Priory of St Mary Overie (now Southwark Cathedral).

St Mary-le-Bow

Cheapside, EC2 (7248 5139). St Paul's tube/Bank tube/DLR. **Open** 6.30am-6pm Mon-Thur; 6.30am-4pm Fri; closed Sat, Sun. **Map** p404 P6.
Wren's graceful white tower and spire (1670-3), topped by a huge dragon weathercock, is one of the architect's finest works. German bombers put paid to the original interior; what you see now is a post-war reconstruction. The tradition that only those born within earshot of these church bells can claim to be a true Cockney probably dates from the 14th century, when the bells first rang the City's nightly curfew. The crypt of the original Norman church survives (its arches, or 'bows', give the church its name) and is now home to **The Place Below** restaurant (*see p215*).

St Mary Woolnoth

Lombard Street, EC3 (7626 9701). Bank tube/DLR. **Open** 8am-5pm Mon-Fri; closed Sat, Sun. **Map** p405 Q6.
Wulnoth, a Saxon noble, is believed to have founded this church on the site of a Roman temple to Concord. It was rebuilt many times,

most recently by Hawksmoor in 1716-17, and its tiny but beautifully proportioned interior, based on the Egyptian Hall of Vitruvius, is one of the architect's finest. Edward Lloyd, in whose coffee shop Lloyd's of London was founded, was buried here in 1713. When Bank station was built between 1897 and 1900, the church was undermined, the dead removed from the vaults and lift shafts sunk directly beneath the building.

St Stephen Walbrook

39 Walbrook, EC4 (7283 4444). Mansion House or Monument tube/Bank tube/DLR/Cannon Street tube/rail. **Open** 10am-4pm Mon-Thur; 10am-3pm Fri; closed Sat, Sun. **Map** p404 P6.
Arguably Wren's finest parish church, St Stephen Walbrook was a practice run for many of the ideas that he brought to fruition in St Paul's. Its cross-in-square plan surmounted by a central dome creates a marvellous feeling of space and light and is an ingenious use of the relatively cramped site. Although badly damaged in the Blitz, the church has been superbly restored; largely thanks to the support of Lord Palumbo, who commissioned the amorphous, Roman travertine central altar by Henry Moore. The rector, Prebendary Dr Chad Varah, founded the Samaritans here in 1953.

Holborn & Clerkenwell

A winning combination of history and hedonism.

Holborn

Maps p399 & p401
Holborn tube.

The character of Holborn – pronounced 'Hó-bun' and named for the long-vanished Holebourne river, a tributary of the not-so-long-ago-vanished Fleet that ran along today's Farringdon Road – owes something to the three districts that surround it: commercial Covent Garden, learned Bloomsbury and the money-mad City. However, it's primarily defined by the straggling, anachronistic Inns of Court scattered across the area. The four remaining Inns of Court, home to countless legal types and something of a spiritual home for British justice, were situated here to symbolise the law's role as mediator in the historical battle for power between the City and royal Westminster.

In the Inns of Court, members of the legal profession wander safely out of touch with reality, bewigged but serious, selling British justice. Amble around **Lincoln's Inn** and **Gray's Inn**, and sample the joys of passing 'by unexpected ways, into its unexpected avenues, into its magnificent ample squares, its classic green recesses', as essayist Charles Lamb put it at the end of the 18th century. The alleys and open spaces of the Inns remain a blessed haven from the choking fumes of central London, though be warned: most of the buildings are open only by appointment, some just for group tours, so call before you make the trip.

Around Aldwych

The western flank of modern Holborn is formed by the uncompromising car-filled conduit of **Kingsway**, carved out of slum-lined streets in the early 1900s in an attempt to relieve traffic congestion, and culminating in the crescent of **Aldwych**. The handsome Meridien Waldorf hotel, built here soon afterwards, and One Aldwych, one of London's newest and most stylish luxury hotels, face a trio of unashamedly Imperial buildings: India House, Australia House and Bush House, once intended to be a huge trade centre and now home to the BBC's much-loved World Service.

Between here and the Thames lies **King's College**, its hideous 1960s buildings sitting uncomfortably with Robert Smirke's graceful

The leafy **Middle Temple**. *See p97.*

1829-31 originals. Infinitely easier on the eye, though, is William Chambers' grandiose late 18th-century **Somerset House** (*see p98*), beautifully restored and now open again to the public (*see p98* **Rebirth, marriages & deaths**) and home to the **Courtauld Gallery**, the **Gilbert Collection** and the **Hermitage Rooms** (for all, *see p97*).

Two nearby curiosities are worth a glance. On **Temple Place** is one of a handful of still-functioning cabmen's shelters. These rather dainty, green-painted sheds are a legacy of the Cabmen's Shelter Fund, set up in 1874 to provide cabbies with an alternative to pubs in which to hide from the elements and get a hot meal and (non-alcoholic) drink. And around the corner on **Strand Lane** is the 'Roman' bath, reached via an alley off Surrey Street. David Copperfield took many a cold plunge here. The interior can be viewed through a window if you don't manage to pass by during its official opening times (10am-12.30pm Mon-Fri).

Back on the Strand are the churches of St Mary-le-Strand (James Gibbs' first public building; built 1714-17) and St Clement Danes (*see p97*), both isolated on traffic islands. Samuel Johnson was a regular and 'solemnly devout' member of the congregation at the latter. Just north of here loom the suitably imposing neo-Gothic **Royal Courts of Justice** (*see p97*), opened in 1882 by Queen Victoria. The stress of the commission was such that the architect GE Street's crowning achievement brought him to an early grave.

The fearsome bronze griffin in the middle of the road near here marks the site of **Temple Bar** and the official boundary of the City, past which the Queen cannot stray without the Lord Mayor's permission. Just beyond here is the church of St Dunstan in the West (*see p98*) and the 17th-century Prince Henry's Room (*see below*), while just south of the Strand – and, to be pedantic, actually located just inside the borders of The City – are **Middle Temple** (Middle Temple Lane, EC4; call 7427 4800 for details on the variable opening hours) and **Inner Temple** (Inner Temple Treasury Office, EC4; group tours of the hall, costing £10, can be booked on 7797 8250). Built around a maze of courtyards and passageways, they're especially atmospheric when gaslit after dark.

Courtauld Gallery

Somerset House, Strand, WC2 (7848 2526/ www.courtauld.ac.uk). Covent Garden or Temple tube (closed Sun). **Open** 10am-6pm Mon-Sat; noon-6pm Sun. **Admission** £4; £3 concessions; free under-18s; *Joint ticket with Gilbert Collection* £7; £5-£6 concessions. **Credit** MC, V. **Map** p401 M7.

Housed in the superb 18th-century **Somerset House** (*see p98*), the Courtauld represents the sum of several donated private collections. At its heart are the paintings of textile magnate Samuel Courtauld, which account for the bulk of the Impressionist and post-Impressionist works and which include the likes of Manet's *A Bar at the Folies-Bergère* and a version of his *Le Déjeuner sur l'Herbe*, Cézanne's *The Card Players* and Gauguin's *Nevermore*. This collection is augmented largely by the munificence of Count Antoine Seilern, who gave the institute a wealth of 14th- to 20th-century paintings, resulting in a roomful of Rubens and a group of wonderful early Flemish and Italian paintings. Highlights include Fra Angelico's *Man of Sorrows*, Cranach's *Adam and Eve* and Quentin Metsys' almost-translucent *Virgin and Child with Angels*.

Gilbert Collection

Somerset House, Strand, WC2 (7240 4080/ www.gilbert-collection.org.uk). Covent Garden or Temple tube (closed Sun). **Open** 10am-6pm Mon-Sat; noon-6pm Sun (last entry 5.15pm). **Admission** £4; £2-£3 concessions; free students, under-18s. Free to all 10am-2pm Mon. *Joint ticket with Courtauld Gallery* £7; £5-£6 concessions. **Credit** AmEx, MC, V. **Map** p401 M7.

The South Building of **Somerset House** (*see p98*) is now the home of London's newest museum of decorative arts. The three-pronged collection of London-born Arthur Gilbert is made up of over 800 items, part of which focuses on a fabulous array of exquisitely ornate gold boxes for containing snuff (powdered tobacco, the fashionable addiction of the 17th and 18th centuries). Elsewhere, the collection takes in European silverware and Italian mosaics and micromosaics (intricate mosaics formed from impossibly tiny bits of opaque coloured glass).

Hermitage Rooms

Somerset House, Strand, WC2 (information 7845 4630/ticketmaster 7413 3398/ www.hermitagerooms.co.uk). Covent Garden or Temple tube (closed Sun). **Open** 10am-6pm Mon-Sat; noon-6pm Sun. **Admission** £6; £4 concessions. **Credit** MC. V. **Map** p401 M7.

Opened in November 2000, the Hermitage Rooms in **Somerset House** (*see p98*) plays host to rotating exhibitions from the world famous State Hermitage Museum in St Petersberg. Displayed in rooms decorated in the style of the Hermitage, new exhibitions will arrive every six to ten months, with the opening display, Treasures of Catherine the Great, running until September 2001. The £6 admission price is a little steep, but it's reassuring to know that for each ticket sold, £1 goes straight to the underfunded State Hermitage. Advance booking is advisable.

Prince Henry's Room

17 Fleet Street, EC4 (7936 4004). Temple tube (closed Sun). **Open** 11am-2pm Mon-Sat; closed Sun. **Admission** free. **Map** p404 N6.

Built in 1611 and named in honour of James I's eldest son, this is one of the few City buildings to have survived the Great Fire, with oak panelling and plaster ceiling intact. It now houses a collection of Samuel Pepys memorabilia.

Royal Courts of Justice

Strand, WC2 (7947 6000/www.open.gov.uk). Temple tube (closed Sun). **Open** 9.30am-1pm, 2-4.30pm Mon-Fri; closed Sat, Sun. No court cases during Aug & Sept recess. **Admission** free. **Map** p399 M6.

Anyone is free to take a pew at the back of any of the 88 courts. It's a fascinating and somehow reassuring experience to thus exercise one's democratic right to witness the creaky British justice system in action. The interior of the building is as impressive as the façade, and also houses a coffee shop and a small exhibition of legal garb.

St Clement Danes

Strand, WC2 (7242 8282). Temple tube (closed Sun). **Open** 8.30am-4.30pm Mon-Fri; 9am-3.30pm Sat; 9am-12.30pm Sun. **Map** p399 M6.

The curious name of this Wren church – which boasts a tower extension by James Gibbs on top, and a controversial statue of Arthur 'Bomber' Harris outside; the church has been renovated as a stately central church for the RAF since being gutted during the Blitz – may date back to its use by Danes married to English wives, who were allowed to stay behind when Alfred the Great expelled most of their countrymen from the kingdom. Its name is immortalised in the children's nursery rhyme 'Oranges and lemons, Say the bells of St Clement's'; the bells still ring out the tune, and children at St Clement Danes Primary School are given an orange and a lemon after the annual service. A pity, then, that the church in the rhyme almost certainly wasn't this one: in fact, it was most likely St Clement Eastcheap, near to the wharves where citrus fruit used to be unloaded.

Rebirth, marriages and deaths

The recent transformation of **Somerset House** has returned one of London's grandest edifices to the public. It was originally a Tudor palace built by Edward Seymour, the first Duke of Somerset and brother of Henry VIII's third wife Jane. The palace stood close by two vital links between the City and Westminster Palace: the Strand and the Thames, which was then London's major thoroughfare and the fastest route between the two. The Crown appropriated the site after Edward's execution in 1552 and granted it to Princess Elizabeth, later Queen Elizabeth I.

By the 1770s, the palace had become a temporary residence for royalty, digs for foreign ambassadors and the centre of society events. However, it was also in danger of collapse. King George III gave the nod for its total demolition, and approved the construction of William Chambers' neo-classical design.

The project took a quarter of a century to complete, and Chambers himself did not live to see the finished article. But the end result was stunning. The building became home to the Navy Board, to seats of learning such as the Royal Academy of the Arts and, eventually, to the Inland Revenue and the Register of Births, Marriages and Deaths.

Somerset House was closed to the public for almost a century. But following a millennial makeover, it's now possible to stroll through the Strand entrance and enjoy the attractive grove of dancing water jets in the courtyard, the first major public fountain commissioned in London since Trafalgar

St Dunstan in the West

Fleet Street, EC4 (7242 6027). Chancery Lane tube.
Open 10am-2pm Tue; 2-6pm Sat; 9am-2pm Sun; occasional concerts on Fri. **Map** p404 N6.
The first mention of this church was in 1185, but the present early Gothic-revival building dates only from 1831-3, when a widening of Fleet Street required it to shift slightly northwards. John Donne was rector here (1624-31); Izaak Walton (whose *Compleat Angler* was published in the churchyard in 1653) held the bizarrely named posts of 'scavenger, questman and sidesman' (1629-44); and Samuel Pepys popped in one day in 1667 to hear a sermon and unsuccessfully try to fondle one of the local maidens ('… at last I could perceive her to take pins out of her pocket to prick me if I should touch her again').

Around Lincoln's Inn Fields

The winding streets to the west of the courts bear the names of several of the now-defunct Inns of Chancery, such as **New Inn** and **Clement's Inn**, and are home to the one-time cradle of left-wing agitation, the LSE (London School of Economics). Nearby, at 13 Portsmouth Street, is the Old Curiosity Shop, the supposed – though this is much disputed – inspiration behind the Dickens novel of the same name. It dates from about 1567.

The broad expanse of **Lincoln's Inn Fields** is London's largest square and Holborn's focal point. On the north side of the square is **Sir John Soane's Museum** (*see p99*); on the south side are the various **Museums of the Royal College of Surgeons** (*see below*); and to the east are the daunting buildings of the Inn itself. On a guided tour of Lincoln's Inn's Old Hall and Great Hall (Lincoln's Inn Fields, WC2; call 7405 1393 for details on times and tours), it's possible to relive scenes from *Bleak House*, Dickens' ferocious attack on the legal system: virtually nothing has changed.

Chancery Lane, running up from the Strand to High Holborn – site of Mid-City Place, an ambitious new steel and glass office block – is home to the Public Records Office and the Law Society. At its northern end are the weird, subterranean shops of the London Silver Vaults (*see p229*), selling everything from silver spoons to antique clocks. Around the corner, towards Holborn Circus, teeter the overhanging, half-timbered Tudor buildings of **Staple Inn**, one of the former Inns of Chancery. Across the road, by the ancient Cittie of Yorke pub, is an alley leading into the most northerly of the Inns of Court, **Gray's Inn**. The last Inn to be founded (in 1569), its Hall – group tours of which can be arranged on 7458 7800 – contains a superb screen, said to be made from the wood of a galley from the Spanish Armada.

Museums of the Royal College of Surgeons

35-43 Lincoln's Inn Fields, WC2 (7869 6560/ recorded information 7869 6563/www.rcseng.ac.uk). Holborn tube. **Open** 10am-5pm Mon-Fri; closed Sat, Sun. **Admission** free; donations encouraged. **Map** p399 M6.
The Royal College of Surgeons runs four museums under one roof: the **Hunterian**, the **Odontological**, and the **Wellcome Museums of Pathology** and **Anatomy** (open by appointment only). The former

Square's in 1845. Waterloo Bridge has a glass-and-steel footbridge leading directly on to the River Terrace, with a café and views to Westminster and St Paul's. And the Victoria Embankment entrance leads through the Great Arch that was at one time the central watergate into the Thames.

As for the buildings themselves, the Inland Revenue remains in the East and West Wings, but the **Courtauld Gallery**, **Gilbert Collection** and **Hermitage Rooms** (for all, *see p97*) all provide cultural sustenance for visitors on a daily basis. Add in a fine restaurant (the Admiralty), a café, a nicely stocked shop and the breathtaking grandeur of the courtyard – which, in a truly inspired move, was temporarily covered with an ice rink during winter 2000; here's hoping it becomes an annual event in the capital – and you have one of London's most quietly wonderful new attractions. It seems the millennium was good for something after all.

Somerset House

Strand, WC2 (7845 4600/www.somerset-house.org.uk). Covent Garden or Temple tube (closed Sun). **Open** 10am-6pm Mon-Sat; noon-6pm Sun (last entry 5.15pm). **Admission** free. **Credit** *Shop* MC, V. **Map** p401 M7.

is the most impressive, and consists of a collection of anatomical and pathological specimens bought by the British government in 1799 from John Hunter (1728-93). It's also not for those with weak stomachs. Tall glass-fronted display cabinets hold jars of (human and animal) organs, along with foetuses at different stages of development. The skeleton of the 'Irish Giant' and a dwarf woman are also on display.

Meanwhile, the Odontological Museum has jaws, casts and skulls, plus the famous Waterloo teeth, extracted from corpses on the field of battle to replace those lost by the living. Dental and surgical instruments reinforce the value of anaesthetics.

Sir John Soane's Museum

13 Lincoln's Inn Fields, WC2 (7405 2107/ www.soane.org). Holborn tube. **Open** 10am-5pm Tue-Sat; 6-9pm 1st Tue of every month; closed Mon, Sun. **Admission** free; donations appreciated. **Guided tours** 2.30pm Sat (£3; free concessions). **Map** p399 M5. An extraordinary place, this, and a wonderful testament to the collecting tendencies of its founder, architect Sir John Soane. The word 'eclectic' doesn't do justice to the wild jumble of treasures stuffed, much as they were in Soane's time, into the house he reconstructed himself. It's chaos, but a wonderful chaos. Cantonese chairs sit near vases dating from the fourth century BC; a tiny study is made smaller by the assortment of marble bits and pieces glowering from the walls; another wall is covered by Hogarth's *Rake's Progress* series, but then opens up to reveal a stash of Piranesi drawings… Oh, and there's a huge 3,300-year-old Egyptian sarcophagus downstairs.

The overall effect is stunning, especially on the first Tuesday of the month, when the house is lit by candles. Tickets for the excellent guided tours go on sale at 2pm in the library dining room, on a first-

come first-served basis. All in all, this is one of our favourite London museums; give generously, and hopefully it will be able to realise its plans of opening the house next door – also owned by Soane – as a full add-on to the present museum in 2003.

Clerkenwell & Farringdon

Map p402

Chancery Lane or Farringdon tube.

North and east of Holborn lies the cosy little neighbourhood of **Clerkenwell**. In the 12th century, a hamlet grew up here around the religious foundations of the Priory of St John of Jerusalem, the long-gone St Mary's Nunnery and, from the 14th century, the Carthusian monastery of Charterhouse (now a posh OAP home). The original Clerk's Well, first mentioned in 1174 and long thought lost, was rediscovered by chance in 1924, and can now be viewed through the window of 14-16 Farringdon Lane.

Over the centuries, a strong crafts tradition grew up in Clerkenwell, as French Huguenots and other immigrants settled to practise their trades away from the City guilds. The area was thought 'an esteemed situation for gentry' until the early 19th century, when population pressure and increasing dilapidation led to an influx of Irish, and then Italian, immigrants, looking for cheap accommodation. (Evidence of the once 10,000-strong Italian community can still be seen in St Peter's Italian Church, on Clerkenwell Road, and L Terroni & Sons, the excellent deli next door.) Radicals were also attracted. Lenin edited 17 editions of the

Café society in **Clerkenwell**. See p99.

Bolshevik paper *Iskra* from a back room (which has been preserved) in the Marx Memorial Library at no.37A Clerkenwell Green.

By the late 19th century, the district had become a 'decidedly unsavoury and unattractive locality': prime Dickens territory. The vice-sodden rookeries of **Saffron Hill** were depicted in *Oliver Twist*, while **Bleeding Heart Yard**, off Greville Street, was where Arthur Clennam became a partner in the engineering firm of Doyce and Clennam in *Little Dorritt*, and where the ineffectual Mr Pancks tried to collect rent from his impecunious tenants.

In nearby **Ely Place**, David Copperfield met Agnes Wakefield and renewed his friendship with Tommy Traddles. This fascinating enclave was once the site of the Bishop of Ely's London palace; all that remains is the delightful church of St Etheldreda (which contains a good lunchtime café; *see below*). The private, gated road, now lined by Georgian houses, is crown property and remains outside the jurisdiction of the City of London. Pub-lovers should not miss the Olde Mitre Tavern, on this site since 1546, secreted up a narrow alley off Ely Place. West of here, the long-established, no-nonsense **Leather Lane Market** sells clothes, food and dodgy videos, and supports a number of cheap caffs. Running parallel is **Hatton Garden**, now the centre of London's diamond trade.

Astonishingly, it wasn't until the end of the 1980s that property developers wised up to the attractions of an area so close to the City and the West End, and Clerkenwell underwent a property boom. Along with it has come a vast improvement in the area's nightlife, which, ten or 15 years ago, was non-existent. **St John Street** is home to terrific restaurant St John (no.26; *see p192*), plus hip bar Cicada (no.126; *see p218*). Meanwhile, running almost parallel, Farringdon Road offers pioneering gastropub the Eagle (no.159; *see p218*), while ever-hip eaterie Moro (*see p212*) sits nicely in Exmouth Market. Clubbers, too, are well served by the area: aside from the long-established Turnmills, it boasts newcomer Fabric, arguably London's best club (for both, *see p281*), in among a clutch of hip watering holes, such as Fluid and Mint (for both, *see p218*).

The tourism potential of the district has also been exploited, albeit quietly. There's now a heritage walk, as well as the 16th-century **St John's Gate and Museum of the Order of St John** (*see below*). However, the spooky **House of Detention** attraction is closed for an indefinite period pending a court ruling on a complicated property dispute. Call 7253 9494 in 2002 to find out when – if ever – it will reopen.

Museum and Library of the Order of St John

St John's Gate, St John's Lane, EC1 (7253 6644/ www.sja.org.uk/history). Farringdon tube/rail. **Open** 9am-5pm Mon-Fri; 10am-4pm Sat; closed Sun. *Guided tours* 11am, 2.30pm Tue, Fri, Sat. **Admission** free; donations requested. **Map** p402 O4.

The surviving 1504 gateway was once the entrance to the Priory of St John of Jerusalem, founded in the 12th century, and is now the HQ of the British Order of St John. Beside the gate is a small museum tracing the history of the Order from the days of the crusading Knights Hospitallers, to the more mundane but more useful work of today's St John Ambulance Brigade. The Chapter Hall, Council Chamber, Old Chancery, new church and Norman crypt (the only remaining part of the original building) can only be seen on the guided tours. All that remains of the priory's original circular church is its outline, traced in cobbles, in St John's Square, just north of the gate.

St Etheldreda

Ely Place, EC1 (7405 1061). Chancery Lane tube. **Open** 7.30am-7pm daily. **Admission** free. **Map** p402 N5.

Britain's oldest Catholic church (built in the 1250s) is the only surviving building of the Bishop of Ely's London residence. The simple chapel, lined with the statues of local martyrs, is London's sole remaining example (excepting parts of Westminster Abbey) of Gothic architecture from the reign of Edward I. The strawberries once grown in the gardens were said to be the finest in the city (and received plaudits in Shakespeare's *Richard III*); every June the church holds a 'Strawberrie Fayre' in Ely Place.

Sightseeing

Bloomsbury & Fitzrovia

Art, literature and one of the best museums on the planet.

Bloomsbury

Map p399

Chancery Lane, Holborn or Tottenham Court Road tube/Euston or King's Cross tube/rail.

Boundaried by Euston Road, Gray's Inn Road, Theobald's Road/Bloomsbury Way and Gower Street, Bloomsbury is an area with heavyweight literary and academic associations. The name comes from 'Blemondisberi', or 'the manor of (William) Blemond', who acquired the area in the early 13th century. It remained largely rural until the fourth Earl of Southampton built **Southampton** (now **Bloomsbury**) **Square** around his house in the 1660s.

The construction of Southampton Square marked the start of a trend and many more followed. Among them were Bloomsbury's only surviving complete Georgian square, **Bedford Square** (1775-80), once the haunt of publishers, and enormous **Russell Square** (laid out in 1800), dominated by the red-brick-and-terracotta fantasy of the Russell Hotel and boasting a handy café in the square gardens.

But though the area had become residential by the mid-19th century, it was never one of London's more fashionable districts. And it's this fact that perhaps explains why Bloomsbury came to be dominated by large institutions. Chief among them is the **British Museum** (*see below*), though the University of London runs it a close second. Made up of various colleges, some in Bloomsbury and some outside, its 130-metre (210-foot) tower atop the 1930s Senate House looms massively over the Malet Street campus like an Orwellian Ministry of Truth. Many of the buildings in Bloomsbury's fine Georgian squares contain offshoots of the university, including the **Percival David Foundation for Chinese Art** and the **Petrie Museum of Egyptian Archaeology** (for both, *see p105*).

On the whole, though, Bloomsbury is less populous than it at first might appear: many of the apparently residential properties in the area today are, in fact, super-smart offices, such as those in 1820s **Gordon Square**. Few original houses remain in the square, but it's still the area most closely associated with the **Bloomsbury Group** (*see p103* **Triangles, circles and squares**). Further east are some of Bloomsbury's most charming corners, including

The villagey charm of **Woburn Walk**.

pedestrianised **Woburn Walk** (off Upper Woburn Place), with its bow-windowed shops and cafés. Just as appealing are the small-scale eateries and shops lining **Marchmont Street**, the pleasant kids' park of **Coram's Fields**, the fine pubs on **Lamb's Conduit Street** (the Lamb is recommended; *see p219*) and **Dickens' House** on Doughty Street (*see p104*), the author's only surviving London residence.

Traffic-packed **Southampton Row**, leading down to Holborn, forms Bloomsbury's lower backbone. Try the noisy, old-fashioned Princess Louise, on the corner of High Holborn and Newton Street, for a pint, or lunch in the quiet October Gallery Café on **Old Gloucester Street** before browsing the second-hand books at Skoob (*see p232*) in the curious, pedestrianised, colonnaded **Sicilian Avenue**.

British Museum

Great Russell Street, WC1 (7636 1555/ recorded information 7323 8783/disabled information 7637 7384/minicom 7323 8920/ www.thebritishmuseum.ac.uk). Holborn, Russell Square or Tottenham Court Road tube. **Open** *Galleries* 10am-5.30pm Mon-Wed, Sat, Sun; 10am-8.30pm Thur, Fri. *Great Court* 9am-9pm Mon-Wed;

9am-11pm Thur-Sat; 9am-6pm Sun. **Admission** free; donations appreciated. *Temporary exhibitions* prices vary; phone for details. **Map** p399 K5.

The British Museum is easily London's number one tourist attraction, and it's not difficult to see why. This is one of only two institutions in the world – the other being the 14-museum Smithsonian in Washington, DC – that fulfil the Enlightenment concept of gathering together all branches of human knowledge in what is basically a real-life encyclopaedia.

The museum's beginnings can be traced to royal physician Dr Hans Sloane's 'cabinet of curiosities' (bequeathed to the nation in 1753), a substantial miscellany of books, paintings, classical antiquities and stuffed animals. Over the next century, the plunder of empire, including the Elgin Marbles and various

massive Egyptian monuments, overwhelmed the storage space. In 1847, Robert Smirke designed the present impressive neo-classical edifice, with its grand colonnaded façade and ample interior.

But with more than five million visitors a year and an ever-expanding list of exhibits, the museum found it increasingly hard to justify the massive expanse at its centre – almost two acres – around the edge of the Reading Room, that lay occupied only by bookstacks belonging to the British Library. The museum's 250th anniversary (actually in 2003) seemed like a fitting time to resolve the situation. The first part of the plan was the long-delayed move of the **British Library** to Euston Road in 1998 (*see p106*), which freed up 40 per cent of the building's space. Work then began on Norman Foster's

Triangles, circles and squares

Though its foundations were laid at Cambridge University, it wasn't until sisters Vanessa and Virginia Stephen moved to 46 Gordon Square that the **Bloomsbury Group** became a reality. The girls and their husbands, Clive Bell and Leonard Woolf, were the focus of the social circle, which soon came to incorporate many of their friends and neighbours. Shedding stuffy Victorianism, and its inherent taboos about art, society and sexuality, the Bloomsberries celebrated freedom of expression and the avant-garde. Bohemian thinkers, they opposed imperialism abroad and materialism at home, instead supporting pacificism and internationalism.

In various houses around Bloomsbury, Virginia and Leonard Woolf (who eventually came to live at 52 Tavistock Square), Vanessa and her critic husband Clive (who left the 46 Gordon Square property and moved to Sussex in 1916), historian Lytton Strachey (at 51 Gordon Square), painter Duncan Grant (who made his home at 22 Fitzroy Square) and economist John Maynard Keynes (a later resident of 46 Gordon Square) flounced about practising GE Moore's belief that 'by far the most valuable things... are... the pleasures of human intercourse and the enjoyment of beautiful objects'.

The group's shared contempt for the conventional was reflected in their art and literature. The Omega Workshop, founded at 33 Fitzroy Square by critic and painter Roger Fry in 1913, produced artistic objects for everyday use, while the literature also took on new styles and challenged the conventional. Virginia Woolf incorporated fashionable Freudian theories of the time into

her text with her 'stream of consciousness' technique in *Mrs Dalloway*; in *Orlando*, she confronted issues of women's freedom, femininity and androgyny.

To its friends, Bloomsbury offered a safe and inspirational clique, but to those who were excluded – DH Lawrence was patronised by the group and, later, cast out entirely – it represented insular elitism and social snobbery. The group, too, became as famous for their tangled personal relations as they were for their art, swapping sexual partners yet bound together by platonic friendships. In the words of Lytton Strachey, the group was made-up of 'women in love with buggers, and buggers in love with womanisers'. Virginia Woolf had an affair with fellow author Vita Sackville-West, an affair her husband Leonard apparently encouraged. As Dorothy Parker commented of this artistic circle of friends, 'they loved in triangles, and lived in squares'.

There was a revived interest in the Bloomsbury Group after Woolf's death in the 1960s, and curiosity barely seems to have diminished since. Aside from the Blue Plaques that scatter the area, commemorating the group's old residences and haunts, Virginia has even been honoured – albeit in dubious fashion – with a burger restaurant named after her in Russell Square. It seems that whether it's discussion over their disputable talents, their more tangible contribution to artistic style in the 20th century, or just a fascination with a way of life that was arguably a century ahead of its time, people will likely be reading, writing and talking about the Bloomsberries for centuries to come.

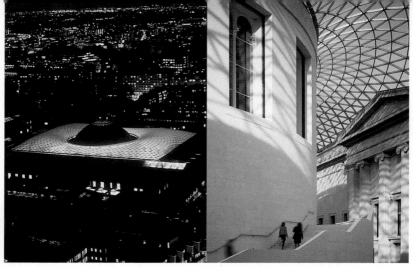

The new Great Court at the **British Museum** has met with universal acclaim. *See p101.*

£100-million **Queen Elizabeth II Great Court**, which opened in December 2000. And a stunning construction it is, too. Topped off with a roof made from steel and 3,312 panes of glass, it's the largest covered public space in Europe, and looks it.

The centrepiece is still the **Reading Room**, restored to its original splendour and open to the public for the first time. The **Joseph Hotung Great Court Gallery** (room 35) doubles capacity for temporary exhibits; the **Concourse Gallery** includes 12 sculptures from various cultures featured elsewhere in the museum. Below the Great Court sit the **Sainsbury African Galleries** (room 25): their opening in March 2001 signals the return of ethnography to the museum after 30 years away, a return that will be completed in 2003 when the **Wellcome Gallery of Ethnography** opens to the public. Also below the Great Court is the **Clore Centre for Education**, with two auditoria for lectures, film and video, plus conferences and concerts, and the **Ford Centre for Young Visitors**, which offers special facilities for kids, parents and teachers.

However, and to its credit, the museum has realised the potential of the Great Court as a public space (a potential extended to the museum's forecourt, which has at last been closed to traffic). The extended hours and the inclusion of cafés and restaurants in the Great Court are inspired ideas. In addition, the original Smirke façades have been restored and the south portico reinstated. And it's this last point that's been the source of much controversy. Despite of an order to use Portland stone in an effort to match the rest of the construction, a builder bought a cheaper (and visually lighter) variety. Unfortunately, reconstruction work was almost finished before anybody noticed the difference, causing a press furore. And sure, the difference is noticeable and hardly ideal, but it's nowhere near as nasty as its critics would have you believe.

When visiting the museum, the cardinal rule is simple: don't try to see everything. Even if it were physically possible to do so, you'd end up with nothing but glazed eyes, throbbing feet and only the haziest of memories of your visit. Instead, focus your attention on specific areas of interest. If you're not sure what you want to see, buy one of the excellent souvenir guides (£5) and take your pick of the highlights, or try one of the four suggested tours on the £1 leaflets. Alternatively, book one of the 90-minute tours of the museum's top treasures at the information desk (£7) or join one of the free 'Eye Openers' tours, which concentrate on one aspect of the museum's collections (such as 'Europe: Medieval to Modern' or 'Treasures of the Islamic World'). For a cheat-sheet of highlights, *see p106* **An hour in…** .

Work is continuing on projects that are scheduled to open in time for the museum's 250th anniversary in 2003. Aside from the aforementioned Wellcome Gallery of Ethnography, the **King's Library** is being restored with an eye to a 2003 opening, while the new **British Museum Study Centre** should also open in stages at the same time. All this modernisation is long overdue, as is the concurrent dragging of the behind-the-scenes organisational structure into the 21st century. But when it's complete, it will surely confirm the British Museum's status as the finest institution of its type in the world.

Dickens' House

48 Doughty Street, WC1 (7405 2127/ www.dickensmuseum.com). Chancery Lane or Russell Square tube. **Open** 10am-5pm Mon-Sat; closed Sun. **Admission** £4; £3 concessions; £2 5-15s; £9 family. **Credit** *Shop* AmEx, MC, V. **Map** p399 M4.
This Georgian terrace house is the sole survivor of Charles Dickens's many London residences. He was able to move into this elegant street on the strength of the phenomenal success of *The Pickwick Papers*, and penned *Oliver Twist* and *Nicholas Nickleby*

Dickens' House. *See p104.*

during his two-and-a-half-year stay here. Only the drawing room has been restored to its original state, but the house is packed with Dickensabilia, including portraits of the author and his family, his desk bars from the Marshalsea Prison where his father was incarcerated for debt and the room in which his sister-in-law, 16-year-old Mary Hogarth (with whom he had fallen in love), died. Every Wednesday night from April to July, a one-man show, 'The Sparkler of Albion', brings the author and his characters to life.

Percival David Foundation of Chinese Art

53 Gordon Square, WC1 (7387 3909/ www.soas.ac.uk). Euston Square, Goodge Street or Russell Square tube/Euston tube/rail. **Open** 10.30am-5pm Mon-Fri; closed Sat, Sun. **Admission** free; donations appreciated (under-14s must be accompanied by an adult). **Map** p399 K4.

In short, the finest collection of Chinese ceramics outside China, as well as an extensive library of East Asian and Western books relating to Chinese art and culture. The permanent collection – 1,700 pieces dating mainly from the 10th to 18th centuries – is housed on the first and second floors, with temporary exhibitions on the ground floor. Aficionados will be drawn to the very rare Ru and Guan wares and the unique pair of blue-and-white Yuan dynasty temple vases (1351), while curiosity-seekers should look out for the late 17th-century Dehua ware figure of Guanyin with a swastika hanging on his chest.

Petrie Museum of Egyptian Archaeology

University College London, Malet Place, WC1 (7679 2884/www.petrie.ucl.ac.uk). Goodge Street tube. **Open** 1-5pm Tue-Fri; 10am-1pm Sat; closed Mon, Sun. **Admission** free; donations appreciated. **Map** p399 K4.

William Flinders Petrie is regarded as the father of scientific archaeology, and the collection of Egyptian artefacts that he bequeathed to UCL in 1933 is well worth picking your way through the campus to witness. Displayed in glass cabinets, Petrie's horde includes the oldest piece of clothing in the world (from 2800 BC) and an array of Roman mummy portraits as well as a dazzling collection of the minutae of Egyptian life, from jewellery and ceramics to games and grooming accessories. Macabre exhibits include an exhumed pot-burial and the coiffured head of a mummy with eyebrows and lashes still intact.

St George Bloomsbury

Bloomsbury Way, WC1 (7405 3044). Holborn or Tottenham Court Road tube. **Open** 9.30am-5.30pm Mon-Fri; 10.30am-12.30pm Sun; closed Sat. **Map** p399 L5.

A classical portico leads from the smoke-blackened exterior of this episcopal Hawksmoor church (1716-31) into its genteelly flaking interior (a restoration is planned). Despite its sky-blue ceiling and gilding, there's a mournful air to the place. George I, looking inappropriately heroic in a Roman toga, surmounts the remarkable tiered steeple, inspired by Pliny's description of the Mausoleum at Halicarnassus. There are some concerts in summer (1.10pm Tue) and services on Sundays, often with opera singers.

St Pancras New Church

Euston Road, NW1 (7388 1461). Euston tube/rail. **Open** 1-2.30pm Tue; 9am-2pm, 3-5pm Wed-Fri; 9am-11am Sat; 8am-7pm Sun; closed Mon. **Admission** free.

This fascinating construction was built in 1822 at a cost of £89,296: at the time, it was the most expensive church since St Paul's. Its spectacular exterior was inspired by the design of the Ionic Temple of Erectheum in Athens and its main features, the Caryatid porches, are used as entrances to the burial vaults. The interior is less ornate but does feature a series of beautiful 19th-century stained-glass windows and an impressive marble font, added in 1887.

Somers Town

The north of Bloomsbury is decisively bounded by the traffic on **Euston Road**. Above here is Somers Town, an area rich in history – parts of it were once bordered by a moat – but now little more than a maze of council estates wracked by poverty and riven by racial divisions.

On the edge of Somers Town, set back a little on the north side of Euston Road, you'll find the utilitarian **Euston Station**, at once the oldest and newest of London's mainline termini. Opened in 1837 and described at the time as 'a railway station without equal', its magnificent classical portico, screen and Great Hall were, criminally, demolished in 1963 to make way for the current structure. Equally controversial has been the new **British Library** (*see p106*), shamed by the building next door, **St Pancras**

An hour in... The British Museum

The must-see exhibits for visitors in a rush

The Great Court: Norman Foster's addition is one of London's finest public spaces

The Lindow Man (Celtic Europe, room 50): Preserved in peat after having been ritually killed 2300 years ago

Sutton Hoo Ship Burial (Middle Ages, room 41): A cache of Anglo-Saxon treasure

Goddess Tara (South-east Asia, room 33): Near-lifesize figure from the eighth century

Rosetta Stone (Egyptian Sculpture, room 4): Part of a terrific Egyptian display

The Elgin Marbles (Parthenon Galleries; room 18): The debate as to who should keep them rages on; for now, they're here

Station. This Victorian glass-and-iron train shed, spanning 73 metres (240 feet) and over 30 metres (100 feet) high at its apex, is fronted by Sir George Gilbert Scott's exuberant High Gothic fairytale of a building, formerly the Midland Grand Hotel, a structure the architect accurately if immodestly described as 'possibly too good for its purpose'. It's now known as St Pancras Chambers: there's a small exhibition about the hotel and the building's future in the lobby (at the west end of the building; open 11.30am-3.30pm Mon-Fri). If you want to see more, fill in a form available in the lobby for one of the occasional guided tours.

Across St Pancras Road is another station, the functional, unlovely **King's Cross**. Much of the surrounding area is seedy – drug dealers and prostitutes predominate – and in desperate need of regeneration, though the Scala nightclub (*see p281*) has managed to imbue the region with a little cool in recent years.

British Library

96 Euston Road, NW1 (7412 7332/www.bl.uk).
Euston Square tube/Euston or King's Cross tube/rail.
Open 9.30am-6pm Mon, Wed, Thur, Fri; 9.30am-8pm Tue; 9.30am-5pm Sat; 11am-5pm Sun. **Admission** free; donations appreciated. **Map** p399 K3.

Whenever traditionalists find themselves losing an argument with forward-thinkers about modern architecture, they know they can always fall back on the British Library as an easy points-scorer. A hideous red-brick construct that cost a fortune and took forever to build, the facilities inside may well be a huge upgrade on what was there before, but from the outside, it's an aesthetic embarrassment.

That said, though, the exhibitions here are, by and large, splendid. Of the permanent displays, the John Ritblat Gallery, housing the Treasures of the British Library, is the most impressive, showcasing the best of the library's vast collection of rare and historic items including the Lindisfarne Gospels (c700) and the Magna Carta (1215), literary manuscripts from Chaucer to Heaney and a collection of scribbled Beatles lyrics. Also of interest are the Workshop of Words, Sounds and Images, a hands-on gallery about the history of book production, and the Philatelic Exhibition, described as 'probably the best permanent display of diverse, classical stamps in the world'.

At the heart of the building is the stunning King's Library, the library of George III, a gift from George IV to the nation in 1823. It's housed in a six-storey glass-walled tower by the café, but you can catch a glimpse even if you're not stopping for refreshments. The Pearson Gallery of Living Words is based around five themes: the Story of Writing, Children's Books, the Scientific Record, Images of Britain and the Art of the Book. It's also used for temporary exhibitions, including, until May 27th 2001, **Treasures of the Ark**, a display of artefacts charting the history of Christianity in Armenia. Phone for times and prices of the guided tours, some of which feature a visit to one of the Reading Rooms (for information about Readers' Tickets call 7412 7677), and for details of events, discussions and lectures held at the library.

Fitzrovia

Maps p398 & p399

Goodge Street, Great Portland Street, Oxford Circus, Tottenham Court Road or Warren Street tube.

Between Gower Street and Great Portland Street, Euston Road and Oxford Street, lies the area that, during the 1930s and 1940s, became known as Fitzrovia. That said, bored hacks and cash-hungry estate agents have lately tried to re-christen the area 'Noho', a horrible name born from *No*rth of *So*ho (if nothing else, it implies that the area south of Soho should be named 'So-so'). Thankfully, it hasn't really stuck.

A long time prior to Noho, though, aspiring and expiring artists headed here to drink away their talent in pubs such as the Fitzroy Tavern

Newman Passage in Fitzrovia.

on **Charlotte Street**. In *Memoirs of the Forties*, Julian Maclaren-Ross recalls being warned by Tambimuttu, Sinhalese editor of *Poetry London*, to 'beware of Fitzrovia… you will stay there always day and night and get not work done ever'. The fact that few have heard of him today suggests he failed to heed the warning.

Today, Fitzrovia's backstreets are oddly quiet. Few tourists venture north of Oxford Street, and fewer local workers stray from the gaggle of no-longer-very-appetising pubs in the area around Charlotte Street (the restaurants here are good, however). The area is, however, slowly reviving as Soho crowds spill northwards into trendy bar-restaurants such as Jerusalem (on **Rathbone Place**), or to the eccentric Spanish bars and eateries on **Hanway Street**, tucked away behind the Virgin Megastore (*see p256*).

Beyond **Pollock's Toy Museum, All Saints Margaret Street** (for both, *see below*), and the omnipresent (620-foot) British Telecom

Tower, sights are few. Still, the area has a certain neglected charm, provided you avoid the scruffy, fume-filled canyon of **Tottenham Court Road**. Barely a century ago, this was a quiet rural road lined by cow sheds; now it's the place to head for electronic goods and computers, and classy furniture and household wares. The southern end of the road has been revived somewhat by the construction of an impressive glass mini-shopping complex, with big-name stores such as Sainsbury's and Boots breathing some life back into the area.

All Saints
Margaret Street, W1 (7636 1788/www.ucl.ac.uk/~ucgbmxd/allss.htm). Oxford Circus tube. **Open** 7am-7pm daily. **Services** phone for details. **Map** p398 J5.
This 1850s church is the work of William Butterfield, whose dread hand scarred countless London churches with his Victorian Gothic 'improvements'. The site of All Saints, however, was too small for Gothic proportions so, instead, he used an extraordinary but surprisingly triumphant mishmash of 14th-century-style details, red brick and humbug-like black stone bands à la Siena Cathedral. Look for the Pre-Raphaelite Minton tile paintings on the walls.

Pollock's Toy Museum
1 Scala Street, W1 (7636 3452/www.pollocks.cwc.net). Goodge Street tube. **Open** 10am-5pm Mon-Sat; closed Sun. **Admission** £3; £1.50 3s-18s; free under-3s. **Credit** *Shop* MC, V. **Map** p398 J5.
Despite the presence of a rare Egyptian clay mouse from 2000 BC, most of the exhibits at this worthwhile museum date from the last two centuries, and include optical toys with such intriguing names as the Phenakistoscope and Heliocinegraphe. The puppet cabinets feature more familiar faces – Sooty and Sweep, Punch and Judy, Muffin the Mule – and a large collection of dolls, plus folk toys from across Europe, India, Africa, China and Japan. It's interesting to witness the evolution of teddy bears: from veteran Eric ('born' 1905) to a decidedly larger and cuddlier specimen only a few years later. Toy theatre performances can be booked for parties of children (minimum 10) and the museum also boasts an appropriately well-stocked toy shop.

Relive your childhood at **Pollock's Toy Museum**.

Marylebone

Away from the bustle of Oxford Street lies a quietly charming London village.

Maps p395 & p398

Baker Street, Bond Street, Edgware Road, Great Portland Street, Marble Arch, Oxford Circus or Regent's Park tube.

Roughly defined by Oxford Street, Edgware Road, Marylebone and Great Portland Street, the ancient manors of Lileston (Lisson) and Tyburn were thoroughly disreputable, violent places by the 14th century. Gallows were set up at Tyburn in 1388 where they remained in use until 1783 (their site is marked by a plaque on the traffic island at the junction of Bayswater and Edgware Roads). Local residents petitioned the Bishop of London for their frequently ransacked church to be moved half a mile away, to a safer site by the Tyburn stream (or bourne). The church, St Mary by the Bourne, eventually gave its name to the entire district, Marylebone.

The small-scale shops, restaurants and pubs along today's snaking **Marylebone Lane** and **Marylebone High Street** create an agreeably laidback, if rather upmarket, small-town ambience in contrast to the frenzy of nearby Oxford Street. Yet this coexists amid a grander, land-that-time-forgot world of sedate Georgian squares and streets.

In the 16th century, the northern half of Marylebone – now Regent's Park – became a royal hunting ground, while the southern section was bought up by the Portman family. Two centuries later, the Portmans developed many of the elegant streets and squares that lend much of this relatively unvisited part of the city its dignified air. One of these squares, **Manchester Square**, is home to the paintings, armour and other goodies of the **Wallace Collection** (*see below*). Nearby is **Harley Street**, renowned since the mid-19th century for its high-charging medical specialists, while the parallel **Wimpole Street** was immortalised by Tennyson in *In Memoriam* as a 'dark unlovely street'. It was from no.50 that Elizabeth Barrett eloped with Robert Browning in 1846; they were secretly married at **St Marylebone Parish Church** on Marylebone Road.

Stately **Portland Place**, leading up to Regent's Park, was the glory of 18th-century London. Although many of its houses have been rebuilt, its spacious proportions have been maintained. At its kink, where it links at **Langham Place** with Nash's **Regent Street**, is the BBC's HQ, Broadcasting House, and the

BBC Experience (*see below*). Next door is Nash's delicate little Thunderbird of a church, **All Souls** (1822-4), much ridiculed in its time for the slenderness of its spire. Over the road is the expensively restored Langham Hilton, the first of London's grand hotels, opened in 1865.

BBC Experience

Broadcasting House, Portland Place, W1 (0870 603 0304/www.bbc.co.uk/experience). Oxford Circus tube. **Open** 11am-6pm Mon; 10am-6pm Tue-Sun. *Last tour* 4.30pm daily. **Admission** *Tour only* £7.50; £4.95 5-16s; £5.95 students; £6.50 OAPs; £19.95 family. **Credit** MC, V. **Map** p398 H5.

Admit it: you've always fancied yourself as a news anchor, haven't you? Or a sports commentator? Or director of *EastEnders*? Come on. You know you have, and so does the BBC. This interactive exhibit brings out the 'I shoulda been in pictures' conceit in everyone. Based in an art deco, Portland-stone construction designed by G Val Myers, this exhibit takes more than an hour to get through, and that's if you hurry. It starts with a film on modern BBC TV followed by a lengthy programme on the history of BBC radio. Both are surprisingly interesting; the latter is, in essence, a recorded history of Britain from 1900 to the mid-1950s. This occasionally sombre education is followed by a giddy enterprise in which tour members record a radio drama, though it merits mention that this is somehow less cheesy than it sounds. After being guided through these sections of the exhibit by endlessly perky staff, you're then left alone to run amok, filming yourself in BBC programmes, directing a show, doing sports voiceovers, and, in general, putting your money where your mouth is.

Wallace Collection

Hertford House, Manchester Square, W1 (7935 0687/www.the-wallace-collection.org.uk). Bond Street tube. **Open** 10am-5pm Mon-Sat; noon-5pm Sun. **Admission** free. **No credit cards. Map** p398 G5.

The hallway and the state drawing room of Sir Richard Wallace's late 18th-century house have been restored to the splendour of his original design, down to the crimson silk hangings and damask curtains. The illegitimate heir of the Marquis of Hertford, Wallace inherited the ardent Francophile's extraordinary collection of furniture (including a writing desk belonging to Marie Antoinette), paintings and porcelain purchased for safe keeping in London after the Revolution. An impressive clutch of Old Masters, including Franz Hals' *The Laughing Cavalier* and Rubens' *Rainbow Landscape*, vie for space with magnificent European and Asian arms and armour and a display of Catherine the Great's crockery.

At one with nature in **Regent's Park**.

The addition of new space at the Wallace, designed and opened in time for its centenary as a museum in 2000, has proved a major boon. The **Watercolour Gallery**, an interactive **Materials and Techniques Gallery** and the entire **Reserve Collection** are all housed in a basement reached via the lovely, glass-roofed Sculpture Garden which, while neither as large or as flashy as that at the British Museum, is still an entirely charming place in which to while away a lunch hour in the company of Stephen Bull's delicious food.

Regent's Park

Regent's Park was laid out between 1817 and 1828 by John Nash (and named for his faithful patron) and remains central London's most well-mannered park. Originally part of the Middlesex Forest, and later a royal hunting ground, the park is lively in summer, with a boating lake (herons live on the islands), three playgrounds, music, tennis courts, a café and an open-air theatre that's been running since 1932 (*see p335*). Strolling in Queen Mary's Gardens within the park, is one of the loveliest ways to waste a summer's evening in the capital.

The **Outer Circle**, the main road running around the park, is over two miles (3.2 kilometres) long. It's bordered to the south by Marylebone Road and Nash's sublimely proportioned Park Crescent, completed in 1818 and originally intended to be a full circus. To the west of the park is the London Central Mosque, built in 1978 to service the spiritual needs of the city's many Muslims, whose shops, cafés and restaurants are a feature of nearby **Edgware Road** and **Bayswater** (*see p180*). To the east are the Palladian mansions of **Cumberland Terrace** (also Nash's handiwork), while the north edge of the park offers up **London Zoo**

(*see below*), the Grand Union Canal and, across Prince Albert Road, Primrose Hill, which affords some of the finest views in the city.

Just below Regent's Park, on the perpetually congested Marylebone Road, are the area's main tourist draws: **Madame Tussaud's** (*see p110*) and the **London Planetarium** (*see below*). Nearby Baker Street is synonymous with junkie-detective Sherlock Holmes, celebrated at the **Sherlock Holmes Museum** (*see p111*).

London Planetarium
Marylebone Road, NW1 (0870 400 3000/ www.madame-tussauds.com). Baker Street tube. **Open** *June-Aug* 10am-5pm daily; *Sept-May* 12.30-5pm Mon-Fri; 10am-5pm Sat, Sun. **Admission** £6.75; £4.65 5-15s; £5.30 OAPs. *Combined ticket with Madame Tussaud's* £14.45; £9.95 5-15s; £11.25 OAPs. **Credit** AmEx, MC, V. **Map** p398 G4.
The Planetarium is slanted largely at the kids, but even particularly bright children may lose interest in the no-really-you're-in-a-big-spaceship schtick. Despite the name, the attraction is actually little more than a cinema with some models of planets in the lobby, a scale that purports to guess your weight with extra gravity, and a 20-minute film about stars beamed onto an domed screen above you. The film isn't bad, though it reveals nothing new to anyone who paid even minimal attention in science class. Bear in mind that it plays every 40 minutes: if you arrive at the wrong time, you could be in for a long wait, and those big models of planets lose their charm quickly. Book ahead to avoid queues, too.

London Zoo
Regent's Park, NW1 (7722 3333/ www.londonzoo.co.uk/londonzoo). Baker Street or Camden Town tube, then 274, C2 bus. **Open** *Nov-Mar* 10am-4pm daily; *Apr-Oct* 10am-5.30pm daily. **Admission** £9; £7 3-14s; £8 concessions. **Credit** AmEx, MC, V. **Map** p398 G2.
The times, as Robert Zimmerman once sung, are a-changing. And few have suffered from changing attitudes as much as the world's zoos. Increased concerns as to the morality of keeping animals in cages for the entertainment of humans has left many zoos needing to reevaluate their roles in order to stay on the right side of public opinion. In this regard, London Zoo is well on its way. The zoo places great emphasis on its conservation and educational programmes, but does so in entertaining fashion, not least in the new **Web of Life** exhibition, aimed at promoting conservation in the natural world. Housed in an environmentally friendly glass pavilion, it features interactive displays and on-show breeding facilities. *See also p272.*

As you might expect, kids love the place, though credit should be given to the staff for their ceaseless enthusiasm and splendidly devised programmes of entertainment. There's a lot here for adults too, though. The gardens are beautifully landscaped – it's easy to spend the best part of a day wandering between the enclosures – and the buildings include some gems of modern architecture: look out for the

Sightseeing

Penguin Pool (1936) by Lubetkin and Tecton, Hugh Casson's Elephant House (1965) and Lord Snowdon's Aviary (1963-4). All in all, between kids, conservationists and courting couples, the zoo is more or less guaranteed to offer customer satisfaction.

Madame Tussaud's

Marylebone Road, NW1 (7935 6861/ *www.madame-tussauds.com). Baker Street tube.* **Open** *May-Sept* 9.30am-5.30pm daily. *Oct-June* 10am-5.30pm Mon-Fri; 9.30am-5.30pm Sat, Sun. **Admission** £11.95; £9.45 OAPs; £8.45 5-15s. *Combined ticket with Planetarium* £14.45; £11.25 OAPs; £9.95 5-15s. **Credit** AmEx, MC, V. **Map** p398 G4.

Let's be fair. There are a few good things about Madame Tussaud's. The Garden Party section at the beginning, for example, is pleasingly (if unintentionally) surreal in the way the dummies are arranged in a casual atmosphere with the sounds of festivities swirling around them. One almost bumps into Whoopi Goldberg and Hugh Grant before realising that they're not real. But, for the most part, this place – one of London's most popular attractions – is expensive and pointless. Quite why people pay this much money to stare at wax dummies of famous people is beyond us. Why are the Beatles perched next to the Queen? What the hell is Bob Geldof (not

A route mastered No.8

Victoria, Hyde Park Corner, Mayfair, Oxford Circus, Holborn, Bank, Liverpool Street, Bethnal Green, Old Ford, Bow Church.

There are few bus routes that link as many disparate areas of London as the no.8. In Victoria, it passes the western boundary of the grounds of Buckingham Palace before heading into opulent Mayfair and the consumer mecca of Oxford Street. It then bisects the old Jewish quarter around Holborn and heads into the centre of the City, then out to the earthy charms of the East End.

Hop on the no.8 on Buckingham Palace Road by Victoria station. You'll travel north along Grosvenor Place, with pretty Green Park to your right, before turning right at Hyde Park corner and proceeding along Piccadilly. Just before the bus reaches the Ritz, it swings left onto Stratton Street and into Mayfair. Despite a shift from residential to commercial usage, Mayfair's architecture remains relatively unchanged since its 18th-century heyday, and a well-bred Georgian air pervades its conspicuously upmarket streets. Remarkably, for such a vast and valuable tract of central London, much of the area is still owned by the Grosvenor family and their trustees, who acquired the land in 1677.

At the top of Stratton Street, the no.8 turns left onto Berkeley Street and then north into Berkeley Square. No nightingales here, but the square is notable for its 30 enormous plane trees, said to have been planted in 1789, that line its central garden, and for the several exclusive design houses that occupy its offices. After passing onto Davies Street at the north-west corner of Berkeley Square, the bus crosses Brook Street, home to the US Embassy and to Eisenhower's World War II headquarters.

At the top of Davies Street is Bond Street station, where the bus turns right. As it emerges on Oxford Street, look left for a glimpse of the spectacular façade of Selfridges department store, with its famous clock, then sit back and enjoy the spectacle as Oxford Street slips past in a blur of bright shop window displays and bustling crowds.

At busy Oxford Circus, the route crosses Regent Street, also home to an impressive array of shops, but continues straight along Oxford Street. At the junction with Tottenham Court Road, it passes Centre Point, a concrete monolith of a office building that's become a useful landmark: it's visible from most parts of central London and is handy as a reference point should you get a little lost.

Beyond Centre Point you'll travel along New Oxford Street, passing the eccentric old umbrella shop James Smith & Sons, and then on to High Holborn. Beyond here, the bus heads to Newgate Street, home to the Central Criminal Court at the Old Bailey. The first Old Bailey Sessions House was erected here in 1539 and the current courts occupy the site of the old Newgate Prison.

At the east end of Newgate Street the bus passes St Paul's station, at which point there's a good (albeit brief) view of Wren's majestic St Paul's Cathedral to your right. As you continue along Cheapside, the bus sweeps past the church of St Mary-le-Bow; only those born within earshot of its bells qualify as true cockneys. Cheapside merges into Poultry; as the bus takes a left at Bank onto Threadneedle Street, keep an eye out on your left for the Bank of England. Another left onto Bishopsgate takes the bus past Liverpool Street station and thenSpitalfields Market, before it heads north-east along Bethnal Green Road, terminating at Bow Church.

looking anything like himself) doing leaning against the wall nearby in a wig that looks like something Tina Turner threw away in 1984? Et cetera.

Some dummies look like their subjects. Princess Di is a dead ringer for herself, for example, as are Elvis and Tony Blair. Others, though, are dreadful. Marilyn Monroe looks like a clothes shop mannequin of a transvestite trying to look like Marilyn Monroe. The Elizabeth Taylor dummy is an insult to poor Liz. And even Gerard Depardieu would admit he was never that thin.

The much vaunted Chamber of Horrors, too, is not scary at all. Having Hitler standing at the door is an interesting touch, but the graphically disembowelled prostitute in the Jack the Ripper section is in poor taste. In the end, for all the shadows and screams, it's just a Chamber of Silliness. A description that could reasonably be applied to the whole museum.

Regent's Park

NW1 (7486 7905/tennis courts 7486 4216/ www.royalparks.co.uk). Baker Street, Camden Town, Great Portland Street or Regent's Park tube. **Open** *Park & Queen Mary's Gardens* 5am-30mins before dusk daily. *Tennis courts* Apr-Oct 9am-dusk daily; May-Sept 8am-dusk. *Playgrounds* 10am-30mins before dusk daily. **Map** p398 G3.

Sherlock Holmes Museum

221B Baker Street, NW1 (7935 8866/ www.sherlock-holmes.co.uk). Baker Street tube. **Open** 9.30am-6pm daily. **Admission** £6; £4 under-16s. **Credit** AmEx, DC, MC, V. **Map** p398 G4. 'Museum' is a misnomer for this facility: it's little more than an excuse to pretend this beloved fictional character existed. And so 221B Baker Street is filled with the kinds of things Sherlock Holmes might have owned. He might have kept a violin just like the one by the fireplace, for example. He may have kept chained handcuffs on the bed near his nice leather case of toiletries. Or not. Whatever.

Pick up a penguin in **London Zoo**. *See p109.*

Atmospherically, it's an interesting if vaguely creepy set-up, sort of like walking into a stranger's house in the 19th century. But then you come across the mannequins acting out scenes from Conan Doyle's books and it all gets too weird. Virtually no information is provided about the displays, which adds to the surreality of it all. What's with the guy with the animatronic snake wrapped around his head, for instance? And what about the man sticking his own head in a wooden box? Unless Sherlock is your favourite literary figure, the ticket price is just too steep for what amounts to a curiosity shop.

Oxford Street & Marylebone High Street

Discreet Marylebone hits snooty Mayfair at **Oxford Street**, with **Marble Arch**, another Nash creation, marking its western extent. This almost apologetically unremarkable monument was intended to be the entrance to Buckingham Palace but, found to be too small, was moved to its current site in 1851 where it now stands, marooned on a traffic island.

London's most famous shopping street is a scruffy, people-packed canyon of uncontrolled commerce. It's also the London street most despised by locals, who abhor the slow-moving traffic – both pedestrian and vehicular – the crowd-induced claustrophobia and the largely unexciting nature of the shops on it. Next to the tourist tat stalls and dodgy geezers flogging counterfeit perfumes on the street are huge department stores (Selfridges, John Lewis, Marks & Spencer *et al*; *see p232*). Filling the middle ground are cheap clothes stores, music shops and high-street favourites such as Gap.

More individual shops can be found back north on **Marylebone High Street**, which has quietly managed to cement its place as one of London's finest, most fashionable shopping thoroughfares. The chances of this happening have been boosted by relatively recent arrivals such as eco-friendly toiletries store Aveda (no.28-29; *see p247*), cool French designer Agnès b (no.41), and Sir Tel's Conran Shop (no.55; *see p245*), showcasing the best of modern furniture and household design, and topped with the fine Orrery restaurant. However, Marylebone High Street is still short on decent food and drink options, with Orrery (*see p206*) and the superlative Italian cooking of Ibla (no.89; *see p200*) the leading exceptions.

Desirable food and drink destinations – formerly not abundant in the area – are multiplying rapidly. Try restaurant-cum-deli Villandry at 170 Great Portland Street, sausage and beer emporium RK Stanley (6 Little Portland Street) or noodle joint Wagamama (101A Wigmore Street; *see p209*).

Mayfair & St James's

London's most moneyed districts hide a wealth of delights.

The late 17th century was a time of great dynamism in London. New districts such as Covent Garden and Soho were laid out, and enjoyed brief vogues as fashionable addresses before the well-to-do looked west for grander residences. The elegant Georgian streets and squares of Mayfair and St James's were part of the next wave, most occupying their current sites by the mid-18th century, but their social cachet, unlike that of their eastern neighbours, has never wavered.

Mayfair

Map p400

Bond Street, Green Park, Hyde Park Corner, Marble Arch, Oxford Circus or Piccadilly Circus tube.

To the casual observer, the huge expanse of space between Oxford Street, Regent Street, Piccadilly and Park Lane can seem little more than a homogeneous mass of mansions. But there is much of interest in this vast area, named Mayfair after the raucous annual fair that moved to the site of today's Curzon Street and Shepherd Market from Haymarket in 1686 and that was suppressed by the local nobs less than a century later for lowering the tone of the 'hood. Today, the narrow streets around **Shepherd Market**, lined with restaurants, pubs and shops (and, secluded in the buildings, prostitutes), make up Mayfair's quirkiest corner. Just south of here, on **Down Street**, distinctive maroon glazed tiles betray the former entrance of a now disused tube station. The Duke of Wellington's London home, **Apsley House** (*see p115*), stands not far away at Hyde Park Corner.

Three great squares dictate the feel of the northern portion of Mayfair: **Hanover Square**, **Berkeley Square** (where no nightingales have sung in living memory) and immense **Grosvenor Square**, second in size only to Lincoln's Inn Fields (*see p98*). Laid out between 1725 and 1731, it has always been a prestigious address, although disappointingly few of its original houses survive. Today, the square is dominated by the US Embassy on the west side, built in 1958-61 by Eero Saarinen. A statue of Franklin D Roosevelt in the centre of the square furthers the American connection, and the Grosvenor Chapel on South Audley Street (where radical MP John Wilkes is buried) is still a favourite with American expats. Nearby are the peaceful Mount Street Gardens, next to the Church of the Immaculate Conception on Farm Street. One of London's few Catholic churches at which a sung Latin mass is celebrated, this splendid Gothic revival building is the British HQ of the Jesuits.

One unlikely Mayfair resident in 1968 was Jimi Hendrix, who lived at 23 **Brook Street**, next door to the house where George Frederick Handel spent the last 35 years of his life. ('I haven't heard much of the guy's stuff, but I dig a bit of Bach now and again,' said Jimi of his neighbour.) The **Handel House Museum** will open on the site later in 2001 (*see p113*).

Not far from here, on Brook Street and **Carlos Place**, are two of Mayfair's poshest and most history-laden hotels: Claridge's and the Connaught. Towards Piccadilly, on **Albemarle Street**, is another classic London hotel, Brown's, from where Alexander Graham Bell made the first successful telephone call in 1876. At no.21, another pioneer, Michael Faraday, is commemorated in the **Faraday Museum** (*see p113*) in the basement of the Royal Institution, which itself boasts a striking classical façade added in 1838 by Lewis Vulliamy.

The eastern side of Mayfair is largely devoted to commerce, albeit of a very upmarket kind, with Savile Row a longtime home to gentlemen's outfitters of a fiercely traditional stamp. At the junction of Savile Row and Vigo Street, old meets new with the venerable firm of Gieves & Hawkes squaring up opposite the iconoclastic tailoring of Ozwald Boateng. Quite what the former thought of the Beatles'

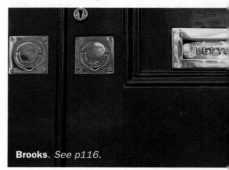

Brooks. *See p116.*

The imposing **US Embassy.** *See p112.*

impromptu final performance on the roof of their Apple Corp HQ at no.3 – now the Building Societies Association – is anyone's guess.

Bond Street is equally famed for its frighteningly opulent yet clinical temples of art, couture, jewellery and antiques. In fact, there is no Bond Street as such, but, rather, **New Bond Street** and **Old Bond Street**. Here, also, are two of London's best-known auction houses – Sotheby's, at 34-35 New Bond Street (7293 5000), and Phillips, at 101 New Bond Street (7629 6602) – and, near the corner of New Bond Street and Grafton Street, one of the capital's ugliest statues: a lifesize Roosevelt and Churchill on a bench. Art fans might also like to cruise the many commercial galleries of **Cork Street** and **Dering Street** (*see p293*), while antique buffs shouldn't miss the Bond Street Antiques Centre (124 New Bond Street; 7493 1854) and Grays Antique Market (*see p229*). Nearby, pedestrianised **South Molton Street** offers more chic and bank-breakingly pricey shops.

A moment's peace from the commercial bustle can be had in the church of St George (1721-4) on **St George Street** near Hanover Square, where Handel regularly played the organ. This was the first London church to have a portico and has long been a favourite venue for society weddings. Sadly, dining options in Mayfair tend towards the unimaginative and extortionate, though there are exceptions: Marco Pierre White's Mirabelle (*56 Curzon Street*) and the renowned south Indian vegetarian cooking at Rasa W1 (*16 Dering Street*) are two prime examples.

Faraday Museum

Royal Institution, 21 Albemarle Street, W1 (7409 2992). Green Park tube. **Open** 9am-5pm Mon-Fri. **Admission** £1. **Map** p400 J7.
The achievements of Michael Faraday, 'father of electricity', are celebrated in this small, ragged but interesting museum in the basement of the building where he was once professor. Exhibits include a re-creation of the lab where Faraday discovered the laws of electromagnetics.

Handel House Museum

25 Brook Street, W1 (7495 1685). Bond Street tube. **Open** *From autumn 2001* 10am-6pm Tue, Wed, Fri, Sat; 10am-8pm Thur; noon-6pm Sun. **Admission** £4.50; £3.50 concessions. **No credit cards**. **Map** p400 J7.
The composer's old Mayfair house is being restored to its original state and opened as a museum this year. The provisional opening date is late October 2001, but always call ahead to check before visiting.

Piccadilly Circus

An unholy coming-together of traffic and commerce, all overseen by some flashy neon advertising hoardings (first erected in 1910), **Piccadilly Circus** is one of central London's pivotal points. The name derives from the speciality of a tailor, Robert Baker, who made his fortune selling stiff collars known as 'picadils' and lived nearby in the early 17th century. The connection is apposite, for the posh shops of Mayfair, Piccadilly and Regent Street have long been a fixture of the area.

But like many of central London's pivotal points, Piccadilly Circus is a mess. Traffic pours in from all directions with little apparent rhyme or reason. Its main feature, a 'statue' of Eros – it's actually a memorial fountain (not a statue) to the philanthropic Lord Shaftesbury, representing the Angel of Christian Charity (not the god of love) – loses much of its grandeur and appeal due to its cramped location on a traffic island. Even the neon signs seem less impressive in the 21st century than they did two decades ago, while the only other defining feature of the square is the inedible pizza served by the slice from cafés on every corner.

The best thing you can say about Piccadilly Circus is that it's unapologetically urban, and that its dirty, slightly seedy hustle and bustle offers up the quintessence of London urban life. However, short of stopping by the late-opening Tower Records or passing through it at 3am in order to flag a black cab on Piccadilly itself, few locals ever feel the need to pass through it, let alone pay it a visit, while tourists are invariably disappointed by the charmless chaos they find upon making its acquaintance.

Two big tourist attractions lie just to the east of the Circus: the bafflingly popular **Rock Circus** (*see p114*) and the **Trocadero** (*see p114*). Leading south from here, **Haymarket**'s associations are with older forms of fun. The market, after which the street is named, traded until 1830; by then, Haymarket was already famed for its theatres (the Theatre Royal opened in 1720, Her Majesty's Theatre in 1705) and notorious for its prostitutes. Today, it's short on charm of any variety.

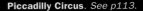

Piccadilly Circus. *See p113.*

Rock Circus

London Pavilion, 1 Piccadilly Circus, W1 (7734 7203). Piccadilly Circus tube. **Open** *Mar-Aug* 10am-8pm Mon, Wed, Thur, Sun; 11am-8pm Tue; 10am-9pm Fri, Sat; *Sept-Feb* 10am-5.30pm Mon, Wed-Sun; 11am-5.30pm Tue. **Admission** £8.25; £7.25 concessions; £6.25 under-16s. **Credit** AmEx, MC, V. **Map** p401 K7.

Only the lack of queues at its front door prevent this hysterically shit tourist trap from garlanding the prize of London's Worst Sight. Having forked out your £8.25, you'll stroll through a tribute to Michael Jackson: a couple of laughable waxworks, some bashed-up album covers and his old trilby and glove. Only it's not actually *his* trilby and glove: rather, it's a trilby and glove 'of the type' worn by Michael Jackson. Hmm. From here, it gets worse. Models and handprints of the stars make up the bulk of the displays, with the odd slab of memorabilia – signed Jimmy Somerville singles! – plopped down in their midsts. It doesn't help, of course, that many of the models are hopeless: Bryan Ferry is a dead ringer for Jimmy Ross, for example, while the Beatles look more like the Rutles. Worst of all, though, is the Cemetery, a jaw-droppingly tasteless 'tribute' to dead rock stars ('Bon Scott. AC-DC. Drank himself to death' reads one fairly typical mock gravestone). All in all, a thoroughly depressing experience, and one to be avoided.

Trocadero

1 Piccadilly Circus, W1 (09068 881100). Piccadilly Circus tube. **Open** 10am-midnight daily. **Admission** free. **Credit** varies. **Map** p401 K7.

Is the Troc cursed? Despite its none-more-central location, no one has ever figured out what to do with it. However, those behind Funland hope their new conceit – a huge amusement arcade, complete with pool hall, dodgems and, eventually, go-karting – will be more successful than the venue's recent incumbents, among them an IMAX cinema and a James Bond-themed ride (both now closed). Take the space-age escalator to the top floor, and then puzzle over how to get out: exits are badly signed, presumably to encourage punters to spend more on the noisy array of arcade games that prop up every wall. Other Troc options include a cinema (the UGC Trocadero; *see p290*), a Scream ride (pay £3 for the 'privilege' of dropping six floors in two seconds) and an Internet café. The ground floor is dominated by shops, among them HMV, Baskin Robbins, Claire's Accessories and a bunch of tacky novelty and souvenir stores hawking everything from Union Jack towels to 'Pecker Party Whistles'.

Regent Street

Curving away north-west from Piccadilly Circus and southwards towards Pall Mall, **Regent Street** was conceived by John Nash in the early 1800s as a dramatic boulevard to clear away slums, improve transport links and connect the Prince Regent's residence, Carlton House, with Regent's Park. His plans were frustrated by a variety of vested interests, but the sweep of the section just north of Piccadilly Circus – known as the Quadrant – impresses, even if the shops at this end definitely don't. Nash also intended Regent Street to act as a *cordon sanitaire* between the scruffs of Soho and the toffs of Mayfair. The distinction still holds good.

Shops 'appropriated to articles of fashion and taste' were a fixture of Regent Street from the beginning. Some of the capital's most famous retailing names – the mock-Tudor department store Liberty (*see p233*), and Hamleys toy store (*see p258*) – still survive amid the encroaching mainstream chains. Here, too, is the Café Royal, at no.68, an ultra-fashionable bohemian hangout for artists and writers a century ago.

Piccadilly & Green Park

Extending from Piccadilly Circus past Green Park to Hyde Park Corner, **Piccadilly** is, along with Oxford Street, one of the ancient roads heading west out of London. Despite the attractions of the street's almost equally ancient emporia – among them Fortnum & Mason (*see p232*) and Hatchards bookshop at no.187, which was founded in 1797 but which has rather had its thunder stolen of late by the new, eight-floor Waterstones bookshop at nos.203-206 – the constant traffic means that more sedate window shopping can be had in the arcades leading off Piccadilly. **Burlington Arcade**, running down the side of Burlington House, now home of the **Royal Academy of Arts** (*see below*), is the most celebrated. Built in 1819 by the house's then-owner, Lord George Cavendish, to stop passers-by throwing rubbish over the wall into his garden, it's today home to some hyper-posh shops that, one imagines, require proof of one's aristocratic heritage in order to allow entry. Regency laws still in effect today state that singing, whistling or hurrying in the arcade are punishable offences. Consider yourself warned.

It's unsurprising, then, that the street is also home to several of London's luxury hotels, chief among them the Ritz. Soon after the hotel opened in 1906, it became a byword for a level of glamour, luxury and extravagance. Putting on the Ritz can be done without forking out for a room by taking afternoon tea in the opulent Louis XVI interior . Those seeking escapism of a more low-key kind should duck in to Wren's delightful **St James's Church** (*see p116*). The churchyard hosts a regular craft market, and the Aroma café next door has good food and outdoor seating in the summer.

Further along Piccadilly – within spitting distance of the Ritz – stands **Green Park**. It's the least grand of all central London's parks, lacking the ornithological delights of St James's

Park to the south-east and the grand expanses of Hyde Park to the north-west. But for that reason, the park – enclosed by Henry VIII, made into a Royal Park by Charles II, and the site of a number of early balloon ascents and firework displays, including that for which Handel composed his *Music for the Royal Fireworks* – is a quiet delight, its underuse by locals leaving it free to be discovered by those simply after a bit of peace and quiet away from the hurly-burly of central London.

Apsley House: The Wellington Museum

149 Piccadilly, W1 (7499 5676). Hyde Park Corner tube. **Open** 11am-5pm Tue-Sun. **Admission** £4.50; £3 students, OAPs, ES40s, disabled; free under-18s. **Credit** AmEx, DC, MC, V. **Map** p400 G8.

This grand house (once known as 'No.1 London' – it was the first building you came to en route from the village of Kensington to London), built by Robert Adam in the 1770s, was the London residence of the Duke of Wellington from 1817 until his death in 1852. His descendants still live here, but ten rooms, restored to their original state, are open to the public, and contain paintings, sculpture, ceramics, silverware and memorabilia belonging to the Iron Duke (so nicknamed not for his indomitable will but for the iron shutters he installed after rioters broke his windows in protest over his Reform Bill). One of the more eccentric touches is a huge 3.4-m (11ft 4-in) statue by Canova of the diminutive Napoleon. The basement contains an exhibition on the Duke's death, including his death mask. An audio guide is included in the entrance fee.

Royal Academy of Arts

Burlington House, Piccadilly, W1 (box office 7300 5959/7300 8000/www.royalacademy.org.uk). Green Park or Piccadilly Circus tube. **Open** 10am-6pm Mon-Thur, Sat, Sun; 10am-8.30pm Fri. **Admission** varies. **Credit** AmEx, MC, V. **Map** p400 J7.

Britain's first art school – it opened in 1768 – the Royal Academy also held the country's first annual open exhibitions of living artists. This persists as the Summer Exhibition (5 June-13 August 2001), which attracts masses of entrants (it's an open exhibition, so, theoretically, anyone has a chance of getting a painting in) and visitors.

Though there is a permanent collection at the RA, only a few works from it are on show at any one time; for others, you must make an appointment with the curator. But in any case, almost everyone who visits does so to see one of the temporary exhibitions: the most visited of any London gallery, booking for them is sometimes a necessity (1999's 'Monet in the 20th Century' was reckoned the most popular art exhibition ever held in Britain). Shows to look out for in 2001 include Botticelli & Dante: Drawings for the Divine Comedy (until 10 June), Ingres to Matisse: The Triumph of French Painting (30 June-23 September), Rembrandt's Women (22

Nun shall pass: Apsley House.

September-16 December 2001) and Frank Auerbach (same dates). Usually, two exhibitions run concurrently, one in the main exhibition spaces and one in the Norman Foster-designed Sackler Galleries.

St James's Church Piccadilly

197 Piccadilly, W1 (7734 4511). Piccadilly Circus tube. **Open** 8am-7pm daily (phone for details of evening events). **Map** p400 J7.

Offering a tranquil haven from the traffic pounding along Piccadilly, this charming Wren church (consecrated in 1684) is, surprisingly, the only church the prolific architect built on an entirely new site. It was also one of the architect's favourites: 'I think it may be found beautiful and convenient'. The limewood reredos, carved by Grinling Gibbons (also responsible for the font and organ case), was much admired by John Evelyn. Aside from providing a ministry, the church also stages an array of concerts (*see p307*), lectures (it's the home of the Blake Society) and markets: an antiques market takes place in the churchyard every Tuesday, with an arts and crafts fair following suit from Wednesday to Saturday.

Maps p400 & p401

Green Park or Piccadilly Circus tube.

Few visitors (and equally few Londoners) venture too far into St James's, which takes as its borders Piccadilly, Haymarket, The Mall and Green Park. And, it's safe to say, that's just the way its habituées like it. If anything, St James's is even posher than Mayfair, its comrade in swank north of Piccadilly. This is a London unchanged for decades, perhaps even centuries: charming in its way, but unreconstructed and snooty with it. Still, you'll find plenty to enjoy and admire; and even, perhaps, plenty at which to laugh.

Much of the comedy – and the snootiness – can be found among the gentlemen's clubs (and they're definitely gentlemen, not men, blokes or geezers) of the area. Not that you'll be allowed in, of course: these temples to self-importance are more exclusive than a year's worth of *Sun* covers. The clubs, most of them on **St James's Street** and **Pall Mall**, evolved from 17th-century coffee houses as meeting places for the gentry, though most date only from the 19th century. Ultra-aristocratic White's (Prince Charles had his stag party here), at 37 St James's Street, is the oldest (founded in 1693); while Brook's (60 St James's Street) boasts a list of past members that includes Charles James Fox, William Pitt and Horace Walpole; the 1832 Reform Act spawned both the 'radical' Reform Club (104 Pall Mall) and the reactionary, right-wing Carlton Club (69 St James's Street). Pass by them all, mull over the goings-on inside, and wonder what happened to the real world.

The material needs of the venerable gents of St James's are met by the anachronistic shops and restaurants of **Jermyn** (pronounced 'jérmun') **Street** and **St James's Street**. If you ignore the fact that well-to-do tourists make up most of the clientele these days, it's still a thrill to see the lovingly crafted quality of the goods and the time-warp shopfronts, among them cigar retailer JJ Fox (19 St James's Street), upmarket cobbler John Lobb (no.6) and Bates the Hatter (21A).

It's doubtful whether the Queen Mother uses either of these establishments, but if she ever saw the need for a Cuban stogie or a pair of £2,000 brogues, she'd only have to take a short walk around the corner from her home at Clarence House on **Stableyard Road**. Its architect, John Nash, was also responsible for the remodelling of St James's Palace in the early 19th century. Built by Henry VIII on the site of St James's Hospital, the palace was one of the principal royal residences for more than 300 years and is still used by Prince Charles and various minor royals; indeed, tradition still dictates that foreign ambassadors to the UK are officially known as 'Ambassador(s) to the Court of St James'. Although the palace is closed to the public, it is possible to explore Friary Court on **Marlborough Road** and attend the Sunday services at the Chapel Royal (October to Good Friday; 8.30am, 11.30am). It was here that Charles I took holy communion on the morning of his execution, and that Victoria and Albert (among many other royals) were married.

Two other notable St James's mansions stand nearby and overlook Green Park. The neo-classical Lancaster House was rebuilt in the 1820s by Benjamin Dean Wyatt for Frederick, Duke of York, and much impressed Queen Victoria with its splendour: on one visit she remarked to her hostess, 'I have come from my house to your palace'. Closed to the public, it's now used mainly for government receptions and conferences. A little further north, on **St James's Place**, is beautiful, 18th-century **Spencer House** (*see p118*), ancestral townhouse of Princess Diana's family and now open as a museum and art gallery.

Across Marlborough Road, the Queen's Chapel was the first classical church built in England. Designed by Inigo Jones in the 1620s for Charles I's intended bride of the time, the Infanta of Castile, the chapel now stands in the grounds of Marlborough House and is only open to the public during Sunday services (Easter to July; 8.30am, 11.30am). The house itself was built by Christopher Wren (both father and son) for Queen Anne's bosom

Almost famous

When asked to recall London statues, most locals name Nelson's Column (or 'our toilet', as the pigeons call it), the Albert Memorial and Eros. These icons of the capital's heritage are so widely known that a myriad of lesser known statues can be easily overlooked; as, indeed, are the people whom they honour.

In Langham Place, Marylebone, W1, stands a bronze sculpture of **Quintin Hogg**, founder of the nearby Polytechnic of Central London. The statue depicts him seated with a boy on either side, one with a football; on the pedestal are inscriptions to his wife, Alice, and dedications to those of the Polytechnic killed in World War I. Born in 1845, Hogg was a social reformer and philanthropist who spent over three decades working with underprivileged children in the capital. The polytechnic, which began life as a run-down building in Regent Street, was created, in his own words, for 'the instruction of artisans and clerks in the principles, and, to some extent, the practice of their breadwinning pursuits'. It's now the University of Westminster.

Another less obvious icon is tenth-century Ukrainian king **St Vlodymyr** (pictured top), a statue of whom is on the corner of Holland Park and Holland Park Avenue. Vlodymyr was responsible, in 988, for the Christianisation of the Ukrainian people, and Kreshchatik Street in Kiev marks the place where the people descended to the Dnipro River to be christened.

A rather sadder monument is that to **William Huskisson** (pictured bottom), President of the Board of Trade, standing in Pimlico Gardens, SW1. Invited to attend the official opening of the Liverpool & Manchester Railway in 1830, Huskisson alighted from his carriage on the Northumbrian to speak with the Duke of Wellington. However, he failed to take into account the approaching presence of another train, the Rocket, which then proceeded to give Huskisson the peculiar and unwelcome distinction of being the first person to be killed in a railway accident.

And then there's the elegant bronze bust of **Sir Joseph Bazalgette** by George Simonds on Victoria Embankment, WC2 (pictured middle). Engraved 'Flumini Vincula Posuit' ('He chained the river'), it's a tribute to one of the greatest civil engineers in London's history. Born in 1819, he was appointed Chief Engineer of the Metropolitan Board of Works in 1855, and, famously, was responsible for the creation of the Thames Embankments, and Battersea, Hammersmith and Putney Bridges. Perhaps more importantly, though, he also revolutionised London's sewerage system. When the Houses of Parliament became so revoltingly pungent after the 'Great Stink' of 1858 that the members demanded a solution, Bazalgette built 83 miles of sewers that prevented raw waste from flowing into the Thames. A London hero if ever there was one.

Sightseeing

Travel light

Forget the black cab and the red double-decker bus. If you were to walk through parts of central London at night, you'd be forgiven for thinking that London's most famous method of transport was a small, yellow, pedal-operated rickshaw.

These odd-looking machines first appeared here in 1998, and have rapidly grown in popularity. That this is so is largely thanks to a company called Bugbugs, a non-profit-making organisation developed with a view to cutting down fuel emissions and providing employment for unskilled labour. There are a couple of competitors operating in the West End but none has yet earned the reputation of Bugbugs.

The best place to pick up one of these mean machines – which may look a little dicey, but which are all fitted with shock absorbers, seat belts, and brakes for maximum safety – is on the corner of Frith Street and Old Compton Street in Soho. They're available from about 7pm until

2am during the week, and until 5am at weekends. Journeys during the day are made by appointment, so you can call to book or visit their website (8675 6577, www.bugbugs.co.uk).

All the drivers are self-employed, so fares vary depending on distance, amount of hills and even the weight of the passengers. It starts at about £2 per person for a local trip within Soho, rising to about £15 up to King's Cross. It may seem steep, but rickshaw driving is no easy work. Riders often only take home a well-earned £18 a day, so if you can find it in your heart and pocket, they'd appreciate a tip.

There is some irony in the fact that while malnourished locals ferry fat British travellers around Bombay, skinny rickshaw drivers are now tugging delighted Japanese tourists around Soho. However, while the world as a whole suffers a fuel crisis, and this town in particular bursts at the seams with traffic, pedal-power could be the pollution solution and the best way forward.

---

chum, Sarah, Duchess of Marlborough, and, as requested, is 'strong, plain and convenient'.

A little like **St James's Square**, in fact. Reached from the west via King Street or The Mall, it was the most fashionable address in London for the 50 years after it was laid out in the 1670s: some seven dukes and seven earls were residents by the 1720s. The Prince Regent was attending a ball at no.16 in 1815 when a bloodied and dirty major arrived to announce the victory at Waterloo, much to the dismay of the hostess who was 'much annoyed with the Battle of Waterloo as it spoilt her party'. Alas, no private houses survive on the square today but among the current occupants is the prestigious London Library, in the north-west corner. This private library was founded by Thomas Carlyle in 1841 in a demonstration of his disgust at the inefficiency of the British Library (a sentiment that many would have recognised until recent times).

Further east, overlooking The Mall, is **Carlton House Terrace**, which was built by Nash in 1827-32 on the site of Carlton House. When the Prince Regent came to the throne as George IV, he decided his home was not

ostentatious enough for his elevated station and levelled what Horace Walpole had once described as 'the most perfect palace' in Europe. The terrace splits at the Duke of York's Column, erected in 1833. Not only did the 'Grand Old Duke' march his 10,000 men to the top of the hill and down again, he also docked them a day's wages to pay for his own monument.

Spencer House

27 St James's Place, SW1 (7499 8620). Green Park tube. **Open** *Feb-July, Sept-Dec 11.45am-4.45pm Sun.* **Admission** *£6; £5 10s-16s (no children under 10).* **Map** p400 J8.

The compulsory guided tours of one of the capital's most splendid Palladian mansions take in eight restored state rooms, which are now used mainly for corporate entertaining. Apart from the its being the ancestral London house of Princess Diana's family, the most notable features of Spencer House are the extravagant murals of the Painted Room, the beautiful painted ceiling in the Great Room, and the impressive collection of 18th-century paintings. James Vardy, James Stuart and Robert Adam all worked on the opulent house, which was completed in 1766 for Earl Spencer.

Soho & Leicester Square

Bohemian, sleazy, lively… welcome to London's sole 24-hour neighbourhood.

Soho

Maps p398-p401
Leicester Square, Oxford Circus, Piccadilly Circus or Tottenham Court Road tube.

It's appropriate that Soho should be boundaried by four Circuses, those of St Giles, Cambridge, Oxford and Piccadilly. For this characterful, unique square mile could, at its best, pass for a circus itself. All human life is here, from the affluent media darlings and movie moguls who work, drink and snort in the area, to the council estate- and housing association-sponsored residents for whom every last penny is to be treasured, via prostitutes, market traders, trendies, dealers, tailors… the list is endless.

That Soho has largely managed to fend off the kind of tourist-led bastardisation suffered by its neighbour, Covent Garden, is a minor miracle. It's at least partially explained, though, by the fact that Soho is still heavily residential, home to some 5,000 people: its habitueés, both those who live there and those who work and play there, are stubborn types. But that said, there isn't any way the developers could do much to the area. The streets are narrow, the buildings mean, and greenery is largely limited to two small squares at opposite ends of Soho.

It's not always been this way. Back in the Middle Ages, the area was used for farming, then found a role in the 16th and 17th centuries as a hunting ground for London's aristocracy. It wasn't until the last quarter of the 17th century that it became residential, when, post-Great Fire, the City became too crowded. Many of the properties erected to cope with the overflow in the late 1600s were the work of builder Richard Frith, who lent his name to Frith Street.

Among the area's first residents were Greek Christians (hence, Greek Street) fleeing Ottoman persecution, and a larger wave of French Protestants (Huguenots) forced out of France by Louis XIV's bigotry. However, despite the speed with which its pastoral history became swallowed up, a nod was paid to the past in the choice of name for the area: when the huntsmen who once frequented it spied their intended target, they would holler 'So-ho!'.

Many early, well-to-do residents left their Soho Square mansions for Mayfair in the early 18th century. In their place came artists, writers, radicals and more foreign immigrants,

Oh so very **Soho Square**.

particularly Italians. John Galsworthy, in *The Forsyte Saga*, summed up Soho of the 19th century as: 'untidy, full of Greeks, Ishmaelites, cats, Italians, tomatoes, restaurants, organs, coloured stuffs, queer names… '

As the resident population dropped in the 20th century, the area became known for its entertainments (legal and otherwise) and cheap restaurants. Jazz came to Soho in the 1950s – the late Ronnie Scott opened his jazz club on Gerrard Street in 1959, moving it to Frith Street six years later – and the sex industry expanded in the 1960s and, especially, the sleazy 1970s (*see p120* **A brief history of sex**).

However, during the 1980s and 1990s, Soho began to turn the corner, spurred on by a boom in gay business (the so-called 'pink pound'). Pubs such as the Golden Lion on Dean Street had long been the haunt of gay servicemen (as well as writer Noel Coward and murderer Dennis Nilsen, who picked up some of his victims in it), but now gay cafés, bars and shops appeared along Old Compton Street, injecting a much-needed vitality and *joie de vivre* into a district that had become the sole province of dirty old men.

That Soho is now more popular than ever is a cause for both celebration and concern. Old Compton Street and surrounds is the closest London gets to a 24-hour culture. Yet the chains are moving in, too, bringing with them those faint-hearts who once found Soho too grimy for their tastes. No lover of cranky, louche old Soho can fail to worry at the sight of queues at the doors of characterless booze barns such as the Pitcher & Piano and All Bar One on Dean Street.

A brief history of sex

What the Red Light District is to Amsterdam and the Reeperbahn is to Hamburg, so Soho is to London: play a word association game with a local, and the chances are that the word 'Soho' will yield 'sex' as your combatant's reply.

That said, few realise sex has been an integral part of Soho for years. By the mid-19th century, the area was known as a centre of prostitution, and a wave of French immigrants in the 1930s added to the prostitute population. But two years after the Wolfenden Committee's report on the sex industry, the 1959 Street Offences Act outlawed soliciting and drove many prostitutes off Soho street corners, from where they had conducted their trade with a nod and a wink.

Despite this, though, Soho's sex industry continued to grow. Throughout the 1960s, as Soho's raffish, naughty reputation rose to new levels, more sex clubs and shops moved in to join the local hookers, now confined to flats and brothels. The artists, writers and bohemian hangers-on who had frequented the area during the 1950s moved on to pastures new, replaced by a new breed of Sohovian: the sex hunter.

By the early 1970s, Soho was truly Sin City. Swathes of east Soho had been given over to some 200 sex shops, porn cinemas, hostess bars and the like. Garish neon signs advertised 'live bed shows' to men who knew what they wanted but, with typical British reserve, didn't complain if they didn't get it. This latter point is important, as almost all the sex establishments promised more than they delivered: for all their inherent dodginess, they were careful to stay within restrictive British laws on obscenity, public decency and alcohol sales. Westminster council turned a blind eye, while the Vice Squad were on the take from club owners, promising to allow them to carry on trading in what amounted to little more than a law-enforced protection racket.

It was only when this latter fact was revealed in a series of prosecutions against corrupt officers that Westminster council decided to crack down and, in 1986, it was granted permission to require each sex-related business to hold a licence. Aside from making the licences massively expensive, the council also released only a limited number, and in next to no time, around 150 of Soho's more insalubrious and licence-less establishments had been raided, prosecuted and closed.

But even today, the sex industry in Soho is far from totally legit. Though there are exceptions – the 40-year-old Sunset Strip on Dean Street is one of 14 licensed strip clubs, along with 16 authorised adult shops – many of the supposed sex clubs in Soho are little better than racketeering crime dens. As in the 1970s and 1980s, punters are lured in on the promise of mischief and naughtiness, only to find that within five minutes, their arm has been twisted into buying a bored-looking, fully-clothed hostess a drink and their two-brew bar bill has topped three or even four figures. The whole experience is about as arousing as being mugged.

Similarly, and much as they have done for 50-plus years, clippers – streetwalking women who take payment in advance on the promise of sex and then mysteriously vanish with the cash – predominate in Soho. In fact, the only girls who actually deliver on their promises in the area can be found, as they were several decades ago, in squalid walk-up flats: cards pinned inside half-open doors advise passing men that a 'model' – strangely decorous local slang for a whore – works upstairs.

But it will take a lot more than the iron fist of local government to rid Soho of the one feature synonymous with its name, and an uneasy truce between the now right-wing council and the devious flesh traders has kept the area's sex industry alive, if hardly flourishing. But even so, neither seem to care that said industry lacks one key attribute. It just ain't sexy.

The heart of Soho

The core of Soho is **Old Compton Street** and its surrounding streets. Here is Soho at its most heterodox and lively: gay bars, off-licences, delis, heaving boozers, pâtisseries and cheap to chic restaurants. The most evocative way to enter Soho, however, is via the arch of the Pillars of Hercules pub leading from Manette Street to Greek Street. The sense of passing through a portal into a different world has entranced many Soho neophytes in the past. Just north of here is shady **Soho Square**, built on land once known as Soho Fields and initially known as King Square (a weather-beaten statue of the king in question, Charles II, stands in the centre). In summer, office workers munch their sandwiches on the grass; while, around the square's edge, London's one remaining French Protestant church and St Patrick's Catholic church provide spiritual nourishment.

The short streets leading down from here to Old Compton Street are brimful of eateries and historical associations. Casanova and Thomas de Quincey once lodged on **Greek Street**, the street on which Josiah Wedgwood had his London showroom. Restaurants L'Escargot (no.48; *see p194*) and the Hungarian Gay Hussar (no.2) have survived the years, as has notorious Soho soak Jeffrey Bernard's favourite hangout, the Coach & Horses (no.29).

Neighbouring **Frith Street** has been home to John Constable, Mozart and William Hazlitt (at no.6, in what is now one of London's most charming hotels; *see p53*). Over the vibrant Bar Italia (no.22) are the rooms where John Logie Baird first demonstrated the wonder of television. The Vietnamese culinary delights of Saigon (no.45; *see p215*) adds to the multicultural feel of the block.

Dean Street, meanwhile, is the site of such famed drinking haunts as the French House (no.49; unofficial HQ of De Gaulle and the Free French during World War II; *see p220*) and the Colony Club (no.41), second homes to Francis Bacon and assorted literary and artistic layabouts from the 1950s, and of the Groucho Club (no.44), a focus for today's arts and media crowd. Karl Marx and his family lived in two cramped rooms over the Quo Vadis restaurant (no.28) from 1851 to 1856.

West of here, work begins to get an equal billing with play. **Wardour Street** has long associations with the film industry and remains home to a number of film production companies, as well as to Sir Terence Conran's Mezzo restaurant (no.100), which stands on the site of the legendary Marquee Club. At the street's southern end is the churchyard of St Anne. Only the early 19th-century tower of the

Sup with the beautiful people at **Bar Italia** on Frith Street.

church survived the Blitz, but it's worth a look to read the memorial slabs of William Hazlitt and the unfortunate Theodore, King of Corsica, who died penniless.

At the eastern end of **Brewer Street**, sex shops, shows and clip joints dominate (though the City Gates Church Christian Fellowship, tucked away on Greens Court, attempts to lend the area a spiritual dimension). Leading south to Shaftesbury Avenue is **Rupert Street** market, majoring in clothes, jewellery and CDs, while to the north is another one of Soho's portals, the tiny arch of Walkers Court. It leads past Paul Raymond's Revuebar into **Berwick Street**, home to several great record and CD shops – not for nothing is it featured on the cover of Oasis's *(What's The Story) Morning Glory?* – and central London's only surviving fruit and veg market (*see p255*).

Branching off west is **Broadwick Street**, birthplace of William Blake and centre of a severe cholera outbreak in 1854. Local doctor John Snow became convinced that the disease was being transmitted by polluted water and had the street's water pump chained up. That Snow was proved correct led to a breakthrough in epidemiology. The doctor is commemorated by a handleless replica water pump and in the name of the street's pub (appropriate, this, as the only locals who survived the outbreak were those who drank beer rather than water).

Six for a pound: **Berwick Street** (*see p121*).

West Soho

The area west of Berwick Street is considerably less interesting than the eastern half of Soho. Sure, Brewer Street is dotted with interesting shops – among them the Vintage Magazine Store (nos.39-43, 7439 8525) and Anything Left-Handed (no.57, 7437 3910) – while Windmill Street is not without its sleazy charm, but much of west Soho is given over to flats and offices and holds little of interest for the visitor.

Still, proof that change can be a good thing arrives on **Carnaby Street** and its surrounding thoroughfares. Hip in the 1960s – it was the epicentre of Swingin' London – it then degenerated into consumer hell, and became overrun with shops selling, for want of a better phrase, total crap. However, though Carnaby Street itself still reeks a little of tourist tat, many of the character-sapping enterprises have bitten the dust and been replaced by hipper retailers, and the area has turned itself around. **Newburgh Street**, in particular, is now home to some notable fashion stores – among them the Levi's-owned Cinch (no.5, 7287 4941), streetwear haven Bond International (no.10, 7437 0079) and the rather smarter but no less fashionable Errol Peake (no.13, 7434 4456) – while both **Foubert's Place** and the bar- and restaurant-dominated **Kingly Street** have more to offer than at any time for years.

Chinatown

Map p401

Leicester Square or Piccadilly Circus tube.

Shaftesbury Avenue, extending from New Oxford Street to Piccadilly Circus, was driven through an area of slums in the 1880s. Over the next 20 years, seven theatres were built along the street; six still stand, and Shaftesbury Avenue is the heart of Theatreland. However, also on the street are a handful of Chinese opticians, herbalists, restaurants and travel agents. This is the northern tip of Chinatown, which extends down below Shaftesbury Avenue to just above Leicester Square.

In the 1950s, many Chinese – mainly from Hong Kong and London's original Chinatown, near the docks in Limehouse – were drawn to **Gerrard Street** and **Lisle Street** by cheap rents. Today, the ersatz oriental gates, stone lions and silly pagoda-topped phone booths suggest a Chinese theme park rather than a genuine community. But though most of the city's Chinese live elsewhere, Chinatown is a close-knit residential and working enclave: beyond the many restaurants (*see p192*), few concessions are made to tourism. Oriental foodies shouldn't miss the amazing New Loon Fung supermarket on Gerrard Street, below the rooms where John Dryden once lived.

Leicester Square

Map p401

Leicester Square or Piccadilly Circus tube.

Leading from Lisle Street to Leicester Square is Leicester Place, home to one of London's cheapest yet most comfortable cinemas, the Prince Charles (*see p292*) and the French Catholic church of Notre Dame de France. This circular symphony in concrete contains some fetching 1960 murals by Jean Cocteau.

Leicester Square itself is one of the city's great tourist meeting points. It started out as a chic aristo hangout in the 17th and 18th centuries, when Leicester House fronted the north side, but the attractions of the theatre and the flesh had taken over by the mid-19th century. Over the years, it became neglected and run-down to the point where the area's only visitors were tourists who didn't know any better, moviegoers drawn by the big cinemas in the square – which today include the Empire, the Warner Village multiplex, and a pair of Odeons that hold most of London's glitzy premieres (for all, *see p290*) – and winos.

However, Westminster Council tarted the place up in the mid-1990s, and today, the convex-cambered square is a far nicer space, albeit one that's done few favours by the undistinguished, monumental buildings that surround it and the abysmal buskers who provide a soundtrack for the passing tourists. Aside from the cinemas and the grassy square itself, the main attractions are the Society of London Theatres' cheap tickets booth, tkts (*see p331* **tkts, please**), popular superclub Home (*see p281*) and, in the north-west corner, the hideous Swiss Centre, where the bizarre, hourly-chiming cowherd clock exerts an inexplicable fascination on the milling masses.

Covent Garden & St Giles's

London's primary pedestrianised neighbourhood is not universally loved by locals, but shopaholics may care to head here before anywhere else.

Covent Garden

Maps p399 & p401

Covent Garden, Leicester Square, Temple or Tottenham Court Road tube.

The designation 'Covent Garden' nowadays refers to anywhere within the bounds of Charing Cross Road, the Strand, Kingsway, High Holborn and Shaftesbury Avenue. The name is a corruption of the 'convent garden' of the Abbey of St Paul at Westminster, which originally stood on the site. In the 1630s, would-be property speculator the Earl of Bedford asked Inigo Jones to develop the centre of Covent Garden into an area 'fitte for the habitacions of *Gentlemen* and men of ability'. Influenced by the Italian neo-classicism of Palladio, Jones designed the bluff, no-nonsense church of **St Paul's** (*see p124*) looking on to tall terraces over an arcaded, three-sided square (none of the original houses survive).

London's first planned square was an immediate hit with the well-to-do, but as the fruit and vegetable market, founded in 1656, grew to uncomfortable proportions, and newer, more exclusive developments sprung up further west, Covent Garden's reputation slumped. Coffee houses, taverns, Turkish baths and brothels thrived: John Cleland's archetypal tart-with-a-heart, Fanny Hill, lodged here for a while. Later, the area's grandiose Victorian gin palaces acted as 'the lighthouses which guided the thirsty soul on the road to ruin'.

Yet throughout these years, Covent Garden remained a fashionable venue for theatre and opera (as celebrated at the **Theatre Museum**; *see p125*). From the time the first **Royal Opera House** (*see p311* **Burn, baby, burn**) opened in Bow Lane in 1732, London's beau monde has gingerly picked its way through the filth and rotting vegetables to enjoy the glittering pleasures of the stage. The Theatre Royal in

Get on the buses at **London's Transport Museum**. *See p124.*

Drury Lane was the other main attraction; it was here that David Garrick revolutionised English theatre. With the Royal Opera House, the area's theatrical reputation has been maintained to this day; and though the fruit and vegetable market has long gone (in 1974, to a new site in Battersea), the Piazza remains a shopping hub thanks to redevelopment led by the now-defunct Greater London Council.

Covent Garden Piazza

The focus of Covent Garden is its pedestrianised piazza, where gift shops, market stalls and street entertainers vie for visitors' attention. The heavily touristy nature of the area – it's hellishly busy most weekends, especially in summer – the influx of chain restaurants and shops and the assorted street entertainers are not to everyone's taste, yet Covent Garden works: even those Londoners who can't stand the place appreciate the need for it. It's one of London's few extensive pedestrianised public spaces, and while it's true that some of the shops and market stalls dispense cheap tat, many do not: check out some of the jewellery on the **Apple Market** stalls in the market building for further evidence. Less appealing is **Jubilee Market** on the south side of the piazza, dominated by tatty souvenir stalls.

And then there's the jewel in the Piazza's crown, the **Royal Opera House**. The long, controversial and expensive redevelopment programme has improved the building no end, and the stunning structure, which features the impressive cast-iron and glass façade of the Floral Hall, links Bow Street with Covent Garden piazza. The building is open to the public throughout the day, for drinks, snacks, full meals and tours (for more, *see p307*).

London's Transport Museum

Covent Garden Piazza, WC2 (7379 6344/ www.ltmuseum.co.uk). Covent Garden tube. **Open** 10am-6pm Mon-Thur, Sat, Sun; 11am-6pm Fri (last entry 5.15pm). **Admission** £5.50; £2.95 concessions; free under-16s when accompanied by an adult. **Credit** MC, V. **Map** p401 L6.

A recent and subtle name change from the London Transport Museum will herald an array of new exhibits in the future, with taxis and water transport to be put under the microscope. But for now, this winning enterprise provides an enlightening history of public transport in the capital from 1820 to the present. It's a tale illuminated by countless exhibits, including a beautiful selection of old buses, trams and cabriolets around which both adults and kids are free to roam. Among the intriguing tidbits we learn along the way are that trams were brought to London by a man whose surname was Train; that the symbol for London Transport is called a roundel and was designed by Frank Pick in the early 20th

Stompin' at the **Savoy**. *See p127.*

century; and that at peak periods, the Underground uses 2% of all electricity in Britain. By and large, it's fascinating stuff, beguilingly presented.

That said, some of the exhibits could do with an update. One display opines that 'London Transport's future remains uncertain' thanks to the reorganisation of London government, when in fact these issues were resolved in 1999. But the positives – the interactive KidZones, the presentations by actors in character, the informative temporary displays, the terrific shop – outweigh the negatives, and this museum is far more fun than it has any right to be. Temporary exhibitions in 2001 include a summer show about buses, aimed at kids, and another on how Londoners have used public transport for their leisure time activities (provisionally slated to start in Sept 2001).

St Paul's

Bedford Street, WC2 (7836 5221). Covent Garden tube. **Open** 9am-4.30pm Mon-Fri; 9am-12.30pm Sun; closed Sat. **Admission** free. **Map** p401 L7.

When the parsimonious 4th Earl of Bedford asked Inigo Jones to build a church on newly developed Covent Garden piazza, he said, 'I would not have it much better than a barn,' to which Jones replied, 'Well then, you shall have the handsomest barn in England.' The result, completed in 1633, was a suitably plain Tuscan pastiche that is, indeed, little more than a huge box inside (refreshingly uncluttered, some might say). With Covent Garden being so intertwined with theatre, it's no surprise that it has long been known as the actors' church. Lining the interior walls of the church are memorials to stars such as Charlie Chaplin, Boris Karloff and Vivien Leigh, interspersed with those of lesser-known, but undoubtedly just as great in their way, entertainers such as Pantopuck the Puppetman.

Theatre Museum

Tavistock Street (entrance off Russell Street), WC2 (7943 4700/www.theatremuseum.org). Covent Garden tube. **Open** 10am-6pm Tue-Sun; closed Mon. **Admission** £4.50; £2.50 concessions; free under-16s, OAPs. **Credit** AmEx, MC, V. **Map** p401 L6.

Appropriately sited near the West End's oldest theatre, Theatre Royal Drury Lane, the basement galleries of the Theatre Museum offer an informative chronology of theatre history. Arranged in aquarium-style tanks lining long, gloomy corridors, the exhibits, including examples of costumes, props and set designs, chart the progress of theatre from the opening of this country's first permanent theatre since Roman times, in 1576 to the recent restoration of the Savoy Theatre and present-day productions. **From Page to Stage** invites younger visitors to explore the creative development of the National Theatre's acclaimed production of *The Wind in the Willows*. Unfortunately, while the presentation is slick, the information (and insight) is limited. In another gallery, **Picturing the Players** exhibits 82 portraits from the Somerset Maugham collection including actors such as David Garrick and Charles Macklin. The acclaimed **Forkbeard – Architects of Fantasy**, an interactive exhibition with props such as a giant eyeball and a 2m (7ft) rabbit with a 'sinister twitching nose', is ostensibly a temporary exhibition, but, having been extended countless times – most recently until at least June 2001 – is fast becoming permanent.

Elsewhere in Covent Garden

East of the piazza, in **Bow Street**, stands the Magistrates' Courts. During the 1750s and 1760s the courts were presided over by novelist and barrister Henry Fielding, and his blind half-brother John ('the blind beak'), who was said to be able to recognise 3,000 thieves by their voices alone. It was Henry who, horrified by the lawlessness and danger of Georgian London, established the Bow Street Runners, precursors of the modern police force. Nearby on Great Queen Street stands the monolithic HQ of the United Grand Lodge of England, otherwise known as **Freemasons' Hall** (*see below*).

Connoisseurs of London pubs should not miss the Lamb & Flag (*see p221*) at 33 Rose Street. Built in 1623, it's one of central London's few surviving wooden-framed buildings. Another delightful echo of the past is the tiny alley of **Goodwin's Court**, running between St Martin's Lane and Bedfordbury, which contains a row of bow-fronted 17th-century houses still lit by clockwork-operated gas street lighting.

However, most locals journey to Covent Garden for the concentration of hip clothes shops, many selling clubby gear, that are a world away from many of the establishments on the Piazza. **Floral Street**, in particular, offers rich pickings for dedicated followers of fashion, with more mainstream chains represented on parallel **Long Acre**. Pedestrianised **Neal Street** has an agreeably offbeat ambience – everything from kites to oriental tea sets can be had here – while **Neal's Yard** (off Shorts Gardens), a hippie haven of health food and natural remedies, is a reminder of the 'alternative' scene that did so much, through its mass squats and demonstrations, to stop the brutal redevelopment of Covent Garden after the market moved to Battersea in 1974.

The consumer heaven continues up **Shorts Gardens** and **Earlham Street** to **Seven Dials**, a onetime hangout for criminals and now a quaint little junction. Taking Earlham Street at Seven Dials will lead you back onto Shaftesbury Avenue and out of Covent Garden.

Freemasons' Hall

Great Queen Street, WC2 (7831 9811/ www.grandlodge-england.org). Covent Garden or Holborn tube. **Open** 10am-5pm Mon-Fri; 10.30-11.30am Sat; closed Sun. **Admission** free. **Map** p399 L6.

You need to book a tour to enter the precincts of this monumental, strangely disturbing art deco edifice, the Grand Lodge of the Freemasons. Though the building includes around 20 temples, the centrepiece is undoubtedly the Grand Temple – possibly the quietest spot in central London – with its beautiful carved doors, superb mosaic ceiling and stained-glass windows. In a bid to update the Masons' notorious reputation for secretiveness, it's also open for concerts and other public events in addition to the guided tours (days and times vary; phone for details).

The Strand

Skirting the south of Covent Garden, the **Strand** (or articleless 'Strand', as it's officially known) has an ancient pedigree. Originally a muddy bridle path, it ran alongside the river until Victoria Embankment was constructed in the 1860s. Built to link the City with Westminster and lined with the palatial homes of the aristocracy from the 13th century, it turns southwards at **Charing Cross**. In front of the railway station is an 1863 monument commemorating the original cross, erected near here by the sorrowful Edward I to mark the passing of the funeral procession of his queen, Eleanor, in 1290. An appealing tradition says that Charing is a corruption of 'Chère Reine', but there was a village of Charing here long before Eleanor's body passed through.

The Strand became as notorious for pickpockets and prostitution as Covent Garden (Boswell recalled how '... last night... I met a monstrous big whore in the Strand, whom I had a great curiosity to lubricate'), but within 100 years Disraeli thought it the finest street in

Europe. The building of the grand **Savoy Hotel**, completed in 1889, enhanced this reputation, though the adjoining Savoy Theatre actually predates the hotel by eight years: it was built by Richard D'Oyly Carte in order to house the light-as-a-feather operas of Gilbert and Sullivan. Despite the location of their theatre, though, the pair didn't immortalise the Strand in song. That distinction is held by Harry Castling and CW Murphy, whose *Let's All Go Down The Strand* became a music hall staple in the early 20th century: 'Oh what a happy land/That's the place for fun and noise/All among the girls and boys/So let's all go down the Strand'.

Today's Strand, brimming with traffic and lined with offices, shops, theatres, and the odd pub and restaurant, still appears grand on a surface level. However, without its former grace and distinction, it's a harsh, rather forlorn place, an impression reinforced by the many homeless people who bed down in its doorways.

The Embankment

From the Strand, pedestrianised Villiers Street leads past Terry Farrell's monster-toy-brick **Embankment Place** development and the claustrophobic but character-packed Gordon's wine bar (*see p221*) to **Embankment**

Gardens and Embankment tube station. All that remains of the grand York House, which stood here from the 13th to the 17th centuries, is the **York Watergate** on Watergate Walk, which once let on to the Thames.

Across from the gardens, sandwiched between the river and the Embankment's constant traffic, is Cleopatra's Needle. Nothing to do with Cleopatra, this 19-metre (60-foot), 186-ton granite obelisk dates from around 1475 BC. Presented to Britain by Egypt in 1819, it didn't make the long journey here until 1878. Buried under the needle are various objects including, bizarrely, photographs of 12 of the best-looking English women of the day. The sphinxes at the base were accidentally replaced facing the wrong way after being cleaned in the early 20th century.

Just down from here, and ostensibly linking Embankment tube station with the Royal Festival Hall, is **Hungerford Bridge**, which, while offering spectacular views of London looking eastwards from its pedestrian walkway, is also dilapidated and unpleasant. In line with London's hilarious inability to complete its millennium projects to anyone's satisfaction (qv the Dome, the late arrival of the London Eye and the long-running, comic saga of the Millennium Bridge, for which *see p32*), a

Sightseeing

Dead and buried

As a church, **St Giles-in-the-Fields** is nothing too special, at least not in a city with so many other more obviously unique houses of worship. The area that surrounds it, too, is not especially pleasant, frequented as it is by vagrants, junkies and other undesirables. That said, the church is not without its charms, among them the graves of some fascinating figures who often fall between the cracks in history's pavement.

One such resident of St Giles's is **Richard Penderell**, whose contribution to history was highly significant, and yet remains little known. In 1651 Charles II, in exile in Scotland after the execution of his father, led a 10,000-strong Scots army to a crushing defeat on Cromwell's parliamentary forces at Worcester. After the battle, fearing capture, Charles hid in a large oak tree at Boscobel, near the battlefield. Penderell was the woodman of Boscobel at the time and guarded the 'royal oak' for several hours as the Roundheads searched for Charles in vain. Nine years later the monarchy was restored and Charles became king.

Cecilius Calvert is another figure on the peripheries of history who lies in St Giles's. The Oxford-educated Calvert became second Lord Baltimore upon the death of his father, inheriting a cool 12 million acres of land in the process. This land became known as Maryland, and Calvert was its first proprietor. Bizarrely, though, he never visited America before his death in 1675 aged 70, remaining in England his whole life and entrusting the governorship of the region to assorted deputies, including his son Charles.

One personality who did visit the lands that bear his name was **William Balmain**, Chief Surgeon of New South Wales, Australia from 1796-1802 and another notable occupant of St Giles's. Balmain joined the navy as a surgeon's mate in 1780 and travelled to Australia on one of the first major voyages to the country in the same year. In 1800, he was granted 222 hectares (550 acres) of land by the Governor of NSW for services rendered. He sold it all within 18 months, but his name seemed to stick and the area, now a suburb of Sydney, is still called Balmain.

revamp of the bridge has been delayed several times and already run way over budget. The planned opening of the new bridge – two walkways either side of the railway bridge – has now been put back to 2002. In other words, don't hold your breath.

Walk over Hungerford Bridge towards the South Bank Centre to enjoy one of the best views of London's riverscape, particularly at night. The huge white New Adelphi building, with the giant clock, stands on the site of the Adam brothers' celebrated Adelphi, built between 1768 and 1772. This terrace of 11 houses over arches and vaults was more of an architectural than commercial success, but it was mindless vandalism that the whole thing was pulled down in 1936.

St Giles's

Directly north-east of Covent Garden is a curious little pocket of London that doesn't appear to sit well with the clear area boundaries around it (it's west of Soho, south of Fitzrovia and, yes, north-east of Covent Garden). However, the name St Giles's seems to fit this triangle as well as any, in honour of the parish church of **St Giles-in-the-Fields**, unknown by many locals but still in use today.

The reason for this area's lack of moniker becomes clear when one examines its tawdry history. A leper colony was established here 900 years ago in the area bordered by Charing Cross Road, New Oxford Street and Shaftesbury Avenue (St Giles being the patron saint of lepers), lasting until the 15th century. It was also on this site that prisoners on their way to be executed at Tyburn were allowed to stop for one last drink before going to the gallows. Think about that as you stop and sup a pint in the Angel pub on **St Giles High Street**, reputedly haunted by the ghosts of those who died nearby.

The 19th century saw St Giles's nosedive further with the emergence of the Rookeries. A small area bordered by St Giles High Street, Bainbridge Street and Dyott Street was overrun with criminals, prostitutes and vagrants who lived cheek by jowl in appalling conditions. It's apposite, then, not only that a hostel for the homeless sits underneath Centre Point, the building on the corner of **Charing Cross Road** and New Oxford Street that dominates the skyline, but also that this top stretch of Charing Cross Road and the streets behind it should still be frequented by drug users and dealers, petty criminals and other disreputable characters: take care if you're walking the streets around **Denmark Street** (home to a great many instrument and sheet music shops and informally known as 'Tin Pan Alley').

The parish church of **St Giles-in-the-Fields**.

The remainder of the Charing Cross Road – south of Denmark Street – is more pleasant, at least for bibliophiles. It's long been dominated by bookshops, something that shows no sign of changing. However, with the addition of Borders (no.120; *see p229*) to the street, the idiosyncratic doyen of the London book trade, Foyles (nos.119-125, *see p229*), is really starting to look its age (it's 97 this year). Still on Charing Cross Road, but south of Shaftesbury Avenue, it's second-hand and specialist book stores that dominate.

St Giles-in-the-Fields

St Giles High Street, WC2 (7240 2532/ www.store.yahoo.com/giles-in-the-fields). Tottenham Court Road tube. **Open** 9am-4pm Mon-Fri; closed Sat; open for services Sun, call for details. **Map** p399 K6.
Founded in 1101, this church was once surrounded by fields. The Great Plague started in the parish of St Giles in 1665; the number of corpses buried here was so high that subsidence caused severe structural damage to the church. Henry Flitcroft's replacement church, influenced by Gibbs's newly completed St Martin-in-the-Fields (*see p130*), is little changed since the 18th century. *See also p127* **Dead and buried**.

Westminster

Where God, Queen and Prime Minister convene.

Maps p400 & p401

Embankment, Piccadilly Circus, Pimlico, St James's Park or Westminster tube/Charing Cross or Victoria tube/rail.

Since Edward the Confessor built his 'West Minster' and palace on the then-marshy Thorney Island, three miles west of the City, in the 11th century, Westminster has been the centre of London's religious and royal life. The first Parliament met in the abbey in the 14th century and politics remains the lifeblood of the distric.

Trafalgar Square

Expansive and somewhat bleak in appearance, **Trafalgar Square** only came into existence 170 years ago, when it was laid out on the site of the demolished King's Mews. Its appearance would undoubtedly be improved if it were not, in effect, a huge traffic island – despite numerous public debating, no one's yet come up with a viable and attractive alternative – and if the pigeons that infest the place were destroyed.

The birds, though, never seem overawed by Trafalgar Square's centrepiece. Surrounded by

Sir Edwin Landseer's splendid lions, **Nelson's Column** commemorates Britain's most famous sailor. The friezes around the base of the 51-metre (171-foot) column, erected in 1843, were cast from metal from French and Spanish cannons captured at the Battle of Trafalgar in 1805. Incidentally, the fourth plinth in the square, which has been empty for over 150 years, will soon be permanently filled. A decision on what will sit atop it will be made in May 2001; until then, a striking untitled work by Rachel Whiteread is in temporary occupancy.

The disappointingly low-key, low-rise buildings on the north side of the square, built in 1832-8, don't seem a grand enough home for the **National Gallery** (*see below*). The adjoining **National Portrait Gallery** (*see p130*) can be accessed around the corner on Charing Cross Road. A more impressive structure, on the north-east corner of the square, is James Gibbs's perky **St Martin-in-the-Fields** (*see p130*).

National Gallery

Trafalgar Square, WC2 (7747 2885/ www.nationalgallery.org.uk). Leicester Square tube/ Charing Cross tube/rail. **Open** 10am-6pm Mon, Tue,

Big Ben. As if you didn't already know. *See p133.*

Thur-Sun; 10am-9pm Wed. *Micro Gallery* 10am-5.30pm Mon, Tue, Thur-Sun; 10am-8.30pm Wed. *Sainsbury Wing* 10am-6pm Mon, Tue, Thur-Sun; 10am-10pm Wed. **Admission** free. *Temporary exhibitions* prices vary. **Map** p401 K7.

Founded in 1824 with just 38 pictures, the National Collection of Paintings has grown into one of the world's greatest museums of western European painting, covering work from the mid-13th century to 1900. The galleries are fairly bright and airy, especially in the Sainsbury Wing, and there is a very active programme of educational and guided talks. In addition, there are free audio guides available and, in the Micro Gallery, you can use computers to devise your own tour or print out favourite paintings.

The earliest works in the gallery's collection are displayed in the Sainsbury Wing. Here, you can see the likes of Bellini's *Portrait of the Doge Leonardo Loredan*, Holbein's *The Ambassador's*, Van Eyck's *The Arnolfini Portrait* and Leonardo's cartoon of *The Virgin and Child with St Anne and St John the Baptist*. In the main building, the collection takes in some of Canaletto's meticulously executed views of Venice, and Constable's quintessentially English *Hay-Wain*. It's also fascinating to compare two Rembrandt self-portraits, one at the age of 34 when he was young and successful, and one at the age of 63, less than a year before his impoverished death. The bright vitality of the impressionist and post-impressionist paintings always draws a crowd to works such as Seurat's *Bathers at Asnières* and Van Gogh's *Sunflowers and Chair*. Temporary exhibitions planned for 2001 include Spirit of an Age: 19th Century Painting from the Nationalgalerie, Berlin (7 Mar-13 May), Vermeer and the Delft School (20 June-16 Sep), and Pisanello (24 Oct-13 Jan 2002).

National Portrait Gallery

2 St Martin's Place, WC2 (7306 0055/www.npg.org.uk). Leicester Square tube/Charing Cross tube/rail. **Open** 10am-6pm Mon-Wed, Sat, Sun; 10am-9pm Thur, Fri. **Admission** free. *Selected exhibitions* £5; £3 concessions . **Map** p401 K7.

The NPG has recently had a facelift to improve its own self-image. A lengthy escalator ride now takes you skywards to enter the main collection at the top of the new Ondaatje Wing. From such lofty heights you can trace the history of the nation in the faces of various key players down the ages. Highlights of this gallery include some of its smallest exhibits, such as a miniature of Thomas Cromwell attributed to Hans Holbein, and a series of Nicholas Hilliard's miniatures that includes a portrait of Sir Walter Raleigh, a fine old dandy with an outrageous ruff. Marcus Gheeraerts' portrait of a waxy Queen Elizabeth I is another stunning painting, as she stands astride England, her feet squashing the small folk of Oxfordshire. The painted portraits of the 20th century look flimsy by comparison, but several photographs – Richard Avedon's Sir Isaiah Berlin and Helmut Newton's Thatcher – hold their own.

An added attraction of the extension is the Portrait, a swanky restaurant with views west beyond Nelson's Column and across a sea of sloping rooftops to Westminster. Among 2001's temporary exhibitions are the photography of Horst P Horst (until 3 June); the BT Amoco Portrait Award (23 June-16 Sept); and Painted Ladies (late 18th- to early 19th-century painting; 11 Oct-6 Jan 2002).

St Martin-in-the-Fields

Trafalgar Square, WC2 (7766 1100/www.stmartin-in-the-fields.org). Leicester Square tube/Charing Cross tube/rail. **Open** 8am-6pm daily. **Map** p401 L7.

A church has stood here since the 13th century, when it was 'in the fields' between Westminster and the City. The present church, designed by James Gibbs (1726), is embellished inside with dark woodwork and ornate Italian plasterwork. Note the Royal Box to the left of the gallery: this is the parish church for Buckingham Palace. Free lunchtime concerts take place here on Mondays, Tuesdays and Fridays at 1.05pm (*see p307*). The crypt contains a café, a gift shop and the London Brass Rubbing Centre.

St James's Park & surrounds

From Trafalgar Square, the grand processional route of **The Mall** (home of the **ICA Gallery**; *see p131*) passes under Admiralty Arch and past St James's Park to the Victoria Memorial in front of **Buckingham Palace** (*see below*) which, up close, seems rather small, squat and unimposing. More satisfying is a wander round the carriages of the **Royal Mews** behind the Palace, or a stroll in **St James's Park**.

In the 17th century, Charles II had the deer park of St James's Palace converted into a garden by French landscape gardener Le Nôtre; and St James's Park was landscaped further by John Nash in the early 19th century. The view of Buckingham Palace from the bridge over the lake is wonderful, particularly at night when the palace is floodlit. The lake itself is now a sanctuary for wildfowl, among them pelicans (fed at 3pm daily), ducks, geese and Australian black swans. There's a playground at the Buck Palace end, and refreshments at a café. Many Londoners – including us, for what it's worth – rate St James's as the loveliest and most intimate of the capital's central parks.

On the south side of the park, the Wellington Barracks, home of the Foot Guards, contains the **Guards' Museum** (*see p131*). Nearby are the fully intact Georgian terraces of Queen Anne's Gate and Old Queen Street

Buckingham Palace & Royal Mews

SW1 (7930 4832/recorded information 7799 2331/credit card bookings 7321 2233/disabled information 7839 1377/www.royal.gov.uk). Green Park or St James's Park tube/Victoria tube/rail. **Open** *6 Aug-30 Sept* 9.30am-4.15pm daily. *Royal Mews* Oct-July noon-4pm (last entry 3.30pm); Aug-Sept 10.30am-4.30pm (last entry 4pm), Mon-Thur; closed Fri-Sun.

Buckingham Palace. See p130.

Admission £11; £5.50 5-16s; £9 OAPs; £27.50 family. *Royal Mews* £4.60; £2.70 5-16s; £3.60 OAPs; £11.80 family. **Credit** AmEx, MC, V. **Map** p400 H9.
Built in 1703 for the Duke of Buckingham, the original Buckingham House was bought by George III and converted into a palace by his son George IV. In 1837, Queen Victoria decided to make Buckingham Palace her home, and it has been the London residence of the royal family ever since. The Royal Standard flies above the palace when the Queen is in London. During August and September, while the royals are on their hols, the State Apartments, used for banquets and investitures, are open to the public. While some of the works of art in the 18 accessible rooms are impressive, there really is little of interest unless you're after tips on how to do up your house with upmarket knick-knackery. Tickets go on sale from 9am on the day at the ticket office on Constitution Hill: to avoid queues, book in advance (note that only £11 tickets are available in advance). The **Queen's Gallery**, featuring highlights of Lizzie's art collection, is closed for remodelling until 2002.

Just around the corner, on Buckingham Palace Road, the **Royal Mews** is home to the royal carriages. The Coronation Coach, the Glass Coach, the immaculately groomed horses and the sleek, black landaus make the Mews one of the capital's better-value collections. Top of the pecking order, though, is Her Majesty's State Coach, a breathtaking double-gilded affair built in 1761. The Mews is closed during Royal Ascot (*see p262*) and on state occasions.

Guards' Museum
Wellington Barracks, Birdcage Walk, SW1 (7414 3271). St James's Park tube. **Open** 10am-4pm daily (last entry 3.30pm). **Admission** £2; £1 concessions; free under 16s; £4 family. **Map** p400 J9.

This small museum records the history of the British Army's five Guards regiments, founded in the 17th century under Charles II. It's mostly made up of uniforms and oil paintings accompanied by stirring martial music, but it also houses a collection of curios including the guards oldest' medal (awarded by Cromwell to officers of his New Model Army at the Battle of Dunbar in 1651) and a bottle of Iraqi whisky captured in the Gulf War. The Guards can be seen in ceremonial action (every day Apr-Aug, every other day Sept-Mar, at 10.50am) performing the change of guard at St James's Palace and Buckingham Palace. The toy soldier shop at the museum is the largest of its kind in London.

ICA Gallery
The Mall, SW1 (box office 7930 3647/membership enquiries 7873 0062/www.ica.org.uk). Piccadilly Circus tube/Charing Cross tube/rail. **Open** noon-7.30pm daily. **Membership** *Daily* £1.50, £1 concessions Mon-Fri; £2.50, £2 concessions Sat, Sun. *Annual* £25; £15 concessions. **Credit** AmEx, DC, MC, V. **Map** p401 K8.
The 52-year-old ICA – it stands for Institute of Contemporary Arts – has a fine track record for promoting young artists from these shores as well as highlighting the importance of more established artists from abroad. Damien Hirst, Helen Chadwick, Gary Hume and the Chapman brothers all had early exposure at the ICA, while artists of the calibre of Bruce Nauman, Charles Ray and Thomas Struth have also shown here. With its spaces separated by a lengthy corridor and a couple of flights of stairs, the ICA's somewhat ramshackle feel ensures that shows here are never slick, but they frequently provoke reaction and debate. A feature of programming in recent years has been the inclusion of contemporary architects, with Future Systems, Rem Koolhaas, Zaha Hadid and Daniel Libeskind all showing over the last few years. Among the events scheduled for 2001 are the Beck's Futures Awards (30 Mar-20 May), and a Mike Nelson show around Nov/Dec.

Whitehall to Parliament Square

Back in Trafalgar Square, Nelson gazes, with his one good eye, down the long, gentle curve of **Whitehall** into the heart of political Britain. Lined up along the street, many of the big ministries maintain at least the façade of heart-of-the-empire solidity. Halfway down the street, the Horse Guards building (try to pass by when the mounted scarlet-clad guards are changing; *see p264*) faces the **Banqueting House** (*see p133*), central London's first classical-style building and the site of Charles I's execution. Near here is Edwin Lutyens's ascetically plain memorial to the dead of both world wars, the **Cenotaph**, and, on **Downing Street**, the anonymous official homes of the prime minister and the chancellor of the exchequer (closed off by iron security gates since 1990). At the end of King Charles Street sits the **Cabinet War Rooms** (*see p133*), the operations centre used by Churchill and his cabinet during World War II air raids.

Parliament Square was laid out in 1868 on the site of what was then a notorious slum, and the architecture here is on a grand scale. **Westminster Central Hall**, with its great black dome, was built on the site of the old Royal Aquarium in 1905-11 and is used for conferences (the first assembly of the United Nations was held here in 1946) as well as for Methodist church services. Following a lengthy facelift, **Westminster Abbey** (*see p134*) is now resplendent in its original pristine white. Similarly shaped but much smaller, **St Margaret's Westminster** (*see p134*) stands in the shadow of the abbey, like a promising child next to an indulgent parent. Both Samuel Pepys and Winston Churchill were married here.

Few buildings in London genuinely dazzle, but the **Houses of Parliament** (*see p133*) are

Sightseeing

Here's looking at you

Have you walked around London today? According to Home Office figures, someone moving around a UK city will be caught on closed-circuit television (CCTV) an average of 300 times a day. Paranoia about being watched is a legitimate concern, as Britain heads rapidly towards a big brother society. CCTV footage is no longer just tabloid television, it's your life: and it's readily available for viewing.

Details of your financial, marital and employment status, your tastes in consumer goods and your personal shopping habits are stored on specially formulated information databases. From the moment you enter London to the time you wave goodbye, your actions are recorded, processed and stored for future use. Regardless of age, social standing or job, someone, somewhere is interested in you. Few can escape. Nothing is sacrosanct.

Buses, trains and stations are rife with equipment tracking your every move. And driving in London, your vehicle is captured by cameras every four minutes, new zoom lens and night vision technology recording information as detailed as number plates and drivers' faces. Once parked, the roving eye follows you in and out of shops, restaurants and bars. Westminster City Council started patrolling Soho and the West End in September 2000 in a 'supervan' sporting nine CCTV cameras, so your audience may be nearer than you think.

Recreational activities attract high viewing figures. Every member of the crowd at a London football match is likely to have their face archived in case trouble breaks out.

Other places where you're likely to be observed are cinemas, clubs, museums and even the London Eye, where two randy teenagers joined the Mile Eye Club in October 2000. Security staff watched CCTV coverage of them getting frisky.

Is this surveillance an infringement of our human rights, or must we accept such operations as part of a national security policy? Originally installed to deter burglary, assault and car theft, most camera systems are, in practice, used to combat 'anti-social behaviour', including littering, urinating in public places and under-age smoking.

After a new wave of government investment in late 2000, it appears that the streets of London will soon be more closely scrutinised than the *Big Brother* house. But crime prevention aside, should you be worried? If petty crime and public peeing aren't your thing, then surely the lens won't zoom in your direction. Right?

Wrong. New technology is being developed to alert police to people who are merely behaving suspiciously or looking furtive. Linger too long in a department store and they'll have you. Push past someone while running for the bus and you'll feel a tap on your shoulder. Give your friend a jovial punch on the arm, and you'll be nicked. Society has lost the battle for personal privacy and now even law-abiding citizens have something to fear. George Orwell could only have dreamed of the sophistication of a big brother with 20:20 vision. If you can't run or hide, then you'll just have to stare him out.

Westminster Abbey. *See p134.*

an exception. Built between 1834 and 1858 by Charles Barry and fancifully decorated by Augustus Pugin, their Disneyland Gothic chutzpah simultaneously raises a smile, a gasp and, perhaps, a chuckle. Although formally still known as the Palace of Westminster, the only surviving part of the medieval royal palace is **Westminster Hall** (and the **Jewel Tower**, just south of Westminster Abbey; *see p134*).

London icon though it is, Parliament's clock tower, **Big Ben**, seems rather stumpy when viewed close up, especially with the London Eye leering down above it from the other side of the river. The tower originally contained a small prison cell; Emmeline Pankhurst, in 1902, was its last occupant. A statue of the suffragette stands in **Victoria Tower Gardens**, by the river on the south side of Parliament. Here, too, is a cast of Rodin's glum-looking *Burghers of Calais* and a splendid Gothic revival drinking fountain. In the shadow of Big Ben, at the end of Westminster Bridge, stands a statue of Boudicca and her daughters gesticulating ambiguously towards Parliament. The Queen of the Iceni was no friend to Londoners, having reduced Roman city to ruins and massacred its inhabitants in AD61.

Banqueting House

Whitehall, SW1 (7930 4179/www.hrp.org.uk). Westminster tube/Charing Cross tube/rail. **Open** 10am-5pm Mon-Sat (last entry 4.30pm) (sometimes closed at short notice; phone to check); closed Sun. **Admission** £3.80; £2.30 5-15s; £3 concessions. **Credit** MC, V. **Map** p401 L8.

The only surviving part of the original Whitehall Palace (destroyed by fire in 1698), Inigo Jones's classically inspired Banqueting House (1619-22) looks perfectly in step with Whitehall buildings 200 years its junior. There's a video and small exhibition in the undercroft, but the chief glory is the first-floor hall, designed for court ceremonials and magnificently adorned with ceiling paintings by Rubens (1635). Charles I commissioned the Flemish artist and diplomat to glorify his less-than-glamorous father James I and celebrate the divine right of the Stuart kings. An audio guide explaining the paintings and the hall's functions is included in the admission price.

Cabinet War Rooms

Clive Steps, King Charles Street, SW1 (7930 6961/ www.iwm.org.uk). St James's Park or Westminster tube. **Open** *Oct-Mar* 10am-6pm, *Apr-Sept* 9.30am-

6pm, daily (last entry 5.15pm). **Admission** £5; £3.60 students, OAPs; £2.30 ES40s; £1.80-£2.50 disabled. **Credit** AmEx, MC, V. **Map** p401 K9.

The austere underground HQ of Churchill's World War II Cabinet has been preserved largely as it was left when it closed down on 16 August 1945. Every book, chart and pin in the Map Room occupies the same space now as it did on VJ day, and Churchill's bedroom still contains the BBC microphones with which he would address the nation. Other highlights include the Transatlantic Telephone Room and an impressive collection of Churchill's private papers and speeches. A guided audio tour offers some interesting information, but sadly fails to convey a feel for the stress, noise and (controlled) chaos that must have filled these rooms at the height of the war.

Houses of Parliament

Parliament Square, SW1 (Commons information 7219 4272/Lords information 7219 3107/ www.parliament.uk). Westminster tube. **Open** (when in session; always phone to check) *House of Commons Visitors' Gallery* from 2.30pm Mon-Wed; 11.30am-7.30pm Thur; 9.30am-3pm Fri; closed Sat, Sun. *House of Lords Visitors' Gallery* from 2.30pm Mon-Wed; from 3pm Thur; from 11am Fri; closed Sat, Sun. **Admission** free. **Map** p401 L9.

The first Parliament was held here in 1275, but Westminster did not become Parliament's permanent home until 1532, when Henry VIII upped sticks to Whitehall. Parliament was originally housed in the choir stalls of St Stephen's Chapel, where members sat facing each other from opposite sides; the tradition continues today. The only remaining parts of the original palace are Westminster Hall, with its hammer-beam roof, and the Jewel Tower (*see below*); the rest burned down in a great fire (1834) and was rebuilt in neo-Gothic style by Charles Barry and Augustus Pugin. The mammouth structure comprises 1,000 rooms, 100 staircases, 11 courtyards, eight bars and six restaurants, none open to the public.

Anyone can watch the Commons or Lords in session from the visitors' galleries. Queueing outside gives you access to the central lobby, and, eventually, the strangers' galleries. If you arrive after 6pm (the chamber sits until at least 10pm Mon-Thur) you shouldn't have to queue. The best spectacle, however, is Prime Minister's Question Time at 3pm on Wednesdays (though you'll need tickets in advance for this; arrange with your MP or embassy). There's no minimum age but children must at least be able to sign their name in the visitors' book.

Parliament goes into recess at Christmas, Easter and during the summer. At these times the galleries are open only for pre-booked guided tours (which are not free). Phone for details of how to book.

Jewel Tower

Abingdon Street, SW1 (7222 2219/www.english-heritage.org.uk). Westminster tube. **Open** *Apr-Sept* 10am-6pm daily; *Oct* 10am-5pm daily; *Nov-Mar* 10am-4pm daily. **Admission** £1.50; 80p 5-16s; £1.10 concessions. **Credit** MC, V. **Map** p401 L9.

Along with Westminster Hall, the moated Jewel Tower is a survivor from the medieval Palace of Westminster. It was built in 1365-6 to house Edward III's gold and jewels (and *not* the Crown Jewels, as a notice outside reiterates). From 1621 to 1864, the tower stored records of the House of Lords. Restored, it now contains an informative if rather plainly presented exhibition, and a livelier video on Parliament past and present.

St Margaret's Westminster

Parliament Square, SW1 (7222 5152/ www.westminster-abbey.org). St James's Park or Westminster tube. **Open** 9.30am-4.30pm Mon-Fri (last entry 3.45pm); 9.30am-2.45pm Sat (last entry 1.45pm); 2-5pm Sun (last entry 4pm). **Services** 11am Sun (phone to check). **Map** p401 K9.

Founded in the 12th century but rebuilt in 1486-1523 and restored many times since, it's easy to overlook this historic church, dwarfed by the adjacent abbey. The impressive east window (1509), in richly coloured Flemish glass, commemorates the marriage of Henry VIII and Catherine of Aragon. Later windows celebrate Britain's first printer, William Caxton, buried here in 1491; explorer Sir Walter Raleigh, executed in Old Palace Yard; and writer John Milton (1608-74), who married his second wife here.

Westminster Abbey

Dean's Yard, SW1 (7222 5152/guided tours 7222 7110/www.westminster-abbey.org). St James's Park or Westminster tube. **Open** *Nave & Royal Chapels* 9.30am-4.45pm Mon-Fri (last entry 3.45pm); 9am-2.45pm Sat (last entry 1.45pm). *Chapter House* Nov-Mar 10am-4pm daily (last entry 3.45pm); Apr-Sep 9.30am-5pm daily (last entry 4.45pm); Oct 10am-5pm (last entry 4.45pm). *Pyx Chamber & Abbey Museum* 10.30am-4pm daily. *College Garden* Apr-Sept 10am-6pm Tue-Thur; closed Mon, Fri-Sun; Oct-Mar 10am-4pm Tue-Thur; closed Mon, Fri-Sun. **Admission** *Nave & Royal Chapels* £5; £2 11-15s; £3 concessions; £10 family. *Chapter House, Pyx Chamber & Abbey Museum* £2.50; £1 with main entrance ticket; free with audio guide. *Audio guide* £2. **Map** p401 K9.

Since Edward the Confessor built his church to St Peter (consecrated in 1065) on the site of the Saxon original, the abbey has been bound up with British royalty. With two exceptions, every king and queen of England, since William the Conqueror (1066) has been crowned here. Many are buried here, too: the royal chapels and tombs include Edward the Confessor's shrine and the Coronation Chair (1296).

Of the original abbey, only the Pyx Chamber (the one-time royal treasury) and the Norman Undercroft remain; the Gothic nave and choir were rebuilt by Henry III in the 13th century; the Henry VII Chapel, with its spectacular fan vaulting, was added in 1503-12; Hawksmoor's west towers completed the building in 1745. The interior is cluttered with monuments to statesmen, scientists, musicians and poets. The centrepiece of the octagonal Chapter House (1253) is its 13th-century tiled floor, while the Little Cloister, surrounding a pretty garden, offers respite from the

crowds, especially during the free lunchtime concerts on Thursdays in July and August. Worth a look, too, are the statues of ten 20th-century Christian martyrs in 15th-century niches over the west door.

If you can avoid the dispiriting tour-group throng, you'll get much more out of a visit: come as early or late as possible or on midweek afternoons, when the coach parties have moved on to St Paul's.

Millbank

Millbank runs along the river from Parliament to Vauxhall Bridge. Just off here is **St John's Smith Square**, built as a church in 1713-28 by Thomas Archer, and now a venue for classical music (*see p307*). This exuberant baroque fantasy has not been without its detractors: Dickens thought it 'a very hideous church with four towers at the corners, generally resembling some petrified monster, frightful and gigantic, on its back with its legs in the air'.

By the river, just north of Vauxhall Bridge, stood the Millbank Penitentiary, an attempt to build a model prison based on the ideas of Jeremy Bentham. But it was a grim place, lasting only 70 years before being demolished and replaced by the rather more enlightened Tate Gallery, now the **Tate Britain** (*see p134*). Overshadowing the Tate is the 240-m (387-ft) high **Millbank Tower** while, over the river, the giant toy-town-building-block bulk of **Vauxhall Cross** is the strangely conspicuous HQ of the internal security service, MI6.

Tate Britain

Millbank, SW1 (7887 8000/www.tate.org.uk). Pimlico tube/ C10, 77A, 88 bus. **Open** 10am-5.50pm daily. **Admission** free. *Special exhibitions* prices vary. **Map** p401 K11.

Since spring 2000, the Tate Britain has honed its responsibility to that of focusing on British art only, from the 16th century to the present day. Since the sailing of the Tate's international modern art collection down river to Bankside and the Tate Modern (*see p77*; shuttle bus and boat services link the two

The not-so-secret **MI6 Building**.

All glass, no wall: the **Channel Four Building**.

sites), the Millbank gallery has been able to stretch out a little to better accommodate the works of artists such as Blake, Constable, Spencer and Bacon. The Clore Gallery extension, meanwhile, continues to house the Turner bequest. The obvious overlap between the two Tates is modern and contemporary British art, and the galleries will undoubtedly play swapsies with works as and when needs arise.

The big news for Tate Britain in 2001 is the Centenary Development, which in October will open up the new Linbury Galleries, increasing exhibiting capacity by 35 per cent. The Linbury Galleries will be largely taken up with temporary shows, and so the gallery's profile as a major exhibition venue will be further enhanced. As for exhibitions in 2001, Tacita Dean (15 Feb-6 May) will run partially concurrently with Stanley Spencer (22 Mar-24 Jun); a recent but now almost forgotten painter, Michael Andrews, will be revived for the summer months (19 Jul-7 Oct); and the last big show of the year will be The Victorian Nude (25 Oct-20 Jan 2002).

Victoria & Pimlico

Victoria Street, stretching from Parliament Square to Victoria Station, links political London with backpackers' London. **Victoria Coach Station** is a short distance away in **Buckingham Palace Road**; **Belgrave Road** provides an almost unbroken line of cheap and fairly grim hotels. The area has seldom stayed the same for long. In the 18th and early 19th centuries, it was dominated by the Grosvenor Canal, but in the 1850s much of this was buried under the new Victoria Station. A century later, many of the shops and offices along Victoria Street were pulled down and replaced by the anonymous blocks that now line it on both sides.

Partly screened by office blocks and set well back from Victoria Street behind its own piazza, **Westminster Cathedral** (*see below*) always comes as a pleasant surprise, coming into view only when you draw level with it. Built between 1896 and 1903, the cathedral's interior has never been finished. Further down Victoria Street, the grey concrete monstrosity

that is the **Department of Trade and Industry** HQ represents 1960s architecture at its near-worst.

Continuing along Victoria Street, you come to **Christchurch Gardens**, burial site of Thomas ('Colonel') Blood, the 17th-century rogue who nearly got away with stealing the Crown Jewels. A memorial is dedicated to the suffragettes, who held their first meetings at **Caxton Hall**, visible on the far side of the gardens and in need of repair. **New Scotland Yard** – with its famous revolving sign – is in Broadway, at the end of Caxton Street. Strutton Ground, on the other side of Victoria Street, is home to a small market. At the other end, Richard Rogers's zippy **Channel Four Building**, with its outside lifts and spindly exterior design, is worth a look (on the corner of Chadwick Street and Horseferry Road).

Pimlico fills the triangle of land formed by Chelsea Bridge, Ebury Street, Vauxhall Bridge Road and the river. Thomas Cubitt built elegant streets and squares here in the 1830s, as he had in Belgravia, albeit on a less grand scale. The cluster of small shops and restaurants around Warwick Way forms the heart of Pimlico, but Belgrave Road, with its rows of solid, dazzling-white terraces, is its backbone. Nearby are many dignified, beautifully maintained townhouses.

Westminster Cathedral

Victoria Street, SW1 (7798 9055/ www.westminstercathedral.org.uk). Victoria tube/rail. **Open** 7am-7pm Mon-Fri, Sun; 8am-7pm Sat. **Admission** free; donations appreciated. *Audio guide* £2.50; £1.50 concessions. **Map** p400 J10.
Britain's premier Catholic cathedral is a delightfully bizarre neo-Byzantine confection, with candy-striped stone and brick bands. The structure was completed in 1903 by John Francis Bentley, but the decoration still isn't finished, and the domes are bare. Nevertheless, the columns and mosaics (made from over 100 kinds of marble) are magnificent; the nave is the widest in Britain, Eric Gill's sculptures of the Stations of the Cross (1914-18) are especially fine and the view from the 83-metre (273-feet) Campanile Bell Tower is superb.

You're nicked: **New Scotland Yard**.

Knightsbridge & South Kensington

Shop among the nobs, wander through parks and mooch around the museums.

Sightseeing

Knightsbridge

Maps p395-p397, p400

Knightsbridge or South Kensington tube.

The village of Knightsbridge was once renowned for its taverns and notorious for its highwaymen. The only danger of daylight robbery today comes from the inflated prices of the exclusive shops along **Sloane Street** and **Brompton Road**. Whether or not there's any truth in the suspiciously literal legend that a fight between two knights on a bridge over the now-subterranean Westbourne river (near Albert Gate in **Hyde Park**) gave the area its name, there's no doubt that Knightsbridge today is as posh as London gets.

The majority of visitors get no further than a devotional visit to that fabled temple of retailing, Harrods (*see p232*). But, if it's Knightsbridge cachet you're after, follow the ladies-who-lunch up the road to the hipper Harvey Nichols (food and fashion are its strengths; *see p232*), where the Fifth Floor restaurant (*see p205*) continues to be *the* shop-and-scoff destination for those who consider 'work' to be deciding whether to wear the Christian Lacroix or Dolce & Gabbana number today. The Fifth Floor Café, and a branch of Wagamama, in the basement, are the other commendable options at Harvey Nick's, and the whole experience is absolutely fabulous. If your lunch budget is closer to £5 than £50, you'll be relieved to discover one of London's bargain Stockpot restaurants on nearby Basil Street, where it has been serving up ludicrously cheap, if basic, grub since 1956.

Harrods – can get a little busy.

The fashion triangle of Sloane Street, Brompton Road and **Beauchamp** (pronounced, heaven knows why, 'bee-chum') **Place** contains just about every big couture name on the planet. If the staggering price tags don't freeze you to the spot, the icy stares of the cooler-than-thou assistants surely will.

Hyde Park & Kensington Gardens

Maps p394 & p395

High Street Kensington, Hyde Park Corner, Knightsbridge, Lancaster Gate, Marble Arch or Queensway tube.

Knightsbridge (the street), leading westward via Kensington Road into Kensington High Street, borders the largest of London's royal parks. One-and-a-half miles long and just under a mile wide – and, incidentally, the first royal park to be opened to the public, in the early 17th century – Hyde Park soon developed a reputation as a fashionable place to see and be seen, despite being plagued by highwaymen and duelling nobles. Queen Caroline, a keen landscape gardener, was behind the damming of the Westbourne river to form the park's central feature, the Serpentine, in the 1730s.

Joseph Paxton's magnificent Crystal Palace stood between the lake and the Prince of Wales Gate, and served as the venue for the 'Great Exhibition of the Works and Industry of All Nations' in 1851. Although phenomenally successful and visited by over six million people in less than six months – contrast with the abject failure of the Millennium Dome – the palace was dismantled and rebuilt in south-east London in 1854; it burned down in 1936.

Today, Hyde Park's distractions are equally numerous: lounging in a deckchair, playing softball, boating on the lake, trotting a horse down Rotten Row (a corruption of 'route du roi', which William III laid out from the West End to Kensington Palace), watching soldiers of the Household Cavalry emerge from their barracks to ride through the park to Horse Guards Road for the **Changing of the Guard** (*see p264*

Take time out in **Kensington Gardens**.

Frequent events) every morning at 10.28am (9.28am on Sundays), listening to the Sunday soapbox orators revive the flagging British tradition of free speech at Speakers' Corner near Marble Arch. However, its relative lack of vegetation can give it a barren appearance during the bleaker months. On royal anniversaries and other special occasions, a 41-gun salute is fired in the park, opposite the Dorchester Hotel in Park Lane.

Merging into Hyde Park is **Kensington Gardens**. The attraction of **Kensington Palace**'s (*see below*) extensive gardens – John Evelyn thought them 'very delicious' – was part of the reason that William and Mary bought the house. Although the gardens now merge into Hyde Park, they were, in the early 18th century, laid out in a distinct formal Dutch style; they now have a considerably more natural appearance. Wander through the sunken garden, take tea at the Orangery, or gaze at the paintings in the **Serpentine Gallery** (*see below*). The huge Round Pond in the middle is a focus for little boys (most of them over 40) sailing their model boats. Close to the Long Water is the Peter Pan statue. Also for children, look out for Elfin Oak, puppet shows in summer and two playgrounds (one off Broad Walk and one near Black Lion Gate).

Hyde Park

W2 (7298 2100). Hyde Park Corner, Knightsbridge, Lancaster Gate, Marble Arch or Queensway tube. **Open** 5am-midnight daily. **Map** p395.

Kensington Gardens

W2 (7298 2100). Bayswater, High Street Kensington, Lancaster Gate or Queensway tube. **Open** dawn-dusk daily. **Map** p394 & p395.

Kensington Palace

W8 (7937 9561/www.hrp.org.uk). Bayswater, High Street Kensington or Queensway tube. **Open** 10am-4pm daily. **Admission** £8.50; £6.10 5-15s; £6.70 concessions; £26.10 family. **Credit** AmEx, MC, V. **Map** p394 B8.

Living by the river at Whitehall aggravated William III's asthma, so, in 1689, he and Mary, looking for a new home, bought this modest Jacobean mansion then known as Nottingham House. Wren and Hawksmoor (and, later, William Kent) were drafted in to redesign the building, which remained the favoured royal residence until the reign of George III (he preferred Buckingham House). The future Queen Victoria was born in the palace in 1819, and it has latterly been known as the last home of Princess Di (only one of a number of royal residents). The palace is open for tours of the State Apartments, including the room where Queen Victoria was baptised, the King's Gallery with its fine 17th-century paintings, and the royal dress collection.

Serpentine Gallery

Kensington Gardens (near Albert Memorial), W2 (7402 6075/www.serpentinegallery.org). Lancaster Gate or South Kensington tube. **Open** 10am-6pm daily. **Admission** free. **Map** p395 D8.

The Serpentine has pursued an independent and lively curatorial policy that has won it many regular visitors. It's housed in a tranquil former tea pavilion with French windows looking out on to Hyde Park, imbuing the exhibitions with varying qualities of natural light (depending on the British weather, of course). The first exhibition in 2001 will be a joint venture with the V&A: at the Serpentine, Hans Haacke will display objects chosen from the V&A's collection, while a selection of artists, including Marc Quinn and Andreas Selano, will exhibit their work amid the museum's collection. Later in the year at the Serpentine, Rachel Whiteread is scheduled for a summer slot, with Doug Aitkin and, in a rare UK appearance, Richard Artschwager both lined up for autumn.

Belgravia & Brompton

Maps p397 & p400

Hyde Park Corner, Knightsbridge, Sloane Square or South Kensington tube.

East of Sloane Street, west of Grosvenor Place and north of Eaton Square lies **Belgravia**. Until it was developed by Lord Grosvenor and Thomas Cubitt in the 1820s, the area comprised

Sightseeing

open fields and was popular as a site for duels. As soon as the first grand stucco houses were raised, Belgravia established a reputation as a highly exclusive, largely residential district. It retains so today, although the judgment of Disraeli that Belgravia was 'monotonous… and so contrived as to be at the same time insipid and tawdry' might be echoed by anyone who has found themselves lost in this curiously characterless embassyland. Characterful relief is provided in the Grenadier pub (*see p222*), in Old Barrack Yard, off Wilton Row, once frequented by the Duke of Wellington and said to be haunted by the ghost of one of his officers, beaten to death for cheating at cards.

The area known as **Brompton**, meanwhile, sits west of Belgravia, bounded approximately by Sloane Street, King's Road, Sloane Avenue and Brompton Road. The area is very similar to Belgravia, and, outside of the **London Oratory** (*see below*), provides little in the way of sights, unless jealously ogling the beautiful houses of local rich folk is your idea of fun.

London Oratory

Thurloe Place, Brompton Road, SW7 (7808 0900). South Kensington tube. **Open** 6.30am-8pm daily. **Admission** free (donations appreciated) **Map** p397 E10.

The second largest Catholic church in the city – only Westminster Cathedral tops it – the London Oratory makes for an awesome, daunting spectacle whether you're a believer or not. Built in 1880-4 to the designs of little-known architect Herbert Gribble after an open competition, and known to most Londoners as the Brompton Oratory, it's a shameless attempt to imitate a florid Italian baroque church, both outside and in; indeed, many of the ornate internal decorations predate the building, including Mazzuoli's late 17th-century statues of the apostles, which previously stood in Siena Cathedral. All in all, it's an anachronistic but fascinating place in which to spend a half-hour or so, both from architectural and sociological perspectives. During the Cold War, the church was used by the KGB as a dead letter box.

South Kensington

Maps p396 & p397

Gloucester Road or South Kensington tube.

Prince Albert's greatest legacy to the nation barely south of Knightsbridge is the area commonly known as South Kensington. With the £186,000 profit of the 1851 Great Exhibition, and a matching government grant, he oversaw the purchase of 35 hectares (87 acres) of land for the building of institutions to 'extend the influence of Science and Art upon Productive Industry'. Although the Prince didn't live to see the completion of

London Oratory, once popular with the KGB.

'Albertopolis', the scheme was an unqualified success. Concentrated in this small area are Imperial College, the Royal Geographical Society, the Royal College of Art, the Royal College of Music (which contains a small museum), plus the heavyweight museum triumvirate of the **Science Museum**, the **Natural History Museum** (for both, *see p139*) and the **Victoria & Albert Museum** (*see p140*).

Albert is commemorated by the Roman-influenced **Royal Albert Hall**, venue for the annual 'Proms' concerts (*see p263 and p309*), and, opposite, the extravagant **Albert Memorial** on the edge of Hyde Park. This grandiose memorial was finally unveiled by|the Queen in October 1998 after a decade-long restoration programme. Designed by Sir George Gilbert Scott and finished in 1872, it centres around a gilded Albert, holding a copy of the catalogue of the 1851 Great Exhibition. It is hard to believe that the modest German Prince, who explicitly said, 'I would rather not be made the prominent feature of such a monument', would have approved of the finished product, or the fact that its restoration cost £11 million (£3 million under budget, and completed a year earlier than expected). Guided tours of the

memorial can be booked on 7495 0916 or
www.tourguides.co.uk; they allow you to get
closer to the memorial and examine, in
particular, the superbly crafted and
wonderfully detailed marble frieze of 168
leading literary and artistic figures.

The well-to-do residential area of South
Kensington stretches down to meet Chelsea
somewhere around Fulham Road. Near its
northern end, at no.81, stands the unique,
exuberant, art nouveau **Michelin Building**,
designed by Espinasse for the tyre
manufacturers in 1905. It now houses
book publishers, the beautiful, if pricey,
Bibendum restaurant (*see p204*) and Sir
Terence Conran's design shrine, the **Conran
Shop** (*see p245*). Fulham Road, lined with
swish antique shops, bars and restaurants
(**Wok Wok** at no.140 is good for a bowl of
noodles), continues down to Chelsea's football
ground, **Stamford Bridge**, and on through
Fulham towards Putney Bridge.

Natural History Museum

*Cromwell Road, SW7 (7942 5000/www.nhm.ac.uk).
South Kensington tube.* **Open** 10am-5.50pm Mon-Sat;
11am-5.50pm Sun. *Guided tours* hourly 11am-4pm
daily. **Admission** £7.50; £4.50 concessions; free
OAPs & under-16s. **Free** for all after 4.30pm Mon-
Fri; after 5pm Sat, Sun, public holidays. **Credit**
AmEx, MC, V. **Map** p397 D10.

Don't even think about getting round it all in an
afternoon, or even a whole day. But similarly, don't
let the daunting size of this world-class museum –
whose collection runs to a staggering 68 million
items – put you off. Opened in 1881 to display the
the natural history specimens of the late Sir Hans
Sloane (as in Sloane Square), it was built to the
grandiose brick-and-terracotta designs of Alfred
Waterhouse on the site of the Great Exhibition of
1851, and is one of London's most stunning buildings from any age.

The museum is ostensibly split into two main
blocks whose names pretty much describe what
they're about. Entered via the main Cromwell
Road entrance – which leads into the magnificent
Central Hall, dominated by a gigantic cast of a
diplodocus – the Life Galleries contain a wealth
of fabulous exhibits. The wonderful Dinosaurs
exhibition (gallery 21), where visitors walk across
a raised 70-metre walkway surrounded by dinosaurs that then doubles back on itself at ground
level, is perhaps the most popular, but both the
Creepy-Crawlies exhibition (adored by kids; gallery
33) and the Mammals section (the most striking
feature of which is a 24-metre wooden model of a
blue whale; galleries 23 and 24) are both excellent
and well-loved by visitors. Among the other highlights in the Life Galleries are some extraordinary
exhibits uncovered by amateur fossil-finder Mary
Anning in the 19th century ('Fossil Marine Reptiles',
gallery 30); an unnerving wooden case packed with

hummingbirds ('Birds', gallery 40); a 'leaf factory'
illustrating photosynthesis in fascinating fashion
('Ecology', gallery 32); and plenty more besides.

The Earth Galleries, which can be entered directly via the smaller Exhibition Road entrance, were
opened a few years back, but the contrast between
their modern, high-tech appearance and the traditional terracotta of the Life Galleries is still striking.
Here you'll find a series of exhibits on volcanoes and
earthquakes (including a recreation of the Kobe
'quake of 1995; gallery 61), a fascinating display entitled Restless Surface that looks at how natural elements change the planet (gallery 62), and Earth's
Treasury (gallery 64), which offers an illuminating
survey of rocks and minerals. All in all, if you can't
find enough here to educate, entertain and entrance
you (and your kids, if you have any) for the duration
of an afternoon, then you're really not trying.

And as if the current museum isn't sizeable
enough, work has now started on the £100-million
Darwin Centre, a new building that will allow the
public greater access to the museum's collections
and laboratories. The first phase of the project,
focusing on the museum's zoological resources, is
scheduled for completion in summer 2002, with
phase two, spotlighting the entomological and
botanical collections, due to open several years later.

Science Museum

*Exhibition Road, SW7 (7942 4454/4455/
www.sciencemuseum.org.uk). South Kensington tube.*
Open 10am-6pm daily. **Admission** £6.95; £3.50
students; free under-16s, OAPs, ES40s, registered
disabled & carer. Free for all after 4.30pm daily.
Credit AmEx, MC, V. **Map** p397 D9.

If you're not thoroughly exhausted after a visit to
one or both of the museums reviewed directly before
and after this one, then a trip here will definitely finish you off. And we mean that in the nicest possible
way, for the Science Museum's sprawling, seven-
floor building is a mine of educational and entertaining exhibits. The showpieces are impressive
enough: Stephenson's Rocket (which sits close to an
earlier steam locomotive, the charmingly named
Puffing Billy), a V2 missile and the Apollo 10
command module being perhaps the most famous.
But there are plenty of other joys here: the extraordinary 1903 red mill engine, which operates
several times a day, highlights the Power display,
while William Grey Walter's somewhat disturbing
Conditioned Reflex Analogue machine, used to
analyse the human brain, is just one of many
oddities in the illuminating new Making The
Modern World gallery. Elsewhere, the Challenge of
Materials, Time Measurement, Health Matters and
Flight displays all yield much of interest for both
adults and children, though you might find the
young 'uns will be too entranced by the basement
Launch Pad, a hands-on technological adventure
playground, and the Flight Lab, where you can test
the principles of flight and ride in a flight simulator,
to go anywhere else in a hurry. That said, kids also

An hour in... The V&A

The must-see exhibits for visitors in a rush

St Thomas à Becket's casket (Medieval Treasury 400-1400, room 43): Built in 1180 for the murdered archbishop

Constable Collection (Henry Cole Wing, rooms 603, 606, 620, 621): The largest collection of works in the world by the great English artist

The Eltenberg Reliquary (Medieval Treasury 400-1400, room 43): Over 700 years old, and of huge historical import

Tippoo's Tiger (Nehru Gallery of Indian Art, room 41): The wildest barrel organ you'll ever see

The Great Bed of Ware (British Galleries; reopening November 2001): If you're really, really tired, this Elizabethan bed, 10 feet 11 inches (3.33m) square, will sleep five

Raphael Cartoons (Raphael Gallery, room 48a): Matt Groening ain't got nothing on these 500-year-old religious paintings

seem to love the exhibits in the brand spanking new Wellcome Wing, a high-tech add-on to the museum that opened in July 2000. Antenna offers up news on recent developments in science; Who Am I? engages visitors keen to find out more about themselves with a series of interactive games and slightly spurious personality tests; Digitopolis attempts to make sense of modern technology in entertaining, hands-on fashion; and the IMAX cinema, one of only two in London, offers some suitably dazzling and disorientating 3-D films.

Victoria & Albert Museum (V&A)

Cromwell Road, SW7 (7938 8500/www.vam.ac.uk). South Kensington tube. **Open** 10am-5.45pm Mon, Tue, Thur-Sun; 10am-10pm Wed. **Admission** £5; free concessions. **Free** for all after 4.30pm daily. £15 season ticket. **Credit** AmEx, MC, V. **Map** p397 E10.
The Victoria & Albert Museum, commonly known as the V&A, houses the world's greatest collection of decorative arts, as well as the national sculpture collection. Founded in 1852 and housed in Aston Webb's immense, sprawling, exceptionally grand building (1890), it offers a staggering cross-cultural view of human achievement. The Art & Design galleries are arranged thematically by place and date, the Materials & Techniques galleries by type of

material. A free guide, available at either entrance, helps with the task of navigating your way around this labyrinth of delights. It's advisable to concentrate on certain areas of interest: it would be foolish – and, probably, physically impossible – to try to cover all 145 galleries on one visit. You might wish to peruse the world's largest collection of art from India outside the subcontinent, take a look at some exquisitely dyed clothing from India, view the finely wrought medieval European reliquaries or have a gander at Korean ceramics from around AD300. The most famous exhibits are, perhaps, the Raphael cartoons, seven almighty designs for tapestries, based on episodes from the Acts of the Apostles, hung together in a vast hall. Of more popular interest are the superb Dress and Jewellery collections.

In addition to the wide array of decorative arts and devotional objects, the V&A also houses a huge photographic archive, and there are regular photographic exhibitions, as well as shows devoted to designers, illustrators and notable artistic periods. Major exhibitions planned for 2001 include Inventing New Britain: the Victorian Vision (5 Apr-29 July); American designer Dale Chihuly (21 June-23 Oct); and Radical Fashion (18 Oct-6 Jan 2002). Note, though, that the V&A's British Galleries are currently undergoing a massive programme of modernisation. They're due to reopen in November 2001, when they will tell the tale of Britain's ascent from a minor off-shore island in 1500 to a major world power and cultural authority in 1900.

The museum shop has a pretty good selection of books and various ornaments and bits of jewellery. The basement café is pricey, but a bit better than your average museum eaterie: the jazz brunch/lunch every Sunday has become an institution (£9.50 including entrance to the museum). However, the best place for coffee during the day is the small café in the Morris and Gamble Rooms.

Daniel Libeskind's much discussed Spiral is due to be constructed as the contemporary wing of the V&A, forming a physical and metaphorical bridge between the museum's past and present. The scheduled completion date is 2004.

Aston Webb's 1890 building for the **V&A**.

Chelsea

I just want to go to Chelsea.

Maps p396 & p397

Sloane Square or South Kensington tube.

The name still has cachet. It may no longer be a 'village of palaces', as it was in the 16th century; it may now be too pricey to support an impoverished but formidably talented artistic community, as it did in the 19th century; the cutting-edge King's Road fashions of the 1960s and punk may have passed into folk memory; the economic boom of the 1980s, which brought the derogatory phrase 'Sloane Ranger' (used to describe the uppity local yuppies) may have passed; but Chelsea still thrives.

This wedge-shaped piece of land between Kensington and the river is now the province of identikit blondes (mobile phones glued to their ears, noses held high), of venerable *grandes dames*, and of the odd well-to-do writer (the century-old Chelsea Arts Club, at 143 Old Church Street, remains as popular as ever). It is the maintenance of this arts connection, together with abundant shopping opportunities, that give Chelsea a life and spark that districts like nearby Knightsbridge – where wealth is the sole god – can only envy.

Chelsea's central axis is the ever-vibrant **King's Road**. Once the private royal route to Hampton Court (hence the name), it stretches south-west from snooty **Sloane Square**, becoming more downmarket as it rounds the bend at World's End, and then, as New King's Road, proceeding all the way to Putney Bridge.

The arts and commerce stare each other in the face in Sloane Square, where upmarket department store Peter Jones – housed in one of Britain's first glass-curtain buildings, built in the 1930s – faces the **Royal Court** theatre (*see p330*). Many of George Bernard Shaw's plays premièred here, along with John Osborne's *Look Back in Anger* and Arnold Wesker's *Roots*. Following a much-needed refurbishment, the theatre continues to pioneer new works.

But it's shopping that has long been King's Road's *raison d'être*, and fashion remains dominant. Though the chains have moved in, many boutiques survive, providing relatively affordable garb for a mainly youthful market. Just beyond the King's Road kink is Vivienne Westwood's World's End clothes store (no.430), with its backward-spinning clock and sloping floor. Known as Sex in the mid-'70s, it was here that the look of punk was born.

The ever-fashionable **King's Road**.

Antiques are also much in evidence in the area: try the excellent Antiquarius (nos.131-141; *see p229*). Contemporary household desirables are available from Habitat (no.206) and Heal's (no.234; *see p245*). But the most welcome development of recent years on King's Road is Sir Terence Conran's Bluebird gastrodome (no.350; *see p205 and p244*), combining a restaurant, a café, a shop and a fabulous food hall. Gourmets would also do well to head for the selection of eating spots in the peaceful Chelsea Farmers' Market on Sydney Street, near Kensington and Chelsea Town Hall.

By the river

Chelsea's non-commercial attractions, and historical and artistic associations, are found between King's Road and the river. Just south of the huge Lots Road Power Station – which provides much of the juice for the London Underground network – is the slightly spooky **Chelsea Harbour** development. Lavish apartments for the super-rich, a hotel, offices, unapproachably swish designer shops and a handful of restaurants cluster around the fleet of mega-yachts in the marina. But where are all the people?

More rewarding sightseeing is provided further north on **Cheyne** ('chain-ee') **Walk**, where handsome, blue plaque-spattered houses testify to the extraordinary concentration of artistic and literary talent that was drawn to the area in the 19th century. George Eliot lived the last few weeks of her life at no.4; Dante Gabriel Rossetti, Algernon Charles Swinburne and George Meredith moved into no.16 (Queen's House) in 1862, where Rossetti kept a small but noisy menagerie, much to the irritation of his neighbours; and Henry James lived and died in Carlyle Mansions. Other distinguished residents of the street include Mrs Gaskell (no.93), James McNeill Whistler (no.96), Hilaire Belloc (no.104) and JMW Turner (no.119). Nearby, Oscar Wilde lovingly decorated his house at 16 Tite Street (now no.34) in whites, yellows, reds and blues, a house he left behind when he was arrested at the Cadogan Hotel, 75 Sloane Street. The rather more sober-minded historian, Thomas Carlyle, entertained the Victorian great and good at his home at 24 Cheyne Row, now open to visitors as **Carlyle's House** (*see below*).

The first big-name resident in Chelsea was that man for all seasons, Thomas More, who fell foul of axe-happy Henry VIII in 1535 for refusing to acknowledge the King's divorce from Catherine of Aragon. More's manor house has long since disappeared, but a gilt-faced statue of the 'scholar, saint, statesman' sits outside **Chelsea Old Church** (*see below*), where he built his own chapel, stoically gazing at the traffic pounding along Chelsea Embankment.

Past the delightful walled **Chelsea Physic Garden** (*see p143*) on Royal Hospital Road is the impressive **National Army Museum** (*see p143*), offering an unexpectedly accessible insight into military life over the centuries. After a lifetime of service, a lucky few veterans might find themselves passing their twilight years next door in Wren's majestic **Royal Hospital Chelsea** (*see p143*). Part of the hospital's grounds were once the location of **Ranelagh Gardens**, celebrated during the 18th century as a favourite haunt of pleasure-seeking toffs ('You can't set your foot without treading on a Prince, or Duke of Cumberland,' as Horace Walpole wrote). Canaletto's painting of the gardens – where the eight-year-old Mozart gave a concert in 1764 – hangs in the National Gallery.

It's worth bearing in mind that most of the area is poorly served by the tube, so unless you're prepared for a long walk from the station at Sloane Square, take a bus.

Post pre-Raphaelite housing: **Cheyne Walk**.

Carlyle's House

24 Cheyne Row, SW3 (7352 7087). Sloane Square tube/11, 19, 22, 39, 45, 49, 219 bus. **Open** *Apr-Oct* 11am-5pm Wed-Sun; closed Mon, Tue. *Nov-Mar* closed. **Admission** £3.50; £1.75 5s-16s. **Map** p397 E12.

Such was the contemporary renown of the 'Sage of Chelsea', the historian Thomas Carlyle, that within a few years of his death in 1881, the red-brick Queen Anne house where he'd lived since 1834 had been converted into a museum by public subscription. In the care of the National Trust since 1930, it is now watched over by a live-in custodian who will regale visitors with stories of the many eminent visitors Carlyle and his feisty wife Jane entertained here, including Dickens, Thackeray, George Eliot and Ruskin. The roomy yet modest house remains much as it was in the Carlyles' time; it's easy to imagine the tempestuous couple in residence. Carlyle and Tennyson would smoke by the chimney in the basement kitchen so Jane didn't have to endure the smell.

Chelsea Old Church

Cheyne Walk, Old Church Street, SW3 (7352 5627/ www.domini.org/chelsea-old-church). Sloane Square tube/11, 19, 22, 49, 319 bus. **Open** 2pm-5pm Tue-Fri; 8am-1pm, 2-7pm, Sun; closed Mon. **Admission** free; donations appreciated. **Map** p397 E12.

It doesn't look very old from the outside, but All Saints (as it's also known) traces its origins back to 1157. World War II bombing all but flattened the church (which was rebuilt in the 1940s and '50s). However, the interior has a few points of interest, among them the south chapel, built in 1528 by Sir Thomas More for his own private worship; a font from 1673; monuments to local families such as the Lawrences and the Cheynes; and a memorial to Henry James. Henry VIII is said to have married Jane Seymour in the church before their state wedding.

Chelsea Physic Garden

66 Royal Hospital Road (entrance in Swan Walk),
SW3 (7352 5646/www.cpgarden.demon.co.uk).
Sloane Square tube/11, 19, 22, 239, 319 bus.
Open *1 Apr-28 Oct* noon-5pm Wed; 2-6pm Sun;
closed Mon, Tue, Thur-Sat. *Nov-Mar* closed.
Admission £4; £2 5-16s, concessions (not incl
OAPs). **Credit** *shop only* MC, V. **Map** p397 F12.
Proof that London is a city of joyous, contradictory
surprises, the perfectly peaceful Chelsea Physic
Garden sits just off the noisy, traffic-clogged Chelsea
Embankment. Established in 1673, the garden was
developed by Sir Hans Sloane in the early 18th century for 'the manifestation of the glory, power and
wisdom of God, in the works of creation'. Today, it's
primarily a research and educational facility (hence
the limited opening hours), but even the uninitiated
will make enlightening discoveries. Among the dye
plants you'll find woad, which pre-Roman Britons fer-
mented in stale urine to produce a violent blue face
paint. In the greenhouses are the types of yams from
which modern contraceptives and steroids were syn-
thesised, as well as meadowsweet, source of the active
ingredient of aspirin, discovered in 1899. The gardens
enjoy a microclimate, as evidenced by some of the
trees – olive and cork among them – found growing
here. Guided tours are held if there is enough demand;
otherwise, there are two self-guided tours.

National Army Museum

Royal Hospital Road, SW3 (7730 0717/
www.national-army-museum.ac.uk). Sloane
Square tube/11, 19, 239 bus. **Open** 10am-5.30pm
daily. **Admission** free. **Map** p397 F12.
An admirable attempt to make the history of the
British soldier accessible for the non-martially
inclined. Permanent exhibits include Redcoats, a
new gallery that tells the story of the British soldier
from the archers of Agincourt in 1415 to the redcoats
of the American revolution in 1792; The Victorian
Soldier, which traces the history of the British Army
in peace and war from 1816 to 1914 across the world;
The Road to Waterloo, which features a huge model
of the battle complete with 75,000 mini-soldiers and
three specially commissioned films; The Nation in
Arms, which charts the history of the Army in two
world wars and includes reconstructions of a trench
in Flanders and a landing craft off Normandy; and
The Modern Army, with exhibitions on the Gulf
War and Bosnia, where you can brush up on army
slang and test your map-reading skills. All this is
done with lifesize figures of soldiers from different
eras, plus film footage and memorabilia, and more
quirky exhibits such as the skeleton of Napoleon's
beloved Arab stallion, Marengo. The Art Gallery
contains portraits by Reynolds and Gainsborough.

Royal Hospital Chelsea

Royal Hospital Road, SW3 (7730 5282). Sloane
Square tube/11, 19, 22, 137, 211, 239 bus.
Open *Museum, chapel & hall* 10am-noon,
2-4pm, Mon-Sat; *May-Sept also* 2-4pm Sun.
Admission free. **Map** p397 F12.

The grandest old folks' home in the country, the
Royal Hospital was inspired by Louis XIV's Hôtel
des Invalides in Paris. Charles II wanted an equally
splendid home for his veteran soldiers and, in 1682,
commissioned Christopher Wren to construct the
present structure around three courtyards. 'Quiet
and dignified and the work of a gentleman,' in the
words of Thomas Carlyle, the hospital is still home
to around 400 ex-servicemen, whose uniforms of
navy blue (for everyday wear) and scarlet (for ceremonial occasions) are nationally recognised: indeed,
to mark the millennium, a new statue depicting a
Chelsea pensioner in uniform was erected at the hospital's north front. Visitors can peek at the harmonious, barrel-vaulted chapel, with its florid depiction
of the *Resurrection* by Sebastiano Ricci over the
altar, and the equally fine hall opposite, still in use
as the pensioners' refectory. In the central, south-
facing courtyard stands a bronze statue of Charles
II in Roman garb by Grinling Gibbons (1676), gazing across the grounds (which host the Chelsea
Flower Show every May, *see p261*) and the river to
Battersea Power Station. On Oak Apple Day (29
May), pensioners parade in the courtyard and dress
the statue in oak foliage to commemorate the King's
birthday and his escape from the Battle of Worcester
when he hid in the Boscobel Oak. The interesting
museum has a collection of medals, and records of
the hospital dating back to its foundation.

The beautiful **Chelsea Physic Garden**.

North London

It's far from grim up north, where sights and scenery jostle for attention.

Camden

Camden Town or Chalk Farm tube.

Camden Town, an area that – in the vernacular, at least – stretches from Victorian politician Richard Cobden's statue at **Mornington Crescent**, up **Camden High Street** to the borders of **Chalk Farm**, has undergone a sea change in the past 30 years. From 1816, when the Regent's Canal and, later, the railway were laid out, the area became built up with cheap lodging houses, which had a reputation for rough characters. After 1905, artist Walter Sickert, who lodged at Mornington Crescent and **Fitzroy Street**, led the so-called Camden Town Group, who rebelled against highbrow and symbolist composition.

Irish and, after 1945, Greek Cypriots, migrated to Camden; traces of the latter are still visible in the scattered Greek tavernas and cafés, and the Greek Orthodox church near the Royal Veterinary College (founded in 1791) on

A super supermarket: **Sainsbury's**.

Royal College Street. Until the late 1960s, this was still a slum area; a surge in property prices, coupled with Camden's popularity with London's hippies as a (relatively) cheap bohemian hangout – it's no coincidence that the struggling actors in the film *Withnail & I* live here – brought the place into new repute. Then the professional classes and media celebs such as Alan Bennett and Michael Palin moved in, renovating houses in some of Camden's lovely crescents. The influx of money shows itself in buildings such as Nicholas Grimshaw's hi-tech Sainsbury's supermarket on **Camden Road**.

But to say that Camden is not to everyone's taste is akin to suggesting that the British weather is a little changeable, or that the London traffic can get a wee bit slow from time to time. You'll either love or hate Camden, depending on your character, your patience and – crucially – the day and time you choose to visit. Go during the week and during the day and you'll find a high street awash with litter, framed by a host of unremarkable shops and takeaway food vendors. Go at night and you'll find a spreadeagled selection of pubs and clubs with little in common save an NW1 postcode.

But go during the weekend and you'll see the best and worst of Camden. For it's on the weekend – and, specifically, Sunday – that Camden's enormously popular market (*see p252*) reaches full-on fever pitch. The streets are uncomfortably crowded – with irksome youths handing out promotional literature and cackling winos as much as with visitors – but the market area, up by the lock, is positively claustrophobic. It's London's fourth most popular tourist 'attraction', and it shows.

And all for what? Some of the goods here are worth the trek, particularly the collectibles in the Stables market, the decent second-hand books, and the homewares in the main Market Hall at Camden Lock. But there's far too much hippy, ethnicky nonsense on offer here, much of it overpriced, not to mention a scary array of touristy junk and vile, already-out-of-date fashion. And when you're stuck in a horrible crush here on a Sunday afternoon, bearings lost and will to live rapidly evaporating, it's hard not to come to the conclusion that Camden is becoming – some would say already become – what Carnaby Street was a decade ago: an area defeated by its own popularity and

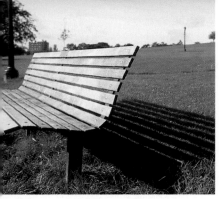

Take a seat at **Primrose Hill**.

once-upon-a-time hipness, the life sucked out of it by the inevitable market forces that apply themselves to any construct of coolness and destroy it with a graceless, undignified zeal.

That said, there are other sides to Camden than the market. The **Jewish Museum** (*see below*) on Albert Street, just off **Parkway**, is an unheralded gem; and a reflection, along with a variety of restaurants and bars, of the area's cultural diversity. To these ends, try the hip Caribbean Mango Room (*see p192*), the irreverent moules-frites minimalism of Belgo Noord (72 Chalk Farm Road, NW1, 7267 0718) or top-rank gastropub, the Engineer (65 Gloucester Avenue, NW1, 7722 0950). If it's a scorcher outside, cool down with one of the sorbets or ice-creams at Marine Ices, opposite Chalk Farm tube.

Close by is the famous Roundhouse on **Chalk Farm Road**, originally a turning point for trams, then (in the 1960s) a music venue, and now a multipurpose venue for everything from exhibitions and plays to circuses and gigs. The maze of tunnels underneath the Roundhouse – aka the undercroft – is presently being converted into a creative arts centre, a process that should be complete by 2002.

Jewish Museum, Camden

129-131 Albert Street, NW1 (7284 1997/ www.jewmusm.ort.org). Camden Town tube. **Open** 10am-4pm Mon-Thur; 10am-5pm Sun; closed Fri, Sat. **Admission** £3.50; £2.50 OAPs; £1.50 concessions; free under-5s. **Credit** MC, V. This highly impressive museum offers an extensive look into the Jewish religion in Britain. One of a pair of partnered museums (the other is in Finchley, for which *see p152*), the Camden branch includes three galleries that combine to tell the story of the history of Jews in this country. Upstairs is a display of objects used in religious ceremonies including Hanukkah lamps and an incredible 16th-century Venetian synagogue ark. The staff here are very helpful, willingly taking the time to explain the dis-plays to visitors.

Around Camden

Moving north from Camden, green relief is provided by charming **Primrose Hill** and, at the edge of Hampstead Heath, **Gospel Oak,** from which the kite-flyers of **Parliament Hill** are a short walk away. As Camden has grown, it seems to have swallowed its neighbours. Fat cat retail outlets have moved in, causing small local shops in neighbouring areas to suffer. **Kentish Town** has now become a series of bargain stores and cheap eateries, linking Camden to **Highgate** and **Tufnell Park**. There have been, nevertheless, benefits from the social elevation of its southern neighbour, such as the ceaseless conversions of traditional London boozers into modern 'gastropubs'. Travel along Highgate Road, past one of London's busiest music venues, the **Forum** (*see p312*), and stop for nosh and a pint at the **Vine** or the **Bull & Last** (at nos.86 and 168 respectively).

South and east of Camden, meanwhile, the **Camley Street Natural Park** offers a much-needed injection of bucolic charm amid the railway sheds and gas works. The **Regent's Canal** runs along one side of the park; enthusiasts should visit the nearby **Canal Museum** (*see below*).

Canal Museum

12-13 New Wharf Road, N1 (7713 0836/ www.canalmuseum.org.uk). King's Cross tube/rail. **Open** 10am-4.30pm Tue-Sun; closed Mon. **Admission** £2.50; £1.25 concessions; free under-8s. **Credit** MC, V. **Map** p399 L2. The warehouse housing this small museum on the Regent Canal's Battlebridge Basin was built in the 1850s by an Italian immigrant, Carlo Gatti, who made his fortune importing ice from Norway. The blocks were carried from the docks on canal boats and stored here in huge ice wells. The museum tells the story of Gatti and the families who made their living on the canals, and supplements the permanent displays with lectures and temporary exhibitions.

St John's Wood

St John's Wood or Swiss Cottage tube.

To the west of Regent's Park is St John's Wood, a wealthy enclave containing the world's most famous cricket ground, **Lord's.** Aside from providing a home to the **MCC Museum** (*see p146*), it's worth visiting if only to see the stunning NatWest Media Centre (*see p31*), one of the most extraordinary new constructions in the capital; kudos to Lord's for being brave enough to build it. Of course, you could always stop by to actually watch some cricket (*see p325*).

Sightseeing

Grove End Road leads from here into **Abbey Road**, made famous by the Beatles when it was still called EMI Studios (no.3). The zebra crossing outside is always busy with Japanese and American tourists scrawling their names on the wall. Further north is the former paint factory that's now home to the **Saatchi Gallery** (*see below*).

Lord's Tour & MCC Museum

Marylebone Cricket Club, Lord's, St John's Wood Road, NW8 (7432 1033/www.lords.org). St John's Wood tube/13, 46, 82, 113, 274 bus. **Open** *Guided tours* (phone for availability) *Oct-Mar* noon, 2pm daily; *Apr-Sept* 10am, noon, 2pm daily. **Admission** *Guided tours* £6.50; £5 concesssions; £4.50 5-15s; free under-5s. **Credit** MC, V.

Cricket fans will be delighted by this entertainingly anecdotal exhibition, and even those with no previous interest in the game should find something of interest. Among the paintings, photographs and significantly battered bats on display here, there's a reconstruction of the shot that killed a passing sparrow in 1936, complete with stuffed bird and the ball. The Ashes reside here, too, and will be contested in this country again by England and Australia in 2001 (*see p262* **Ashes to ashes**). The guided tour allows visitors to view the ground from the Mound stand, and continues with a lingering wander through the pavilion, the visitors' dressing room and the historic Long Room.

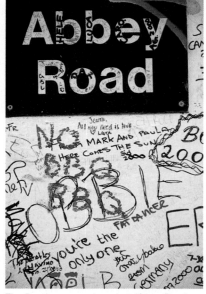

The Beatles remembered at **Abbey Road**.

Saatchi Gallery

98A Boundary Road, NW8 (information 7624 8299/ 7328 8299). St John's Wood or Swiss Cottage tube/ 139, 189 bus. **Open** *During exhibitions* noon-6pm Thur-Sun; closed Mon-Wed. **Admission** £5; £3 concessions; free under-12s. **Credit** MC, V.

The whitewashed warehouse-like interior of the Saatchi Gallery plays host to loosely themed shows of work from ad man Charles Saatchi's collection, bought up from the major centres of contemporary western art. Saatchi mostly concentrates on the USA, Germany and the UK, but last year's Eurovision took in Holland, Switzerland, Finland, and Spain. The following exhibitions, Ant Noises 1 and 2, rechecked the artists involved in the RA's Sensation exhibition, such as Tracey Emin, Sarah Lucas, Damien Hirst and Gavin Turk, artists with whom Saatchi is most associated. Richard Wilson's 20:50, an installation in sump pump oil and galvanised steel, is the sole fixture at this gallery (in an adjacent room), and alone makes a visit worthwhile.

Hampstead

Golders Green or Hampstead tube/Hampstead Heath rail.

Insular, villagey Hampstead has long been popular with the literati and chattering classes. Pope and Gay took the waters here during its brief time as a spa; Wilkie Collins, Thackeray and Dickens drank at Jack Straw's Castle on **North End Way**; and Keats strolled on the Heath with Coleridge and Wordsworth. Much of Keats's best work was composed in his house in **Wentworth Place**; it was in its garden that he heard his nightingale. Happily, Hampstead's hilly geography has prevented the sort of urbanisation that Camden has suffered, and it remains, together with **Highgate**, a haven for much of London's (monied) intelligentsia and literary bigwigs. It's entirely appropriate that Hampstead's MP is ex-actress Glenda Jackson.

Hampstead tube stands at the top of the steep High Street, lined with opulent but unexciting shops and bars. Running north, and further uphill, from here is **Heath Street**. Don't miss the dark and inviting Louis Pâtisserie (no.32) for tea and fabulously sticky mittel-European cakes. Just off the southern end of Heath Street is **Church Row**, one of Hampstead's most beautiful streets, with twin lines of higgeldy-piggeldy terraces leading down to **St John at Hampstead**, where painter John Constable and his wife lie at rest in the sylvan graveyard. Close by, on **Holly Hill**, is Hampstead's nicest pub, the Hollybush (*see p223*); while another minute's climb brings you to **Fenton House** (*see p148*) on Hampstead Grove, with its fine porcelain and paintings. The celestially inclined might like to gaze skyward at the nearby **Hampstead Scientific Society**

Go directly to jail

Outside the Old Bailey, the Central Criminal Courts, there is a Blue Plaque stating that it is the site of Newgate, once the most notorious of all of London prisons where famous people were incarcerated or executed. There are many such places in London, too numerous to detail here, that act as reminders of an inhuman, squalorous and corrupt penal system. But if you were touring the Houses of Parliament or fashionable Clerkenwell, you might think about a detour to study their more shameful histories.

Next time you shop at the **Army and Navy** in Victoria Street, remember the unfortunate vagrants and petty offenders as they endured hard labour on that site when it was still the Tothill Fields Bridewell. You can see an engraving of the women at work and undergoing punishment there in Hogarth's *The Rake's Progress*. 'Bridewell' was a general term for a House of Correction after the Bridewell near Blackfriars, once been a palace owned by Henry VIII. Nearby, Tothill Fields Prison was a huge site with granite walls, where prisoners were forced to work together but forbidden to communicate. Although there were about 500 small cells, more than 900 women and boys under 16 were accommodated there. Today, **Westminster Cathedral** stands on the very foundations laid for the prison.

Going to the **Tate Britain**? It was built on part of the site of the vast Millbank Penitentiary. Constructed hexagonally within an octagonal wall in pentagonal blocks, it was

such a maze, it confused even the warders. Prisoners were reformed with hard work, but also from here thousands of convicts were transported to Australia. Bernard, the landlord of the nearby **Morpeth Arms**, will tell you how they were marched under his pub to embark at the Vauxhall Bridge pier, where a plaque still commemorates them.

Across town, then if you're eating in chic Clerkenwell, you'll be close to the **Mount Pleasant** postal sorting office. This was where Coldbath Fields once stood: the Clerkenwell House of Correction, and the all-male counterpart of the Tothill Fields Bridewell. Prisoners, many of whom were there simply for being unable to pay fines, were required to operate treadmills that ground nothing at all, and to carry large cannon balls round and round a yard.

Hardly half-a-mile away was the **Clerkenwell House of Detention**, where army deserters were held and prisoners awaited trial or for someone outside to pay surety, money to assure good behaviour when released. Hundreds of failed suicides were also detained there, since suicide was once a crime. The site was rebuilt as a large school at the end of the 19th century and is now being converted from a state primary school into luxury flats. Its most famous prisoner, or rather escapee, was the legendary Jack Sheppard, who cheated the hangman. It also held cab drivers who overcharged and gave poor service. Perhaps they weren't such bad places after all.

Sightseeing

Observatory (Lower Terrace; 8346 1056). On Hampstead's southern fringes is the house where Sigmund Freud lived the last year of his life, having fled Nazi persecution in Vienna in 1938 (now the **Freud Museum**; *see p148*). Nearby is **Camden Arts Centre** (*see below*), with its eclectic programme of exhibitions.

East of Heath Street is a maze of attractive streets that shelters **Burgh House** on New End Square (a Queen Anne house that now houses a small museum) and **2 Willow Road** (*see p148*), a modernist house built by Hungarian-born Ernö Goldfinger for himself in the 1930s. Nearby, off Keats Grove, is **Keats' House** (*see p148*). Around the corner, on South Hill Park, Ruth Ellis shot her former boyfriend outside the Magdala pub in 1955 (look for the bullet holes in the wall), and became the last woman to be hanged in Britain.

Camden Arts Centre

Arkwright Road, corner of Finchley Road, NW3 (7435 2643). Finchley Road tube. **Open** 11am-7pm Tue-Thur; 11am-5.30pm Fri-Sun; closed Mon. **Admission** free. **No credit cards.**

Camden's community arts centre holds three spaces that host contemporary exhibitions and one historical show a year. There is a programme of talks by artists, usually responding to the current exhibitions. In 2001, New Contemporaries, the work of recently graduated artists, will return (21 June-19 Aug). Doris Salcedo, a sculptor based in Colombia, will be showing a new installation with a political/spiritual bent (14 Sept-11 Nov), along with Jose Dávila, a young Mexican artist. Douglas Huebler, one of the players in New York's conceptualist movement of the 1960s and '70s, follows on from this (Nov/Dec). The gallery will be closing for refurbishment for a year from May or June 2002; call nearer the time for full details.

Fenton House

Hampstead Grove, NW3 (7435 3471). Hampstead tube. **Open** *Mar* 2-5pm Sat, Sun. *Apr-Oct* 2-5pm Wed-Fri; 11am-5pm Sat, Sun (last entry 4.30pm). *Nov-Feb* closed. **Admission** £4.30; £2.15 5s-15s. **No credit cards.**

This gem of a house, built in 1693 in William and Mary style, is one of the earliest and largest houses in Hampstead. It houses the excellent Benton Fletcher Collection of Early Keyboard Instruments, which can be heard in action during the summer at fortnightly baroque concerts (phone for details). Other exhibits include a quirky range of pottery poodles in the Rockingham Room. The four attic rooms have retained the atmosphere of a 17th-century property with impressive views over London. Entry to the garden (one side is beautifully landscaped; the other contains an orchard and vegetable patch) is free.

Freud Museum

20 Maresfield Gardens, NW3 (7435 2002/ www.freud.org.uk). Finchley Road tube/Finchley Road & Frognal rail. **Open** noon-5pm Wed-Sun; closed Mon, Tue. **Admission** £4; £2 concessions; free under-12s. **Credit** AmEx, MC, V.

This modest home on a quiet, wooded street looks unspectacular from the outside, and is, generally, unspectacular on the inside as well. Before his death in 1939, Sigmund Freud, the father of modern psychotherapy, spent a year here after fleeing the Nazis in Austria. Perhaps that limited amount of time explains why the house feels so sparse and reveals so little about the man. The ground floor houses a reproduction of Freud's Vienna study, as reflected in a photo hanging on the wall. A selection from his collection of art and antiquities is also displayed. The upstairs is devoted to the belongings of his daughter Anna, a child analyst who lived here until her death. A short video offers a little more insight into the family, but, overall, this is for serious fans only.

Keats' House

Wentworth Place, Keats Grove, NW3 (7435 2062/ www.keatshouse.org.uk). Hampstead tube/24, 46, 168 bus. **Open** phone to check. **Admission** free. **No credit cards.**

Keats wrote some of his best-loved poems and fell in love with Fanny Brawne while living in this cutesy Regency cottage (1818-20). A plum tree in the garden marks the site of the original tree beneath which he is thought to have penned his *Ode to a Nightingale*. Cabinets contain original manuscripts, and visitors can nose around the poet's bedroom, living room and kitchen. A five-year programme of restoration means the house will be closed until 1 May 2001 for repair work, as well as during winter 2001.

2 Willow Road

2 Willow Road, NW3 (7435 6166/www.nationaltrust. org.uk). Hampstead tube/Hampstead Heath rail. **Open** *Mar* noon-5pm Sat. *Apr-Oct* noon-5pm Thur-Sat; closed Mon-Wed, Sun. *Nov-15 Dec* noon-5pm Sat only (last entry 4pm). Closed 15 Dec-Feb. **Admission** £4.30; £2.15 5-15s. **No credit cards.**

Ernö Goldfinger's pioneering piece of domestic architecture looks as striking today as it did when it was built in 1939. Its purchase by the National Trust was a brave move, but one that has paid off. Before being taken on an informative guided tour of the house, visitors watch a video explaining Goldfinger's philosophy of design described as 'structural rationalism'. This was the Goldfinger family home and still contains much of its original contents including furniture he designed himself, plus a collection of 20th-century art. Hour-long tours run every 45 minutes from 12.15pm to 4pm.

Hampstead Heath

The 800-acre **Heath** (*see below*) is Hampstead's chief glory. A Sunday tramp across its varied landscapes is essential therapy for any jaded Londoner, while a dip in the swimming ponds to the east and south of the heath, and a picnic at one of the summer lakeside concerts at **Kenwood House** at the heath's northern tip (*see p149*) are equal institutions.

Not far from Kenwood is the old Spaniard's Inn pub (haunted, it is said, by the ghost of a highwayman). To the west lies the weatherboarded pub Jack Straw's Castle (named after one of the leaders of the 1381 Peasants' Revolt) and **Whitestone Pond**, where grown men play with model boats. Ignore, if you wish, the gay men cruising the **West Heath**'s leafy undergrowth, and head to **Golders Hill Park**, with its small menageries of deer, goats and birds. Or, if you want utter tranquillity, follow the long stone walkway on the left behind the new housing development on North End Way (coming up from Jack Straw's Castle) until you stumble upon the all-but-secret **Hill Garden** with its goldfish pond and collections of plants and rare trees set in landscaped grounds. On a clear day, the views from here are superb.

Hampstead Heath

NW3 (Parliament Hill 7485 4491/Golders Hill 8455 5183). Belsize Park or Hampstead tube/Gospel Oak or Hampstead Heath rail/24, 46, 168, 214, C2, C11 bus. **Open** 24hrs daily.

The rolling, semi-landscaped Heath has something for everyone. You can jog, stroll, sunbathe, picnic, swim in the ponds or Parliament Hill Lido (*see p323*), walk the dog, play football, fish, or fly a kite from atop Parliament Hill. Alternatively, sit and admire the views, which, on a clear day, take in the whole of central London. There are band concerts on summer Sunday afternoons on Golders and Parliament hills, as well as bowls (7284 3779) and guided walks (7482 7073). Visit **Kenwood House** to see the wonderful **Iveagh Bequest** (*see p149*) collection of paintings, and look for one of Kenwood's real hidden treasures: the beautifully restored **Romany Buckland Caravan**, in a small building near the

Coach House restaurant. On Saturdays in summer, thousands make their way to Kenwood for lakeside concerts (*see p309*). Funfairs are held at the upper and lower ends of the Heath on the Easter, May and August Bank Holidays (*see p265*). A diary of events on the Heath is available at information points.

Kenwood House/Iveagh Bequest
Kenwood House, Hampstead Lane, NW3 (8348 1286/www.english-heritage.org). Hampstead tube/ Golders Green tube, then 210 bus. **Open** Apr-Sept 10am-6pm Mon, Tue, Thur, Sat, Sun; 10.30am-6pm Wed, Fri. Oct 10am-5pm Mon, Tue, Thur, Sat, Sun; 10.30am-5pm Wed, Fri. Nov-Mar 10am-4pm Mon, Tue, Thur, Sat, Sun; 10.30am-4pm Wed, Fri. **Admission** free (donations appreciated). **No credit cards**.

This elegant mansion overlooking the Heath from its northern fringe was rebuilt in classical style for the Earl of Mansfield by Robert Adam in 1767-9 and bequeathed to the nation in 1927. Today, the chief attraction is the Iveagh Bequest, a collection of paintings that takes in works by Reynolds, Turner and Van Dyck, plus a Rembrandt self-portrait tucked into a darkened corner of the Dining Room and a rare Vermeer (*The Guitar Player*). Botticelli, Guardi and a couple of classic flirtatious Bouchers round out this wonderful collection. The sumptuous library is also worth a gawp. Restoration to the windows may cause some disruption throughout spring 2001.

Highgate

Archway or Highgate tube.

East of Hampstead Heath, and perched on a hill of its own, is graceful Highgate. Once a remote settlement, impassable in winter snows, the area gets its name from an old tollgate that once stood on the site of the **Gate House** pub on the High Street; dinky shops now predominate. There are fine views from the top of **Highgate Hill**. At the foot of the hill, it's said that Dick Whittington, on the point of leaving town, heard the Bow bells peel out 'Turn again Whittington, thrice Lord Mayor of London Town'. This momentous and entirely fictitious event is commemorated on the Whittington Stone, near the eponymous hospital.

The idyllic **Waterlow Park**.

North of Highgate tube station, **Highgate Wood** and **Queen's Wood** offer shady walks plus refreshments in the former at Oshobasho Café (closed on Mondays). Highgate's best known sight is **Highgate Cemetery** on Swain's Lane (*see below*), one of London's great burial grounds. Adjoining the cemetery is beautiful **Waterlow Park** (7272 2825), complete with ponds, trees, a mini-aviary, tennis courts, a putting green and a garden café in the 16th-century Lauderdale House. Further down Swain's Lane, you can peep through the Gothic entrance to **Holly Village**, a private village built in 1865, complete with its own village green. Hornsey Lane, on the other side of Highgate Hill, leads you to the **Archway** (or 'Suicide Bridge'), a Victorian viaduct built high over what is now the A1 and offering vertiginous views of the City and East End.

Highgate Cemetery
Swain's Lane, N6 (8340 1834). Archway tube/C11, 271 bus. **Open** East Cemetery Apr-Oct 10am-5pm Mon-Fri; 11am-5pm Sat, Sun. Nov-Mar 10am-4pm Mon-Fri; 11am-4pm Sat, Sun. West Cemetery tours Apr-Oct noon, 2pm, 4pm, Mon-Fri; 11am, noon, 1pm, 2pm, 3pm, 4pm, Sat, Sun. Nov-Mar 11am, noon, 1pm, 2pm, 3pm, Sat, Sun. **Admission** East Cemetery £2. West Cemetery tour £3. **No credit cards**.

One of north London's most beautiful and unusual sights, Highgate Cemetery is justifiably famous. Divided into two halves, the West Cemetery can be visited only as part of a guided tour, but it is well worth the visit. The eastern half is notable primarily because Karl Marx is buried there. But the western section is simply beautiful, with long pathways winding through tall tombs and gloomy catacombs. Some of the funerary architecture here is remarkably elaborate, while the layout of the cemetery as a whole is, at times, breathtaking. Not to be missed is the spooky vastness of Egyptian Avenue and the enormous mausoleum of 17th-century businessman Julius Beer. Others who rest here include chemist Michael Faraday and celebrated fighter Tom Sayers. Note that under-8s are not allowed on the tours, and photography is only allowed with a £2 permit.

Islington

Map p402
Angel or Highbury & Islington tube.

Islington's fortunes have ebbed and flowed over time. Henry VIII owned several houses here and liked to hunt nearby. In the 19th century, it was known for its smart shopping streets, theatres and music halls, but its fortunes plummeted in the early 20th century and the area became run-down.

These days Islington is decidedly of two parts. Like so much of London, its Georgian squares and Victorian terraces have been

A quiet moment at **Camden Passage**.

gentrified in the past 25 years, and rising property prices have succeeded in pushing out some of its poorer population. The middle classes are appropriately served by Camden Passage's antique shops, assorted bijou restaurants, an independent cinema (the Screen on the Green; see p291), music at the gorgeous Victorian Union Chapel (see p316), and theatre at the King's Head (see p335) and, until refurbishment work forced them to vacate their Islington premises for the duration of 2001, the Almeida (see p333). It's easy to forget that Islington and its chic Canonbury and Highbury neighbours are close to ramshackle housing projects like **Essex Road**'s Marquess Estate.

Islington is best taken at a stroll. Start at Angel tube station, and walk along **Upper Street**, past the glass façade of the Business Design Centre and the adjacent Hilton hotel, along the side of the triangular Green and up to Highbury. This way, you'll take in the shops – such as the art deco lamps at Out of Time (21 Canonbury Lane) and the vinyl delights of Reckless Records (79 Upper Street) – and allow yourself a bite to eat at restaurants as varied as Alsatian eaterie Schnecke (see p197) or Modern European spot Granita (p205).

But before striking out for **Highbury** and beyond, sample the architectural delights of Regency **Canonbury Square** and **Compton Terrace**, both well-maintained pieces of architectural history. The square, once home to George Orwell (no.27) and Evelyn Waugh (no.17A), houses the **Canonbury Tower**, which affords great views (telephone the Canonbury Academy on 7359 6888 to arrange admission). This is Islington's oldest monument, with possibly Roman foundations. Restored in 1907, two of the tower's rooms contain Elizabethan oak panels. Also on the square is the dedicated **Estorick Collection of Modern Italian Art** (see below).

Highbury Fields, at the north end of Upper Street, was where 200,000 Londoners fled to escape the Great Fire of 1666, and where one of the first protests against gay discrimination took place in 1970, an event commemorated with a plaque on the public toilet (the protest, not the Great Fire). Beyond here, on the way to Finsbury Park, lies compact Highbury Stadium, home to Arsenal football club (see p326): nicknamed 'the Gunners', the team's origins lie in south London's Woolwich munitions works.

Estorick Collection of Modern Italian Art

39A Canonbury Square, N1 (7704 9522/ www.estorickcollection.com). Highbury & Islington tube/rail/271 bus. **Open** 11am-6pm Wed-Sat; noon-5pm Sun; closed Mon, Tue. **Admission** £3.50; free under-16s; £2.50 concessions.

Housed in a Georgian listed building, this museum opened in 1998 to display Eric and Salome Estorick's predictably esoteric collection of modern Italian art. Work by members of the Futurist movement – Balla, Boccioni, Severini and Soffici among them – are well represented, alongside figurative artists such as Modigliani and the work of metaphysical/surrealist painter de Chirico. Temporary shows relating to modern Italian art are also hosted, and varying amounts of the museum are given over to accommodating them. The first temporary show of 2001 is Futurism and Photography (until 22 Apr), which will take up most of the wall space. Besides its galleries, the Estorick Collection houses a library of some 2,000 books on modern Italian art and a pleasant terrace café.

Dalston & Stoke Newington

Dalston: Dalston Kingsland rail/30, 38, 56, 67, 149, 242, 243, 277 bus. Stoke Newington: Stoke Newington rail/73 bus.

Bishopsgate in the City passes through Shoreditch and becomes Kingsland High Street, otherwise known as the A10, the busy main road that runs out through Dalston, Stoke Newington, past the Hassidic enclave of Stamford Hill, via Tottenham and out of London altogether.

A route mastered No.73

Victoria, Hyde Park Corner, Marble Arch, Oxford Circus, Euston, King's Cross, Islington, Newington Green, Stoke Newington; often extended to Stamford Hill and Tottenham.

The 73 is one of the most famous bus routes in London. It's also one of the easiest to follow. The bus leaves Victoria and works its way up the swanky Park Lane, with Hyde Park to the east and moneyed Mayfair over to the west. A twist and turn leads the bus around Marble Arch – which law dictates can only be passed through by the Royal Family and the King's Troop Royal Horse Artillery, though no one will be too upset if you skip through it – and down the length of Oxford Street; stop off to visit the shops if you really must.

A left turn up the technology-dominated consumer thoroughfare of Tottenham Court will eventually take the bus onto the Euston Road, and the borders of north London. Euston, St Pancras and King's Cross stations all offer routes out of the capital, but stick with the bus as it wends its way up the shabby Pentonville Road and you'll end up at the Angel and, in turn, Islington. Neither central nor burdened with the masses of visitors of central London, you can slip through the famous antique markets or boutiques unobstructed before settling into the local hobby: people-watching.

Begin by crossing Upper Street and sauntering down to the Camden Passage Antiques Market, a great place to find a keepsake. Many of the pieces in this enclosed market have the look of museum pieces, but bargains can be found in some shops on Charlton Place and in the open-air street market (*see p228*). Many shops focus on certain areas of expertise: one shop only sells antique greeting cards, another amber jewellery, and several others solely prints or engravings.

Eating options in the area are many, varied and cheap. For a taste of Afghanistan stop in at the cafeteria-style Afghan Kitchen (*see p189*), or head to Argentinian restaurant La Piraqua (176 Upper Street, N1, 7354 2843) for the best steak found in London for under £10. After eating, saunter Peter's Street from Essex Road to the Grand Union Canal where you can either follow it along into Essex (not recommended) or find an old canal pub for a few drinks. If this doesn't appeal, the Screen

on the Green (*see p291*) offers a nostalgic venue to catch a film, though tall people will have difficulty getting their legs into the seats. There are also local history walks through Islington that describe the 1,000-year history of the Borough, from being the last hamlet before Smithfield to being the home of Tony Blair. Look in the latest issue of *Time Out* to find out what's on.

Or, alternatively, jump back on the 73 and head onwards down the Essex Road, Islington's shabbiest quarter, towards Newington Green. Hop out here and turn left up Green Lanes for some of the best Turkish food in London, or stay on the bus as it wends its way up Albion Road to Stoke Newington. The locals up in N16 have long been pigeonholed as the sort of people who'd love to live in Islington but can't afford it, and there's an element of truth in that: the area's more bohemian than its near-neighbour, but just as liberal and eccentric. Swan around on Church Street, visiting one of the several bookstores or stopping for a bite at one of the many fine eateries that clutter the street, and you'll realise the area has a character all its own. An entirely pleasant one it is, too: an evening in Stokey is, almost inevitably, an evening well spent.

Though scruffy and, at times, intimidating, **Dalston** is a vibrant place: there are several kosher shops, including the round-the-clock Bagel Bakery at 13-15 Ridley Road, and, along the same road, bustling market stalls selling Afro-Caribbean vegetables. Lots of the small cafés and late-night restaurants reflect the Turkish influx into the area.

Middle-class house buyers started moving in to **Stoke Newington** in a big way after 1980. Green spaces can be found at **Clissold Park** (which includes a small zoo and tearooms) and the rambling old boneyard of **Abney Park Cemetery**, which took over from Bunhill Fields as a burial ground for dissenters and Nonconformists; General Booth, founder of the Salvation Army, is buried here. Attractive, villagey Stoke Newington Church Street contains a number of good restaurants: **Rasa** (no.55) is famed for its superlative vegetarian south Indian cooking, and the hippie café **Blue Legume** (no.101) has a great laid-back vibe. The **Vortex** (no.139; *see p319*) combines jazz venue, café, wine bar and bookshop in one atmospheric building.

Further north

Moving towards the northern perimeter of London, dull suburban streets are enlivened by the immigrant communities that have made them their home. **Golders Green**, **Hendon** (where the impressive **Royal Air Force Museum** is located; *see below*) and **Finchley** have large Jewish communities; you'll still find plenty of Jewish restaurants and shops selling kosher delicacies. Finchley is home to London's second **Jewish Museum** (*see below*), to go with the one in Camden (for which, *see p145*). Golders Green is also the focus of a growing population of Chinese and Japanese City workers. There has been a Jewish cemetery on Hoop Lane since 1895; cellist Jacqueline du Pré is buried here. Across the road, the fires of **Golders Green Crematorium** have consumed hundreds of notable bodies, including those of TS Eliot, Marc Bolan and Anna Pavlova.

Tottenham and **Haringey** retain a strong Greek Cypriot and Turkish Cypriot identity. Both areas are fun for the sweet-toothed wanting to try a few honey-soaked pastries, or the fabulous kebab shops of Green Lanes. **Cricklewood**'s Indian population has also contributed a marvellous array of shops, stocking all kinds of sugary goodies. **Muswell Hill**'s prime attraction is the giant glass-house of **Alexandra Palace**, within **Alexandra Park** (*see below*), with its wonderful views.

Alexandra Park & Palace

Alexandra Palace Way, N22 (park 8444 7696/ information 8365 2121/boating 8889 9089/ www.alexandrapalace.com). Wood Green tube/ Alexandra Palace rail/W3, W7, 84A, 144, 144A bus. **Open** *Park 24hrs daily.*

The views over London from Alexandra Palace, at the top of this steeply sloping park, are impressive on a clear day. The Palace, informally known as Ally Pally, once housed the BBC's first television studio. Now, it's an entertainment and exhibition centre with an indoor ice rink. The park's public gardens have plenty of kids' attractions and sports facilities, including a pitch-and-putt course. There are bank holiday funfairs (*see p265*) and a free fireworks display on Bonfire Night (5 Nov, but usually held on the nearest Saturday).

Jewish Museum, Finchley

80 East End Road, N3 (8349 1143/ www.jewmusm.ort.org). Finchley Central tube/13, 82, 112, 143, 260 bus. **Open** 10.30am-5pm Mon-Thur; 10.30am-4.30pm Sun; closed Fri, Sat. **Admission** £2; £1 concessions; free under-12s. **No credit cards.**

Located in the Sternberg Centre for Reform Judaism, the museum's Finchley branch may lack the gilt-edged splendour of its NW1 sibling (*see p145*), but it compensates with its fascinating displays on many aspects of Jewish social history. On two levels, there is a functional sewing workshop, detailing sweatshop life at the turn of the century, plus arte-facts on East End life and practical information for refugees from Germany. Upstairs, a Holocaust exhibition follows the life of Leon Greenman, a British Jew who, alone of his family, survived Auschwitz. This branch also has a 12,000-strong photographic archive, augmented by 2,000 oral history tapes.

Royal Air Force Museum

Grahame Park Way, NW9 (8205 2266/recorded information 8205 9191/www.rafmuseum.org.uk). Colindale tube/Mill Hill Broadway rail/32, 226, 292, 303 bus. **Open** 10am-6pm daily. **Admission** £7.50; £4.90 concessions; free under-16s accompanied by an adult, OAPs, registered disabled. **Credit** MC, V.

Hendon Aerodrome bills itself as the birthplace of aviation in Britain and here you can see how baby has grown. The hi-tech Phantom jet dwarfs the Spitfire and Hurricane fighters that won the Battle of Britain. You can have a close look at these on a guided tour (book in advance). The main hangar houses planes plucked from aviation history. Opposite you'll find the harbingers of the terrible rain from Bomber Command. There's also a Red Arrows flight simulator, a 'touch and try' Jet Provost cockpit and a walk-through Sunderland flying boat. The museum plans to expand by one third in the next few years with the addition of two new buildings, the 'Landmark' building, which will form the museum's new entrance, and a Grade II-listed air-craft hangar that's being moved directly from its original site. Both are scheduled to open in 2003.

East London

Museums and markets help make up London's own, unique Eastern promise.

Peal here: the 430-year-old **Whitechapel Bell Foundry**.

Whitechapel & Spitalfields

Maps 10 & 12

Aldgate, Aldgate East, Shoreditch or Whitechapel tube.

Whitechapel has always been the City's poor neighbour. Situated on the main route from London to Essex, it was first developed as a home for bell-founders and other metalworkers who were expelled from the City for being too noisy; the Whitechapel Bell Foundry (established 1570) and Gunmakers' Company Proof House still survive in **Fieldgate Street** and **Commercial Road** respectively. By Victorian times, the area was wretchedly poor, a contemporary social historian describing it as 'a shocking place... an evil plexus of slums that hide human creeping things'. Only crime – and, in particular, prostitution – thrived.

Poverty meant low rents, an attraction for the waves of immigrants who've enriched the area over the last few centuries. First, it was French Protestant refugees, the Huguenots, in the early 18th century; then the Irish and Germans in the early 19th century; Jewish refugees from eastern Europe from 1880 to 1914; and then, as the Jews prospered and moved north, Indians and Bangladeshis, who between the 1950s and 1970s took over textile businesses on Commercial Street and Commercial Road.

The best way to enter the heart of the East End is to take the 15 bus through the City (*see p159* **A route mastered**) and get off at **Aldgate East** at the stop between Goulston Street and Old Castle Street (look out for Tubby Isaacs' jellied eel stall – established 1919 – by the Aldgate Exchange pub). **Commercial Street**, which sweeps off to the left through Spitalfields towards **Shoreditch**, is largely a wide swathe of Victorian warehouses. Halfway up it is the covered **Spitalfields Market** (*see p256*). An organic market is now held where the old fruit and veg market (established in 1682) left off, surrounded by traders who enjoy a thriving weekend trade in books, music, clothes, household accessories and arts and crafts. The market is currently under threat from developers who want to build offices on three-fifths of the site. However, after a High Court ruling in December 2000 throwing out planning permission previously granted by the local council, the scheme is up in the air, and the market, happily, lives to fight another day, at least for now.

After dark, this stretch of Commercial Street – highlighted by Hawksmoor's **Christ Church Spitalfields** (*see below*) opposite – has a Hell's Kitchen look about it, with prostitutes standing along the kerb. The sex trade, though, is only doing its best to preserve tradition in the area, much like the nearby Ten Bells pub. It was here that Jack the Ripper met several of his prostitute victims before butchering them on nearby streets. Today, the pub gains regular custom from the many Ripper walking tours that stop in every night, but also from the local city gents who stop by earlier in the evening to take in an array of strippers. Irony's not even a start.

Fournier Street, which runs alongside Christ Church to link Commercial Street with Brick Lane, is altogether more respectable: a reminder of the Huguenots, whose skill at silk weaving brought them prosperity in the East End. Their tall houses, with distinctive shutters and ornate, jutting porches, line the street. Similar houses are to be found in nearby **Elder Street** and **Folgate Street**, where the unique, recreated Georgian residence, **Dennis Severs' House** (*see below*), can be distinguished by its flickering gas flames over the front door.

Christ Church Spitalfields

Commercial Street, E1 (7247 7202). Aldgate East tube/Liverpool Street tube/rail/67 bus. **Open** *Services 10.30am Sun; phone for details of other times.* **Map** p403 S5.
Hawksmoor's Christ Church is best seen at night, when its floodlit bulk looms above the warehouses of Commercial Street. Built in 1714 to provide a place of worship for the Huguenot silk-weavers, it fell into disrepair and is currently undergoing restoration (mainly on the inside), though it remains open.

Dennis Severs' House

18 Folgate Street, E1 (7247 4013/ www.dennissevershouse.co.uk). Liverpool Street tube/rail. **Open** *noon-2pm Mon; Mon evenings (times vary, phone to book); 2-5pm 1st Sun of mth; or by appointment (phone to book).* **Admission** £7 Sun; £10 Mon. **Map** p403 R5.
Half-museum, half-piece of performance art, this place must be experienced to be understood. The eccentric Mr Severs, who died in 2000, converted this vast terraced house (built in 1724) into a tribute to London living through the ages. Each floor represents a different era, so as you climb the stairway you travel back in time from the early 1900s to the 1800s to an 18th-century tenement at the top. Interestingly, the experience here goes beyond appearances. Guests are even discouraged from looking at the decorations, and are urged, instead, to sit, close their eyes, and smell and listen. If you're open-minded enough, it's a wonderful experience. But do bear in mind that staff are deadly serious about protecting the mood here: ringing mobile phones may be ferociously confiscated.

Brick Lane

Once, the two main reasons for visiting **Brick Lane** and the immediate area were Brick Lane Market (*see p252*) and the plethora of cheap curry restaurants. Many of the latter are, alas, uninspiring these days, though notable exceptions are (at the basic end of the scale) Sweet & Spicy (no.40) and (rather posher) Le Taj (no.134). Brick Lane's Jewish heritage survives in the 24-hour Beigel Bake at no.159, while the Pride of Spitalfields in Heneage Street is one of the few good old-fashioned pubs remaining in this area. Several younger, trendier brasseries and bars have struck roots in the area, the best known being the Vibe Bar (no.91). These additions reflect the changing face of Brick Lane's social mix as it heads into the 21st century. Hip folk come to the area to catch the latest in designer furniture, clothing and art since the Truman Brewery opened up to entrepreneurs cut from a savvier, artier pattern than their '80s forebears.

Whitechapel Road

Fieldgate Street, running behind the huge East London Mosque, is worth a detour for a look at the grim, derelict, Victorian bulk of Tower House, built as a hostel for the homeless. Stalin and Lenin stayed here while attending the Fifth Congress of the Russian Social Democratic Labour Party in nearby Fulbourne Street. The Elephant Man, Joseph Merrick, was exhibited at what is now the Bombay Saree House, before Sir Frederick Treves, a surgeon at the **Royal London Hospital** opposite, spotted him and provided a home for him in the hospital buildings. The hospital is topped by a helipad and contains a museum with a section on Merrick plus a general rundown on the history of medicine and the hospital itself (*see p155*).

Crime dominates the area. George Cornell was shot dead by Ronnie Kray in May 1966 at the Blind Beggar pub (*see p160* **Crime time**), while **Sidney Street**, which leads off Whitechapel Road opposite Cambridge Heath Road, was the site of a famous siege on 3 January 1911. Several anarchists barricaded themselves into a house and took potshots at the police and soldiers outside before the house caught fire. Two charred bodies were recovered but the gang's leader, the enigmatically named Russian Peter the Painter, was never found.

For decades, the alley at **Wood's Buildings** (down the side of the Bombay Saree House, across Whitechapel Road from the Royal London Hospital) led to what was arguably the most desolate spot in the whole of the East End: an almost-forgotten tract of land, dominated by

With its large ground-floor gallery and skylit upper gallery, the Whitechapel is one of London's best exhibition spaces. Over the years it has maintained a continually challenging programme; recent years have seen themed shows such as 2000's Protest and Survive, and major one-person exhibitions on artists such as Rosemarie Trockel and Jeff Wall. This year, the gallery's Centenary Exhibition (mid-March-mid-May) will display key works that have been shown over its 100-year history, with other celebratory events held alongside it. Los Angeles-based artists Toba Khedoori and Raymond Pettibon are planned for the summer months (22 June-19 Aug).

Shoreditch & Hoxton

Map p403
Old Street tube/rail.

Shoreditch was formed at the intersection of two Roman roads: **Old Street**, running east-west, and **Kingsland Road**, running north-south. Not quite the City or the East End, the place seems uncertain of its identity, and its main focal point, around Old Street station, is dour. But it has seen more cheerful times. James Burbage founded London's first theatre on the corner of **Great Eastern Street** and **New Inn Yard**. Called, simply, The Theatre, it lasted barely 20 years before decamping to Southwark and becoming the Globe (*see p75*). The same year, 1598, Ben Jonson, then Britain's foremost playwright after Shakespeare, fought actor Gabriel Spencer at Hoxton Fields (now **Hoxton Square**) and killed him. As he was a clergyman, Jonson escaped the gallows, but had his left thumb branded.

Hoxton is the section of Shoreditch north of Old Street and west of Kingsland Road. From Victorian times until the outbreak of World War II, it was known chiefly for its overcrowded slums and its music halls. Both features have since disappeared under unappealing blocks of flats, but an influx of artists, musicians and other bohemian types in recent years has given the area an unexpected if arrogant chic. Centred around **Hoxton Square**, home of the Lux Cinema (*see p292*), cool bars are now legion in Hoxton (*see p223-5*), yet shops and other basic facilities remain conspicuous by their absence and the whole area is still pretty unpleasant. Nearby is the **Geffrye Museum** (*see below*).

Geffrye Museum
Kingsland Road, E2 (7739 9893/recorded information 7739 8543/www.geffrye-museum.org.uk). Liverpool Street tube/rail, then 149 bus/ Old Street tube/rail, then 243 bus. **Open** 10am-5pm Tue-Sat; noon-5pm Sun; closed Mon. **Admission** free (under-8s must be accompanied by an adult). **Map** p403 R3.

The **Blind Beggar**. *See p154.*

a huge, ruined Victorian school. It was here that Jack the Ripper claimed his first victim. The school may now have been converted into luxury flats, but the view back along the alley towards Whitechapel Road is still tinglingly Dickensian. However, be aware that the old East End is disappearing with alarming rapidity: catch it while you can.

Back towards the city, the art nouveau **Whitechapel Art Gallery** (*see below*) on Whitechapel High Street specialises in contemporary art. The lobby of Whitechapel Public Library is adorned with a painted-tile depiction of the hay market that was held in the High Street for 300 years until its abolition in 1928. A modest clothing market continues to thrive further along Whitechapel Road.

Royal London Hospital Archives & Museum
St Philip's Church, Newark Street, E1 (7377 7608). Whitechapel tube. **Open** 10am-4.30pm Mon-Fri. **Admission** free.
Joseph Merrick, aka the Elephant Man, was a first patient, then exhibit at the Royal London Hospital in the late 1880s. Part of the hospital's museum is devoted to this tragic figure. The rest charts the history of the hospital, and nursing and medicine in general, including a section on heroic nurse Edith Cavell, executed by the Germans in 1915 for helping Allied soldiers to escape from occupied Belgium.

Whitechapel Art Gallery
80-82 Whitechapel High Street, E1 (7522 7888/ recorded information 7522 7878/ www.whitechapel.org). Aldgate East tube/15, 25, 253 bus. **Open** 11am-5pm Tue, Thur-Sun; 11am-8pm Wed; closed Mon. **Admission** free. **Map** p405 S6.

Sightseeing

These beautiful almshouses, built in 1715, were converted into a museum of furniture and interior design in 1914 and are now one of London's most fascinating and delightful museums. A series of rooms, reconstructed in period style, amounts to an informative and atmospheric voyage through the ages of British domestic interiors from the Elizabethan era to the present day; not least in winter, when the rooms are charmingly garnished with period Christmas decorations. The 20th-century rooms and exhibits are displayed in a 1998 extension to the almshouses, with Edwardian, 1930s and 1960s living rooms and a 1990s loft conversion arranged in a loop around a sinuous, skeletal staircase leading down to the **Geffrye Design Centre**, a showcase gallery for contemporary designer-makers based locally in the East End, educational art rooms, and a cosy temporary exhibition gallery, which in 2001 will offer up At Home with Plastics (mid Apr-mid July) and London Furniture 1660-1715 (Nov-Mar 2002). Conferences, workshops, lectures and events for children enliven proceedings still further.

In summer, free jazz and world music concerts are given on the front lawns. A bright, airy restaurant separating the old and new sections of the museum looks out over the walled herb garden, which provides a pleasant 'outdoor room' in fine weather to go alongside the series of period garden rooms that opened in 1999. All in all, a delightful enterprise.

Look in on the **Geffrye Museum**. See p155.

Bethnal Green & Hackney

Bethnal Green tube/rail/Hackney Central or Hackney Downs rail.

In Victorian times, **Bethnal Green** was the poorest district in London. And though the area was transformed in the 20th century, with wholesale slum clearance and the building of huge council estates, the area remains impoverished. The **Bethnal Green Museum of Childhood** (*see below*), originally the east London branch of the V&A, opened in 1872. Almost as ancient is the art deco inlaid Anglo-Italian caff E Pellicci (332 Bethnal Green Road), run by the friendly Pellicci family for a century and now open again after a fire.

Hackney, to the north, was originally an extended village, popular in the 15th and 16th centuries with merchants who wanted to live near, but not too near, the City. Hackney's oldest house, **Sutton House** (*see p157*), dates from this period. In his diary entry for 11 June 1664, Pepys records that he went 'with my wyfe only to take ayre, it being very warm and pleasant, to Bowe and Old Ford; and thence to Hackney. There... played at shuffle board, ate cream and good cherries'. The rural idyll continued until the 19th century, when the area's market gardens were buried under terraced houses and workshops, themselves to be replaced by housing estates after World War II.

Hackney is best approached selectively. **Columbia Road** (*see p255*) and **Ridley Road** have fine markets; the former also has a number of pottery shops specialising in terracotta. **Mare Street** offers the **Hackney Empire** (8985 2424), in its heyday one of London's great music halls and still a popular theatre. Constantly under threat due to lack of funding, a campaign led by comic Griff Rhys Jones has gone a long way towards securing the lovely old theatre's future in time for its centenary in 2001. **Hackney Central Hall** opposite was built as a Methodist meeting hall in 1907. In March 2001, it will reopen as Ocean, a music venue (*see p313*). A Technology and Learning Centre, due to open in 2002, is being built on the south side of the Town Hall Square, incorporating a Central Library, offices, and a new site for the Hackney Museum (8986 6914).

Bethnal Green Museum of Childhood

Cambridge Heath Road, E2 (8983 5200/recorded information 8980 2415/www.vam.ac.uk). Bethnal Green tube/rail. **Open** 10am-5.50pm Mon-Thur, Sat, Sun; closed Fri. **Admission** free (under-8s must be accompanied by an adult).

A mixture of the nostalgic and the bizarre, this museum features an exhaustive array of dolls, trains and puppets. The best of the lot are the enormous,

Brick Lane Beigel Bake. *See p154.*

elaborate, multi-levelled dolls' houses, which are astonishing to behold. Evidently, children had the gift of imagination before television was invented to take it all away. Displayed in large glass cases, the dolls – some of which are centuries old – are interesting, albeit in a slightly macabre way. Some have mature faces and are dressed in fantastic costumes, while others are naked and hanging forlornly from cupboard walls. It's a good thing Suntan Barbie is there to show us how far we've come in children's toys: from baby dolls to voluptuous, long-legged dolls in bikinis. Less for kids, and more for doll-loving adults walking down memory lane.

Sutton House

2 & 4 Homerton High Street, E9 (8986 2264).
Bethnal Green tube, then 253, 106, D6 bus/Hackney
Central rail. **Open** *Historic rooms Feb-Nov* 11.30am-
5.30pm Wed, Sun (last entry 5pm); closed Mon, Tue,
Thur-Sat. Closed Dec, Jan. **Admission** £2.10; 60p
5s-16s; £4.80 family. **Credit** MC, V.
This National Trust-owned red-brick Tudor mansion is the oldest house in east London, and was built in 1535 for Henry VIII's first secretary of state. It opened as a community centre in the late 1980s after a fierce debate over its future that led to the superb restoration now on view. There are Tudor, Jacobean and Georgian interiors, as well as the Edwardian

chapel and medieval foundations in the cellar. It also boasts what is possibly London's oldest loo: a 16th-century 'garderobe'. There's even a protected wall of graffiti, believed to have been done by squatters in the early '80s. The café and shop are open all year.

Docklands

Assorted stops on the Docklands Light Railway.

The history of London's **Docklands**, which stretches east from Tower Bridge to the Isle of Dogs and beyond, is the history of Britain in microcosm. As the British Empire expanded in the 18th and 19th centuries, so did the traffic along the River Thames, as ships arrived laden with booty from all corners of the globe. Different docks were built to specialise in various types of cargo: rum and hardwood at West India Docks on the **Isle of Dogs**; wool, sugar and rubber at **St Katharine's Dock** by Tower Bridge; ivory, coffee and cocoa at London Docks in **Wapping**. During World War II, the docks suffered heavy bombing (including 57 consecutive nights of firebombing), but by the 1950s they had again reached full capacity.

When it came, the end was sudden. The collapse of the Empire, a series of crippling strikes and, above all, the introduction of deep-water container ships led to the closure, one by one, of all of London's docks from Tower Bridge to Barking Creek between 1967 and 1984. (In September 2001, the **Museum in Docklands** (*see p160*) will open, charting the history of the docks and the port of London.)

Since then, though, efforts have been made to spruce up the area. In 1981, the Conservative government set up the London Docklands Development Corporation (LDDC) with a brief to regenerate the eight-and-a-half square miles (2,200 hectares) of derelict land by building new offices and homes and attracting new businesses. Accused from the outset of favouring wealthy outsiders over the needs of local people, the LDDC came badly unstuck in the recession of the early 1990s, when developers found themselves with brand new buildings yet no one to move into them. Since then, the situation has improved: the population of Docklands had increased from 39,400 in 1981 to 77,000 by the time the organisation ceased operation in March 1998. Its responsibilities have been taken over by other new bodies.

Docklands remains one of the most intriguing areas of London to visit, and it's becoming more accessible. New, imaginatively designed pedestrian bridges across the water-filled docks have made the place more people-friendly. The Docklands Light Railway (DLR) was joined in 1999 by the stations of the long-awaited Jubilee Line extension.

Sightseeing

St Katharine's

Just east of Tower Bridge on the north bank of the Thames, St Katharine's once housed over 1,000 cottages, a brewery and the 12th-century church of St Katharine, all of which were demolished (without compensation) to make way for a grandiose new docklands development scheme in 1828. **St Katharine's Dock**, which was built over the old settlement, remained open until 1968, re-emerging in 1973 as the first of the Docklands redevelopments. **St Katharine's Haven** is now a yacht marina; one corner of the dock houses a squadron of russet-sailed, turn-of-the-century barges. The restaurants, cafés and pubs around the dock pull in tourists by the coachload.

Wapping

In 1598, London historian John Stowe described **Wapping High Street** as a 'filthy strait passage, with alleys of small tenements or cottages… built and inhabited by sailors' victuallers'. Today, it is a quiet thoroughfare – though not without charm – hemmed in on either side by warehouses (those in **Wapping Wall** are the most spectacular) and new flats.

The river at Wapping, to the east of St Katharine's, brims with history. Until well into the 19th century, convicted pirates were taken at low tide to **Execution Dock** (near the River Police station, at Wapping New Stairs), hanged, and left there in chains until three tides had washed over them. The Captain Kidd pub (108 Wapping High Street) commemorates one of the most famous recipients of this brand of rough justice: Kidd had been dispatched by the government to capture pirates in the Indian Ocean but decided to become one himself.

Another historic pub, the Town of Ramsgate (62 Wapping High Street), is where bloodthirsty Judge Jeffreys, who sent scores of pirates to Execution Dock, was himself captured as he tried to escape to Hamburg disguised as a sailor (he died in the Tower of London). 'Colonel' Blood was also caught here after attempting to steal the Crown Jewels in 1671. Dating from 1520, the Prospect of Whitby (57 Wapping Wall; *see p225*) is the oldest and most famous of the Wapping riverside pubs; Pepys, Dickens, Whistler and Turner were all regulars. The White Swan & Cuckoo (corner of Wapping Lane and Prusom Street) lacks a riverside view, but is friendly and serves good food.

The streets north of **The Highway** are working-class tenements, and have a colourful past. A large mural at St George's Town Hall on **Cable Street** commemorates the battle between local people and fascist blackshirts,

led by Sir Oswald Mosely, on 4 October 1936. The march, meant to intimidate the local Jewish population, was abandoned and the blackshirts were never seen in such numbers again in the East End. The church of St George-in-the-East, just off The Highway on **Cannon Street Road**, was built in 1714-29 to the designs of Hawksmoor. Although the interior was rebuilt after the Blitz, the exterior and monumental tower are typical of the architect.

Limehouse

Sandwiched between Wapping and the Isle of Dogs, Limehouse was named after the medieval lime kilns that once stood here. But, like Wapping, Limehouse's prosperity came from the sea. In 1610, a census revealed that half the working population were mariners, and Limehouse later became a centre for shipbuilding. The straw-coloured **Sail Makers' & Ship Chandlers' Building** still stands at 11 West India Dock Road.

The importance of Limehouse is reflected in the immense size of **St Anne's Limehouse** (corner of Commercial Road and Three Colt Street). Built between 1712 and 1724 in what were then open fields, this is probably Hawksmoor's most dramatic creation. The clock tower is the second highest in Britain after Big Ben, and was built by the same makers.

Britain's first wave of Chinese immigrants, mainly seamen, settled in Limehouse in the 19th century. Their influence survives in some of the street names (**Ming Street, Canton Street**) and in the few Chinese restaurants that remain around **West India Dock Road**. In Victorian times, Limehouse was notorious for its gambling and drug dens (Oscar Wilde's Dorian Gray comes here to buy opium) and it features in stories by Sax Rohmer (creator of oriental villain Fu Manchu) and Sir Arthur Conan Doyle. Dickens knew Limehouse well: he regularly visited his godfather in Newell Street and used the tiny, dark, and still superb, Grapes Inn (76 Narrow Street; *see p225*) as the model for the Six Jolly Fellowship Porters in *Our Mutual Friend* (1865).

Isle of Dogs

For many people, the Isle of Dogs *is* Docklands. Redevelopment has been at its most intense here, focusing on **Canary Wharf**. Cesar Pelli's rocket-shaped 244-metre (800-foot) tower is the tallest building in the UK and has dominated the London skyline since it was erected in 1991. The only pity is that owing to fear of IRA attack – a bomb at South Quay in February 1996 caused a huge amount of damage and killed two people –

A route mastered No.15

Paddington, Marble Arch, Oxford Circus, Piccadilly Circus, Trafalgar Square, Aldwych, St Paul's, Cannon Street, Tower of London, Aldgate, Limehouse, then Poplar, Blackwall (DLR) (not evenings), Canning Town (evenings), Upton Park, East Ham.

Made famous by the breathtaking Victorian engineering of Isambard Kingdom Brunel and a fictional Peruvian bear with a penchant for marmalade sandwiches, Paddington is the starting point for the number 15 bus whose eventual destination is the East End. After setting off along Praed Street, the bus turns right into Edgware Road, with its profusion of Middle Eastern shops and restaurants, and heads south towards Hyde Park. Turning left onto Oxford Street, it sweeps past Marble Arch on the right and continues past the grand Selfridges store to Oxford Circus, then heads south along Regent Street.

At Piccadilly Circus, look left for the Shaftesbury Memorial Fountain, with its famous figure of Eros. The first London statue cast in aluminium, it's actually intended to represent the angel of Christian charity, rather than the ancient Greek god of love. From here, you'll be led along Haymarket and through Trafalgar Square, past the enormous National Gallery on the left and the 145-foot Nelson's Column, erected in 1839-42 as a monument to Horatio's last and greatest victory at Trafalgar. The colossal lions that guard the base of the column are a favourite with tourists; as, strangely, are the innumerable pigeons that patrol the square scavenging food.

Exiting Trafalgar Square past the attractive church of St Martin-in-the-Fields, the bus turns onto the Strand, passing Charing Cross station on the right. Along this broad thoroughfare, you'll pass, on the north side, the Adelphi Theatre, built in 1804, and, on the south, the brilliant art nouveau-fronted Savoy Hotel. Crossing into the Aldwych, the bus passes One Aldwych, one of London's finest hotels, as well as the BBC's headquarters at Bush House.

Whipping out of the Aldwych, the historic tea importer R Twining & Co can be seen on the right, opposite the Royal Courts of Justice. Meanwhile, on an island between the two, is the Temple Bar Monument, marking the end of the Strand and the beginning of Fleet Street and the boundary between Westminster and the City of London. Behind this stretch of Fleet Street on both sides are the four Inns of Court, establishments for legal education founded in the 15th century.

As the number 15 winds down Fleet Street (once the centre of London's newspaper trade but now a quiet, rather forlorn thoroughfare) and into Ludgate Circus, straight ahead the vast dome of St Paul's Cathedral forms one of the most imposing views in London. As you climb Ludgate Hill, its west porch entrance dominates the view. Opposite St Paul's south porch is the delicate and still unopened Millennium Bridge across to Bankside.

From here, the bus proceeds along Cannon Street into the heart of the city, past Sir Christopher Wren's 17th-century Monument to the Great Fire (which offers great views over the Thames and Tower Bridge) and then on to Tower Hill. The Tower of London is the most perfect medieval fortress in Britain and a must-see attraction. William I built his first fortress on this site shortly after the battle of Hastings in 1066, since when the building has been expanded and improved by countless successive monarchs. Today, it's one of London's most popular tourist destinations, home to the Crown Jewels, the Yeoman Warders (or Beefeaters) and the famous Tower ravens, though the royal family long since abandoned it as a residence.

Beyond the Tower, the number 15 heads east along Commercial Road, built in the early 19th century for the transportation of goods from the new East and West India docks to the edge of the City, through Limehouse, Westferry and Blackwall before terminating in East Ham, just a few hundred yards, oddly enough, from the home of West Ham football club.

the public aren't allowed access to enjoy the view from the top. Still, the sight of the tower through the glass-domed roof of Canary Wharf DLR station is spectacular in itself, and almost makes up for the disappointment at not being able to ride the elevator to the top.

There's little about the Isle that isn't subject to dispute. Some insist that it isn't an island at all, but a peninsula (though the main section of West India Docks effectively splits it in two) and no one can agree on whether 'Dogs' refers to the royal kennels that were once kept here or

Crime time

The dodgy dealings, double-crosses, scams and swindles of the villainous East End gangsters have taken on almost mythical proportions in our urban history. What with old crim 'Mad' Frankie Fraser appearing on chat shows – he even offers minibus tours of the East End at www.madfrankiefraser.co.uk; progress, eh? – and the success of films such as *Lock, Stock and Two Smoking Barrels* and *Gangster No.1*, if you're a bit of a dodgy geezer with a sordid past, chances are Guy Ritchie is at this minute beating a path to your door begging you to sell your story.

Even the savage beatings and bloodthirsty murders committed by these self-confessed 'hard bastards' seem to be gilded in glamour: they were only killing their own, right? Perhaps this fascination can be put

down to morbidity being embedded within human nature, but it's even better if the charismatic perpetrators of these acts are more worried about losing their 22-carat bracelets or getting bloodstains on their Savile Row suits than blowing off their victim's head. But let's face it: what these cheeky Cockney chappies were getting up to wasn't really that nice. At all.

The most famous of this ilk are, of course, the Kray twins, Ronnie and Reggie, many of whose haunts can still be visited today. Born in Stene Street in Hoxton on 24 October 1933 to Violet (whose father was a bare knuckle boxer) and Charlie (who knocked on doors buying silver and gold to sell on at a profit), they were embroiled in the underground East End from birth.

whether it's a corruption of the dykes that were built by Flemish engineers in the 19th century. Above all, argument continues to rage over whether the Isle of Dogs is a crucible of economic progress or a monstrous adventure playground for big business.

The best way to see Docklands is from the overhead Docklands Light Railway. At the undeveloped southern end of the Isle is Mudchute City Farm, a big hit with kids. **Island Gardens**, at the very tip, offers an unparalleled view across the Thames towards Greenwich. Alternatively, since the completion of the Jubilee Line extension, you could arrive in one of the most expansive (and expensive)

stations in the world; the Foster-designed **Canary Wharf** station, resplendent in glass and steel, is said to be as long as Canary Wharf Tower itself is high. Nearby, at West India Quay, is the new **Museum in Docklands**, due to open in September 2001 (*see below*).

Museum in Docklands

Warehouse No.1, West India Quay, Docklands, E14. (www.museumindocklands.org.uk). **Open** *From Sept 2001; hours subject to change* 10am-6pm Mon-Sat; noon-6pm Sun. **Admission** phone for details. **Credit** MC, V.

Located in a Grade I-listed warehouse and due to open in September 2001, this £16.5-million museum will chart the history of the Port of London and Docklands

In 1939, the Krays moved to 178 Vallance Road, a ghetto of gambling dens and dodgy dealers. Thus began their rite of passage. By the age of 23, the twins had organised a protection racket and were known as The Firm. As well as their Double R Club in Bow Road, the pair established an illegal gambling den behind the Bow Police Garage at 8 Wellington Way.

For those of you with a bloodthirsty streak, the Blind Beggar pub on Whitechapel Road is definitely worth nipping into for a swift pint. It was here, in 1966, that Ronnie Kray shot George Cornell in the head with a 9mm Mauser pistol, having spent the day drinking in the Lion on Tapp Street (you can make it a pub crawl by adding in a third Kray haunt, the shabby Grave Maurice on the Whitechapel Road). Over in Stoke Newington a few years later, in the basement flat at 97 Evering Road, the pair murdered Jack 'The Hat' McVitie, an event – when the trigger of Reggie's gun jammed, Ronnie restrained him while Reggie stabbed him to death – that led to the brothers being jailed for life.

With Hoxton and Shoreditch now achingly trendy, as media types and their entourage flood to bars and pubs in the area, it's well worth remembering how Ronnie and Reggie would approach East End proprietors in their heyday. 'Keep your business aggro free – The Firm Security Service, guaranteed, extended warranty. Special introductory offer – if you don't take it within seven days, we'll throw in aggro – free.' It would have left Hoxtonites choking on their Sea Breezes.

with an array of multi-media presentations, including reconstructed scenes, engravings and artefacts. Tracing the history of the docks chronologically, the galleries will detail Roman trading activities, the medieval port, colonial expansion and the success of the East India Company, Thames shipbuilding, and 20th-century decline and regeneration.

Mile End, Bow & Stratford

Bow Church, Bow Road or Mile End tube/ Stratford tube/rail.

Mostly common land until the 16th century, **Mile End** experienced a minor population explosion in the 1800s as industrialisation

took hold. The area never really experienced the ravages of poverty suffered by neighbouring Whitechapel and Bethnal Green. Nevertheless, it was here that the **Trinity Almshouses** were built in 1695 (near the junction with Cambridge Heath Road) for '28 decayed masters and commanders of ships'. Look out for the model galleons, on either side of the entrance. In the 1860s, William Booth founded the Salvation Army in Mile End.

To the south-west, **Mile End Park** borders Copperfield Road, home to the **Ragged School Museum** (*see p162*) and Matt's Gallery (*see p296*). A £25-million development scheme has begun to completely revitalise the park, which will, when work is completed by 2002, be divided up into separate themed areas: an Arts Park, complete with an outdoor exhibition space; a Sports Park, incorporating Mile End Stadium and a go-karting course; and an Ecology Park, billed as a cross between a nature park and a science museum and due to open in spring 2001. Piers Gough's 25-metre (82-foot) wide **Green Bridge** now provides a link between the two sides of the park.

To the north of Mile End is **Victoria Park** (8533 2057), a welcome slice of green stretching towards Hackney. Fringed by the Hertford Union Canal, it's a useful detour for those weary of Hackney's plains of cement. At the main Sewardstone Road entrance, look out for the deranged-looking Dogs of Alcibiades, which have stood here since 1912. The park's large ponds and tearooms provide it with an atmosphere reminiscent of Regent's Park.

Bow, to the east, has played a major role in the growth of London. In the 12th century, the narrow Roman bridge over the River Lea at Old Ford was supplemented by a new bridge downriver. Its bow shape gave the whole area its name. Grain was transported by boat from Hertfordshire and unloaded at mills along the river. In the 19th century, new factories sprang up, notably the Bryant and May match factory, scene of a bitter but ultimately successful match-girls' strike in 1888. A quarter of a century later, Bow struck another blow for women's rights when Sylvia Pankhurst, sister of Emmeline, launched the East London Federation of Suffragettes.

Stratford ('street by the ford') was formed north of the 12th-century bridgehead. A wealthy Cistercian monastery, Stratford Langthorne Abbey, helped put Stratford on the map. The abbey was dissolved by Henry VIII in 1538, but by then Stratford's prosperity was ensured, thanks to the development of early industries such as gunpowder manufacture. In the mid-19th century, much of the area was covered by railway lines and marshalling

Sightseeing

yards, and Stratford remains a busy transport nexus, boasting a railway, tube and DLR station and a decidedly odd-looking bus station.

Modern Stratford has a busy, well-defined centre, focused on Broadway, where an obelisk commemorates 19th-century philanthropist Samuel Gurney. Look for the distinctive green dome and globe of the Transport and General Workers Union building in **West Ham Lane**, then head through the big indoor shopping centre to **Gerry Raffles Square**. Here the Stratford Picture House faces the venerable Theatre Royal Stratford East (*see p335*), due to reopen in spring 2001 with a new neighbour: Stratford Circus, an arts centre with five spaces that will host 2,000 performances a year.

Ragged School Museum
48-50 Copperfield Road, E3 (8980 6405/ www.raggedschoolmuseum.org.uk). Mile End tube. **Open** 10am-5pm Wed, Thur; 2-5pm 1st Sun of mth; closed Mon, Tue, Fri, Sat. **Admission** free.
Sparse and limited though it is, this museum is still a compelling affair. Designed to educate the public about ragged schools – a Victorian invention to educate poor children – it also commemorates the development of east London. A ground-floor exhibit explains the history of the Tower Hamlets that eventually become the eastern boroughs; the first floor is devoted to a recreation of a Victorian ragged school classroom; and the top floor is designed like a 19th century home. The latter pair may prove more interesting for children than adults, but the displays on the ground floor offer enough to satisfy.

Walthamstow
Walthamstow tube/rail.

The name comes from the Old English word 'Wilcumestowe': a place where guests are welcome. It's a description that still applies today: Walthamstow is noticeably friendly. Its borders are ancient ones: **Epping Forest** to the north, **Walthamstow Marshes** to the west. The first settlers lived here in the Bronze Age, when the whole area was still thickly forested. In medieval times, much of the forest was cleared and replaced by farmland. It wasn't until the 19th century that Walthamstow became a wholly urban area, though most of its largely working-class population has been spared the tenements and tower blocks that litter other parts of east London.

Walthamstow has two main thoroughfares. The narrow **High Street** contains the longest and, after Brixton, most varied market in London. **Walthamstow Market** stretches for more than a mile and is lined by inexpensive shops. The second thoroughfare is undulating **Hoe Street**, consisting of a drab selection of kebab shops and mini-marts, although the Dhaka Tandoori (no.103) is rather good.

Lloyd Park contains the Waltham Forest Theatre and a variety of imported water birds. The aviary and manicured bowling green, frequented by white-clad elderly locals, make it particularly pleasant on a sunny summer's

Politics with an architectural difference: **Walthamstow Town Hall**. See p163.

afternoon. The 18th-century building with its back imperiously turned to the park is the **William Morris Gallery** (*see below*). From here, a short walk up Forest Road will be amply rewarded by the dramatic view of the art nouveau **Walthamstow Town Hall**, one of the most startling pieces of municipal architecture in London. Its beautiful proportions, green-and-gold clock tower and circular reflecting pool have graced many a film and TV production; indeed, in pre-glasnost days, it was frequently called to stand in for Moscow or Leningrad.

The area's oldest buildings can be found in a well-concealed enclave known as **Walthamstow Village**. Vestry Road is the site of the **Vestry House Museum** (*see below*) and the Monoux Almshouses, built in 1795 and 'endowed for ever… for the use of six decayed tradesmen's widows of this parish and no other'. The squat exterior of nearby St Mary's Church conceals a modest but tranquil interior. Timbered **Ancient House**, opposite the churchyard, was once a farmhouse. Restored in 1934, it sags like an unsuccessful fruit cake. The Village continues along Orford Road, with its Italian restaurants and cosy pub.

Vestry House Museum

Vestry Road, E17 (8509 1917/www.lbwf.gov.uk/vestry/vestry.htm). Walthamstow Central tube/rail. **Open** 10am-1pm, 2-5.30pm Mon-Fri; 10am-1pm, 2-5pm Sat; closed Sun. **Admission** free. **No credit cards.**
This diminutive but charming museum offers a fascinating photographic history of Walthamstow, as well as focusing on two of the area's favourite sons: Alfred Hitchcock, from Leytonstone, and Frederick Bremer, designer of Britain's first motor car (the 1894 vehicle is on display). Strangely, there's nothing about Britain's first powered flight, by AV Roe over Walthamstow Marshes in 1909. The costume and toy sections are well worth a look.

William Morris Gallery

Lloyd Park, Forest Road, E17 (8527 3782/www.lbwf.gov.uk/wmg). Walthamstow Central tube/rail, then 34, 97, 215, 257 bus. **Open** 10am-1pm, 2-5pm Tue-Sat; 1st Sun of every mth; closed Mon. **Admission** free. **Credit** MC, V.
Opened to the public exactly 50 years ago last year, this was the childhood home of influential late-Victorian designer, craftsman and socialist William Morris. In four rooms on the ground floor, Morris's biography is expounded through his work and political writings. Upstairs are galleries devoted to his associates – Burne-Jones, Philip Webb and Ernest Gimson – who assisted in contributing to the considerable popularity Morris's style retains today. There are also paintings by one-time apprentice to Morris, Frank Brangwyn.

Leyton & Leytonstone

Leyton or Leytonstone tube.

Badly bombed during World War II, **Leyton**'s post-war development has been haphazard, and it lacks the cohesion and charm of neighbouring Walthamstow. Much of the land originally consisted of marshy, fertile farmland, and during the 18th century the area was best known for its market gardening. The inevitable industrialisation of the mid-19th century led to much of the marshland being covered by railways and gas works, and to a downturn in the area's fortunes as the population swelled with low-paid railway workers. The proliferation of discount supermarkets and second-hand furniture and electrical shops testifies to the fact that Leyton remains one of London's poorer areas. Its best-known 'attraction' is its endearingly underachieving football team, **Leyton Orient** (*see p326*).

Leytonstone, to the east of Leyton, took its name from a milestone on the Roman road from the City to Epping Forest. The petrol station on the corner of Leytonstone High Road is on the site of a greengrocer's shop where Alfred Hitchcock spent his early childhood. Late in life, he recalled how, following some forgotten mischievousness, his father gave him a note and told him to take it to Harrow Green police station nearby. The sergeant on duty read the note and then locked the future Master of Suspense in a cell for 20 minutes, explaining, 'This is what we do to naughty boys.'

Further east

Although the London Docklands Development Corporation remit to revive the London Docks extended well to the east of the Isle of Dogs, there is little to interest visitors beyond **Blackwall. Canning Town**, huddled next to the River Lea, lost its main industry as early as 1912, with the closure of the Thames Ironworks and Shipbuilding Company on Bow Creek. Much of the area was flattened by German bombers, and ugly post-war housing estates did nothing to revive the area's fortunes. Neighbouring **Newham** fared even worse: the collapse of a tower block, Ronan Point, in 1968 caused several deaths. **Beckton**, to the east, has been more fortunate, with better-than-average new housing. South of Beckton, **London City Airport** was opened in 1987, using the long, narrow quay between Royal Albert Dock and George V Dock as a runway for short-haul airliners (there's a good view of the airport from the DLR).

South London

North Londoners may sneer, but there's charm aplenty below the river.

Charlton, Woolwich & Eltham

In centuries past, few travellers relished the prospect of a journey along the Old Dover Road. At **Shooters Hill**, in particular, the road was steep and the countryside wild; this was a favourite spot for footpads and highwaymen to lie in wait for easy prey. Robbers who were caught were themselves shown no mercy: they were hanged at a gallows at the bottom of Shooters Hill and their bodies displayed on a gibbet at the summit. In 1661, Samuel Pepys recorded that he 'rode under a man that hangs at Shooters Hill, and a filthy sight it was to see how the flesh is shrunk from his bones'.

Charlton was a nearby village, built around the Jacobean manor **Charlton House** (*see below*). Nearby **Hornfair Park** is tucked away at the corner of a housing estate; **Maryon Park**, used in Antonioni's film *Blow-Up* and closer to the river, is more pleasant. Nearby is the **Thames Barrier**, which stretches between Silvertown on the north bank and Woolwich on the south (*see p165* **Opening the floodgates**).

Woolwich itself attracts fewer visitors than its more glamorous neighbour Greenwich, although it does have plenty to offer, including an above-average shopping centre. Long, pedestrianised **Powis Street** also boasts two spectacular buildings at the river end: the ruddy Edwardian Central Stores building and, opposite, the creamy-tiled, art deco Co-Op.

The character of Woolwich has been shaped by military and naval associations. Woolwich Arsenal was established in Tudor times as the country's main source of munitions. Over the centuries it spread to colossal proportions: at its peak, during World War I, the site stretched 32 miles (52 kilometres) along the river and employed 72,000 people. When it closed down in 1967, much of the land was used to build a new town, **Thamesmead**. **Woolwich Garrison**, historic home of the Royal Artillery, remains, and boasts the longest Georgian façade in the country. It's best seen from Woolwich Common or from Grand Depot Road, where the remains of the **Royal Garrison Church of St George** have been left as consecrated ground after being hit by a flying bomb in 1944 (the end walls and altar still stand). Military aficionados should look forward to the 2001 opening of a new museum, **Firepower** (*see p165*).

Henry VIII established the Royal Dockyard at Woolwich in 1512, initially so his new flagship, the *Great Harry*, could be built there. It closed in 1869 and moved to Chatham. Downstream from the Woolwich Ferry terminal, the stretch of river known as Gallions Reach was the scene of the Thames' worst-ever shipping accident. In 1878, a crowded pleasure steamer, the *Princess Alice*, was struck broadside by a collier, with the loss of some 700 lives.

The **Woolwich Ferry** has existed since the 14th century; the old paddle steamers were replaced by diesels as late as 1963. (There is also a foot tunnel.) Today, the seating area outside the Waterfront Leisure Centre, next to the terminal, is a fine spot to watch a great river at work. Railway enthusiasts might like to take the ferry across the river to the **North Woolwich Old Station Museum** (*see p166*).

Despite being despoiled by numerous bleak housing estates, there are a surprising number of green spaces in this part of south-east London, connected by the excellent **Green Chain Walk** (call 8921 5028 for maps, or log on to www.greenchain.com). It takes in wonderful ancient woodlands such as **Oxleas Wood** (easily accessible from Falconwood rail station), a couple of miles south of Woolwich. A mile and a half south-west of here was the site of the now-restored **Eltham Palace** (*see below*).

Charlton House

Charlton Road, SE7 (8856 3951). Charlton rail/53, 54, 380, 442 bus. **Open** 9am-11pm Mon-Fri; 9am-5.30pm Sat; closed Sun. **Admission** free.
The finest Jacobean house in London, and possibly in the country, red-brick Charlton House was built in 1612 as a retirement gift for Adam Newton, tutor to James I's son Prince Henry. It's not known for sure who the architect was, though John Thorpe is the most likely contender. The orangery, on the other hand, is almost certainly the work of Inigo Jones. The building now enjoys a useful if humdrum existence as a community centre and public library.

Eltham Palace

off Court Road, Eltham, SE9 (8294 2577/ www.english-heritage.org.uk). Eltham rail.
Open *Apr-Sept* 10am-6pm Wed-Fri, Sun. *Oct* 10am-5pm Wed-Fri, Sun. *Nov-Mar* 10am-4pm Wed-Fri, Sun. Closed Mon, Tue, Sat all year round.
Admission *House & grounds* £6; £4.50 concessions; £3 5-16s. *Grounds only* £3.60; £2.70 concessions; £1.80 5-16s. **Credit** MC, V.

Although there was a royal palace on this site from the late 13th to the mid-17th century, the name Eltham Palace is a little inappropriate for the wonderful homage to the 1930s that stands here today. It's true that the oldest part of the building, the 15th-century Great Hall, is a remnant of the royal palace, but the joy of this house is the art deco interior.

In the mid-1930s, the once-grand hall was a crumbling relic. Stephen Courtauld, a patron of the arts, bought the wreck and, with the aid of gifted architects and designers, grafted a country home on to the old hall. In characteristic deco style, the interior plays with geometry, line and contrasts of light and dark, from the deep wooden veneers to the truly modern concrete and glass dome in the light-filled entrance hall. The gardens are splendid, with views across to the city and out to the greenery of Kent. The palace is a 20-minute walk from Eltham station.

Firepower

Royal Arsenal, Woolwich, SE18 (8855 7755/ www.firepower.org.uk). **Open** *From May 21 2001; hours subject to change* 10am-5pm daily. **Admission** phone for details. **Credit** phone for details.
Replacing the old Museum of Artillery, this £15-million attraction, due to open in May 2001, charts the history of the Royal Regiment of Artillery. The

Opening the floodgates

Succeeding where King Canute failed, and costing a cool £535 million when it was completed in 1982, the Thames Barrier is London's first line of defence against devastating surge tides and one of the world's modern engineering marvels. Stretching like sci-fi sentinels across the river at Woolwich Reach, south-east London, the barrier's nine piers anchor massive steel gates that are raised from the riverbed several times a year in order to avert flooding in London's low-lying areas.

Protective barrages across the river were proposed as far as back as 1907, but it wasn't until the great flood of 1953, when 300 people drowned and 65,000 hectares of farmland were flooded with sea water, that the government decided to act. It was 12 years before consent was given for construction to begin on the barrier, chosen from 41 proposals because it minimised interference with the river's flow and posed no headroom restrictions.

The statistics are staggering. Half a million tonnes of concrete were laid along the 1,716-foot wide river, divided by nine piers founded on solid chalk 50 feet below the river. Six openings suitable for shipping traffic were made, along with four smaller openings. The four largest steel gates are 200 feet wide and weigh 1,500 tonnes. When raised from their flat resting place, each is as high as a five-storey building. As well as the world's largest movable flood barrier, 11.5 miles of new defences that scale a height of 23 feet were built on the riverbanks to the east, with similar work carried out at the mouth of the estuary. In all, 4,000 men and women worked on the barrier over the course of eight years leading up to its official opening by Queen Elizabeth II almost two decades ago.

While surge tides – 'humps' of water that cross the Atlantic and, pushed by north winds, sweep into the North Sea, the English Channel and, finally, up the Thames – were the primary reason for the construction of the barrier, global warming has emphasised its role. The high water level at London Bridge has risen by about 75 centimetres each century due to a combination of melting polar ice caps, the tilting of the British Isles towards Europe and man's encroachment on the river; and environmentalists estimate sea levels will continue to rise globally at around a metre every century.

The Barrier is raised for a test each month, and it's worth timing a visit to the fascinating Visitors' Centre on the south bank to see this extraordinary and unique 'attraction' in action. Just keep your fingers crossed that it only has to be raised for testing purposes...

Thames Barrier Visitors' Centre

1 Unity Way, SE18 (8305 4188/ www.environment-agency.gov.uk). North Greenwich tube/Charlton rail/riverboats to & from Greenwich Pier (8305 0300) & Westminster Pier (7930 3373)/177, 180 bus. **Open** *10am-5pm Mon-Fri; 10.30am-5.30pm Sat, Sun.* **Admission** *£3.40; £2 5-16s, OAPs; £7.50 family.* **Credit** *MC, V.*

museum will be centred around 'Field of Fire', a multi-media presentation that aims to recreate the experiences of artillery gunners in the 20th century, from World War I to Bosnia: expect plenty of loud noises and bright lights. The Gunnery Hall will feature a series of static displays illustrating the development of artillery weapons in the 20th century, while the interactive Real Weapon gallery will allow visitors to learn the principles of targeting, including the benefits of direct and indirect fire. All in all, there should be much more to Firepower than the ragged uniforms and massed medals of your average regimental museum.

North Woolwich Old Station Museum

Pier Road, E16 (7474 7244/www.newham.net/ museums). Beckton DLR/North Woolwich rail/ Woolwich Dockyard or Woolwich Arsenal rail, then foot tunnel to North Woolwich Pier. **Open** *Jan-Nov* 1-5pm Sat, Sun; closed Mon-Fri. *Dec* closed. *School holidays* phone for details. **Admission** free.

Dedicated to the London & North Eastern Railway, this museum is at its best on the first Sunday of each month during summer, when the Coffee Pot and Pickett steam engines chug up and down outside. Inside, trains, tickets, station signs and a 1920s ticket office are on display. For railway enthusiasts, it's well worth the journey to this otherwise charmless part of London.

Cross the Meridian in **Greenwich**.

Greenwich & Blackheath

Greenwich was the playground of kings and queens. Henry VIII and his daughters Mary I and Elizabeth I were born here, and Greenwich Palace, then called Placentia, was Henry's favourite residence. It was at Greenwich that Sir Walter Raleigh supposedly laid his cloak over a puddle so Elizabeth I wouldn't get her feet wet.

After the Tudors, the palace fell on hard times. Under Oliver Cromwell, it became first a biscuit factory, then a prison. In 1660, the newly restored Charles II embarked on an ambitious scheme to return Greenwich to its former glory. Work began on a new palace, but only one riverside wing was ever built. William and Mary, who succeeded Charles, preferred the royal palaces at Kensington and Hampton Court and ordered Sir Christopher Wren to design another wing for the unfinished building, to create the Royal Naval Hospital. Better known today as the **Old Royal Naval College** (the Navy moved out in 1998; *see p169*), this is the great façade you see from the river today, with a gap to allow an unobscured view of **Queen's House** behind (*see p169*), now part of the **National Maritime Museum** (*see p168*). Maritime Greenwich was designated a UNESCO World Heritage Site in 1997, and rightly so.

The nicest way to arrive at Greenwich is by river to Greenwich Pier where you'll disembark in the shadow of the **Cutty Sark** (*see p168*). The new **Greenwich Tourist Information Centre** (0870 608 2000) is based in Pepys House beside the *Cutty Sark*, and provides full details on sights and transport in the area. On the other side of the ship will be **Greenwich Reach**, a leisure and retail development slated for completion in 2004 that will include a ten-screen cinema, bars, restaurants, luxury flats and the city's first central cruise liner terminal.

Greenwich is a busy, traffic-ridden place. Visitors flood in every weekend to peruse the arts and crafts stalls of sprawling **Greenwich Market** (*see p253*). But punters aren't spoiled for choice when it comes to eateries in the area. Many fill up at Goddard's Ye Old Pie House at 45 Greenwich Church Street, which has been serving home-baked pies since 1890; Time at 7A College Approach and the North Pole at 131 Greenwich High Road are two decent alternatives.

The church of **St Alfege Greenwich** (1712-18), on Greenwich High Road, takes its name from the Archbishop of Canterbury who was martyred on the site by marauding Vikings in 1012, after courageously refusing to sanction a demand for ransom that would have secured his release. The church is normally open to visitors at weekends.

Oh buoy, showing visitors the way to the **National Maritime Museum**. *See p168.*

A Thames-side walkway by the *Cutty Sark* takes you past the riverside front of the Old Royal Naval College to the Trafalgar Tavern, built directly on to the river and a favourite of literary chums Dickens, Thackeray and Collins (Dickens set the wedding feast here in *Our Mutual Friend*). Tiny **Crane Street**, on the far side of the pub, leads you to the bizarre, white, castellated Trinity Hospital, which, since 1617, has been home to '21 retired gentlemen of Greenwich'. Despite its proximity to the town centre, it's one of the most peaceful spots anywhere on the urban Thames. The path continues until it reaches the Cutty Sark Tavern, dating from 1695. Seats outside give a good view of still-active wharfs downstream.

The remains of 20 Saxon grave mounds and a Roman temple may have been identified within its precincts, but the beautiful riverside **Greenwich Park** (8858 2608) is more famous for its Tudor and Stuart history. Henry VIII was born at Greenwich Palace and it remained his favourite residence, surrounded by a park for hunting and hawking. In 1616, James I commissioned Inigo Jones to rebuild the Tudor palace. The result was **Queen's House** (*see p169*), England's first Palladian villa. In the 1660s, it was redesigned by André Le Nôtre, who landscaped Versailles, but Charles II's plan for a new palace was later adapted to become the **Old Royal Naval College** (*see p169*).

Crowning the hill at the top of the park are the **Royal Observatory** (*see p169*) and Flamsteed House, both designed by Wren. Temporally speaking, it's the centre of the planet. Greenwich Mean Time, introduced in 1890, sets the world's clocks. Visitors can straddle the Greenwich Meridian Line and stand in the eastern and western hemispheres simultaneously. Each day since 1833, the red time-ball on the north-eastern turret of the observatory has dropped at 1pm as a signal to shipmasters on the river to adjust their chronometers.

At the southern end of the park stands the 18th-century **Ranger's House** (closed for refurbishment throughout 2001; phone 8853 0035 from 2002 to find out when it will reopen), which, when open, shows a range of paintings from Jacobean to contemporary times. It's still worth a short detour for the exterior.

Visitors wishing to avoid the long hike up the hill can take advantage of the Shuttle Bus (8859 1096), a royal blue minibus that meets the boats at Greenwich Pier to transport visitors up through Greenwich Park stopping at the National Maritime Museum and the Royal Observatory. Tickets for the hop-on, hop-off service are valid all day and cost £1.50 for adults and 50p for children.

A long road, **Maze Hill**, runs south from Trafalgar Road, forming the eastern boundary of Greenwich Park. At the top of the hill, at the corner of Maze Hill and Westcombe Park Road, is the castle-like house built by the architect-playwright John Vanbrugh, who lived here from 1719 to 1726. From here, the view back towards the Old Royal Naval College and the City is superb. On Croom's Hill, west of the park, is the simply titled **Fan Museum** (*see p168*).

Back north and sticking out into the Thames, Greenwich Peninsula is famous as the site of the **Dome**. Closed on 31 December 2000, it had been home to the Millennium Experience, a series of attractions intended to amount to 'the most spectacular millennial event anywhere in the world'. What it turned out to be, in most people's eyes, was a spectacular waste of cash. Despite being the most visited attraction in the country last year, the Dome failed by half to achieve its insanely high target figures, and the attraction made significant financial losses and required several hefty hand-outs from the government simply to remain open, on top of the initial £758 million it cost to build.

While it seems certain that history will not be kind to the Millennium Experience, the future of the building itself was less certain in early 2001, as proposals to sell it off for conversion into a business park were dogged by accusations of cronyism. Even after death, the project continues to create controversy.

Perhaps the true legacy of the Dome, though, is that it provided the motivation to turn a huge slab of wasteland into a habitable residential development. The £250-million **Millennium Village**, a high-tech, environmentally friendly plot of 1,400 properties built on an adjacent site on Greenwich Peninsula, received its first residents on 15 December 2000.

Cutty Sark

King William Walk, SE10 (8858 3445/ www.cuttysark.org.uk). Cutty Sark DLR/Greenwich DLR/rail. **Open** 10am-5pm daily (last entry 4.30pm). **Admission** £3.50; £2.50 concessions; £8.50 family; free under-5s. *Combined ticket with National Maritime Museum & Royal Observatory* £12; £9.60 concessions; £2.50 under-16s. **Credit** MC, V.
The world's only surviving tea and wool clipper, Hercules Linton's 1869 vessel broke speed records. Visitors are free to roam the beautifully restored decks and crew's quarters, and gaze up at the rigging. Inside are collections of prints and naval relics, the world's largest collection of carved and painted figureheads, plus a number of hands-on exhibits, such as a knot-tying board and a hammock, aimed at younger visitors. On summer weekends, there are shanty singers and popular costume storytelling sessions, reliving life aboard the ship.

Fan Museum

12 Crooms Hill, SE10 (8305 1441/www.fan-museum.org). Cutty Sark DLR/Greenwich DLR/rail. **Open** 11am-5pm Tue-Sat; noon-5pm Sun; closed Mon. **Admission** £3.50; £2.50 concessions; free under-7s. Free OAPs, disabled 2-5pm Tue.
Credit MC, V.
One of only two permanent exhibitions of hand-held folding fans in the world, this unexpectedly fascinating museum is housed in two converted Georgian townhouses. True to their coy usage, only part of the huge collection is on view at one time: their elasticity necessitates periodic rest. The fans are displayed by theme, such as design, provenance or social history. Among the exhibitions planned for 2001 is

Ahoy! It's the **Cutty Sark**.

Japanese Fans (until 24 June), which will include a collection of 'export' fans created for the European market in the 18th and 19th centuries.

National Maritime Museum

Romney Road, SE10 (8858 4422/information 8312 6565/www.nmm.ac.uk). Cutty Sark DLR/Greenwich DLR/rail. **Open** 10am-5pm daily. **Admission** £7.50; £6 concessions; free under-16s, OAPs. *Combined ticket with Cutty Sark & Royal Observatory* £12; £9.60 concessions; £2.50 under-16s, over-60s.
Credit AmEx, MC, V.
Following a £20-million Lottery-funded redevelopment in 1997, this ever-expanding, ever-improving museum has thrown off its old-fashioned image and emerged as a modern attraction with something to offer even the most jelly-legged land-lubber. Its themed galleries combine traditional exhibits with interactive elements so as to be entertaining and educational in equal measure. The galleries, arranged around three sides of the vast central atrium, Neptune Court, are not meant to be seen in any particular order, and you may do well to ignore the bewildering colour-coded floor plan and explore the museum at your leisure.

On level one, the **Explorers** gallery examines pioneering sea travel, from early Polynesian and Viking voyages to the vain, imperialist drive of later European exploration. **Passengers** looks at the more passive participants in marine expeditions, concentrating on the mass migration of the early

20th century, while **Maritime London** brings old prints and lithographs together with video installations to help reconstruct London's nautical past and explore the city's current role as the financial hub of the shipping industry. Next door, **Rank & Style** looks at the way in which climate and class affect Naval uniform styles. Upstairs, the new **Seapower** exhibition concentrates on the Navy and sea trade in the 20th century, from World War I to the Gulf War, while in the next gallery, **Trade & Empire** is a worthy examination of some of the less glorious episodes in Britain's maritime history.

Level three is home to **All Hands** and **The Bridge**, two hands-on, interactive galleries where younger visitors can learn how to send a distress signal using Morse code, flags or radio, or try their hands at steering a Viking longboat, a paddle steamer and a modern passenger ferry. Despite the lure of these new exhibitions, the **Nelson Gallery**, a comprehensive monument to this country's most celebrated naval hero, and the 17th- and 18th-century models in the **Ship of War** exhibition, continue to prove just as popular with adults and kids. **South**, a fascinating exhibition charting the four major expeditions in the race for the South Pole, is also open on this level until 30 September 2001.

Old Royal Naval College

King William Walk, SE10 (8269 4747/ www.greenwichfoundation.org.uk). Cutty Sark DLR/ Greenwich DLR/rail. **Open** *10am-5pm daily (last entry 4.15pm).* **Admission** *£3; £2 concessions; free accompanied under-16s. Free for all from 3.30pm daily.* **No credit cards**.

Probably the finest example of monumental classical architecture in England, work begun on Wren's spectacular riverside buildings in 1696. The college is split in two in order to give an unimpeded view of **Queen's House** (*see below*) from the river, and vice versa. Originally a grand almshouse for former Royal Navy seamen, the building was adapted for use as a Naval college in 1873. But after 125 years in residence, the Navy vacated the buildings in 1998 and the University of Greenwich took up residence. The spectacular Painted Hall (decorated by James

In a flap at the **Fan Museum**. *See p168.*

Thornhill in 1708-27) and the chapel are open to the public, as before, and a space has been opened up for temporary exhibitions. Events planned for 2001 include the Millennium Crown Jewels, a collection of perfect facsimiles of crown jewels from all over Europe that looks set to stay on display all year.

Queen's House

Romney Road, SE10 (8312 6565). Cutty Sark DLR/ Greenwich DLR/rail. **Open** *From April 2001 10am-5pm daily.* **Admission** *call for details.* **Credit** AmEx, DC, MC, V.

Furnished as it would have been in the 17th century, the Queen's House was one of the first truly classical buildings in Britain. It was designed by Inigo Jones in 1616 for James I's wife, Anne of Denmark, but she died before it was finished and the house was completed at the order of Queen Henrietta Maria in 1629. The house is closed until April 2001, when it will reopen with A Sea of Faces, an exhibition of over 130 portraits of sea captains and shipwrights from the 17th century to the present day, including work by the likes of Reynolds and Hogarth.

Royal Observatory

Greenwich Park, SE10 (8312 6565/ www.rog.nmm.ac.uk). Cutty Sark DLR/Greenwich DLR/rail. **Open** *10am-5pm daily.* **Admission** *£6; £4.80 concessions; free under-16s, OAPs. Combined ticket with Cutty Sark & National Maritime Museum £12; £9.60 concessions; £2.50 under-16s, OAPs.* **Credit** AmEx, DC, MC, V.

The Royal Observatory was founded in 1675, when Charles II appointed the first Astronomer Royal, John Flamsteed, with the task of finding out 'the so much desired longitude of places for the perfecting of the art of navigation'. It is appropriate, then, that the museum devotes several galleries to tell of the search for a means of determining longitude at sea, including a collection of absurd instruments that failed to solve the problem and, of course, the one that finally did, John Harrison's ingenious marine chronometer. The rest of the museum includes exhibits on the development of more accurate timepieces and an extensive history of the buildings as a working Observatory, including the Octagon Room, a faithful restoration of Sir Christopher Wren's original interior design for Flamsteed House.

Blackheath

Maze Hill brings you to the edge of windswept **Blackheath**. Blackheath Village, on the far side of the heath, lies just beyond the **Princess of Wales** pub, where the first ever rugby union club, Blackheath FC, was founded in 1858. The fieldstone **All Saints Church** stands nearby, its unusually tall, sharp spire giving the building the shape of a witch's hat.

Blackheath Village exudes middle-class values. **The Paragon**, a crescent on the edge of the heath, lined with prestigious colonnaded houses, was built in the late 18th century with

the express purpose of attracting the right sort of people to the area when it was still struggling to lose its reputation as a no-go area, plagued by highwaymen. Allowed to fall into disrepair in the 1920s and 1930s, and badly bombed during World War II, the crescent has since been restored to its original state.

Rotherhithe

Upriver from Greenwich, the Thames curves past **Deptford**, where the Royal Naval Yards once built the warships with which Britain controlled the world's seas, to **Rotherhithe**. Pepys knew Rotherhithe as Redriffe, though both names may derive from the Anglo-Saxon words 'redhra' and 'hyth': 'mariner's haven'. The old name still holds good: Rotherhithe is relatively undisturbed by visitors, with superb views across the river and one of the best riverside pubs in London. The Mayflower (117 Rotherhithe Street; *see p226*) dates from 1550 and was built on piles so it stands directly over the river. It was given its name when *The Mayflower* docked here in 1620 before heading to America. Its captain, Christopher Jones, is buried in **St Mary's Rotherhithe** (*see below*).

St Mary's Rotherhithe

St Marychurch Street, SE16 (7231 2465). Rotherhithe tube. **Open** 7am-6pm Mon-Thur; 8am-6pm Sat, Sun; closed Fri. **Admission** free.
A gem of a church, built in 1715 by local sailors and watermen. Today, thanks to acts of burglary and vandalism, the interior can only be viewed through glass, under the watchful eye of a video camera. The communion table in the Lady Chapel and two bishop's chairs were made from timber salvaged from the warship *Fighting Temeraire*, the subject of Turner's painting hanging in the National Gallery.

Camberwell, Peckham & Dulwich

Much of south London is stigmatised as a dull, amorphous sprawl. But this (predominantly north Londoner) prejudice masks a patchwork of communities of character and charm.

Sandwiched between Brixton and Peckham, **Camberwell** was a country village until the mid-19th century. Mendelssohn lived here briefly, and his 'Spring Song', written in 1842, was originally entitled 'Camberwell Green' after the former village green next to what is now the junction of Camberwell Road and Denmark Hill. Camberwell's best feature is **Camberwell Grove**, a steep hill lined with tall Georgian houses. Its golden-lit drawing rooms, reminiscent of Henry James novels, are an enticing sight at dusk. At the eastern end of

Camberwell Church Street, **St Giles Church**, built to the designs of Sir George Gilbert Scott (1844), has grown mossy over the years and, with its 72-metre (210-foot) spire, now seems embarrassingly big for its surroundings.

Like many districts of south London, **Peckham** was a rural idyll until the Industrial Revolution. It was a favourite stopping place for cattle drovers on their way to markets in the City; they would leave their herds grazing on the common, **Peckham Rye**, while they refreshed themselves at the inns along **Peckham High Street**. As a child, William Blake saw a vision of angels on the Rye, and in her novel *The Ballad of Peckham Rye* (1960), Muriel Spark refers, without irony, to 'the dusky scope of the Rye's broad lyrical acres'.

The Victorian terraces that feature in the novel have now mostly gone, replaced by monolithic council estates and tower blocks that recently found an unwanted spot in the public consciousness after a 10-year-old boy was murdered nearby. Ironically, he had just been to a class at the building many felt would help revitalise the area, the new £5-million **Peckham Library** (*see p31*), the focus of an attractive new public square and park.

West of here, long **Lordship Lane** is the main thoroughfare through more sedate **Dulwich**. **Dulwich Park**, with its dramatic view of the Crystal Palace TV transmitter (in **Crystal Palace Park**; *see below*), and adjoining **Dulwich Village** lie at the southern tip of Lordship Lane. Dotted with modern sculpture, the grounds of **Dulwich Picture Gallery** (*see p172*) are a pleasant place in which to sit. The rarefied atmosphere of the Village, with its distinctive dark brick, is as great a contrast to Peckham as you could imagine. Heading south out of the Village, College Road is lined with fine detached houses. At **Dulwich Common**, palatial, red-brick **Dulwich College** greets you, serene in its verdant grounds. Old boys include PG Wodehouse and Raymond Chandler. Close by is the marvellously eccentric **Horniman Museum** (*see p172*).

Built to house the 1851 Great Exhibition, the all-glass **Crystal Palace** was originally erected in Hyde Park (*see p136*). After the Exhibition closed, the building was moved to Sydenham, where it was used for exhibitions, plays and concerts. The extensive grounds contained an amusement park and, dotted here and there, life-sized models of dinosaurs. In 1936, the Crystal Palace caught fire and burned to the ground; the small but informative **Crystal Palace Museum** (8676 0700, open 11am-5pm Sun only), housed in the old engineering school where John Logie Baird invented television, chronicles the history of

Sightseeing

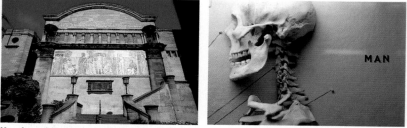
Horniman Museum (left). Not very horny man in a museum (right).

the palace. The model dinosaurs, which survived the blaze and are now classified as listed buildings, are a reminder of how quirky the whole place was in its heyday. Views from the park – which contains the **National Sports Centre** (*see p328*) – are stunning.

Dulwich Picture Gallery

Gallery Road, SE21 (8693 5254/ www.dulwichpicturegallery.org.uk). North Dulwich or West Dulwich rail. **Open** 10am-5pm Tue-Fri; 11am-5pm Sat, Sun; closed Mon. **Admission** £4; £3 OAPs; free all other concessions. Free for all Fri. **Credit** MC, V.

A prime example of the trend towards adding modern extensions to classic buildings, the eminently lovely Dulwich Picture Gallery was reopened by the Queen in May 2000 to great acclaim. Designed by Sir John Soane in 1811, it has been revamped by Rick Mather Architects (the firm behind the proposed redevelopment of the South Bank; *see p71*) with the addition of a café, educational facilities and extra space for temporary exhibitions. 2001 will see temporary shows devoted to the work of Spanish Golden Age artist Bartolomé Esteban Murillo (until 13 May) and Howard Hodgkin (26 June-19 Aug), and some choice cuts from Sir Hickham Bacon's noted collection of watercolours (19 Sept-6 Jan 2002), alongside the museum's splendid permanent collection of European Old Masters.

Horniman Museum

100 London Road, SE23 (8699 1872/recorded information 8699 2339/www.horniman.demon.co.uk). Forest Hill rail/63, 122, 176, 185, 312, 352, P4 bus. **Open** 10.30am-5.30pm Mon-Sat; 2-5.30pm Sun. **Admission** free; donations appreciated. **No credit cards**.

It's a testament to this idiosyncratic museum that it's well worth the journey from central London. The essence of 19th- century tea merchant Frederick Horniman's endearingly peculiar collection is on view in the natural history hall. Here, an immense stuffed walrus presides gruffly over an eclectic display of other specimens. The surprising Apostle's Clock enacts a famous episode from the Gospels daily at 4pm. Equally interesting is the **Living Waters Aquarium**, which demonstrates the life

in a river on its way to the sea. But the most popular gallery is **African Worlds**, a large space devoted to African art and sculpture including several Egyptian mummies and a spectacular 6.1m (20ft) high tribal mask. In summer, the formal and sunken gardens with fine views are an added attraction, as is the small zoo containing farmyard animals.

Due to a major redevelopment programme, the museum will close until 30 April 2001. When the work is completed, the Horniman will feature a new world cultures gallery, a hands-on gallery and a new temporary exhibition space (due to open in spring 2002), plus a new space for the vast musical instruments collection (scheduled for autumn 2002), a new education section, shop and a café.

Stockwell, Kennington & Vauxhall

Stockwell was, at one time, a medieval manor, with the manor house on the site of present-day Stockwell Gardens, off Stockwell Road. Until the feverish house- and railway-building of the 1840s, Stockwell remained a country village. South Lambeth Common, on which cattle used to graze, has now been reduced to the scrap of green bearing the clock tower and war memorial outside Stockwell tube station.

St Mark's Church, between Prima Road and Camberwell New Road, was built in 1824 on the site of a gallows; many of the Jacobites who fought in the 1745 rebellion were hanged, drawn and quartered here. Nearby **Kennington Park** was originally Kennington Common. In the 18th and 19th centuries, preachers – among them John Wesley – addressed large audiences here. The nearby **Foster's Oval** (*see p325*) is the home of Surrey County Cricket Club.

The continuation of Kennington Lane beyond the junction with Kennington Road brings you to some of south London's most delightful streets: **Cardigan Street**, **Courtney Street** and **Courtney Square** are lined with clean, neat, light-brown terraced houses, all dating from 1914. The rather unexpected glimpse of the Palace of Westminster from Cardigan Road is a reminder of how close the area is to central London.

Vauxhall lies between Kennington and the Thames. The wasteland bounded by Tyers Street, Goding Street and Glasshouse Walk is all that remains of the 18th-century pleasure park, **Vauxhall Gardens**. Henry Fielding's novel *Amelia* and Thackeray's *Vanity Fair* give a taste of the Gardens at their peak; these days, it's a depressing adjunct to any trip south.

Imperial War Museum

Lambeth Road, SE1 (7416 5000/www.iwm.org.uk). Lambeth North tube/Elephant & Castle tube/rail. **Open** 10am-6pm daily. **Admission** £5.50; £4.50 concessions; £2.75 disabled; free under-16s, OAPs. Free for all 4.30-6pm daily. **Credit** AmEx, MC, V. **Map** p404 N10.

The early 19th century's most famous lunatic asylum, known as Bedlam, now houses the country's memorial to the wars of the 20th century. A rotating clock-hand in the basement symbolises the cost of war in terms of human lives, an estimated body count that has already passed 100 million.

In the vast atrium, you can see pristine restored and cut-away examples of a selection of hardware, including a Polaris, a V2 rocket and a Spitfire. The museum has recently had a £17 million five-storey extension that now houses a two-floor permanent exhibition on the Holocaust. The documents, artefacts, photographs and survivors' testimonies make for a moving display.

The lower ground floor galleries hold the excellent four-part permanent exhibition of the history of warfare in the 20th century. Two of the most popular 'experiences' are The Blitz and The Trench, which do a good job of bringing history to life while avoiding vicarious thrills. Secret War, on the first floor, attempts to shed light on the clandestine world of espionage from 1909 to the present day. Exhibits range from Brezhnev's uniform to an original German 'Enigma' encrypting machine. The second floor is devoted to art collections, including the huge

Buy or sell at **Brixton Market**.

Gassed painted in 1919 by John Singer Sargent, and works by CRW Nevinson and Stanley Spencer.

Temporary exhibition-wise, the 1940s House display, with its full-scale recreation of a typical wartime home, has proved popular and had its run extended to the end of August 2001. A hands-on exhibition, aimed particularly at children, looking at the history of British submarines opens in April 2001, and a Spanish Civil War exhibition starts in October.

Brixton

Brixton has existed for around a thousand years, of which the first 985 or so were relatively uneventful. The small settlement in the early 19th century underwent development between the 1860s and 1890s, as railways and trams linked it with the heart of London. At the turn of the century, the character of Brixton began to alter, as large houses built 100 years earlier were turned into flats and boarding houses popular with theatre people.

Brixton's ethnic identity changed during the 1940s and '50s, with the arrival of immigrants from the West Indies. A generation later, economic decline and hostility between the black community and the police led to the riots of 1981, 1985 and 1995. Yet today, the mood in Brixton is ostensibly upbeat. Problems (particularly drug-related) certainly remain, and this contributes to a volatile edge that's prone to sparking up now and again. But an influx of youngish, middle-class residents with a bit of money to burn has fuelled some of the nightlife enterprises that continue to spring up around the centre of Brixton, and given it a rather cool kudos.

By day, Brixton is fairly unassuming but after work things ease into their stride. Cinema-goers congregate outside the Ritzy (*see p292*), and drinking and dancing joints such as the Dogstar (*see p226*), the Isobar and the Fridge Bar (*see p281*) start to fill, while Fujiyama and the Satay Bar get their first cocktail- and saki-sipping, noodle- and rice-eating punters. Food options include the crypt-ensconced vegetarian Bah Humbug (*see p215*) and the exemplary Caribbean cuisine of the rum-soaked Brixtonian Havana Club (*see p192*).

That said, though, much of the area is still run-down and grimy. Emerging from the tube station to a chorus of shouts from incense-sellers, *Big Issue* vendors, drunks and the multitude of religious groups with a hankering for a hold on your soul can be quite a shock for the unwary. There's plenty more noise, chaos and colour in evidence in **Brixton Market** (*see p252*), which offers the widest selection of African and Caribbean food in Europe, as well as everything from wigs to ironing boards. It sprawls between Electric Avenue and Brixton

Station Road. The former was so named in the 1880s when it became the first street in the area to be lit by electricity. More serene attractions of the area include hilly **Brockwell Park**, 15 minutes' walk from the tube, with its 1930s-built lido (*see below* **Bathe in glory**).

Clapham

Clapham has two centres: **Clapham Junction**, technically part of Battersea, and **Clapham Common**. Until the railways arrived, Clapham Junction was a country crossroads, with the Falcon providing refreshment for travellers. Nowadays, it offers respite for shoppers: the department store opposite, **Arding & Hobbs**, has been serving the area since 1885. With more than 2,500 trains passing through every day, Clapham Junction is one of the busiest stations in the world.

Northcote Road, which heads south, is awash with shops, bars and restaurants, plus a fine market. **Battersea Rise**, leading towards

the Common, is an arty stretch, also with a huge choice of eateries. The road eventually becomes **Clapham Common North Side**, the eastern reaches of which contain tall, stately houses with enviable views of the Common. A flat, grassy expanse within a triangle of roads, **Clapham Common** is somewhere between a park and a wild place; its bleak atmosphere has never been more vividly evoked than in Graham Greene's *The End of the Affair*. After dark, parts of the Common become gay cruising grounds.

The streets around the north end of Clapham Common have rapidly poshed up with fine new bars and restaurants, perhaps to try and compete with **Clapham Old Town**, just north-east of the Common. This latter spot, despite being a little snobby, is worth a visit, if only to take in the villagey atmosphere. At its central point, attractive 18th-century pubs face on to an approximate square (complete with a small, countryish bus terminus). The 88 bus, rather self-consciously styled 'The Clapham Omnibus', starts its pleasantly circuitous route from here.

Bathe in glory

Lidos were once a major part of London life, an echo of a time when Romans introduced bathing for pleasure. There are few left now, but perhaps the best and certainly the hippest is the **Brockwell Lido**, on the fringes of one of south London's loveliest leafy expanses, Brockwell Park.

Brockwell Lido – the word 'lido', incidentally, is derived from a 17th-century beach resort near Venice – was built in the 1930s amid a national mania for 'healthy public resorts'. It also provided relief on rare hot summer days for those who could not travel to the coast. The fitness craze of the '30s soon gave way to wartime restraint and the popularity of lidos fell. But by the '50s, the tide had turned, and the masses came out to bathe in the post-war boom.

When Thatcher's Britain tightened the screws on council coffers, dozens of lidos closed and fell into disrepair. Between 1984 and 1994, ten shut in London alone, the closure of Brockwell Lido leaving 250,000 Lambeth borough residents without a major outdoor recreation area. In 1993, squatters moved in and gave the empty pool shell a new lease of life as a venue for alternative parties, concerts, theatre performances and even film screenings.

A year later, two former council employees struck a deal with the Lambeth Council to

reopen the lido on a seven-year lease. They pulled the weeds, spruced up the changing rooms and introduced night swimming and theme dinner nights in the wonderful art deco Brixton Beach Café. In addition, a winter programme was put in place, including music and drama courses for children, massage, yoga and meditation.

The community came back in droves. On hot summer days, up to 2,000 people passed through the turnstiles. Dreadlocked Brixton boys strutted alongside high-ranking Dulwich public servants, single mothers and their children splashed in the 50-metre pool, and gays soaked up the sunshine amid women bathing topless.

With the lease due to expire in May 2001, the future of the complex was unclear as this guide was being prepared. The lido's management was in negotiations with the council in a bid to keep open what has again become one of the few truly communal meeting points in South London. Here's hoping they succeed.

Brockwell Lido

Dulwich Road, Herne Hill, SE24 (7274 3088/ www.thelido.co.uk). Herne Hill rail. **Open** *May-Sept 6.45-10am; noon-7pm Mon-Fri; 11am-7pm Sat, Sun.* **Admission** *Morning* £2; £1.50 children. *Afternoon* £4; £2.50 children.

Natural high: **Wetland Centre**. *See p176.*

Holy Trinity Church, on the edge of the common, was known in the 19th century as the HQ of the Clapham Sect, a group of wealthy Anglicans – among them William Wilberforce, the anti-slavery campaigner – who advocated 'muscular Christianity'. The church was rebuilt after being hit by a V2 in 1945.

Battersea

In Saxon times, **Battersea** was a small settlement known as Batrices Ege (Badric's Island), bounded by the Thames to the north and marshes to the south. Known for centuries as a centre for market gardening – part of it is still called Lavender Hill – the character of Battersea changed dramatically with the Industrial Revolution. In the 19th century, scores of factories sprang up, and the area was covered by a dense network of railway lines.

Battersea is still best approached by rail. The journey from Victoria station will give you the greatest view of its best-known landmark, Sir Giles Gilbert Scott's gargantuan **Battersea Power Station** (built 1929-33). Closed in 1983, it has been subject to innumerable development plans in recent years, but in late 2000, Parkview International was finally granted planning permission to convert it into a vast riverside business and entertainment complex including 6,500 square metres of office space, 700 hotel rooms, a 2,000-seat theatre, a multiplex cinema and residential accommodation.

Battersea has long been a favourite spot for artists and writers: the old **Battersea Bridge** was the subject of Whistler's moody *Nocturnes*; Turner used to paint the river and its sunsets from **St Mary's Battersea**. **Battersea Park** (8871 7530), meanwhile, has a bloody history: in 1671 Colonel Blood hid in reeds near what is now the boating lake, waiting to shoot King Charles II as he bathed (Blood's nerve failed him); and in 1829, the Duke of Wellington

fought a pistol duel here with Lord Winchilsea, who had accused him of treason for introducing the Catholic Emancipation Bill.

Opened as a park in 1858 by Queen Victoria, it was conceived as a means of keeping the lower orders orderly with healthful recreation. These days its patrons are more mixed, though still generally well behaved. Its most famous feature, **Festival Gardens**, was one of the attractions of the 1951 Festival of Britain. There are sports facilities and playgrounds, a boating lake, a café, a children's zoo, Bank Holiday funfairs and other events throughout the year. The Peace Pagoda by the Thames was built by Japanese monks and nuns in 1985 to commemorate Hiroshima Day. A massive £12-million restoration includes the restoration of the sub-tropical gardens, the elegant promenade along the Thames and the Festival Gardens.

Putney, Barnes, Mortlake & Kew

Originally a fishing and farming community, **Putney** ('Putta's landing') can claim to be London's first suburb. Thomas Cromwell was the most senior among the scores of Tudor courtiers who bought homes in the village and travelled to their jobs in the royal palaces around west London. Away from the narrow, busy High Street, it's a peaceful spot, especially if you head west from the bridge along the Embankment, with its ubiquitous canoe trailers hitched to Land Rovers. The annual **Boat Race** (*see p261*) is held between here and Mortlake.

Striking inland across the base of the Putney peninsula eventually brings you to **Mortlake**. On the main road, Queen's Ride, crosses a railway line at **Barnes Common**. On the western side of the humpbacked bridge, there's a spindly tree invariably decorated with flowers and other offerings to Marc Bolan. On 16 September 1977, the T-Rex singer's Mini collided with the tree, killing him instantly. Since May 2000, Barnes has also been the setting for the **WWT Wetland Centre** (*see p176*), a unique mosaic of wetland habitats created from scratch from the Thames Water Barn Elm reservoirs and water works.

Kew is all but synonymous with **Kew Gardens** (more properly known as the **Royal Botanic Gardens**; *see p176*), the world's principal botanical research centre. Lichfield Road takes you to Kew Road and one of the gardens' entrances. A few hundred metres to the north is the old-fashioned Maids of Honour tea shop (288 Kew Road), with its fine home-made cakes and pastries, **Kew Green**, with

Sightseeing

its cricket ground surrounded by pubs, and, in a corner, long, low, elegant **St Anne's Church**, built for Queen Anne in 1714. Its interior, with fine stained glass, is superbly clear and bright.

Royal Botanic Gardens (Kew Gardens)

Richmond, Surrey (8332 5000/recorded information 8940 1171/www.rbgkew.org.uk). Kew Gardens tube/rail/Kew Bridge rail/riverboat to Kew Pier. **Open** 9.30am daily; closing times vary according to time of year: 4.30pm midwinter-7.30pm midsummer. **Admission** £5 adults; £3.50 concessions; £2.50 5-16s; £13 family; free under-5s. **Credit** MC, V.

Covering a 120-hectare (300-acre) site next to the Thames, Kew Gardens is filled with every imaginable variety of tree, shrub and flower. The gardens were developed in the 17th and 18th centuries in the grounds of the 17th-century Dutch-style **Kew Palace** (closed for restoration until at least early 2002) and were landscaped by 'Capability' Brown. In the late 18th century, under the direction of Sir Joseph Banks, botanists collected specimens from all continents to be planted at Kew to form the basis of the gardens' extraordinary botanical collections. It's now a world-renowned centre for horticultural research and boasts the world's largest collection of orchids. A good option for first-time visitors is to take the 'Kew Explorer' road train from its stop by the Victoria Gate for a 35-minute tour of the gardens. The Explorer stops at all the main sights and a ticket (£2.50; £1.50 concessions) can be used to hop on and off throughout the day.

Among the gardens' highlights are its immense glasshouses, the most famous of which is the steamy **Palm House** (Decimus Burton and Richard Turner, 1848), the finest surviving glass-and-iron structure in the country. Climb to the gallery for a bird's eye view of the dense, dripping foliage, or descend to a display of marine life in the basement. From here, Cherry Walk leads to the **Temperate House** (also by Burton), the largest ornamental glasshouse in the world. The specimens are arranged geographically and include the world's largest indoor plant, the Chilean wine-palm. Near the gardens' main gate, the impressive **Princess of Wales Conservatory** recreates ten different climates for a dizzying variety of species.

In addition to the glasshouses, don't miss the **Marianne North Gallery**, which displays paintings by this extraordinary Victorian artist and traveller; the **Great Pagoda** by William Chambers (1762) near the Lion Gate; and the **Japanese Gateway & Landscape**. Located opposite the Palm House, Museum No.1 houses the **Plants & People** exhibition, exploring humankind's reliance on plants. There are also numerous cafés, restaurants and shops dotted around the gardens. To enjoy Kew at its best, however, wander along pathways away from the more obvious tourist attractions, enjoying the views from the **Riverside Walk** or the seclusion of the woods at the south-west end.

In 2001, Kew will host a Japanese garden festival in the summer, an autumn harvest festival, and a range of Christmas activities.

WWT Wetland Centre

Queen Elizabeth's Walk, SW13 (8409 4400/ www.wetlandcentre.org.uk). Hammersmith tube, then 33, 72, 209, 283 bus/Barnes rail then 33, 72 bus. **Open** *Apr-Sept* 9.30am-6pm daily. *Oct-Mar* 9.30am-5pm daily (last entry 1hr prior to closing). **Admission** £6.75; £5.50 OAPs; £5.25 students; £4.25 under-16s. **Credit** MC, V.

Created by the Wildfowl and Wetlands Trust (WWT) on the site of four redundant Thames Water reservoirs, the Wetland Centre is a unique 422-hectare (105-acre) complex of lakes, reedbeds, ponds, grasslands and mudflats that attracts an abundance of birds and other wildlife. Londoners who don't 'do' the countryside will be reassured by the tarmacked paths and interactive displays in the two wetland exhibition areas, while serious birdwatchers will twitch with delight at the prospect of observing more than 130 species of birds ducking and diving in the wild reserve. The Peter Scott Visitors' Centre houses a discovery centre, a gallery, a shop and a café, while the Observatory affords a stunning view of the main lake. CCTV screens and hides allow a closer look at our feathered friends in action.

Wimbledon

Just as most people think of Kew as its gardens, most non-Londoners equate **Wimbledon** with its two-week tennis tournament (*see p324* **Netting a Wimbledon ticket**) or with the cuddly, litter-collecting Wombles. For the rest of the year, the place is left to its own devices. **Wimbledon Broadway** is dominated by the huge **Centre Court** shopping centre, and, further east, **Wimbledon Theatre**, an entertaining example of Edwardian architecture at its most feverish.

Points mean prizes at **Wimbledon**. See p177.

Beyond lies **Wimbledon Common**, a huge, partially wooded expanse, criss-crossed with paths and horse tracks; it's easy to get lost here. The windmill towards the north-east corner dates from 1817; Baden-Powell wrote part of *Scouting for Boys* while living in it during 1908. The museum it now houses is closed during winter, though the large tearoom is open all year round. **Putney Vale Cemetery**, in the north-east corner of the Common (accessible from Roehampton Vale), is one of the largest graveyards in London. Lillie Langtry was buried here in 1929.

On the east side of the common, the disused **Bluegate Gravel Pit** forms an idyllic lake, whose peace and quiet is barely disturbed by the murmur of traffic on Parkside. Cross the road and go down Calonne Road to discover Wimbledon's biggest surprise. Amid prime south London suburbia (all pre-war villas and new Rovers at rest) is a fully fledged Thai Buddhist temple, the **Buddhapadipa Temple**. Visitors are free to look around (1-6pm Sat; 8.30-10.30am, 12.30-6pm, Sun). Close by is the All England Lawn Tennis Club and the **Wimbledon Lawn Tennis Museum** (*see below*). Next door, **Wimbledon Park** has public tennis courts and a large boating lake.

Wimbledon Lawn Tennis Museum

Centre Court, All England Lawn Tennis Club, Church Road, SW19 (8946 6131/ www.wimbledon.org/museum). Southfields tube/39, 93, 200 bus. **Open** 10.30am-5pm daily; spectators only during championships. **Admission** £5; £4 concessions; free under-5s. **Credit** MC, V.

From the lawns of Victorian England to the multi-million pound sport of today, more than 150 years of social and sporting history are encapsulated in this well designed museum. More interesting than the rows of cases filled with racquets and balls are a mock-up of an Edwardian tennis party and the section on tennis since 1968, with touch-screen commentaries on past and present stars and videos of past championships. The place is packed with unusual information, but only fanatics will thrill at the array of personal memorabilia, such as some of Pat Cash's headbands and Boris Becker's autograph.

Richmond

It's not so difficult to envisage **Richmond** as the busy, cramped English country town it once was, though the rural calm has long since been supplanted by heavy traffic and the roar of low-flying jets approaching Heathrow. Until the early 16th century, the whole area was called Sheen, receiving its new name when Henry VII acquired the local manor house and named it after his earldom in Yorkshire. Elizabeth I spent the last few summers of her life at Richmond and died there in 1603, but Richmond Palace fell into neglect, and all that remains is a gateway on **Richmond Green**. Bigger and rather less appealing than Kew Green, but enlivened at one end by the twin-cupola'd Richmond Theatre, it's best reached from alley-like **Brewer's Lane**, with its rows of antique shops. The church of St Mary Magdalene, in Paradise Road, is worth a look for its combination of architectural styles dating from 1507 to 1904.

Despite its period look, **Richmond Riverside**, near **Richmond Bridge**, was built in the 1980s, the mock Georgian-style façades concealing ordinary offices and flats. The Victorian town hall houses the library, tourist office and the **Museum of Richmond** (*see below*). But ultimately, Richmond is a place for enjoying the Great Outdoors. With the exception of Epping Forest, **Richmond Park** is the last vestige of the great oak forests that surrounded London until medieval times. It's ideal for rambling, cycling and riding, and is also home to much wildlife, most famously red and fallow deer (*see p178* **Oh, deer**). Notable buildings in the park include **Pembroke Lodge** (now a café), the childhood home of philosopher Bertrand Russell, and the fine Palladian villa, **White Lodge**. Don't miss the exquisite **Isabella Plantation**, a woodland haven landscaped with a stream, ponds and spectacular floral displays.

In 1727, the poet James Thomson exclaimed of **Richmond Hill**: 'Heavens! What a goodly perspective spreads around, of hills and dales and woods and lawns and spires and glittering towns and gilded streams.' The view has changed little, except that the glittering towns have merged to form a glittering city. Close to the top of Richmond Hill, the **Terrace Gardens** descend steeply towards the river. If the river isn't flooding, follow its course towards **Petersham** and **Ham**. The Thames is at its most tranquil here and, in the early morning and evening, **Petersham Meadows** are impossibly pastoral: brown cattle grazing on water meadows beside the misty river.

Museum of Richmond

Old Town Hall, Whittaker Avenue, Richmond, Surrey (8332 1141/www.museumofrichmond.com). Richmond tube/rail. **Open** *May-Sept* 11am-5pm Tue-Sat; 1-4pm Sun; closed Mon. *Nov-Apr* 11am-5pm Tue-Sat; closed Mon, Sun. **Admission** £2; £1 concessions; free under-16s. **No credit cards.**

The focus may be on Richmond's popularity as a royal resort, but this museum also traces the area's history from its role as a prehistoric settlement (weapons and other implements frequently turn up in the river) to life in the town during World War II. The staff are friendly and well informed.

Further south

Following the Thames south from Richmond (a delightful walk or bike ride) takes you close to a clutch of fine country villas. **Marble Hill House** and neighbouring **Orleans House** square up across the river to **Ham House** (for both, *see below*). Past **Twickenham** (home to the **Museum of Rugby**; *see p179*) is Horace Walpole's idiosyncratic home, **Strawberry Hill**, before the river reaches the busy shopping centre of **Kingston** and curves around to **Hampton Court Palace** (*see below*).

Ham House

Ham, Richmond, Surrey (8940 1950/ www.nationaltrust.org.uk/southern). Richmond tube/rail, then 371 bus. **Open** *House Apr-Oct 1-5pm Mon-Wed, Sat, Sun; closed Thur, Fri. Nov-Mar closed. Gardens 11am-6pm/dusk Mon-Wed, Sat, Sun; closed Thur, Fri.* **Admission** £6; £3 5-15s; £15 family. *Garden only* £2; 75p 5-15s. **Credit** AmEx, MC, V.
The uniqueness of this handsome, red-brick, riverside mansion is due to the original 17th-century furniture, paintings and decor that still adorn its rooms. From the house, water meadows lead down to the Thames, while the formal gardens are currently being restored to their original state. Part of the grounds is known as the wilderness, an area that is in fact a carefully planted, almost maze-like section, divided into garden rooms.

Hampton Court Palace

East Molesey, Surrey (8781 9500/www.hrp.org.uk). Hampton Court rail/riverboat from Westminster or Richmond to Hampton Court Pier (Apr-Oct). **Open** *Palace Apr-Oct 10.15am-6pm Mon; 9.30am-6pm Tue-Sun. Nov-Mar 10.15am-4.30pm Mon; 9.30am-4.30pm Tue-Sun (last entry 45mins before closing). Park dawn-dusk daily.* **Admission** *Palace, courtyard, cloister & maze* £10.50; £7 5-15s; £8 concessions; £31.40 family; free under 5s. *Maze only* £2.50; £1.60 5-15s. **Credit** AmEx, MC, V.
Yup, it's pricey, but, as you can easily spend the best part of a day wandering the corridors and gardens of Hampton Court, it's also value for money. In 1514, the powerful Cardinal Wolsey started to build up Hampton Court as his country seat. After his fall from favour in 1529, Henry VIII took over the palace, adding the fabulous vaulted ceiling of the **Chapel Royal**, which took 100 men nine months to complete. In the 1690s, William and Mary commissioned Wren to rebuild the **State Apartments** in classical

Oh, deer

On a stroll through the vast wilds of **Richmond Park**, you'll probably pass cyclists, joggers, horseriders and beer drinkers. All before 11am. The park boasts 12 kilometres of 'shared use leisure path', a pony school and a public golf course, but it's primarily famous for the families of deer that roam around its 1,012 hectares (2,500 acres), oblivious to human recreation. In fact, if bucks, does and roes are not chilling out among the oaks or feeding in the ferns, they're stopping the traffic to cross the road and visit fellow herds. Road signs give the deer right of way, clearly indicating that they are the presiding monarchs in this royal park.

The park itself, a blissfully under-exploited gem cushioned comfortably between Richmond, Ham, Sheen, Kingston and Roehampton, was created in 1637, when Charles I, who had a passion for hunting, took it upon himself to enclose a great tract of countryside as his own personal hunting park. Thankfully, obstinate locals, who resented the loss of such a large amount of land, fought the king through the courts and he was eventually forced to grant public access to the park. It's said that resentment resulting from this incident was a factor in the decision to execute the king 10 years later.

With the trigger-happy Charles out of the way, the deer were safe and soon became a dominant feature of the landscape. Despite the abundance of wildlife – badgers, rabbits and even parrots – that inhabits the huge and tranquil expanse of parkland, none draws such a crowd as the antlered population. But nature-lovers and dogs, be warned: in mid- to late autumn, the rutting season begins and it becomes unwise to approach the deer. Signs are posted to remind visitors to steer clear of the ruminants themselves and not to allow dogs, as it quaintly puts it, to 'worry' the deer.

Richmond Park was declared a Site of Special Scientific Interest in 1992 and designated a National Nature Reserve in May 2000, meaning that the deer can now, once and for all, sleep easy. It's ironic that Charles's enclosure of the area, done for the purpose of hunting deer and seen as tyrannical at the time, has undoubtedly helped prevent a retail park springing up here in later years, and has ultimately ensured the preservation of the site and its inhabitants.

Richmond Park

Richmond, Surrey (8948 3209). Richmond tube/rail, then 371 bus. **Open** *Mar-Sept 7am-dusk daily. Oct-Feb 7.30am-dusk daily.*

Hampton Court Palace.
Gritty and urban it ain't. *See p178.*

Renaissance style (the **King's Apartments**, badly damaged by fire in 1986, have been restored).

Sensibly, the palace has been split into six bite-size tours. Highlights include the Henry VIII's hammer-beam-roofed **Great Hall**, **Renaissance Picture Gallery**, and the **Tudor Kitchens**. The latter is the most fun part of the whole palace, as period-dressed minions make 16th-century dishes, turn meat on a spit and chat to visitors. Elsewhere, costumed guides lead tours and there's foolery several times a day in **Clock Court**, overlooked by the magnificent Astronomical Clock, made for Henry VIII in 1540 by Nicholas Oursian.

The extensive gardens are an attraction in themselves. Look out for the **Great Vine**, which is the oldest-known vine in the world. It was probably planted by 'Capability' Brown around 1770 and still produces an annual crop of 230-320kg (500-700lbs) of black grapes, sold to visitors. Another must-see, or rather, must-get-lost-in, is the famous maze.

Marble Hill House

Richmond Road, Twickenham, Middx (8892 5115/ www.english-heritage.org.uk). Richmond tube/rail/ 33, 90, 290, H22, R70 bus. **Open** *Apr-Oct 10am-6pm daily. Nov-Mar 10am-4pm Wed-Sun, closed Mon, Tue.* **Admission** *£3.30; £2.50 concessions; £1.70 5-15s; free under 5s.* **Credit** MC, V.

Marble Hill House, overlooking the Thames in Marble Hill Park, is a perfect Palladian villa. It was built for Henrietta Howard, the mistress of George II, and later occupied by Mrs Fitzherbert, George IV's secret wife. The interior Cube Hall has beautiful moulded decoration, and the house has been immaculately restored with original Georgian furnishings and paintings. On Sunday evenings in summer, there are concerts in the park (*see p309*).

Museum of Rugby/ Twickenham Stadium

Gate K, Twickenham Rugby Stadium, Rugby Road, Twickenham, Middx (8892 8877/www.rfu.com). Hounslow East tube, then 281 bus/Twickenham rail. **Open** *Museum 10am-5pm Tue-Sat; 2-5pm Sun (last entry 4.30pm); closed Mon. Tours 10.30am, noon, 1.30pm, 3pm Tue-Sat; 3pm Sun.* **Admission** *Combined ticket £6; £4 concessions; £19 family.* **Credit** MC, V.

Fans of the game will find lots to interest and delight them in this carefully collated and beautifully presented museum. Rugby tots will enjoy the interactive exhibits, including a real scrum machine, while old-timers can listen to early radio commentary and muse on the days when players still wore bow ties. The highlight, however, is the excellent stadium tour: it's hard to be unimpressed by the stunning view from the top of the North Stand, and diehard fans will be thrilled by the chance to run through the players' tunnel onto the hallowed turf.

Orleans House

Riverside, Twickenham, Middx (8892 0221/ www.richmond.gov.uk/depts/opps/leisure/arts/ orleanshouse). St Margaret's rail. **Open** *Apr-Sept 1-5.30pm Tue-Sat; 2-5.30pm Sun; closed Mon. Oct-Mar 1-4.30pm Tue-Sat; 2-4.30pm Sun, closed Mon.* **Admission** free.

Built in 1710 for James Johnston, William III's secretary of state for Scotland, this was later home to the exiled Duke of Orléans, hence the name. The building was demolished in 1926, with the exception of the Octagon, an eight-sided turret that had formed part of the west wing. A gallery was subsequently built on the site of the main house, and both it and the Octagon are used for exhibitions.

West London

Forget the tinseltown fantasy, and find out if west is really best.

Paddington & Bayswater

Maps p394 & p395
Bayswater, Lancaster Gate or Queensway tube/
Paddington tube/rail.

The name Paddington derives from the ancient Anglo-Saxon chieftain Padda, but most contemporary Londoners associate the area, which sits to the north of Hyde Park, with the railway station and its magnificent cathedral-like iron girder roof, designed by Isambard Kingdom Brunel in 1851. It was the building of the station, along with the Grand Junction Canal (1801), that precipitated the population boom in Paddington and Bayswater in the mid-19th century: the area was previously considered off residential limits thanks to the infamous Tyburn gallows near present-day Marble Arch.

Despite another dip in fortune in the early 20th century, when the district became synonymous with prostitution, poverty and neglect, Bayswater and Paddington are now relatively prosperous, owing to their centrality and the popularity of their classic Victorian stuccoed townhouses. There's also an agreeably cosmopolitan ambience thanks to Middle Eastern, Greek and Jewish communities. But although tourist hotels and hostels abound, the **Alexander Fleming Laboratory Museum** (*see below*) in St Mary's Hospital is as close as the area comes to conventional attractions. The station itself was given a new lease of life a couple of years ago by an ambitious £63 million overhaul, the centrepiece of which is the Lawn, a swanky glass-and-steel space with shops, cafés and airline check-in desks for passengers taking the Heathrow Express (*see p356*).

Queensway is the heart of Bayswater, but, despite some decent restaurants (particularly Chinese; *see p192*), it's a bit of a gaudy tourist trap. The palatial Whiteley's mall labours under the ignominy of being one of Adolf Hitler's favourite buildings, but it makes up for this with a number of cafés, an eight-screen cinema (*see p292*) and an assortment of shops.

A left turn at the north end of Queensway opens up the richer pickings of **Westbourne Grove**, where there are some excellent Middle Eastern and African eateries such as the Sudanese Mandola (*see p212*). As the road continues westward towards Portobello Road and Notting Hill, antique shops begin

Little Venice. *See p181.*

to proliferate. Look out also for London's most stylish public toilet (a big green-tiled triangular structure), complete with its own upmarket flower stall, Wild at Heart (*see p242*), at the junction with **Colville Road**.

Alexander Fleming Laboratory Museum

St Mary's Hospital, Praed Street, W2 (7725 6528). Paddington tube/rail/7, 15, 27, 36 bus. **Open** 10am-1pm Mon-Thur. *By appointment* also 2-5pm Mon-Thur; 10am-5pm Fri. **Admission** £2; £1 concessions. **No credit cards. Map** p395 D5.

On 3 September 1928, when a Petri dish of bacteria became contaminated with a mysterious mould, Alexander Fleming realised something peculiar was going on. His chance discovery of penicillin had momentous consequences, and this re-creation (in the very same room) of his laboratory is backed up with displays and a video providing insights into his life and the role of penicillin in the fight against disease.

Maida Vale, Kilburn & Queen's Park

Kilburn, Kilburn Park, Maida Vale, Queen's Park or Warwick Avenue tube.

North of the divisive Westway lie Edgware Road, Maida Vale, Kilburn and Queen's Park. **Edgware Road** follows the course of ancient Watling Street, a traffic-clogged thoroughfare redeemed only by some of London's best kebab shops courtesy of the thriving local Middle Eastern community (try Patogh; *see p204*).

Maida Vale, named after the British victory against the French at the Battle of Maida in southern Italy in 1806, is an affluent area characterised by Edwardian purpose-built flats, and prettified immeasurably by the locks around **Little Venice**. You can walk from here along the canals to **London Zoo** (*see p271*), or even take a boat. **Kilburn High Road**, meanwhile, is well known for its pubs, patronised primarily by Irish expats. Kilburn is also a good place for bargain shopping, and its mainly Afro-Caribbean and Irish populations are well served by one of London's more enterprising local arts complexes, the Tricycle (*see p335*). Slightly further north, **Queen's Park** is a sanctuary away from the bedlam of Kilburn High Road and offers a children's playground, a pitch-and-putt golf course beside six well-maintained hard tennis courts, and a good café.

Notting Hill

Map p394

Notting Hill Gate or Westbourne Park tube.

Despite its depiction in the movie named after it, and the subsequent wave of tourists and arthouse sorts that it's attracted, Notting Hill is still one of London's best places for weekend strolling. It's easy to find your space among the media whores and bohemian roués, and there's plenty of potential for eating, drinking and sipping chai in this trendy enclave.

But it was not ever thus. Until a wave of white stuccoed buildings mapped out Notting Hill in the early and mid-1800s, there was little but piggeries in the area (the racecourse that once stood on what is now the corner of Kensington Park Gardens and Ladbroke Grove having been closed after only a few years). But the district's fortunes declined in the 20th century, becoming solidly white and working class until the 1950s, when an influx of West Indian immigrants were forced to live in hideous properties owned by slum landlord Peter Rachman. Riots, incited by white racists, followed in 1958, and it was only in the late 1980s that the area became prosperous again.

Notting Hill Gate itself is little more than a busy through road, although it does boast two cinemas: the Gate and the Notting Hill Coronet (for both, *see p292*), the latter being one of the last cinemas in London where you can smoke. Around the corner on Pembridge Road over the Prince Albert pub is the tiny Gate Theatre (*see p335*), one of the best pub-theatres in town.

However, when people talk about Notting Hill they really mean **Portobello Road**. This narrow, snaking thoroughfare, most famed for its market (*see p255*) and antique shops, forms the spine of the neighbourhood. There are cafés, bars, restaurants, curiosity shops and delis, many of which have been patronised by the same people for decades. The section around Westbourne Park Road and Talbot Road, together with the northern end of Kensington Park Road, was made famous and, perhaps, now destroyed by the Hugh Grant/Julia Roberts film. Further up Portobello Road, under the Westway, there is a massive free-for-all flea market of modish second-hand clothes, shoes and accessories on Fridays and Saturdays.

At the north end of Portobello Road past another series of cafés lies **Golborne Road**, a great place to buy Portuguese and Moroccan groceries and patisserie. The other main feature of Golborne Road is Trellick Tower, seen as a hideous carbuncle by some and by others as a seminal piece of modern architecture. Built in 1973 by Ernst Goldfinger (Ian Fleming hated his

Sightseeing

Kensal Green Cemetery. *See p182.*

work so much he used his name for the notorious Bond villain), it was the tallest residential block in the country at the time, and is distinguished by a separate lift shaft linked to the main building by concrete corridors. (*See also p149* **2 Willow Road**.)

Up at the top of Ladbroke Grove, past the gigantic Sainsbury's superstore, is Kensal Green Cemetery on Harrow Road. Opened in 1833, it's a huge and beautiful resting-place for many a famous Londoner: Thackeray, Trollope and Brunel, were joined in 1997 by London's most celebrated drinker, Jeffrey Bernard.

Kensington & Holland Park

Maps p394-p397
High Street Kensington or Holland Park tube.

No doubt to the delight of its heritage-conscious upper-class residents, Kensington is mentioned in the Domesday Book of 1086. In the 17th century the district grew up around Holland House (1606) and Campden House (1612) and was described by one historian in 1705 as a place 'inhabited by gentry and persons of note, with an abundance of shopkeepers and artificers'. This is still the case with both aspects of Kensington in evidence around the **High Street**. A lively mix of chain stores and individual shops stretches along the busy main road while the nearby streets and squares are lined by large townhouses. The most famous of the squares, **Kensington Square**, sports a generous display of plaques denoting residents of distinction, such as William Makepeace Thackeray (no.16) and John Stuart Mill (no.18).

Kensington Square is just behind the art deco splendour of Barker's department store (built 1905-13). Next door, on the sixth floor of the former Derry & Toms, is one of Europe's largest roof gardens (accessed from the entrance on Derry Street). Over the road from here, at the foot of **Kensington Church Street**, is the church of St Mary Abbots, distinguished by the tallest steeple in London (85 metres, or 250 feet) and the secluded gardens to its rear.

Kensington Market was finally closed in 2000, leaving a gap in the body-jewellery and second-hand jeans market. Opposite the site is trendy store Urban Outfitters (*see p237*), and in nearby Kensington Church Street there's an array of antique shops. And further west down the High Street there's an Odeon cinema, opposite which, behind a small wood of flagpoles, lurks the Commonwealth Institute, a monument to flimsy 1950s design.

Behind the Institute is **Holland Park**, one of the most romantic parks in London. Beautiful woods and formal gardens surround the reconstructed Jacobean **Holland House**, named after an early owner, Sir Henry, Earl of Holland. The house suffered serious bomb damage during World War II and only the ground floor and arcades survived; the restored east wing contains the most romantically sited youth hostel in town, while the summer ballroom has been converted into a stylish contemporary restaurant, the Belvedere. Open-air theatre and opera under an elegant canopy are staged in the park during the summer (*see p335*), and for children, there's an adventure playground with tree-walks and rope swings, while tame rabbits, squirrels and peacocks patrol the grounds. The Kyoto Japanese Garden provides a tranquil retreat from the action.

Among the historic houses worth a visit are **Leighton House** (*see below*), the 19th-century home of the painter Lord Leighton. However, Linley Sambourne House, home of Edward Linley Sambourne, cartoonist for the satirical magazine *Punch*, is closed for a couple of years.

Leighton House
12 Holland Park Road, W14 (7602 3316). High Street Kensington tube. **Open** 11am-5.30pm Mon,Wed-Sun; closed Tue. **Admission** free; donations appreciated.
Located on a quiet Kensington side street, Leighton House was designed by one-time president of the Royal Academy, Frederic Lord Leighton (1864-79), in collaboration with George Aitchison. Leighton spent much of his life travelling the world, and it is from the East that the house takes most of its inspiration; its most striking feature is the exotic Arab Hall, added in 1879, and based on a Moorish palace in Palermo, Sicily. The audio tour gives an anecdote-filled insight into Leighton's life. A charge is levied for guided tours (noon Wed, Thur); phone for details.

Leighton, himself a distinguished artist, collected a variety of Victorian works of art by his contemporaries that are now on permanent display. The house also hosts a varied programme of temporary exhibitions throughout the year.

Earl's Court & Fulham

Maps p396 & p397
Earl's Court, Fulham Broadway or West Brompton tube.

Earl's Court changed from hamlet to built-up urban area with the arrival of the Metropolitan Railway in 1860, and from 1914 many of its imposing houses were subdivided into flats. To this day, it remains a district where many have lived but few have settled.

Once known as Kangaroo Valley, thanks to Antipodean trekkers seeking cheap rooms in its warren of bedsits and budget hotels, Earl's Court has always had a seedy, though not dangerous, reputation. In the late 1970s and

1980s it became the gay centre of London, with the action centering most famously on the Coleherne pub (on the corner of Brompton and Coleherne Roads). One of England's more famous dominatrixes, Lindy St Clair (aka Miss Whiplash), set up parlour on Eardley Crescent until bankrupted by the Inland Revenue. Freddie Mercury also lived around here, at Garden Lodge, 1 Logan Place, and Earl's Court retains a strong gay vibe. The area is, perhaps, more widely known as the site of the hulking **Exhibition Centre**, opposite the tube station. The 1937 structure, in its time the largest reinforced concrete building in Europe, was used as an internment camp in World War II.

The pleasantly laid-out **Brompton Cemetery** is sometimes exploited for sexual encounters (the proximity to graves presumably sharpening the experience), although an unmolested stroll, perhaps searching for the grave of Emmeline Pankhurst, is perfectly possible. The peace is only broken on Saturday afternoons when Chelsea FC are playing at home: the massive bulk of their Stamford Bridge stadium overlooks the tombs.

Neighbouring **Parsons Green** and **Fulham** are home to a more established and affluent population with aspirations of Chelsea living. Parsons Green is centred around a small green that once – of course – supported a parsonage. Residents will be relieved to know that it was considered the aristocratic part of Fulham even in 1705 when Bowack pronounced it to be inhabited by 'Gentry and persons of Quality'.

Despite the posh Hurlingham Sports Club and the Queen's (Tennis & Rackets) Club, which hosts the Stella Artois pre-Wimbledon tournament, there is one place in Fulham you can enter without a massive bank balance: **Fulham Palace** (*see below*). Next door, Bishop's Park offers beautiful leafy walks by the side of one of the prettiest stretches of the Thames.

Fulham Palace

Bishop's Avenue, off Fulham Palace Road, SW6 (7736 3233). Putney Bridge tube/220, 74 bus. **Open** *Museum Mar-Oct* 2-5pm Wed-Sun; closed Mon, Tue. *Nov-Feb* 1-4pm Thur-Sun; closed Mon-Wed. **Admission** *Museum* £1; 50p concessions; free under-16s. *Guided tours* £3; free under-16s.
From 704 until 1973, Fulham Palace was official residence of the Bishops of London. The present brick house is a mishmash of periods and architectural styles; the oldest part is from 1480, while William Butterfield's neo-Gothic chapel is relatively recent, dating from 1866. The quirky museum, which traces the building's history, counts a mummified rat among its exhibits. The lovely grounds are open daily, but to see the palace interior go on one of the informative tours, held twice a month in summer and monthly in winter (Sundays; phone for dates).

Shepherd's Bush & Hammersmith

Goldhawk Road, Hammersmith or Shepherd's Bush tube.

The approach to **Shepherd's Bush** from Holland Park Avenue is marked by Shepherd's Bush roundabout, with the Thames Water Tower springing out of its centre. The tower, which looks like a state-of-the-art toilet cistern, is in fact a 15-metre (50-foot) surge pipe for London's underground ring main. Designed by students at the Royal College of Art, it doubles as a huge barometer.

Shepherd's Bush Common once formed the centre of what was, 150 years ago, a 'pleasant village'. The name Shepherd is thought to be a personal one, but a more quaint story ascribes the origin of the name Shepherd's Bush to the habit of shepherds watching sheep on the green while hiding in thorn bushes. Now, however, the Common is a scruffy traffic island overlooked by one of London's ugliest edifices: the Shepherd's Bush shopping centre. This eyesore is currently being transformed into a cinema.

All is not gloom in W12, however, for this is home to one of London's most prestigious new-writing theatres, the Bush (*see p333*), and the neighbouring Shepherd's Bush Empire (*see p313*). Shepherd's Bush market, between **Shepherd's Bush** and **Goldhawk Road** tubes, is one of west London's busiest and, unlike Portobello Road, is very much geared to the local (Afro-Caribbean) population.

Shepherd's Bush and neighbouring White City are the main base of BBC TV. Television Centre on Wood Lane can be identified by its massive rooftop satellite dishes. Nearby is **Loftus Road**, the home of Queens Park Rangers FC. The wide open spaces of Wormwood Scrubs to the north are marred by one of London's most famous and forbidding Victorian jails, but less than a mile down Goldhawk Road is **Ravenscourt Park**, a much more agreeable space with an adventure playground and a number of tennis courts.

Hammersmith, south of Shepherd's Bush, is less depressing than its neighbour, but, on a similar note, is best known for its huge traffic interchange and the stone-clad corporate monstrosity of the **Broadway Centre**. The district is not, however, without its more notable architectural landmarks. There's the **Olympia Exhibition Centre** on Hammersmith Road, and the brown, ship-shaped curiosity called the London Ark, the city's first energy-saving, eco-friendly building (which ironically, leans across one of the city's least eco-friendly roadways, the A4). Then there's the London Apollo, formerly the Hammersmith Odeon, where many a famous

Sightseeing

rock band has gigged. Finally, the knobbly Hammersmith Bridge, built in 1824 with a span of 144m (422ft), was London's first suspension bridge (currently closed to traffic; it's great for promenading). Lower Mall, running along the river from the bridge, is a pleasant spot for a stroll or a pint at one of several riverside pubs, of which the Dove (see p227) is the pick.

Nor is Hammersmith without culture. On the main shopping route of **King Street** stands the Lyric theatre (see p335), while the Riverside Studios (see p292 and p335) on **Crisp Road** is a three-theatre contemporary arts centre with a gallery and repertory cinema.

Chiswick

Turnham Green tube/Chiswick rail.

A leafy suburb coveted by BBC execs, actors and minor celebs, Chiswick is in a world of its own. Turning your back on the tarmacked swoops of Hammersmith and walking west by the river from Hammersmith Bridge, **Chiswick Mall** gives off a different vibe. Lining this mile-long riverside stretch is an assortment of grand 17th-

to 19th-century townhouses with be-flowered, wrought iron verandas. The nearby Fuller's Griffin Brewery on Chiswick Lane South has stood on the same site since the 17th century and offers tours that include a full tasting session (8996 2063; tours at 11am, noon, 1pm and 2pm, Mon, Wed-Fri; £5). Chiswick Mall ends at the church of St Nicholas. Only the ragstone tower of the original 15th-century building remains; the rest of the church is 19th century. Gravestones commemorate local painters Hogarth and Whistler, but they are buried elsewhere.

Other Chiswick attractions include the Palladian magnificence of **Chiswick House** (see p185) and **Hogarth's House** (see p185). Further west is the **Kew Bridge Steam Museum** (see p185), and next door is the **Musical Museum** (see p186), one of the west's best kept little secrets. South of here, overlooking Kew Gardens from the opposite side of the river, is **Syon House** (see p186). A cutesy riverside promenade, just east of Kew Bridge on the north side of the river, runs by the mini-village of Strand-on-the-Green, and takes in three of the best pubs in the area.

Small but perfectly formed

For such a small strip of land – arching the bend of the Thames at twee Twickenham, it clocks in at only five acres – **Eel Pie Island** has had a busy past. It's also had a long one: the island's human colonisation seems to date back to at least some neolithic settlements, and its riverbed has thrown up axes, flint flakes and a bronze spearhead, plus some iron age coins.

Variously referred to in medieval texts as Twickenham Ayte, Gose (or Goose) Eyte and Church Ayte, the island seems to have earned its current name from the Tudor period, when it also served as a bowling alley. Apparently, watermen spoke so highly of the eel pies from this small ait that Henry VIII sped to sample the dish. He was so impressed that he insisted on receiving the first pie of each season, an event then celebrated in the ritual 'landing of the pie'.

A 'Mistress Mayo' is traditionally cited as the chef whose pies so tickled the royal gullet. Certainly, Mayo is the chef whose pies won fame, but she was the 19th-century proprietress of the Eel Pies Hotel that served as the court in one form or another from 1830 until it burnt down in 1971. The hotel, and its pies, attracted thousands of visitors

in Victorian London. Picnics would be drawn up on the lawns surrounding the hotel, and dancing would run through to the early hours. Dickens and JMW Turner were regular visitors.

Fashions moved on, though, and while the hotel struggled in the 20th century, the arrival of boatyards and wooden homes saw the growth of a resident community. Facing bankruptcy, the hotel opened a club at the suggestion of Arthur Chisnall, a social anthropologist looking for a sample study group. Little can he have known what he'd started. The jazz and R&B club soon boasted an impressive membership of some 30,000 and an even more impressive gig roster. The Rolling Stones, the Who, the Yardbirds, the Small Faces and Black Sabbath all played; Rod Stewart and Elton John first met here, playing in an ad hoc backing band for Long John Baldry; while Jeff Beck, originally just a member, became renowned for his jamming and founded the Tridents in the early 1960s.

The club was an oasis of the unholy trio of sex, drugs and rock 'n' roll, but the club also supported its members. Self-help groups were formed with leading educationalists, truanting teenagers would be encouraged back to

Opulent **Chiswick House**.

Chiswick House

Chertsey Road, W4 (8995 0508/www.english-heritage.org.uk). Turnham Green tube, then E3 bus to Edensor Road/Chiswick rail or Hammersmith tube/rail, then 190 bus. **Open** *Apr-Sept* 10am-6pm daily. *Oct* 10am-5pm daily. *Nov-Mar* 10am-4pm Wed-Sun; closed Mon, Tue (last entry 30mins before closing).* **Admission** £3.30; £2.50 concessions; £1.70 5-16s. **Credit** MC, V.

Lord Burlington's 1727 design for Chiswick House is based on Palladio's Villa Capra (the Rotonda) in Vicenza. The spectacular interior is decked out in ostentatious baroque splendour, with the lavish Blue Velvet Room winning the fiercely contested prize for most over-the-top decor. The attractive formal gardens are peopled with statues, temples and obelisks as well as a seasonal population of living picnickers. Handel, Jonathan Swift and Alexander Pope were all guests here.

Hogarth's House

Hogarth Lane, Great West Road, W4 (8994 6757). Turnham Green tube/Chiswick rail. **Open** *Apr-Oct* 1-5pm Tue-Fri; 1-6pm Sat, Sun; closed Mon. *Nov, Dec, Feb, Mar* 1-4pm Tue-Fri; 1-5pm Sat, Sun; closed Mon. *Jan* closed. **Admission** free. **No credit cards**.

Hogarth's country retreat has been fully restored to its 18th-century condition and provides wall space for over 200 of the social commentator's prints, though his most famous work, *The Rake's Progress*, is a copy (the original is in Sir John Soane's Museum; *see p99*).

Kew Bridge Steam Museum

Green Dragon Lane, Brentford, Middx (8568 4757/www.kbsm.org.uk). Gunnersbury tube/Kew Bridge rail/65, 237, 267, 391 bus. **Open** 11am-5pm daily. **Admission** *Mon-Fri* £3; £1 5-15s; £2 concessions; £7 family. *Sat, Sun* £4; £2 5-15s; £3 concessions; £10.50 family. **Credit** MC, V.

A Victorian riverside pumping station, close to the north end of Kew Bridge, is now home to this museum of water supply. The Water for Life exhibition details the history of London's use and abuse of the world's most precious commodity and includes a unique walk-through sewer experience. At 3pm on weekends one of the largest working steam engines in the world, the 229cm (90in) Cornish Beam engine

education, and, by the time the club closed in 1967, they had financially supported 20 people through college. The subsequent hippy colony was finally expelled by the police in 1971, and the hotel burned down.

Eel Pie Island is now a tight mix of wood-panelled bungalows, boatyards and artists' studios, messily arranged across the crescent-shaped island with nature conservation areas at each tip. Towards the western end, tugs undergo repairs in dry docks, with houseboats and artists' studios – the island has a long-established arts community here, some of whom exhibit in the Par Ici gallery on Church Street – further beyond that.

Besides the 120 inhabitants, the island's wooded ends also boast bats, Japanese knotweed and Himalayan balsam, with, at the last count, one centipede and two millipede species. Tawny owls have been known to settle there, too. A wander around the island is, by necessity, brief, but you do feel a community proud of its spirit, liberated by its separation from the mainland. Jazzman George Melly once wrote, 'I liked the sound of Eel Pie Island. It seemed to go with "Gut Bucket" or "Honky Tonk". It had the right feel to it. It not only sounded right. It looked right too.' Whatever it had then, it still has now. It always has.

The manic **Musical Museum**.

(built in 1845 for use in the tin mines), stirs ponderously into motion. Like the working waterwheel and five other steam engines, it has been restored by enthusiastic volunteers to its former working order.

Musical Museum

368 High Street, Brentford, Middx (8560 8108). Gunnersbury tube/Brentford Central or Kew Bridge rail. **Open** *Apr-Oct*, Sat, Sun, 2-5pm; closed Mon-Fri. *Nov-Mar* closed. **Admission** £3.20; £2.50 concessions. **No credit cards**.
This museum allows visitors to experience the fascinating world of automatic musical instruments, which are played and explained during an hour-and-a-half demonstration. Run on a voluntary basis, the museum can only open from April to October due to heating problems, but there are plans to expand to new, purpose-built premises in the near future.

Syon House

Syon Park, Brentford, Middx (8560 0883/ www.syonpark.co.uk). Gunnersbury tube, then 237, 267 bus. **Open** *14 Mar-31 Oct* 11am-5pm Wed, Thur, Sun, Bank Holiday Mon (last entry 4.15pm); closed Mon, Tue, Fri, Sat. Closed Nov-Mar 13. **Admission** £6.25; £5.25 concessions; £15 family; free under-5s. **Credit** varies, check for details.
Once a wealthy monastery, Syon was established by Henry V and used by Henry VIII as a prison for his wife Katherine Howard while she awaited execution. Home of the Percy family since the 1590s, Robert Adam remodelled the inside in 1761, creating one of the most lavish interiors in London. Among the many paintings on display are works by Gainsborough, Lely, Reynolds and Van Dyck. The riverside gardens, modelled by 'Capability' Brown, contain an impressive 19th-century conservatory, a miniature steam train, a garden centre, the London Butterfly House and the Aquatic Experience, with fish, reptiles, amphibians, birds and small mammals in their natural habitats. All sights have their own admission prices above and beyond entry to the house and gardens. For more on Syon Park, *see p270* **Park royal**.

Further west

A couple of miles west of Chiswick is the suburb of **Ealing**, famous for Ealing Studios, the oldest site of continuous film production in Britain. The area is a one-stop option for shopping (the Broadway Centre lies at its heart), eating and drinking, plus it boasts a large selection of museums and parks. Especially worth a visit is **Walpole Park**, home to Pitshanger Manor (*see below*) and the annual Ealing Jazz Festival.

Further west still, in the middle of gigantic **Osterley Park**, is Osterley House (*see below*), yet another Robert Adam revamp.

Just north of here are the colour and curries of **Southall**, which, like many previously sleepy parts of west London, has been given a new lease of life by Indian immigrants. The mainly Punjabi community offers a great opportunity to sample authentic north Indian cuisine in the cheap restaurants that line the Broadway (*see p199*). Visit on a Sunday, when the locals stroll among the market stalls and sari stores.

To the north, **Wembley** has been similarly enlivened by the mainly Gujarati community, although this district is better known as the home of the famous stadium (*see p328*). Plans to demolish the old stadium were in limbo at the beginning of 2001, and the proposed new venue looks set to miss its scheduled 2004 opening.

Nearby **Neasden** is another piece of sprawling suburbia, once satirised by the Monty Python team. Then a Hindu sect built the multi-billion-rupee Shri Swaminarayan Mandir, replicating the Akshardam outside Ahmedabad in Gujarat, western India. Constructed in 1995, the temple required 5,000 tons of marble and limestone and employed 1,500 sculptors for an enterprise unprecedented in this country since building the cathedrals in the Middle Ages. Visitors are welcome, though dress discreetly.

Osterley House

Osterley Park, off Jersey Road, Isleworth, Middx (8232 5050/recorded information 01494 755566/ www.nationaltrust.org.uk). Osterley tube. **Open** *Park* 9am-dusk daily. *House 31 Mar-4 Nov* 1-4.30pm Wed-Sun; closed Mon, Tue. **Admission** *House* £4.30; £2.15 5-15s; £10.50 family.
Osterley House was built for Sir Thomas Gresham (founder of the Royal Exchange) in 1576 but transformed by Robert Adam in 1761. His revamp is dominated by the imposing colonnade of white pillars before the courtyard of the house's red-brick body. The splendour of the state rooms alone makes the house worth the visit, but the still-used Tudor stables, the vast parkland walks and the ghost said to be lurking in the basement add to Osterley's allure.

Pitshanger Manor & Gallery

Walpole Park, Mattock Lane, Ealing, W5 (8567 1227/www.ealing.gov.uk/pitshanger). Ealing Broadway tube/rail. **Open** 10am-5pm Tue-Sat; closed Mon, Sun. **Admission** free.
A beautiful Regency villa situated in the idyllic surroundings of Walpole Park. Sir John Soane, architect of the Bank of England, rebuilt most of the house in 1801-3 using highly individual ideas in design and decoration. Among the exhibits worth seeing is the Hull Grundy Martinware collection of pottery. There is an art gallery adjacent to the museum where contemporary exhibitions are held, plus a lecture and workshop programme for all ages.

Eat, Drink, Shop

Feature boxes

LI SAUCE
(Forts)

rée, is ready to
ogs, hamburgers,
ios, spicy taste.

à partir de piments
préparation pour
pizza, hot dog,
hose qui peut lui

Nes maduredos al
asta, pizza, perros
en pualquiere cosa

0 24463 06116

Restaurants

London's myriad eateries cover every corner of the culinary globe. Even Britain.

Terrifically tasty Tex Mex can be enjoyed at **Cactus Blue**. *See p189*.

London being one of the world's greatest cities, it's perhaps unsurprising that it should boast such a terrific array of restaurants. But even habituées and devotees of London's dining circuit express amazement at how much it has improved over the last decade or so. Britons are now more clued-up about food than ever before, a fact reflected in the dazzling quality and dizzying variety of food being served in every corner of the city. There are still exceptions to the rule, of course, but choose carefully – we'd modestly suggest using this section as a good place to start – and you'll have a terrific time.

DOS AND DON'TS

Pleasingly, dining out in London is an informal affair. Few places have strict dress codes, but as a rule, the pricier the restaurant, the smarter the clientele. And besides, half the fun of dining at the likes of La Tante Claire is the 'event' nature of the evening out: dress up and enjoy it.

Although not all London restaurants insist on reservations, it certainly doesn't do any harm to make them; we'd suggest booking ahead if at all possible. While some London eateries are entirely non-smoking and others allow smoking anywhere, the most common arrangement in all but the smallest operations is for staff to set aside sections of the restaurant for smokers. If you're particularly passionate either way, be sure to mention it when you book.

Restaurants are one of the few areas of British life where tipping is standard practice; ten to 15 per cent is usual. Some places add service automatically, so double-check the bill or you may tip twice. Be wary of places that include service in the bill but leave the space for

gratuities empty on your credit card slip. And try and tip in cash, as some restaurants do not pass on credit card tips to their table staff.

We've listed a range of main course prices for all the restaurants in this section, except for those places that only serve set menu meals; where that's the case, we've listed those prices

The best Restaurants

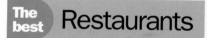

For breaking the bank in style
La Tante Claire (*see p198*).

For those without a bank to break
Viet Hoa (*see p215*).

For surreptitious star-spotting
The Ivy (*see p206*).

For Britain's old national dish
Rock & Sole Plaice (*see p194*).

For Britain's new national dish
Café Spice Namaste (*see p199*).

For a taste of the States
Arkansas Café (*see p189*).

For an absolutely fabulous meal
The Fifth Floor at Harvey Nichols (*see p205*).

For something completely different
Afghan Kitchen (*see p189*).

instead. But bear in mind that restaurants can (and often do) change their menus at any time without giving notice, and so these prices should only be used as guidelines. For child-friendly restaurants, see p272; for Internet cafés, see p369; and for more information on all aspects of eating out in London, buy the annual *Time Out Eating & Drinking Guide* (£9).

Afghan

Afghan Kitchen
35 Islington Green, Islington, N1 (7359 8019). Angel tube. **Open** noon-3.30pm, 5.30-11pm Tue-Sat; closed Mon, Sun. **Main courses** £4.50-£7. **No credit cards. Map** p402 O2.
Delicious, cheap Afghan food is served in this pint-sized diner overlooking Islington Green. Communal tables are the norm and the menu is short, but everything on it is very impressive. Western music and decor prevent an authentic atmosphere, however.

American

Arkansas Café
Unit 12, Old Spitalfields Market, 107 Commercial Street, Spitalfields, E1 (7377 6999). Aldgate East tube/Liverpool Street tube/rail. **Open** noon-2.30pm Mon-Fri; noon-4pm Sun; dinner by arrangement. **Main courses** £4-£12.50. **Credit** DC, MC, V. **Map** p403 R5.
The food at this affable American café is basic but terrific, with steak, burgers and chicken the order of the day. Staff can also do whole barbecued pigs and sheep to order for dinners or delivery.

Cactus Blue
86 Fulham Road, Chelsea, SW3 (7823 7858/ www.cactusblue.com). South Kensington tube. **Open** 5.30-11.45pm Mon-Fri; noon-11.45pm Sat; noon-11pm Sun. **Main courses** £9.95-£14.95. **Credit** AmEx, DC, MC, V. **Map** p397 D11.
Cactus Blue offers a sophisticated take on a Tex Mex theme. The menu offers mainly classic dishes, but cooked with a little more invention and served with a little more panache than usual. There's live music on Tuesday, Wednesday and Sunday nights.

Dakota
127 Ledbury Road, Notting Hill, W11 (7792 9191/ www.hartfordgroup.co.uk). Notting Hill Gate tube/ 52 bus. **Open** noon-3.30pm, 7-11pm Mon-Sat; noon-3.30pm, 7-10.30pm Sun. **Main courses** £10-£16. **Credit** AmEx, MC, V.
It's hard not to be impressed by the Notting Hill outpost of this chain, from the room's off-white cool ambience to the stunning modern south-western American food. Sibling restaurants **Montana** (125-129 Dawes Road, Fulham, SW6, 7385 9500), **Idaho** (13 North Hill, Highgate, N6; 8341 6633), **Canyon** (Riverside, Richmond, 8948 2944) and **Utah** (18 High Street, Wimbledon, 8944 1909) continue the good work elsewhere.

Argentinian

Gaucho Grill
19 Swallow Street, Mayfair, W1 (7734 4040). Piccadilly Circus tube. **Open** noon-3pm, 5-11pm Mon-Fri; noon-11pm Sat; noon-10.30pm Sun. **Main courses** £7.50-£32.50. **Credit** AmEx, DC, MC, V. **Map** p400 J7.

Take your seats at **Idaho.**

British food? You know the **Rules**. See p192.

The main attraction at this smart, adult-oriented cellar restaurant is steak: in fact, you'd be hard-pushed to find any better at any restaurant in London. Dishes are stripped down to the bare essentials, emphasising the quality of ingredients and cooking. A real treat.

Belgian

Belgo Centraal
50 Earlham Street, Covent Garden, WC2 (7813 2233/www.belgo-restaurants.com). Covent Garden tube. **Open** noon-11.30pm Mon-Sat; noon-10.30pm Sun. **Main courses** £8.95-£16.95. **Credit** AmEx, DC, MC, V. **Map** p399 L6.
An industrial lift leads up to this stylish subterranean beer hall, which resembles a cross between the set of *Alien* and a noisy crypt. The food is basic but brilliant Belgian fare, and the massive variety of beers are a big draw. There are branches in Camden and Notting Hill.

Brazilian

Rodizio Rico
111 Westbourne Grove, Bayswater, W2 (7792 4035). Bayswater or Notting Hill Gate tube. **Open** 6.30-11pm Mon-Fri; 12.30-4.30pm, 6.30-11pm Sat; 12.30-11.30pm Sun. **Main courses** £11 (vegetarian); £16.90 two courses. **Credit** AmEx, MC, V. **Map** p394 B6.
There's no menu at this extraordinary Brazilian steakhouse, but for £16.90 you'll get hot starters, free range at the salad bar and then as much meat as you can eat, served up on sabres by men in outrageous trousers.

British

Boisdale
13 & 15 Eccleston Street, Belgravia, SW1 (7730 6922/www.boisdale.co.uk). Victoria tube/rail. **Open** noon-2.30pm, 7-11pm Mon-Fri; 7-11pm Sat; closed Sun. **Main courses** £11.95-£24.90. **Credit** AmEx, DC, MC, V. **Map** p400 H10.
This popular Franco-Scottish cigar-and-whiskey bar-restaurant – no, really – serves hearty, reliable fare (roast haggis with mash and neeps, and fish and chips in beer batter and the like) over the bar or in its cosy restaurant. Over 200 whiskies are also on offer, and bar snacks are available until 1am.

Greenhouse
27A Hay's Mews, Mayfair, W1 (7499 3331/3314/www.capitalgrp.co.uk). Green Park tube. **Open** noon-2.30pm, 6.30-11pm Mon-Fri; 6.30-11pm Sat; 12.30-3pm, 7-10pm Sun. **Main courses** £15-£19. **Credit** AmEx, DC, MC, V. **Map** p400 H7.
The Greenhouse has long been a prime example of substance over style. The interior is dull, but the service is good and – most importantly – the food, while pricey, is exceptional.

Lindsay House
21 Romilly Street, Soho, W1 (7439 0450). Leicester Square or Piccadilly Circus tube. **Open** noon-2.30pm, 6-11pm Mon-Fri; 6-11pm Sat; closed Sun. **Main courses** (lunch only) £16-£25. **Set dinner** £43 three courses; £62 eight courses. **Credit** AmEx, DC, MC, V. **Map** p399 K6.
Irish chef Richard Corrigan is a man with a vision, and his constantly evolving modern British cooking is never less than interesting and often outstanding. The townhouse setting is unusual and intimate.

Rules

*35 Maiden Lane, Covent Garden, WC2 (7836 5314/
www.rules.co.uk). Covent Garden tube/Charing
Cross tube/rail.* **Open** noon-11.30pm Mon-Sat;
noon-10.30pm Sun. **Main courses** £16.95-£18.95.
Credit AmEx, DC, MC, V. **Map** p401 L7.
As well as being enormously popular, Rules is also
London's oldest restaurant (founded in 1798). You
may have to wait a little while for your food to arrive
at busy times, but it's only this popular because it's
so reliably good. Game and fish are specialities.

St John

*26 St John Street, Clerkenwell, EC1 (7251 0848/
www.stjohnrestaurant.co.uk). Farringdon tube/rail.*
Open *Bar* 11am-11pm Mon-Fri; 6-11pm Sat; closed
Sun. *Restaurant* noon-3pm, 6-11pm Mon-Fri; 6-11pm
Sat; closed Sun. **Main courses** *Bar* £3.50-£12.
Restaurant £9.80-£13.40. **Credit** AmEx, DC, MC, V.
Map p402 O5.
The decor is stark, but the food at St John couldn't
be more satisfying. It's big on offal, but don't despair
if innards aren't your thing: there are plenty of alternatives on the menu, including an interesting starter
of razor clams and superb plaice and samphire. You
can also eat at the bar.

Veronica's

*3 Hereford Road, Bayswater, W2 (7229 5079).
Bayswater tube.* **Open** noon-3pm, 6-11.30pm
Mon-Fri; 6-11.30pm Sat; closed Sun. **Main
courses** £10.50-£17.50. **Credit** AmEx, DC, MC, V.
Map p394 B6.
Veronica Shaw's unique restaurant serves historic
British dishes, including a couple based on Roman
recipes. The results are generally successful and the
experience enjoyable and educational.

Burmese

Mandalay

*444 Edgware Road, Paddington, W2 (7258 3696/
www.bcity.com/mandalay).* *Edgware Road tube.*
Open noon-3pm, 6-11pm Mon-Sat; closed Sun.
Main courses £3.90-£6.90. **Credit** AmEx, DC,
MC, V. **Map** p395 E4.
The road to Mandalay may be the traffic-choked
Edgware Road, but the warmth of Dwight and Gary
Ally's welcome and the quality of their cooking
ensure satisfied stomachs and smiles on faces.

Caribbean

Brixtonian Havana Club

*11 Beehive Place, Brixton, SW9 (7924 9262/
www.brixtonian.co.uk). Brixton tube/rail.*
Open noon-3pm, 7-10.30pm Mon-Thur, Sun;
noon-3pm, 7-11pm Fri, Sat. **Main courses** £12.50.
Credit MC, V.
Despite its location down a tiny sidestreet, the
Brixtonian Havana Club continues to lure the
punters. It's a lively bar/restaurant that does a great
line in cocktails and accomplished Caribbean/'Black
British' cooking.

Golden Harvest.

Mango Room

*10 Kentish Town Road, Camden, NW1 (7482
5065). Camden Town tube.* **Open** 6pm-midnight
Mon; noon-3pm, 6pm-midnight Tue-Sun.
Main courses £8-£11. **Credit** MC, V.
Lifting London's Caribbean food out of the region of
home cooking, the lovely Mango Room is also as cool
a bar/restaurant as Camden has to offer.

Chinese

See also p203 **Singapore Garden.**

Golden Harvest

*17 Lisle Street, Chinatown, WC2 (7287 3822).
Leicester Square or Piccadilly Circus tube.* **Open** noon-
2.45am daily. **Main courses** £5.50-£20. **Minimum**
£5 from 5pm. **Credit** MC, V. **Map** p401 K7.
The food in this unpretentious restaurant has a clar-
ity and freshness that makes it one of our favourites
in Chinatown. The seafood hot-pot at £20 a head (not
on the English language menu) is worth every penny.

Hunan

*51 Pimlico Road, Pimlico, SW1 (7730 5712).
Sloane Square tube.* **Open** noon-2.30pm, 6-11pm
Mon-Sat; closed Sun. **Main courses** £5-£150.
Credit AmEx, MC, V. **Map** p400 G11.
Named for a Chinese province famed for its spicy
and fragrant food, Hunan is unique among Chinese
restaurants in London for its cuisine. Be bold and
ask maître d' Mr Peng to devise a feast for you, and
insist on genuine full-blooded spicing.

Mandarin Kitchen

14-16 Queensway, Bayswater, W2 (7727 9012).
Queensway tube. **Open** noon-midnight daily.
Main courses £4.90-£25. **Credit** AmEx, DC,
MC, V. **Map** p394 C6.
Packed every night with smart Cantonese professionals, this longstanding restaurant has some of the best seafood in London; the lobster is superb.

Mr Kong

21 Lisle Street, Chinatown, WC2 (7437 7341/
9679). Leicester Square or Piccadilly Circus tube.
Open noon-3am daily. **Main courses** £6-£24.
Minimum £7 after 5pm. **Credit** AmEx, DC, MC, V.
Map p401 K7.
The dining room may be somewhat cramped, but the staff at Mr Kong are friendly and the food is excellent. Stick to the specials menu for unusual Cantonese dishes such as squid with shrimp paste.

New Diamond

23 Lisle Street, Chinatown, WC2 (7437 2517).
Leicester Square or Piccadilly Circus tube.
Open noon-3am daily. **Main courses** £8-£25.
Minimum £5.50-£22. **Credit** AmEx, DC, MC, V.
Map p401 K7.
Mel Brooks' favourite Chinese restaurant doesn't look flash, but it does knock out some of the most subtle and delicious sauces in the capital. Its late opening hours are also a bonus.

New Four Seasons

84 Queensway, Bayswater, W2 (7229 4320).
Bayswater or Queensway tube. **Open** noon-11.30pm
Mon-Sat; noon-11pm Sun. **Main courses** £4.30-£28.
Credit AmEx, MC, V. **Map** p394 C6.
Always a good bet for a hearty Cantonese meal, though you may have to queue for a table. The great specials list contains the kind of dishes that most restaurants confine to their Chinese-language menus.

Oriental

Dorchester Hotel, 55 Park Lane, Mayfair, W1
(7317 6328). Hyde Park Corner or Marble Arch
tube. **Open** noon-2.30pm, 7-11pm Mon-Fri; 7-11pm
Sat, Sun. **Main courses** £17.50-£38. **Credit** AmEx,
DC, MC, V. **Map** p400 G7.
It's pricey and blandly formal, but if only the highest standards of cooking will do, the Dorchester's Oriental is the one. The MSG-free policy is laudable.

Dim sum

London is one of the best places in the world to try one of the highlights of Cantonese cuisine, dim sum. These small, delicate dumplings and snacks are served from midday through the afternoon (never after 6pm) at low prices: expect to pay around £10 a head for a decent selection.

Golden Dragon

28-9 Gerrard Street, Chinatown, W1 (7734
2763). Leicester Square or Piccadilly Circus tube.
Open noon-11.30pm Mon-Thur; noon-midnight Fri,
Sat; 11am-11pm Sun. *Dim sum* noon-5pm Mon-Sat;

11am-5pm Sun. **Main courses** £6-£25.
Minimum £10. **Credit** AmEx, DC, MC, V.
Map p401 K7.
Chinatown's premier dim sum restaurant serves reliably excellent snacks in the noisy bustling atmosphere much loved by Chinese diners-out.

Harbour City

46 Gerrard Street, Chinatown, W1 (7439 7859).
Leicester Square or Piccadilly Circus tube.
Open noon-11.30pm Mon-Thur; noon-midnight
Fri, Sat; 11am-10.30pm Sun. *Dim sum* noon-5pm
Mon-Sat; 11am-5pm Sun. **Main courses** £4.50-
£18. **Minimum** £5. **Credit** AmEx, DC, MC, V.
Map p401 K7.
Outstanding dim sum are served at this otherwise so-so Cantonese eaterie, including such rarely found treats as ducks' tongues in black bean and chilli sauce.

Royal China

13 Queensway, Bayswater, W2 (7221 2535).
Queensway tube. **Open** noon-11pm Mon-Thur;
noon-11.30pm Fri, Sat; 11am-10pm Sun. *Dim*
sum noon-5pm Mon-Sat; 11am-5pm Sun.
Main courses £6-£80. **Credit** AmEx, DC, MC,
V. **Map** p394 C7.
Undoubtedly the finest dim sum in London: exquisite in flavour and presentation, and incredibly cheap. Come during the week for a quiet, leisurely meal: Sundays are more hectic, and queues are long.

Fish

fish!

Cathedral Street, Borough Market, Bankside, SE1
(7836 3236/www.fishdiner.co.uk). London Bridge
tube/rail. **Open** 11.30am-2.45pm, 5.30-10.30pm Mon-
Sat; noon-3.30pm Sun. **Main courses** £8.50-£15.95.
Credit AmEx, DC, MC, V. **Map** p404 P8.
While, to a certain extent, fish! is about being perky and in your face, it's also about great seafood and a good time. So good, in fact, that it has expanded into new branches in and out of London.

J Sheekey

28-32 St Martin's Court, Covent Garden, WC2
(7240 2565). Leicester Square tube. **Open** noon-3pm,
5.30pm-midnight Mon-Sat; noon-3.30pm, 5.30pm-
midnight Sun. **Main courses** £9.50-£28.75.
Credit AmEx, DC, MC, V. **Map** p401 K7.
Looking and feeling very much like The Ivy Mark II (it has the same owners; *see p205*), J Sheekey offers the same classy dining experience (with a fish bias) marred by the same sittings policy.

Livebait

21 Wellington Street, Covent Garden, WC2 (7836
7161/www.santeonline.co.uk). Covent Garden tube.
Open noon-3pm, 5.30-11.30pm Mon-Sat; closed Sun.
Main courses £14.95-£28. **Credit** AmEx, DC,
MC, V. **Map** p401 L7.
The strengths that originally fuelled Livebait's success remain. The seafood is impeccably fresh, the menu is flexible and interesting, and the service is engaged and intelligent.

Eat, Drink, Shop

Fish & chips

Rock & Sole Plaice

47 Endell Street, Covent Garden, WC2 (7836 3785/ www.rockandsoleplaice.com). Covent Garden tube. **Open** 11.30am-10pm Mon-Sat; 11.30am-9pm Sun. **Main courses** £3-£13. **Credit** MC, V. **Map** p399 L6.

Open since 1871, Rock & Sole Plaice claims to be the oldest chippie in London. The claim is unsubstantiated, but what the hell: since the sad demise of the Upper Street Fish Shop in Islington, it's certainly the best place in the centre of town to sample the national dish.

Seashell

49-51 Lisson Grove, Marylebone, NW1 (7224 9000). Marylebone tube/rail. **Open** noon-2.30pm, 5-10.30pm Mon-Fri; noon-10.30pm Sat; closed Sun. **Main courses** £7.95-£14.95. **Credit** AmEx, MC, V. **Map** p395 E4.

Being a more upmarket establishment, Seashell has a creditably long wine list to accompany its gourmet fish and chips. The fish cakes are always worth a try.

French

Chez Bruce

2 Bellevue Road, Wandsworth Common, SW17 (8672 0114). Wandsworth Common rail. **Open** noon-2pm, 7-10.30pm Mon-Thur; noon-2pm, 6.30-10.30pm Fri; 12.30-2.30pm, 6.30-10.30pm Sat; 12.30-3pm Sun. **Set lunch** (Mon-Sat) £21.50 three courses; (Sun) £25 three courses. **Set dinner** £27.50 three courses. **Credit** AmEx, DC, MC, V.

Its location, opposite Wandsworth Common, is a pleasant one, but it's the combination of Bruce Poole's superlative cooking and the relaxed front-of-house operation that makes this restaurant special.

Chez Lindsay

11 Hill Rise, Richmond, Surrey (8948 7473). Richmond tube/rail. **Open** 11am-11pm Mon-Sat; noon-10pm Sun. **Main courses** £3.95-£17.50. **Credit** MC, V.

Bringing a surprisingly authentic slice of Brittany to Richmond, Chez Lindsay specialises in gallettes, crêpes and other regional dishes, including moules à la St Malo and terrine Breton. Its Breton ciders are unmissable.

Club Gascon

57 West Smithfield, Clerkenwell, EC1 (7253 5853). Barbican tube/Farringdon tube/rail. **Open** noon-2pm, 7-10pm Mon-Fri; 7-10.30pm Sat; closed Sun. **Main courses** £5-£12. **Credit** MC, V. **Map** p402 O5.

Specialising in the earthy cuisine of south-west France, Club Gascon is refreshing and unique among London's French restaurants. The beguiling regional food is served in tapas-sized portions, encouraging diners to experiment. The wine bar next door, Cellar Gascon, is also well worth a visit.

The Criterion

224 Piccadilly, St James's, W1 (7930 0488). Piccadilly Circus tube. **Open** noon-2.30pm, 6-11.30pm Mon-Sat; 5.30-10.30pm Sun. **Main courses** £15.50-£23.50. **Credit** AmEx, DC, MC, V. **Map** p401 K7.

Marco Pierre White's showcase restaurant has a stunning interior, with opulent ceilings of burnished gold and neo-classical paintings set in marble walls, and an equally alluring menu.

L'Escargot

48 Greek Street, Soho, W1 (7437 2679/ www.whitestarline.org.uk). Tottenham Court Road tube. **Open** *Ground floor* 12.15-2.15pm, 6-11.30pm Mon-Fri; 6-11.30pm Sat; closed Sun. *Picasso Room* noon-2.15pm, 7-11pm Tue-Fri; 7-11pm Sat; closed Mon, Sun. **Main courses** *Ground floor* £12.95-£16.95. **Set lunch** *Picasso Room* £29.50 three courses. **Set meal** *Picasso Room* £42 three courses. **Credit** AmEx, DC, MC, V. **Map** p399 K6.

A Soho fixture for 70 years, this famed eating spot still has a special aura. The modern but ungimmicky food has moved with the times, though it's pricey.

Roussillon

16 St Barnabas Street, Pimlico, SW1 (7730 5550/ www.roussillon.co.uk). Sloane Square tube. **Open** noon-2.15pm, 6.30-10.30pm Mon-Fri; 6.30-10.30pm Sat; closed Sun. **Set lunch** £15 two courses; £18 three courses. **Set dinner** £29 two courses; £35 three courses; £35 (vegetarian), £42 four courses; £50 seven courses. **Credit** AmEx, DC, MC, V. **Map** p400 G11.

Old-school scran at the **Rock & Sole Plaice**.

Eat, Drink, Shop

A lot of bottle

The capital has always provided a veritable cornucopia of eateries, catering for appetites as varied as its citizens. But in the last ten years, dining out in London has enjoyed something of a renaissance; whether for work or leisure, the act of eating out has become more fashionable and (in many cases) more affordable than ever. This boom has gone hand-in-hand with the rise of TV überchefs such as Gary Rhodes, Gordon Ramsey and the monstrous Jamie 'Pukka!' Oliver. However, with the exception of the slightly sozzled Keith Floyd, not much is ever told of the joys of wine while you dine.

Wine has become more integral to the British dining experience than ever before, and seems to have finally managed to shake off its dated image. Memories of *Abigail's Party*-esque couples sipping a glass of Blue Nun and nibbling on cheese and pineapple may have done wonders for sales at the time, but they also set back the growth of the wine industry in this country about two decades. Thankfully, though, tastes have moved on, as has the unavoidable translation of the phrase 'wining and dining' into images of tipsy aristos slurping claret in St James's gentlemen's clubs.

Although tastes may have moved on, only a small percentage of diners have total confidence in their ability to perfectly pair wine with food in a restaurant. At the top end of the market, sommeliers (head wine waiters) fulfil this function, and are to be found at most of London's prestigious dining dens. If money is no object, **1837** (Brown's Hotel, 33 Albermarle Street, Mayfair, W1, 7408 1837)

has just about the best cellar in London; and in general, it's hard to go wrong with any of the restaurants listed under **Haute Cuisine** (see p198). Also worth investigating – and, in general, less stuffy – are those listed under **Modern European** (p204), particularly **Bibendum** (see p204), **Clarke's** (see p205) and **Odette's** (see p206). For diners who don't want to dress up, the most bohemian of this bunch is **Andrew Edmunds** (see p204).

But for those who don't want a discussion with a wine waiter, however laid-back the atmosphere, try one of the growing band of restaurants where the wines are listed by style. At **Bank** (see p204), for example, they come in categories ranging from 'light and crisp' through to 'full and firm'. **Pasta Plus** (62 Eversholt Street, Somers Town, NW1, 7383 4943) offers a budget version of this service: next to each dish on the menu are numbers corresponding to those on the wine list.

Combining the food and wine of a country pays dividends, too. To this end, try French restaurants **Chez Bruce** (see p194); **Club Gascon**, which has a wine bar of its own, **Cellar Gascon** (see p194); and **RSJ**, which specialises in wines from the Loire (13A Coin Street, South Bank, SE1, 7928 4554). Alternatively, head to Italians **Enoteca Turi**, **Isola** or **Zafferano** (for all, see p200); or explore the much-improved wines of Greece at **The Real Greek** (see p197).

But wherever you decide to dine, don't be afraid to ask the waiter for a recommendation: he or she will usually be happy to oblige. Things are so much more relaxed these days, and waiters are more inclined to be helpful than snooty. The pay-off should be a meal to remember, with wine to match.

Eat, Drink, Shop

Georgian

Little Georgia

2 Broadway Market, London Fields, E8 (7249 9070). Bethnal Green tube, then 106 bus/26, 48, 55, 236 bus. **Open** 6.30-10.30pm Tue-Sat; 1-4pm Sun; closed Mon. **Main courses** £7.50-£9.50. **Credit** MC, V.

Little Georgia has the delightful air of a neighbourhood restaurant, with decoration provided by restrained ethnic adornments. The food, with its robust, rounded flavours and textures, is superb, and the service is relaxed and attentive.

Global

Bali Sugar

33A All Saints Road, Notting Hill, W11 (7221 4477/www.thesugarclub.co.uk). Westbourne Park tube. **Open** 12.30-3pm, 6.30-11pm daily. **Main courses** £13.10-£17.90. **Credit** AmEx, DC, MC, V.

Plain walls and stripped wood floors offer little distraction from Bali Sugar's complex and imaginative fusion dishes. A multitude of Pacific Rim and European flavours are blended with skill and verve at this fine Notting Hill eaterie.

The Lavender

171 Lavender Hill, Clapham, SW11 (7978 5242). Clapham Junction rail. **Open** noon-11.30pm Mon-Sat; noon-10.30pm Sun. **Main courses** £7-£11. **Credit** AmEx, MC, V.

Always cheerful, friendly and buzzy, we've yet to have a bad meal at the Lavender. The modern global food is imaginative and skillfully executed, and it's also very good value.

Greek

Halepi

48-50 Belsize Lane, Belsize Park, NW3 (7431 5855). Belsize Park or Swiss Cottage tube. **Open** 6-11pm Mon-Fri; noon-3pm, 6-11pm Sat; noon-11pm Sun. **Main courses** £6.95-£24. **Credit** AmEx, DC, MC, V.

At last, it's official: there *is* such a thing as a modern Greek Cypriot restaurant. The contemporary minimal decor complements a long and ambitious menu that aspires to be cutting edge. What's more, it generally succeeds.

The Real Greek

15 Hoxton Market, Hoxton, N1 (7739 8212/ www.therealgreek.co.uk). Old Street tube/rail/26, 48, 55, 149, 242 bus. **Open** noon-3pm, 5.30-10.30pm Mon-Sat; closed Sun. **Main courses** £8-£15.90. **Credit** MC, V. **Map** p403 R3.

This converted pub offers Greek food like you won't find anywhere else in town. Theodore Kyriakou's cooking is a little hit and miss, but, when on form, the Real Greek demonstrates just how moribund most of the capital's Hellenic eateries are.

Unique food can be had at **The Real Greek**.

Unusually for a French restaurant, Roussillon takes special care of vegetarians, offering a six-course 'Garden' menu that's free of meat. Omnivores need not panic, however, as it also offers sublime 'Sea' and 'Land' menus for fish and meat eaters.

Schnecke

80-82 Upper Street, Islington, N1 (7226 6500/ www.schnecke-restaurants.com). Angel tube. **Open** noon-midnight Mon-Sat; noon-10.30pm Sun. **Main courses** £5.99-£10.99. **Credit** AmEx, DC, MC, V. **Map** p398 J6.

The decor may have some kitsch touches, but the food at this Alsatian eaterie is taken very seriously. The showpiece of the menu is the tarte flambée, which is like a thin, rectangular pizza and is available with sweet or savoury toppings.

Eat, Drink, Shop

Haute cuisine

Haute equals posh, generally. Expect formality in decor and service, high prices and classic, superlative food, so dress up and live it up.

Cheznico at Ninety Park Lane

90 Park Lane, Mayfair, W1 (7409 1290). Hyde Park Corner or Marble Arch tube. **Open** noon-2pm, 7-11pm Mon-Fri; 7-11pm Sat; closed Sun. **Main courses** (lunch only) £13.50-£26. **Set dinner** £56 three courses; £65 eight courses; £75 ten courses. **Credit** AmEx, DC, MC, V. **Map** p400 G7.
Rich, luxurious flavours, colours and textures are the hallmarks of Nico Ladenis's cooking, which combines classic French cuisine with adroit touches of Asia and the Middle East. The atmosphere at this Mayfair drawing room is formal yet relaxed.

Gordon Ramsay

68-9 Royal Hospital Road, Chelsea, SW3 (7352 4441). Sloane Square tube. **Open** noon-2pm, 6.45-10pm Mon-Fri; closed Sat, Sun. **Set lunch** £30 three courses. **Set dinner** £60 three courses (from à la carte menu), £75 seven courses. **Credit** AmEx, DC, MC, V. **Map** p397 F12.
Since his acrimonious parting from Aubergine in 1998, Ramsay's profile has increased dramatically. The Michelin two-star chef continues to serve exquisite food, but service can be rather brusque.

La Tante Claire

The Berkeley, Wilton Place, Knightsbridge, SW1 (7823 2003). Knightsbridge tube. **Open** 12.30-2pm, 7-11pm Mon-Fri; 7-11pm Sat; closed Sun. **Main courses** £23-£35. **Minimum** £50 dinner. **Credit** AmEx, DC, MC, V. **Map** p400 G8.
Sophisticated restaurants don't get much more relaxed than La Tante Claire; and the food doesn't get much better, either. Pierre Koffman's food mecca delivers on almost every level; go and be amazed.

Pied à Terre

34 Charlotte Street, Fitzrovia, W1 (7636 1178/ www.pied.a.terre.co.uk). Tottenham Court Road tube. **Open** 12.15-2.15pm, 7-10.45pm Mon-Fri; 7-10.45pm

Tea for two

The big attraction of traditional afternoon tea is a chance to snoop inside hotels at which you'll never get to stay. The hotels are in on this, too, so you don't have to be a millionaire or a Hollywood star to gain entry. Dress codes of jacket and tie for men are the main rules at the Ritz, the Savoy and Claridge's. Other hotels may have this rule but they don't appear to enforce it; check when phoning to book. As for the food: quality scones, clotted cream, jam, cakes and sandwiches for around £20 (and often more) may sound expensive, but you're also paying for being treated like royalty in luxurious surroundings for up to two hours.

For the glitziest interior, go to the **Waldorf Meridien**, but for the cosiest setting, try **Brown's**. For top-notch tea and sandwiches, **The Lanesborough** impresses, though the tastiest pastries and the best pianist can be found at **The Dorchester**. The best-value tea in town is at the low-key **Basil Street Hotel**, while the service at **Claridge's** can't be beaten. **The Ritz**, of course, is the most popular: you'll need to book about three months in advance for a weekend.

Basil Street Hotel *Basil Street, Brompton, SW3 (7581 3311). Knightsbridge tube.* **Tea served** 3.30-5.45pm daily. **Credit** AmEx, DC, MC, V. **Map** p397 F9.
Brown's *33-4 Albemarle Street, Mayfair, W1 (7518 4108). Green Park tube.* **Tea served** two seatings: 3pm, 4.45pm, Mon-Fri; first come first served Sat, Sun. **Credit** AmEx, DC, MC, V. **Map** p400 J7.
Claridge's *Brook Street, Mayfair, W1 (7629 8860). Bond Street tube.* **Tea served** 3-5.30pm daily. **Credit** AmEx, DC, MC, V. **Map** p398 H6.
The Dorchester *54 Park Lane, Mayfair, W1 (7629 8888). Hyde Park Corner tube.* **Tea served** 3-6pm daily. *High tea* 5-8pm daily. **Credit** AmEx, DC, MC, V. **Map** p400 G7.
The Lanesborough *Hyde Park Corner, Belgravia, SW1 (7259 5599). Hyde Park Corner tube.* **Tea served** 3.30-6pm daily. **Credit** AmEx, DC, MC, V. **Map** p400 G8.
The Ritz *Piccadilly, St James's, W1 (7493 8181). Green Park tube.* **Tea served** 2-6pm daily; reserved sittings at 3.30pm, 5pm. **Credit** AmEx, DC, MC, V. **Map** p398 J7.
St James, Fortnum & Mason *181 Piccadilly, St James's, W1 (7734 8040).* **Tea served** 3-5pm Mon-Sat. **Credit** AmEx, DC, MC, V. **Map** p400 J7.
The Savoy *Strand, Covent Garden, WC2 (7836 4343). Charing Cross tube/rail.* **Tea served** 3-5.30pm daily. **Credit** AmEx, DC, MC, V. **Map** p401 L7.
Waldorf Meridien *Aldwych, Holborn, WC2 (7836 2400). Covent Garden or Temple tube.* **Tea served** 3-5.30pm Mon-Fri. **Tea dance** 2.30-5pm Sat; 4-6.30pm Sun. **Credit** AmEx, DC, MC, V. **Map** p401 M7.

Sat; closed Sun. **Set lunch** £19.50 two courses; £23 three courses. **Set dinner** £39.50 two courses; £50 three courses; £65 eight-course tasting. **Minimum** £19.50 lunch. **Credit** AmEx, DC, MC, V. **Map** p398 J5. The frosted glass frontage of Pied à Terre gives nothing away from the outside. Step inside, though, and sample some terrific food at the hands of the ingenuous waiters. An accomplished restaurant.

Stefano Cavallini Restaurant at the Halkin

Halkin Hotel, 5-6 Halkin Street, Belgravia, SW1 (7333 1234). Hyde Park Corner tube. **Open** 12.30-2.30pm, 7-10.30pm Mon-Fri; 7-10.30pm Sat; 7-10pm Sun. **Main courses** £24-£30. **Credit** AmEx, DC, MC, V. **Map** p400 G9. This elegant dining room is one of London's finest. The à la carte menu (divided into antipasti, pasta and rice and meat and fish main courses) is expensive, but the set lunch is one of the best deals in town.

Indian

Central London is not well equipped with Indian restaurants, and the few good ones come at a price. For an authentic subcontinental culinary and cultural experience, visit one of the unglamorous but vibrant centres of Indian London: Wembley, Southall or Tooting. Sunday lunchtime is the best time to join in the snacking: take the tube to Tooting Broadway and cruise Upper Tooting Road and Tooting High Street; the train to Southall and head along The Broadway; or the tube to Alperton or Wembley Central and stroll down Ealing Road.

Café Spice Namaste

16 Prescot Street, Whitechapel, E1 (7488 9242). Aldgate East or Tower Hill tube. **Open** noon-3pm, 6.15-10.30pm Mon-Fri; 6.30-10.30pm Sat; closed Sun. **Main courses** £7.95-£13.95. **Credit** AmEx, DC, MC, V. **Map** p405 S7. Never afraid to combine the traditional with the distinctly untraditional, Cyrus Todiwala's imaginative cooking shows just how exquisite and extraordinarily diverse modern Indian cooking can be.

Gifto's Lahore Karahi

162-4 The Broadway, Southall, Middx (8813 8669/ www.gifto.com). Southall rail/207 bus. **Open** noon-11.30pm Mon-Fri; noon-midnight Sat, Sun. **Main courses** £1.60-£7.90. **Credit** AmEx, DC, MC, V. Southall's premier Pakistani restaurant is a lively, exuberant place where the team of chefs – karahis or tandoori skewers in hand – produce a command performance from their open kitchen.

Karahi King

213 East Lane, North Wembley, Middx (8904 2760). North Wembley tube/245 bus. **Open** noon-midnight daily. **Main courses** £3.50-£12. **No credit cards.** The out-of-the-way location and cramped surroundings have never proved a deterrent to the hordes of

locals – young African-Asians and others – who continue to flock to this lively restaurant to enjoy some of the best Karahi cooking in town.

Kastoori

188 Upper Tooting Road, Tooting, SW17 (8767 7027). Tooting Broadway tube. **Open** 6-10.30pm Mon, Tue; 12.30-2.30pm, 6-10.30pm Wed-Sun. **Main courses** £3.50-£5.50. **Credit** MC, V. The best known of the several East African Gujarati restaurants along this busy road, Kastoori is notable for its innovative food and friendly, helpful service. The Kastoori special thali is particularly impressive.

Porte des Indes

32 Bryanston Street, Marylebone, W1 (7224 0055/ www.blueelephant.com). Marble Arch tube. **Open** noon-2.30pm, 7-11.30pm Mon-Fri; 7-11.30pm Sat; noon-3pm, 7-10.30pm Sun. **Main courses** £8.50-£19.20. **Credit** AmEx, DC, MC, V. **Map** p395 F6. A former Edwardian ballroom provides possibly the grandest setting for an Indian restaurant in London, and the imaginative menu comes close to matching the surroundings. Service, however, is inconsistent.

Quilon

41 Buckingham Gate, Westminster, SW1 (7821 1899). St James's Park tube. **Open** noon-2.30pm, 6-11pm Mon-Fri; 6-11pm Sat; closed Sun. **Main courses** £5.95-£18.95. **Credit** AmEx, DC, MC, V. **Map** p400 J9. Seafood is prominent at this excellent eaterie, which takes its name from a town in the Kerala region. However, the best deal is to be had at lunchtime: two courses, from the full menu, cost £12.50, with three courses clocking in at just £15.95; both are bargains.

Rasa Samudra

5 Charlotte Street, Fitzrovia, W1 (7637 0222). Goodge Street tube. **Open** noon-3pm, 6-11pm Mon-Sat; 6-11pm Sun. **Main courses** £6.20-£11. **Credit** AmEx, DC, MC, V. **Map** p398 J5. By far the most expensive (and ambitious) of Siva Das Sreedharan's three-strong Rasa group, this is the place to come for exemplary Keralan seafood cooking. Unusual and exquisite.

Tamarind

20 Queen Street, Mayfair, W1 (7629 3561/ www.tamarindrestaurant.com). Green Park tube. **Open** noon-3pm, 6-11.30pm Mon-Fri; 6-11.30pm Sat; noon-2.30pm, 6-10.30pm Sun. **Main courses** £5.80-£15. **Credit** AmEx, DC, MC, V. **Map** p400 H7. One of London's finest Indian restaurants is housed in one of the city's most beautifully decorated basements. Chef Atul Kochhar's assured touch with the best and freshest ingredients ensures a culinary treat and the staff are almost unnervingly attentive.

Vama

438 King's Road, Chelsea, SW10 (7351 4118/ www.vama.co.uk). Sloane Square tube, then 11, 22, 211 bus. **Open** noon-3pm, 6.30-11.30pm Mon-Sat; noon-3pm, 6.30-10.30pm Sun. **Main courses** £6.35-£12.50. **Credit** AmEx, DC, MC, V. **Map** p397 D12.

Eat, Drink, Shop

One of the most reliable of the new-wave high-class Indian restaurants: we've yet to receive a complaint about it and we've yet to be served a bad dish.

Zaika

257-9 Fulham Road, Chelsea, SW3 (7351 7823). South Kensington tube/14 bus. **Open** noon-2.30pm, 6.30-10.30pm Mon-Fri, Sun; 6.30-10.30pm Sat. **Main courses** £9.95-£21.50. **Credit** AmEx, MC, V. **Map** p397 D11.
Operating from restrained, classy premises, Zaika's Vineet Bhatia excels at creating Indian classics with a twist, such as lamb biriani with a pastry crust.

Italian

Assaggi

The Chepstow, 39 Chepstow Place, Notting Hill, W2 (7792 5501). Notting Hill Gate tube. **Open** 12.30-2.30pm, 7.30-11pm Mon-Sat; closed Sun. **Main courses** £15.95-£18.75. **Credit** AmEx, DC, MC, V. **Map** p394 B6.
So highly esteemed is this small restaurant that diners often have to book about a month in advance. The prices are reasonable, but the somewhat rudimentary decor doesn't seem quite in tune with the impeccable standards of the imaginative food.

Enoteca Turi

28 Putney High Street, Putney, SW15 (8785 4449). East Putney or Putney Bridge tube/Putney rail/14 bus. **Open** 12.30-2.30pm, 7-11pm Mon-Fri; 7-11pm Sat; closed Sun. **Main courses** £12.50-£15.50. **Credit** AmEx, DC, MC, V.
Matching wines with food is a special feature of the mouth-watering menu at this deservedly popular restaurant. Several wines are served by the glass and each dish comes listed with a suggested wine.

Ibla

89 Marylebone High Street, Marylebone, W1 (7224 3799/www.ibla.co.uk). Baker Street, Bond Street or Regent's Park tube. **Open** noon-2.30pm, 7-10.30pm Mon-Fri; 7-10.30pm Sat; closed Sun. **Set lunch** £15 two courses; £18 three courses. **Set meal** £30 three courses; £35 four courses. **Credit** AmEx, DC, MC, V. **Map** p398 G5.
An elongated S-shape provides the unusual setting for this modern yet refreshingly untrendy Italian. The regularly changing set-price menu scores highly for quality and presentation.

Isola

145 Knightsbridge, Knightsbridge, SW1 (7838 1044). Knightsbridge tube. **Open** noon-3pm, 6pm-midnight Mon-Sat; noon-3pm, 6-10.30pm Sun. **Main courses** £18-£22.50. **Credit** AmEx, DC, MC, V. **Map** p395 F9.
Oliver Peyton's Isola is his most mature restaurant to date. With Bruno Loubet in the kitchen, this is Italian cooking of the highest refinement and quality (and cost). The restaurant won the Best Interior Design gong at the *Time Out* Eating and Drinking Awards 2000.

Oliver Peyton's stunning **Isola**.

Passione

10 Charlotte Street, Fitzrovia, W1 (7636 2833/ www.passione.com). Goodge Street tube. **Open** 12.30-2.30pm, 7-10.30pm Mon-Fri; 7-10.30pm Sat; closed Sun. **Main courses** £14.50-£17.50. **Credit** AmEx, DC, MC, V. **Map** p398 J5.
Passione, in defiance of its name, emits a cool, calm civility and serves up beautifully executed classic Italian dishes. The quality of ingredients is impeccable and their handling is assured.

Vasco & Piero's Pavilion

15 Poland Street, Soho, W1 (7437 8774). Oxford Circus or Tottenham Court Road tube. **Open** noon-3pm, 6-11pm Mon-Fri; 7-11pm Sat; closed Sun. **Main courses** £11.50-£16. **Credit** AmEx, DC, MC, V. **Map** p398 J6.
This reliable old Soho stager delivers carefully executed dishes in a pleasingly cosy atmosphere. The service is very friendly, even if not you're one of the celeb regulars.

Zafferano

15 Lowndes Street, Belgravia, SW1 (7235 5800). Knightsbridge tube. **Open** noon-2.30pm, 7-11pm Mon-Sat; noon-2.30pm, 7-10.30pm Sun. **Set lunch** *Mon-Fri* £18.50 two courses; £21.50 three courses. **Set meal** (dinner, Sat-Sun lunch) £29.50 two courses; £35.50 three courses; £39.50 four courses. **Credit** AmEx, DC, MC, V. **Map** p397 F9.
This Belgravia operation might be a little pricey, but it's also one of London's best Italian restaurants. The food is nigh-on faultless, from imaginative pastas to more unusual dishes like sweetbreads in a Sicilian-style sweet and sour sauce.

Pizzerias

Of the chains, **Pizza Express** (with branches all over the city) remains the best. Other good bets within central London include **Condotti** (4 Mill Street, Mayfair, W1, 7499 1308), **Pizza on the Park** (11-13 Knightsbridge, SW1, 7235 5273), the **Soho Pizzeria** (16-18 Beak Street, Soho, W1, 7434 2480), the **Purple Sage** (92 Wigmore Street, Marylebone, W1, 7486 1912), **Spiga** (84-86 Wardour Street, Soho, W1, 7734 3444) and **La Spighetta** (43 Blandford Street, Marylebone, W1, 7486 7340).

Japanese

K-10

20 Copthall Avenue, The City, EC2 (7562 8510/ www.k10.net). Liverpool Street or Moorgate tube/rail. **Open** 11.30am-3pm, 5-10pm Mon-Fri; closed Sat, Sun. **Main courses** £1-£3.50. **Credit** AmEx, DC, MC, V. **Map** p405 Q6.
The rise of the kaiten epitomises the rising popularity of Japanese food in London, and K-10 is perhaps the best. Elegant decor and a innovative menu mix and mingle to make for a splendid enterprise.

Kulu Kulu

76 Brewer Street, Soho, W1 (7734 7316). Piccadilly Circus tube. **Open** noon-2.30pm, 5-10.30pm Mon-Fri; noon-4pm, 5-10.30pm Sat; closed Sun. **Main courses** £1.20-£10. **Credit** MC, V. **Map** p400 J7.
A no-nonsense conveyor-belt sushi bar with thoroughly authentic, keenly priced, gimmick-free grub.

Matsuri

15 Bury Street, Mayfair, SW1 (7839 1101/ www.matsuri-restaurant.com). Green Park or Piccadilly Circus tube. **Open** noon-2.30pm, 6-10.30pm Mon-Sat; closed Sun. **Main courses** £13-£30. **Credit** AmEx, DC, MC, V. **Map** p400 J7.

Guess what's on the menu at **Pizza Express**.

Matsuri avoids the stuffiness of some top-notch Japanese places while matching all in the quality of food and service. There's a great range of sushi, but teppanyaki is the speciality, and the greater part of the restaurant is laid out for that purpose.

Nobu

Metropolitan Hotel, 19 Old Park Lane, Mayfair, W1 (7447 4747). Hyde Park Corner tube. **Open** noon-2.15pm, 6-10pm Mon-Thur; noon-2.15pm, 6-11pm Fri; 6-11pm Sat; 6-9.30pm Sun. **Main courses** £1.50-£27. **Credit** AmEx, DC, MC, V. **Map** p400 H8.
Nobu co-owner (with Robert De Niro) Matsuhisa Nobuyuki has lived in Japan, Peru and the US, a fact reflected in a menu that melds the basics of Japanese cuisine with the food of the Americas. The result of this culinary daring is superb and unique.

Ramen Seto

19 Kingly Street, Soho, W1 (7434 0309). Oxford Circus tube. **Open** noon-3pm, 6-10pm Mon-Sat; closed Sun. **Main courses** £4.50-£6.80. **Credit** MC, V. **Map** p398 J6.
A good range of noodles and some excellent value lunches, including tempura and sashimi, make this friendly restaurant popular with tourists, trendies and local office workers alike.

Yo! Sushi/Yo! Below

52 Poland Street, Soho, W1 (7287 0443/ www.yosushi.com). Oxford Circus tube. **Open** noon-midnight daily. **Main courses** £1.50-£3.50. **Credit** AmEx, DC, MC, V. **Map** p398 J6.
Yo! Sushi boasts a wealth of novelties, including the world's longest sushi conveyor belt (60m/176ft), sushi-making machines and robotic drinks trolleys. The food is only decent, but for fun this place is hard to beat. Yo! Below is more of a drinking den, though basic sushi and noodle dishes are available.

Yumi

110 George Street, Marylebone, W1 (7935 8320). Baker Street, Bond Street or Marble Arch tube. **Open** 5.30-10.30pm daily. **Main courses** £10-£22. **Credit** AmEx, DC, MC, V. **Map** p398 G5.
It's pricey, but Yumi (pronounced 'yoo-mee') is a top-class restaurant that rarely fails to deliver. The food is beautifully fresh and artfully presented, and the staff are as refined as the cooking.

Jewish & Kosher

Six-13

19 Wigmore Street, Marylebone, W1 (7629 6133.www.six13.com). Bond Street tube. **Open** noon-3pm, 5.30-11pm Mon-Thur, Sun; 11.30am-3.30pm Fri (summer only); 11.30am-1pm winter); 8-11pm Sat (winter only). **Main courses** £10-£21.50. **Credit** AmEx, DC, MC, V. **Map** p398 G5.
The menu at this new restaurant might be kosher, but the food isn't traditionally Jewish: chef Stephen Collins has assimilated the best of Ashkenazi and Sephardi into his menu. Unique among London restaurants, and worth seeking out.

Eat, Drink, Shop

Solly's

148A Golders Green Road, Golders Green, NW11 (ground floor & takeaway 8455 2121/first floor 8455 0004). Golders Green tube. **Open** *Ground floor* 11am-11pm Mon-Thur, Sun; 11am-3pm Fri; 1hr after Sabbath-1am Sat. *First floor* 6.30-11.30pm Mon-Thur; noon-11pm Sun; winter also 1hr after Sabbath-11pm Sat; closed Fri. **Main courses** £8.50-£15. **Credit** AmEx, MC, V.

The upstairs dining room at this well-known kosher-supervised Lebanese Jewish restaurant is decked out in Middle Eastern style, with murals, rugs and ornate hanging lamps. A well-executed menu and attentive service ensure a great evening out.

Korean

Greater London's main concentration of Korean restaurants is in New Malden, 20 minutes from Waterloo by train; try **Chisshine** (74 Burlington Road, New Malden, 8942 0682).

Han Kang

16 Hanway Street, Fitzrovia, W1 (7637 1985). Tottenham Court Road tube. **Open** noon-3pm, 6-11pm Mon-Sat; closed Sun. **Main courses** £5-£15. **Credit** AmEx, MC, V. **Map** p399 K5.

A tatty backstreet linking Tottenham Court Road to Oxford Street is not the most glamorous location, but Han Kang's winning formula of great food, service and ambience ensures its continued success.

Kaya

42 Albemarle Street, Mayfair, W1 (7499 0622). Green Park or Piccadilly Circus tube. **Open** noon-3pm, 6-11pm Mon-Sat; 6-11pm Sun. **Main courses** £6.50-£43. **Credit** AmEx, DC, MC, V. **Map** p400 J7.

Kaya is London's most stylish Korean restaurant. Waitresses dressed in traditional costumes shuffle along to Korean folk music, and serve up impressive, authentic dishes such as *pibimbap*.

Malaysian & Indonesian

Melati

21 Great Windmill Street, Soho, W1 (7437 2745). Piccadilly Circus tube. **Open** noon-11.30pm Mon-Thur, Sun; noon-12.30am Fri, Sat. **Main courses** £5.65-£7.95. **Credit** AmEx, MC, V. **Map** p401 K7.

Perennially popular, Melati has been serving good Indonesian food for decades. Expect authentic cooking in generous portions.

Selasih

114 Seymour Place, Marylebone, W1 (7724 4454/www.selasih.co.uk). Edgware Road tube. **Open** noon-3pm, 6-10.30pm Mon-Sat; 6-10.30pm Sun. **Main courses** £3.95-£8.95. **Credit** AmEx, DC, MC, V. **Map** p395 F5.

The high ceiling and decorative mouldings in Selasih's main dining room provide a suitable backdrop for its exquisite Indonesian cooking. Service is friendly and prices reasonable, too.

Singapore Garden

83 Fairfax Road, Belsize Park, NW6 (7624 8233). Swiss Cottage tube/South Hampstead rail. **Open** noon-2.45pm, 6-10.45pm Mon-Thur, Sun; noon-2.45pm, 6-11.15pm Fri, Sat. **Main courses** £5.50-£27.50. **Credit** AmEx, DC, MC, V. **Map** p395 F5.

Chefs from China and Vietnam serve Malaysian, Cantonese, Thai and Singaporean dishes in a bright modern dining room at this top-class restaurant.

Singapura

31 Broadgate Circle, The City, EC2 (7256 5044/www.singapuras.co.uk). Liverpool Street tube/rail. **Open** 11.30am-9.30pm Mon-Fri; closed Sat, Sun. **Main courses** £7.50-£13.95. **Credit** AmEx, DC, MC, V. **Map** p403 Q5.

Formerly known as Suan Neo, Singapura's take on Singaporean cuisine is pricey – especially if you want the full freedom of the menu – but meritorious, even if service can be a little wayward.

Mediterranean

Bistro 190

190 Queen's Gate, South Kensington, SW7 (7581 5666). Gloucester Road or South Kensington tube. **Open** 7am-midnight Mon-Fri; 7.30am-midnight Sat; 7.30am-11.30pm Sun. **Main courses** £9.50-£14.95. **Credit** AmEx, DC, MC, V. **Map** p397 D9.

The airy dining room of this charming bistro offers ideal surroundings in which to enjoy simple, but accomplished dishes such as spatchcock with chorizo and wild mushroom risotto.

Snow's on the Green

166 Shepherd's Bush Road, Hammersmith, W6 (7603 2142). Hammersmith tube. **Open** noon-3pm, 6-11pm Mon-Fri; 6-11pm Sat; noon-3pm Sun. **Main courses** £10.50-£14.50. **Credit** AmEx, DC, MC, V.

The extensive menu at Sebastian Snow's sunny and serene restaurant encompasses adventurous dishes, such as roast sea scallops with buckwheat linguine, as well as Mediterranean classics.

Middle Eastern

Fairuz

3 Blandford Street, Marylebone, W1 (7486 8108). Baker Street tube. **Open** noon-11.30pm daily. **Main courses** £8.95-£16. **Credit** AmEx, DC, MC, V. **Map** p398 G5.

Warmly hued and intimate, Fairuz serves first-rate, classic Lebanese cooking without the haughty formality of some of its rivals.

Maroush

21 Edgware Road, Marylebone, W1 (7723 0773). Marble Arch tube. **Open** noon-2am daily. **Main courses** £12. **Minimum** £48 after 10pm. **Credit** AmEx, DC, MC, V. **Map** p395 F6.

A great place for a night out, Maroush provides entertainment in its dimly-lit basement dining room, as well as first-class Lebanese cuisine.

Eat, Drink, Shop

Patogh

8 Crawford Place, Marylebone, W1 (7262 4015).
Edgware Road tube. **Open** noon-midnight daily.
Main courses £5-£9.50. **No credit cards.**
Map p395 E5.
This delightful, informal restaurant offers good, no-
nonsense cooking that attracts a young, largely
Persian clientele.

Modern European

The cutting edge of modern cuisine in London.
Classical European cooking usually provides
the base, but ingredients and inspiration are
pillaged from around the world.

Alastair Little

49 Frith Street, Soho, W1 (7734 5183). Tottenham
Court Road tube. **Open** noon-3pm, 6-11pm Mon-Fri;
6-11pm Sat; closed Sun. **Main courses** £17.50.
Credit AmEx, DC, MC, V. **Map** p399 K6.
Alastair Little's small, informal restaurant is a Soho
institution. The menu is dominated by nicely rendered, gutsy, Italian-style cuisine, while attractive
modern art subtly enlivens the pared-down interior.

Andrew Edmunds

46 Lexington Street, Soho, W1 (7437 5708). Oxford
Circus or Piccadilly Circus tube. **Open** 12.30-3pm,
6-10.45pm Mon-Fri; 1-3pm, 10.45pm Sat; 1-3pm,

6-10.30pm Sun. **Main courses** £7.50-£12.50.
Credit AmEx, MC, V. **Map** p398 J6.
This informal bistro is tiny, with a loyal and large
following of thirtysomething Soho workers, but for
simple, well-executed dishes, a wonderful wine list
and a cosy atmosphere, it's worth the squeeze.

Bank

1 Kingsway, Holborn, WC2 (7379 9797/
www.bankrestaurant.co.uk). Covent Garden or Holborn
tube. **Open** 7.30-10.30am, noon-3pm, 5.30-11pm
Mon-Fri; 11.30am-3.30pm, 5.30-11pm Sat; 11.30am-
3.30pm, 5.30-9.30pm Sun. **Main courses** £9.50-
£22.50. **Credit** AmEx, DC, MC, V. **Map** p399 M6.
Huge, noisy and overcrowded, Bank serves food
around the clock. With pasta and risotto at £10-£13
and Bank fish and chips at £18.50, it can be pricey,
although the prix fixe offers better value.

Bibendum

Michelin House, 81 Fulham Road, Chelsea, SW3
(7581 5817/www.bibendum.co.uk). South Kensington
tube. **Open** noon-2.30pm, 7-11pm Mon-Fri;
12.30-3pm, 7-11pm Sat; 12.30-3pm, 7-10.30pm Sun.
Main courses £14.50-£24.50. **Credit** AmEx, DC,
MC, V. **Map** p397 E10.
Housed in the former HQ of the Michelin tyre company, Conran's Bibendum offers classic French-based
cuisine. It may have lost some of its original lustre,
but it's still a pretty faultless operation.

Let them entertain you

As well as some of the world's finest
dining, London also offers plenty of less
weighty choices. If a night at the opera's
not an option, **Sarastro** (126 Drury Lane,
Covent Garden, WC2, 7836 0101), in the
heart of Theatreland, lets you dine while
someone else sings for your supper.
Performers emerge from the wings to
serenade diners at intervals through the
evening. An ingenious design – diners can
peer down on the entertainment from
balconies – and heavy use of gilt and
chandeliers combine to give an appropriate
Italianate feel. When we visited, £30 yielded
a filling three-course set menu. Bravo.

But if arias while you eat is a bit highbrow,
how about dinner with the King? The **Elvis
Gracelands Palace** (881-3 Old Kent Road,
Peckham, SE15, 7639 3961) has been an
insitution ever since owner Paul Chan's
impersonations – he's known throughout the
country as the Chinese Elvis – came to the
attention of the tabloids. The food, though
acceptable, is incidental to the floorshow, as
'Elvis' (circa jump suit and kung-fu posturing),
plays the crowd like, well, like the King.

Diners, mostly in big groups, invariably end
up dancing on the tables. And 'Elvis' loves
every minute of it. On one occasion, as the
over-hyped pretend Presley blocked the only
exit, reluctant to let his audience escape, a
diner grabbed the mike from his hand and
shouted into it, 'Elvis! Leave the building!'
Top fun.

Anything to ward off a cold in London has
to be good, and **Garlic & Shots** (14 Frith
Street, Soho, W1, 7734 9505) will give you
enough oral ammo to keep most bugs at bay,
not to mention vampires. The restaurant does
what it says on the tin – and how. A paean to
the powerful root, it has a huge range of
drinks from garlic vodka to garlic beer (non-
garlic wines are also available, though this is
kind of missing the point), and also offers a
simple but tasty menu featuring garlic steak
and garlic-encrusted chicken. Stagger in from
the chill, down a bloodshot – vodka, garlic,
chilli and tomato juice – and, as your arteries
thaw, check out the Dr Crippen meets Ozzy
Osborne decor. There's a crypt-like bar
downstairs and, if you can stand the light,
outside tables at the rear.

Pay a visit to **Bank**. *See p204.*

Bluebird

350 King's Road, Chelsea, SW3 (7559 1000/ www.conran.com). Sloane Square tube, then 19, 22, 319 bus. **Open** noon-3pm, 6-11pm Mon-Fri; 11am-3.30pm, 6-11pm Sat; 11am-3.30pm, 6-10pm Sun. **Main courses** £8.50-£29.50. **Credit** AmEx, DC, MC, V. **Map** p397 D12.

This former garage is now a Conran-owned gastro-complex consisting of a large but very pretty restaurant, a bar, a café, a fruit and veg stall, a food shop and a cook shop. The buzzy first-floor restaurant is a relaxing spot for weekend brunch.

Clarke's

124 Kensington Church Street, Kensington, W8 (7221 9225/www.sallyclarke.com). Notting Hill Gate tube. **Open** 12.30-2pm, 7-10pm Mon-Fri. **Main courses** (lunch only) £14. **Set dinner** £44 four courses. **Credit** AmEx, DC, MC, V. **Map** p394 B7.

The freshness of the ingredients dictates the daily changing menu here. At lunch there's an element of choice, but dinner here means accepting Clarke's choice for the evening, so phone first if you're a fussy eater. Wonderful food, great service.

The Fifth Floor

Harvey Nichols, Knightsbridge, SW1 (7235 5250). Knightsbridge tube. **Open** noon-3pm, 6.30-11.30pm Mon-Fri; noon-3.30pm, 6.30-11.30pm Sat; 6.30-11.30pm Sun. **Main courses** £4.50-£20.50. **Credit** AmEx, DC, MC, V. **Map** p397 F9.

Cocooned by a glass wall from the din of Harvey Nicks' fifth floor café is this relaxed, well-mannered modern European restaurant. The food is consistently impressive, the wine list is a beauty and the service is easy and agreeable.

French House Dining Room

First floor, French House, 49 Dean Street, Soho, W1 (7437 2477). Piccadilly Circus or Tottenham Court Road tube. **Open** noon-3pm, 6-11.15pm Mon-Sat; closed Sun. **Main courses** £8.50-£14. **Credit** AmEx, DC, MC, V. **Map** p399 K6.

An inimitable, unmissable slice of Soho, this tiny lacquered room is always packed with relaxed regulars who lap up expertly rendered dishes such as guinea fowl and lentils from the daily changing menu.

The Glasshouse

14 Station Parade, Kew, Surrey (8940 6777). Kew Gardens tube/rail. **Open** noon-2.30pm, 7-10.30pm Mon-Thur; noon-2.30pm, 6.30-10.30pm Fri, Sat; 12.30-3pm Sun. **Main courses** £15. **Credit** AmEx, MC, V.

A pleasantly decorated, light-filled dining room and friendly staff helps make this a supremely comfortable and welcoming restaurant. The menu is also excellent, packed with unfussy, gimmick-free dishes.

Granita

127 Upper Street, Islington, N1 (7226 3222). Angel tube/Highbury & Islington tube/rail. **Open** 6.30-10.30pm Tue; 12.30-2.30pm, 6.30-10.30pm Wed-Sun; closed Mon. **Main courses** £10.95-£14.95. **Credit** MC, V. **Map** p402 O3.

This simple restaurant is still the best in Islington. Stand-out dishes include asparagus chargrilled with sweet potato, dill and sour cream, and spinach fatayer with feta, cos, olive and parsley salad.

The Ivy

1 West Street, Covent Garden, WC2 (7836 4751). Covent Garden or Leicester Square tube. **Open** noon-3pm, 5.30pm-midnight Mon-Sat; noon-3.30pm, 5.30pm-midnight Sun. **Main courses** £10.75-£36.50. **Credit** AmEx, DC, MC, V. **Map** p399 K6.

Be prepared to book six weeks in advance to get a peak-time table at this beautifully restrained thespians' favourite. Well-drilled staff serve dishes such as corned beef hash and upmarket fish and chips from a menu that sticks to a well-loved formula.

Eat, Drink, Shop

Odette's

130 Regent's Park Road, Primrose Hill, NW1 (7586 5486). Chalk Farm tube. **Open** *Wine bar* 12.30-2.30pm, 5.30-10.30pm Mon-Sat; 12.30-2.30pm Sun. *Restaurant* 12.30-2.30pm, 7-11pm Mon-Fri; 7-11pm Sat. **Main courses** £10.50-£18.50. **Credit** AmEx, DC, MC, V.

With its gorgeous display of gilded mirrors upstairs, and cosy pockets of space downstairs, Odette's offers a delightfully old-fashioned, intimate evening. Happily, the quality of the food (not to mention a superb wine list) more than matches the setting.

Orrery

55 Marylebone High Street, Marylebone, W1 (7616 8000/www.orrery.co.uk). Baker Street or Regent's Park tube. **Open** noon-3pm, 7-11pm daily. **Main courses** £14.50-£26. **Credit** AmEx, DC, MC, V. **Map** p398 G4.

Cafés, coffees & light lunches

London is now better supplied with quality cafés (from trad to trendy), coffee shops, soup bars and lunch pit stops than ever. If all you want is a shot of caffeine and a slice of cake, fast-growing chains **Aroma**, **Caffè Nero**, **Coffee Republic**, **Costa** and **Starbucks** have branches all over the centre of town. Ground-breaking sandwich chain **Prêt à Manger** has spawned a sea of other, similarly smart and modern operations, **Eat** chief among them.

The South Bank & Bankside

Konditor & Cook *Young Vic, 66 The Cut, SE1 (7620 2700). Southwark tube/Waterloo tube/rail.* **Open** 8.30am-11pm Mon-Fri; 10.30am-11pm Sat; closed Sun. **Credit** MC, V. **Map** p404 N8.

Divine cakes from its own bakery and global grub are the attractions at this popular café.

The City

See also **The Place Below** (*p215*), the **Arkansas Café** (*p189*) and **The Quiet Revolution** (*p215*).

Holborn & Clerkenwell

Goodfellas *50 Lamb's Conduit Street, WC1 (7405 7088). Holborn tube.* **Open** 8am-7pm Mon-Fri; 10am-6pm Sat; closed Sun. **Map** p399 M4.

Great sandwiches and an enormously popular lunchtime buffet (11.30am-2pm).

Saints' *1 Clerkenwell Road, EC1 (7490 4199). Barbican tube.* **Open** 8am-6pm Mon-Fri (no hot food after 4pm); closed Sat, Sun. **Map** p402 O4.

A cheap and cheery lunch spot, though service can sometimes be slow.

Bloomsbury & Fitzrovia

Coffee Gallery *23 Museum Street, WC1 (7436 0455). Holborn or Tottenham Court Road tube.* **Open** 8.30am-5.30pm Mon-Fri; 10am-5.30pm Sat; closed Sun. **Afternoon tea served** 3-5.30pm. **Set tea** £3.40. **Credit** MC, V. **Map** p399 L5.

Light lunches, coffee and superior cakes in this jolly, bright café handily near the British Museum.

October Gallery Café *24 Old Gloucester Street, WC1 (7242 7367). Holborn tube.* **Open** 12.30-2.30pm Tue-Fri; closed Mon, Sat, Sun. **Map** p399 L5.

Global cooking and global art in a quiet gallery tucked away behind Holborn.

Pâtisserie Deux Amis *63 Judd Street, WC1 (7383 7029). Russell Square tube/King's Cross tube/rail.* **Open** 9am-5.30pm Mon-Sat; 9am-1.30pm Sun. **Map** p399 L3.

An oasis of sophistication in a drab area, offering filled baguettes, cakes, pastries and a Mediterranean ambience.

Marylebone

Delizioso *90B Cleveland Street, W1 (7383 0497). Great Portland Street tube.* **Open** 8am-5pm Mon-Fri; closed Sat, Sun. **Map** p398 J4.

Marylebone's Delizioso is a cut above the usual sandwich bar.

Pâtisserie Valerie *105 Marylebone High Street, W1 (7935 6240). Baker Street or Bond Street tube.* **Open** 7.30am-7pm Mon-Fri; 8am-7pm Sat; 9am-6pm Sun. **Credit** AmEx, MC, V. **Map** p398 G5.

This elegant café offers toothsome snacks and savouries, and fabulous cakes and tarts.

Mayfair & St James's

Madison's *171 Piccadilly, W1 (7629 4991). Green Park or Piccadilly Circus tube.* **Open** 7am-7pm Mon-Fri; 9am-7pm Sat, Sun. **Credit** AmEx, DC, MC, V. **Map** p401 J7.

A chic coffee house with imaginative food.

Victory Café *Basement, Gray's Antiques Market, South Molton Lane, W1 (7495 6860). Bond Street tube.* **Open** 10am-5.30pm Mon-Fri; closed Sat, Sun. **Map** p398 H6.

A quirky 1950s-style café in the depths of an antiques market. Food is more up to date.

The most understated – and underrated – of Sir Terence Conran's London restaurant portfolio. The decor is very much à la Conran but the cooking is light years away from the production-line experience found at some of his other kitchens.

Oxo Tower Restaurant

Barge House Street, South Bank, SE1 (7803 3888).
Blackfriars or Waterloo tube/rail. **Open** *Brasserie*
noon-3.30pm, 5.30-11.30pm Mon-Sat; 6-10.30pm Sun. *Restaurant* noon-3pm, 6-11pm Mon-Fri; noon-3.30pm, 6-11pm Sat; noon-3.30pm, 6.30-10.30pm Sun. **Main courses** *Brasserie* £7-£17. *Restaurant* £11-£25. **Credit** AmEx, DC, MC, V. **Map** p404 N7.
The food here is of a high standard, but hope the fab views over the Thames distract you from the sky-high prices. That said, the set meal at the Brasserie includes a glass of house wine and coffee.

Going underground at the **Café in the Crypt**.

Soho

For dim sum, *see p193. See also* **Mildred's** (*p215*), **Kulu Kulu** (*p201* and **Ramen Seto** (*p200*).

Bar Italia *22 Frith Street, W1 (7437 4520). Leicester Square or Tottenham Court Road tube.* **Open** 24hrs daily. **Map** p399 K6.
Evergreen, ever-open Italian coffee bar.

EAT *16A Soho Square, W1 (7222 7200). Tottenham Court Road tube.* **Open** 7am-6pm Mon-Fri; 10am-5pm Sat; closed Sun. **Map** p399 K6.
Outstanding sarnies, muffins, cookies, coffees and other lunchables at this growing chain.

Maison Bertaux *28 Greek Street, W1 (7437 6007). Leicester Square, Piccadilly Circus or Tottenham Court Road tube.* **Open** 9am-8pm daily. **Map** p399 K6.
A wonderfully lost-in-time French café with exquisite pastries and a priceless ambience.

Pâtisserie Valerie *44 Old Compton Street, W1 (7437 3466). Leicester Square or*
Tottenham Court Road tube. **Open** 7.30am-8pm Mon-Fri; 8am-8pm Sat; 9.30am-7pm Sun. **Map** p399 K6.
Wonderful savoury flans, cakes and pastries are found at this massively popular haunt.

Star Café *22 Great Chapel Street, W1 7437 8778). Tottenham Court Road tube.* **Open** 7am-4pm Mon-Fri; closed Sat, Sun. **Map** p399 K6.
A cosy oasis just off Oxford Street, offering pastas, salads and five daily specials.

Covent Garden & St Giles's

See also **Rock & Soul Plaice** (*p193*), **World Food Café** (*p215*) and **Food for Thought** (*p215*).

Neal's Yard Beach Café *13 Neal's Yard, WC2 (7240 1168). Covent Garden tube.* **Open** 11am-7pm daily. **Map** p399 L6.
A colourful spot for brunchy snacks and great milkshakes.

Photographers' Gallery Café *5 Great Newport Street (7831 1772). Leicester Square tube.* **Open** 11am-5.30pm Mon-Sat; noon-5.30pm Sun. **Map** p401 K6.
Healthy lunchtime snacks and photography exhibitions at this nice spot.

Knightsbridge & South Kensington

Gloriette Pâtisserie *128 Brompton Road, SW3 (7589 4750).* **Open** 7am-7pm Mon-Sat; 9am-6pm Sun. **Credit** MC, V. **Map** p397 E9.
A tiny, cosy place in which to tuck into Austrian sweets, pastries and exquisite cakes.

Westminster

Café in the Crypt *Crypt of St Martin-in-the-Fields, Duncannon Street, WC2 (7839 4342). Charing Cross tube/rail.* **Open** *Coffee bar* 10am-8pm Mon-Wed; 10am-10.30pm Thur-Sat; noon-8pm Sun. *Buffet* noon-3.15pm, 5-7.30pm, daily; 8.30-10.30pm Thur-Sat. **Map** p401 K7.
An atmospheric spot, in the crypt of a church, dishing out good salads and sandwiches.

Eat, Drink, Shop

The People's Palace

Royal Festival Hall, South Bank, SE1 (7928 9999/ www.peoplespalace.co.uk). Waterloo tube/rail. **Open** noon-3pm, 5.30-11pm daily. **Main courses** £13.50-£17.50. **Credit** AmEx, DC, MC, V. **Map** p401 M8.

The dining option of choice if you're taking advantage of the entertainment at the South Bank Centre. There's a hint of airport lounge about the interior, but the mainly Med-influenced menu is reliable, the wine list is well chosen and the river views are fab.

Quaglino's

16 Bury Street, St James's, SW1 (7930 6767/ www.conran.com). Green Park or Piccadilly Circus tube. **Open** *Bar* 11.30am-1am Mon-Thur; 11.30am-2am Fri, Sat; noon-11pm Sun. *Restaurant* noon-2.30pm, 5.30pm-midnight Mon-Thur; noon-2.30pm, 5.30pm-1am Fri, Sat; noon-2.30pm, 5.30-11pm Sun. **Main courses** £13-£24. **Credit** AmEx, DC, MC, V. **Map** p400 J7.

Quag's sunken dining room, polished and gleaming, looks as good as ever and the upmarket comfort food usually passes muster, but diners can feel they're just part of an impersonal culinary machine.

Smiths of Smithfield

67-77 Charterhouse Street, Farringdon, EC1 (7236 6666/www.smithsofsmithfield.co.uk). Farringdon tube/rail. **Open** *Bar* 7am-11pm Mon-Fri; 10.30am-11pm Sat; 10.30am-10.30pm Sun. *Dining Room* noon-3pm, 6-11pm Mon-Fri; 6-11pm Sat; closed Sun. *Top Floor* noon-3pm, 6-11pm Mon-Fri; 6-11pm Sat; noon-4pm, 6-10.30pm Sun. **Main courses** *Dining Room* £9.50-£10.50. *Top Floor* £15-£26. **Credit** AmEx, DC, MC, V. **Map** p402 O5.

An unfailingly contemporary eaterie close by the meat market, Smiths is most things to most people. The ground-floor bar/café offers some terrific fry-ups among its treats, with the upstairs brasserie and dining room serving a mix of British and European dishes under the direction of John Torode.

Stephen Bull

5-7 Blandford Street, Marylebone, W1 (7486 9696). Bond Street tube. **Open** 12.15-2.30pm, 6.30-10.30pm Mon-Fri; 6.30-10.30pm Sat; closed Sun. **Main courses** £9.95-£16. **Credit** AmEx, DC, MC, V. **Map** p398 G5.

One of the founding fathers of Mod Euro cooking in London, Bull continues to serve outstanding food in his modern, comfortable restaurant. Stand-out dishes include haggis fritters with curry gravy, and duck tournedos with red onion tarte tatin. A real treasure, and a serious bargain.

Sugar Club

21 Warwick Street, Soho, W1 (7437 7776/ www.thesugarclub.co.uk). Oxford Circus or Piccadilly Circus tube. **Open** noon-3pm, 6-10.30pm Mon-Sat; 12.30-3pm, 6-10pm Sun. **Main courses** £13.80-£19.90. **Credit** AmEx, DC, MC, V. **Map** p400 J7.

Fusion cooking is a dangerous game, but when it works, the results can be dazzling. The conveniently central Sugar Club is one of the most successful exponents of this eclectic approach, its menu veering between Europe and Asia. Through and through, a very impressive operation.

Teatro

93-107 Shaftesbury Avenue, Soho, W1 (7494 3040). Piccadilly Circus tube. **Open** noon-3pm, 6-11.45pm Mon-Fri; 6-11.45pm Sat; closed Sun. **Main courses** £12.75-£19.75. **Credit** AmEx, DC, MC, V. **Map** p399 K6.

Owned by ex-footballer Lee Chapman and actress Leslie Ash, Teatro is luvvie heaven, but the food is impressive and the wine list extensive and well chosen, if a little pricey.

North African

Momo

25 Heddon Street, Mayfair, W1 (7434 4040). Piccadilly Circus tube. **Open** noon-2.30pm, 7-11pm Mon-Sat; noon-2.30pm, 6.30-10.30pm Sun. **Main courses** £9.75-£17. **Credit** AmEx, DC, MC, V. **Map** p400 J7.

Momo has survived its original hype to emerge as one of London's best North African restaurants. The decor is as wonderful as the food, with a stone interior, candlelight and Arabic carved wooden screens. The bar downstairs is members only, but Mô, the tearoom next door, is more welcoming.

Original Tajines

7A Dorset Street, Marylebone, W1 (7935 1545). Baker Street tube. **Open** 12.30-3pm, 6-11pm Mon-Fri; 6-11pm Sat; closed Sun. **Main courses** £8.95-£11.95. **Credit** MC, V. **Map** p398 G5.

An popular, unpretentious restaurant that serves big portions of authentic North African food and some splendid Moroccan wines.

Oriental

Birdcage

110 Whitfield Street, Fitzrovia, W1 (7383 3346). Goodge Street or Warren Street tube. **Open** noon-2.30pm, 6-11.15pm Mon-Fri; 6-11.15pm Sat; closed Sun. **Set lunch** £19.50 two courses; £26.50 three courses. **Set dinner** £32.50 two courses; £38.50 three courses. **Credit** AmEx, DC, MC, V. **Map** p398 J4.

Sculptures, ornithological knick-knacks and slide projections are part of the decor at this visually incredible restaurant. Michael von Hruschka's fusion cooking is also unusual and often stunning.

Itsu

118 Draycott Avenue, Chelsea, SW3 (7584 5522/ www.itsu.com). South Kensington tube/49 bus. **Open** noon-11pm Mon-Sat; noon-10pm Sun. **Main courses** £2.50-£4.50. **Credit** AmEx, MC, V. **Map** p397 E10.

East meets west at this relaxed conveyor-belt eaterie. Food is a sushi hybrid (almost an oriental tapas) and is served in colour-coded dishes. Help yourself to the likes of spicy crab wrap and prawn sushi with pesto.

A cut above the usual pub grub: the **French House Dining Room**. *See p205.*

Silks & Spice

23 Foley Street, Fitzrovia, W1 (7636 2718). Goodge Street or Oxford Circus tube. **Open** noon-11pm Mon-Fri; 5.30-11pm Sat; 5.30-10.30pm Sun. **Main courses** £4.50-£11.95. **Credit** AmEx, DC, MC, V. **Map** p398 J5.
A chain of 'Thai-Malaysian café-bar-restaurants', Silks & Spice is one of the most reliable oriental joints in town. The decor is warm-toned and the cooking varied and assured. Check the phone book for details of branches.

Vong

Berkeley Hotel, Wilton Place, Knightsbridge, SW1 (7235 1010/www.jean-georges.com). Hyde Park Corner or Knightsbridge tube. **Open** noon-2.30pm, 6-11.30pm Mon-Fri; 11.30am-2pm, 6-11.30pm Sat; 11.30am-2pm, 6-10.30pm Sun. **Main courses** £14.50-£31.50. **Credit** AmEx, DC, MC, V. **Map** p400 G8.
Like Nobu, Vong is an import from New York, and, again, the cooking (a Thai/French fusion) has travelled very well. It's pricey, but save up and treat yourself: and don't pass on the stunning desserts.

Wagamama

101A Wigmore Street, Marylebone, W1 (7409 0111/ www.wagamama.com). Bond Street or Marble Arch tube. **Open** noon-11pm Mon-Sat; 12.30-10pm Sun. **Main courses** £4.85-£7.35. **Credit** AmEx, DC, MC, V. **Map** p398 G6.
Having become something of a London institution (see the phone book for branches), the Wagamama empire shows no signs of waning. Health- and money-conscious diners pack the long tables and slurp bowls of ramen and plates of noodles. You may have to queue, but it's worth the wait.

Pie & mash

It may lack finesse and any kind of visual appeal, but the last bastions of London's indubitably unique indigenous cuisine – pies, eels and mash – do offer delicious stomach-fillers at laughably low prices. Two of the finest purveyors of the old-school Cockney fare are **G Kelly** (414 Bethnal Green Road, Bethnal Green, E2, 7739 3603) and **Manze's** (87 Tower Bridge Road, Bermondsey, SE1; 7407 2985).

Polish

Patio

5 Goldhawk Road, Shepherd's Bush, W12 (8743 5194). Goldhawk Road or Shepherd's Bush tube. **Open** noon-3pm, 6pm-midnight Mon-Fri; 6pm-midnight Sat, Sun. **Main courses** £4-£8.20. **Credit** AmEx, DC, MC, V.
The quality of the cooking is sky-high and the prices are rock-bottom at this welcoming 'lounge/diner'. Standards such as blinis and carp Polish-style are served up by relaxed, friendly staff in comfortable surroundings.

Eat, Drink, Shop

Wódka

12 St Alban's Grove, Kensington, W8 (7937 6513/www.wodka.co.uk). Gloucester Road or High Street Kensington tube. **Open** 12.30-2.30pm, 7-11.15pm Mon-Fri; 7-11.15pm Sat, Sun. **Main courses** £8.90-£13.90. **Credit** AmEx, DC, MC, V. **Map** p396 C9.

Wódka delivers traditional Polish dishes with a pleasingly progressive slant, innovatively combining classic hearty soups, stuffed cabbage and the like with unexpected ingredients such as olives and couscous.

Portuguese

Golborne Road, W10 is home to the best of the Portuguese *pastelarias* (pâtisseries).

O Cantinho de Portugal

137 Stockwell Road, Stockwell, SW9 (7924 0218). Stockwell tube/Brixton tube/rail/2, 322, 345 bus. **Open** 10am-midnight daily. **Main courses** £6-£9. **Credit** MC, V.
Choose between the light, modern restaurant and the shiny bar area at O Cantinho de Portugal, with green

Restaurants by area

The South Bank & Bankside

fish! (Fish, *p193*); **Oxo Tower Restaurant** (Modern European, *p207*); **People's Palace** (Modern European, *p208*); **Quiet Revolution** (Vegetarian, *p215*); **Tas** (Turkish, *p215*).

The City

K-10 (Japanese, *p201*); **The Place Below** (Vegetarian, *p215*); **Singapura** (Malaysian, *p203*).

Holborn & Clerkenwell

Bank (Modern European, *p204*); **Club Gascon** (French, *p194*); **Gaudí** (Spanish, *p212*); **Moro** (Spanish, *p212*); **St John** (British, *p192*); **Smiths of Smithfield** (Modern European, *p208*).

Bloomsbury & Fitzrovia

Birdcage (Oriental, *p208*); **Han Kang** (Korean, *p203*); **Passione** (Italian, *p200*); **Pied à Terre** (Haute cuisine, *p198*); **Rasa Samudra** (Indian, *p199*); **Silks & Spice** (Oriental, *p209*).

Marylebone

Fairuz (Middle Eastern, *p203*); **Ibla** (Italian, *p200*); **Maroush** (Middle Eastern, *p203*); **Original Tajines** (North African, *p208*); **Orrery** (Modern European, *p205*); **Patogh** (Middle Eastern, *p204*); **Porte des Indes** (Indian, *p199*); **Purple Sage** (Pizzerias, *p201*); **Seashell** (Fish & chips, *p194*); **Selasih** (Indonesian, *p203*); **Six-13** (Jewish & Kosher, *p201*); **La Spighetta** (Pizzerias, *p201*); **Stephen Bull** (Modern European, *p208*). **Wagamama** (Oriental, *p209*); **Yumi** (Japanese, *p201*).

Mayfair & St James's

Cheznico at Ninety Park Lane (Haute cuisine, *p198*); **Condotti** (Pizzerias, *p201*); **The Criterion** (French, *p194*); **Gaucho Grill** (Argentinian, *p189*); **Greenhouse** (British, *p191*); **Kaya** (Korean, *p203*); **Matsuri**

Rasa. *See p199.*

(Japanese, *p201*); **Momo** (North African, *p208*); **Nobu** (Japanese, *p201*); **Oriental** (Chinese, *p193*); **Quaglino's** (Modern European, *p208*); **Sofra Restaurant** (Turkish, *p213*); **Tamarind** (Indian, *p199*).

Soho & Chinatown

Alastair Little (Modern European, *p204*); **Andrew Edmunds** (Modern European, *p204*); **L'Escargot** (French, *p194*); **French House Dining Room** (Modern European, *p205*); **Golden Dragon** (Dim Sum, *p193*); **Golden Harvest** (Chinese, *p192*); **Harbour City** (Chinese, *p193*); **Hunan** (Chinese, *p192*); **Kulu Kulu** (Japanese, *p201*); **Lindsay House** (British, *p191*); **Melati** (Indonesian, *p203*); **Mildred's** (Vegetarian, *p215*); **Mr Kong** (Chinese, *p193*); **New Diamond** (Chinese, *p193*); **Pizza Express** (Pizzerias, *p201*); **Ramen Seto** (Japanese, *p201*); **Saigon** (Vietnamese, *p215*); **Soho Pizzeria** (Pizzerias, *p201*); **Spiga** (Pizzerias, *p201*); **Sri Siam** (Thai, *p212*); **Sugar Club** (Modern European,

Eat, Drink, Shop

tiles, bright lights and droning TV. Tapas might include pig's ear salad. An authentic Iberian experience in the heart of Portuguese territory.

The interior here is dark-hued and candlelit, with portraits of Russian aristos adorning the walls, while the menu is long and comprised mainly of traditional Russian dishes, including a range of cavier.

Russian

Nikita's
65 Ifield Road, Chelsea, SW10 (7352 6326). Earl's Court or West Brompton tube. **Open** 7.30-11.30pm Tue-Sat; closed Mon, Sun. **Main courses** £8.50-£14.95. **Credit** MC, V. **Map** p396 C12.

South African

Springbok Café
42 Devonshire Road, Chiswick, W4 (8742 3149/ www.springbokcafecuisine.com). Turnham Green tube. **Open** 6.30-11pm Mon-Sat; closed Sun. **Main courses** £8.75-£15.75. **Credit** DC, MC, V.

p208); **Teatro** (Modern European, *p208*); **Vasco & Piero's Pavilion** (Italian, *p200*); **Yo! Sushi/Yo! Below** (Japanese, *p201*).

Covent Garden & St Giles's
Belgo Centraal (Belgian, *p191*); **Food for Thought** (Vegetarian, *p215*); **The Ivy** (Modern European, *p205*); **J Sheekey** (Fish, *p193*); **Livebait** (Fish, *p193*); **Rock & Sole Plaice** (Fish & chips, *p194*); **Rules** (British, *p192*); **Thai Pot** (Thai, *p212*); **World Food Café** (Vegetarian, *p215*).

Westminster
Quilon (Indian, *p199*).

Knightsbridge & South Kensington
Bistro 190 (Mediterranean, *p203*); **The Fifth Floor** (Modern European, *p205*); **Isola** (Italian, *p200*); **Pizza on the Park** (Pizzerias, *p201*); **La Tante Claire** (Haute cuisine, *p198*); **Vong** (Oriental, *p209*).

Belgravia & Pimlico
Boisdale (British, *p191*); **Roussillon** (French, *p194*); **Stefano Cavallini Restaurant at the Halkin** (Haute cuisine, *p199*); **Zafferano** (Italian, *p200*).

Chelsea
Bibendum (Modern European, *p204*); **Bluebird** (Modern European, *p205*); **Busabong** (Thai, *p212*); **Cactus Blue** (American, *p189*); **Gordon Ramsay** (Haute cuisine, *p198*); **Itsu** (Oriental, *p208*); **Nikita's** (Russian, *p211*); **El Rincón** (Spanish, *p212*); **Vama** (Indian, *p199*); **Zaika** (Indian, *p200*).

North London
Afghan Kitchen (Islington, Afghan, *p189*); **Granita** (Islington, Modern European, *p205*); **Halepi** (Belsize Park, Greek, *p197*); **Istanbul Iskembecisi** (Stoke Newington, Turkish, *p213*); **Iznik** (Highbury, Turkish, *p213*); **Mango Room** (Camden, Caribbean, *p192*); **Odette's** (Primrose Hill, Modern European, *p206*); **Schnecke** (Islington, French, *p197*);

Singapore Garden (Belsize Park, Malaysian, *p203*); **Solly's** (Golders Green, Jewish & Kosher, *p203*).

East London
Arkansas Café (Spitalfields, American, *p189*); **Café Spice Namaste** (Whitechapel, Indian, *p199*); **G Kelly** (Bethnal Green, Pie & mash, *p209*); **Green Papaya** (Hackney, Vietnamese, *p215*); **Little Georgia** (London Fields, Georgian, *p197*); **The Real Greek** (Hoxton, Greek, *p197*); **Viet Hoa** (Shoreditch, Vietnamese, *p215*).

South London
Bah Humbug (Brixton, Vegetarian, *p215*); **Brixtonian Havana Club** (Brixton, Caribbean, *p192*); **Chez Bruce** (Wandsworth, French, *p194*); **Chez Lindsay** (Richmond, French, *p194*); **Enoteca Turi** (Putney, Italian, *p200*); **The Glasshouse** (Kew, Modern European, *p205*); **Kastoori** (Tooting, Indian, *p199*); **The Lavender** (Clapham, Global, *p197*); **Manze's** (Bermondsey, Pie & mash, *p209*); **O Cantinho de Portugal** (Stockwell, Portuguese, *p210*).

West London
Assaggi (Notting Hill, Italian, *p200*); **Bali Sugar** (Notting Hill, Global, *p197*); **Cambio de Tercio** (Earl's Court, Spanish, *p212*); **Clarke's** (Kensington, Modern European, *p205*); **Dakota** (Notting Hill, American, *p189*); **The Gate** (Hammersmith, Vegetarian, *p215*); **Gifto's Lahore Karahi** (Southall, Indian, *p199*); **Karahi King** (Wembley, Indian, *p199*); **Mandalay** (Paddington, Burmese, *p192*); **Mandarin Kitchen** (Bayswater, Chinese, *p193*); **Mandola** (Notting Hill, Sudanese, *p212*); **New Four Seasons** (Bayswater, Chinese, *p193*); **Patio** (Shepherd's Bush, Polish, *p209*); **Rodizio Rico** (Bayswater, Brazilian, *p191*); **Royal China** (Bayswater, Chinese, *p193*); **Snow's on the Green** (Hammersmith, Mediterranean, *p203*); **Springbok Café** (Chiswick, South African, *p211*); **Tawana** (Bayswater, Thai, *p212*); **Veronica's** (Bayswater, British, *p192*); **Wódka** (Kensington, Polish, *p210*).

Eat, Drink, Shop

London's only exclusively South African restaurant offers such rare delights as peppered kudu, Plettenberg Bay linefish and zebra samosas. The quality of the cooking, however, has much more to offer than mere novelty, and the staff are delightful.

Spanish

Cambio de Tercio

163 Old Brompton Road, Earl's Court, SW5 (7244 8970). Gloucester Road tube. **Open** 12.30-2.30pm, 7-11.30pm Mon-Sat; 12.30-2.30pm, 7-11pm Sun. **Main courses** £12.50-£14.90. **Credit** AmEx, MC, V. **Map** p396 C11.

This stylish restaurant out in the wilds of Earl's Court is a fine example of sophisticated modern spanish food. Diego Ferrer's cooking is innovative but still true to its roots.

El Rincón

2A Pond Place, Chelsea, SW3 (7584 6655). South Kensington tube. **Open** 6-11pm Mon-Sat; closed Sun. **Set dinner** £14.50 one course; £20.50 two courses; £24.50 three courses. **Credit** AmEx, MC, V. **Map** p397 E11.

Chef Anton Escalera's modern take on Spanish cuisine garnered raves when it opened in late 2000, and not without good reason. The food here is exquisite: try the snails starter, and then follow it with the suckling pig.

Gaudí

63 Clerkenwell Road, Clerkenwell, EC1 (7608 3220/ www.turnmills.co.uk). Farringdon tube/rail/55, 243 bus. **Open** noon-2.30pm, 7-10.30pm Mon-Fri; closed Sat, Sun. **Main courses** £16-£17.25. **Credit** AmEx, DC, MC, V. **Map** p402 N4.

The grandiose Gaudí-esque decor of convoluted metalwork and multicoloured tiling is matched by the food of Nacho Martínez Jiménez, whose cooking, firmly rooted in traditional Spanish styles, shows great flair.

Moro

34-6 Exmouth Market, Clerkenwell, EC1 (7833 8336). Farringdon tube/rail. **Open** 12.30-2.30pm, 7-10.30pm Mon-Fri; 7-10.30pm Sat; closed Sun. **Main courses** £10.50-£14.50. **Credit** AmEx, DC, MC, V. **Map** p402 N4.

The mass of attention it's received since its 1997 opening has not bred complacency at Moro. The service remains an exemplary mix of friendliness and efficiency and the cooking continues to hit the right note. Between lunch and dinner, you can get tapas at the bar.

Sudanese

Mandola

139-141 Westbourne Grove, Notting Hill, W11 (7229 4734). Notting Hill Gate tube/23 bus. **Open** noon-11.30pm Mon-Sat; noon-10.30pm Sun. **Main courses** £9.50-£10.50. **Credit** MC, V. **Map** p394 A6.

This pleasant Sudanese restaurant now extends over three rooms, attractively decorated in warm, bright colours. The food is tasty and freshly prepared, and the bring-your-own-booze policy (corkage is £1) helps to keep the bill low.

Thai

Busabong

1A Langton Street, Chelsea, SW10 (7352 7414/ 7517/www.busabong.co.uk). Sloane Square tube, then 11, 22 bus. **Open** noon-2.45pm, 6-11.15pm daily. **Main courses** £7.95-£15.95. **Credit** AmEx, MC, V. **Map** p397 D13.

A soothing oriental design makes for a relaxing, elegant backdrop to the clear, precise flavours of the consistently first-rate cooking at this splendid Chelsea restaurant.

Sri Siam

16 Old Compton Street, Soho, W1 (7434 3544). Leicester Square or Tottenham Court Road tube. **Open** noon-3pm, 6-11.15pm Mon-Sat; 6-10.30pm Sun. **Main courses** £6.80-£10.50. **Credit** AmEx, DC, MC, V. **Map** p399 K6.

A minimalist Thai restaurant may usually be a contradiction in terms in London, but Sri Siam's woodstrip floors and brightly painted walls are a refreshing setting for reliable food, including an impressively long vegetarian menu.

Tawana

3 Westbourne Grove, Bayswater, W2 (7229 3785). Bayswater, Queensway or Royal Oak tube. **Open** noon-3pm, 6-11pm daily. **Main courses** £4.95-£17.95. **Credit** AmEx, DC, MC, V. **Map** p394 B6.

Kitted out like a vision of colonial Asia à la Somerset Maugham, Tawana's unobtrusive service, languid atmosphere and exemplary food make it one of London's best Thais. Weekend diners should note that it's always packed on Saturdays.

Thai Pot

1 Bedfordbury, Covent Garden, WC2 (7379 4580/ www.thaipot.co.uk). Covent Garden tube/Charing Cross tube/rail. **Open** noon-3pm, 5.30-11.15pm Mon-Sat; closed Sun. **Main courses** £5-£9. **Credit** AmEx, DC, MC, V. **Map** p401 L7.

The high ceilings and cream walls help this stylish Thai maintain a light, airy feel, even when it's crowded out almost to capacity. The menu is predictable but accomplished, with the curries particularly recommended.

Turkish

Surprisingly, many of London's best Turkish restaurants are the unreconstructed kebab houses serving north London's Turkish community. Choose carefully, and a walk along Green Lanes or Stoke Newington Road in N16 can be a culinary revelation.

Istanbul Iskembecisi

*9 Stoke Newington Road, Stoke Newington, N16
(7254 7291/www.londraturk.com/istanbuliskembecisi).
Dalston Kingsland rail then 30, 38, 56, 149 bus.*
Open noon-5am daily. **Main courses** £5-£8.50.
No credit cards.
The signature dish here, *iskembe* (an odd concoction
of tripe in warm milk with chilli flakes), may not be
to everyone's taste, but the selection of meze is fabulous and the solicitous service will please everyone.

Iznik

*19 Highbury Park, Highbury, N5 (7354 5697).
Highbury & Islington tube/rail/19 bus.* **Open** 10am-
3.30pm, 6.30-11pm daily. **Main courses** £7.25-
£9.50. **Credit** MC, V.

Exotically decorated like a bazaar or souk, Iznik's
food is equally reverent of Turkish culture and
includes rarely seen, labour-intensive Ottoman lamb
dishes. It's also excellent value.

Sofra Restaurant

*18 Shepherd Market, Mayfair, W1 (7493 3320).
Green Park tube.* **Open** noon-midnight daily.
Main courses £5.75-£16. **Credit** AmEx, MC, V.
Map p400 H8.
Due to its popularity with well-heeled tourists and
local office workers, this restaurant often feels quite
cramped, but the food is high-quality and the ser-
vice accommodating. If it is too busy, though, check
the phone book for details of the other Sofras in
Mayfair, Marylebone and Covent Garden.

Grease is the word

A couple of sausages, fried. A pair of eggs,
fried. A few rashers of bacon, fried. Large
dollops of mushrooms and tomatoes, both
fried. A scoop of baked beans, a slap of black
pudding and a wodge of bubble and squeak.
Garnish with two slices of fried bread, and
serve with two slices of toast and a large mug
of lukewarm milky tea.

The uninitiated may think this description is
the chemical formula
for heart disease.
And the uninitiated
would be absolutely
right. However, it is
also one way – the
proper way, at least
according to builders
and truck drivers the
length and breadth
of the country – of
starting the day in
England.

Sadly, in these
days of personal
vanity and health
awareness,
it's becoming
increasingly difficult
to find a good English fried breakfast in
London. Most of those served in the capital's
hotels are sanitised beyond recognition, and
often don't appear to have been fried. And
reprehensible shifts in fashion have seen the
traditional greasy breakfast overtaken in
popularity by dull cereals, soggy croissants
and horrendously overpriced, underfilled
bagels. (If bagels are your thing, by the way,
head to the 24-hour **Brick Lane Beigel Bake**,
159 Brick Lane, Spitalfields, E1, 7729 0616.
Accept no substitute.)

Still, a few valiant caffs are upholding the
grand tradition of the fried breakfast.
Generally speaking, the further out of central
London you go, the better the fry-up. The
Beano Café (6 Caledonian Road, King's
Cross, N1, 7837 6782), the **Full Monty** (57
Stroud Green Road, Finsbury Park, N4, 7561
0474), **E Pellicci's** (322 Bethnal Green Road,
Bethnal Green, E2, 7739 4873), **Mona Lisa**
(417 King's Road,
Chelsea, SW10,
7376 5447),
Mario's Café
(6 Kelly Street,
Camden, NW1,
7284 2066) and
the **Borough Café**
(11 Park Street,
Bankside, SE1,
7407 5048) all
knock up heart-
stoppingly good –
and, to be frank,
just plain heart-
stopping – fried
breakfasts, while
the fry-ups served at
the **River Café** (Putney Bridge Road, Putney,
SW6) are nigh-on legendary. But for the
biggest concentration of fine greasy spoons,
head to Smithfield Market in EC1, where an
assortment of cafés vie for the attentions of
the local meat traders and truck drivers. For
a twist, wash it down with a pint at the early-
opening **Fox & Anchor** pub (*see p218*). You
won't be able to move for about three hours,
but rest easy in the knowledge that you've
sampled one of only a few remaining British
culinary traditions.

Tas

33 The Cut, Bankside, SE1 (7928 2111). Southwark tube/Waterloo tube/rail. **Open** noon-11.30pm Mon-Sat; noon-10.30pm Sun. **Main courses** £5.45-£14.90. **Credit** AmEx, MC, V. **Map** p404 N8.
This airy, glass-fronted restaurant offers Turkish food with a twist, rather than the standard classic dishes. Expect the likes of mussel soup with coriander and ginger, and inventive seafood and casseroles.

Vegetarian

Aside from those listed below, other good restaurants for vegetarians include **Roussillon** (*see p194*), **Mandola** (*see p212*) and **Sri Siam** (*see p211*). In addition, most Thai and Turkish places also have fine meat-free ranges.

Bah Humbug

The Crypt, St Matthew's Church, Brixton Hill, SW2 (7738 3184/www.bahhumbug.co.uk). Brixton tube/rail. **Open** 5-11pm Mon-Thur; 5-11.30pm Fri, Sat; 11am-10.30pm Sun. **Main courses** £8-£12.50. **Credit** MC, V.
Located in the cavernous crypt of St Matthew's Church, Bah Humbug is invariably packed with Brixton trendies who come for the vibe and for some fine, filling grub with which to accompany the ever-flowing drink.

Food For Thought

31 Neal Street, Covent Garden, WC2 (7836 0239). Covent Garden tube. **Open** noon-8.30pm Mon-Sat; noon-5pm Sun. **Main courses** £2.50-£5.80. Minimum £2.50 noon-3pm, 6-7.30pm. **No credit cards. Map** p399 L6.
Particularly busy at lunchtimes, this unlicensed wholefood eaterie serve veggie classics such as stir-frys, vegetable bakes, stews and quiches. The menu changes daily, but tends to stick to the staples.

The Gate

51 Queen Caroline Street, Hammersmith, W6 (8748 6932/www.gateveg.co.uk). Hammersmith tube. **Open** noon-3pm, 6-10.45pm Mon-Fri; 6-10.45pm Sat; closed Sun. **Main courses** £7.25-£9.50. **Credit** AmEx, DC, MC, V.
Tucked away in a quiet, leafy church courtyard, the Gate's sunflower-yellow walls and stripped-wood floor are a civilised setting in which to enjoy the elaborate, imaginative but not over-ambitious globally inspired menu. Probably London's best vegetarian restaurant.

Mildred's

58 Greek Street, Soho, W1 (7494 1634). Leicester Square or Tottenham Court Road tube. **Open** noon-11pm Mon-Sat; closed Sun. **Main courses** £5.30-£6.50. **No credit cards. Map** p399 K6.
A Soho institution, Mildred's is always busy and you can usually expect to have to share a table. The short menu lacks imagination, but the food (stir-fry, beanburgers, falafel etc) is tasty and wholesome.

The Place Below

St Mary-le-Bow, Cheapside, The City, EC2 (7329 0789/www.theplacebelow.co.uk). St Paul's tube/Bank tube/DLR. **Open** 11.30am-2.30pm Mon-Fri; closed Sat, Sun. **Main courses** £5.50-£7.50. **Credit** MC, V. **Map** p404 P6.
Deep within the Norman crypt of the St Mary-le-Bow church (see also p95), this canteen-style café offers a welcome retreat from the bustle of City life, as well as some outstanding vegetarian sustenance.

Quiet Revolution

49 Old Street, The City, EC1 (7253 5556/ www.quietrevolution.co.uk). Old Street tube/rail. **Open** 8am-5pm Mon-Fri; 10am-2pm Sat, Sun. **Main courses** £3.95-£5.95. **Credit** MC, V. **Map** p402 P4.
Tucked away towards the Barbican end of Old Street, Quiet Revolution serves food that is not quite 100% veggie, but that is 100% organic and almost entirely delicious. Soups are a particular forte.

World Food Café

Neal's Yard Dining Room, First floor, 14 Neal's Yard, Covent Garden, WC2 (7379 0298). Covent Garden or Leicester Square tube. **Open** 11.30am-3.45pm Mon-Fri; noon-5pm Sat; closed Sun. **Main courses** £5.85-£7.85. **Credit** MC, V. **Map** p399 L6.
One of the best choices for veggie food in the centre of town, the Whole Food Café is a reliable source of fresh, adventurous and wholesome dishes. The atmosphere is friendly and relaxed.

Vietnamese

Green Papaya

191 Mare Street, Hackney, E8 (8985 5486). Bethnal Green tube/rail/D6, 253, 277 bus. **Open** 11am-midnight Mon-Sat, 11am-11.30pm Sun. **Main courses** £4.50-£6.95. **Credit** MC, V.
Appetising food (including a separate vegetarian section), friendly staff and a back garden that's the perfect place for an alfresco meal in summer make this one of London's finest Vietnamese joints.

Saigon

45 Frith Street, Soho, W1 (7437 7109). Leicester Square tube. **Open** noon-11.30pm Mon-Sat; closed Sun. **Main courses** £3.50-£9.75. **Credit** AmEx, DC, MC, V. **Map** p399 K6.
The long-established Saigon is as civilised an introduction to the food of Vietnam as you'll find in town. For an all-round taster, the set meals are good value.

Viet Hoa

70-72 Kingsland Road, Shoreditch, E2 (7729 8293). Old Street tube/Bus 26, 48, 55, 67, 149, 242. **Open** noon-3.30pm, 5.45-11.30pm daily. **Main courses** £4.80-£6.90. **Credit** MC, V.
This huge, unpretentious restaurant is equally popular with suits and trendies. Deservedly so, too, for while the decor may not be much to write home about, the quality of the food is consistently high and the prices remarkably low. The atmosphere is relaxed and buzzy and service is efficient.

Eat, Drink, Shop

Pubs & Bars

London's watering holes offer a window into the soul of the city, past, present and even future. It's just a shame they aren't open past 11pm.

Tradition is, of course, important. But though London still boasts more than its fair share of old-fashioned, old-school and, in many cases, just plain old pubs, the scene has changed. Most under-30s don't go to pubs any more: instead, they go to bars (*never* pubs), whether of the generic chain variety (of which more in a moment) or the super-cool Soho/Hoxton style. Bored with darts, pool and menus consisting of variants on pie 'n' chips, they've found solace in a new breed of clean, airy hangouts where the menu features not steak pie but tagliatelle and smoked salmon, where the music is supplied not by a broken tape deck behind the bar but by a DJ in front of it, and where the atmosphere is not one of quiet contemplation but of lairy jollity to a soundtrack of raucous, half-shouted conversations.

That said, the homogenisation of London's drinking scene is cause for concern. Over the last decade, the big breweries have made it their business to strip away the character and individuality of many London pubs and replace them with a generic, flat-packed, stripped-pine decor or a spurious theme (*see p227* **Breaking the chains**). And despite the fact that everyone in the UK agrees it's a good idea – yes, even the politicians – there still hadn't been any extension of Britain's opening hours by early

2001. Pubs and bars are still required by law to close at 11pm (10.30pm on Sundays), though a limited number of bars do have late licences that allow them to serve as late as 3am: the biggest concentrations of late-opening spots are in Soho, Shoreditch and Hoxton, Brixton and Covent Garden.

Central London

The South Bank & Bankside

Anchor Bankside

34 Park Street, SE1 (7407 1577). London Bridge tube/rail. **Open** 11am-11pm Mon-Sat; noon-10.30pm Sun. **Credit** AmEx, MC, V. **Map** p404 P8.
A historic (if slightly touristy) riverside inn that offers atmospheric, odd-shaped rooms, a Thames-side terrace and the knowledge that Dr Johnson wrote part of his dictionary on the premises.

Auberge

1 Sandell Street, off Waterloo Road, SE1 (7633 0610). Waterloo tube/rail. **Open** noon-midnight Mon-Fri; noon-11pm Sat; closed Sun. **Credit** AmEx, DC, MC, V. **Map** p404 N8.
A discreet side entrance admits you to this vaguely ecclesiastical-feeling café/bar specialising in Belgian beers, the best bar within a striking distance of Waterloo station. There's a restaurant upstairs.

Cynthia's Cyberbar

4 Tooley Street, SE1 (7403 6777/www.cynbar.co.uk). London Bridge tube/rail. **Open** 12.30pm-2am Mon-Wed; 12.30pm-3am Thur-Sat; closed Sun. **Credit** AmEx, DC, MC, V. **Map** p405 Q8.
Located near the London Dungeon, Cynthia's is far more entertaining than its tourist-trap neighbour. Cocktails are poured and mixed by two huge robots (no, really) in an outrageously kitschy setting.

Market Porter

9 Stoney Street, SE1 (7407 2495). London Bridge tube/rail. **Open** 6-8.30am, 11am-11pm Mon-Sat; noon-10.30pm Sun. **Credit** AmEx, MC, V. **Map** p408 P8.
Serving a mix of Borough Market traders (hence the early opening) and commuters, the Market Porter is a gem, mixing olde worlde decor, a friendly vibe and some rare, lovely beers to near-perfection.

Royal Oak

44 Tabard Street, SE1 (7357 7173). Borough tube/ London Bridge tube/rail. **Open** 11am-11pm Mon-Fri; closed Sat, Sun. **Credit** MC, V. **Map** p404 P9.

The best Bars

For a trip back in time
Grapes (*see p225*).

For stylish Soho cool
Lab (*see p220*).

For a view over the capital
Twentyfour (*see p218*).

For a terrific gastropub lunch
The Westbourne (*see p227*).

For cocktails with class
American Bar (*see p221*).

For an eco-friendly pint
Duke of Cambridge (*see p223*).

Strange but true

● **Crocker's Folly** (24 Aberdeen Place, Maida Vale, NW8, 7286 6608), a lavish, marble-encrusted Victorian masterpiece, was built by Frank Crocker in the belief that a major railway terminus was going to be built there. However, it was built at Marylebone instead and an understandably distraught Crocker, his huge investment wasted, threw himself off the top.

● The London pub with the oldest licence? It's probably the **White Hart** (191 Drury Lane, Covent Garden, WC2, 7831 0791). Women have been drinking here since 1201, when it was also a nunnery.

● On the other hand, the oldest pub in the city is also its oldest building. The **Hoop & Grapes** (*pictured*; 47 Aldgate High Street, The City, EC3, 7265 5171) dates from the late 1500s, though its foundations were laid three centuries earlier. The current building survived the Great Fire, but only just: it was extinguished on its doorstep.

● Not all pubs in London are expansive, high-ceilinged All Bar One-type spots. Take the **Cock** (22 Fleet Street, The City, EC4, 7353 3454), for example, one of the narrowest pubs in London. The Cock was actually moved in the late 19th century from the other side of the road in order to make way for the building of a new branch of the Bank of England. A branch, incidentally, that is itself now a pub.

● One Good Friday two centuries ago, a mother made traditional hot cross buns for her returning sailor son at the **Widow's Son**, east of the city in Bow (75 Devons Road, Bow, E3, 7515 9072). But her boy never returned. Now, every year, a bun is baked and a Royal Navy sailor adds it to the collection.

● The cellar beneath the **Morpeth Arms** (58 Millbank, Westminster, SW1, 7834 6442) is said to be haunted by the ghost of a prisoner at Millbank Penitentiary, which stood next door. The man died after getting lost in the labyrinthine vaults under the pub while trying to escape transportation. It's not known whether anyone ever expired in the basement of the **Viaduct Tavern** (126 Newgate Street, The City, EC1, 7606 8476), but it, too, was once a prison. Ask nicely and the landlord will show you around.

● **Dirty Dick's** (202 Bishopsgate, The City, EC2, 7283 5888), meanwhile, was established in honour of Nathaniel Barley, an 18th-century City ironmonger who fell to pieces after being jilted, refusing to wash and leaving his cats lying around the house after they'd died. Upon Barley's death, his possessions were bought by an eccentric landlord and shown off in this pub. Sadly, the cats have since been packed away, and the decor these days is rather more bland.

Hidden away in the Borough, ten minutes from the river, this old-style pub will remind keen TV viewers of the Queen Vic in *EastEnders*. A treasure of a pub: try one of the sturdy Harvey's ales for full effect.

The City

Black Friar

174 Queen Victoria Street, EC4 (7236 5474). *Blackfriars tube/rail.* **Open** 11.30am-11pm Mon-Fri; noon-5pm Sat; closed Sun. **Credit** AmEx, MC, V. **Map** p404 O6.

This unique, cheese-shaped tavern boasts tremendous decor – think art nouveau monastery – and an atmosphere far more agreeable than those found in many of its cocksure City counterparts.

Jamaica Wine House

St Michael's Alley, off Cornhill, EC3 (7626 9496). *Bank tube/DLR.* **Open** 11am-11pm Mon-Fri; closed Sat, Sun. **Credit** AmEx, DC, MC, V. **Map** p405 Q6.

This one-time haunt of London's rum merchants that dates back to the 17th century is, happily, a theme-free drinking hole, despite its resemblance to a BBC Victorian costume drama set.

Old Cheshire Cheese

145 Fleet Street, EC4 (7353 6170). Blackfriars tube/rail. **Open** 11.30am-11pm Mon-Fri; noon-3pm, 6-11pm Sat. **Credit** AmEx, DC, MC, V. **Map** p404 N6.
One of the oldest pubs in London, the labyrinthine Cheese has a storied history: both Dickens and Johnson drank here, as did every journo worth his salt when the newspaper industry was based around here. These days, it's a dimly-lit, atmospheric pub.

Tsunami

1 St Katherine's Way, E1 (7488 4791). Tower Hill tube. **Open** 11am-11pm Mon-Fri; 6-11pm Sat; closed Sun. **Credit** AmEx, DC, MC, V. **Map** p405 S7.
A sleek cocktail bar (with cocktails by London's grand doyen of barmen, Dick Bradsell) handy both for City folk and those visiting the Tower of London, Tsunami is both cool and welcoming.

Twentyfour

Level 24, Tower 42, 25 Old Broad Street, EC2 (7877 2424). Bank tube/DLR/Liverpool Street tube/rail. **Open** noon-11pm Mon-Fri; closed Sat, Sun. **Credit** AmEx, DC, MC, V. **Map** p402 N5.
The fine cocktails and comfortable furnishings are all well and good. But as you're supping in this 24th-floor bar, look out through the windows over the metropolis. You'll feel like the king of the world.

Holborn & Clerkenwell

Bleeding Heart Tavern

Bleeding Heart Yard, off Greville Street, EC1 (7242 8238). Chancery Lane tube/Farringdon tube/rail. **Open** noon-11pm Mon-Fri; closed Sat, Sun. **Credit** AmEx, DC, MC, V. **Map** p402 N5.
Restored in recent years to its 1746 origins, this popular, jolly, informal and occasionally chaotic wine bar (with a smarter dining area) has a tremendous list, with plenty of choice under £15 a bottle.

Cicada

132-136 St John Street, EC1 (7608 1550). Farringdon tube/rail. **Open** noon-11pm Mon-Fri; 6-11pm Sat; closed Sun. **Credit** AmEx, DC, MC, V. **Map** p402 O5.
Cicada's pleasingly butch, modernist interior is a fine space, with rough-hewn surfaces and big windows. Pan-oriental food is available in the bar and restaurant. Trendy, but laid-back.

The Eagle

159 Farringdon Road, EC1 (7837 1353). Farringdon tube/rail. **Open** noon-11pm Mon-Sat; noon-5pm Sun. **No credit cards. Map** p402 N4.
London's trail-blazing gastropub continues to be absurdly popular: arrive early if you want any hope of a seat. The quality of the mainly Med dishes is high, and many wines are available by the glass.

Fluid

40 Charterhouse Street, EC1 (7253 3444/ www.fluidbar.com). Farringdon tube/rail. **Open** noon-midnight Tue, Wed; noon-2am Thur, Fri; 7pm-2am Sat; 7pm-midnight Sun; closed Mon. **Credit** AmEx, DC, MC, V. **Map** p402 O5.
Heaven knows what the seen-it-all-before traders at nearby Smithfield make of Fluid. However, young Clerkenwell trendies adore its mix of hip decor, fine Japanese food, obscure beers and retro video games.

Fox & Anchor

115 Charterhouse Street, EC1 (7253 5075). Farringdon tube/rail. **Open** 7am-11pm Mon-Fri; closed Sat, Sun. **Credit** AmEx, MC, V. **Map** p402 O5.
The beer is good at this old school boozer, and food is top-of-the-range butties with the emphasis on fried flesh. Early opening draws a mix of workers at nearby Smithfield market and clubbers on comedown.

Jerusalem Tavern

55 Britton Street, EC1 (7490 4281). Farringdon tube/rail. **Open** 11am-11pm Mon-Fri; closed Sat, Sun. **Credit** AmEx, MC, V. **Map** p402 O5.
All Farringdon's media circus seems to squeeze into this tiny rparlour with original fires, partitioned cubicles and distempered walls. A major reason is the terrific beers from St Peter's Brewery in Suffolk.

Mint

182-186 St John Street, EC1 (7253 8368/ www.mintbar.co.uk). Farringdon tube/rail. **Open** 11am-midnight Mon-Sat; closed Sun. **Credit** AmEx, DC, MC, V. **Map** p402 O5.
The design of Mint is striking, to say the least: all curved lines and bold colours. However, it's matched by the cool vibe (often helped along by DJs), decent cocktails and good-value food.

Na Zdrowie

11 Little Turnstile, WC1 (7831 9679). Holborn tube. **Open** noon-11pm Mon-Fri; closed Sun. **Credit** MC, V. **Map** p399 M5.
Set on the south side of the Holborn-Bloomsbury border, Na Zdrowie will appeal to lovers of all things Polish. For most drinkers, that list begins and ends with vodka, with the bargain stews aiding digestion.

Bloomsbury & Fitzrovia

Bradley's Spanish Bar

42-44 Hanway Street, W1 (7636 0359). Tottenham Court Road tube. **Open** 11am-11pm Mon-Sat; closed Sun. **Credit** MC, V. **Map** p399 K6.
A gloriously mad bar over two tiny floors behind Oxford Street, Bradley's is highlighted by its kitschy Spanish memorabilia, discerning drinkers resourceful enough to have found the place, and the all-vinyl jukebox, the best in London.

Duke of York

7 Roger Street, WC1 (7242 7230). Chancery Lane or Russell Square tube. **Open** noon-11pm Mon-Fri; 6-11pm Sat; closed Sun. **Credit** MC, V. **Map** p399 M4.

Iberia as you've never seen it before, downstairs at **Bradley's Spanish Bar**. *See p218.*

Tucked away down a mews, the Duke of York makes a virtue of its old-fashionedness while bringing drinkers into the modern world with a daring food menu. Cosy and friendly, it's a lovely lunch stop.

The Lamb

Lamb's Conduit Street, WC1 (7405 0713). Holborn or Russell Square tube. **Open** 11am-11pm Mon-Sat; noon-4pm, 7-10.30pm Sun. **Credit** MC, V. **Map** p399 M4.
The Lamb is among the best of all the pubs operated by Young's brewery. A grand Victorian boozer that's survived the years well, it's as strong an argument in favour of tradition as you're likely to find.

Truckles of Pied Bull Yard

off Bury Place, WC1 (7404 5338/www.davy.co.uk). Holborn tube. **Open** 11am-10pm Mon-Fri; 11.30am-3pm Sat; closed Sun. **Credit** AmEx, DC, MC, V. **Map** p399 L5.
One of the chain of Davy's wine bars, Truckles boasts a spacious two-floor interior and an attractive paved courtyard. All the classic bottles are sold, from claret to sherry to port. Good grub rounds things off.

Marylebone

The Chapel

48 Chapel Street, NW1 (7402 9220). Edgware Road tube. **Open** noon-11pm Mon-Sat; noon-3pm, 7-10.30pm Sun. **Credit** AmEx, DC, MC, V. **Map** p395 E5.
This award-winning bar has a simple, bare-boarded interior, a pleasant shaded garden, plenty of wines by the glass, good cask-conditioned ales and excellent food.

Dover Castle

43 Weymouth Mews, W1 (7580 4412). Regent's Park tube. **Open** 11.30am-11pm Mon-Fri; noon-11pm Sat; closed Sun. **Credit** MC, V. **Map** p398 H5.
A damn fine pub with good cheap Sam Smith's beer. Tucked away in a little mews, the Dover Castle has plenty of inviting nooks and bags of atmosphere.

Mash

19-21 Great Portland Street, W1 (7637 5555). Oxford Circus tube. **Open** *Bar* 11am-1am Mon-Fri; noon-1am Sat; closed Sun. **Credit** AmEx, DC, MC, V. **Map** p398 J5.
The modish Mash makes for a great detour from the bustle of Oxford Circus. With fun decor (including a gloriously comfortable leatherette couch), occasional DJs and exquisite microbrewed beer this is a fine bar.

Windsor Castle

29 Crawford Place, W1 (7723 4371). Edgware Road tube. **Open** 11am-11pm Mon-Sat; noon-10.30pm Sun. **Credit** MC, V. **Map** p395 F5.
Unintentionally, this is one of the kitschiest bars in London. Royal memorabilia covers the walls, the bartenders are almost embarrassingly chipper, and it's the haunt of the Handlebar Club, a group of men with handlebar moustaches. Bonkers but fab.

Mayfair & St James's

Che

23 St James's Street, SW1 (7747 9380). Green Park tube. **Open** 11am-11pm Mon-Fri; 5-11pm Sat; closed Sun. **Credit** AmEx, DC, MC, V. **Map** p400 J8.

...nky set, Che is London's finest cigar ...tart at £8, and are best washed down ...ish Martini in this plush establishment.

...ge's Bar
...ge's Hotel, Brook Street, W1 (7629 8860/
...w.savoygroup.com). Bond Street tube.
Open 11am-11pm Mon-Sat; noon-10.30pm Sun.
Credit AmEx, DC, MC, V. **Map** p400 H6.
Evergreen aristo hotel Claridge's opened a stunning new art deco bar to celebrate its centenary in 1998, designed by David Collins (Madonna's decorator). Dress up and bring a credit card.

Ye Grapes
16 Shepherd Market, W1 (7499 1563). Green Park tube. **Open** 11am-11pm Mon-Sat; noon-10.30pm Sun.
Credit MC, V. **Map** p400 H8.
Unlike most Mayfair pubs, Ye Grapes draws drinkers from all social strata. The decor is olde worlde (the red velvet tying in nicely with Shepherd Market's hidden sex trade) and the atmosphere lively.

Soho & Leicester Square

Alphabet
61-63 Beak Street, W1 (7439 2190). Oxford Circus tube. **Open** noon-11pm Mon-Fri; 4.30-11pm Sat; closed Sun. **Credit** MC, V. **Map** p400 J6.

Line 'em up at **Freedom**.

Still the best bar in west Soho, and one of only a few that has learned how to balance self-conscious hipness with un-selfconsciously polite service. If you can't remember how to get home, worry not: there's a map of London printed on the floor.

Coach & Horses
29 Greek Street, W1 (7437 5920). Leicester Square tube. **Open** 11am-11pm Mon-Sat; noon-10.30pm Sun.
No credit cards. Map p399 K6.
Made famous by perpetually drunk columnist Jeffrey Bernard (it was his local) and by the legendary if now rather pantomimic rudeness of its landlord, Norman Balon, the Coach remains Soho's greatest drinking den. Eccentric, bohemian and quite unique.

Cork & Bottle
44-46 Cranbourn Street, WC2 (7734 6592). Leicester Square tube. **Open** 11am-midnight Mon-Sat; noon-10.30pm Sun. **Credit** AmEx, DC, MC, V. **Map** p401 K7
This 30-year-old basement wine bar is one of the city's finest, and the best watering hole on or near Leicester Square. Brave the discomfort – it's often very busy – for the superb wine list and good food.

Freedom
60-66 Wardour Street, W1 (7734 0071). Leicester Square tube. **Open** 11am-3am Mon-Sat; noon-midnight Sun. **Credit** AmEx, DC, MC, V. **Map** p399 K6.
It's no longer as hip as it once was, but Freedom is now a far more pleasant place for a drink or six. A terrifically mixed crowd up for a good time mingle over an assortment of beers, cocktails and DJs.

French House
49 Dean Street, W1 (7437 2799). Leicester Square tube. **Open** noon-11pm Mon-Sat; closed Sun. **Credit** AmEx, DC, MC, V. **Map** p399 K6.
This tiny pub has maintained its bohemian spirit while most of Soho has lost it. A longtime haunt of writers and artists (Dylan Thomas and Francis Bacon among them), it's loud, lairy and unforgiving to bores. And that's meant as a compliment.

Lab
12 Old Compton Street, W1 (7437 7820). Leicester Square or Tottenham Court Road tube.
Open noon-midnight Mon-Sat; 4-10.30pm Sun.
Credit AmEx, MC, V. **Map** p399 K6.
Knowingly retro, modishly raffish and winner of the *Time Out* Best Bar award for 2000, the two-floor Lab has found its niche among Soho's hip hangouts with ease. Here's where to get in with the in-crowd.

Pop
14 Soho Street, W1 (7734 4004). Tottenham Court Road tube. **Open** 5pm-3.30am Mon-Thur; 5pm-4am Fri; 8pm-5am Sat; 5-11.30pm Sun. **Credit** AmEx, DC, MC, V. **Map** p399 K6.
An impossibly loud and colourful bar on the fringes of Soho, Pop is not for the feint of heart. The young at heart, though, will love its glammy, designer take on pop culture, and rightly so.

Not even cameras can see straight after a glass or nine at **Gordon's**.

Covent Garden & St Giles's

American Bar
*Savoy Hotel, Strand, WC2 (7836 4343/
www.savoygroup.co.uk). Charing Cross tube/rail.*
Open 11am-11pm Mon-Sat; noon-3pm, 7-10.30pm
Sun. **Credit** AmEx, DC, MC, V. **Map** p401 L7.
This art deco period piece is surprisingly relaxed for
the cocktail bar of a posh hotel. The drinks are first
class – the first Martini to be served in Britain was
mixed here – and come with endlessly replenished
crisps and olives. Dress smart or you won't get in.

Angel
*61 St Giles High Street, WC2 (7240 2876).
Tottenham Court Road tube.* **Open** 11am-11pm Mon-
Sat; noon-10.30pm Sun. **Credit** MC, V. **Map** p399 K6.
The trendy bars are closing in, but this admirably
scruffy, multi-roomed trad pub (with tables outside
in the garden) remains deservedly popular. It's a
Sam Smith's pub, so the beer is astonishingly cheap.

Detroit
*35 Earlham Street, WC2 (7240 2662/
www.detroit-bar.com). Covent Garden tube.*
Open 5pm-midnight Mon-Fri; 6pm-midnight Sat;
closed Sun. **Credit** AmEx, DC, MC, V. **Map** p399 L6.
One of many painfully hip Covent Garden hangouts,
Detroit distinguishes itself with pleasant table service, decent cocktails and some above-average food.
DJs provide the background noise.

Freedom Brewing Company
*41 Earlham Street, WC2 (7240 0606/
www.freedombrew.com). Covent Garden tube.*
Open 11am-11pm Mon-Sat; noon-10.30pm Sun.
Credit AmEx, MC, V. **Map** p399 L6.
Looking not unlike a pristine steamship engine
room, this sizeable basement bar (formerly the Soho
Brewing Company) is distinguished by its home-
brewed beers and above-average food in the restaurant. There's a branch at 14-16 Ganton Street, W1.

Fuel
*41 Earlham Street, WC2 (7836 2137). Covent Garden
tube.* **Open** 11am-11pm Mon-Sat; noon-10.30pm Sun.
Credit AmEx, DC, MC, V. **Map** p401 L6.
Red, brown and blue enliven the stone cellar of this
former fruit store on Earlham Street. There are pizzas for the peckish, beers and wines for the thirsty,
and a mixed clientele.

Gordon's
*47 Villiers Street, WC2 (7930 1408). Embankment
tube/Charing Cross tube/rail.* **Open** 11am-11pm
Mon-Sat; closed Sun. **Credit** MC, V. **Map** p401 L7.
Atmosphere is everything at this deliberately raffish basement wine bar. Chow down on some basic
nosh, all the better with which to soak up the range
of wines and sherries.

Lamb & Flag
*33 Rose Street, WC2 (7497 9504). Covent Garden
tube.* **Open** 11am-11pm Mon-Thur; 11am-10.45pm
Fri, Sat; noon-10.30pm Sun. **No credit cards.**
Map p401 L7.
In the 17th century, Dryden was beaten up at this
small, rickety pub up a side alley; now it's a popular meeting place and one of the only decent pubs in
Covent Garden. Upstairs is quieter, but not much.

Westminster & Pimlico

Boisdale
15 Eccleston Street, SW1 (7730 6922/
www.boisdale.co.uk). Victoria tube/rail. **Open** *Back*
Bar noon-11pm Mon-Fri; closed Sat, Sun. Macdonald
Bar noon-1am Mon-Fri; 7pm-1am Sat; closed Sun.
Credit AmEx, DC, MC, V. **Map** p400 H10.
The bar at this great Franco-Scottish restaurant has
the largest collection of malt whiskies in London,
plus equally impressive ranges of champagnes and
cigars. A veritable oasis in this bar-starved area.

Red Lion
48 Parliament Street, SW1 (7930 5826).
Westminster tube. **Open** 11am-11pm Mon-Sat;
noon-7pm Sun. **Credit** MC, V. **Map** p401 L9.
Though the Marquis of Granby (41 Romney Street)
and the Westminster Arms (9 Storey's Gate) attract
a few parliamentary refugees, the venerable Red
Lion is the most politically charged of Westminster's
pubs. See how many MPs you can recognise.

Knightsbridge & South Kensington

Grenadier
Old Barrack Yard, off Wilton Row, SW1 (7235
3074). Hyde Park Corner or Knightsbridge tube.
Open noon-11pm Mon-Sat; noon-10.30pm Sun.
Credit AmEx, DC, MC, V. **Map** p400 G9.
Famed Bloody Marys, monster sausage baguettes,
a 200-year-old pewter bar and the ghost of one of the
Duke of Wellington's soldiers (flogged to death for
cheating at cards) are among the draws here.

The Library
Lanesborough Hotel, Hyde Park Corner, SW1 (7259
5599/www.lanesborough.com). Hyde Park Corner
tube. **Open** 11am-11pm Mon-Sat; noon-10.30pm
Sun. **Credit** AmEx, DC, MC, V. **Map** p400 G8.
The Lanesborough's book-lined bar has an old-fashioned air at odds with the rest of the lavishly decorated hotel. Both cocktails and service are excellent,
though unless you're smartly attired, you won't be
permitted to sample either.

Nag's Head
53 Kinnerton Street, SW1 (7235 1135). Hyde Park
Corner or Knightsbridge tube. **Open** 11am-11pm
Mon-Sat; noon-10.30pm Sun. **No credit cards.**
Map p400 G9.
A charming chatterbox of a pub where staff are
friendly and newcomers are made to feel welcome. In
summer, lack of space means drinkers end up spilling
from the aesthetically faultless pub out into the mews.

Chelsea

Builder's Arms
13 Britten Street, SW3 (7349 9040).
South Kensington or Sloane Square tube.
Open 11am-11pm Mon-Sat; noon-10.30pm Sun.
Credit MC, V. **Map** p397 E11.

The decor – hunting lodge meets *fin de millennium*
living room – won't be to everyone's taste, but we
like both it and the friendly atmosphere at this posh,
builder-free boozer in the heart of Chelsea.

Orange Brewery
37 Pimlico Road, SW1 (7730 5984). Sloane Square
tube. **Open** 11am-11pm Mon-Sat; noon-10.30pm Sun.
Credit AmEx, DC, MC, V. **Map** p400 G11.
The beers at this microbrewery make it well worth
the trek, even if the place itself looks a bit too done-
up in a tied-house makeover sort of way.

Phene Arms
9 Phene Street, SW3 (7352 3294). Sloane Square
or South Kensington tube. **Open** 11am-11pm
Mon-Sat; noon-10.30pm Sun. **Credit** AmEx, DC,
MC, V. **Map** p397 E12.
This excellent boozer, midway between King's Road
and Chelsea Embankment, is full of character, and
has a fine terrace. It's also George Best's local.

North London

25 Canonbury Lane
25 Canonbury Lane, Islington, N1 (7226 0955).
Highbury & Islington tube/rail/Canonbury rail.
Open 5-11pm Mon-Thur; 4-11pm Fri, Sat; n
oon-11pm Sun. **Credit** MC, V.
The name of the bar means you should be able to
remember the address; if and when you get there,
you'll find an adventurous mix of cocktails, some
fine foody fare and a warm decor.

Wind down at the **Albion**. *See p223.*

The Albion
10 Thornhill Road, Barnsbury, N1 (7607 7450).
Angel tube/Highbury & Islington tube/rail.
Open 11am-11pm Mon-Sat; noon-10.30pm Sun.
Credit AmEx, DC, MC, V. **Map** p402 N1.
Ivy cascades down the broad front of this delightful evergreen local in Barnsbury (north-west of Islington). In summer, the beer garden makes for a wonderful drinking spot.

Bar Vinyl
6 Inverness Street, Camden, NW1 (7681 7898)
Camden Town tube. **Open** 11am-11pm Mon-Sat;
11am-10.30pm Sun. **No credit cards.**
The crowd, young and trendy, is often cliquey here, but there is usually a good, albeit loud atmosphere. Food is good, impressively varied and cheap. DJs spin a mix of techno, funky house and breaks.

Bierodrome
173-174 Upper Street, Islington, N1 (7226 5835/
www.belgo-restaurant.com). Angel tube/Highbury &
Islington tube/rail. **Open** noon-midnight Mon-Sat;
noon-10.30pm Sun. **Credit** MC, V. **Map** p402 O1.
Owned and operated by the people behind Belgo, Bierodrome gets by on high-falutin' design and a loud but happy atmosphere. The range of 200 beers should appease most palates.

The Clifton
96 Clifton Hill, St John's Wood, NW8 (7372 3427).
St John's Wood tube. **Open** 11am-11pm Mon-Sat;
noon-10.30pm Sun. **Credit** AmEx, MC, V.
A smart, trad establishment in a fine St John's Wood house. The tables on the leafy front terrace make this an agreeable summer hangout, while the conservatory ensures it is a pub for all seasons.

Duke of Cambridge
30 St Peter Street, Islington, N1 (7359 3066).
Angel tube. **Open** 5-11pm Mon; noon-11pm Tue-Sat;
noon-10.30pm Sun. **Credit** AmEx, MC, V.
This spacious, friendly gastropub would probably merit mention here even without the characteristic that truly defines it: the Duke of Cambridge is an organic boozer, with wines, beers and excellent food all as untampered with as can be.

The Flask
14 Flask Walk, Hampstead, NW3 (7435 4580).
Hampstead tube. **Open** 11am-11pm Mon-Sat;
noon-10.30pm Sun. **Credit** V.
Defiantly old school, the Flask is one of Hampstead's finest watering holes. Grizzled locals sup pints alongside young bucks in a space that proves there is room for tradition on today's super-modernised bar scene.

Hollybush
22 Holly Mount, Hampstead, NW3 (7435 2892).
Hampstead tube. **Open** 11am-11pm Mon-Sat;
noon-10.30pm Sun. **Credit** MC, V.
If you're after quiet conversation and an unspoilt bar full of nooks and crannies, away from the ostentation of Hampstead village, head to this hidden gem.

Bierodrome, a temple to the brewski.

Lansdowne
90 Gloucester Avenue, Primrose Hill, NW1
(7483 0409). Camden Town or Chalk Farm tube.
Open noon-11pm Mon-Sat; 12.30-4pm, 7-10.30pm
Sun. **Credit** MC, V.
The pick of the Primrose Hill pubs, the Lansdowne garnered its reputation a while back for the quality of its cuisine. The adventurous, hearty fare makes a nice accompaniment to the well-chosen beers.

Shakespeare
57 Allen Road, Stoke Newington, N16 (7254 4190).
Bus 73. **Open** noon-2pm, 5-11pm Mon-Fri;
noon-11pm Sat; noon-10.30pm Sun. **No credit cards.**
This untainted pub is frequented by locals for whom the rowdiness of Bar Lorca – Stoke Newington's other notable boozer – is way too much trouble.

East London

Cantaloupe
35-42 Charlotte Road, Shoreditch, EC2 (7613 4411/
www.cantaloupe.co.uk). Liverpool Street or Old
Street tube/rail. **Open** 11am-midnight Mon-Fri;
noon-midnight Sat; noon-10.30pm Sun.
Credit AmEx, MC, V. **Map** p403 R4.
Once a *Time Out* Best Bar award-winner, Cantaloupe is still cantering along nicely. The real trendies have shuffled over to more of-the-moment local hangouts, leaving the loud, fun bar to people unafraid to say the wrong thing or wear the wrong haircut.

Eat, Drink, Shop

The wonder of waxy's...

WAXY O'CONNOR'S
LONDON ®

Waxy O'Connor's has gained world wide acclaim for its spectacular surroundings, traditional, wholesome food and warm hospitality.

Four bars on five different levels, including the amazing Church Bar, offer the ultimate friendly environment in the heart of London's West End.

Open   12 noon - 11 pm Monday - Friday
11 am - 11 pm Saturday
12 noon - 10:30 pm Sunday

14-16 Rupert Street,
London, W1D 6DD
Tel: (020) 7287 0255
Fax: (020) 7287 3962
Email: london@waxyoconnors.co.uk
Web: www.waxyoconnors.co.uk

Here's where you'll find us...

Grapes

76 Narrow Street, Limehouse, E14 (7987 4396).
West Ferry DLR. **Open** noon-3pm, 5.30-11pm
Mon-Fri; 7-11pm Sat; noon-3pm, 7-10pm Sun.
Credit AmEx, DC, MC, V.
Established in 1583, rebuilt in 1720, the character-
ful Grapes – which claims to have been mentioned
by Dickens in *Our Mutual Friend* – is many people's
pick of the traditional East End riverside pubs.

Great Eastern Dining Room

*54-56 Great Eastern Street, Shoreditch, EC2 (7613
4545). Old Street tube/rail.* **Open** noon-midnight
Mon-Fri; 6pm-midnight Sat; closed Sun.
Credit AmEx, DC, MC, V. **Map** p403 R4.
Maddeningly hip – hey, it's in Shoreditch, so how
can it be anything but? – take your pick here from
the basement cocktail bar (Below 54) or the more
relaxed, traditional space upstairs.

Home

*100-106 Leonard Street, Shoreditch, EC2 (7684
8618). Old Street tube/rail.* **Open** 5.30pm-midnight
Mon-Sat; 2-10.30pm Sun. **Credit** AmEx, MC, V.
Map p403 Q4.
The most chilled of the Hoxton/Shoreditch bars,
Home is best enjoyed from the comfort of one of the
massive leather sofas that pass as decor in here.
Louche and lovely, it's not to be confused with the
club of the same name (for which, *see p281*).

Pride of Spitalfields

3 Heneage Street, Spitalfields, E1 (7247 8933).
Aldgate East tube. **Open** 11am-11pm Mon-Sat; noon-
10.30pm Sun. **Credit** AmEx, DC, MC, V. **Map** p403 S5.
Tucked away off Brick Lane around the point where
Whitechapel morphs into Spitalfields, frequented by
a mix of students, labourers, businessmen and pensioners, the Pride gets by on atmosphere alone: the
decor here is hideous, but that's not really the point.

Prospect of Whitby

57 Wapping Wall, Wapping, E1 (7481 1095).
Wapping tube. **Open** 11.30am-3pm, 5.30-11pm
Mon-Fri; 11.30am-11pm Sat; noon-10.30pm Sun.
Credit AmEx, DC, MC, V.
A stunningly preserved pub that dates back to 1520
and was last remodelled in 1777, the former Devil's
Tavern also comes with some terrific views of the
river. Not even the gawping tourists who now make
up much of its clientele can ruin the atmosphere.

Shoreditch Electricity Showrooms

39A Hoxton Square, Hoxton, N1 (7739 6934).
Old Street tube/rail. **Open** noon-11pm Mon-Wed;
noon-midnight Thur; noon-1am Fri, Sat;
noon-10.30pm Sun. **Credit** MC, V. **Map** p403 R3.
Location is everything in modern-day Shoreditch
and Hoxton, and this bar has a cracker: right on
Hoxton Square (and close to another hip hangout,
the **Hoxton Square Bar & Kitchen** at no.2).
Drinkers are super-cool – or, at least, they think they
are – and the downstairs bar is more comfortable
than the frequently heaving street-level space.

291

291 Hackney Road, Bethnal Green, E2 (7613 5676).
*Liverpool Street or Old Street tube/rail/26, 48, 55
bus.* **Open** 6.30pm-midnight Tue, Wed; 6.30pm-2am
Thur-Sat; noon-6pm Sun; closed Mon. **Credit** MC, V.
A remarkable conversion from a neo-Gothic church
on the borders of Bethnal Green and Hackney, 291
also boasts a gallery and a fine restaurant on top of
its stylish, vibey bar. A great addition to the area,
and well worth the trek.

South London

Bread & Roses

*68 Clapham Manor Street, Clapham, SW4 (7498
1779). Clapham Common or Clapham North tube.*
Open 11am-11pm Mon-Sat; noon-10.30pm Sun.
Credit MC, V.
The first home of the Workers' Beer Company, the
Bread & Roses is a kind of modern-day working
men's club for south London's New Labourites. Still,
they're mostly very friendly, and both beer and food
are well up to scratch.

Brixtonian Havana Club

*11 Beehive Place, Brixton, SW9 (7924 9262/
www.brixtonian.co.uk). Brixton tube/rail.* **Open**
noon-2.30am daily. **Credit** MC, V.
More than 300 types of rum and killer cocktails are
dispensed from behind the bar of this exuberant,
high-ceilinged bar and restaurant.

Cheers. The **Brixtonian Havana Club**.

Dogstar

389 Coldharbour Lane, Brixton, SW9 (7733 7515/ www.dogstarbar.co.uk). Brixton tube/rail.
Open noon-2.30am Mon-Thur; Sun; noon-4am Fri, Sat. **Credit** AmEx, MC, V.
The bar that set the Brixton renaissance in motion, the Dogstar's unforgiving mix of hangover-inducing alcohol abuse, tinnitus-inducing music and sweat-inducing temperatures is as popular with the area's young things as ever.

Drawing Room & Sofa Bar

103 Lavender Hill, Battersea, SW11 (7350 2564). Clapham Junction rail. **Open** 6pm-midnight Mon-Fri; noon-midnight Sat, Sun. **Credit** MC, V.
It's all in the name: the Drawing Room & Sofa Bar is so laid back during the day as to be catatonic. After dark, though, it livens up with local well-to-dos and ne'er-do-wells enjoying the louche, ragged comfort.

Mayflower

117 Rotherhithe Street, Rotherhithe, SE16 (7237 4088). Rotherhithe tube/188, P11, P13 bus.
Open noon-11pm Mon-Sat; noon-10.30pm Sun.
Credit AmEx, DC, MC, V.
The Pilgrim Fathers' ship moored here at the start of its fateful journey, and, with its creaking wooden floors, small, wood-panelled rooms and narrow passages, you get the feeling that the pub has hardly changed at all since then.

The Plug

90 Stockwell Road, Stockwell, SW9 (7274 3879/ www.theplug.co.uk). **Open** noon-midnight Mon-Wed, Sun; noon-2am Thur; noon-3am Fri, Sat. **Credit** MC, V.
Part pub, part bar, part club, the Plug is all things to all people. To most, though, its liveliness on weekends is evidence of Stockwell's up-and-coming status.

Prince of Wales

48 Cleaver Square, Kennington, SE11 (7735 9916). Kennington tube. **Open** noon-3pm, 5-11pm Mon-Fri; 5-11pm Sat; 5-10.30pm Sun. **Credit** MC, V.
The Prince of Wales, set in a gorgeous and slightly exclusive Kennington square, is a simply lovely pub: the decor old-fashioned, the lighting low – including some candles – the staff friendly and the atmosphere relaxed and easy. Just about perfect.

Sand

156 Clapham Park Road, Clapham, SW4 (7622 3022). Clapham Common tube. **Open** 5pm-2am Mon-Sat; 5pm-1am Sun. **Credit** MC, V.
A little slice of Hoxton transmuted across the river, Sand has picked up some of the south London slack with aplomb. Expect DJs to put an end to any ambitions towards conversation, as hip young things suck down beers and cocktails until the early hours.

Time

7A College Approach, Greenwich, SE10 (8305 9767). Cutty Sark DLR/Greenwich rail. **Open** noon-11pm Mon-Sat; noon-10.30pm Sun. **Credit** AmEx, MC, V.

Named, presumably, for the Greenwich Meridien, Time brings a bit of much-needed style and artsiness to the area, with the added bonus of fine food and rotating exhibitions on the walls.

Trafalgar Tavern

Park Row, Greenwich, SE10 (8858 2437/ www.trafalgartavern.co.uk). Cutty Sark DLR/ Greenwich or Maze Hill rail. **Open** 11.30am-11pm Mon-Sat; noon-10.30pm Sun. **Credit** MC, V.
The Trafalgar's history is long and fascinating, a fact only partly evidenced by the array of celeb snapshots on one wall of this large, old-fashioned watering hole. The pick of Greenwich's riverside pubs.

West London

Albertine

1 Wood Lane, Shepherd's Bush, W12 (8743 9593). Shepherd's Bush tube. **Open** 11am-11pm Mon-Fri; 6.30-11pm Sat; closed Sun. **Credit** MC, V.
No spirits, no cocktails and only one beer on the menu: yep, the Albertine is a wine bar and proud of it. Still, it has every reason to be proud, as this cosy, candlelit spot is a lovely diversion in an area without a great many decent hangouts.

Anglesea Arms

35 Wingate Road, Hammersmith, W6 (8749 1291). Goldhawk Road or Ravenscourt Park tube. **Open** 11am-11pm Mon-Sat; noon-10.30pm Sun. **Credit** DC, MC, V.
The Anglesea is noted far and wide for the quality of its food, but it's also a terrific pub in its own right: comfortable, relaxed and altogether amiable.

Archery Tavern

4 Bathurst Street, Paddington, W2 (7402 4916). Lancaster Gate tube. **Open** 11am-11pm Mon-Sat; noon-10.30pm Sun. **Credit** AmEx, MC, V.
Map p395 D6.
A textbook example of a traditional London boozer. Though there's a TV for sports matches, there's no muzak: just good ales, good conversation and a good mix of punters.

Churchill Arms

119 Kensington Church Street, Kensington, W8 (7727 4242). High Street Kensington or Notting Hill Gate tube. **Open** 11am-11pm Mon-Sat; noon-10.30pm Sun. **Credit** MC, V. **Map** p394 B8.
Thai food, Irish football posters and Churchill memorabilia leads to a splendidly confused ambience at this Kensington boozer.

The Cow

89 Westbourne Park Road, Notting Hill, W2 (7221 0021). Westbourne Park or Royal Oak tube. **Open** noon-11pm Mon-Sat; noon-10.30pm Sun. **Credit** AmEx, MC, V. **Map** p394 B5.
If you can stomach the braying drinkers who frequent Tom Conran's tiny local, then be sure to leave room for the excellent food, a cut above the usual pub fare.

Breaking the chains

Given that London is a capital city, with all the multicultural diversity that implies, the rise and rise of your local neighbourhood chain pub on every other street is a phenomenon that would raise a few eyebrows in other capitals of the world. But visit any borough and walk down any main thoroughfare and you'll be presented with all manner of **All Bar Ones**, **Pitcher & Pianos** or **Slug & Lettuces** within whose walls you can safely savour some all too familiar decor and not once have cause to remember whereabouts in the city – or, for that matter, the country – you are.

While the archaic licensing laws have prevented London catching up with the rest of the world in terms of an all-night party atmosphere, the chain pubs can also take some of the responsibility for removing the colour from Londoners' and visitors' drinking hours. It may be easy to woo a bunch of suits to an emporium in which they can be assured they will have the same hassle-free Friday night they experienced last week, but it's also an impersonal touch in a city where – before 11pm, at least – the options are actually limitless.

If, as is often touted, the city's attraction is deeply rooted in the fact that it's made up of many villages, each one with its own atmosphere, style and character, then to stumble on yet another **O'Neills** in an unfamiliar part of town detracts from the plethora of surprising discoveries that makes living in or visiting a city so pleasurable. In short, there is less to discover if everything looks the same.

As if to prove it, even those apparently untouchable areas such as Soho, still regarded as the hippest area for nightlife in the West End, have recently seen the high street chain bar springing up within their confines, simultaneously knocking a touch of local flavour out of the way. The anonymity these places bring with them also extends to the anonymous bar staff; there's a distance between customer and server that comes from the impersonality of the chain itself. In other words, this is McDonald's for the casual drinker.

Our advice? Steer clear and find your tipple of choice in a more personable environment. This is a capital city, after all.

The Dove
19 Upper Mall, Hammersmith, W6 (8748 5405).
Hammersmith tube. **Open** 11am-11pm Mon-Sat;
noon-10.30pm Sun. **Credit** AmEx, MC, V.
Three small, low-ceilinged rooms huddle round the tiny central bar of this unspoilt 300-year-old tavern that proudly eschews the paraphernalia of heritage theme pubs. A small terrace looks over the Thames.

Elbow Room
103 Westbourne Grove, W2 (7221 5211/
www.elbow-room.co.uk). Bayswater, Notting
Hill Gate or Westbourne Park tube/7, 23, 52 bus.
Open noon-11pm Mon-Sat; noon-10.30pm Sun.
Credit DC, MC, V. **Map** p394 B6.
A pool hall like no other, with an industrial look but a relaxed feel. The long bar area widens out to the pool tables at the rear. As many people come here to drink – and nibble snacks – as to shoot some stick. There's a branch in Chapel Market, Islington, N1.

Jacs
48 Lonsdale Road, Notting Hill, W11 (7792 2838).
Notting Hill Gate tube. **Open** 6-11pm Tue-Sat;
7-10.30pm Sun; closed Mon. **Credit** MC, V.
Map p394 A6.
Jacs is surprisingly approachable given its status as one of Notting Hill's hippest hangouts. The decor is chaotic, though intentionally so, and the crowd hip without bragging too much about it.

The Westbourne
101 Westbourne Park Villas, Notting Hill, W2
(7221 1332). Royal Oak tube. **Open** 5-11pm Mon;
noon-11pm Tue-Fri; 11am-11pm Sat; 11am-10.30pm
Sun. **Credit** AmEx, DC, MC, V. **Map** p394 B5.
A phenomenally popular gastrobar, where the good food is matched by the beer selection. By day, it's relaxed and civilised; by night, the front terrace heaves with west London's trendiest.

White Horse
1-3 Parsons Green, Fulham, SW6 (7736 2115/
www.whitehorsesw6.com). Parsons Green tube.
Open 11am-11pm Mon-Sat; 11am-10.30pm Sun.
Credit AmEx, MC, V.
This invariably heaving pub provides a spectacular range of beers (60 bottled varieties, including wheat beers, smoked beer from Bavaria and a few Trappist ales) and at least six real ales on tap.

White Swan
Riverside, Twickenham, Middx (8892 2166).
Twickenham rail. **Open** *Apr-Sept* 11am-11pm
Mon-Sat; noon-10.30pm Sun. *Oct-Mar* 11am-3pm,
5.30-11pm Mon-Thur; 11am-11pm Fri, Sat;
noon-10.30pm Sun. **Credit** MC, V.
A local landmark, the centuries-old White Swan is a terrific, characterful haunt cherished by locals. It looks out over Eel Pie Island, London's most unique settlement (*see p184*).

Eat, Drink, Shop

Shops & Services

Credit cards at the ready...

SHOPPING DISTRICTS

Oxford Street and **Regent Street** are the mainstays for high street shopping with the flagship branches of most major UK and international chains pretty much shared between them. Other busy shopping areas include Neal Street and the Piazza in **Covent Garden**, **King's Road**, where you can expect to find plenty of high-fashion and more quirky, independent shops and **Knightsbridge**, which boasts two high-class department stores in Harrods and Harvey Nichols.

If you prefer the convenience of a one-stop mall, **Bluewater**, off junction 2 of the M25 at Greenhithe in Kent (08456 021021), is Europe's largest, incorporating a vast array of upmarket shops, more than 40 restaurants plus a 12-screen cinema. Alternatively, at junction 30/31 of the M25, at West Thurrock, Essex, there's **Lakeside** (01708 869933), which is slightly smaller and less polished, but perfectly adequate nevertheless.

For information on consumer rights, *see p364.*

LATE OPENING

Stores in central London are open late one night of the week (usually until 7pm or 8pm). Those in the West End (Oxford Street to Covent Garden) stay open late on Thursdays, while Wednesday is late opening in the chi-chi Chelsea/Knightsbridge/Kensington triangle. In addition, some shops are open on Sundays, especially in the weeks leading up to Christmas.

Antiques

In addition, there are myriad stalls, both indoor (open Tue-Sat) and outdoor (open Wed and Sat only), at **Camden Passage** in Islington (www.antiquescamdenpassage.co.uk).

Admiral Vernon

141-9 Portobello Road, Notting Hill, W11 (7727 5242/www.portobello-antiques.co.uk). Notting Hill Gate tube. **Open** 5am-5pm Sat. **Credit** varies. **Map** p394 A6.
The busiest arcade on Portobello Road, the Admiral Vernon boasts specialists in advertising art, 17th-to 19th-century porcelain and antique textiles among its numerous concessions.

Alfie's Antiques Market

13-25 Church Street, Marylebone, NW8 (7723 6066/www.ealfies.com). Edgware Road tube/ Marylebone tube/rail. **Open** 10am-6pm Tue-Sat; closed Mon, Sun. **Credit** varies. **Map** p395 E4.
The basement of this sprawling multi-floor arcade is packed with 19th-century furniture, antique textiles, jewellery and accessories. On the upper levels you might find French country furniture, Clarice Cliff pottery and '60s furniture and lighting.

Well read: the **Riverside Walk Market.** *See p229.*

Antiquarius

131-41 King's Road, Chelsea, SW3 (7351 5353). Sloane Square tube/19, 22, 319 bus. **Open** 10am-6pm Mon-Sat; closed Sun. **Credit** varies. **Map** p397 F11.

Specialities among the hundred or more dealers at this Chelsea arcade include glassware, classic luggage, silverware and costume jewellery.

Grays Antiques Market & Grays in the Mews

58 Davies Street & 1-7 Davies Mews, Mayfair, W1 (7629 7034/www.graysantiques.com). Bond Street tube. **Open** 10am-6pm Mon-Fri; closed Sat, Sun. **Credit** varies. **Map** p398 H6.

The front hall has the biggest collection of antique jewellery in London. There are also silverware dealers, selling pieces ranging from Roman to Victorian. The Mews has cheaper but no less desirable collectibles, particularly tin-plate toys.

London Silver Vaults

Chancery House, 53-64 Chancery Lane, Holborn, WC2 (7242 3844). Chancery Lane tube. **Open** 9am-5.20pm Mon-Fri; 9am-12.50pm Sat. **Credit** AmEx, MC, V. **Map** p399 M5.

These fascinating subterranean vaults, home to over 40 dealers, are packed with antique and modern silver. With prices from £20 to £20,000-plus, you should find something to suit you. Some traders also specialise in clocks and watches or jewellery.

Bookshops

The **Riverside Walk Market** (10am-5pm Sat, Sun and irregular weekdays) on the South Bank under Waterloo Bridge is always worth a browse: it's generally a haven of outrageously cheap paperbacks. The big bookstore chains – **Waterstone's**, **Books Etc** and **Borders** – have branches all over London; the largest are listed below.

General

Books Etc

263 High Holborn, Holborn, WC1 (7404 0261). Holborn tube. **Open** 9am-7pm Mon-Fri; closed Sat, Sun. **Credit** AmEx, MC, V. **Map** p399 K6.

Another of London's bookish chains, Books Etc's star has rather been on the wane since the arrival of Borders. That said, the selection of stuff here should appease most literary palates.

Borders

203 Oxford Street, Soho, W1 (7292 1600/www.borders.com). Oxford Circus tube. **Open** 8am-11pm Mon-Sat; noon-6pm Sun. **Credit** AmEx, MC, V. **Map** p398 J6.

This US chain has a comprehensive range of books, from fiction and poetry to textbooks and manuals, plus a café, magazine racks and music and video sections. It's particularly strong on American imports.

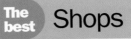

The best Shops

For four floors of fashion
Top Shop/Top Man (*see p234*).

For a right proper pampering
The Refinery for the boys (*see p247*), The Sanctuary for the girls (*see p247*).

For life's little luxuries
Fortnum & Mason (*see p232*).

For protection from the elements
James Smith & Sons (*see p248*).

For exotic ingredients
Brixton Market (*see p252*).

For exotic undergarments
Agent Provocateur (*see p239*).

For piling on the pounds
Pâtisserie Valerie (*see p243*).

For taking them back off again
Fresh & Wild (*see p244*).

For togs for toddlers
Daisy & Tom (*see p235*).

For the name alone
eat my handbag bitch (*see p245*).

Foyles

113-19 Charing Cross Road, Soho, WC2 (7437 5660/www.foyles.co.uk). Tottenham Court Road tube. **Open** 9am-6pm Mon-Wed, Fri, Sat; 9am-7pm Thur; closed Sun. **Credit** AmEx, MC, V. **Map** p399 K6.

A vast range of titles with hard-to-find publications a speciality. Thankfully, books are no longer shelved by publisher, but (more conventionally) by author.

Waterstone's

203-6 Piccadilly, St James's, W1 (7851 2400/www.waterstones.co.uk). Piccadilly Circus tube. **Open** 10am-11pm Mon-Sat; noon-6pm Sun. **Credit** AmEx, DC, MC, V. **Map** p400 J7.

With over a million titles on sale, this Piccadilly branch of Waterstone's is the largest bookshop in Europe, boasting a restaurant, cafés, bars, an Internet area and a gallery space.

Specialist

Books for Cooks

4 Blenheim Crescent, Notting Hill, W11 (7221 1992/www.booksforcooks.com). Ladbroke Grove tube. **Open** 9.30am-6pm Mon-Sat; closed Sun. **Credit** AmEx, DC, MC, V.

The shelves at this west London enterprise are stacked floor to ceiling with books on all aspects of food and diet. In keeping with the theme, there's even a small café.

Children's Book Centre

237 Kensington High Street, Kensington, W8 (7937 7497/www.childrensbookcentre.co.uk). High Street Kensington tube. **Open** 9.30am-6.30pm Mon, Wed, Fri, Sat; 9.30am-6pm Tue; 9.30am-7pm Thur; noon-6pm Sun. **Credit** AmEx, MC, V. **Map** p396 A9.

In addition to its 20,000 titles for ages 0-13, the Children's Book Centre also carries activity games, puzzles, videos, cassettes and character toys.

Cinema Bookshop

13-14 Great Russell Street, Fitzrovia, WC1 (7637 0206). Tottenham Court Road tube. **Open** 10.30am-5.30pm Mon-Sat; closed Sun. **Credit** MC, V. **Map** p399 K5.
London's best ranges of film books and paraphernalia, including biographies, movie guides, stills and screenplays.

You're booked

The makers of the film *Notting Hill* were not just being whimsical when they chose to have Hugh Grant dithering between Julia Roberts and his bookshop. London is not only the home to many screen stars: it's also peppered with small, independent book retailers. Many sell a mix of new and used books, often devoted to specialist themes, in an attempt to differentiate themselves from the might of the chains, while others are devoted entirely to dusty warrens of tattered second-hand books. The acknowledged elite, though, are the antiquarian bookshops scattered across London, dedicated purveyors of manuscripts, engravings, leather-bound tomes, first editions and rare imprints.

A good place to start is **Henry Sotheran** just off Piccadilly (2-5 Sackville Street, Mayfair, W1, 7439 6151), where a handsome ground floor room of wall-lined, glass-fronted cabinets packed with antiquarian books is supplemented by a downstairs print gallery. Another favourite is **Maggs Brothers** (50 Berkeley Square, Mayfair, W1, 7493 7160). Arguably the most prestigious of them all, it sells pre-20th-century manuscripts and first editions, especially literature and travel. For charm, Cecil Court, a small alley off the west side of Charing Cross Road, injects a little bit of Montmartre into London's West End. Here you can find a number of specialist book, poster and print shops devoted to, among many subjects, ballet, travel and Italiana.

Many antiquarian booksellers have been forced to move out of their traditional premises by soaring rents and have found refuge in cellars, up narrow stairwells or above shops. One such refugee is **Bertram Rota** (31 Long Acre, Covent Garden, WC2, 7836 0723), who left its lovely old premises a few years to make way for a cheap imported clothing emporium. Rota, however, still offers a huge selection of first editions, with an emphasis on English literature.

Another way in which London antiquarian booksellers have sought to combat costs has been to combine and offer their wares on a single site where the inveterate browser can while away the hours sampling the merchandise. The best of these is **Biblion** (1-7 Davies Mews, Mayfair, W1, 7629 1374) behind Bond Street station, where a wide variety of booksellers exhibit their stock. The real beating heart of London's book trade, though, is to be found in the Bloomsbury area where a number of fine bookshops are clustered around the British Museum, among them **Unsworths Booksellers**, **Ulysses** (for both, *see p232*) and **Gekoski** (Pied Bull Yard, 15A Bloomsbury Square, Bloomsbury, WC1, 7404 6676).

Despite a number of excellent websites, the dry surf of the Internet has not yet swamped the variety of London's antiquarian bookshops. Animated discussions with a learned bookseller about the exact year of a first edition, the thrill of the find and, above all, the delving in the shelving, will never be substituted. Even Hugh, given the choice between Julia's perfect spine and that of a morocco-bound first folio, could be forgiven for thinking twice.

Hark back to the golden age of the silver screen at the **Cinema Bookshop**. *See p230.*

Daunt Books
83-4 Marylebone High Street, Marylebone, W1 (7224 2295). Baker Street or Bond Street tube.
Open 9am-7.30pm Mon-Sat; 11am-6pm Sun.
Credit MC, V. **Map** p398 G5.
The varied stock and knowledgeable staff at this lovely travel bookshop make it the first choice for many seasoned travellers.
Branch: 193 Haverstock Hill, Belsize Park, NW3 (7794 4006).

Edward Stanford
12-14 Long Acre, Covent Garden, WC2 (7836 1321/ www.stanfords.co.uk). Covent Garden or Leicester Square tube. **Open** 9am-7.30pm Mon, Wed, Thur, Fri; 9.30am-7.30pm Tue; 10am-7pm Sat; noon-6pm Sun. **Credit** MC, V. **Map** p401 L5.
Maps and globes are a speciality here, but there are also great ranges of travel literature and guides.

Forbidden Planet
71-5 New Oxford Street, St Giles's, WC1 (7836 4179). Tottenham Court Road tube.
Open 10am-6pm Mon-Wed, Sat; 10am-7pm Thur, Fri; closed Sun. **Credit** AmEx, MC, V. **Map** p399 L5.
This sci-fi, fantasy and horror emporium stocks comics, mags, books and collectibles.

Gay's the Word
66 Marchmont Street, Bloomsbury, WC1 (7278 7654/www.gaystheword.co.uk). Russell Square tube. **Open** 10am-6.30pm Mon-Sat; 2-6pm Sun. **Credit** AmEx, DC, MC, V. **Map** p399 L4.
London's only exclusively gay and lesbian bookshop is located in the heart of Bloomsbury and offers a broad stock including fiction, biography, travel literature and sex manuals, shelved by genre.

Silver Moon Women's Bookshop
64-8 Charing Cross Road, Covent Garden, WC2 (7836 7906/www.silvermoonbookshop.co.uk). Leicester Square tube. **Open** 9.30am-7.30pm Mon-Fri; 10am-6.30pm Sat; noon-6pm Sun. **Credit** AmEx, MC, V. **Map** p401 K6.
'Europe's largest women's bookshop' offers two floors of books and magazines by, for and about women and women's issues.

Sportspages
Caxton Walk, 94-6 Charing Cross Road, St Giles's, WC2 (7240 9604/www.sportspages.co.uk). Leicester Square tube. **Open** 9.30am-7pm Mon-Sat; noon-6pm Sun. **Credit** AmEx, DC, MC, V. **Map** p401 K6.
Football dominates at Sportspages, but the books, fanzines, magazines and videos cover most sports.

Talking Books Shop
11 Wigmore Street, Marylebone, W1 (7491 4117/ www.talkingbooks.co.uk). Bond Street tube.
Open 9.30am-5.30pm Mon-Fri; 10am-5pm Sat; closed Sun. **Credit** AmEx, MC, V. **Map** p398 G6.
A massive selection of spoken-word CDs and tapes.

Zwemmer Media Arts
80 Charing Cross Road, Covent Garden, WC2 (7240 4157/www.zwemmer.com). Leicester Square tube. **Open** 10am-6.30pm Mon-Wed, Fri; 10am-8pm Thur; 10am-6pm Sat; closed Sun. **Credit** AmEx, DC, MC, V. **Map** p401 K6.
Zwemmer is a byword for books on the arts. This branch specialises in photography and cinema.

Antiquarian/second-hand

Skoob

*15 Sicilian Avenue, Bloomsbury, WC1 (7404 3063/
www.skoob.com). Holborn tube.* **Open** 10.30am-
6.30pm Mon-Sat; noon-5pm Sun. **Credit** AmEx,
MC, V. **Map** p399 L5.
One of London's most comprehensive second-hand
bookshops, Skoob caters for students, academics
and those with special interests. Prices are low.

Ulysses

*40 Museum Street, Bloomsbury, WC1 (7831 1600).
Tottenham Court Road tube.* **Open** 10.30am-6pm
Mon-Sat; closed Sun. **Credit** AmEx, DC, MC, V.
Map p399 L5.
One of London's foremost dealers in 20th-century
literature and modern first editions, mostly fiction
and poetry.

Unsworths Booksellers

*12 Bloomsbury Street, Bloomsbury, WC1 (7436
9836/www.unsworths.com). Tottenham Court Road
tube.* **Open** 10am-8pm Mon-Sat; noon-8pm Sun.
Credit AmEx, DC, MC, V. **Map** p399 K5.
Antiquarian books, general second-hands, remain-
dered and out-of-print titles, review copies and current releases, all at 50% or more below list price.

Woburn Book Shop

*10 Woburn Walk, Bloomsbury, WC1 (7388 7278).
Russell Square tube/Euston tube/rail.* **Open** 11am-
6pm Mon-Fri; 11am-5pm Sat; closed Sun. **Credit** MC,
V. **Map** p399 K3.
The friendly owners of this fascinating Bloomsbury
bookshop gear the stock to their own personal
interests. Thus, politics, philosophy, sociology and
history dominate.

Newsagents

A Moroni & Son

*68 Old Compton Street, Soho, W1 (7437 2847).
Piccadilly Circus or Tottenham Court Road tube.*
Open 7am-8pm daily. **Map** p399 K6.
A small but invaluable shop in the heart of Soho
packed to the rafters with international newspapers
and periodicals.
Branch: 308 Regent Street, Marylebone, W1
(7580 3835).

Department stores

Dickens & Jones

*224-44 Regent Street, Mayfair, W1 (7734 7070/
www.houseoffraser.co.uk). Oxford Circus tube.*
Open 10am-6.30pm Mon, Tue; 10am-7pm Wed, Fri,
Sat; 10am-8pm Thur; noon-6pm Sun. **Credit** AmEx,
DC, MC, V. **Map** p398 J6.
Though it does carry ranges of sensible, high-
quality furniture and home goods, D&J is mainly
devoted to clothing and beauty. Women's fashion
tends towards classic designers such as Jasper

Conran and Betsey Johnson, while the underrated
menswear department includes Kenzo, Burberry
and London's only Crombie concession.
Branches: George Street, Richmond, Surrey (8940
7761). *Army & Navy Stores* 101 Victoria Street,
Westminster, SW1 (7834 1234). *DH Evans* 318
Oxford Street, Marylebone, W1 (7629 8800). *Barkers
of Kensington* 63 Kensington High Street,
Kensington, W8 (7937 5432).

Fortnum & Mason

*181 Piccadilly, St James's, W1 (7734 8040/
www.fortnumandmason.co.uk). Piccadilly Circus
tube.* **Open** 10am-6.30pm Mon-Sat; closed Sun.
Credit AmEx, DC, MC, V. **Map** p400 J7.
Though undeniably anachronistic, F&M continues
to thrive, selling *la style anglaise* to hordes of eager
tourists and preserving a slice of *Brideshead
Revisited* Britain. The ground floor houses the
famous food hall, while classic womenswear (Jean
Muir *et al*) and the quintessential attire of the
English gent are to be found on the first and third
floors respectively. The fourth floor contains furniture and homeware, while the basement is the place
to go for made-to-order hampers.

Harrods

*87 Brompton Road, Knightsbridge, SW1 (7730
1234/www.harrods.com). Knightsbridge tube.*
Open 10am-7pm Mon-Sat; closed Sun.
Credit AmEx, DC, MC, V. **Map** p397 F9.
With its armies of liveried doormen and panoply of
branded merchandise, Harrods sometimes feels more
like a theme park than a shop. That said, though,
Britain's most famous department store is still
pretty impressive: its magnificently decadent food
halls and panoramic range of goods (exotic animals
to medieval instruments) remind you why hordes of
tourists continue to pour in, while 60 fashion departments provide ample ammo for the style-conscious
shopper. However, beware the out-of-date dress code:
anyone arriving wearing shorts, torn jeans or even a
rucksack will receive a swift rebuttal.

Harvey Nichols

*109-25 Knightsbridge, Knightsbridge, SW1
(7235 5000). Knightsbridge tube.* **Open** 10am-7pm
Mon, Tue, Sat; 10am-8pm Wed-Fri; noon-6pm Sun.
Credit AmEx, DC, MC, V. **Map** p397 F9.
The spiritual home of London's fashion junkies,
Harvey Nicks devotes three floors to designer labels,
including Alexander McQueen, Stella McCartney,
Joseph and Alberta Ferrari. There's an extensive
beauty department (of course), a chic homeware collection and a stylish food hall. On the fifth floor, a
restaurant and bar provide respite from the shopping,
but don't stop until you're looking absolutely fabulous. The window displays, too, are legendary.

John Lewis

*278-306 Oxford Street, Marylebone, W1 (7629
7711/www.johnlewis.co.uk). Oxford Circus tube.* **Open**
9.30am-6pm Mon-Wed, Fri; 10am-8pm Thur; 9am-6pm
Sat; closed Sun. **Credit** MC, V. **Map** p398 H6.

Computer Exchange.

The most family-orientated and down-to-earth of London's department stores is also probably its best. Always strong on areas that the other stores neglect (such as homewares and haberdashery), JL also boasts a comprehensive and vastly underrated electronics section and a good range of stylish, functional clothing. Its famed 'never knowingly undersold' policy means prices, as a rule, are an absolute steal. **Branches**: Brent Cross Shopping Centre, Brent Cross, NW4 (8202 6535); Wood Street, Kingston, Surrey (8547 3000).

Liberty
214-20 Regent Street, Soho, W1 (7734 1234/ www.liberty.co.uk). Oxford Circus tube. **Open** 10am-6.30pm Mon-Wed; 10am-8pm Thur, Fri; 10am-7pm Sat; noon-6pm Sun. **Credit** AmEx, DC, MC, V. **Map** p398 J6.
The Arts and Crafts heritage and faux-Tudor building give Liberty a certain quaint charm, but the store hasn't rested on its laurels and has garnered a reputation for the funkiest women's fashion in London. Most other departments – especially accessories, furniture, fabrics and jewellery – offer an above-average selection of goods, while the small space of the cosmetics department, on the ground floor, is intelligently filled with a mix of cult and big names.

Marks & Spencer
458 Oxford Street, Marylebone, W1 (7935 7954/ www.marks-and-spencer.com). Bond Street or Marble Arch tube. **Open** 9am-8pm Mon-Fri; 9am-7pm Sat; noon-6pm Sun. **Credit** AmEx, MC, V. **Map** p398 G6.
A bastion of consumer necessities, M&S does socks, underwear and ready-made meals like no one else in Britain. It's fallen behind in several other areas in recent years, however, and its drab, utilitarian fashions and conservative homeware, though good-quality and reasonably priced, are frequently passed over for their lack of flair. It's hard to believe the British public will desert trusty old M&S, though,

and exciting new lines like the 'Salon Rose' underwear by the Agent Provocateur (*see p239*) team suggest the tide is beginning to turn.
Branches are numerous: check the phone book.

Selfridges
400 Oxford Street, Marylebone, W1 (7629 1234/ www.selfridges.co.uk). Bond Street or Marble Arch tube. **Open** 10am-7pm Mon-Wed; 10am-8pm Thur, Fri; 9.30am-7pm Sat; noon-6pm Sun. **Credit** AmEx, DC, MC, V. **Map** p398 G6.
Since its £100 million makeover, Selfridges has shrugged off its frumpy old image and achieved the rare feat of having a real sense of style and colour while remaining open to all. The fashion department is cutting edge but not intimidating, and the food hall luxurious without being extortionate. It also boasts London's largest cosmetics hall, a spectacular toy department and a number of in-store restaurants that range from sprawling family-orientated affairs to hip little coffee bars. In short, this is a proper city department store: grand, impressive and universal.

Electronics

Tottenham Court Road, W1, boasts a glut of electronics and computer shops. It's best to know what you're after and shop around for the best prices: staff are notoriously pushy.

Computers & games

Two other good stockists of games are **Virgin Megastore** and **HMV** (for both, *see p256*).

Computer Exchange
32 Rathbone Place, Fitzrovia, W1 (7636 2666/ www.cex.co.uk). Tottenham Court Road tube. **Open** 10am-7pm daily. **Credit** MC, V. **Map** p399 K5.
New, used and imported games and PC software, plus second-hand hardware (including a great retro section with consoles from 1970 onwards).

Gultronics

52 Tottenham Court Road, Fitzrovia, W1 (7637 1619/mail order 7436 3131/www.gultronics.co.uk). Tottenham Court Road tube. **Open** 9am-6pm Mon-Wed, Fri, Sat; 9am-7pm Thur; closed Sun. **Credit** AmEx, MC, V. **Map** p399 K5.

A decent range of PCs, though prices are not always the cheapest in town.

Branches are numerous: check the phone book.

Micro Anvika

245 Tottenham Court Road, Fitzrovia, W1 (7636 2547/www.microanvika.co.uk). Goodge Street or Tottenham Court Road tube. **Open** 9.30am-6pm Mon-Wed, Fri, Sat; 9.30am-6.30pm Thur; 11am-5pm Sun. **Credit** AmEx, DC, MC, V. **Map** p399 K5.

Central London's leading Mac specialist (it also sells PCs, incidentally) offers reasonably priced computers but rather expensive software.

Branches are numerous: check the phone book.

Hi-fi

Hi-Fi Experience

227 Tottenham Court Road, Fitzrovia, W1 (7580 3535/www.hifilondon.co.uk). Tottenham Court Road tube. **Open** 10am-7pm Mon-Fri; 9am-6pm Sat; closed Sun. **Credit** AmEx, DC, MC, V. **Map** p399 K5.

This hi-fi and home cinema equipment offers eight demo rooms and expert staff.

Richer Sounds

2 London Bridge Walk, Borough, SE1 (7403 1201/www.richersounds.com). London Bridge tube/rail. **Open** 10am-6pm Mon-Wed, Fri; 10am-7pm Thur; 10am-5pm Sat; closed Sun. **Credit** MC, V. **Map** p405 Q8.

Decent hi-fi separates at rock-bottom prices.

Branches are numerous: check the phone book.

Photography

Jessops

63-9 New Oxford Street, St Giles's, WC1 (7240 6077/www.jessops.com). Tottenham Court Road tube. **Open** 9am-6pm Mon-Wed, Sat; 9am-8pm Thur; 9am-7pm Fri; 11am-5pm Sun. **Credit** AmEx, DC, MC, V. **Map** p399 L5.

Jessops caters for professionals and amateurs alike with its great range of keenly-priced cameras, plus film processing and a repairs service.

Branches are numerous: check the phone book.

Snappy Snaps

23 Garrick Street, Covent Garden, WC2 (7836 3040). Leicester Square tube. **Open** 8.30am-6pm Mon-Fri; noon-5pm Sat; closed Sun. **Map** p401 L7.

An outstanding high-street film processing chain, offering the full gamut of developing services. The processing service offered in selected branches of Boots (*see p257*) is also above average.

Branches are numerous: check the phone book.

Fashion

Budget

Oxford Street is the main hunting ground for bargain seekers. Try **New Look** (nos.175 & 309; 7499 8497) for trashy, glitzy streetwear; **Tribe** (nos.67-71; 7494 1798) for sub-designer lads' kit; or **Jeffrey Rogers** (Unit G6, The Plaza, 120 Oxford Street; 7580 5545) for decent womenswear.

H&M

261-71 Regent Street, Marylebone, W1 (7493 4004/www.hm.com). Oxford Circus tube. **Open** 10am-7pm Mon-Wed, Sat; 10am-8pm Thur, Fri; noon-6pm Sun. **Credit** AmEx, MC, V. **Map** p400 J7.

The Swedish chain has recently added a range of hip, utilitarian menswear to its stylish budget-priced womenswear and functional kids' clothing.

Branches are numerous: check the phone book.

Miss Selfridge

221 Oxford Street, Soho, W1 (7434 0405). Oxford Circus tube. **Open** 10am-8pm Mon-Sat; noon-6pm Sun. **Credit** AmEx, MC, V. **Map** p398 G6.

From the people who brought you Selfridges (*see p233*) comes this funky chain for trendy young things. Disposable fashion at disposable prices.

Branches are numerous: check the phone book.

Top Shop/Top Man

214 Oxford Street, Marylebone, W1 (7636 7700/www.topshop.co.uk). Oxford Circus tube. **Open** 9am-8pm Mon-Wed, Fri, Sat; 9am-9pm Thur; noon-6pm Sun. **Credit** AmEx, DC, MC, V. **Map** p398 J6.

The world's biggest fashion store offers rails of bargain streetwear, clubwear and catwalk knock-offs, plus a café and a men's and women's hairdressers.

Branches are numerous: check the phone book.

Zara

118 Regent Street, Mayfair, W1 (7534 9500/www.inditex.com). Oxford Circus or Piccadilly Circus tube. **Open** 10am-7pm Mon-Wed, Fri, Sat; 10am-8pm Thur; noon-6pm Sun. **Credit** AmEx, DC, MC, V. **Map** p400 J7.

Clothes that convey designer quality and style without the price. The stock tends to be chic and classic rather than throwaway trendy.

Children

See also p258 **Cheeky Monkeys**.

Baby Gap/Gap Kids

146-8 Regent Street, Mayfair, W1 (7287 5095/www.gap.com). Oxford Circus or Piccadilly Circus tube. **Open** 9.30am-7pm Mon-Wed, Fri, Sat; 9.30am-8pm Thur; noon-6pm Sun. **Credit** AmEx, MC, V. **Map** p400 J7.

Functional and hard-wearing clothes for the wee ones in your life.

Branches are numerous: check the phone book.

Daisy & Tom
*181 King's Road, Chelsea, SW3 (7352 5000).
Sloane Square tube, then 11, 19, 22 bus/49 bus.*
Open 10am-6pm Mon-Sat; noon-6pm Sun.
Credit AmEx, MC, V. **Map** p397 E12.
This children's department store stocks toys, games, books and kids' clothing.

Jigsaw Junior
*97 Fulham Road, Chelsea, SW3 (7823 8915). South
Kensington tube.* **Open** 10am-6pm Mon-Sat; noon-
6pm Sun. **Credit** AmEx, MC, V. **Map** p397 D11.
Floral dresses and fashion-conscious denim and
khakis for young girls with moneyed parents.
Branches are numerous: check the phone book.

Trotters
*34 King's Road, Chelsea, SW3 (7259 9620/
www.trotters.co.uk). Sloane Square tube.* **Open** 9am-
6.30pm Mon, Tue, Thur-Sat; 9am-7pm Wed; 10am-
6pm Sun. **Credit** AmEx, MC, V. **Map** p397 F11.
A great range of trendy kids' clothes and shoes, plus
a hairdresser and a children's library.
Branch: 127 Kensington High Street, Kensington,
W8 (7937 9373).

Fetish

Regulation
*17A St Alban's Place, Islington, N1 (7226
0665/www.regulation-ltd.com). Angel tube.*
Open 10.30am-6.30pm Mon-Sat; noon-5pm Sun.
Credit AmEx, MC, V. **Map** p402 O2.
Regulation is packed with one of London's best selections of men's fetish clothing and bondage equipment, including leatherwear, rubber and strap-work.

Mid-range

Egg
*36 & 37 Kinnerton Street, Belgravia, SW1
(7235 9315). Hyde Park Corner or Knightsbridge
tube.* **Open** 10am-6pm Tue-Sat; closed Mon, Sun.
Credit AmEx, MC, V. **Map** p400 G9.
Low-tech clothing and homewares with an individ-
ualistic and organic look.

French Connection
*99-103 Long Acre, Covent Garden, WC2 (7379
6560/www.frenchconnection.com). Covent Garden
tube.* **Open** 10.30am-7pm Mon-Wed, Fri, Sat;
11am-8pm Thur; noon-6pm Sun. **Credit** AmEx, DC,
MC, V. **Map** p401 L6.
A popular high-street chain offering stylish men's
and women's clothes, plus its own range of toiletries.
Branches are numerous: check the phone book.

Gap
*30-31 Long Acre, Covent Garden, WC2 (7379
0779/www.gap.com). Covent Garden tube.*
Open 10am-8pm Mon-Fri, 10am-7pm Sat; noon-6pm
Sun. **Credit** AmEx, MC, V. **Map** p401 L6.
Casual, good-quality separates for men and women.
Branches are numerous: check the phone book.

Hobbs
*Unit 17, The Market, Covent Garden, WC2 (7836
9168). Covent Garden tube.* **Open** 10.30am-7pm
Mon-Fri, Sat; 10am-7.30pm Thur; noon-5.30pm
Sun. **Credit** AmEx, DC, MC, V. **Map** p401 L7.
Hobbs is dominated by the kind of classic casuals
favoured by mildly boho mothers and college types.
Branches are numerous: check the phone book.

Jigsaw
*126-7 New Bond Street, Mayfair, W1 (7491
4484/www.jigsaw-online.com). Bond Street tube.*
Open 10am-6.30pm Mon-Wed, Fri, Sat; 10am-
7.30pm Thur; closed Sun. **Credit** AmEx, MC, V.
Map p398 H6.
It may have fallen behind a little in the high-fashion
stakes, but Jigsaw still offers slick modern tailoring
and quality fabrics: classic with a twist, if you will.
Branches are numerous: check the phone book.

Karen Millen
*22-3 James Street, Covent Garden, WC2 (7836
5355). Covent Garden tube.* **Open** 10am-7pm
Mon- Wed, Fri, Sat; 10am-8pm Thur; noon-6pm
Sun. **Credit** AmEx, DC, MC, V. **Map** p399 K6.
Smart, sophisticated and fashion-conscious, Karen
Millen focuses on suits, dresses and party gear.
Branches are numerous: check the phone book.

Kookaï
*Unit 13, The Market, Covent Garden, WC2
(7379 1318/www.kookai.co.uk). Covent Garden tube.*
Open 10am-7pm Mon-Wed, Fri, Sat; 10am-8pm
Thur; noon-6pm Sun. **Credit** AmEx, DC, MC, V.
Map p401 L7.
Catwalk-conscious, sophisticated and distinctly
youthful women's clothing. Sizes are small (8-14)
and prices are reasonable.

Mango
*8-12 Neal Street, Covent Garden, WC2 (7240 6099/
www.mango.es). Covent Garden tube.* **Open** 10am-
7pm Mon- Wed, Fri, Sat; 10am-8pm Thur; noon-6pm
Sun. **Credit** AmEx, DC, MC, V. **Map** p396 B9.
Catwalk-inspired numbers made from decent material and sold at nice prices.

Monsoon
*5 James Street, Covent Garden, WC2 (7379
3623/www.monsoon.co.uk). Covent Garden
tube.* **Open** 10am-8pm Mon-Sat; 11am-6pm Sun.
Credit AmEx, DC, MC, V. **Map** p401 L6.
Inspired by Chinese or Indian designs, Monsoon's
clothes have a strong, ethnic look, with lots of bead-
work and embroidery.

Oasis
*13 James Street, Covent Garden, WC2 (7240 7445/
www.oasis-stores.com). Covent Garden tube.*
Open 10am-7pm Mon-Wed, Fri-Sun; 10am-8pm
Thur; **Credit** AmEx, DC, MC, V. **Map** p401 L6.
Youthful, funky and relatively cheap, Oasis picks
up on every catwalk trend and translates it to suit
the purse of the girl next door.
Branches are numerous: check the phone book.

PANDORA

**Dress Agency/Consignment Shop
Armani to Zikha**

"Have you ever wondered how some woma
always manage to look smartly dressed.
Natural style, money to burn?"

They have discovered the secret of second h
clothes shopping.

PANDORA,
London's leading Dress Agency.
Approximately 5,000 items; huge collection;
· suits · dresses · hats · shoes · accessories
All the top designer labels, all in perfect condit

**16-22 Cheval Place,
Knightsbridge,
London SW7 1ES
Open 9am-6pm
Mon-Sat
Tel (020) 7589 5289**

**PANDORA is a
minute from Harrods –
ideal for buyers
and sellers**

Ted Baker

1-4 Langley Court, Covent Garden, WC2 (7497 8862/www.tedbaker.co.uk). Covent Garden tube. **Open** 10am-7pm Mon-Fri; 9.30am-6.30pm Sat; noon-5pm Sun. **Credit** AmEx, DC, MC, V. **Map** p401 L6.
Ted Baker has managed to give its hip, youthful menswear and womenswear semi-designer status, with prices to match.
Branch: 7 Foubert's Place, Soho, W1 (7437 5619).

Second-hand

Blackout II

51 Endell Street, Covent Garden, WC2 (7240 5006/www.blackout2.com). Covent Garden tube. **Open** 11am-7pm Mon-Fri; 11.30am-6.30pm Sat; closed Sun. **Credit** AmEx, DC, MC, V. **Map** p399 L6.
This emporium of 1950s-'80s clothes has sequinned gowns and glam frocks for the ladies, Hawaiian shirts and 1960s suits for the gentlemen.

Cornucopia

12 Upper Tachbrook Street, Pimlico, SW1 (7828 5752). Victoria tube/rail. **Open** 11am-6pm daily. **Credit** MC, V. **Map** p400 J7.
An overcrowded little shop with a huge stock of 20th-century clothing in varying states of repair. It's also particularly strong on accessories.

Oxfam Originals

26 Ganton Street, Soho, W1 (7437 7338). Oxford Circus tube. **Open** 11.30am-7pm Mon-Sat; closed Sun. **Credit** MC, V. **Map** p398 J6.
Fashionably retro and vintage clothing comes priced highly at this arm of the charity chain.
Branches: 123A King's Road, Chelsea, SW3 (7351 7979); 22 Earlham Street, Covent Garden, WC2 (7836 9666).

Pandora

16-22 Cheval Place, Knightsbridge, SW7 (7589 5289). Knightsbridge tube. **Open** 9am-6pm Mon-Sat; closed Sun. **Credit** AmEx, MC, V. **Map** p397 E9.
One of London's best known dress agencies, Pandora is a must for those with the taste – but not necessarily the wallet – for the top designer labels.

Street

Bond International

10 Newburgh Street, Soho, W1 (7437 0079/www.bondinternational.com). Oxford Circus tube. **Open** 10.30am-6pm Mon-Sat; closed Sun. **Credit** AmEx, MC, V. **Map** p398 J6.
Bond sells a raft of baggy threads by brands such as Silas, Oeuf, Tender Loin and Stussy to wannabe b-boys and fly-girls.

Carhartt

56 Neal Street, Covent Garden, WC2 (7836 5659/www.carhartt.com). Covent Garden tube. **Open** 11am-6.30pm Mon-Wed, Fri, Sat; 11am-7pm Thur; noon-5pm Sun. **Credit** MC, V. **Map** p399 L6.

Carhartt offers both men and women a functional but stylish range of workwear separates that can be endlessly mixed and matched.

Diesel

43 Earlham Street, Covent Garden, WC2 (7497 5543/www.diesel.com). Covent Garden tube. **Open** 10am-6pm Mon-Wed, Fri-Sun; 10am-8pm Thur. **Credit** AmEx, MC, V. **Map** p399 L6.
A self-consciously cool Italian street-cum-designer label specialising in denim and hip, retro men's and women's separates.

The Dispensary

25 Pembridge Road, Notting Hill, W11 (7221 9290/www.dispensary.co.uk). Notting Hill Gate tube. **Open** 10.30am-6.30pm Mon-Sat; closed Sun. **Credit** AmEx, MC, V. **Map** p394 A7.
An ultra-trendy but sometimes overpriced store offering a mixture of retro, catwalk and street styles.
Branches: *Womenswear* 9 Newburgh Street, Soho, W1 (7287 8145). *Menswear* 15 Newburgh Street, Soho, W1 (7734 4095); 200 Kensington Park Road, Notting Hill, W11 (7727 8797).

Duffer of St George

29 Shorts Gardens, Covent Garden, WC2 (7379 4660). Covent Garden or Leicester Square tube. **Open** 10.30am-7pm Mon-Sat; 1-5pm Sun. **Credit** AmEx, DC, MC, V. **Map** p399 L6.
Its own-brand clothes are impossibly cool in their own right, but Duffer also carries all the latest labels.

Shop

4 Brewer Street (basement), Soho, W1 (7437 1259). Leicester Square or Piccadilly Circus tube. **Open** 10.30am-6.30pm Mon-Fri; 11am-6.30pm Sat; closed Sun. **Credit** AmEx, MC, V. **Map** p400 J7.
Shop offers a mixture of funky and feminine with a host of labels, including Hysteric Glamour and Earl Jean, plus its own range of Shopgirl lingerie.

Urban Outfitters

36-8 Kensington High Street, Kensington, W8 (7761 1001/www.urban.com). High Street Kensington tube. **Open** 10am-7pm Mon-Wed, Fri, Sat; 10am-8pm Thur; noon-6pm Sun. **Credit** AmEx, MC, V. **Map** p396 A9.
A one-stop super-shop catering for all your lifestyle needs, with trendy, affordable clobber (including Uniform, Final Home and Generic Costume), cosmetics, gadgets, magazines and homewares all under one roof.

Suit hire

Moss Bros

88 Regent Street, Mayfair, W1 (7494 0666/www.mossbros.com). Oxford Circus or Piccadilly Circus tube. **Open** 9am-6pm Mon-Wed, Fri; 9am-7pm Thur; 11am-5pm Sun. **Credit** AmEx, DC, MC, V. **Map** p400 J7.
Everything from dinner jackets and morning suits to top-hat and tails.
Branches are numerous: check the phone book.

Eat, Drink, Shop

Designs for life

London's high-falutin', high-end, high-fashion clothing emporia tend to be concentrated in and around two main areas: Mayfair and Chelsea/South Kensington/Knightsbridge; below is a basic list. Most shops are open 10am-6pm Monday to Saturday, with many Knightsbridge and South Kensington stores staying open until 7pm on Wednesday and the West End shops opening until 7pm on Thursday. If you're looking for a wide range of labels under one roof, try **Harvey Nichols**, **Harrods** (for both, *see p232*), **Liberty** or **Selfridges** (for both, *see p233*).

Chelsea, SW3
Sloane Square tube.
King's Road: Joseph (sale shop), World's End (Vivienne Westwood).

Covent Garden, WC2
Covent Garden tube.
Floral Street Agnès B, Jones, Paul Smith.

Knightsbridge, SW1, SW7
Knightsbridge tube.
Sloane Street Alberta Ferretti, Armani, Chanel, Christian Dior, Gucci, Hermès, MaxMara, Tommy Hilfiger.

Mayfair, W1
Bond Street tube.
Avery Row: Paul Smith (sale shop).
Brook Street: Comme des Garçons, Pleats Please (Issey Miyake).
Conduit Street: Alexander McQueen, Issey Miyake, Moschino, Krizia, Vivienne Westwood, Yohji Yamamoto.
Davies Street: Vivienne Westwood.
New Bond Street: Burberry, Calvin Klein, Donna Karan, Collezioni Armani, Emporio Armani, Fenwick, Louis Vuitton, Miu Miu, Nicole Farhi, Ralph Lauren, Tommy Hilfiger, Yves Saint Laurent.
Old Bond Street: Anna Molinari Blumarine, Dolce & Gabbana, DKNY, Gianni Versace, Joseph, Prada.
South Molton Street: Browns.

South Kensington, SW1, SW3
South Kensington tube.
Brompton Road: Emporio Armani, Issey Miyake, Betty Jackson, Paul Costelloe.
Draycott Avenue: Betsey Johnson, Galerie Gaultier.
Fulham Road: Voyage.
Sloane Avenue: Paul Smith.

Joseph.

Issey Miyake.

Underwear

Marks & Spencer (see p233) also sells good quality, affordable undies, and has recently gone all raunchy with a range designed by Agent Provocateur. See also p248 **A world away**.

Agent Provocateur

6 Broadwick Street, Soho, W1 (7439 0229/ www.agentprovocateur.com). Oxford Circus tube. **Open** 11am-7pm Mon-Sat; closed Sun. **Credit** AmEx, MC, V. **Map** p398 J6.
Agent Provocateur sells women's lingerie with 1950s pin-up appeal, as well as its own perfume.

Unusual sizes

High & Mighty

81-3 Knightsbridge, Knightsbridge, SW1 (7589 7454/www.highandmighty.co.uk). Knightsbridge tube. **Open** 10am-6.30pm Mon-Fri; 10am-6pm Sat; closed Sun. **Credit** AmEx, DC, MC, V.
Larger (17in-21in collar), broader (44in-60in chest) and taller (over 6ft 2in) men have an extensive range from which to choose, including jeans, casuals and suits.
Branches: 145-7 Edgware Road, Paddington, W2 (7723 8754); The Plaza, 120 Oxford Street, Fitzrovia, W1 (7436 4861).

French & Teague

69 Gloucester Avenue, Camden, NW1 (7483 4174/ www.sixteen47.com). Camden Town or Chalk Farm tube. **Open** 10am-6pm Mon-Wed, Fri, Sat; 10am-7pm Thur; closed Sun. **Credit** MC, V.
This classic and successful designer line, founded by comic Dawn French and designer Helen Teague, offers chic day- and eveningwear in sizes 16-32.

Fashion accessories & services

See also p248 **A world away**.

General

Accessorize

Unit 22, The Market, Covent Garden, WC2 (7240 2107/www.accessorize.co.uk). Covent Garden tube. **Open** 10am-8pm Mon-Sat; 11am-7pm Sun. **Credit** AmEx, DC, MC, V. **Map** p401 L6.
Keenly priced items for glamming up any outfit, including purses, jewellery and scarves.
Branches are numerous: check the phone book.

American Retro

35 Old Compton Street, Soho, W1 (7734 3477/ www.americanretro.com). Leicester Square tube. **Open** 10.30am-7.30pm Mon-Fri; 10.15am-7pm Sat; closed Sun. **Credit** AmEx, DC, MC, V. **Map** p399 K6.
Pumping music, funky decor and shelves packed with all manner of kitsch knick-knacks, fashion and home accessories make Retro an upbeat experience.

Antoni & Alison

43 Rosebery Avenue, Clerkenwell, EC1 (7833 2002/ www.antoniandalison.co.uk). Farringdon tube/rail/ 19, 38, 341 bus. **Open** 10.30am-6.30pm Mon-Fri; noon-4pm Sat; closed Sun. **Credit** AmEx, MC, V. **Map** p402 N4.
Punky, playful designs on badges, clothing, bags and jewellery are offered at this super-hip store.

Emma Bernhardt

301 Portobello Road, Notting Hill, W10 (8960 2929/www.emmabernhardt.co.uk). Ladbroke Grove tube. **Open** 10.30am-5.30pm Tue-Fri; 10.30am-6.30pm Sat; closed Sun, Mon. **Credit** MC, V. **Map** p394 A6.
Plastic heaven, Emma Bernhardt offers kitchenware, storage and lots of quite useless but fabulous cheap and chic kitschery from Mexico.

Dry cleaning, laundries & repairs

Buckingham Dry Cleaners

83 Duke Street, Mayfair, W1 (7499 1253). Bond Street tube. **Open** 8am-6pm Mon-Fri; 9.30am-12.30pm Sat; closed Sun. **Credit** AmEx, MC, V. **Map** p398 G6.
Unbeatable for quality of cleaning and service.

Danish Express

16 Hinde Street, Marylebone, W1 (7935 6306). Bond Street tube. **Open** 8.30am-5.30pm Mon-Fri; 9.30am-12.30pm Sat; closed Sun. **Credit** AmEx, DC, MC, V. **Map** p398 G5.
Danish Express has a same-day service on items received before 10am, and attractive prices to boot.

Michael's Shoe Care

7 Southampton Row, Bloomsbury, WC1 (7405 7436). Holborn tube. **Open** 8am-6.30pm Mon-Fri; closed Sat, Sun. **Credit** AmEx, DC, MC, V. **Map** p399 M5.
Michael's offers a range of shoe repairs, including re-heeling and shoe-dyeing, plus scarves, umbrellas and briefcases.
Branches are numerous: check the phone book.

Hats

See also p248 **A world away**.

Fred Bare

14 Lamb Street, Spitalfields, E1 (7247 9004). Liverpool Street tube/rail. **Open** 10am-5pm Mon-Fri, Sun; closed Sat. **Credit** MC, V. **Map** p400 J7.
A mix of cosy pull-ons and extravagant occasion-wear is offered at this fine Spitalfields spot.

Stephen Jones

36 Great Queen Street, Covent Garden, WC2 (7242 0770). Covent Garden or Holborn tube. **Open** 11am-6pm Mon-Wed, Fri; 11am-7pm Thur; also by appointment. **Credit** AmEx, DC, MC, V. **Map** p400 J7.
For cutting-edge, crafted fashion statements, few can rival Jones. Prices range from £70 to £250.

Eat, Drink, Shop

Jewellery

Angela Hale
5 The Royal Arcade, 28 Old Bond Street, Mayfair, W1 (7495 1920/www.angelahale.co.uk). Green Park tube. **Open** 10am-6pm Mon-Sat; closed Sun. **Credit** AmEx, MC, V. **Map** p400 J7.
Hale has deco and '50s-style costume jewellery, from beaded bracelets to chunky cufflinks and tiaras.

Argenta
82 Fulham Road, Chelsea, SW3 (7584 4480/ www.argenta.co.uk). South Kensington tube. **Open** 9.30am-5.30pm Mon-Fri; 9.30am-5pm Sat; closed Sun. **Credit** AmEx, MC, V. **Map** p397 D11.
A wide range of contemporary jewellery and watches, including over 1,000 wedding rings.

Electrum Gallery
21 South Molton Street, Mayfair, W1 (7629 6325). Bond Street tube. **Open** 10am-6pm Mon-Sat; noon-6pm Sun. **Credit** AmEx, DC, MC, V. **Map** p398 H6.
More like an art gallery than a shop, Electrum sells sparkling contemporary jewellery.

Frontiers
37 & 39 Pembridge Road, Notting Hill, W11 (7727 6132). Notting Hill Gate tube. **Open** 11am-6.30pm Mon-Sat; 11am-4.30pm Sun. **Credit** AmEx, DC, MC, V. **Map** p394 A7.
Specialising in old and new jewellery from Asia and North Africa, Frontiers is packed with exotic items.

Great Frog
10 Ganton Street, Soho, W1 (7439 9357/ www.greatfrog.com). Oxford Circus tube. **Open** 10.30am-6.30pm Mon-Sat; closed Sun. **Credit** AmEx, DC, MC, V. **Map** p398 J6.
From the plain gothic to the downright scary, Great Frog does chunky silver jewellery in skull and insect form, plus friendlier moonstone and amethyst items.

Into You
144 St John Street, Finsbury, EC1 (7253 5085/ www.into-you.co.uk). Angel tube/Farringdon tube/rail. **Open** noon-7pm Tue-Sat; closed Mon, Sun. **Credit** MC, V. **Map** p402 O3.
A top-notch tattoo and piercing outfit with five artists offering classic designs and expert piercing.

Janet Fitch
37A Neal Street, Covent Garden, W1 (7240 6332). Covent Garden tube. **Open** 10.30am-7pm Mon-Sat; noon-6pm Sun. **Credit** AmEx, DC, MC, V. **Map** p399 L6.
This small chain stocks work by 300 or so contemporary designers.
Branches are numerous: check the phone book.

Lesley Craze Gallery/Craze 2
34-5 Clerkenwell Green, Clerkenwell, EC1 (Lesley Craze Gallery 7608 0393/Craze 2 7251 0381/ www.lesleycrazegallery.co.uk). Farringdon tube/rail. **Open** 10am-5.30pm Mon-Sat; closed Sun. **Credit** AmEx, MC, V. **Map** p402 N4.

This gallery/shop is divided into two: Lesley Craze Gallery displays precious metal pieces by up to 100 designers, while Craze 2 works in mixed media.

Tiffany
25 Old Bond Street, Mayfair, W1 (7409 2790/ www.tiffany.com). Green Park tube. **Open** 10am-5.30pm Mon-Sat; closed Sun. **Credit** AmEx, DC, MC, V. **Map** p400 J7.
Seriously romantic and seriously pricey, but if you've seen the film, you'll know all but the most depleted of wallets can afford some kind of Tiffany trinket.

Wright & Teague
1A Grafton Street, Mayfair, W1 (7629 2777/ www.wrightandteague). Green Park tube. **Open** 10am-6pm Mon-Wed, Fri, Sat; 10am-7pm Thur; closed Sun. **Credit** AmEx, MC, V. **Map** p400 J7.
Contemporary jewellery, with a particular emphasis on crosses and hearts. Inscriptions are also popular, especially on the chunky silver pieces.

Leather goods

Bill Amberg
10 Chepstow Road, Notting Hill, W2 (7727 3560). Notting Hill Gate or Westbourne Park tube. **Open** 10am-6pm Mon, Tue, Thur-Sat; 10am-7pm Wed; closed Sun. **Credit** AmEx, MC, V. **Map** p394 A5.
Timeless designs with universal appeal. Bags are the mainstay of Amberg's business, but he also makes home accessories and furniture (by commission).

Mulberry
11-12 Gees Court, St Christopher's Place, Marylebone, W1 (7493 2546/www.mulberry-england.co.uk). Bond Street tube. **Open** 10am-6pm Mon-Wed, Fri, Sat; 10am-7pm Thur; closed Sun. **Credit** AmEx, DC, MC, V. **Map** p398 H6.
Purveyors of the classic landed gentry look, Mulberry offers quintessentially English clothing, homewares, leather luggage and accessories.
Branches are numerous: check the phone book.

Osprey
11 St Christopher's Place, Marylebone, W1 (7935 2824). Bond Street tube. **Open** 11am-6pm Tue, Wed, Fri, Sat; 11am-7pm Thur; closed Mon, Sun. **Credit** AmEx, MC, V. **Map** p398 H6.
Somewhere between high-street and designer, Osprey carries reasonably priced, handmade leather bags and accessories.

Shoes

If you really want to treat your feet, try two of the biggest names in fashion shoes: **Jimmy Choo** (20 Motcomb Street, SW1; 7235 0242) and **Manolo Blahnik** (49-51 Old Church Street, SW3; 7352 3863). For something rather more trad, try **John Lobb** (*see p116*).

Camper

39 Floral Street, Covent Garden, WC2 (7379 8678/
www.camper.es). Covent Garden tube. **Open**
10.30am-7pm Mon-Sat; noon-6pm Sun. **Credit**
AmEx, DC, MC, V. **Map** p401 L6.
Stylish, fashionable shoes from Majorca.

Dr Marten Department Store

1-4 King Street, Covent Garden, WC2 (7497 1460/
www.drmartens.com). Covent Garden tube. **Open**
10am-7pm Mon-Wed, Fri, Sat; 10am-8pm Thur; noon-
6pm Sun. **Credit** AmEx, MC, V. **Map** p401 L7.
World-famous, hard-as-nails footwear and clothing
is offered at DM's Covent Garden megastore.

Natural Shoe Store

21 Neal Street, Covent Garden, WC2 (7836 5254/
www.naturesko.com). Covent Garden tube.
Open 10am-6pm Mon, Tue; 10am-7pm Wed-Fri;
10am-6.30pm Sat; noon-5.30pm Sun. **Credit** AmEx,
DC, MC, V. **Map** p399 L6.
Environmentally friendly and cruelty-free shoes in
a range of styles. Vegan shoes are also available.
Branch: 325 King's Road, Chelsea, SW3 (7351 3721).

Office

57 Neal Street, Covent Garden, WC2 (7379 1896/
www.officelondon.co.uk). Covent Garden tube.
Open 10am-7pm Mon-Wed, Fri, Sat; 10am-8pm

Say it at **Wild at Heart**. *See p242.*

Thur; 10.30am-7pm Sat; noon-6pm Sun.
Credit AmEx, MC, V. **Map** p399 L6.
Fashionable footwear for all occasions, from the
smart and sober to the impossibly trendy.
Branches are numerous: check the phone book.

Patrick Cox

129 Sloane Street, Chelsea, SW1 (7730 8886).
Sloane Square tube. **Open** 10am-6pm Mon, Tue,
Thur-Sat; 10am-7pm Wed; 11am-5pm Sun.
Credit AmEx, MC, V. **Map** p397 F10.
Cox produces a range of mainly '60s inspired styles,
but he's still best known for his 'wannabe' loafers.

Shellys

266-70 Regent Street, Marylebone, W1 (7287
0939/www.shellys.co.uk). Oxford Circus tube.
Open 10am-7pm Mon-Wed, Fri; 10am-8pm Thur;
9.30am-7pm Sat; noon-6pm Sun. **Credit** AmEx, DC,
MC, V. **Map** p398 J6.
Shoes, boots and trainers for both sexes, from
casual and functional to glam and impractical.
Branches are numerous: check the phone book.

Tailors

Ozwald Boateng

9 Vigo Street, Mayfair, W1 (7734 6868). Piccadilly
Circus tube. **Open** 10am-6pm Mon-Sat; closed Sun.
Credit AmEx, MC, V. **Map** p400 J7.
Boateng's trademarks are his tapered trousers and
electric-lined, high-closing jackets. Bespoke suits
start at around £1,800.

Timothy Everest

32 Elder Street, The City, E1 (7377 5770).
Liverpool Street tube/rail. **Open** 9am-6pm Mon-Fri;
9.30am-3pm Sat; closed Sun; also by appointment.
Credit AmEx, DC, MC, V. **Map** p403 R5.
Tailor to Posh and Becks, Everest keeps a close eye
on trends and responds accordingly, but he can still
make a perfectly good traditionally cut suit.

Watches

City Clocks

31 Amwell Street, Islington, EC1 (7278 1154/
www.cityclocks.co.uk). Angel tube. **Open** 8.30am-
5.30pm Tue-Fri; 9.30am-2.30pm Sat; closed Mon,
Sun. **Credit** AmEx, DC, MC, V. **Map** p402 N3.
This shop can repair most watches, including
quartz, new and antique mechanical and some electric. **CR Frost & Son** (60-62 Clerkenwell Road,
EC1; 7253 0315) is another good repairer.

Simon Carter

15 Quadrant Arcade, 80-82 Regent Street, Mayfair,
W1 (7287 4363/www.simoncarter.net). Oxford
Circus or Piccadilly Circus tube. **Open** 10am-6.30pm
Mon-Sat; closed Sun. **Credit** AmEx, MC, V.
Map p400 J7.
Aside from his famous cufflinks, Carter's thing is
retro-style watches, from steel chronometers to
leather-strapped classics. Prices start at £89.

Eat, Drink, Shop

A taste of home

There's something about London that makes the visitor yearn for a taste of home. After all, there are only so many English fry-ups and cod-and-chips anyone can stomach. Fortunately, homesick hunter-gatherers are never far from satisfaction, with dozens of outlets specialising in goodies from almost every part of the globe.

Some cultures are so established in London that entire markets have grown to satisfy their appetites. The most vibrant of these community shopping festivals include **Brixton Market** (*see p252*), with a superb choice of Afro-Caribbean comestibles; **Brick Lane**, E1, the epicentre of Punjabi and Bangladeshi expats; **Ealing Road** in Wembley, where Indian Hindus and Muslims buy sweets and spices; and, of course, **Chinatown** in the West End.

But there are plenty more where they came from; in fact, where most people come from. Stroll along **South Street**, **Southall Market** and you could be in any sub-continental bazaar. Spaniards conquer their epicurial urges at the ever-popular **Brindisi** (Borough Market, Bankside, SE1, 8772 1600): watch as traditional dishes are prepared, then make a selection from mounds of sausage, peppers, cheeses, hams and oils. **Green Lanes**, N4 services a large Turkish community, with dozens of speciality shops and supermarkets open daily and several trading late.

Middle Eastern tastes are met along Edgware Road, north of Marble Arch, with several well-stocked groceries and **Bestway**, a 24-hour general store (107 Edgware Road, Marylebone, W2, 7723 6793). **Tooting High Street**, between Tooting Bec and Broadway, also has a wide choice of halal butchers and vegetable and spice specialists. **Golders Green Road** is kosher corner for London's huge Jewish community, though the legendary 24-hour **Brick Lane Beigel Bake** (*see p213* Grease is the word) keeps 'em coming back.

La Fromagerie (30 Highbury Park, Highbury, N5, 7359 7440) has a delectable range of cheeses from Europe, but with an emphasis, *naturellement*, on produce from across the Channel. If the Romans had conquered London and left only **Carluccio's** megadeli (28A Neal Street, Covent Garden, WC2, 7240 1487), that'd be legacy enough. **German Wurst & Delicatessen** (*pictured*; 127 Central Street, EC1, 7250 1322) specialises in authentic Teutonic sausage. And Aussies will be happy to collect armfuls of Burger Rings and Caramello Koalas from the **Australia Shop** (26 Henrietta Street, Covent Garden, WC2, 7836 2292).

The Swatch Store

313 Oxford Street, Mayfair, W1 (7493 0237/ www.swatch.com). Bond Street or Oxford Circus tube. **Open** 10am-7pm Mon-Wed, Fri, Sat; 10am-8pm Thur; noon-6pm Sun. **Credit** MC, V. **Map** p398 H6.
The full range of over 160 Swatch designs is available at this Oxford Street outlet, at prices from £17.95 to £75.
Branch: 104-6 Long Acre, Covent Garden, WC2 (7836 7868).

Florists

See also p255.

Wild at Heart

49A Ledbury Road, Notting Hill, W11 (7727 3095). Notting Hill Gate or Westbourne Park tube. **Open** 8.30am-7pm Mon-Sat; closed Sun. **Credit** AmEx, MC, V. **Map** p394 A6.

The hot-pinks, strong scents and lime-green flowers at this thoroughly modern florist hold a strong attraction for the denizens of Notting Hill.

Wild Bunch

17 Earlham Street, Covent Garden, WC2 (7497 1200). Covent Garden tube. **Open** 9.30am-7.30pm Mon-Sat; closed Sun. **Credit** MC, V. **Map** p399 K6.
Wild Bunch runs the length of seven stalls and has a greater variety of flowers than most fancy florists you'd care to name.

Woodhams at One Aldwych

1 Aldwych, Holborn, WC1 (7300 0777/ www.woodhams.co.uk). Covent Garden or Temple tube/Charing Cross tube/rail. **Open** 10am-6pm Mon-Fri; 10am-5pm Sat; closed Sun. **Credit** AmEx, DC, MC, V. **Map** p401 M6.
Housed within the effortlessly stylish One Aldwych hotel is this gleaming, perfumed shrine to the ultra-modern school of flower arranging.

A massive selection of bottled (and some draught) beer from Britain, Belgium and Germany is offered at this friendly store.

Food & drink

For department-store food halls, *see p232*. For fish, *see p193* **fish!**.

Bakeries & pâtisseries

For other café-pâtisseries, *see p206* **Cafés, coffees & light lunches**.

& Clarke's

122 Kensington Church Street, Kensington, W8 (7229 2190/www.sallyclarke.com). Notting Hill Gate tube. **Open** 8am-8pm Mon-Fri; 9am-4pm Sat; closed Sun. **Credit** AmEx, MC, V. **Map** p394 B8.
A foodie heaven, this neatly countrified shop alongside Sally Clarke's renowned restaurant offers a choice of some 35 breads, plus delicious cakes and pâtisseries and luxurious deli fare.

Konditor & Cook

22 Cornwall Road, South Bank, SE1 (7261 0456). Waterloo tube/rail/27 bus. **Open** 7.30am-6.30pm Mon-Fri; 8.30am-2.30pm Sat; closed Sun. **Credit** MC, V. **Map** p404 N8.
K&C's exquisite cakes and pastries are baked on the premises. The goodies from other producers include bread from **& Clarke's** (*see above*).
Branch: 10 Stoney Street, Bankside, SE1 (7407 5100).

Pâtisserie Valerie

44 Old Compton Street, Soho, W1 (7437 3466/www.patisserievalerie.co.uk). Tottenham Court Road tube. **Open** 7.30am-8pm Mon-Sat; 9.30am-7pm Sun. **Credit** AmEx, DC, MC, V. **Map** p399 K6.
Established in 1926, Soho's most famous pâtisserie and tearoom is packed with creamy gateaux, chocolates, gooey pastries and fruit tarts.
Branches are numerous: check the phone book.

Beer

The Beer Shop

14 Pitfield Street, Hoxton, N1 (7739 3701/www.pitfieldbeershop.co.uk). Old Street tube/rail. **Open** 11am-7pm Mon-Fri; 10am-4pm Sat; closed Sun. **Credit** MC, V. **Map** p403 Q4.

Cheese shops

Neal's Yard Dairy

17 Shorts Gardens, Covent Garden, WC2 (7240 5700). Covent Garden tube. **Open** 9am-7pm Mon-Sat; 10am-5pm Sun. **Credit** MC, V. **Map** p399 L6.
This renowned shop has done wonders to increase the profile of British cheeses. Some of those offered are seasonal, but classics such as Montgomery's Cheddar and Colston Bassett Stilton sell so well they never leave.
Branch: 6 Park Street, Bankside, SE1 (7378 8195).

Coffee & tea

Algerian Coffee Stores

52 Old Compton Street, Soho, W1 (7437 2480/www.algcoffee.co.uk). Leicester Square or Piccadilly Circus tube. **Open** 9am-7pm Mon-Sat; closed Sun. **Credit** AmEx, MC, V. **Map** p399 K6.
Established in 1887, this shop boasts a wonderfully varied range of coffees and an equally impressive array of teas, sourced all over the world.

The Tea House

15A Neal Street, Covent Garden, WC2 (7240 7539). Covent Garden tube. **Open** 11am-7pm Mon-Wed; 10am-7.30pm Thur; 10am-7pm Fri, Sat; noon-6pm Sun.* **Credit** AmEx, MC, V. **Map** p399 L6.
The Tea House has a range of some 60 teas from most of the world's producer countries, including Russia and Turkey.

R Twining & Co

216 Strand, Covent Garden, WC2 (7353 3511/www.twinings.com). Temple tube/Charing Cross tube/rail. **Open** 9.30am-4.45pm Mon-Fri; closed Sat, Sun. **Credit** AmEx, DC, MC, V. **Map** p399 M6.
The world's most famous tea merchant was established on these premises in 1706 and continues to sell a dazzling array of teas. There's also a small museum of the firm's history.

Crack open a cold one courtesy of **The Beer Shop**.

Confectioners

Godiva

247 Regent Street, Mayfair, W1 (7495 2845/
www.godiva.com). Oxford Circus tube.
Open 9.30am-7pm Mon-Sat; noon-6pm Sun.
Credit AmEx, DC, MC, V. **Map** p398 J6.
One to avoid if you're counting the calories, this
Mayfair chocolatier sells luxurious handmade and
hand-finished Belgian chocs. Seasonal goodies are
a speciality.
Branches are numerous: check the phone book.

Rococo

321 King's Road, Chelsea, SW3 (7352 5857/
www.rococochocolates.com). Sloane Square tube.
Open 10am-6.30pm Mon-Sat; noon-5pm Sun.
Credit AmEx, MC, V. **Map** p397 D12.
A cute little Chelsea den for chocoholics, Rococo
specialises in delicious handmade chocs but also
stocks organic bars and Valrhona, the Rolls Royce
of chocolate.

Delicatessens

Bluebird

350 King's Road, Chelsea, SW3 (7559 1000/
www.conrad.com). Sloane Square tube, then 11, 19,
22, 49, 211, 319, 345 bus. **Open** 9am-8pm
Mon-Wed; 9am-9pm Thur-Sat; noon-6pm Sun.
Credit AmEx, DC, MC, V. **Map** p397 D12.
Sir Terence Conran's spacious food hall is a gastro-
nomic delight, packed with a fab array of gourmet
provisions and incorporating a bakery, a cheese-
monger and a fishmonger.

Carluccio's

28A Neal Street, Covent Garden, WC2 (7240
1487/www.carluccios.com). Covent Garden tube.
Open 11am-7pm Mon-Sat; noon-6pm Sun.
Credit AmEx, MC, V. **Map** p399 L6.
This high-quality (with prices to match) Italian deli
sells luxurious pasta, breads, oils and vegetables.
Branches are numerous: check the phone book.

Villandry

170 Great Portland Street, Marylebone, W1 (7631
3131/www.villandry.com). Great Portland Street
tube. **Open** 8.30am-10pm Mon-Sat; 9am-4pm Sun.
Credit AmEx, MC, V. **Map** p398 H5.
This stunning food store is piled high with rare and
expensive delicacies from across the world. For
those occasions when you absolutely, positively
have to have French organic vegetables.

Health & organic food

See also p256 **Spitalfields Market**.

Fresh & Wild

49 Parkway, Camden, NW1 (7428 7575/
www.freshandwild.com). Camden Town tube.
Open 8am-9.30pm daily. **Credit** MC, V.

A superb, highly appetising selection of healthy
organic food is offered at this terrific Camden store,
which also boasts a juice bar and a takeaway section if you're in a hurry.
Branches are numerous: check the phone book.

Planet Organic

42 Westbourne Grove, Bayswater, W2 (7221 7171/
www.planetorganic.com). Bayswater or Queensway
tube. **Open** 9.30am-8pm Mon-Sat; noon-6pm Sun.
Credit AmEx, MC, V. **Map** p394 B6.
Most supermarket needs are covered at this popular, pioneering west London staple. Organic produce
is sourced where possible, and all stock is otherwise
additive-free.
Branch: 22 Torrington Place, Fitzrovia, WC1
(7436 1929).

International

See p242 **A taste of home**.

Wines & spirits

For everyday use, **Oddbins** (branches all over
London; it's online at www.oddbins.co.uk) is
hard to beat, though supermarket chains such
as Sainsbury's and Safeway have improved
their alcohol selections no end in recent years
and can cater for most needs.

Gerry's

74 Old Compton Street, Soho, W1 (7734 4215).
Leicester Square or Tottenham Court Road tube.
Open 9am-6.30pm Mon-Fri; 9am-5.30pm Sat; closed
Sun. **No credit cards**. **Map** p399 K6.
Spirits and liqueurs from all corners of the globe,
sold by friendly staff who will happily explain away
some of the more unique bottles on their shelves. A
favourite of London's cocktail barmen and -women.

Milroy's of Soho

3 Greek Street, Soho, W1 (7437 9311/
www.milroys.co.uk). Tottenham Court Road
tube. **Open** 11am-7pm Mon-Sat; closed Sun.
Credit AmEx, DC, MC, V. **Map** p399 K6.
The only whisky shop in London, Milroy's has a
huge selection (over 400) of whiskies from Scotland,
Ireland and America.

Furniture

The Conran Shop

Michelin House, 81 Fulham Road, Chelsea, SW3
(7589 7401/www.conran.co.uk). South Kensington
tube. **Open** 10am-6pm Mon, Tue, Fri; 10am-7pm
Wed, Thur; 10am-6.30pm Sat; noon-6pm Sun.
Credit AmEx, MC, V. **Map** p398 G5.
Holding a wealth of classic modern and contempo-
rary furniture, Conran's design mecca is proof
positive that you can buy style.
Branch: 55 Marylebone High Street, Marylebone,
W1 (7723 2223).

The write stuff: **Paperchase**.

eat my handbag bitch

*6 Dray Walk, Old Truman Brewery, 91-5
Brick Lane, Spitalfields, E1 (7375 3100/
www.eatmyhandbagbitch.co.uk). Aldgate East tube/
Liverpool Street tube/rail.* **Open** 11am-7pm daily.
Credit MC, V. **Map** p403 S5.
Despite the name, this is actually a rather serious if
incredibly fashionable modern design shop.

Habitat

*196 Tottenham Court Road, Fitzrovia, W1
(7631 3880/www.habitat.net). Goodge Street tube.*
Open 10am-6pm Mon-Wed; 10am-8pm Thur;
10am-6.30pm Fri; 9.30am-6.30pm Sat; noon-6pm
Sun. **Credit** AmEx, DC, MC, V. **Map** p398 J4.
Habitat continues to go from strength to strength.
Its directional biannual collections mean it pioneers
the latest look from season to season.
Branches are numerous: check the phone book.

Heal's

*196 Tottenham Court Road, Fitzrovia, W1
(7636 1666/www.heals.co.uk). Goodge Street tube.*
Open 10am-6pm Mon-Wed; 10am-8pm Thur;
10am-6.30pm Fri; 9.30am-6.30pm Sat; noon-6pm
Sun. **Credit** AmEx, DC, MC, V. **Map** p399 K5.
Heal's gear is not exactly cutting edge, but it is clas-
sic, high quality and still very much in fashion.
Branch: 234 King's Road, Chelsea, SW3 (7349 8411).

Purves & Purves

*220-4 Tottenham Court Road, Fitzrovia, W1
(7580 8223/www.purves.co.uk). Goodge Street
or Warren Street tube.* **Open** 9.30am-6pm Mon,
Wed, Fri, Sat; 10am-6pm Tue; 9.30am-7.30pm
Thur; closed Sun. **Credit** AmEx, MC, V.
Map p398 J4.
With one shop devoted to furniture and one to acces-
sories, P&P takes a fun look at modern design (think
Alessi, Starck and plastic in bright colours).

Gifts & stationery

In addition to the shops listed below, most of
London's large museums have excellent gift
shops, in particular **London's Transport
Museum** (*see p124*), the **British Museum**
(*see p101*), the **V&A** (*see p140*) and the **Tate
Modern** (*see p77*).

BBC World Service Shop

*Bush House, Strand, Covent Garden, WC2 (7557
2576/www.bbc.co.uk/worldservice). Temple tube/
Charing Cross tube/rail.* **Open** 10am-6pm Mon-Fri;
10am-5.30pm Sat; closed Sun. **Credit** AmEx, MC, V.
Map p401 M6.
A wide range of BBC merchandise, plus books on a
variety of arts and media subjects.

Mysteries

*9-11 Monmouth Street, Covent Garden, WC2
(7240 3688/www.mysteries.co.uk). Covent Garden or
Tottenham Court Road tube.* **Open** 10am-6pm Mon-
Sat; closed Sun. **Credit** MC, V. **Map** p399 L6.
Swimming with incense and dreamy music, this new
age shop stocks everything from books on paganism to crystals and phrenology heads.

Neal Street East

*5 Neal Street, Covent Garden, WC2 (7240 0135).
Covent Garden tube.* **Open** 11am-7pm Mon-Wed;
10am-7.30pm Thur; 10am-7pm Fri, Sat; noon-6pm
Sun. **Credit** AmEx, MC, V. **Map** p399 L6.
London's leading ethnic emporium has a huge range
of Oriental and South American goods, including
clothing, jewellery, books, homewares and gifts.

Paperchase

*213 Tottenham Court Road, Fitzrovia, W1 (7467
6200). Goodge Street tube.* **Open** 9.30am-6.30pm
Mon, Wed, Fri, Sat; 10am-6.30pm Tue; 9.30am-
7.30pm Thur; noon-6.30pm Sun. **Credit** AmEx,
MC, V. **Map** p399 K5.
A stationery chain with more style than most. This
three-floor flagship branch has a vast selection of
notebooks, writing books, pens, greetings cards and
the like, plus an extensive art materials department.
Branches are numerous: check the phone book.

The Pen Shop

*199 Regent Street, Mayfair, W1 (7734 4088/
www.penshop.co.uk). Oxford Circus tube.* **Open**
9.30am-6pm Mon, Tue, Fri, Sat; 10am-6pm Wed;
9.30am-7pm Thur; closed Sun. **Credit** AmEx, DC,
MC, V. **Map** p400 J7.

Eat, Drink, Shop

Pens by Lamt, Waterman, Cross, Shaeffer and Parker, plus Yard O Led's distinctive silver pens and Mont Blanc's chic black models.
Branch: 10 West Mall, Liverpool Street Station, The City, EC2 (7628 4416).

The Tintin Shop

34 Floral Street, Covent Garden, WC2 (7836 1131). Covent Garden tube. **Open** 10am-5.30pm Mon-Sat; closed Sun. **Credit** AmEx, DC, MC, V. **Map** p401 L6.
A tiny shop entirely devoted to Hergé's much loved reporter. The stock includes key-rings, stationery, collectibles, plus, of course, the full range of books.

Health & beauty

Beauty services

The Green Room

21 Earl's Court Road, Kensington, W8 (7937 6595). High Street Kensington tube. **Open** 9am-9pm Mon-Thur; 9am-6pm Fri, Sat; 10am-5pm Sun. **Credit** AmEx, MC, V. **Map** p396 A9.
A chain of right-on salons that uses the Body Shop's natural, cruelty-free products alongside its own. Facials, massage and manicures are among the treatments on offer.
Branches are numerous: check the phone book.

The Refinery

60 Brook Street, Mayfair, W1 (7409 2001/ www.the-refinery.com). Bond Street tube. **Open** 10am-7pm Mon, Tue; 10am-9pm Wed-Fri; 9am-6pm Sat; 11am-4pm Sun. **Credit** AmEx, MC, V. **Map** p398 H6.
One for the gents (it's men only, except in the ground-floor shop), the smart, pricey Refinery offers a selection of spa, skincare and hairdressing services over three floors in the heart of Mayfair.

The Sanctuary

12 Floral Street, Covent Garden, WC2 (08700 630300/www.thesanctuary.co.uk). Covent Garden tube. **Open** *Health spa* 10am-6pm Mon, Tue, Sun; 9.30am-10pm Wed-Fri; 9.30am-8pm Sat. *Gym* 7am-9.30pm Mon-Fri; 10am-5pm Sat, Sun. **Credit** AmEx, DC, MC, V. **Map** p401 L6.
If you can't jet off to a secluded Greek island, this famous women-only retreat is the next best thing. Recline in the luxurious Koi Carp relaxation lounge, drift in the Atrium swimming pool and enjoy a slice of gateau in the Palm restaurant. Admission is £58-£68 a day, or £35 for an evening visit (Wed-Fri only).

SPAce.NK

127-31 Westbourne Grove, Notting Hill, W11 (7727 8002). Notting Hill Gate tube. **Open** 10am-7pm Mon-Wed, Sat; 10am-9pm Thur, Fri; 11am-5pm Sun. **Credit** AmEx, MC, V.
The truly ugly name (the 'ce' is silent) belies a rather beautiful, serene operation offering all manner of treatments to moneyed Londoners who love to be pampered. *See p248.*

Cosmetics & herbalists

Aveda Institute

28-9 Marylebone High Street, Marylebone, W1 (7224 3157/www.aveda.com). Baker Street or Bond Street tube. **Open** 9.30am-7pm Mon-Fri; 9am-6pm Sat; closed Sun. **Credit** AmEx, MC, V. **Map** p398 G5.
At the forefront of holistic skincare in the UK, Aveda's lotions and potions are made with 97% natural ingredients. It's not cheap, but you get what you pay for.
Branches are numerous: check the phone book.

Crabtree & Evelyn

6 Kensington Church Street, Kensington, W8 (7937 9335/www.crabtree-evelyn.com). High Street Kensington tube. **Open** 10am-6pm Mon-Wed, Fri, Sat; 10am-7pm Thur; 11am-5pm Sun. **Credit** AmEx, MC, V. **Map** p394 B8.
Fanciful, feminine toiletries and gifts, beautifully packaged in old-fashioned, bijou boxes and bottles.
Branches are numerous: check the phone book.

Jo Malone

150 Sloane Street, Sloane Square, SW1 (7730 2100/www.jomalone.co.uk). Sloane Square tube. **Open** 10am-6pm Mon-Tue, Fri, Sat; 10am-7pm Wed, Thur; closed Sun. **Credit** AmEx, MC, V. **Map** p397 E10.
Skincare products don't come more chic than these. Smartly styled and highly covetable goodies. Forget the flowers: say it with scents.
Branches 24 Threadneedle Street, The City, EC3 (7444 1999).

Lush

Units 7 & 11, The Market, Covent Garden, WC2 (7240 4570/www.lush.co.uk). Covent Garden tube. **Open** 10am-7pm Mon-Sat; noon-6pm Sun. **Credit** AmEx, MC, V. **Map** p401 L7.
Cheese-like slabs of natural soap, fruity scents and food-themed bath-treats are the Lush specialities.
Branches: 123 King's Road, Chelsea, SW3 (7376 8348); 40 Carnaby Street, Soho, W1 (7287 5874).

Neal's Yard Remedies

15 Neal's Yard, Covent Garden, WC2 (7379 7222/www.nealsyardremedies.com). Covent Garden tube. **Open** 10am-6pm Mon; 10am-7pm Tue-Fri; 10am-5.30pm Sat; 11am-5pm Sun. **Credit** AmEx, MC, V. **Map** p399 L6.
Legendary for its alternative health and beauty products, this tiny store is crammed with trademark blue glass bottles filled with wonderful-smelling skin, hair care and bath concoctions.
Branches are numerous: check the phone book.

Penhaligon's

16-17 Burlington Arcade, Piccadilly, Mayfair, W1 (7629 1416/www.penhaligons.co.uk). Green Park or Piccadilly tube. **Open** 9.30am-5.30pm Mon-Sat; closed Sun. **Credit** AmEx, DC, MC, V. **Map** p400 J7.
Quintessentially English Victorian-style toiletries and grooming products for men and women.

Eat, Drink, Shop

A world away

Trawling the colossal retail palaces of Oxford Street for overpriced sportswear and throwaway fashion is not everyone's idea of retail therapy. For each of those for whom a high-tech, one-stop mall equals heaven on Earth, there is another who prefers the attentive service and expertise of a traditional, independent outlet. And such discerning shoppers will no doubt be pleased to note that London does not want for specialist, eccentric and archaic shops.

G Smith & Sons.

Much of the interior and exterior of **James Smith & Sons** looks much as it did when the shop opened in 1857. But more notable than its appearance, though, is Smith's peculiar speciality: it deals exclusively in canes, walking sticks and umbrellas. From floor to ceiling, the shop is packed with sticks of all descriptions; once you've picked one out, the personable staff will even cut it to size while you wait.

And what better to go with your brand new cane than a brand new hat? Tucked behind London's most trad department store, Fortnum & Mason, is a quintessentially English headwear retailer, **Bates The Hatter**. Opened in 1902, it's another shop relatively

untouched by modernity, both in appearance and products. The dusty, dark wooden shelves and cabinets are brimming with all manner of hats, from humble tweed gatsbys to prim bowlers and luxurious silk toppers.

Of course, tradition and luxury often go hand in hand, and nowhere is this theory more comprehensively proven than at **Rigby & Peller**. Though the shop front of the corsetière may look a little down at heel, the uniformed doormen and smart, old fashioned interior tell a different, more accurate tale. Here you'll be treated like royalty – quite literally; R&P are corsetières to the Queen – as you make your choice from a range of sumptuous off-the-peg or made-to-measure under- and outerwear.

Space.NK

4 Thomas Neal Centre, 37 Earlham Street, Covent Garden, WC2 (7379 7030/www.spacenk.co.uk). Covent Garden tube. **Open** *10am-7pm Mon-Wed, Fri, Sat; 10am-7.30pm Thur; noon-5pm Sun.* **Credit** AmEx, MC, V. **Map** p399 L6.
Despite the high prices, this is the place to come for cutting-edge cosmetics and the latest catwalk trends.
Branches are numerous: check the phone book.

Hairdressers

Fish

30 D'Arblay Street, Soho, W1 (7494 2398/ www.fishweb.co.uk). Oxford Circus or Tottenham Court Road tube. **Open** *10am-7pm Mon-Wed, Fri; 10am-8pm Thur; 10am-5pm Sat; closed Sun.* **Credit** MC, V. **Map** p399 K6.
This hip Soho salon has a unisex clientele and staff. Stylists keep an eye on the surrounding street action for the latest trends.

Essensuals

34 Southampton Street, Covent Garden, WC1 (7631 3114/www.essensuals.co.uk). Covent Garden tube/Charing Cross tube/rail. **Open** *9am-8pm Mon-Fri, 9am-7pm Sat; noon-6pm Sun.* **Credit** AmEx, MC, V. **Map** p401 L7.

Run by last year's 'London Hairdresser of the Year', Essensuals' salons are aimed at a young, hip clientele. Cuts start at £34, colourings at £60.
Branch: 149 King's Road, Chelsea, SW3 (7631 3114).

Vidal Sassoon

60 South Molton Street, Mayfair, W1 (7491 8848/ www.vidalsassoon.co.uk). Bond Street tube. **Open** *10.30am-6.30pm Mon-Wed; 10.30am-6.45pm Thur; 10.30am-5.15pm Fri; 9am-5.15pm Sat; closed Sun.* **Credit** AmEx, MC, V. **Map** p398 H6.
Sassoon's still known for his precision cutting, a style that moves in and out of fashion with predictable regularity. Cuts start at £45, though you will get a thorough consultation.
Branches are numerous: check the phone book.

Opticians

Kirk Originals

36 Earlham Street, Covent Garden, WC2 (7240 5055/www.kirkoriginals.com). Covent Garden tube. **Open** *10.30am-6.30pm Mon-Wed, Fri, Sat; 10.30am-7pm Thur; closed Sun.* **Credit** AmEx, MC, V. **Map** p399 L6.
Kirk makes frames in limited editions of between two and 250 (numbered) copies, so you know you're getting a true original. Designs are witty and retro.

For luxury of a different kind, try the aged tobacconist **G Smith & Sons**. Though smoking is roundly frowned upon these days, the spectacle and aroma of a well stocked tobacconist is something that even a non-smoker can enjoy.

For those who do partake of the weed, an Elysium of loose tobacco, cigars, cigarettes and (a particular speciality) snuff awaits.

For those who would rather come away from their shopping trip with something a little more tangible than the smell of tobacco, **Stanley Gibbons International** is well worth a try. Philately may not be everyone's idea of a stimulating pastime, but if you're looking for a souvenir with a little more class than a tacky teddy bear in a bearskin, you could do much worse than a Royal Mail first day cover.

James Smith & Sons Walking Sticks
53 New Oxford Street, St Giles's, WC1 (7836 4731). Holborn or Tottenham Court Road tube. **Open** 9.30am-5.25pm Mon-Fri; 10am-5.25pm Sat; closed Sun. **Credit** MC, V. **Map** p399 L5.

Bates the Hatter *21A Jermyn Street, St James's, SW1 (7734 2722). Piccadilly Circus tube.* **Open** 9am-5.30pm Mon-Fri; 9.30am-4pm Sat; closed Sun. **Credit** AmEx, MC, V. **Map** p400 J7.

Rigby & Peller *2 Hans Road, Brompton, SW3 (7589 9293). Knightsbridge tube.* **Open** 9.30am-6pm Mon, Tue, Thur-Sat; 9.30am-7pm Wed; closed Sun. **Credit** AmEx, MC, V. **Map** p397 F9.

G Smith & Sons *74 Charing Cross Road, Covent Garden, WC2 (7836 7422). Leicester Square tube.* **Open** 9am-6pm Mon-Fri; 9.30am-5.30pm Sat; closed Sun. **Credit** AmEx, MC, V. **Map** p401 K7.

Stanley Gibbons International *399 Strand, Covent Garden, WC2 (7836 8444). Charing Cross tube/rail.* **Open** 8.30am-6pm Mon-Fri; 9.30am-5.30pm Sat; 10am-4pm Sun. **Credit** AmEx, MC, V. **Map** p401 L7.

Vision Express
263-265 Oxford Street, Mayfair, W1 (7409 7880/ www.visionexpress.co.uk). Oxford Circus tube. **Open** 9.30am-8pm Mon-Sat; noon-6pm Sun. **Credit** AmEx, MC, V. **Map** p398 H6.
Specs while you wait. Vision Express offers 20-minute eye tests and spectacles within the hour. **Branches** are numerous: check the phone book.

Hobbies

See also p248 **A world away**.

The Bead Shop
21A Tower Street, Covent Garden, WC2 (7240 0931). Leicester Square tube. **Open** 1-6pm Mon; 10.30am-6pm Tue-Fri; 11.30am-5pm Sat; closed Sun. **Credit** AmEx, MC, V. **Map** p399 K6.
A panoramic range of glass, wooden and ceramic beads, plus pliers, wire, thread, clasps and the like.

Beatties
202 High Holborn, Holborn, WC1 (7405 6285/ www.beatties.net). Holborn tube. **Open** 9am-6pm Mon-Fri; 9am-5.30pm Sat; 11am-5pm Sun. **Credit** AmEx, MC, V. **Map** p399 L5.
Toys, model kits and model railways, plus all the necessary (and unnecessary) accoutrements. **Branches** are numerous: check the phone book.

London Dolls' House Company
Unit 29, The Market, Covent Garden, WC2 (7240 8681). Covent Garden tube. **Open** 10.30am-7pm Mon-Sat; noon-5pm Sun. **Credit** AmEx, MC, V. **Map** p401 L7.
Remarkably detailed Victorian-style dolls' houses and a wide range of handmade furniture.

Spink & Son
69 Southampton Row, Bloomsbury, WC1 (7563 4000/www.spink-online.com). Holborn or Russell Square tube. **Open** 9.30am-5.30pm Mon-Fri; closed Sat, Sun. **Credit** AmEx, MC, V. **Map** p400 J8.
Britain's foremost authority on coins and medals.

Home accessories

See also **The Conran Shop** *(p244)*, **Purves & Purves**, **Heal's** and **Habitat** (for all, *see p255*).

After Noah
121 Upper Street, Islington, N1 (7359 4281/ www.afternoah.com). Angel tube. **Open** 10am-6pm Mon-Sat; noon-5pm Sun. **Credit** AmEx, MC, V. **Map** p402 O1.
Restored second-hand and retro furniture and accessories. Some stock has a distinctly art deco flavour. **Branch**: 261 King's Road, Chelsea, SW3 (7351 2610).

Designers Guild

267-71 & 275-7 King's Road, Chelsea, SW3 (7351 5775/www.designersguild.com). Sloane Square tube, then 11, 19, 22 bus. **Open** 9.30am-5.30pm Mon, Tue; 10am-6pm Wed-Sat; noon-5pm Sun (nos.267-71 only). **Credit** AmEx, MC, V. **Map** p397 E12.

Three floors of modernist furniture and accessories, tableware and bedlinen, plus an espresso bar.

David Wainwright

28 Rosslyn Hill, Hampstead, NW3 (7431 5900). Hampstead tube. **Open** 10am-7pm Mon-Sat; 11am-7pm Sun. **Credit** AmEx, DC, MC, V.

Accessories from Indonesia, India, China and Tibet, both old and new.

Branches: 251 Portobello Road, Notting Hill, W11 (7792 1988); 63 Portobello Road, Notting Hill, W11 (7727 0707).

Divertimenti

45-7 Wigmore Street, Marylebone, W1 (7935 0689/www.divertimenti.co.uk). Bond Street tube. **Open** 9.30am-6pm Mon-Wed, Fri; 9.30am-7pm Thur; 9.30am-6pm Sat; closed Sun. **Credit** AmEx, DC, MC, V. **Map** p398 G6.

Over 5,000 items of seriously cool cookware are offered in these fine stores.

Branch: 139-41 Fulham Road, Chelsea, SW3 (7581 8065).

Elephant Furniture

230 Tottenham Court Road, Fitzrovia, W1 (7637 7930). Goodge Street or Tottenham Court Road tube. **Open** 10am-6.30pm Mon-Fri; 10am-6pm Sat; 11am-5pm Sun. **Credit** MC, V. **Map** p399 K5.

Upholstery and imported furniture and accessories that are several grades above the average, from coffee tables to rice baskets.

Branch: 169-71 Queensway, Bayswater, W2 (7467 0630).

Holding Company

241-5 King's Road, Chelsea, SW3 (7352 1600/ www.theholdingcompany.co.uk). Sloane Square tube, then 11, 19, 22 bus. **Open** 10am-6pm Mon, Tue, Thur, Fri; 10am-7pm Wed, Sat; noon-6pm Sun. **Credit** AmEx, MC, V. **Map** p397 D12.

Innovative, inspiring storage ideas are the stock in trade of the Holding Company, who offer everything you could ever need to keep your affairs in order.

Shops by area

The South Bank & Bankside

Borough Market (Markets, *p255*); **Gabriel's Wharf & Oxo Tower** (Home accessories, *p251*); **Konditor & Cook** (Food & drink, *p243*).

The City

Leadenhall Market (Markets, *p253*); **Petticoat Lane Market** (Markets, *p253*); **Timothy Everest** (Fashion accessories & services, *p241*).

Holborn & Clerkenwell

Antoni & Alison (Fashion accessories & services, *p239*); **Beatties** (Hobbies, *p249*); **Books Etc** (Bookshops, *p229*); **Into You** (Fashion accessories & services *p240*); **Lesley Craze Gallery/Craze 2** (Fashion accessories & services, *p240*); **London Silver Vaults** (Antiques, *p229*); **Woodhams at One Aldwych** (Florists, *p242*).

Bloomsbury & Fitzrovia

Cinema Bookshop (Bookshops, *p230*); **Computer Exchange** (Electronics, *p233*); **Contemporary Applied Arts** (Home Accessories, *p251*); **Elephant Furniture** (Furniture, *p250*); **Gay's the Word** (Bookshops, *p231*); **Gultronics** (Electronics, *p234*); **H&M** (Fashion, *p239*); **Habitat** (Furniture, *p245*); **Heal's** (Furniture, *p245*); **Hi-Fi Experience** (Electronics, *p234*); **HMV** (Music shops, *p256*); **Hobgoblin Music**

Borough Market.

(Music instruments, *p256*); **Michael's Shoe Care** (Fashion accessories & services, *p239*); **Micro Anvika** (Electronics, *p234*); **Paperchase** (Gifts & stationery, *p245*); **Purves & Purves** (Furniture, *p245*); **Skoob** (Bookshops, *p232*); **Spink & Son** (Hobbies, *p249*); **Ulysses** (Bookshops, *p232*); **Unsworths Booksellers** (Bookshops, *p232*); **Virgin Megastore** (Music stores, *p256*); **Woburn Book Shop** (Bookshops, *p232*).

Marylebone

Alfie's Antiques Market (Antiques, *p228*); **Aveda Institute** (Health & beauty, *p247*); **Boosey & Hawkes** (Musical instruments, *p256*); **Danish Express** (Fashion accessories & services, *p239*); **Daunt Books** (Bookshops, *p231*); **DH Evans** (Department stores, *p232*); **Divertimenti** (Home accessories, *p250*); **John Lewis** (Department stores, *p232*); **H&M** (Fashion, *p234*); **Marks & Spencer**

Muji

187 Oxford Street, Soho, W1 (7437 7503/
www.muji.co.jp). Oxford Circus tube.
Open 10am-7pm Mon-Wed, Sat; 10am-8pm Thur;
10am-7.30pm Fri; noon-6pm Sun. **Credit** AmEx,
DC, MC, V. **Map** p399 K6.
The Japanese 'no brand goods' store offers a
range of stylish accessories, from cardboard and
polypropylene storage to kitchen and tableware.
Branches are numerous: check the phone book.

Space

214 Westbourne Grove, Notting Hill, W11 (7229
6533/www.spaceshop.co.uk). Notting Hill Gate
tube. **Open** 10am-6pm Mon-Sat; closed Sun.
Credit AmEx, MC, V.
Contemporary furniture and accessories, from
Vietnamese lacquer vases to embroidered silk bedlinen, are the specialities here.

Crafts

See also p240 **Lesley Craze Gallery/**
Craze 2/C2+.

Contemporary Applied Arts

2 Percy Street, Fitzrovia, W1 (7436 2344/
www.caa.org.uk). Tottenham Court Road or Goode
Street tube. **Open** 10.30am-5.30pm Mon-Sat; closed
Sun. **Credit** AmEx, MC, V. **Map** p399 K5.
Contemporary Applied Arts is one of the most
important showcases for new work in the decorative
and applied arts in Britain.

Crafts Council Gallery Shop

44A Pentonville Road, Islington, N1 (7806
2559/www.craftscouncil.org.uk). Angel tube.
Open 11am-5.45pm Tue-Sat; 2-5.45pm Sun; closed
Mon. **Credit** AmEx, MC, V. **Map** p402 N2.
The place to go to get an overview of the best in
British crafts and applied arts, as well as for pick-
ing up original, high quality gifts.
Branch: Victoria & Albert Museum, Cromwell Road,
South Kensington, SW7 (7589 5070).

Gabriel's Wharf & Oxo Tower

Upper Ground, South Bank, SE1 (recorded
information 7401 2255/www.oxotower.co.uk).
Waterloo tube/rail. **Open** 11am-6pm Tue-Sun;
closed Mon. **Credit** varies. **Map** p404 N7.

(Department stores, *p233*); **Mulberry**
(Fashion accessories & services, *p240*);
Niketown (Sport, *p258*); **Osprey** (Fashion
accessories & services, *p240*); **Selfridges**
(Department stores, *p233*); **Shellys** (Fashion
accessories & services, *p241*); **Talking
Books Shop** (Bookshops, *p231*); **Top
Shop/Top Man** (Fashion, *p234*); **Villandry**
(Food & drink, *p244*).

Mayfair & St James's

Angela Hale (Fashion accessories & services,
p240); **Baby Gap/Gap Kids** (Fashion, *p234*);
Black Market (Music shops, *p257*);
Buckingham Dry Cleaners (Fashion
accessories & services, *p239*); **Dickens &
Jones** (Department stores, *p232*); **Electrum
Gallery** (Fashion accessories & services,
p240); **Fortnum & Mason** (Department
stores, *p232*); **Godiva** (Food & drink *p244*);
Grays Antiques Market & Grays in the Mews
(Antiques, *p229*); **Hamleys** (Toys, games &
magic, *p258*); **Harold Moores Records** (Music
shops, *p257*); **Jigsaw** (Fashion, *p235*);
Lillywhite's (Sport, *p258*); **Moss Bros**
(Fashion, *p237*); **Ozwald Boateng** (Fashion
accessories & services, *p241*); **Penhaligon's**
(Health & beauty, *p247*); **The Pen Shop** (Gifts
& stationery, *p245*); **The Refinery** (Health &
beauty, *p247*); **Simon Carter** (Fashion
accessories & services, *p241*); **The Swatch**

Store (Watches, *p242*); **Tiffany & Co** (Fashion
accessories & services, *p240*); **Tower
Records** (Music shops, *p256*); **Vidal Sassoon**
(Health & beauty, *p248*); **Vision Express**
(Opticians, *p249*); **Warner Brothers Studio
Store** (Toys, games & magic, *p258*);
Waterstone's (Bookshops, *p229*); **Wright &
Teague** (Fashion accessories & services,
p240); **Zara** (Fashion, *p234*).

Soho

Agent Provocateur (Fashion, *p239*); **Algerian
Coffee Stores** (Food & drink, *p243*); **American
Retro** (Fashion accessories & services,
p239); **Berwick Street Market** (Markets,
p255); **Bond International** (Fashion, *p237*);
Borders (Bookshops *p229*); **Daddy Kool**
(Music shops, *p257*); **Fish** (Health & beauty,
p248); **Foyles** (Bookshops, *p229*); **Great Frog**
(Fashion accessories & services, *p240*);
Liberty (Department stores, *p233*); **Milroy's
of Soho** (Food & drink, *p244*); **A Moroni &
Son** (Newsagents, *p232*); **Miss Selfridges**
(Department stores, *p234*); **Mr CD** (Music
shops, *p257*); **Muji** (Home accessories,
p251); **Oxfam Originals** (Fashion, *p237*);
Pâtisserie Valerie (Food & drink, *p243*);
Reckless Records (Music shops, *p257*);
Selectadisc (Music shops, *p257*);
Shop (Fashion, *p237*); **Sister Ray** (Music
shops, *p257*).

▶

Despite the prominence of the restaurant atop this riverside building, a lot of people are still unaware that the lower floors of the Oxo Tower contain workshop-retail spaces occupied by independent designers producing a stylish and varied range of work. Near the tower, at Gabriel's Wharf, are several more craft shop/workshop units housing, among others, some excellent jewellers.

Markets

General

Brick Lane Market

Brick Lane (north of railway bridge), Cygnet Street, Sclater Street, E1; Bacon Street, Cheshire Street, Chilton Street, E2. Aldgate East or Shoreditch tube or Liverpool Street tube/rail. **Open** 8am-1pm Sun; closed Mon-Sat. **Map** p403 S5.

You'll find a massive range of goods on sale at this sprawling, ever-entertaining East End institution, including meat, fruit and veg, electrical goods, tools, bicycles, clothing (great streetwear and second-hand gear), jewellery and household goods. A trip here is a quintessential London morning out; whatever you do, don't miss it.

Brixton Market

Electric Avenue, Pope's Road, Brixton Station Road, Brixton, SW9. Brixton tube/rail. **Open** 8am-6pm Mon, Tue, Thur-Sat; 8am-3pm Wed; closed Sun.

Brixton boasts Europe's largest collection of Afro-Caribbean foodstuffs. Head for Electric Avenue or the Granville and Market Row arcades for the best of the provisions, including fab fish. There are also record stalls, second-hand clothes and bric-a-brac.

Camden Market

(7284 2084). Camden Town or Chalk Farm tube. **Camden Market** *Camden High Street, junction with Buck Street, NW1.* **Open** 9am-5.30pm Thur-Sun; closed Mon-Wed. **Camden Lock Market** *Camden Lock Place, off Chalk Farm Road, NW1.* **Open** 10am-6pm Sat, Sun; indoor stalls 10am-6pm Tue-Sun; closed Mon. **Stables Market** *off Chalk Farm Road, opposite junction with Hartland Road, NW1.* **Open** 8am-6pm Sat, Sun; closed Mon-Fri. **Camden Canal Market** *off Chalk Farm Road, south of junction with*

▶ ## Shops by area (continued)

Covent Garden & St Giles's

Accessorize (Fashion accessories & services, *p239*); **Andy's Guitar Centre & Workshop** (Musical instruments, *p256*); **Apple Market** (Markets, *p255*); **BBC World Service Shop** (Gifts & stationery, *p245*); **The Bead Shop** (Hobbies, *p249*); **Blackout II** (Fashion, *p237*); **Camper** (Fashion accessories & services, *p241*); **Carhartt** (Fashion, *p237*); **Carluccio's** (Food & drink, *p244*); **Diesel** (Fashion, *p237*); **Dr Marten Department Store** (Fashion accessories & services, *p241*); **Duffer of St George** (Fashion, *p237*); **Edward Stanford** (Bookshops, *p231*); **Essensuals** (Health & beauty, *p248*); **Forbidden Planet** (Bookshops, *p231*); **French Connection** (Fashion, *p235*); **Gap** (Fashion, *p235*); **Hobbs** (Fashion, *p235*); **Janet Fitch** (fashion accessories & services, *p240*); **Jessops** (Electronics, *p234*); **London Doll's House Company** (Hobbies, *p249*); **Lush** (Health & beauty, *p247*); **Karen Millen** (Fashion, *p235*); **Kirk Originals** (Health & beauty, *p248*); **The Kite Store** (Sport, *p258*); **Kookaï** (Fashion, *p235*); **Mango** (Fashion, *p235*); **MDC Classic Music** (Music shops, *p257*); **Monsoon** (Fashion, *p235*); **Mysteries** (Gifts & stationery, *p245*); **Natural Shoe Store** (Fashion accessories & services, *p241*); **Neal Street East** (Gifts & stationery, *p245*); **Neal's Yard Dairy** (Food & drink, *p243*); **Neal's Yard Remedies** (Health & beauty, *p247*); **Oasis** (Fashion, *p235*); **Office** (Fashion accessories & services, *p241*); **The Sanctuary** (Health & beauty, *p247*); **Silver Moon Women's Bookshop** (Bookshops, *p231*); **Snappy Snaps** (Electronics, *p234*); **Space NK Apothecary** (Health & beauty, *p247*); **Sportspages** (Bookshops, *p231*); **Stephen Jones** (Fashion accessories & services, *p239*); **The Tea House** (Food & drink, *p243*); **Ted Baker** (Fashion, *p237*); **The Tintin Shop** (Gifts & stationery, *p247*); **Turnkey & Soho Soundhouse** (Musical instruments, *p256*); **R Twining & Co** (Food & drink, *p243*); **Wild Bunch** (Florists, *p242*); **YHA Adventure Shop** (Sport, *p258*); **Zwemmer Media Arts** (Bookshops, *p231*).

Westminster

Davenport's Magic Shop (Toys, games & magic, *p258*).

Knightsbridge & South Kensington

Harrods (Department stores, *p232*); **Harvey Nichols** (Department stores, *p232*); **High & Mighty** (Fashion, *p239*); **Pandora** (Fashion, *p237*); **Tridias** (Toys, games & magic, *p258*).

Belgravia & Pimlico

Cornucopia (Fashion, *p237*); **Egg** (Fashion, *p235*).

Chelsea

Antiquarius (Antiques, *p229*); **Argenta** (Fashion accessories & services, *p240*); **Benjamin Pollock's Toy Shop** (Toys, games & magic *p258*); **Bluebird** (Food & drink, *p244*); **The Conran Shop** (Furniture, *p244*); **Daisy &**

Castle Haven Road, NW1. **Open** 10am-6pm Sat, Sun; closed Mon-Fri. **Electric Market** *Camden High Street, south of junction with Dewsbury Terrace, NW1.* **Open** 9am-5.30pm Sat, Sun; closed Mon-Sat. Camden Market is now London's fourth biggest tourist attraction. Street fashion and retro clothes dominate the main market, while Camden Lock maintains its crafts heritage. It's usually busy and, at times, claustrophobic.

Greenwich Market

Cutty Sark DLR/Greenwich DLR/rail. **Antiques Market** *Greenwich High Road, SE10.* **Open** 9am-5pm Sat, Sun; closed Mon-Fri. **Central Market** *off Stockwell Street, SE10.* **Open** *Outdoor* 7am-6pm Sat; 7am-5pm Sun; closed Mon-Fri. *Indoor (Village Market)* 10am-5pm Fri, Sat; 10am-6pm Sun; closed Mon-Thur. **Crafts Market** *College Approach, SE10.* **Open** *Antiques* 7.30am-5pm Thur; closed Mon-Wed, Fri-Sun. *General* 9.30am-5.30pm Fri-Sun; closed Mon-Thur. **Food Market** *off Stockwell Street, SE10.* **Open** 10am-4pm Sat; closed Mon-Fri, Sun.
A covered crafts market filled mainly with objects that straddle a line between skilled craftswork and tourist tat, plus a more interesting, Camden-esque

Central Market with high-quality second-hand clothing, music stalls and bizarre junk shop ephemera. Sundays here are another London tradition.

Leadenhall Market

Whittington Avenue, The City, EC3. Bank or Monument tube. **Open** 7am-4pm Mon-Fri; closed Sat, Sun. **Map** p405 Q6.
It's not a traditional London market, but Leadenhall Market, whose retailers include clothes shops Jigsaw and Hobbs and foodie paradises Butcher & Edmonds and RS Ashby, is worth visiting alone for the beautiful Victorian arcade in which it's situated.

Petticoat Lane Market

Middlesex Street and around, The City, E1. Liverpool Street tube/rail. **Open** 9am-2pm Sun. *Wentworth Street* also 10am-2.30pm Mon-Fri; closed Sat. **Map** p405 R6.
A far cry from trendy Brick Lane, this East End classic may be one of London's most famous markets, but hip it ain't. There are still bargains to be had, though, including good-quality household goods, jewellery, furnishings and cheap clothes.

Tom (Fashion, *p235*); **Designers Guild** (Home accessories, *p250*); **Holding Company** (Home accessories, *p250*); **Jigsaw Junior** (Fashion, *p235*); **Jo Malone** (Health & beauty, *p247*); **Patrick Cox** (Fashion accessories & services, *p241*); **Rococo** (Food & drink, *p244*); **Trotters** (Fashion, *p235*).

North London

After Noah (Islington, Home accessories, *p249*); **Camden Market** (Camden, Markets, *p252*); **Camden Passage** (Islington, Antiques, *p228*); **City Clocks** (Islington, Fashion accessories & services, *p241*); **Crafts Council Gallery Shop** (Islington, Home accessories, *p251*); **David Wainwright** (Hampstead, Home accessories, *p250*); **French & Teague** (Camden, Fashion, *p239*); **Fresh & Wild** (Camden, Food & drink, *p244*); **Mole Jazz** (King's Cross, Music shops, *p257*); **Ray Man** (Camden, Musical instruments, *p256*); **Regulation** (Islington, Fashion, *p235*); **Skate Attack** (Kentish Town, Sport, *p258*).

East London

The Beer Shop (Hoxton, Food & drink, *p243*); **Brick Lane Market** (Spitalfields, Markets, *p252*); **Columbia Road Flower Market** (Bethnal Green, Markets, *p255*); **eat my handbag bitch** (Spitalfields, Furniture, *p245*); **Fred Bare** (Spitalfields, Fashion accessories & services, *p239*); **Spitalfields Market** (Spitalfields, Markets, *p256*); **Walthamstow Market** (Walthamstow, Markets, *p255*).

South London

Bermondsey Market (Bermondsey, Markets, *p255*); **Brixton Market** (Brixton, Markets, *p252*); **Greenwich Market** (Greenwich, Markets, *p253*); **Richer Sounds** (Borough, Electronics, *p234*).

West London

& Clarke's (Kensington, Food & drink, *p243*); **Admiral Vernon** (Notting Hill, Antiques, *p228*); **Bill Amberg** (Notting Hill, Fashion accessories & services, *p240*); **Books for Cooks** (Notting Hill, Bookshops, *p229*); **Boots** (Bayswater, Pharmacies, *p257*); **Cheeky Monkeys** (Ladbroke Grove, Toys, games & magic, *p258*); **Children's Book Centre** (Kensington, Bookshops, *p230*); **Crabtree & Evelyn** (Kensington, Health & beauty, *p247*); **The Dispensary** (Notting Hill, Fashion, *p237*); **Early Learning Centre** (Hammersmith, Toys, games & magic, *p258*); **Emma Bernhardt** (Notting Hill, Fashion accessories & services, *p239*); **The Green Room** (Kensington, Health & beauty, *p247*); **Honest Jon's** (Ladbroke Grove, Music shops, *p257*); **Intoxica!** (Ladbroke Grove, Music shops, *p257*); **Planet Organic** (Bayswater, Food & drink, *p244*); **Portobello Road Market** (Notting Hill, Markets, *p255*); **Rough Trade** (Notting Hill, Music shops, *p257*); **Space/SPAce.NK** (Notting Hill, Home accessories/Health & beauty, *p251/p248*); **Urban Outfitters** (Kensington, Fashion, *p237*); **Wild at Heart** (Notting Hill, Florists, *p242*); **Zafash** (Earl's Court, Pharmacies, *p258*).

Eat, Drink, Shop

Leadenhall Market. *See p253.*

Portobello Road Market

Portobello Road, Notting Hill, W10, W11; Golborne Road, W10. Ladbroke Grove, Notting Hill Gate or Westbourne Park tube. **Open** *Antiques Market* 4am-6pm Sat; closed Mon-Fri, Sun. *General Market* 8am-6pm Mon-Wed; 9am-1pm Thur; 7am-7pm Fri, Sat; closed Sun. *Organic Market* 11am-6pm Thur; closed Mon-Wed, Fri-Sun. *Clothes & Bric-a-Brac Market* 7am-4pm Fri; 8am-5pm Sat; 9am-4pm Sun; closed Mon-Thur. *Golborne Road Market* 9am-5pm Mon-Sat; closed Sun. **Map** p394 A6.
There's something for everyone at this lengthy street mart. The choice of antiques is huge, although prices have always been high, and you'll also find some of west London's cheapest fruit, veg and flowers. What it's probably most famous for, though, is its achingly hip new and vintage clothes stalls.

Walthamstow Market

Walthamstow High Street, Walthamstow, E17. Walthamstow Central tube/rail. **Open** 8am-6pm Mon-Sat; closed Sun.
Walthamstow's answer to the East End's Petticoat Lane claims to be Europe's longest daily street market, with 450 stalls selling cheap clothing, fruit and veg, and household bits and bobs. As trad as they come.

Antiques

See also above **Camden**, **Greenwich** and **Portobello Road** markets.

Bermondsey (New Caledonian) Market

Bermondsey Square, Bermondsey, SE1. Bermondsey tube. **Open** 5am-2pm Fri (starts closing around noon); closed Mon-Thur, Sat, Sun. **Map** p405 Q10.
This market is a mecca for serious collectors and attracts dealers from all over the South-east. Most of the good stuff has gone by 9am.

Crafts

Apple Market

North Hall, Covent Garden Market, Covent Garden, WC2 (7836 9136/www.coventgardenmarket.co.uk). Covent Garden tube. **Open** 10.30am-7pm daily. **Credit** varies. **Map** p400 L8.
A decent (but pricey) range of handmade arts and crafts, antiques and collectibles. The separately run Jubilee Market in Jubilee Hall, on the south side of Covent Garden Piazza, is interesting on Mondays when the usual tourist tosh is replaced by antiques.

Flowers

Columbia Road Flower Market

Columbia Road (between Gosset Street & the Royal Oak pub), Bethnal Green, E2. Old Street tube/rail/ 26, 48, 55 bus. **Open** 8am-1pm Sun; closed Mon-Sat. **Map** p403 S3.
Without question the prettiest street market in town. Flowers, shrubs, bedding plants and other horticultural delights are spread in all directions and roundabout shops stock flowers and garden accessories.

Food

Berwick Street Market

Berwick Street & Rupert Street, Soho, W1. Leicester Square or Piccadilly Circus tube. **Open** 8am-6pm Mon-Sat; closed Sun. **Map** p398 J6.
The best and cheapest selection of fruit and veg in central London can be found here, one of the last parts of Soho with a genuinely seedy feel. There are also good cheese, fish, bread, and herb and spice stalls.

Borough Market

Borough Market, between Borough High Street, Bedale Street, Winchester Walk & Stoney Street, Borough SE10 (www.londonslarder.org.uk). London Bridge tube/rail. **Open** noon-6pm Fri; 9am-4pm Sat; closed Mon-Thur, Sun. **Map** p404 P8.
This superb farmers' market, nicknamed London's Larder, recently started opening to the public every weekend. There are some good cut flowers, as well as quality coffees, fruit, veg and meat. A number of traders specialise in organic produce.

Eat, Drink, Shop

Berwick Street Market. *See p255.*

Organic

Spitalfields Market
65 Brushfield Street, Spitalfields, E1 (7377 1496).
Liverpool Street tube/rail. **Open** 10am-4pm Mon-Fri;
closed Sat; 10am-5pm Sun. **Map** p403 R5.
Crafts and antiques stalls are set up through the
week, but on Friday and, particularly, Sunday, the
market comes alive with a dozen or so organic producers selling relishes, pickles, herbs and spices,
breads and cakes, and fruit and vegetables.

Musical instruments

Denmark Street, WC2, has long been the
commercial mecca for musos of a rock bent.

Andy's Guitar Centre & Workshop
27 Denmark Street, St Giles's, WC2 (7916 5080/
www.andysguitarnet.com). Tottenham Court Road
tube. **Credit** AmEx, DC, MC, V. **Map** p399 K6.
London's most famous stockist of vintage guitars
takes up five floors of rehearsal room-type space,
with a basement for electrics and amps.

Boosey & Hawkes
295 Regent Street, W1 (0800 731 4778/7580
2060/www.boosey.com/musicshop). Oxford Circus
tube. **Open** 9.30am-6pm Mon-Fri; 10am-5pm Sat;
closed Sun. **Credit** AmEx, DC, MC, V. **Map** p398 J6.

Boosey and Hawkes are specialists in classical and
jazz sheet music.

Hobgoblin Music
24 Rathbone Place, Fitzrovia, W1 (7323
9040/www.hobgoblin.com). Tottenham Court Road
tube. **Open** 10am-6pm Mon-Sat; closed Sun. **Credit**
AmEx, DC, MC, V. **Map** p399 K5.
A suitably laid-back, cosy acoustic and folk instrument specialist.

Ray Man
54 Chalk Farm Road, Camden, NW1 (7692 6261/
www.raymaneasternmusic.co.uk/enter). Camden
Town or Chalk Farm tube. **Open** 10.30am-6pm Tue-
Sun; closed Mon. **Credit** AmEx, MC, V.
Ray Man contains an intriguing variety of ancient
instruments from China, India and Africa, including
mandolins, sitars and Chinese banjos.

Turnkey & Soho Soundhouse
114-16 Charing Cross Road, St Giles's, WC2 (7379
5148/www.turnkey.demon.co.uk). Tottenham Court
Road tube. **Open** 10am-6pm Mon-Wed, Fri, Sat;
10am-7pm Thur; closed Sun. **Credit** AmEx, MC, V.
Map p399 K6.
Three floors of electronic equipment, including key-
boards, guitars, amps, PAs, computer gear midis
and recording equipment.

Music shops

Megastores

HMV
150 Oxford Street, Fitzrovia, W1 (7631 3423/
www.hmv.co.uk). Oxford Circus tube. **Open** 9am-8pm
Mon-Sat; noon-6pm Sun. **Credit** AmEx, DC, MC, V.
Map p398 J6.
The ground floor holds rock, pop and soul sections;
in the basement are jazz, soundtrack, classical, spoken word and world music; and on the first floor
you'll find an impressive selection of games, consoles and peripherals.
Branches: 360 Oxford Street, Mayfair, W1 (7514
3600); Trocadero, 18 Coventry Street, St James's, W1
(7439 0447).

Tower Records
1 Piccadilly Circus, Mayfair, W1 (7439 2500/
www.towerrecords.co.uk). Piccadilly Circus tube.
Open 9am-midnight Mon-Sat; noon-6pm Sun.
Credit AmEx, DC, MC, V. **Map** p400 J7.
What Tower lacks in sheen it makes up for in content: you'll find in-depth selections of soul and dance
music, reggae, jazz and classical, plus an unusual
and very welcome classic vinyl section.
Branches are numerous: check the phone book.

Virgin Megastore
14-16 Oxford Street, Fitzrovia, W1 (7631 1234/
www.virgin.com). Tottenham Court Road tube.
Open 9.30am-9pm Mon-Sat; noon-6pm Sun.
Credit AmEx, MC, V. **Map** p399 K6.

The biggest of all the megastores, Virgin has branched out somewhat with its stock, although music still dominates. As well as the usual dance, reggae, and rock and pop sections, Virgin has a good selection of classical music and also sells videos, comics, books, flights and mobile phones.
Branches: 225-9 Piccadilly, St James's, W1 (7930 4208); King's Walk Shopping Centre, King's Road, Chelsea, SW3 (7591 0957).

Specialist music shops

Dive into Hanway Street, which cuts the corner of Oxford Street and Tottenham Court Road, for some quality second-hand sounds: at no.22 there's **On the Beat**, at no.36 **Division One**. Soho's Berwick Street is also a music mecca – **Selectadisc** (no.34) and **Sister Ray** (no.94) are particularly strong on indie, **Reckless Records** (no.30) is good for mainstream, there's Jamaican music at **Daddy Kool** (no.12) and general cut-price CDs at **Mr CD** (no.80).

Black Market
25 D'Arblay Street, Soho, W1 (7437 0478/ www.blackmarket.co.uk). Oxford Circus tube.
Open 11am-7pm Mon-Sat; closed Sun.
Credit AmEx, MC, V. **Map** p399 K6.
A tiny corridor, with nodding DJs behind the counter. Strong on imported house and drum 'n' bass.

Join the dots at **Boosey & Hawkes**.
See p256.

Harold Moores Records
2 Great Marlborough Street, Soho, W1 (7437 1576/www.hmrecords.co.uk). Oxford Circus tube.
Open 10am-6.30pm Mon-Sat; noon-6.30pm Sun.
Credit MC, V. **Map** p398 J6.
Moores holds a gargantuan range numbering 60,000 LPs (downstairs) and CDs (upstairs) of classical music and opera. The staff are knowledgable.

Honest Jon's
276 & 278 Portobello Road, Ladbroke Grove, W10 (8969 9822/www.honestjons.co.uk). Ladbroke Grove tube. **Open** 10am-6pm Mon-Sat; 11am-5pm Sun.
Credit AmEx, DC, MC, V. **Map** p394 A6.
Eclectic and self-consciously cool, Honest Jon's specialises in jazz, fusion, soul, reggae and dance.

Intoxica!
231 Portobello Road, Ladbroke Grove, W11 (7229 8010/www.intoxica.co.uk). Ladbroke Grove tube. **Open** 10.30am-6.30pm Mon-Fri; 10am-6.30pm Sat; noon-5pm Sun. **Credit** AmEx, DC, MC, V.
Map p394 A6.
Considered by many to be the best second-hand record shop in London, Intoxica! is particularly strong on '60s and '70s rock, funk and soul, garage, rockabilly, ska, punk and new wave.

MDC Classic Music
437 Strand, Covent Garden, WC2 (7240 2157/ www.mdcmusic.co.uk). Charing Cross tube/rail.
Open 9am-7pm Mon-Sat; noon-6pm Sun.
Credit AmEx, MC, V. **Map** p401 L7.
This commercially-minded store pushes big names such as Kiri Te Kanawa and the Three Tenors.
Branches are numerous: check the phone book.

Mole Jazz
311 Gray's Inn Road, King's Cross, WC1 (7278 0703/www.molejazz.co.uk). King's Cross tube/rail.
Open 10am-6pm Mon-Thur, Sat; 10am-8pm Fri; closed Sun. **Credit** AmEx, DC, MC, V.
Map p399 M3.
Nostalgia, bebop, free jazz, male and female vocal, trad and avant garde are covered in all formats: CDs, records, books and videos.

Rough Trade
130 Talbot Road, Notting Hill, W11 (7229 8541/ www.roughtrade.com). Ladbroke Grove or Notting Hill Gate tube. **Open** 10am-6.30pm Mon-Sat; 1-5pm Sun. **Credit** AmEx, MC, V. **Map** p394 A5.
If you're looking for obscure American post-rock, Japanese noisecore, the free-est of free jazz and anarchic fanzines, this is the place to come.
Branch: 16 Neal's Yard, Covent Garden, WC2 (7240 0105).

Pharmacies

Boots
75 Queensway, Bayswater, W2 (7229 9266/ www.boots.co.uk). Baywater or Queensway tube.
Open 9am-10pm Mon-Sat; 2-10pm Sun. **Credit** AmEx, MC, V. **Map** p394 C6.

Eat, Drink, Shop

Britain's leading chain of chemists has branches all over London.
Branches are numerous: check the phone book.

Zafash
233-5 Old Brompton Road, Earl's Court, SW5 (7373 2798). Earl's Court tube. **Open** 24hrs daily. **Credit** AmEx, MC, V. **Map** p396 B11.
London's sole 24-hour pharmacy.

Sport

The Kite Store
48 Neal Street, Covent Garden, WC2 (7836 1666). Covent Garden tube. **Open** 10am-6pm Mon-Wed, Fri; 10am-7pm Thur; 10.30am-6pm Sat; closed Sun. **Credit** AmEx, MC, V. **Map** p399 L6.
Kites and other flying gadgets, such as boomerangs and ultimate frisbee disks.

Lillywhite's
24-36 Lower Regent Street, St James's, SW1 (7930 3181). Piccadilly Circus tube. **Open** 10am-8pm Mon-Sat; noon-6pm Sun. **Credit** AmEx, DC, MC, V. **Map** p401 K7.
London's über-sports shop has all the major sports covered, with soccer, tennis, skiing and other outdoor pursuits particularly well represented.

Niketown
236 Oxford Street, Marylebone, W1 (7612 0800/ www.nike.com). Oxford Circus tube. **Open** 10am-7pm Mon-Wed; 10am-8pm Thur-Sat; noon-6pm Sun. **Credit** AmEx, MC, V. **Map** p398 J6.
Three stories of sports gear and streetwear from the giant multinational. A themed shopping experience.

Skate Attack
95 Highgate Road, Kentish Town, NW5 (7485 0007/www.skateattack.com). Kentish Town tube. **Open** 9.30am-6pm Mon-Fri; 9am-6pm Sat; closed Sun. **Credit** AmEx, MC, V.
The largest skate shop in Europe holds everything a skater could need, from beginners' in-line skates to professional ice hockey boots.

YHA Adventure Shop
14 Southampton Street, Covent Garden, WC2 (7836 8541/www.yhaadventure.co.uk). Covent Garden tube. **Open** 10am-6pm Mon, Tue; 10.30am-6pm Wed; 10am-7pm Thur, Fri; 9am-6.30pm Sat; 11am-5pm Sun. **Credit** AmEx, DC, MC, V. **Map** p401 L7.
The Youth Hostel Association's shop has a fine range of walking and camping gear.

Toys, games & magic

It's also worth trying the toy and game departments of **Debenhams** (334-48 Oxford Street, W1; 7580 3000), **Harrods**, **John Lewis** (for both, *see p232*) and **Selfridges** (*see p233*). For computer games, *see p233*. For young children, *see p235* **Daisy & Tom**.

Benjamin Pollock's Toy Shop
44 The Market, Covent Garden, WC2 (7379 7866/ www.pollocks-coventgarden.co.uk). Covent Garden tube. **Open** 10.30am-6pm Mon-Sat; noon-5pm Sun. **Credit** AmEx, MC, V. **Map** p401 L7.
This delightful Covent Garden shop specialises in quaint, old-fashioned toys and games.

Cheeky Monkeys
202 Kensington Park Road, Ladbroke Grove, W11 (7792 9022/www.cheekymonkeys.com). Ladbroke Grove tube. **Open** 9.30am-5.30pm Mon-Fri; 10am-5.30pm Sat; closed Sun. **Credit** MC, V. **Map** p394 A6.
If fantasy is your child's forte, head here. The dressing up outfits here are copious and lavish; there's also traditional toys, plastic novelties and baby gifts.
Branches: 24 Abbeville Road, Clapham, SW4 (8673 5215); 1 Bennett Court, Bellevue Road, Wandsworth, SW17 (8672 2025).

Davenport's Magic Shop
7 Charing Cross Underground Shopping Concourse, Strand, WC2 (7836 0408). Charing Cross tube/rail. **Open** 9.30am-5.30pm Mon-Fri; 10.15am-4pm Sat; closed Sun. **No credit cards.** **Map** p401 L7.
Davenport's selection of tricks, books and videos have made it popular with pros and amateurs alike.

Early Learning Centre
Unit 7, King's Mall, Hammersmith, W6 (8741 2469/ www.elc.co.uk). Hammersmith tube. **Open** 9am-5.30pm Mon-Sat; 11am-5pm Sun. **Credit** AmEx, MC, V.
An aptly named chain that makes safe, fun educational toys and games for young children.
Branches are numerous: check the phone book.

Hamleys
188-96 Regent Street, Mayfair, W1 (7494 2000/www.hamleys.com). Oxford Circus tube. **Open** 10am-8pm Mon-Fri; 9.30am-8pm Sat; noon-6pm Sun. **Credit** AmEx, DC, MC, V. **Map** p400 J7.
The chaotic Hamleys is struggling to maintain its self-described image as 'the finest toy shop in the world'. The stock, spread over five floors, is comprehensive, with electronic games and consoles, hobbies, models, board games, dolls and bears in plentiful supply.
Branch: Unit 3, The Market, Covent Garden, WC2 (7240 4646).

Tridias
25 Bute Street, South Kensington, SW7 (7584 2330/www.tridias.co.uk). South Kensington tube. **Open** 9.30am-6pm Mon-Fri; 10am-6pm Sat; closed Sun. **Credit** MC, V. **Map** p397 D10.
Tridias has plenty of wooden toys and models and a good selection of crafts and rainy-day activities.

Warner Brothers Studio Store
178-82 Regent Street, Mayfair, W1 (7434 3334/ www.wbstudiostore.com). Oxford Circus tube. **Open** 10am-8pm Mon-Sat; noon-6pm Sun. **Credit** AmEx, DC, MC, V. **Map** p400 J7.
Bugs, Daffy, Porky are emblazoned across every toy, novelty, garment and utensil you care to mention.

Arts & Entertainment

By Season

From Punch and Judy to Pearly Kings, London's calendar is full and fulfilling.

London is a city with a great sense of occasion. Its hectic schedule of annual events is packed with celebrations, commemorations, historic contests and archaic rituals. But for all its associations with the starchy traditions of royalty and government, you'll be pleased to find that London's year includes just as much humour and humiliation as it does pomp and ceremony. In fact, about the only thing you can be sure of, from season to season, is the rain.

This chapter concentrates on the best of London's regular annual events; there are scores more advertised in the national press and *Time Out* magazine. For some events you need to book in advance (sometimes several months in advance), some will charge admission on the day/night, while others are free; it's a good idea to phone and check. All the dates given below were correct at the time of going to press, but always double-check nearer the time.

Details of other cultural festivals are listed elsewhere in the book. For **dance**, *see p287* **Festivals**; for **film**, *see p291* **Festivals**; and for **music**, *see p309* and *p319*. Many of the big

museums and galleries, such as the **National Gallery** (*see p129*) and **British Museum** (*see p101*), hold regular talks, films, discussions and other events. Phone the individual institutions for details. And for a list of public holidays in the UK, *see p378*.

Spring 2001

Ideal Home Exhibition

Earl's Court Exhibition Centre, Warwick Road, Earl's Court, SW5 (box office 0870 606 6080/ groups 0870 241 0272). Earl's Court tube.
Date 15 Mar-8 Apr 2001. **Map** p396 A11.
The biggest consumer show in Britain draws huge crowds. Everything from complete, full-scale houses to humble household utensils is displayed.

St Patrick's Day

Date 17 Mar 2001.
London has the third largest Irish population of any city in the world behind New York and Dublin. There are no extravagant, organised events, but head up to Kilburn (NW6) and you'll find plenty of boisterous Irish jubilation, to be sure.

To be a **London Marathon** man – or woman – you've got to apply early. *See p261.*

Head of the River Race

on the Thames, from Mortlake, SW14, to Putney, SW15 (01932 220401/www.horr.co.uk). Mortlake rail (start), Hammersmith tube (mid-point) or Putney Bridge tube (finish). **Date** 17 Mar 2001.

Less well-known than the Oxford-Cambridge race, the HORR is just as impressive. It takes place over the same 4¼-mile (6.8km) course, but in the opposite direction, with over 400 boat crews competing for the best time. Turn up about half an hour before the 9.45am start from Mortlake to get a good spot; the best views are to be had at Hammersmith Bridge or at the finish line at Putney.

Oxford & Cambridge Boat Race

on the Thames, from Putney, SW15, to Mortlake, SW14. Putney Bridge tube (start), Hammersmith tube (mid-point) or Mortlake rail (finish). **Date** 24 Mar 2001.

The 2001 boat race will be the 147th contested by Oxford and Cambridge Universities. Huge crowds line the 4¼-mile (6.8km) course from Putney to Mortlake, with the riverside pubs in Mortlake and Hammersmith the most popular vantage points. The race starts at 1.30pm.

London Harness Horse Parade

Battersea Park, Albert Bridge Road, Battersea, SW11 (01733 234451). Battersea Park or Queenstown Road rail/97, 137 bus. **Date** 16 Apr 2001.

This traditional parade of working horses and their various commercial and private carriages has toured Battersea Park every Easter Monday since 1886.

London Marathon

Greenwich Park to Westminster Bridge via the Isle of Dogs, Victoria Embankment & St James's Park (7620 4117/www.london-marathon.co.uk). **Date** 22 Apr 2001.

Around 35,000 starters – including celebs, record-breakers and fancy-dressed fundraisers – run the 26.2 miles of this, the world's biggest road race. To run it yourself, apply by the October before the race: your name will be entered into a ballot and you'll have a straight 50/50 chance of being allowed to run.

Museums & Galleries Month 2001

various venues (7233 9796/www.may2001.org.uk). **Date** 1 May-3 June 2001.

Museums and galleries around the country will be staging special events and activities, with exhibitions and welcome days.

May Fayre & Puppet Festival

St Paul's Church Garden, Covent Garden, WC2 (7375 0441). Covent Garden tube. **Date** 13 May 2001. **Map** p401 L7.

A free festival celebrating Punch and Judy and the art of puppetry, from 10.30am to 5.30pm.

Chelsea Flower Show

grounds of Royal Hospital, Royal Hospital Road, Chelsea, SW3 (recorded information 7649 1885/ tickets 0870 906 3781/www.rhs.org.uk). Sloane Square tube. **Date** 22-25 May 2001. **Map** p397 F12.

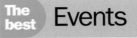

Events

For ancient rivalries
Oxford & Cambridge Boat Race (*see above*), or The Ashes (*see p263*).

For spotting toffs
Henley Royal Regatta (*see p263*).

For archaic royal rituals
Swan Upping on the Thames (*see p263*).

For a cracking hangover
Great British Beer Festival (*see p263*).

For English eccentricity
Great Spitalfields Pancake Day Race (*see p266*).

A huge, world-famous gardening extravaganza by the river. The first two days are solely for members of the Royal Horticultural Society.

Victoria Embankment Gardens Summer Events

Victoria Embankment Gardens, Villiers Street, Westminster, WC2 (7375 0441). Embankment tube. **Date** 27 May-22 July 2001. **Map** p401 L7.

Organised by Alternative Arts, this series of free open-air events close to the river includes an Open Air Dance Festival, the Move It Mime Festival, the Midsummer Poetry Festival (June) and the Summer Season of Street Theatre (July). Phone for details of individual events.

Summer

Royal Academy Summer Exhibition

Royal Academy, Burlington House, Piccadilly, Mayfair, W1 (7300 8000/www.royalacademy.org.uk). Green Park or Piccadilly Circus tube. **Date** 4 June-12 Aug 2001. **Map** p400 J7.

Every year, around 10,000 works are submitted by artists of all styles and standards – from members of the Academy to enthusiastic amateurs – for inclusion in the Summer Exhibition. The work is then judged by a panel of eminent Academicians and around 1,000 entries are chosen for display. Quality is, of course, wildly mixed.

Beating Retreat

Horse Guards Parade, Whitehall, Westminster, SW1 (7930 4466). Westminster tube/Charing Cross tube/ rail. **Date** 6, 7 June 2001. **Map** p401 K8.

For those who like loud circumstance with their pomp, the 'Retreat' is beaten on drums by the Mounted Bands of the Household Cavalry and the Massed Bands of the Guards Division in a colourful musical ceremony. Festivities begin at 7pm.

Arts & Entertainment

Ashes to ashes

Arguably the second most famous trophy in British sport (only the FA Cup is more instantly recognisable), **the Ashes** were borne from – what else? – English sporting failure some 119 years ago at the Oval cricket ground, about a mile south of the river. In August 1882, England played Australia in just the second test match in England (the first had been held two years previously, also at the Oval). After skittling the visitors out for a meagre 63, England limped to a not-much-better 101. Australia's second-innings score of 122 left England needing 85 to win, easy meat under most circumstances. But Aussie fast bowler FR Spofforth, who'd claimed seven wickets in the first innings, once again tore the heart out of the English order. The home side collapsed to 77 all out, and Australia had won.

The next day, the *Sporting Times* published a spoof obituary. 'In affectionate remembrance of English Cricket,' wrote Reginald Brooks, 'which died at the Oval on 28th August 1882, deeply lamented by a large circle of sorrowing friends and acquaintances, RIP. The body will be cremated and the Ashes taken to Australia.' When the English team journeyed down under a month later, they were presented with an urn purporting to claim said Ashes. Opinions differ wildly as to what's actually in the pot, though many believe that it is the burned remains of a bail used in the Melbourne Test match (not, as popular opinion would have it, a charred bail used at the fateful Oval game).

The schtick stuck, and, ever since, England and Australia have played each other for the Ashes. In fact, thanks to English intransigence, the real Ashes remain firmly ensconced at Lord's: the Australians are only permitted to take home a replica when they triumph in the biennial five-match series, which will be played again in England this summer.

And triumph they usually do. To this day, the final Test of every summer is held at the Oval, and usually serves as a painful reminder that the home team are not much better off than they were on that fateful afternoon in 1882. This summer will show whether England's dramatic improvement in form during 2000 was anything other than a blip on the radar. Touch wood...

Derby Day

Epsom Downs Racecourse, Epsom Downs, Surrey (01372 470047/www.epsomderby.co.uk). Epsom Town Centre or Tattenham Corner rail, then shuttle bus. **Date** 9 June 2001.

The most important flat race of the season, the Derby has a carnival atmosphere all its own. A number of stands and spectator enclosures offer varying degrees of comfort and visibility, which depend on how much you are prepared to pay. *See also p327.*

Trooping the Colour

Horse Guards Parade, Whitehall, Westminster, SW1 (7414 2479). Westminster tube/Charing Cross tube/rail. **Date** 16 June 2001. **Map** p401 K8.

The celebration of the Queen's official birthday (as opposed to the day on which she actually was born, 21 April) begins when she leaves Buckingham Palace at 10.45am and travels to Horse Guards Parade, arriving at 11am. The round trip brings her back to the palace around midday, when she takes to the balcony to watch a Royal Air Force flypast before a gun salute is fired in Green Park. Joining the thronging crowds on either side of The Mall is your best bet to get a view of it all.

Royal Ascot

Ascot Racecourse, Ascot, Berks (01344 622211). Ascot rail. **Date** 19-22 June 2001.

Royal Ascot is as much society do as it is sporting occasion. The Queen attends on Ladies' Day (21 June).

Covent Garden Flower Festival

Covent Garden Market, Covent Garden, WC2 (09064 701777/www.cgff.co.uk). Covent Garden tube. **Date** 20-24 June 2001. **Map** p401 L7.

This annual exhibition is free to the public and in-cludes floral installations, demonstrations, fashion shows and street performers.

Wimbledon Lawn Tennis Championships

PO Box 98, Church Road, Wimbledon, SW19 (8944 1066/recorded information 8946 2244/www.wimbledon.org). Southfields tube/Wimbledon tube/rail. **Date** 25 June-8 July 2001.

The one the players want to win, and the fans want to watch. *See p324* **Netting a Wimbledon ticket**.

City of London Festival

venues in and around the City, EC2 (information 7377 0540/box office 7638 8891/www.city-of-london-festival.org.uk). **Date** 26 June-12 July 2001.

A programme of world class arts events in some of the City's finest buildings, this festival primarily features classical, jazz and world music.

Henley Royal Regatta

Henley Reach, Henley-on-Thames, Oxfordshire (01491 572153/www.hrr.co.uk). Henley-on-Thames rail. **Date** 4-8 July 2001.

Toffs on boats, basically, as the British upper-middle classes row about in ineffably posh Henley.

Greenwich & Docklands International Festival

various venues near the Thames at Greenwich & Docklands (8305 1818/www.festival.org). **Date** 6-15 July 2001.

Dance, theatre and music are offered at various locations on either side of the river at this fine event.

Swan Upping on the Thames

various points along the Thames (7236 1863/ 7236 7197). **Date** 16-22 July 2001.

In this archaic ceremony, groups of herdsmen, presided over by the Queen's Keeper of the Swans, round up, divide up and then mark all the cygnets on the Thames as belonging to the Queen, the Vintners' or the Dyers' livery companies. You can watch the action from towpaths along the way. The route and departure time change daily; phone for details.

The Ashes

Lord's, St John's Wood Road, St John's Wood, NW8 (7289 1611/www.lords.org). **Date** 19-23 July 2001.

The second Test of the historic Ashes cricket series against Australia is to be played at Lord's in July. The fifth and final Test is also in London, at the Oval on 23-27 Aug 2001 (7582 7764). *See also p325, and p262* **Ashes to ashes**.

BBC Sir Henry Wood Promenade Concerts

Royal Albert Hall, Kensington Gore, South Kensington, SW7 (7765 5575/box office 7589 8212/ www.bbc.co.uk/proms). Gloucester Road, Knightsbridge or South Kensington tube/9, 10, 52 bus. **Date** 20 July-15 Sept 2001. **Map** p397 D9.

The Proms is the world's greatest music festival, presenting over 70 concerts – an average of over one a day – spanning an impressive variety of composers (most stuff is classical) and repertoire. *See also p309.*

Great British Beer Festival

Olympia, Hammersmith Road, Kensington, W14 (01727 867201/www.camra.org.uk). Kensington (Olympia) tube. **Date** 31 July-4 Aug 2001.

Organised by CAMRA, the Campaign for Real Ale, this beerfest offers up over 300 traditional British ales and ciders, plus a range of international beers.

Summer Rites

Brockwell Park, Herne Hill, SW2 (7278 0995). Brixton tube/Herne Hill rail. **Date** 5 Aug 2001.

A burgeoning, gay-oriented festival, taking in a funfair, bars, market stalls, loads of live performances and disco tents run by top London clubs. At the time of going to press, the organisers were considering staging a 'straight' event on Sunday 6 August.

Notting Hill Carnival

Notting Hill, W10, W11 (8964 0544). Ladbroke Grove, Notting Hill or Westbourne Park tube. **Date** 26-27 Aug 2001.

Staged on the Sunday and Monday of August Bank Holiday weekend, the Notting Hill Carnival is Europe's biggest street party, attracting more than a million revellers over the two days. A massive

Arts & Entertainment

Their Royal Highnesses on their thrones at the **State Opening of Parliament**. *See p265.*

costume parade, live music and plenty of sound systems are among the attractions, but you likely won't be able to get anywhere near them, so busy does it get on the main carnival drag. The crowds can be very uncomfortable; the toilet facilities are woefully inadequate; and, while certain disturbances – including two murders in 2000 – may have been overplayed by the press, muggings and pickpocketing are far from rare, so leave your valuables at home.

Autumn

Chelsea Antiques Fair
Chelsea Old Town Hall, King's Road, Chelsea, SW3 (01444 482514). Sloane Square tube. **Date** 14-23 Sept 2001. **Open** 11am-8pm Mon-Fri; 11am-7pm Sat; 11am-5pm Sun. **Admission** £5; free under-18s. **Map** p397 E12.
A twice-yearly festival (also held 16-25 Mar 2002), where anyone with a budget from £20 to £50,000 should find something of interest.

Thames Festival
on the Thames, between Waterloo Bridge & Blackfriars Bridge (7928 8998). **Date** 15, 16 Sept 2001.
This enjoyable festival celebrates the river with a funfair, a food village, live entertainment and, in the early evening, a stunning river procession and fireworks display. Worth a look.

Great River Race
on the Thames, from Richmond, Surrey, to Island Gardens, E14 (8398 9057). **Date** 15 Sept 2001.
More than 250 'traditional' boats compete in this 22-mile (35km) 'marathon', aiming to scoop the UK Traditional Boat Championship. The race sets off from Ham House, Richmond, and ends at Island Gardens, near Greenwich.

London Open House
various venues in London (0900 160 0061/ www.londonopenhouse.org). **Date** 22-23 Sept 2001.
A unique event providing free access to buildings of architectural and cultural interest that are normally closed to the public. Around 500 buildings participate each year with anything from the hulking Bank of England building to individual rooms in private homes on show. A snooper's paradise.

Horseman's Sunday
Church of St John & St Michael, Hyde Park Crescent, Paddington, W2 (7262 1732). Edgware Road tube/Paddington tube/rail. **Date** 23 Sept 2001. **Map** p395 E6.
Dating from 1969, when local riding stables feared closure and held an open-air service to protest, a vicar on horseback blesses more than 100 horses before the animals trot through Hyde Park.

Pearly Kings & Queens Harvest Festival
St Martin-in-the-Fields, Trafalgar Square, Westminster, WC2 (7766 1100/www.pearlies.co.uk). Charing Cross tube/rail. **Date** 7 Oct 2001. **Map** p401 L7.
Dressed in traditional costumes, pearly kings and queens gather at 3pm for a thanksgiving service. *See also p11* **Pearls of wisdom**.

Punch and Judy Festival
Covent Garden Piazza, Covent Garden, WC2 (7836 9136). Covent Garden tube. **Date** early Oct 2001 (call for details). **Map** p401 L7.

Frequent events

Ceremony of the Keys
Tower of London, The City, EC3 (7709 0765). Tower Hill tube. **Date** daily. **Maximum** *Apr-Oct* party of 7. *Nov-Mar* party of 15. **Map** p405 R7.
The ceremony of locking the entrances to the Tower of London dates back 700 years and starts at precisely 9.53pm every evening, when the Chief Warder leaves the Byward Tower. It's all over just after 10pm, when the last post is sounded. Apply in writing with a stamped self-addressed envelope two months in advance.

Changing of the Guard
Buckingham Palace, Horse Guards & St James's Palace, SW1. Green Park or St James's Park tube/Victoria tube/rail. **Ceremonies** *Buckingham Palace Apr-Aug*

11.15am daily. *Sept-Mar* alternate days. **Map** p400 H9. *Horse Guards* 11am Mon-Sat; 10am Sun. **Map** p401 K8.
The most spectacular ceremony is at **Buckingham Palace**. On guard-changing days, the new guard and its regimental band line up in the forecourt of Wellington Barracks, Birdcage Walk, from 10.45am. It's usually one of the five regiments of Foot

Gather in Covent Garden to watch Punch and Judy duff each other up, but you'll have to telephone first for the exact date.

Trafalgar Day Parade

Trafalgar Square, Westminster, WC2 (7928 8978/ www.sea-cadets.org). Charing Cross tube/rail. **Date** 21 Oct 2001. **Map** p401 K7.
A parade of 500 sea cadets with marching bands and musical performances commemorates Nelson's victory at the Battle of Trafalgar (21 October 1805). It all ends with the laying of a wreath at the foot of Nelson's Column.

State Opening of Parliament

House of Lords, Palace of Westminster, Westminster, SW1 (7219 4272). Westminster tube. **Date** early/mid-Nov 2001. **Map** p401 L9.
The Queen officially reopens Parliament after the summer recess in a ceremony that has changed little since the 16th century. It's a private (though televised) affair, but the public gets a chance to see the Queen as she arrives and departs in her Irish or Australian State Coach, attended by the Household Cavalry. As she enters the House of Lords, a gun salute is fired. Phone nearer the time for the exact date.

London Film Festival

National Film Theatre, South Bank, SE1 (7928 3535/box office 7928 3232/www.lff.org.uk). Embankment tube/Waterloo tube/rail. **Date** early Nov 2001 (call for details). **Map** p401 M8.
One of the biggest film festivals in the world, the LFF screens over 150 British and international features at cinemas across the capital over a two-week period. Centring on the National Film Theatre and the Odeon West End, the festival attracts star actors and directors and offers a great opportunity to the public to see new films at decent prices. For more on other film festivals, *see p291* **Festivals**.

London to Brighton Veteran Car Run

starting at Serpentine Road, Hyde Park, W2 (01753 681736). Hyde Park Corner tube. **Date** 4 Nov 2001. **Map** p395 E8.
Limited to an average speed of 20mph (32kmph), a procession of vintage motors aims to reach Brighton before 4pm. The start (7.30am) at Hyde Park has a great sense of occasion, but if you can't get there, join the crowds lining the rest of the route (via Westminster Bridge).

Bonfire Night

Date 5 Nov 2001.
Every year Britain celebrates the failure of the Gunpowder Plot of 1605, when Guy Fawkes attempted to blow up James I and his Parliament. People across the country get together to burn a 'guy' (an effigy of Fawkes) on a giant bonfire and set off loads of fireworks. Most public displays are held on the weekend nearest to 5 Nov; among the best held in London are those at Primrose Hill, Alexandra Palace and Crystal Palace.

Lord Mayor's Show

various streets in the City (7606 3030). **Date** 10 Nov 2001.
A ceremony that dates back to the signing of the Magna Carta in 1215, under the conditions of which the newly elected Mayor must be presented to the monarch or their justices for approval. Leaving at 11am, the Lord Mayor, accompanied by a procession of 140 floats, travels from Mansion House through

Guards in their scarlet coats and bearskin hats. At 11.27am they march, accompanied by a band, to the palace for the changing of the sentries, who stand guard in the palace forecourt. Note that the ceremony may be cancelled in very wet weather. At **Horse Guards** in Whitehall (the official entrance to the royal palaces, it's the Household Cavalry who mount the guard (10am-4pm daily); they ride to Whitehall via The Mall from Hyde Park for an 11am changeover.

Funfairs

Alexandra Park *Muswell Hill, N22 (8365 2121). Wood Green tube/Alexandra Palace rail/W3 bus.* **Dates** selected public holidays (*see p378*) throughout the year; phone for details.
Hampstead Heath *NW3 (7485 4491 for a leaflet detailing events in the park throughout the year). Belsize Park or Hampstead tube/Gospel Oak or Hampstead Heath*

rail/24, C11 bus. **Dates** selected public holidays (*see p378*) throughout the year; phone for details.

Gun Salutes

Hyde Park, W2 & the Tower of London, EC3. **Date** 6 Feb (Accession Day); 21 Apr (Queen's birthday); 2 June (Coronation Day); 10 June (Trooping the Colour, *see p262*); 4 Aug (Queen Mother's birthday); State Opening of Parliament (*see above*). If the date falls on a Sunday, salutes are fired on the following Monday. **Map** p405 R7.
Cannons are primed on royal occasions for gun salutes. The King's Troop of the Royal Horse Artillery makes a mounted charge through **Hyde Park**, sets up the guns and fires a 41-gun salute (at noon, except for the State Opening of Parliament) opposite the Dorchester Hotel. Not to be outdone, at the **Tower of London**, the Honourable Artillery Company fires a 62-gun salute at 1pm.

Arts & Entertainment

Enter the dragon at the **Chinese New Year Festival**.

the City to the Royal Courts of Justice on the Strand. There, the new Lord Mayor swears vows before returning to Mansion House by 2.20pm. The merriment ends with fireworks launched from a barge moored between Waterloo and Blackfriars bridges.

Remembrance Sunday Ceremony
Cenotaph, Whitehall, Westminster, SW1.
Westminster tube/Charing Cross tube/rail.
Date 11 Nov 2001. **Map** p401 L8.
The Queen, the Prime Minister and other dignitaries lay wreaths at the Cenotaph – Britain's national memorial to 'the Glorious Dead' – and observe a minute's silence (at 11am) in honour of those who gave their lives in both World Wars. Afterwards, the Bishop of London takes a service of remembrance.

Christmas Lights & Tree
Covent Garden, WC2 (7836 9136); Oxford Street, W1 (7629 2738); Regent Street, W1 (7491 4429); Bond Street, W1 (7821 5230); Trafalgar Square, SW1 (7211 2109). **Date** Nov-Dec 2001.
Each year, in thanks for Britain's role in liberating Norway from the Nazis, the Norwegian people make a gift of a giant fir tree, which is then erected in Trafalgar Square. The main shopping streets boast impressive festive displays; the lights on Regent Street are invariably switched on by some jobbing celebrity (early Nov), but those on St Christopher's Place, W1, Bond Street, W1, and Kensington High Street, W8, are often more charming.

Winter

International Showjumping Championships
Olympia, Hammersmith Road, Kensington, W14 (7370 8202/www.olympiashowjumping.com).
Kensington (Olympia) tube. **Date** 19-23 Dec 2001.
An annual jamboree for equestrian enthusiasts, with events ranging from international riders' competitions to the Shetland Pony Grand National. There are also over 100 trade stands.

New Year's Eve Celebrations
Date 31 Dec 2001.
It's anyone's guess as to what might happen in London for New Year. After a hugely successful (if incredibly busy) fireworks event for the Millennium, typical British pig-headedness on various people's parts meant that a similar event proposed to see in 2001 had to be cancelled. As for 2002, it's very much a case of wait and see. Or not, as the case may be.

London International Boat Show
Earl's Court Exhibition Centre, Warwick Road, Earl's Court, SW5 (information 01784 472222/ www.bigblue.org.uk). Earl's Court tube. **Date** 3-13 Jan 2002. **Map** p396 A11.
The latest in boats, equipment and holidays make up one of London's most popular events.

London International Mime Festival
various venues (7637 5661/www.mimefest.co.uk).
Date 12-27 Jan 2002.
There's more to mime than Marcel Marceau. This visual theatre festival encompasses animation, puppetry, circus performance and more.

Chinese New Year Festival
around Gerrard Street, Chinatown, W1 (7439 3822). Leicester Square or Piccadilly Circus tube.
Date 20 or 27 Jan 2002; phone for confirmation. **Map** p401 K7.
The high point of the Chinese calendar sees Chinatown buzzing with stalls selling crafts and delicacies, and dragons snaking their way through the streets, gathering gifts of money and food.

Great Spitalfields Pancake Day Race
Spitalfields Market, entrance on Commercial Street or Brushfield Street, Spitalfields, E1 (7375 0441).
Map p403 R5. **Date** 26 Feb 2002.
On the day before Lent and its 40 days of fasting comes Shrove Tuesday, aka Pancake Day. Would-be tossers should phone a few days in advance.

Arts & Entertainment

Children

Keeping the littl'uns happy in London is child's play.

There's something to suit every type of child in the capital, whether they're into sporty outdoor fun in parks or playgrounds, indoor crafts and activities, or anything and everything in between. For details of current events and activities related to kids, check London's monthly magazine for parents, *Kids Out*.

Grand days out

You can pick the kind of day you want to give the kids depending on the area of London you're in. For family days out, central London and the surrounding areas are usually the best, but there are also a few quirky places in the city's less densely populated areas.

The South Bank & Bankside p69

The pride of the South Bank has to be the **British Airways London Eye** (*see p69*), where the relentless queueing has proved worth it for the chance to step into a rotating capsule that soars 135 metres above London. At the **London Aquarium** (*see p70*), around an hour and a half is needed to learn all about the world's oceans, as well as rainforests, tropical freshwater, seashores and beaches, spot sharks and all manner of sea-dwelling life. From here, it's a ten-minute walk should get you to the **BFI London IMAX Cinema** (*see p292*), which shows 3D films throughout the year and also offers children's parties. The **National Film Theatre** (*see p292*) has Junior NFT film sessions, showing films for kids on weekends and weekday afternoons, while Gabriel's Wharf, a little further east, has shops, cafés and events throughout the year, including the **Coin Street Festival** (*see p319*) and the **Blazing Music Festival**, both held in summer.

A short distance from the South Bank, the Bankside area has got bigger and better over the last year or so, with more and more open spaces and increased access to the riverside. The **Tate Modern** (*see p77*) has free foyer events and activities for families: these include the Start tours (£1) , which involve being kitted out with a map of the galleries and a kitbag with games and puzzles. At **Shakespeare's Globe** (*see p75*), aspiring thespians aged eight to 11 can take part in workshops that serve as an introduction to Shakespeare through drama,

The reconstructed flagship **Golden Hinde**.

storytelling and art. For kids with a yen for the sea, the nearby **Golden Hinde** (*see p74*), a reconstructed 16th-century flagship, offers kids Tudor and Elizabethan workshops and the chance to live like a sailor of yesteryear. Similarly, the **HMS Belfast** (*see p74*), Europe's largest surviving World War II warship, is moored on the Thames close to London Bridge, and organises birthday party facilities on request (7940 6320). Among Bankside's other options is the **London Dungeon** (*see p78*).

The City p81

The City is not the most child-oriented area of London. However, if your kid(s) have plenty of puff, then take a visit to **St Paul's Cathedral** (*see p84*) and climb to the dome for some breathtaking views. **Tower Bridge** and the **Tower of London** (for both, *see p92*) are kid-friendly winners, and the **Museum of London** (*see p91*) never fails to impress. Also, perhaps surprisingly, the **Bank of England Museum** (*see p86*) has proved to be a refreshingly educational landmark in the middle of London's financial district, offering an excellent display of London's monetary history with moving models, past and present legal tender and a mini-cinema, all for free. Just hope that it doesn't get the wee ones thinking about extra pocket money...

Piccadilly Circus p113

There are plenty of attractions under the bright lights of Piccadilly Circus. Inside the Trocadero, there are shops, cafés and a relentless array of slot machines, games and virtual reality rides, all part of **Funland** (*see p114*). The **Rock Circus** (*see p114*) may not be as popular as its more famous benefactor, Madame Tussaud's, but kids like its mix of wax and memorabilia. **Planet Hollywood** is another stop-off point for the type of burgers perhaps eaten by the rich and famous, while nearby **Chinatown** and **Leicester Square** (*see p122*) are also options, especially if you're a sucker for crowds.

Covent Garden p123

There's always something bright and colourful going on in the streets surrounding Covent Garden, which are usually filled with street entertainers. The fine **Theatre Museum** (*see p125*) gives a history of Theatreland and also offers workshops, while the recently (if subtly) renamed **London's Transport Museum** (*see p124*) has themed zones for all ages, including the under-fives, and is a good family venue.

Just south of Covent Garden, the recently reopened **Somerset House** (*see p98*) has a lovely courtyard in which to sit in and have a picnic, as well as a fantastic fountain display which sets off a summer visit nicely. Free family entertainment takes place at weekends and ranges from music and workshops to walks and talks.

Trafalgar Square p129

Quite aside from the perennially popular pigeons in the square, the **National Gallery** (*see p130*) has excellent (free) trails for kids to follow, looking at paintings along the way. The **National Portrait Gallery** (*see p130*) next door will give visitors a chance to put faces to names, from Samuel Beckett to David Beckham. From here, you can take the Mall to get to **Buckingham Palace** and **St James's Park** (for both, *see p130*), which has a huge range of waterfowl. Or, if you want to stick close to the square, try the excellent Café in the Crypt at **St Martin-in-the-Fields** (*see p130*), which has a Brass Rubbing Centre.

Greenwich p166

The gardens at Greenwich would be alone enough to take the wind out of a small child's sails, but with the whole area to enjoy, plus a range of museums and Blackheath to explore, they should be thoroughly and happily exhausted. The **Cutty Sark** (*see p168*), the world's only surviving tea and wool clipper, has restored decks for visitors to explore as well as the crew's quarters. Summer weekends offer costume storytelling sessions and workshops. The **National Maritime Museum** (*see p168*) incorporates the Old Royal Observatory, where planetarium days mean looking at the moon and the stars, and the Queen's House Museum. The NMM also boasts an interactive Bridge, where kids can try 'steering' a range of boats.

Boat trips

Trips run along the **Regent's Canal** in north London between Little Venice and London Zoo (phone the London Waterbus Company on 7482 2550 or Jason's Trip on 7286 3428 for details) as well as along the **Thames** between Hampton Court in the west and the Thames Barrier in the

Information

For more information on activities related to kids, see *Kids Out* magazine, available at all good newsagents or on subscription by calling 01454 620070. For local events, contact the relevant borough council, whose numbers are all in the phone book.

Kidsline

7222 8070. **Open** *Termtime* 4-6pm Mon-Fri; closed Sat, Sun. *School holidays* 9am-4pm Mon-Fri; closed Sat, Sun.
Information on films, shows, attractions and activities geared towards children.

Parentline

0808 800 2222/ www.parentlineplus.org.uk.
Open 9am-9pm Mon-Fri; 9.30am-5pm Sat; 10am-3pm Sun.
A free, confidential parent helpline.

Simply Childcare The Register

7701 6111/www.simplychildcare.com.
A fortnightly childcare listings magazine.

east, calling at all points and piers on the way (various companies run this route; phone 7345 5122 for details). For more on boats, *see p359*.

Museums & collections

Often the first choice for a museum visit, the major attractions at the **Science Museum** (*see p139*) include the Launch Pad, with hands-on activities for all ages. Science Nights and sleepovers take place for eight- to 11-year-olds who want to explore the museum after dark. The newest attraction is the Wellcome Wing, which opened in the summer of 2000 and includes an IMAX cinema (*see p274*).

Nearby, the **Natural History Museum** (*see p139*) has a fantastic wealth of environmental information, from the cretaceous period until the present. A huge reconstructed dinosaur skeleton hogs the main entrance hall, and there are plenty of interactive galleries including Investigate, which allows all ages to try out microscopes and other scientific equipment.

The Young Friends of the **British Museum** (YFBM; *see p101*), meanwhile, is found within the mammoth Bloomsbury building, and offers events and activities specifically for children aged eight to 15. An annual fee (£15) allows entry to the Sunday Club, which offers holiday events, behind-the-scenes visits and free entry to all paying exhibitions. Egyptian sleepovers take place from time to time.

A division of the **V&A** (*see p140*), the **Bethnal Green Museum of Childhood** (*see p156*) contains a huge number of dolls, trains, cars, books and puppets. A selection of educational toys are good for play and, on Saturdays, free one-hour art workshop sessions take place for children aged three and above. For £1, there are regular 'soft play Sundays' in an indoor play area for under-eights.

Off the beaten track, the **Bruce Castle Museum** in Tottenham deals with the history of the local community, but also has a new Inventor Centre with interactive exhibits and 20 acres of surrounding parkland. It's an excellent space for families in the summer, and free kids' activities on Saturdays and Sundays, 2-4pm.

And don't forget the **Courtauld Gallery** (*see p97*), which reopened at Somerset House in 1998. As well as housing a small collection dating from the early Renaissance period to the present, the venue offers kids' drop-in sessions for seven- to 12-year-olds on the first Saturday of each month. Meanwhile, the **London International Gallery of Children's Art** (LIGCA) is the city's only gallery devoted to works of art by children from around the world, and offers weekly classes and occasional workshops.

Bruce Castle *Haringey Museum and Archives, Church Lane, off Lordship Lane, Tottenham, N17 (8808 8772). Wood Green tube, then 243 bus.* **Open** 1-5pm Wed-Sun; closed Mon, Tue. **Admission** free.
LIGCA *O² Centre, 255 Finchley Road, West Hampstead, NW3 (7435 0903). Finchley Road tube.* **Open** 4-6pm Tue-Thur; noon-6pm Fri-Sun; closed Mon. **Admission** free; donations appreciated.

Parks & green spaces

Park life is always a must for kids, and whether their chosen green space is fantastically over-populated during the summer, or has become an off-season haven of peaceful serenity during the winter months, there's usually a good reason for hanging out in any one of London's parks.

Of the most popular, **Regent's Park** (*see p109*) has two boating lakes (one for children), three playgrounds, an open-air theatre and the 36-acre **London Zoo** (*see p109*), while **Kensington Gardens** (*see p136*) features the Round Pond for sailing model boats, two playgrounds and puppet shows in the summer. **Hampstead Heath** and **Parliament Hill** (*see p147*) are great for views and kite-flying, while at **Richmond Park** (*see p178* **Park life**), kids can cycle, spot the herds of red and fallow deer or visit the Isabella Plantation, a woodland with a stream, ponds and flower displays. Down south, **Battersea Park** (*see p175*) has a good adventure playground and a small children's zoo (*see p272*), and **Victoria Park** (*see p162*) in east London has a central playground, tennis courts, a bowling green and an animal enclosure. For sporting activities available in the major parks, *see p321*.

Camley Street Natural Park

12 Camley Street, King's Cross, NW1 (7833 2311). King's Cross tube/rail. **Open** *Summer* 9am-5pm Mon-Thur; 11am-5pm Sat, Sun; closed Fri. *Winter* 9am-5pm or dusk Mon-Thur; 10am-4pm Sat, Sun; closed Fri. **Admission** free.
Don't be put off by the fact that this award-winning natural park overlooks the metal towers of the King's Cross waste transfer station: it's still a great place, whether for activities organised by the London Wildlife Trust, or for hanging out and spying the likes of newts, birds and coloured dragonflies.

Crystal Palace Park

SE19 (park 8778 9496/museum 8676 0700). Crystal Palace rail/buses 2, 3, 63, 108B, 122, 157, 227. **Open** *Park* dawn-dusk daily. *Museum* 11am-2pm Sun. **Admission** free.
Though it's best known for its National Sports Centre (*see p328*; a mini-gym is available for kids, call 8778 0131) and its concert bowl, it's the famous dinosaur park with original sculptures from 1854 that really draws the kids. A maze, two playgrounds, a boating lake and a dry ski-slope are also found here.

Highgate Wood
Muswell Hill Road, Highgate, N6 (8444 6129).
Highgate tube. **Open** 7.30am-1hr before dusk daily.
Highgate Wood offers nature trails, a supervised playground, a nature hut, loads of space for walking or lounging, and the veggie Oshobasho Café with large and small food portions for kids and adults.

Supervised play areas

Kids Active
Information 7731 1435.
Kids Active has playgrounds across London where disabled and able-bodied children can play safely, supervised by fully trained staff.

Indoor adventure playgrounds

Burgess Community Playground
Albany Road, Camberwell, SE5 (7277 1371).
Elephant & Castle tube/rail. **Open** *Termtime*
3.30-7.30pm Tue-Fri; 11am-5.30pm Sat; closed
Mon, Sun. *School holidays* 10.30am-6pm Mon-Fri;
11am-5.30pm Sat; closed Sun. **Admission** free.
This indoor and outdoor adventure playground is suitable for kids aged from five to 15. Activities include swings, slides, sandpits, a football pitch and a small tennis court, table tennis, arts and crafts, cooking and basketball. Burgess Kart Track is also available for kids aged between eight and 16. With petrol-driven, single- and twin-seat karts, beginners are welcome and tuition is always available. The track is open every day except Sunday.

Kimber BMX/Adventure Playground
Kimber Road, Southfields, SW18 (8870 2168).
Southfields tube. **Open** *Termtime* 3.30-7pm Tue-
Fri; 11am-6pm Sat; closed Mon, Sun. *School holidays*
11am-6pm Mon-Sat; closed Sun. **Admission** free.
A BMX track – with BMX bikes for hire – is the chief attraction at this playground. Among the alternatives are rope swings, monkey bars, a basketball court and indoor activities (table-tennis, arts and crafts and a kitchen where kids can try out their culinary skills).

Monkey Business
*222 Green Lanes, The Triangle, Palmers Green, N13
(8886 7520). Palmers Green tube.* **Open** 10am-7pm
daily; closed Wed termtimes. **Admission** £2.75/hr.
Monkey themes rule at this indoor adventure playground, which includes a monkey tree house, ball ponds, Tarzan ropes, net climbs, tube slides, a twizzle maze, an aerial runway, a spook room, a party room, a lounge, a toddler area and a café. Phone for details of special birthday parties.

Park royal

Entering Syon Park, you'd be forgiven for thinking you'd stumbled upon a secret garden. Well-manicured lawns, neatly trimmed hedges and the odd wandering peacock add to a sense of being in a royal retreat, while a central lake framed by weeping willows and snoozing ducks add to the pleasures of escaping central London (note, though, the signs warning adults that their children should be supervised, as the lake is unguarded). On top of this, the Butterfly House is an excellent attraction: queues form during the summer for those wanting to sit among the free flying exotic butterflies that have now, most likely,

become as jaded to visitors as the pigeons in Trafalgar Square. An adjacent insect exhibition includes tropical beetles, scorpions and a Mexican bird-eating spider, all thankfully secured within their respective glass cabinets.

Syon Park & London Butterfly House
*Syon Park, Brentford, Middlesex (8560 0883/
www.syonpark.co.uk/Butterfly House 8560
0378/recorded information 8560 7272/
www.butterflies.org.uk/Snakes and Ladders
8847 0946/www.snakesandladders.co.uk/
Aquatic Experience 8847 4730/www.aquatic-
experience.org). Gunnersbury tube then 237,
267 bus.* **Open** *Syon Park House & Gardens
14 Mar-31 Oct* 11am-5pm Wed, Thur, Sun,
Bank Holiday Mon (last entry 4.15pm); closed
Mon, Tue, Fri, Sat. Closed Nov-Mar 12.
London Butterfly House May-Sept 10am-
5.30pm daily. Oct-Apr 10am-3.30pm daily.
Snakes and Ladders 10am-6pm daily (last
entry 5.15pm). *Aquatic Experience* Mar-Sept
10am-5.30pm daily. Oct-Feb 10am-4.30pm
daily. **Admission** £2.25-£6.25; free-£5.25
concessions (price varies by attraction).
Credit varies by attraction.

You lookin' at me? Inquisitive meerkats in **Battersea Park Children's Zoo**. *See p272.*

Spike's Madhouse

Crystal Palace National Sports Centre, Ledrington Road, Crystal Palace, SE19 (8778 9876/ www.crystalpalace.co.uk). Crystal Palace rail. **Open** *School holidays* noon-5pm Mon-Fri; 10.30am-5pm Sat, Sun. **Admission** £2/hr.

An indoor playground designed especially for kids aged between two and 13. Four storeys of activities include ballpools, scramble nets, slides, rope swings and biff 'n' bash bags. *See also p269.*

Swimming

There are swimming pools and leisure centres all over London. Below we list some of the best for children, as well as two venues – the Dolphin and Swimming Nature – specialising in classes. By law, a maximum of two children under the age of five per adult are allowed into a public pool. For more pools, *see p323.*

Dolphin Swimming Club *ULU Pool, Malet Street, Bloomsbury, WC1 (8349 1844/ http://members.tripod.co.uk/swimminglessons). Russell Square tube/Euston tube/rail.* **Open** 9.15am-2.45pm Sat, Sun; closed Mon-Fri. **Admission** course of 11 30min lessons £203.50 individual; £101.75 two in a group; £66 five in a group. **Map** p399 K4.

Finchley Lido *Great North Leisure Park, High Road, Finchley, N12 (8343 9830). East Finchley or Finchley Central tube.* **Open** 6.45-8.30am, 9am-6.30pm Mon; 6.45am-9.30pm Tue, Thur, Fri; 6.45am-8pm Wed; 9am-4.30pm Sat, Sun. *Last entry* 30 mins before closing. **Admission** £2.70; £1.35-£1.95 concs; free under-5s.

Latchmere Leisure Centre *Burns Road, Clapham, SW11 (7207 8004). Clapham Common tube, then 345 bus/Clapham Junction rail, then 49, 319, 344 bus.* **Open** 7am-9.30pm Mon-Thur, Sun; 7am-6pm Fri; 7am-7.30pm Sat. **Admission** £2.40 9am-5pm; £2.60 6-9pm; £1.80 5-16s; free under-5s, disabled.

Swimming Nature *Various venues in London (bookings 8968 0590/www.swimmingnature.co.uk).* **Open** *Administration* 9.30am-5.30pm Mon-Fri; 9.30am-1pm Sat; closed Sun. **Admission** *Individual lessons* £20.50/half-hr. *Courses* £39.60-£246/term.

Waterfront Leisure Centre *High Street Woolwich, Woolwich, SE18 (8317 5000). Woolwich Arsenal rail/177, 180, 472 bus.* **Open** 7am-11pm Mon-Fri; 9am-10pm Sat; 9am-9.30pm Sun. *Wet & Wild Adventure Park* 3-8pm Mon-Fri; 9am-5pm Sat, Sun. **Admission** £1.25-£4.10; 80p-£3 children (additional charge for activities).

Animal encounters

Animal encounters are not too hard to come by in London. Aside from London Zoo and a good smattering of animal enclosures in the city's parks, animal-loving kids are spoilt for choice by the assorted city farms in and around the capital. Here they can commune with the likes of pigs, geese and cattle, and learn about farming in the process. For a full list, phone or write to the Federation of City Farms & Community Gardens (at The Green House, Hereford Street, Bedminster, Bristol BS3 4NA, 0117 923 1800, www.farmgarden.org.uk).

An elephant encounter at **London Zoo**.

Battersea Park Children's Zoo

Battersea Park, Battersea, SW11 (8871 7540).
Sloane Square tube then 19, 137 bus/Battersea Park
or Queenstown Road rail. **Open** *Apr-Sept* 10am-5pm
daily (last entry 4.30pm). *Oct-Mar* 11am-3pm Sat,
Sun. **Admission** approx £1.80; 90p concessions; free
under-2s. **Map** p397 F13.

A small zoo near the river, with pony rides, a llama,
a hillside infested with meerkats, monkey cages, and
a variety of small animals, including pygmy goats,
rabbits and an adorable pot-bellied pig. The zoo also
opens during school half-term in February and
October. To book a weekend birthday party contact
Splodge on 7350 1473/1477.

College Farm

45 Fitzalan Road, Finchley, N3 (8349 0690).
Finchley Central tube/bus 13, 26, 82, 143, 260.
Open 10am-6pm daily. **Admission** £1.50; £1.25
concessions, 75p under 16s.

At one time College Farm was a major dairy farm
for express dairies and a provider of milk for city
folk, but these days it's more of a petting farm, much
loved by urban north Londoners. Donkeys,
Highland cattle, a horse, pigs, rabbits and sheep are
all found here, while the small farm café, open on
Sunday afternoons, is a good stop-off point for tea,
coffee and home-made cakes.

Hackney City Farm

1a Goldsmiths Row, Bethnal Green, E2 (7729 6381/
www.hackneycityfarm.org.uk). Bethnal Green tube/
Cambridge Heath rail/bus 26, 48, 55. **Open** 10am-
4.30pm Tue-Sun; closed Mon. **Admission** free.

This farm, just off the traffic-laden Hackney Road,
has an education department that organises tours
for groups who can meet the residents (saddleback
pigs, geese, turkeys, sheep and cattle among them).
There is also a very popular summer playscheme.

London Zoo

Regent's Park, NW1 (7722 3333/
www.londonzoo.co.uk). Camden Town tube, then
274 bus. **Open** *Nov-Feb* 10am-4pm daily. *Mar-Oct*
10am-5.30pm daily. **Admission** £9; £7 3-14s;
£8 concessions; free under-4s. **Credit** AmEx, MC, V.
Map p398 G2.

This 36-acre conservation centre has more than 600
species including invertebrates, reptiles, fish, birds,
lions, tigers, gorillas, elephants, giraffes and bears.
For children's activities, Rampage at London Zoo is
held from 10am to 1pm daily except Sunday, featuring art activities, zoo tours, games, fancy dress and
playtimes for children aged five and over, all supervised and tutored by professionals. There are no sessions during January, but this is compensated for by
the extended hours during April and the summer
months, when activities include volleyball and other
sports in Regent's Park. Prices start from around £15
per day and birthday parties can also be arranged
(phone 7722 5909 for details). See p109.

Eating with kids

Babe Ruth's

172-176 The Highway, Wapping, E1 (7481 8181/
www.baberuths.com). Shadwell tube/DLR/D1, 100
bus. **Meals** noon-11pm Mon-Thur; noon-midnight
Fri, Sat; noon-10.30pm Sun. **Credit** AmEx, MC, V.
This family-friendly sports eatery has games galore
and a children's menu (with puzzles on the back) for
£7.99. Kids can slam-dunk in the mini-basketball
court or play table football and arcade games.
Branch: O² Centre, Finchley Road, West
Hampstead, NW3 (7433 3388).

Belgo

Belgo Centraal, 50 Earlham Street, Covent Garden,
WC2 (7813 2233/www.belgo-restaurants.com).
Covent Garden tube. **Meals** noon-11.30pm Mon-
Thur, noon-midnight Fri, Sat; noon-10.30pm Sun.
Credit AmEx, DC, MC, V. **Map** p399 L6.
These trendy Belgian restaurants feature a colour-
in 'Mini Belgo' menu for under-12s (max two kids
per adult) where children eat free at any time. Kids
choose from either fish-fingers or chicken nuggets
served with a salad and fries or mash and followed
by ice cream, plus a fizzy drink or juice.
Branches are numerous: check the phone book.

The Big Easy

332-4 King's Road, Chelsea, SW3 (7352 4071).
Sloane Square tube, then 11, 19, 22 bus.
Meals noon-midnight Mon-Thur; noon-12.30am
Fri, Sat; noon-11.30pm Sun. **Credit** AmEx, MC, V.
Map p397 D12.

All day, every day, one child under eight can eat for
free if they are with an adult, whose subsequent kids
dine for £3.95. The kids' menu features the likes of
burgers and chicken fingers, while adult mains cost
from £4.95 for burgers to £19.95 for lobster. Crayons,
booster seats and high chairs are available; book
these – and your table – in advance on weekends.

Fatboy's Diner

Spitalfields Market, Spitalfields, E1 (7375 2763).
Aldgate East tube/Liverpool Street tube/rail.
Meals 10am-4pm Mon-Fri; 10am-6pm Sat;
9am-7.30pm Sun. **No credit cards. Map** p403 R5.
Step back in time at this gleaming, original 1950s
diner, serving beautifully chunky chips, authentically meaty burgers and gorgeous milkshakes. The
kids' menu has meals for around £3. Staff can
arrange children's parties on Saturdays.

Maxwell's

8-9 James Street, Covent Garden, WC2 (7836
0303/www.maxwells.co.uk). Covent Garden tube.
Meals 11am-midnight daily. **Credit** AmEx, DC,
MC, V. **Map** p401 L6.
Staff take their seasons seriously here, donning
appropriate costumes at Christmas, Halloween and
Thanksgiving to keep everyone in the swing of
things. Children get a special set menu, and there are
colourings and quizzes to keep them happy.
Branches are numerous; check the phone book.

Rainforest Café

Trocadero, 20 Shaftesbury Avenue, St James's, W1
(7434 3111/www.therainforestcafe.co.uk). Piccadilly
Circus tube. **Meals** noon-10pm Mon-Thur; noon-
10.30pm Fri (subject to change); 11.30am-7.45pm Sat;
11.30am-10.30pm Sun. **Credit** AmEx, MC, V.
Map p401 K7.
Cascading waterfalls, thunder, lightning, the sounds
of wild animals… and set children's menus from
£7.95, with the food taking its influences from
Mexico, Asia and the Caribbean. Party bags, cakes,
face painters and games can all be part of a visit.

Smollensky's on the Strand

105 Strand, Covent Garden, WC2 (7497 2101/
www.smollenskys.co.uk). Charing Cross tube/rail.
Meals noon-midnight Mon-Wed; noon-12.30am
Thur-Sat; noon-11pm Sun. **Credit** AmEx, DC, MC, V.
Map p401 L7.
Soft lighting, succulent steaks and live piano jazz
are what the adults go for, but kids make straight
for the 'mini me' menu (£5.25), with steak, breaded
chicken, hot dogs and the like. Drinks and desserts
are separate and cost around £2.25. This branch has
Punch and Judy shows on Saturdays and a magician on Sundays (2.30pm).
Branch: O² Centre, 255 Finchley Road, West
Hampstead, NW3 (7431 5007).

RK Stanleys

6 Little Portland Street, Fitzrovia, W1 (7462
0099/www.rkstanleys.co.uk). Oxford Circus tube.
Meals noon-3.30pm, 5.30pm-midnight Mon-Fri;
6pm-midnight Sat; closed Sun. **Credit** AmEx, MC, V.
Map p398 J5.
Eat diner-style at this informal British restaurant
specialising in slap-up sausage and mash dinners.
The plush red banquette seating and unlimited
ketchup are a hit with kids, as is the separate children's menu (£4.50). Baby-changing facilities and
highchairs are available.

The best Kids' stuff

Best for getting your feet wet
Waterfront Leisure Centre (*see p271*).

Best for country living
College Farm (*see p272*).

**Best for blinding you
with science**
Science Museum IMAX Cinema (*see p274*).

Best for learning by ear
The Gong Club (*see p273*).

Best for stylish dining
Smollensky's on the Strand (*see p273*).

Yo Sushi!

52 Poland Street, Soho, W1 (7287 0443/
www.yosushi.co.uk). Oxford Circus tube. **Meals**
noon-midnight daily. **Credit** AmEx, DC, MC, V.
Map p398 J6.
Colourful dishes, a robotic drinks trolley and a conveyor belt for the food make this a culinary adventure playground for kids. Special easy-to-use
chopsticks and clip-on baby seats make it family-
friendly, and the kids' menu includes fish fingers,
smiley potato croquettes and chicken nuggets.
Under-12s eat free from Monday to Friday, and fun
packs are available.

Entertainment

The Gong Club

Royal Festival Hall, South Bank, SE1 (bookings 7960
4242/information 7921 0848). Embankment tube/
Waterloo tube/rail. **Date** 2-3.30pm Sats during
termtime. **Admission** £25/term. **Map** p401 M8.
At the Gong Club, children aged seven and over can
learn to play the instruments that make up the
Gamelan while learning about Java and its customs.
Instruments include perennial kids' favourites, such
as drums and gongs, and all music is taught by ear.

Everyman Cinema

5 Holly Bush Vale, Hampstead, NW3
(information 7435 1600/bookings 7431 1777/
www.everymancinema.com). Hampstead tube.
Admission £10; £5 accompanying adults.
Everyman Kids is a fantastic new initiative put
together in association with Film Education and
Natural Nylon, a production company formed by
Ewan McGregor, Jude Law, Sadie Frost and other
Brit thespians *du jour*. Designed to offer education
and entertainment to film-loving children, Saturday
mornings combine a screening with an educational
workshop, open to all, aged eight to 12, under-8s with
accompanying parents.

Arts & Entertainment

'Mmmm. Dinner...' A Victorian dinosaur sculpture in **Crystal Palace Park**. *See p269.*

Science Museum IMAX Cinema

*Wellcome Wing, Science Museum, Exhibition
Road, South Kensington, SW7 (7942 4454/4455/
www.sciencemuseum.org.uk). South Kensington
tube.* **Admission** *Before 4.30pm museum & film*
£12; £8 students; £5.75 concessions. *After 4.30pm
(admission to museum is free)* £6.75; £5.75
concessions, students. **Time** *Shows* hourly
10.45am-4.45pm Mon-Fri; extra show 5.45pm Sat,
Sun. **Credit** AmEx, DC, MC, V. **Map** p397 D9.
Housed within the space-age Wellcome Wing of the
Science Museum, this cinema has 2- and 3-D films
for kids of all ages who can try to reach out and
touch the spectacular sights that unfold before them.

National Film Theatre

*South Bank, SE1 (7928 3232/www.bfi.org.uk/nft).
Waterloo tube/rail.* **Admission** £6.50; £5 concessions;
£1 off members. **Credit** AmEx, MC, V. **Map** p401 M7.
Matinées for children are held every Saturday at 3pm
with workshops to accompany the screenings at 2pm.

Puppet Theatre Barge

*Blomfield Road, Little Venice, W9 (7249 6876/
www.movingstage.co.uk). Warwick Avenue
tube.* **Performances** *Termtime* 3pm Sat, Sun.
School holidays 3pm daily. **Admission** £6.50;
£6 concessions. **Credit** MC, V. **Map** p395 D4.
Moored at Henley, Marlow and Richmond from June
to October, and Little Venice in the winter, this
unique floating marionette theatre stages regular
family shows and performances for adults.

Unicorn Theatre for Children

*Unicorn at the Pleasance Theatre, Carpenters Mews,
North Road, Islington, N7 (7700 0702/box office
7609 8753/www.unicorntheatre.com). Caledonian
Road tube.* **Performances** *Termtime* 10.15am,

1.30pm Tue-Fri (phone to check); 11am, 2.30pm Sat;
2.30pm Sun; closed Mon. *School holidays* phone to
check. **Admission** £5-£10. **Credit** AmEx, MC, V.
Founded in 1948, London's oldest professional children's theatre has left Great Newport Street and is at
the Pleasance Theatre for the foreseeable future. It's
adventurous programme of commissioned plays and
entertainment is aimed at children aged four to 12.

Taking a break

Childminders

*6 Nottingham Street, Marylebone, W1 (7935
3000/2049/www.babysitter.co.uk).* **Open** 8.45am-
5.30pm Mon-Thur; 8.45am-5pm Fri; 9am-4.30pm Sat;
closed Sun. **Map** p398 G5.
A large agency with over 1,500 babysitters, mainly
nurses, nannies and infant teachers (all with references) who live all over London and the suburbs.

Pippa Pop-ins

430 Fulham Road, Chelsea, SW6 (7385 2458).
Open 8am-7pm Mon-Fri; closed Sat, Sun.
Fees sessions from £28. **Credit** MC, V.
This nursery school and kindergarten run by NNEB-
and Montessori-trained nursery teachers and nan-
nies offers parties, holiday activities and a crêche.
Branch: 165 King's Road, Fulham, SW6 (7385 2458).

Universal Aunts

*Daytime childminding 7738 8937/evening babysitting
7386 5900.* **Open** 9.30am-5pm Mon-Thur; 9.30am-
4pm Fri; closed Sat, Sun. **Rates** *Childminding* from
£6/hr. *Babysitting* from £5/hr. **No credit cards**.
This London agency, founded in 1921, can provide
reliable people to babysit, meet children from trains,
planes or boats, or take them sightseeing.

Clubs

You can dance till you're dizzy eight days a week in London's clubland.

Scala: a newish kid on the block. *See p278.*

There are probably more places to dance in London than ever before. In the last couple of years four large-scale super-venues (*see p278* **Larging it**) and more than a dozen smaller clubs have opened, and late-opening club bars continue to proliferate. Clubbing is now an essential part of mainstream British culture, but as well as the more commercial options, there's always a new scene – or even a 'new' retro scene – bubbling up.

UK garage and two-step, the thriving breakbeat, tech-house and electro scenes, new Brit house and the resurgence of hip hop culture have all kept alive the city's reputation for innovation. Any future developments will surely be a fusion of the many different musical cultures jostling for attention on the city's dancefloors. Go out in London and you might come across the latest hotbed of musical experimentation and find that it's only a few doors away from the most unapologetically glamorous superclub.

In the descriptions that follow we've focused on the actual venues, but be aware that in most places the precise music and style of a club will usually be different from night to night. We've highlighted particular nights worth looking out for, but for full details check out the extensive weekly club listings in *Time Out* magazine. You'll also find events promoted on radio, on flyers and in specialist club magazines. The more underground scenes are harder to infiltrate, though hanging around in record shops and tuning in to pirate radio are good places to start. Expect to pay about £2-£5 to get into a club between Sunday and Thursday, and £6-£12 on Fridays and Saturdays.

Clubs

UP AT THE BIG HOUSE

All this diversity is fine, but it's house music that usually packs dancefloors at weekends. The most famous dance club in London is still the **Ministry of Sound**. Situated south of the river near the Elephant and Castle, it looks like a prison yard from the outside, yet draws all-night dancers like moths to a flame. Big-name guest DJs from the USA and the UK spinning house and garage are the principal attraction, but the sheer energy and enthusiasm of the place can take your breath away.

However, Ministry is no longer unchallenged in the superclub stakes. **Scala**, **Home** and **Fabric** (*see p278*) have a combined capacity of 7-8,000, and with the impending arrival of new venues such as **Ocean** in Hackney (March 2001; *see p313*) and **Pacha London** (May 2001), Londoners have a great deal more choice of venues large enough to boast impressive sound systems and major visiting DJs.

The End is the most sophisticated dance venue in the heart of London, a cutting-edge homage to minimal styling and maximum sound quality. It's hosted by Mr C and fellow recording artists Layo & Bushwacka, who are often seen on the decks, and it boasts a monthly series of the best funky techno, drum 'n' bass and deep house parties in London, not to mention the indie-rock-dance session Trash on Mondays. Smart toilets and proper air-conditioning also set it apart, and the club has a bar and restaurant, AKA (*see p279*) next door.

The recently expanded Turnmills in Farringdon is famous for its 'underground' dance nights, but it has more nooks and crannies than your granny's cupboards and plenty of space to sit and chill. The Gallery, Friday's full-on housey party, and the electro breakbeat revelry at Headstart and London Calling on Saturdays are both jammed. The latter closes at 3.30am, to be followed by Trade, a marathon, mainly gay ten-years-and-counting event that continues for the next ten hours until Sunday afternoon (*see p279*).

Heaven, a maze of bars, dancefloors and corridors behind Charing Cross station, had a major refit recently. It's London's most famous gay venue (*see p278*); 'straight' clubbers are only likely to test its charms at monthly parties such as Bedrock on Thursdays, or at the popular mixed-gay There on Fridays, where hard house meets new breakbeats.

Other major dance venues worth checking out include the Fridge in Brixton (*see p278*), Bagleys Studios in King's Cross (*see p278*), the Colosseum in Vauxhall, and the Glasshouse by the river in Blackfriars, all of which have at least three dancefloors.

DRESSED TO KILL
If you're looking for a nightclub where you can dress up and party in style, the West End's Café de Paris and Browns fit the bill, while the Roof Gardens in Kensington is probably the most beautiful club location in the city. All are popular with people of all ages, and all encourage smart attire.

The Café de Paris, a classic 1920s ballroom, has a lovely balcony and a restaurant. Browns is a sleek and chic two-floor club in Holborn that has long been known as a haunt of celebs and location for after-show parties. Members are favoured (non-members need to inform the club in advance, preferably by fax), as they are at the Roof Gardens, where non-members are admitted on Thursdays and Saturdays (the £40 admission sounds steep but includes a three-course dinner). It boasts three stunning garden areas in addition to the restaurant and dancefloor.

However, the places to go if you're all dressed up with, er, nowhere to go, are Rock, a recent arrival for cosmopolitan party people, and the Emporium. Rock opened in 1999, but unlike the superclubs which also opened that year, its reputation is built on exclusivity; the chance to party in style (that's slick 1970s lounge style) along with a host of celebrities and Euro hedonists. The Emporium, a spacious Ibizan-style club just off Regent Street, is (also) a celeb hangout and once had to refuse a request to hold a private party for Prince (or should that be The Artist?) as it was too busy.

London clubs are notorious for the length of their queues and the whimsy of their door policies, although at most dance clubs, the latter hardly applies any more. The best approach is to phone in advance to ask about dress requirements and the best time to arrive, and be patient, polite and persistent.

WEST END WHIRLS
Dozens of bars, cafés, clubs and restaurants are situated around Soho and Covent Garden; the best way to explore is to cruise around on foot, although a few venues stand out. Bar Rumba, one of the best dance clubs in town, plays host to a series of excellent one-nighters: Monday has jazz, funk and drum 'n' bass; Tuesday, Latin; it's deep house on Wednesday; drum 'n' bass on Thursday; funky disco-house classics on Friday; and soulful garage on Saturday. Each night is among the best of its type. Equally popular is the Wag, a stylish club on three floors that similarly plays host to a wide variety of music. Midweek sees indie-rock nights, and Friday an '80s and '90s retro session. Blow Up, though, is one of the best parties around on Saturday, a night that takes its inspiration from '60s soul and pop, but that plays all kinds of lounge and big beat too.

The Velvet Room on Charing Cross Road, is a luxuriously appointed club bar that also hosts a top drum 'n' bass Wednesday-nighter (Swerve) and a great techno and deep house night on Thursdays (Ultimate BASE). Stylish club clothes should normally guarantee admission. In the heart of Soho, Madame Jo Jo's is one of London's most atmospheric sleazy-chic venues, with drag queens behind the bar and a capricious musical selection.

Home (*see p278*) has shifted the nightlife focus back on to Leicester Square, where huge discos like Equinox mostly cater to suburbanites and clueless tourists, but Sound is also doing its bit for the much-maligned square. Carwash spins its mirrorball and sparkles here every Saturday, the best disco (and disco house) night in town, but one for which you must dress the part (ie as glittery as an extra from *Saturday Night Fever*). And there's even a classy blue velvet chill out room.

Talking of classy, the **Hanover Grand**, with its balconied dancefloor and groovy bar down a sweeping staircase , is home to the best midweek R&B and hip hop at Fresh 'n' Funky on Wednesdays, and seriously trendy dance nights on Thursdays, Fridays and Saturdays, when only the most gorgeous club-people are likely to get past the style police on the door. **Legends**, also in Mayfair, is sleek and modern. The restaurant and bar upstairs have a huge window on to the street and a dressed-up crowd bops to house beats at weekends.

WEST IS BEST

If you're staying in west or south-west London, then **Subterania** is an excellent night-time destination. DJs spin funky sounds at the weekend to a trendy west London crowd; both Friday's Rotation and Saturday's Soulsonic are hard to get into unless you arrive early (and be sure to dress up for the latter). The congenial **Notting Hill Arts Club** is a whitewashed basement packing in local trustafarians and clubbed-out drinkers. It accommodates a real range of events, from jam sessions and indie rock in midweek to Patrick Forge's Inspiration Information (Fridays). Sundays is when Everything But The Girl's Ben Watt co-hosts and DJs at Lazy Dog, a fortnightly deep house session that barks, wags its tail and wants its tummy scratched all at the same time.

NORTH LONDON NIGHTS

After being hailed as the coolest place on earth a couple of years ago, the loft-loungers' paradise of Hoxton and Shoreditch is now filled with trendy bars and eateries, many of which encourage late drinking with DJs and a dancefloor (*see p281* **Boho in Shoho**).

Away from here, most of the nocturnal action north of the West End happens around King's Cross and Camden. Despite its location, in the wastelands behind King's Cross, the **Cross** has a reputation for great weekend dance parties, including Renaissance, Serious, Work and L'Amour, when the brick arches shake to the latest glammy house grooves. During 2000, it expanded to three dancefloors, and the garden area was enlarged. It's worth the cab fare, but like so many of these clubs, it's already a hit with the dressed-up (but not too self-conscious) locals, so arriving early is always a smart move.

Across a small car park is **Bagley's Studios**, a pioneering warehouse party venue, now renovated into a warren of inter-connected rooms that rock to large-scale house and garage bashes, including Saturday's Freedom. Also in grubby King's Cross is the **Scala** (*see p279*).

Camden Palace, a huge old music hall, was transformed into a multi-level inferno of sound and light back in the early '80s. It's showing its age now but is still worth visiting, if only for Tuesday's indie-rock club Feet First and some of the special events on Saturdays.

SOUTHSIDE STEPPING

There's a thriving nightlife scene in and around Brixton. The biggest venue is the **Fridge**, a former theatre that's hardly glamorous but that can look spectacular with clever use of visuals. Saturday features monthly parties, while Fridays major on tough, uplifting trance at the all-nighter Escape From Samsara. Right opposite the Fridge is **Mass**, a three-room nightclub high up a circular stairwell in a converted church. It's a great space, boasting a series of cutting-edge monthly line-ups at nights like Funkt, Movement and Khz, but often less in the way of atmosphere thanks to rather undramatic sound and sweaty lack of air-con.

Smaller in scale but not in ambition are the club bars. The **Dogstar** on Coldharbour Lane has set the trend: there's free entry for most of the night, and it attracts some of London's most interesting DJs. The **Fridge Bar** (adjacent to the Fridge) adopts a more global dance perspective, with a dark basement dancefloor that generates an old-school funky-sweaty party atmosphere. The **Living Room**, at the start of the distinctly dodgy Coldharbour Lane – just act like you're supposed to be there and you shouldn't have any problems – is a swanky club-bar-restaurant on two floors with DJs adding fresh and cool sounds for Brixton's twenty- and thirtysomethings. It's a sister bar to the nearby Dogstar, as is the **Redstar** a couple of miles away in Camberwell, a wonderful club with massive windows overlooking Camberwell Green and superb DJ line-ups that's usually free. It's all about lounging as well as 'larging' it, so if you're in south-east London, try it out.

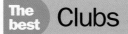

The best Clubs

Bar Rumba
High quality musical diversity. *See p276.*

The Cross
Stylish partying (and outdoors, too). *See p277.*

The End
Underground music, superclub standards. *See p276.*

Arts & Entertainment

Larging it

Typical. You wait ages for a superclub and then three come along at once. In fact, so dramatically did the Scala, Home and Fabric increase London's dancefloor capacity during 2000 that sceptics were asking whether they could all survive. Well, so far there have been no worries, as all three new venues have packed in the punters.

The **Scala** (capacity 800; cost to open £1.8 million), a former cinema, was first out of the box, coming to life in the spring of '99. In 2001, its diet of live gigs and one-off parties – hip hop, hard house, UK garage, whatever – will be supplemented by a new deep and tech-housey party on Saturdays.

The seven-storey nightpalace **Home** (2,700; £9 million) would be a very different club were it not smack in the middle of tourist-oriented, local-unfriendly Leicester Square. Still, it does have elegant design, the appropriately named sixth-floor ViewBar, excellent sound systems and very fine resident DJs and club nights in its favour, as well as a steady stream of guest DJs including mega-jocks such as Danny Tenaglia. Look out for Highrise on a Thursday, a seductive blend of progressive house, funky breakbeats and more.

Fabric (2,500; £9.8m million), a bold adaptation of 15 brick arches, opened to great acclaim in October 1999 and quickly became the city's most impressive venue for serious dancing. Clubbers know there'll be three unpretentious floors of top DJs, world-class sound and facilities and quality beats, whether it's progressive house, jump-up drum 'n' bass, breakhouse or club classics. Music policy concentrates on more underground sounds, with an emphasis on DJs who appeal to the clubland cognoscenti as well as home-grown underground stars. And thanks to its unique 'Bodysonic' main dancefloor – the whole floor is a giant sub-bass loudspeaker – on a visit to Fabric, you'll really feel the earth move.

Club venues

Bagley's Studios *King's Cross Freight Depot, off York Way, King's Cross, N1 (7278 2777/ www.bagleys.net). King's Cross tube/rail.* Map p399 L2.

Bar Rumba *36 Shaftesbury Avenue, Soho, W1 (7287 2715/www.barrumba.co.uk). Piccadilly Circus tube.* Map p401 K7.

Browns *4 Great Queen Street, Covent Garden, WC2 (7831 0802). Holborn tube.* Map p399 L6.

Café de Paris *3 Coventry Street, St James's, W1 (7734 7700/www.cafedeparis.com). Leicester Square or Piccadilly Circus tube.* Map p401 K7.

Camden Palace *1A Camden High Street, Camden, NW1 (7387 0428/www.camdenpalace.com). Camden Town or Mornington Crescent tube.*

Cargo *83 Rivington Street, EC2 (7739 3440). Old Street tube/rail.* Map p403 R4.

Colosseum *1 Nine Elms Lane, Nine Elms, SW8 (7720 3609). Vauxhall tube/rail.*

The Cross *Goods Way Depot, off York Way, King's Cross, N1 (7837 0828/www.the-cross.co.uk). King's Cross tube/rail.* Map p399 L2.

Emporium *62 Kingly Street, Soho, W1 (7734 3190/ www.emporiumlondon.com). Oxford Circus tube.* Map p398 J6.

The End *18 West Central Street, St Giles's, WC1 (7419 9199/www.the-end.co.uk). Holborn or Tottenham Court Road tube.* Map p399 L6.

Equinox *Leicester Square, WC2 (7437 1446). Leicester Square tube.* Map p401 K7.

Fabric *77A Charterhouse Street, Clerkenwell, EC1 (7490 0444/www.fabriclondon.com). Farringdon tube/rail.* Map p402 O5.

Fridge *Town Hall Parade, Brixton Hill, SW2 (7326 5100/www.fridge.co.uk). Brixton tube/rail.*

Glasshouse *The Mermaid Building, Puddle Dock, off Upper Thames Street, EC4 (7680 0415). Blackfriars tube/rail.* Map p404 O7.

Hanover Grand *6 Hanover Street, Mayfair, W1 (7499 7977/www.hanovergrand.com). Oxford Circus tube.* Map p398 J6.

Heaven *Under the Arches, off Villiers Street, WC2 (7930 2020/www.heaven-london.com). Charing Cross tube/rail.* Map p401 L7.

Herbal *12-14 Kingsland Road, Hoxton, E2 (7613 4462). Old Street tube/rail.* Map p403 R3.

Home *1 Leicester Square, WC2 (7909 0000/ information 0900 102 0107/www.homecorp.com). Leicester Square tube.* Map p401 K7.

Legends *29 Old Burlington Street, Mayfair, W1 (7437 9933/www.legends.co.uk). Piccadilly Circus tube.* Map p399 K6.

Mass *at The Brix, St Matthew's Church, Brixton Hill, Brixton, SW2 (7737 1016). Brixton tube/rail.*

Ministry of Sound *103 Gaunt Street, Walworth, SE1 (7378 6528/www.ministryofsound.co.uk). Elephant & Castle tube/rail.* Map p404 O10.

93 Feet East *150 Brick Lane, Spitalfields, E2 (7247 3293). Aldgate East tube.* Map p403 S5.

Plastic People *147-149 Curtain Road, Shoreditch, EC2 (7739 6471). Old Street tube/rail.* Map p403 R4.

Rock *Hungerford House, Victoria Embankment, WC2 (7976 2006). Embankment tube.* Map p401 L7.

Roof Gardens *99 Kensington High Street (entrance in Derry Street), Kensington, W8 (7937 7994). High Street Kensington tube.* Map p396 B9.

Scala *275 Pentonville Road, King's Cross, N1 (7833 2022/www.scala-london.co.uk). King's Cross tube/rail.* Map p399 L3.

Fabric – it's fab.

Subterania *12 Acklam Road (under the Westway), Ladbroke Grove, W10 (8960 4590). Ladbroke Grove tube.*

333 *333 Old Street, Hoxton, EC1 (7739 5949). Old Street tube/rail.* **Map** p403 Q4.

Turnmills *63 Clerkenwell Road, Clerkenwell, EC1 (7250 3409/www.turnmills.com). Farringdon tube/rail.* **Map** p402 N4.

Velvet Room *143 Charing Cross Road, Soho, WC2 (7734 4687/www.velvetroom.co.uk). Tottenham Court Road tube.* **Map** p399 K6.

The Wag *35 Wardour Street, Chinatown, W1 (7437 5534/www.wagclub.com). Piccadilly Circus tube.* **Map** p401 K7.

Club bars

The term 'club bar' has been coined to describe a growing number of bars that stay open later than 11pm, lay on DJs and charge for entry after a certain time. By doing all of this, they combine the conversation culture of pubs with the style, fashion and music of clubs. Here are some of our favourites.

AKA

18 West Central Street, St Giles's WC2 (7836 0110). Holborn or Tottenham Court Road tube. **Open** 6pm-1am Tue; 6pm-3am Wed-Fri; 7pm-3am Sat; closed Mon, Sun. **Map** p399 L6.

This highly rated bar and restaurant is an intimate companion to The End (*see p278*) next door, and is incorporated into its club nights on Saturdays. Expect to queue on busy nights.

Bug Bar

The Crypt, St Matthew's Peace Garden, Brixton Hill, Brixton, SW2 (7738 3184). Brixton tube/rail. **Open** 7pm-1am Mon-Thur; 7pm-3am Sat; 7-11pm Sun.

Laid-back yet resolutely alive, the perennially popular Bug Bar has regular entertainment such as bands, stand-ups and DJs.

Dogstar

389 Coldharbour Lane, Brixton, SW9 (7733 7515). Brixton tube/rail. **Open** noon-1am Mon-Thur; noon-3am Fri, Sat; noon-11pm Sun.

The southside club-bar crowd would probably be lost without this vibey and happening converted pub, home to a lot of fine and occasionally properly havin'-it party nights. Depending on the night, it can cost to get in.

Dust

27 Clerkenwell Road, Clerkenwell, EC1 (7490 5120). Farringdon tube/rail. **Open** 11am-11pm Mon-Wed; 11am-midnight Thur, Fri; 6pm-midnight Sat; noon-6pm Sun. **Map** p402 N4.

This classy DJ bar is a clever, simple space clad in wood and coppery paintwork. The drinks and food are pretty good, too.

Embassy Bar

119 Essex Road, N1 (7226 9849). Angel tube/38, 56, 73, 171A bus. **Open** 5-11pm Mon-Thur; 5pm-1am Fri; 2pm-1am Sat; 2-10.30pm Sun. **Map** p402 O1.

The Embassy boasts suave, retro Hollywood-style glamour design and an up-to-the-minute music policy, with guest DJs on Fridays and Saturdays.

Arts & Entertainment

timeout.com

The World's Living Guide

Boho in Shoho

Five years ago, many Londoners wouldn't have been able to find Shoreditch and Hoxton on a map. But now the area, recently (if spuriously) christened Shoho – as in *Sho*reditch and *Ho*xton – has taken over from Soho as the centre of London's freshest nightlife culture. Restaurants like **Cantaloupe** (*see p223*) and clubs like the brilliant Blue Note led the way, providing much-needed entertainment in an area previously famous only for YBAs (Young British Artists) and 'pioneering' loft-dwellers appropriating rundown Victorian warehouses. Though the Blue Note was forced to close, Cantaloupe still thrives. However, it's now surrounded by bar restaurants and club-bar hybrids – **Home** (*see p223*), the **Great Eastern Dining Room** (*see p225*), the **Dragon** (5 Leonard Street, EC2), **Cocomo** (323 Old Street, EC1) and the **Shoreditch Electricity Showrooms** (*see p225*) for funky drinkers – with more opening all the time.

The four-year-old **333** is the lynchpin of the club scene, a charmingly shabby venue that usually has a wonderful variety of entertainment ranged over its three floors – look out for nights like Off-Centre, Revolver and Renegade Pop Party in particular – but over the past year it's got fresh competition from **Plastic People**, **Cargo**, **Herbal** and **93 Feet East**. The former is a wonderful bar that thinks it's a club. Ade, its designer, owner and resident DJ, has ensured it has top-notch sound and air-conditioning in a lovely, intimate space. Cargo opened in December 2000 with three arches that promise MDF (Music, Dance, Food) but it's the eclectic, quality live music seven nights a week that should set it apart.

Herbal is another two-floor club bar that's free most nights and promises anything from dub reggae to Brit house in an environment that offers beers and sympathy on the top floor and a stylish dancefloor below. 93 Feet East, halfway down Brick Lane, is bigger and more ambitious, with a bundle of monthly nights on rotation that, in early 2001, were just finding their feet in a fresh venue.

Fluid

40 Charterhouse Street, Clerkenwell, EC1 (7253 3444). Farringdon tube/rail. **Open** noon-midnight Tue, Wed; noon-2am Thur, Fri; 7pm-2am Sat; closed Mon, Sun. **Map** p402 O5.
A great place to head to if you're on your way to Fabric, Fluid also acts as a nocturnal magnet in its own right, with a succession of successful monthly parties and some lovely sushi.

Form

4-5 Greek Street, Soho, W1 (7434 3323). Tottenham Court Road tube. **Open** 5pm-midnight Mon-Thur: 5pm-2am Fri; 5pm-3am Sat; closed Sun. **Map** p399 K6.
A fresh heart-of-Soho joint with some very groovy dance midweekers. Just the place to warm up or wind down when in W1.

Fridge Bar

1 Town Hall Parade, SW2 (7326 5100). Brixton tube/rail. **Open** 10am-2am Mon-Thur; 10am-4am Fri, Sat; 10am-12.30am Sun.
At weekends, the Fridge Bar functions as a fairly agreeable chill-down session (6-11am) for the club next door. Sometimes laid-back, sometimes packed.

Ion

165 Ladbroke Grove, W10 (8960 1702). Ladbroke Grove tube. **Open** noon-midnight daily.
This DJ bar is tucked almost underneath Ladbroke Grove station, yet is wonderfully light and airy, with a great terrace and a restaurant on the mezzanine.

Medicine Bar

181 Upper Street, Islington, N1 (7704 9536). Highbury & Islington tube/rail. **Open** 5pm-midnight Mon-Thur; noon-1am Fri, Sat; noon-11pm Sun.
A stylish and comfortable Islington hangout that fills with pre-clubbers as the after-work drinkers begin to fade away. Membership may be required.

Pop

14 Soho Street, Soho, W1 (7734 4004). Tottenham Court Road tube. **Open** 5pm-3am Mon-Thur; 5pm-4am Fri; 8pm-5am Sat; 6-11pm Sun. **Map** p399 K6.
A lovely '60s pop art-inspired venue on the north side of Soho Square, home to a diverse mix of groovy and glamorous parties. Dress to impress.

The Social Bar

5 Little Portland Street, Marylebone, W1 (7636 4992). Oxford Circus tube. **Open** noon-midnight Mon-Sat; 5-10.30pm Sun. **Map** p398 J5.
A smart, two-floor drinkery offering fine music nightly, the Social is the place you're most likely to spot a Manic Street Preacher, a Chemical Brother or a drunken record-biz press officer. It serves fine grub such as eggy bread to help soak up the beer.

WKD

18 Kentish Town Road, Camden, NW1 (7267 1869). Camden Town tube/Camden Road rail. **Open** noon-2am Mon-Thur; noon-3am Fri, Sat; noon-1am Sun.
WKD offers varied live music and DJs from 9.30pm daily. The snack food is decent, too.

Comedy

Where to find out why the chicken crossed the road.

The expansion of London's comedy scene happened a long time ago, and the capital's laughtermongers have now settled into a nice little cosy circuit. But while comedy in London is not as exciting and surprising as it was a decade or so ago, it's perhaps never been of a higher quality. Myriad comics ply their trade, and any one night will yield plenty of treats, whether well-known acts or young hopefuls.

The scene, for better or worse, is dominated by the **Comedy Store** and **Jongleurs** (for both, *see p283*), who pack their bills with big acts and charge accordingly. Away from the big players, lie smaller but cheaper – Ivor Dembina, when asked the difference between the Comedy Store and his own **Red Rose** (*see p283*), pithily replied 'Nine quid' – and equally worthwhile

enterprises, such as the **Banana Cabaret**, the **Comedy Café** (for both, *see below*) and **Up The Creek** (*see p284*). Other, still tinier clubs come and go in rooms above pubs on an almost weekly basis; check *Time Out* magazine for listings.

The best Comedy

Comedy Café
The comics' own favourite. 'Nuff said. See p282.

Comedy Store
London's biggest club still delivers the laughs. See p283.

Lee Hurst's Backyard Comedy Club
High-profile acts in a jolly atmosphere. See p283.

Red Rose Comedy Club
Full-length sets and a cheap bar add up to an ace operation. See p283.

Up the Creek
Raucous, lairy and terrific fun. See p284.

Comedy

Major venues

Banana Cabaret
The Bedford, 77 Bedford Hill, Balham, SW12 (8673 8904/www.bananacabaret.co.uk). Balham tube/rail. **Shows** 9pm Fri, Sat; 8.30pm second Sun of mth. **Admission** £10; £8 concessions. **No credit cards.**
The pub in which it's held may have been modernised, but little else changes at the Banana, which rolls on much as it has done for the last 18 years: with great comics and a friendly atmosphere, basically. Its popularity means you should arrive early: by 8.30pm on Fridays and 7.30pm on Saturdays. Post-laughter, a DJ entertains until 2am.

Canal Café Theatre
The Bridge House, Delamere Terrace, Little Venice, W2 (7289 6054/www.newsrevue.com). Royal Oak or Warwick Avenue tube. **Shows** 7.30pm, 9.30pm Mon-Sat; 7pm, 9pm Sun. **Admission** varies; phone for details. *Membership* £1. **Credit** MC, V. **Map** p394 C4.
The Canal Café Theatre hosts a wide range of entertainment, from the topical sketch show *Newsrevue* (Thur-Sun), which started in 1985 – though most of the jokes are slightly newer – to cabarets and serious drama. Food is available until 9.30pm.

Chuckle Club
London School of Economics, Houghton Street, Holborn, WC2 (7476 1672/www.chuckleclub.com). Holborn or Covent Garden tube. **Shows** 7.45pm Sat (during termtime). **Admission** £8; £6 concessions. **No credit cards. Map** p399 M6.
Another long-running club rightly noted for its fine bills and matey atmosphere, the latter helped by its location in a student bar. Still, we suspect that host Eugene Cheese may have changed his name in a bid to get ahead in show business.

Comedy Café
66 Rivington Street, Shoreditch, EC2 (7739 5706/ www.comedycafe.co.uk). Old Street tube/rail. **Shows** 9pm Wed-Sat. **Admission** free Wed; £3 Thur; £10 Fri; £12 Sat. **Credit** MC, V. **Map** p403 R4.
One of only a few purpose-built comedy clubs in London, the Comedy Café is also one of its finest laugh-houses: the line-ups are terrific – the club is a

The world-famous **Comedy Store**.

favourite of many comics – and the ambience matey. Students of human fallibility will find Wednesday's try-out night yields plenty of research material.

Comedy Store

Haymarket House, 1A Oxendon Street, St James's, SW1 (7344 0234/www.thecomedystore.co.uk). Leicester Square or Piccadilly Circus tube. **Shows** 8pm Tue-Sun; also midnight Fri, Sat. **Admission** £11-£15; £8-£12 concessions. **No credit cards. Map** p401 K7.
The first ever Comedy Store night was held in a Soho strip joint in the late 1970s, an inauspicious start for the club that is largely held to have kick-started alternative comedy. The bills now feature big-name stand-ups, with the Comedy Store Players providing improv on Wednesdays and Sundays, and Tuesday's revered Cutting Edge show offering a twist on stand-up.

Cosmic Comedy Club

177 Fulham Palace Road, Hammersmith, W6 (7381 2006/www.cosmiccomedy.co.uk). Hammersmith tube. **Shows** 9pm Tue, Thur; 8.30pm Fri, Sat. **Admission** free Tue; pay what you like Thur; £10 Fri; £12 Sat. **Credit** MC, V.
On Tuesdays, it's untried comics, with bigger acts appearing on Fridays and Saturdays. Thursdays fall in between, with the twist that while entry is free, you must pay to leave (whatever you think the show was worth). Food is available, and there's a disco until 2am on Fridays and Saturdays.

Downstairs at the King's Head

2 Crouch End Hill, Crouch End, N8 (pub 8340 1028/ office 01920 823265). Finsbury Park tube/rail, then W7 bus. **Shows** 8.30pm Wed-Sun. **Admission** free-£7. **No credit cards.**
Huw Thomas is resident host at this admirable and entertaining long-running club, which features a try-out night every Thursday and a mix of bigger names and new acts on Saturdays.

East Dulwich Cabaret

East Dulwich Tavern, 1 Lordship Lane, East Dulwich, SE22 (8299 4138). East Dulwich rail. **Shows** 9pm Mon, Thur, Sat. **Admission** *Mon, Thur* £3; £2 concessions. *Sat* £7; £5 concessions. **No credit cards.**
Mondays at this friendly club co-run by comic Steve Frost offer up established comics trying out new

material in an entertaining if hit-and-miss manner, while Saturdays offers conventional stand-up. On Thursdays, there's a pub quiz with a different comic each week posing the questions; terrific fun it is, too.

Jongleurs

Battersea *Bar Risa, 49 Lavender Gardens, SW11. Clapham Junction rail.* **Bow** *221 Grove Road, E3. Mile End tube.* **Camden** *Dingwalls, Middle Yard, Camden Lock, Chalk Farm Rd, NW1. Camden Town tube.* **Watford** *76 The Parade, Watford, Herts. Watford tube.* **All** *(7564 2500/0870 787 0707/ www.jongleurs.com)* **Shows** *Battersea* 8.45pm Fri; 7.15pm, 11.15pm Sat. *Bow* 8.15pm Fri, Sat. *Camden* 8.45pm Fri; 7.15pm, 11.15pm Sat. *Watford* 8pm Thur-Sat. **Admission** *Battersea, Camden* £14 Fri; £12 Sat. *Watford* £5 Thur; £12 Fri; £13 Sat. *Bow* £12 Fri; £13 Sat. **Credit** AmEx, MC, V.
What All Bar One is to London's pub scene, so is Jongleurs to the capital's comedy circuit. Still, the acts are usually biggish names of a high quality at all four of Jongleurs' London venues: the first-floor hall in Battersea, the purpose-built Bow club, the scruffy Camden site and the 400-capacity Watford operation. Food is available, and there's an after-show disco on every night at Bow and Watford, and on Fridays at Battersea and Camden. Doors close a half-hour before the times listed above; booking is advised.

Lee Hurst's Backyard Comedy Club

231-237 Cambridge Heath Road, Bethnal Green, E2 (7739 3122/www.leehurst.com). Bethnal Green tube. **Shows** 8.30pm Fri, Sat. **Admission** *Fri* £10, £7 concessions. *Sat* £11, £10 advance. **Credit** MC, V.
The Backyard, which opened in September 1998, is owned and operated by comic Lee Hurst, whose industry clout and avowed intention to treat comics with the respect they don't always command in other clubs means that consistently excellent bills are the norm. Food is available here, too, and discos follow the shows.

Meccano Club

The Dove Regent, 65 Graham Street, Islington, N1 (7813 4478/www.themeccanoclub.co.uk). Angel tube. **Shows** 9pm Fri, Sat. **Admission** £6; £5 concessions. **No credit cards. Map** p402 O2.
Another of the comics' favourites, the Meccano has slotted into this new pub venue with speed and aplomb. Up-and-coming names rub shoulders with the up-and-came-already here twice a week.

Red Rose Comedy Club

129 Seven Sisters Road, Finsbury Park, N7 (7281 3051). Finsbury Park tube/rail. **Shows** 9pm Sat. **Admission** £6; £5 concessions. *Membership* £1. **No credit cards.**
Acts at the Red Rose are permitted – encouraged, even – by comic and club founder Ivor Dembina to do long sets rather than just the 20-minute routines allowed by most clubs. As such, this is where to come if you want to see big-name acts without the usual timing constraints.

Arts & Entertainment

Up the Creek

302 Creek Road, Greenwich, SE10 (8858 4581).
Greenwich DLR/rail. **Shows** 9pm Fri-Sun.
Admission *Fri* £10; £6 concessions; £2 local
students. *Sat* £14; £10 concessions. *Sun* £6; £4
concessions; £2 local students. **Credit** AmEx, MC, V.
Eccentric London comedy legend Malcolm Hardee
runs this noisy bearpit of a club. The atmosphere is
unforgiving – especially for new acts – but some sort
of entertainment is guaranteed. There's also food
and a disco until 2am on Fridays and Saturdays.

Other venues

One-off nights in venues that aren't dedicated to
comedy come and go with astonishing rapidity:
always phone to check that the clubs listed
below – all of which take place weekly – are
still operating before setting out.

In addition, look out for the plethora of
comedy events in July, as many comics try out
new shows in the capital before heading north to
Edinburgh for the Fringe Festival the following
month. Chief among the pre-Edinburgh venues
is the **Battersea Arts Centre** (*see p333*),
which stages a whole festival of new shows that
are shortly to make the trip north.

Acton Bearcat *King's Head, Acton High Street,
Acton, W3 (8891 1852).* **Shows** Fri.
Aztec Comedy Club *The Borderland, 47-49
Westow Street, Norwood, SE19 (8771 0885).*
Shows Fri.
Bearcat Club *Turk's Head, Winchester Road, St
Margarets, Twickenham, Middx (8891 1852).*
Shows Sat.
Bound & Gagged Palmers Green *The Fox, 413
Green Lanes, Palmers Green, N13 (8450 4100/
www.boundandgaggedcomedy.com).* **Shows** Fri.
Bound & Gagged Tufnell Park *Tufnell Park
Tavern, 162 Tufnell Park Road, Tufnell Park, N7
(8450 4100/www.boundandgaggedcomedy.com).*
Shows Sat.
Buccaneers Comedy *The Hope, Tottenham
Street, Fitzrovia, W1 (07931 551520).* **Shows** Tue.
Map p398 J5.
Comedy at Soho-Ho *Crown & Two Chairmen,
31 Dean Street, Soho, W1 (07956 996690).*
Shows Sat. **Map** p399 K6.
Comedy Brewhouse *Camden Head, 2 Camden
Walk, Camden Passage, Islington, N1 (7359 0851).*
Shows Fri, Sat. **Map** p402 O2.
Comedy Spot *The Spot, Maiden Lane, Covent
Garden, WC2 (7379 5900).* **Shows** Mon.
Map p401 L7.
Ha Bloody Ha *Ealing Studios (Whitehouse
entrance), Ealing Green, St Mary's Road, Ealing,
W5 (8566 4067).* **Shows** Fri.
Hackney Empire *291 Mare Street, Hackney, E8
(8985 2424).* **Shows** days vary.
Hampstead Comedy Club *The Washington,
England's Lane, Hampstead, NW3 (8299 2601,
3.30-6.30pm Sat only).* **Shows** Sat.
Hen & Chickens Theatre *109 St Paul's Road,
Highbury Corner, N1 (7704 2001).* **Shows** days vary.

The **Chuckle Club**. *See p282.*

Oranje Boom Boom *Upstairs at De Hems,
Macclesfield Street, Chinatown, W1 (7275 0118).*
Shows Wed. **Map** p401 K6.
Tut & Shive Cabaret *The Tut & Shive,
235 Upper Street, Islington, N1 (7359 7719).*
Shows Sun. **Map** p402 O1.

Spoken word

Away from the thriving comedy circuit, London
also has a decent spoken word scene. Regular
nights range from open poetry workshops (see
Time Out's weekly Books section for details) to
Vox 'n' Roll, where authors read from their
books and pick the evening's music. In addition,
London boasts a great many literary festivals,
of which the biggest is September's **The Word**
(7837 2555, www.theword.org.uk), while many
central London bookstores, **Borders** and
Waterstone's among them (for both, *see
p229*) host regular readings by writers with a
book to plug. Below, though, are listed some of
the bigger spoken word clubs and venues.

Apples & Snakes *Battersea Arts Centre, Lavender
Hill, Battersea, SW11 (7223 2223/www.bac.org.uk).*
Shows Fri, fortnightly.
Express Excess *Enterprise, 2 Haverstock Hill,
Chalk Farm, NW3 (7485 2659).* **Shows** Wed.
Poetry Café *22 Betterton Street, Covent Garden,
WC2 (7420 9880/www.poetrysoc.com).* **Shows** Tue;
other nights vary. **Map** p399 L6.
Voicebox *Level 5, Royal Festival Hall, South Bank,
SE1 (7960 4242).* **Shows** nights vary. **Map** p401 M8.
Vox 'n' Roll *Filthy McNasty's, 68 Amwell Street,
Finsbury, EC1 (7837 6067).* **Shows** Wed.
Map p402 N3.

Dance

Let's face the music and…

London has a huge variety of dance shows and classes for those moved by pirouettes, twirls, jigs and spins. Venues such as the **Barbican Centre** (*see below*), the **Royal Opera House** and **Sadler's Wells** (for both, *see p286*) attract the world's best companies, choreographers and dancers to their boards, while the dance schools that operate out of the city's many studios, halls and attics can teach you how to swing, sway, salsa and tango like the stars (*see p288*).

As well as the performances and venues below, check the weekly listings in *Time Out*. The magazine's dance pages include details on a gamut of fringe shows and more 'mainstream' productions, the latter often held at venues not used solely for dance events (such as *Lord of the Dance* at Wembley Arena) or in West End theatres (such as all-conquering blockbuster *The Lion King*, for which *see p332*).

The **London Dance Network** website (www.london-dance.net) comprises some 50 artists, venues, producers and agencies whose brief is to promote awareness of the strength and diversity of dance in London. And try to stop by at **Dance Books**. Located just off the Charing Cross Road at 15 Cecil Court, WC2 (7836 2314), it's the world's sole specialist shop for new and used dance books.

Major venues

Barbican Centre

Silk Street, The City, EC2 (box office 7638 8891/ enquiries 7638 4141/www.barbican.org.uk). Barbican tube/Moorgate tube/rail. **Box office** 9am-8pm daily. **Tickets** £6-£30. **Credit** AmEx, MC, V. **Map** p402 P5.

This arts centre in the heart of the City (*see also p306*) has hosted some excellent shows since it entered the world of dance a few years back. The fourth BITE:01 season (May-Oct 2001) looks set to include Sweden's Cullberg Ballet and the acclaimed choreographer Mats Ek presenting a dramatic interpretation of *Swan Lake*, and Belgium contemporary dance company Rosas, under choreographer Anne Teresa De Keersmaeker, will be performing *I Said I*.

ICA

The Mall, Westminster, SW1 (7930 3647/ membership 7873 0062/www.ica.org.uk). Piccadilly Circus tube/Charing Cross tube/rail. **Box office** noon-9.30pm daily. **Tickets** prices vary; average £8. **Credit** AmEx, DC, MC, V. **Map** p401 K8.

The intimate space of the Institute of Contemporary Arts is the setting for experimental, movement-based theatre and performance with an avant-garde flavour. A balance is struck between emerging talent and established artists. The London International Mime Festival (*see p266*) is a regular visitor each January. Compulsory day membership costs £1-£1.50 extra.

London Coliseum

St Martin's Lane, Covent Garden, WC2 (box office 7632 8300/minicom 7836 7666/www.eno.org). Leicester Square tube/Charing Cross tube/rail. **Box office** 24hrs daily. **Tickets** £3-£58; day tickets on sale to personal callers after 10am Mon-Fri; by telephone from 12.30pm Mon-Fri. **Credit** AmEx, DC, MC, V. **Map** p401 L7.

The beautiful, spacious Coliseum is home to the English National Opera (ENO) for most of the year, and is usually visited by major dance companies over summer and at Christmas. The June-July 2000 ENO season saw a Mark Morris collaboration with Peter Sellars on the staging of John Adams' *Nixon in China*. Restoration work means there will be no summer dance in 2001, but the Christmas season will start as usual in December.

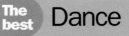

The best Dance

Dance Umbrella

Eclectic, eccentric, exciting and one of London's best arts festivals. *See p287.*

The Place

This terrific contemporary dance theatre reopens in autumn 2001. *See p286.*

Sadler's Wells

Great performances in a wonderfully modern theatre (pictured). *See p286.*

Arts & Entertainment

Sylvie Guillem returns to the **Royal Opera House** in 2001.

The Place

17 Duke's Road, Somers Town, WC1 (7380 1268/ www.theplace.org.uk). Euston tube/rail. **Box office** 10.30am-6pm Mon-Fri; noon-6pm Sat; closed Sun. **Tickets** £7-£12. **Credit** MC, V. **Map** p399 K3.

A venue entirely dedicated to contemporary dance, the Place's theatre is under redevelopment: there'll be no shows until Dance Umbrella in October 2001, which will be followed by new works and, in early 2002, Resolution!. Its facilities, though, remain open and include a dance video library, an information centre, top-notch dance training and classes for all levels of ability, and an excellent vegetarian café.

Riverside Studios

Crisp Road, Hammersmith, W6 (8237 1000/box office 8237 1111). Hammersmith tube. **Box office** noon-9pm daily. **Tickets** £7-£15. **Credit** MC, V.

This leading arts and media centre occasionally hosts British contemporary dance and physical theatre in three auditoria. There's a pleasant bar/café, restaurant and bookshop and wheelchair access to all ground-floor areas. Parts of Dance Umbrella (*see p287* **Dance festivals**) take place here in October and November.

Royal Opera House

Bow Street, Covent Garden, WC2 (box office 7304 4000/enquiries 7240 1200/minicom 7212 9228/ www.royaloperahouse.org). **Box office** 10am-8pm Mon-Sat; closed Sun. **Tickets** £6-£65. **Credit** AmEx, DC, MC, V. **Map** p401 L7.

A magnificent theatre. In addition to the main space (home to the Royal Ballet), there's the Linbury Studio Theatre, seating up to 420 people and staging lunchtime opera and music recitals, and the Clore Studio Upstairs, hosting dance workshops, events and small-scale performances.

During the day, the public has access to the restored Vilar Floral Hall, the Amphitheatre Bar leading to a loggia with a view over Covent Garden Piazza, a shop and a coffee shop; there's also a programme of free lunchtime concerts and events,

exhibitions, daily tours, conferences, study days and improved access for people with disabilities. Ticket prices were cut following the refurbishment, though those for the best seats remain horrendously high. (Note that most of the cheapest tickets are for, not surprisingly, restricted view seats.)

The Royal Ballet's standards of performance can be variable and the programming unadventurous, but you'll have the chance to see stars of the calibre of Sylvie Guillem, Tamara Rojo, Roberto Bolle and Sarah Wildor. In 2001, there's *Romeo and Juliet* in March and April; *Giselle* in April and May; and a 'Stravinsky Staged' season, with *The Firebird, Agon* and *Les Noces*. The summer season, too, promises to be spectacular, with the visit of the Kirov Ballet (11 June-7 July). The repertoire encompasses a new production of *Le Corsaire,* the London premieres of Kenneth MacMillan's *Menon,* and of *Apollo* and *Serenade* by the Kirov, plus performances of *Sleeping Beauty, Swan Lake, Jewels* and *Symphony in C.* In August, the Royal Ballet will present two full-length ballets, *Coppélia* and *Swan Lake,* and a mixed programme in tribute to retiring director Sir Anthony Dowell. Also in August, on its first visit to London, the Opera Ballet of La Scala, Milan will present one week of Sylvie Guillem's production of *Giselle. See also p307.*

Sadler's Wells

Rosebery Avenue, Islington, EC1 (7863 8000/ www.sadlers-wells.com). Angel tube. **Box office** 10am-8.30pm Mon-Sat; closed Sun. **Tickets** £8.50-£37.50. **Credit** AmEx, MC, V. **Map 9 N3** *Peacock Theatre, Portugal Street, off Kingsway, Holborn, WC2 (7863 8222/www.sadlers-wells.com). Holborn tube.* **Box office** noon-8.30pm performance days, 10am-6pm when no performances Mon-Sat; closed Sun. **Tickets** £7.50-£35. **Credit** AmEx, MC, V. **Map** p399 M6.

An institution in the London dance world, Sadler's Wells attracts world-class dance companies to its ultra-modern theatre. Among the scheduled performances for 2001 are Houston Ballet, making its new

Dance festivals

The esteemed **Dance Umbrella** (8741 5881, www.danceumbrella.co.uk), now in its 23rd year, is one of the world's top contemporary dance festivals. Held for five weeks from early October, it features a stimulating mix of proven British and international companies, as well as a number of lesser-known discoveries, at a range venues across London.

The fourth **BITE** season opens in May 2001 and brings an eclectic programme of theatre, dance and music to the Barbican Centre (*see p285*). In 2001, work by acclaimed choreographers Mats Ek and Anne Teresa De Keersmaeker should prove among the highlights.

Each August, the South Bank Centre (*see below*) hosts the month-long **Blitz**. Britain's biggest and most diverse community dance festival, it's a cornucopia of free dance performances, lectures and workshops. Also in August, Sadler's Wells (*see p286*) and Jacksons Lane Dancebase (*see below*) co-present **Mosaics**. This season of small-scale events, with young companies performing new dance and physical theatre, is a veritable dance-athon.

Sadler's Wells debut with a mixed programme, and the UK premiere of *Cleopatra* (3-7 Apr), and the Belgrade Theatre, Coventry presenting Roald Dahl's *The Twits* (17-21 Apr).

Other events later in the year look similarly appealing. Paco Peña's *Musa Gitana* was a hit at the Peacock Theatre in spring 1999, and now this Andalusian story, with all the exuberance and artistry of flamenco, is back in London for a second season (23-28 Apr). The following month, the Birmingham Royal Ballet returns to its original home with David Bintley's two-part ballet cycle featuring the world premiere of *Arthur Part II* (8-12 May), and Canadian-born artistic director Wayne Eagling brings his Dutch National Ballet to Sadler's Wells for the first time with two programmes including work by George Balanchine, Krzysztof Pastor and Hans van Manen (15-19 May). Rambert Dance Company, Britain's oldest dance company, marks its 75th anniversary with a two-week season (12-23 Jun) that includes new works by artistic director Christopher Bruce, Richard Alston and Wayne McGregor.

The considerably smaller Lilian Baylis Theatre is also on site in Islington, though the organisation has also retained its second home, the Peacock Theatre in Holborn, for younger companies and longer runs of more populist fare (tango, flamenco and urban street dance).

South Bank Centre

Belvedere Road, South Bank, SE1 (box office 7960 4242/recorded information 7921 0682/ www.sbc.org.uk). Embankment tube/Waterloo tube/ rail. **Box office** 10am-9pm daily. **Tickets** £5-£60. **Credit** AmEx, DC, MC, V. **Map** p401 M8.

This massive and rather austere arts complex has a wonderful view of the Thames and excellent programming. British and international dance companies perform regularly at its three venues: the massive Royal Festival Hall, the medium-sized Queen Elizabeth Hall and the smaller Purcell Room. Highlights for 2001 include CandoCo, performing pieces by Javier de Frutos and Doug Elkins (May), and the Arc Dance Company, which celebrates its 15th anniversary with a mixed bill that includes the award-winning *Orfeo* (June).

Every August, the SBC hosts the fine free dance festival Blitz; some of the higher-profile Dance Umbrella events can be seen here as well. For both, *see above* **Dance festivals**; and for more on the South Bank Centre, *see p307*.

Other venues

The Bull Theatre

68 High Street, Barnet, Herts (8449 0048). High Barnet tube. **Box office** 10am-8.30pm Tue-Sat; 1-8.30pm Sun; closed Mon. **Tickets** £6-£10. **Credit** MC, V.

The Bull hosts a broad range of dance performances (around two a month), mostly by contemporary and world – especially Asian – dance companies.

Chisenhale Dance Space

64-84 Chisenhale Road, Bow, E3 (8981 6617/ www.chisenhale.demon.co.uk). Bethnal Green or Mile End tube. **Box office** 10am-6pm Mon-Sat; closed Sun. **Tickets** free-£4. **No credit cards**.

A seminal research centre for contemporary dance and movement-based disciplines of a more experimental, work-in-progress nature, the Chisenhale also features a range of activities including workshops. It also hosts a summer school for experienced dancers in collaboration with Greenwich Dance Agency and Independent Dance.

Cochrane Theatre

Southampton Row, Holborn, WC1 (7242 7040). Holborn tube. **Box office** 10am-6pm Mon-Fri; times vary Sat; closed Sun. **Tickets** £4-£15. **Credit** MC, V. **Map** p399 L5.

This small West End theatre programmes dance performances from classical to contemporary.

Jacksons Lane Dancebase

269A Archway Road, Highgate, N6 (8341 4421/ jacksonslane@pop3.poptel.org.uk). Highgate tube. **Open** 10am-10pm daily. **Tickets** £8; £6 concessions. **Credit** MC, V.

This community centre presents an admirable number of dance performances and activities, with lots of contemporary and new dance.

Arts & Entertainment

Laban Centre

Laurie Grove, New Cross, SE14 (8692 4070/ www.laban.co.uk). New Cross or New Cross Gate tube/rail. **Open** 8.30am-5.30pm Mon-Fri; 9am-3.30pm Sat, Sun. **Tickets** £6.50; £5 concessions.

An independent conservatory for contemporary dance training and research that runs undergraduate and postgraduate courses, adult, children's and youth dance classes, specialist short courses and Easter and summer schools. Other facilities at the Laban Centre include a dance library and a studio offering Pilates-based body conditioning. It's also home to the dynamic Transitions dance company, and performances featuring work by emerging contemporary dance choreographers are regularly presented in the Bonnie Bird Theatre. The Centre publishes the excellent *Dance Theatre Journal* (available by mail order).

Studio Theatre

North Westminster Community School, North Wharf Road, Paddington, W2 (7641 8424/ studiot@globalnet.co.uk). Edgware Road tube. **Box office** 10am-5pm Mon-Fri; closed Sat, Sun. **Tickets** £6; £4 concessions. **No credit cards. Map** p395 D5.

This theatre hosts about 20 dance shows a year, from traditional to contemporary. Bullies Ballerinas dance company is resident at the studio.

Danceworks. Ouch.

Dance classes

Dance Attic

368 North End Road, Fulham, SW6 (7610 2055). Fulham Broadway tube. **Membership** £1.50/day; £30/6mths; £50/yr. **Classes** £3-£4. **Map** p396 A12.

This centre in Fulham has a wide range of dance classes, including ballet, jazz, flamenco, lambada, salsa and hip hop, for all levels of expertise. Clappy Hour, every Saturday, is a showcase for singers, dancers and musicians to exhibit their talents (admission is free). Membership is required.

Danceworks

16 Balderton Street, Mayfair, W1 (7629 6183). Bond Street tube. **Membership** £1-£4/day; £25/mth; £90/yr. **Classes** £4-£7. **Map** p398 G6.

Danceworks runs a variety of dance classes including Afro, contemporary, salsa and ballet.

Drill Hall

16 Chenies Street, Fitzrovia, WC1 (7637 8270). Goodge Street tube. **Courses** £25-£60. **Map** p399 K5.

This central fringe venue provides classes in Latin American, tango, lindy hop, t'ai-chi and more.

Greenwich Dance Agency

Borough Hall, Royal Hill, Greenwich, SE10 (8293 9741/http://web.ukonline.co.uk/greenwich.dance). Greenwich rail/DLR. **Classes** £3.50-£5.

Daily professional-level contemporary classes, workshops and occasional intensives run by established artists are offered here.

Islington Arts Factory

2 Parkhurst Road, Holloway, N7 (7607 0561/ www.cerbernet.co.uk/iaf). Caledonian Road or Holloway Road tube/29, 43, 91, 253, 279 bus. **Membership** £3 term; £5 2 terms; £8 annual. **Classes** £3.50-£6.

Classes in ballet, Egyptian, jazz, contemporary, salsa and mime are held at this lively arts centre.

London School of Capoeira

Units 1 & 2, Leeds Place, Tollington Park, Finsbury Park, N4 (7281 2020). Finsbury Park tube/rail. **Classes** 7-9pm Mon, Wed, Fri. **Fees** *Beginners' course* (four lessons) £75; £65 concessions; £55 under-18s. **Map** p399 K3.

Capoeira is a popular fusion of dance, gymnastics and martial arts. Free demonstration sessions are held every Friday (8-10pm), and introductory workshops every month.

Morley College

61 Westminster Bridge Road, Lambeth, SE1 (7450 9232/www.morleycollege.ac.uk). Lambeth North tube. **Membership** £1.50/yr. **Classes** £6-£14 one-day workshop; £7-£43 10 classes. **Map** p401 M9.

A broad portfolio of dance classes and courses at all levels is held at this adult education centre.

Pineapple Dance Studio

7 Langley Street, Covent Garden, WC2 (7836 4004/ www.pineapple.uk.com). Covent Garden tube. **Membership** £1-£4/day; £50-£100/yr. **Classes** £4-£6. **Map** p399 L6.

Centrally located, this popular dance centre boasts a wide choice of classes, with an emphasis on ballet, jazz and commercial genres.

Film

Decent British movies may be few and far between these days, but London's many and varied cinemas offer treats from all over the planet.

It's not only the movies that are American in London cinemas: it's the cinemas themselves. In common with almost everywhere in western Europe, cinemas all over the capital are being converted into multiplexes, often indistinct from one other in all but the level of extortion carried out at the box office (seeing a new movie in central London is as pricey as anywhere in the world). However, in fairness to the chains, they're really no different to McDonald's in that you can at least be sure of what you're getting: in this case, a high technical spec (especially in Leicester Square, home to the biggest cinemas in town), comfy seats, endless ads before the movie and overpriced popcorn. Take it or leave it.

However, despite some organisations' best efforts, the local character hasn't been sapped out of London's movie circuit just yet. In the **National Film Theatre**, whose programme is a mix of new-ish releases, classic flicks and rare gems, the city has one of the best rep cinemas in Europe, while the **Everyman** and the **Ritzy** all offer a welcome change from the flat-packed norm if it's a new release you're after.

For full details on screenings in London, check the comprehensive weekly listings and reviews in *Time Out* magazine. And if you've got kids with you, then be sure to check the movie's classification. Films released in the UK are classified under the following categories: **U** – suitable for all ages; **PG** – open to all; parental guidance is advised; **12** – no one under the age of 12 is admitted; **15** – no one under 15 is admitted; **18** – no one under 18 is admitted.

Cinemas

First-run cinemas

London's first-run cinemas are many and varied. On one hand, there's the fantastic 1,943-seat screen at the **Odeon Leicester Square**; on the other, the five horrendously tiny 60-seat cinemas that make up the **Odeon Mezzanine**. In one corner, multiplexes such as the **Warner Village West End** and **UCI Whiteleys**; in the opposite corner, the **Metro** and **Renoir**, which quietly devote themselves to artier new releases. On one side, the big chains such as **UGC**; opposing them, independent operations like the **Ritzy** and the **Tricycle**.

Prices vary greatly, but, some rules hold firm for almost all first-run cinemas. The closer to Leicester Square you are, the more you'll pay. If you go on Mondays or before 5pm from Tuesday to Friday, you'll likely pay a few quid less for your seat (exact days and times vary from cinema, but we've detailed the reduced prices as 'Early shows' in our listings below). And if you're planning on going to see a big blockbuster flick on the weekend of its release – new films emerge in the UK every Friday – then be sure to book in advance.

The City

Barbican *Silk Street, EC2 (information 7382 7000/bookings 7638 8891/www.barbican.org.uk).* *Barbican tube/Moorgate tube/rail.* **Screens** 2. **Tickets** £6.50; £4.50 concessions. *Early shows* £3.80. **Credit** AmEx, MC, V. **Map** p402 P5.

Bloomsbury & Fitzrovia

Odeon Tottenham Court Road (formerly ABC) *Tottenham Court Road, W1 (0870 505 0007/ www.odeon.co.uk).* *Tottenham Court Road tube.* **Screens** 3. **Tickets** £7; £4.50 concessions. *Early shows* £4.50. **Credit** AmEx, MC, V. **Map** p399 K5.
Renoir *Brunswick Centre, Brunswick Square, WC1 (7837 8402).* *Russell Square tube.* **Screens** 1. **Tickets** £6.50. *Early shows* £4.50; £3 concessions. **Credit** MC, V. **Map** p401 L4.

The best Cinemas

For the all-in, bells 'n' whistles multiplex experience
The **Warner Village West End** (*see p290*).

For a *big* big screen
The **Odeon Leicester Square** (*see p290*).

For bona fide movie buffs
The **National Film Theatre** (*see p292*).

For smokers
The **Notting Hill Coronet** (*see p292*).

For wacked-out weirdness
The **Lux** (*see p292*).

For a post-flick beer
The **Ritzy** (*see p292*).

Arts & Entertainment

Marylebone

Odeon Marble Arch *10 Edgware Road, W2 (0870 505 0007/www.odeon.co.uk). Marble Arch tube.* **Screens** 5. **Tickets** £7.50; £5 concessions (select times). **Credit** AmEx, MC, V. **Map** p395 F6.

Screen on Baker Street *96 Baker Street, NW1 (information 7486 0036/bookings 7935 2772/ www.screencinemas.co.uk). Baker Street tube/ Marylebone tube/rail.* **Screens** 2. **Tickets** £6.50. *Early shows* £4. **Credit** MC, V. **Map** p398 G5.

Mayfair & St James's

Curzon Mayfair *38 Curzon Street, W1 (7465 8865). Green Park or Hyde Park Corner tube.* **Screens** 1. **Tickets** £7.50; £4-£5 concessions (select times). *Early shows* £5. **Credit** AmEx, MC, V. **Map** p400 H8.

ICA Cinema *Nash House, The Mall, SW1 (information 7930 6393/bookings 7930 3647/ www.ica.org.uk). Piccadilly Circus tube/Charing Cross tube/rail.* **Screens** 2. **Tickets** £6.50. *Early shows* £4.50. *Membership* £15-£25/yr, allows £2 off all tickets. **Credit** AmEx, DC, MC, V. **Map** p401 K8.

Odeon Haymarket *48 Haymarket, SW1 (0870 505 0007/www.odeon.co.uk). Piccadilly Circus tube.* **Screens** 1. **Tickets** £6.50-£8. *Early shows* £3.50-£5. **Credit** AmEx, MC, V. **Map** p401 K7.

Odeon Panton Street *(formerly ABC) Panton Street, SW1 (0870 505 0007/www.odeon.co.uk). Piccadilly Circus tube.* **Screens** 4. **Tickets** £6.50-£7; £3-£4.50 concessions (select times). *Early shows* £4.50. **Credit** AmEx, MC, V. **Map** p401 K7.

Odeon Piccadilly *(formerly ABC) Piccadilly, W1 (0870 505 0007/www.odeon.co.uk). Piccadilly Circus tube.* **Screens** 2. **Tickets** £6; £2.80-£4.30 concessions (select times). *Early shows* £4.30. **Credit** AmEx, MC, V. **Map** p400 J7.

Plaza *17-25 Regent Street, W1 (0870 010 2030/ www.uci-cinemas.co.uk). Piccadilly Circus tube.* **Screens** 4. **Tickets** £6, £4 concessions. *Early shows* £4. **Credit** AmEx, MC, V. **Map** p401 K7.

UGC Haymarket *(formerly Virgin) 63-65 Haymarket, W1 (0870 907 0712). Piccadilly Circus tube.* **Screens** 3. **Tickets** £8.50; £5-£6 concessions (select times). **Credit** AmEx, MC, V. **Map** p401 K7.

UGC Trocadero *(formerly Virgin) Trocadero, WC2 (0870 907 0716). Leicester Square or Piccadilly Circus tube.* **Screens** 7. **Tickets** £8.50; £5-£6 concessions. **Credit** AmEx, MC, V. **Map** p401 K7.

Soho & Leicester Square

Curzon Soho *93-107 Shaftesbury Avenue, W1 (information 7439 4805/bookings 7734 2255). Leicester Square or Piccadilly Circus tube.* **Screens** 3. **Tickets** £8; £5 concessions (select times). *Early shows* £5. **Credit** MC, V. **Map** p401 K6.

Empire *Leicester Square, WC2 (information 0870 603 4567/bookings 0990 888990/ www.uci-cinemas.co.uk). Leicester Square or Piccadilly Circus tube.* **Screens** 3. **Tickets** £7.50-£9.50; £5-£6 concessions (select times). *Early shows* £5-£6. **Credit** AmEx, MC, V. **Map** p401 K7.

Metro *Rupert Street, W1 (information 7437 0757/ bookings 7734 1506/www.metrocinema.co.uk). Leicester Square or Piccadilly Circus tube.* **Screens** 2. **Tickets** £6.50; £4 concessions (select times). *Early shows* £4. **Credit** AmEx, DC, MC, V. **Map** p401 K7.

Odeon Leicester Square *Leicester Square, WC2 (0870 505 0007/www.odeon.co.uk). Leicester Square tube.* **Screens** 1. **Tickets** £9.50-£10; £6-£6.50 concessions (select times). *Early shows* £6-£6.50. **Credit** AmEx, MC, V. **Map** p401 K7.

Odeon Mezzanine *adjacent to Odeon Leicester Square, WC2 (0870 505 0007/www.odeon.co.uk). Leicester Square tube.* **Screens** 5. **Tickets** £7.50; £5 concessions (select times). *Early shows* £5. **Credit** AmEx, MC, V. **Map** p401 K7.

Odeon Swiss Centre *10 Wardour Street, W1 (0870 505 0007/www.odeon.co.uk). Leicester Square or Piccadilly Circus tube.* **Screens** 4. **Tickets** £7; £4.50 concessions (select times). *Early shows* £4.50. **Credit** AmEx, MC, V. **Map** p401 K7.

Odeon West End *Leicester Square, WC2 (0870 505 0007/www.odeon.co.uk). Leicester Square tube.* **Screens** 2. **Tickets** £9.50; £6 concessions (select times). *Early shows* £6.* **Credit** AmEx, MC, V. **Map** p401 K7.

Warner Village West End *Leicester Square, WC2 (information 7437 4347/bookings 7437 4343/ www.warnervillage.co.uk). Leicester Square tube.* **Screens** 9. **Tickets** £10; £5-£7 concessions (select times). *Early shows* £7. **Credit** MC, V. **Map** p401 K7.

Covent Garden & St Giles's

Odeon Shaftesbury Avenue *(formerly ABC) 135 Shaftesbury Avenue, W1 (0870 505 0007/ www.odeon.co.uk). Leicester Square or Tottenham Court Road tube.* **Tickets** £7.50; £5 concessions (select times). *Early shows* £5. **Screens** 2. **Credit** AmEx, MC, V. **Map** p399 K6.

Chelsea & South Kensington

Chelsea Cinema *206 King's Road, SW3 (7351 3742). Sloane Square tube.* **Screens** 1. **Tickets** £7-£8. *Early shows* £5; £3 concessions. **Credit** AmEx, MC, V. **Map** p397 E12.

UGC Chelsea *(formerly Virgin) 279 King's Road, SW3 (0870 907 0710). Sloane Square tube, then 11, 19, 22 bus.* **Screens** 4. **Tickets** £8; £5.50 concessions; £5.20 under 15s (select times). **Credit** MC, V. **Map** p397 E12.

Screen on the Green. *See p291.*

Festivals

London Lesbian & Gay Film Festival

National Film Theatre, South Bank, SE1 (7928 3232/www.llgff.org.uk/www.bfi.org.uk). Embankment tube/Waterloo tube/rail. **Dates** 29 Mar-12 Apr 2001. **Map** p401 M7.
Over 60 new and restored films from around the world, plus a plethora of special events, highlight this annual event, which goes on to tour the country after its London run.

Rushes Soho Shorts Festival

venues around Soho, W1 (7851 6207/ www.sohoshorts.com). Leicester Square, Piccadilly Circus or Tottenham Court Road tube. **Dates** 1wk during July/Aug 2001 (check website for exact dates). **Map** p398, p399.
A great enterprise, this, in which 60 or so short films, music videos and idents by new directors are screened for free at venues across Soho, from cafés to cinemas. At the end of the week, prizes are awarded for the pick of the pack.

BBC British Short Film Festival

Empire, Leicester Square, WC2 (8743 8000 x6222/www.britishshortfilmfest.com). Leicester Square tube. **Dates** 1wk during Sept 2001 (check website for exact dates). **Map** p401 K7.

A selection of, yes, British short films: around 300 of them, to be precise. In addition to the Empire screenings, videos are usually shown at Planet Hollywood in Leicester Square.

Latin American Film Festival

Metro, Rupert Street, Chinatown, W1 (7434 3357/www.metrocinema.co.uk). Leicester Square or Piccadilly Circus tube. **Dates** Sept 2001 (call for exact dates). **Map** p401 K7.
This entertaining little festival does exactly what it says on the tin, with a range of new movies from Latin America on offer each autumn.

Raindance

Metro, Rupert Street, Chinatown, W1 (7287 3833/www.raindance.co.uk). Leicester Square or Piccadilly Circus tube. **Date** 2wks during Oct 2001 (call for exact dates). **Map** p401 K7.
Britain's largest festival devoted exclusively to independent film: 85 per cent of the content is produced by first-time directors.

London Film Festival

venues around London (7928 3232/ www.lff.org.uk). **Date** 2wks during Nov 2001 (check website for exact dates).
The biggest of them all. For full details on the LFF, *see p265*.

North London

Everyman Hampstead *5 Hollybush Vale, Hampstead, NW3 (information 7431 1818/bookings 7431 1777/www.everymancinema.com). Hampstead tube.* Screens 1. Tickets £4-£6.50; £4 concessions (select times). *Early shows* £5.50. Credit MC, V.
Odeon Camden Town *Parkway, Camden, NW1 (0870 505 0007/www.odeon.co.uk). Camden Town tube.* Screens 5. Tickets £6.50; £3.50-£4.50 concessions (select times). Credit AmEx, MC, V.
Odeon Swiss Cottage *96 Finchley Road, Swiss Cottage, NW3 (0870 505 0007/www.odeon.co.uk). Swiss Cottage tube.* Screens 6. Tickets £6.50; £3.50-£4.50 concessions (select times). Credit AmEx, MC, V.
Phoenix *52 High Road, Finchley, N2 (information 8883 2233/bookings 8444 6789). East Finchley tube.* Screens 1. Tickets £4.75-£5.50; £3.50 concessions (select times). *Early shows* £3.50; £3 concessions. Credit MC, V.
Screen on the Green *83 Upper Street, Islington, N1 (7226 3520/www.screencinemas.co.uk). Angel tube.* Screens 1. Tickets £6.50. *Early shows* £4. Credit MC, V. Map p402 O2.
Screen on the Hill *203 Haverstock Hill, Belsize Park, NW3 (7435 3366/www.screencinemas.co.uk).*

Belsize Park tube. Screens 1. Tickets £6.50. *Early shows* £4.50. Credit MC, V.
Tricycle Cinema *269 Kilburn High Road, Kilburn, NW6 (information 7328 1900/bookings 7328 1000). Kilburn tube.* Screens 1. Tickets £6.50; £5.50 concessions (select times). *Early shows* £4; £3 concessions. Credit MC, V.

East London

Rio Cinema *107 Kingsland High Street, Dalston, E8 (7254 6677). Dalston Kingsland rail/30, 38, 56, 67, 76, 149, 242, 243 bus.* Screens 1. Tickets £5-£5.50; £3-£4 concessions. *Early shows* £3-£4; £1.50-£3 concessions. Credit MC, V.

South London

Clapham Picture House *76 Venn Street, Clapham, SW4 (information 7498 2242/bookings 7498 3323/www.picturehouse-cinemas.co.uk). Clapham Common tube.* Screens 4. Tickets £6. *Early shows* £5; concessions £4. Credit MC, V.
Greenwich Cinema *180 Greenwich High Road, Greenwich, SE10 (information 01426 919020/ bookings 8293 0101/www.networkcinemas.com). Greenwich rail.* Screens 3. Tickets £5.50; £3.50-£4 concessions (select times). *Early shows* £4.30. Credit MC, V.

Ritzy *Brixton Oval, Coldharbour Lane, Brixton, SW2 (information 7737 2121/bookings 7733 2229). Brixton tube/rail.* **Screens** 5. **Tickets** £6.50; £2.50-£3.50 concessions. *Early shows* £4. **Credit** MC, V.
UGC Fulham Road *142 Fulham Road, Chelsea, SW10 (0870 907 0711). South Kensington tube.* **Screens** 6. **Tickets** £8; £5.50 concessions (select times). **Credit** AmEx, MC, V. **Map** p397 D11.

West London

Gate Cinema *87 Notting Hill Gate, Notting Hill, W11 (7727 4043). Notting Hill Gate tube.* **Screens** 1. **Tickets** £6.50; £3.50 concessions (select times). *Early shows* £3. **Credit** MC, V. **Map** p394 A7.
Notting Hill Coronet *103-105 Notting Hill Gate, Notting Hill, W11 (7727 6705). Notting Hill Gate tube.* **Screens** 2. **Tickets** £6.50; £4 concessions (select times). *Early shows* £4. **Credit** MC, V. **Map** p394 A7.
Odeon Kensington *Kensington High Street, Kensington, W8 (0870 505 0007/www.odeon.co.uk). High Street Kensington tube.* **Screens** 6. **Tickets** £7.80; £4.50-£5 concessions. *Early shows* £5. **Credit** AmEx, MC, V. **Map** p396 A9.
UCI Whiteleys *Second floor, Whiteleys Shopping Centre, Queensway, Bayswater, W2 (0870 010 2030/www.uci-cinemas.co.uk). Bayswater or Queensway tube.* **Screens** 8. **Tickets** £8; £4-£5 concessions (select times). *Early shows* £5.50. **Credit** AmEx, MC, V. **Map** p394 C6.

Repertory & art house cinemas

Where old films go to die, basically, though London's art house circuit also provides a home for new movies that haven't managed to secure a commercial release and all manner of bonkers underground flicks.

In addition to the cinemas listed below, several cinemas listed above in the First run section offer a more limited selection of rep-style fare. Specifically, the **Curzon Soho**, **Everyman**, **Phoenix** and **Rio** all devote their Sunday afternoons to hand-picked oldies; the second screen at the **ICA Cinema** is given over to classics and underground weirdness; and the **Ritzy** mixes in a few old classics and rarely screened treats from around the world in its mostly first-run programme. Conversely, the **Watermans Arts Centre** also shows new releases alongside its repertory selections.

Ciné Lumière *Institut Français, 17 Queensberry Place, South Kensington, SW7 (7838 2144/ 2146/www.institut.ambafrance.org.uk). South Kensington tube.* **Screens** 1. **Tickets** £6; £4.50 concessions; £4 members. *Membership* £18/yr. **Credit** MC, V. **Map** p397 D10.
Lux Cinema *2-4 Hoxton Square, Hoxton, N1 (7684 0201/www.lux.org.uk). Old Street tube/rail.* **Screens** 1. **Tickets** £6; £4 concessions. *Membership* £12-£15/yr, allows £1 off all tickets. **Credit** MC, V. **Map** p403 R3.
National Film Theatre (NFT) *South Bank, SE1 (information 7633 0274/bookings 7928 3232/ www.bfi.org.uk/nft). Embankment tube/Waterloo*

tube/rail. **Screens** 3. **Tickets** £6.50; £5 concessions. *Membership* £11-£15.95/yr, allows £1 off all tickets. **Credit** AmEx, MC, V. **Map** p401 M7.
Prince Charles *Leicester Place, Leicester Square, WC2 (today's films 7734 9127/week's films 0901 272 7007 premium rate/www.princecharlescinema.com). Leicester Square or Piccadilly Circus tube.* **Screens** 1. **Tickets** £1.99-£3.50 non-members; £1.50-£2.50 members. *Membership* £5/yr. **Credit** MC, V. **Map** p401 K7.
Riverside Studios *Crisp Road, Hammersmith, W6 (8237 1111/www.riversidestudios.co.uk). Hammersmith tube.* **Screens** 1. **Tickets** £5; £4 concessions. **Credit** MC, V.
Watermans Arts Centre *40 High Street, Brentford, Middx (8568 1176/www.watermans.org.uk). Kew Bridge rail/Gunnersbury tube, then 237, 267 bus.* **Screens** 1. **Tickets** £3.50-£4.95; £2.75-£3.95 concessions. **Credit** MC, V.

IMAX

Following the closure of the IMAX cinema in the Trocadero, London now has a pair of IMAX cinemas: the brand new IMAX cinema in the Wellcome Wing of the **Science Museum** (*see p139*), which has a capacity of 450 amd is only accessible to museum visitors, and the 480-seater **BFI London IMAX Cinema**, which stands ten storeys high on the South Bank and boasts the biggest film screen in Britain, with 80 million tiny holes allowing high-fidelity sound to filter through into the auditorium.

BFI London IMAX Cinema *Waterloo Bullring, South Bank, SE1 (7902 1234/www.bfi.org.uk/imax). Embankment tube/Waterloo tube/rail.* **Screens** 1. **Tickets** £6.75; £4.75-£5.75 concessions; free under-5s. **Credit** AmEx, MC, V. **Map** p401 M8.
Science Museum IMAX Theatre *Exhibition Road, Knightsbridge, SW7 (0870 870 4868/ www.sciencemuseum.org.uk). South Kensington tube.* **Screens** 1. **Tickets** *Before 4.30pm museum & film* £12; £8 students; £5.75 concessions. *After 4.30pm museum* free. *Film* £6.75; £5.75 concessions. **Credit** AmEx, DC, MC, V. **Map** p397 D9.

The BFI London IMAX Cinema.

Galleries

Art for art's sake, money for God's sake: the boom in British art continues.

Anthony d'Offay. Or, to be precise, his gallery.

Quite aside from its world-class collections of art, both old and modern, London has a thriving contemporary art scene. As well as the major exhibition spaces covered in the Sightseeing section (for a list, *see below*), there are around 150 smaller galleries regularly taking the pulse of contemporary art. The galleries on and around Cork Street in Mayfair form the commercial hub of London's art trade, but it's the rising stars of the east (from Shoreditch to Mile End) that burn the brightest.

Aside from *Time Out* magazine, which has weekly art listings, *New Exhibitions of Contemporary Art* details shows in the capital: it can be picked up at most galleries, and is online at www.newexhibitions.com. Entry to all the galleries below is free unless otherwise stated. Some of the galleries close in August; always phone to check. In addition, major galleries and museums are listed in the Sightseeing chapter, including the **Barbican Art Gallery** (*see p95*), the **Camden Arts Centre** (*see p148*), the **Courtauld Gallery** and the **Hermitage Rooms** *see p97*), the **Dulwich Picture Gallery** (*see p169*), the **Hayward Gallery** (*see p73*), the **ICA** (*see p131*), the **National Gallery** (*see p130*), the **Royal Academy** (*see p115*), the

Saatchi Gallery (*see p146*), the **Serpentine Gallery** (*see p137*), the **Tate Britain** (*see p134*), the **Tate Modern** (*see p77*) and the **Whitechapel Art Gallery** (*see p155*).

Central

Anthony d'Offay
9, 23 & 24 Dering Street, Mayfair, W1 (7499 4100/www.doffay.com). Bond Street or Oxford Circus tube. **Open** 10am-5.30pm Mon-Fri; 10am-1pm Sat; closed Sun. **No credit cards. Map** p398 H6.
Anthony d'Offay has a solid reputation for showing contemporary work of a high calibre. Big names often appear, including Warhol, Lichtenstein and Richter, but the gallery pays close attention to contemporary trends, exhibiting the likes of Ron Muek, Glenn Brown and Chris Cunningham.

Also in the area are **Anthony Reynolds** just down the road (no.5), which focuses on British art, and **Annely Juda**, above the gallery at no.23, who favours abstract and expressionist works.

Eagle
159 Farringdon Road, Farringdon, EC1 (7833 2674). Farringdon tube/rail. **Open** 11am-6pm Wed-Fri; 11am-4pm Sat; closed Mon, Tue, Sun; also by appointment. **No credit cards. Map** p402 N4.

A friendly and relaxed art space, upstairs from the Eagle gastropub (see p218). Exhibitors include Andrew Bick, Tom Hammick and Jeff Gibbons, and the gallery has a small catalogue of its own publications and limited edition artists' books.

Entwistle
6 Cork Street, Mayfair, W1 (7734 6440/ info@entwistle.net). Green Park or Piccadilly Circus tube. **Open** 10am-5.30pm Mon-Fri; 11am-4.30pm Sat; closed Sun. **Credit** MC, V. **Map** p400 J7.
Entwistle specialises in showing young British and American artists. Past exhibitions have ranged from Edward Lipski's sculptures and installations to realist photographic paintings by Jason Brooks.

Frith Street
60 Frith Street, Soho, W1 (7494 1550/ www.frithstreetgallery.co.uk). Tottenham Court Road tube. **Open** 10am-6pm Wed-Fri; 11am-4pm Sat; closed Mon, Tue, Sun. **No credit cards**. **Map** p399 K6.
Frith Street's four interlinked rooms provide an intimate space for exhibitions amid the hurly-burly of Soho. Tacita Dean, Cornelia Parker, John Riddy and Jaki Irvine have all shown in the last year or so.

Gagosian
8 Heddon Street, Mayfair, W1 (7292 8222/ www.gagosian.com). Oxford Circus or Piccadilly Circus tube. **Open** 10am-6pm Tue-Sat; by appointment Mon; closed Sun. **No credit cards.** **Map** p400 J7.
A pristine space, with polished stone floors and smaller rooms in the basement. So far, this major new London gallery has seen the likes of Eric Fischl, Chris Burden and deviant painter Dexter Dalwood.

Lisson
52-4 Bell Street, Marylebone, NW1 (7724 2739/ www.lissongallery.com). Edgware Road tube. **Open** 10am-6pm Mon-Fri; 10am-5pm Sat; closed Sun. **Credit** AmEx, MC, V. **Map** p395 E5.
This elegant gallery is one of the best spaces in London. By and large, the Lisson represents artists of a conceptual/abstract bent, among them Dan Graham, Julian Opie and Anish Kapoor.

Sadie Coles HQ
35 Heddon Street, Mayfair, W1 (7434 2227/ www.sadiecoles.com). Oxford Circus or Piccadilly Circus tube. **Open** 10am-6pm Tue-Sat; closed Mon, Sun. **No credit cards**. **Map** p400 J7.
The atmosphere in this quiet Mayfair cul-de-sac may change thanks to rowdy new neighbour Gagosian. However, Sadie Coles can still hold her end up with a show of talent from US and UK artists such as Raymond Pettibon, Sarah Lucas and Jim Lambie.

Stephen Friedman
25-8 Old Burlington Street, Mayfair, W1 (7494 1434/www.stephenfriedman.com). Green Park or Piccadilly Circus tube. **Open** 10am-6pm Tue-Fri; 11am-5pm Sat; closed Mon, Sun. **No credit cards**. **Map** p399 K6.

Approach with caution. *See p295.*

Stephen Friedman's international clutch of artists includes Stephan Balkenhol, Thomas Hirschhorn, Vong Phaophanit, Kerry Stewart, David Shrigley and Yinka Shonibare.

Waddington Galleries
11 & 12 Cork Street, Mayfair, W1 (7437 8611/ www.waddington-galleries.com). Green Park or Piccadilly Circus tube. **Open** 10am-5.30pm Mon-Fri; 10am-1pm Sat; closed Sun. **No credit cards**. **Map** p400 J7.
Waddington's is one of the major dealers of modern and contemporary art, and paintings by such masters as Picasso, Matisse and Dubuffet occasionally make an appearance.

White Cube
44 Duke Street, St James's, SW1 (7930 5373/ www.whitecube.com). Green Park or Piccadilly Circus tube. **Open** 10am-6pm Tue-Sat; by appointment Mon; closed Sun. **Credit** AmEx, MC, V. **Map** p400 J7.
Now almost as famous as the artists that have exhibited here, Jay Jopling's box-like room has provided a focus for some of the finest work produced in the last ten years. It's a very small space, however, hence the opening of **White Cube²** in Hoxton (see p296). Artists include such luminaries as Damien Hirst, Tracey Emin and Antony Gormley.

East

Anthony Wilkinson Gallery
242 Cambridge Heath Road, Bethnal Green, E2 (8980 2662/www.anthonywilkinsongallery.com). Bethnal Green tube. **Open** 11am-6pm Thur-Sat; noon-6pm Sun; also by appointment. **No credit cards** .
Wilkinson's three rooms are lit by a diffuse light that seems to work to the advantage of the discreet, minimalist work on show. In spirit, it's closest to the Lisson (see above), albeit on a smaller scale and with a tighter budget. The gallery represents the work of David Batchelor, Angela de la Cruz and Glen Baxter, among others.

The Approach
First floor, Approach Tavern, 47 Approach Road, Bethnal Green, E2 (8983 3878). Bethnal Green tube. **Open** noon-6pm Thur-Sun; also by appointment. **No credit cards.**
The upstairs room at The Approach is a haven for the young pretenders of the art world, while the bar below caters mainly for those who are past pretending. It functions as more than just a place to hang paintings on the wall, however, and exhibitions are usually thoughtful.

Chisenhale Gallery
64 Chisenhale Road, Bow, E3 (8981 4518/ www.chisenhale.org.uk). Mile End or Bethnal Green tube/D6, 8, 277 bus. **Open** 1-6pm Wed-Sun; also by appointment. **No credit cards.**
This vast late-Victorian warehouse offers a wonderful forum for adventurous exhibitions. One of 2000's highlights was Ori Gersht's 'Pitch', a 360-degree photo of Wembley Stadium taken from the centre circle prior to kick-off at an England game.

Flowers East
199-205 Richmond Road, Hackney, E8 (8985 3333/www.flowerseast.com). Bethnal Green tube or Hackney Central rail, then 106, 253 bus. **Open** 10am-6pm Tue-Sat; closed Mon, Sun. **Credit** AmEx, MC, V.

Flowers East straddles Richmond Road, with spacious galleries on each side, and now also has a space in the heart of the art world (Flowers Central, 21 Cork Street, Mayfair, W1). The art is predominantly painting, both abstract and figurative.

Gallery Westland Place
13 Westland Place, Hoxton, N1 (7251 6456/ www.westlandplace.co.uk). Old Street tube/rail. **Open** 10am-6pm Mon-Sat; closed Sun. **No credit cards.**
An impressive looking gallery with an expanse of floor space and exposed brickwork, GWP is new on the scene. So far it's spread its net across Britain, up to Scandinavia and over to Germany. If the art isn't to your taste, the cakes from their café should be.

Interim Art
21 Herald Street, Bethnal Green, E2 (7729 4112). Bethnal Green tube. **Open** 11am-6pm Thur-Sun; also by appointment. **No credit cards. Map** p403 R3.
A small, smart space where Maureen Paley mixes US and UK artists. Last year saw a return to Britain of painter Ross Bleckner and the 'Agony and Ecstacy' of Rebecca Warren.

Lux Gallery
First floor, Lux Centre, 2-4 Hoxton Square, Hoxton, N1 (7684 2785/www.lux.org.uk). Old Street tube/rail. **Open** noon-7pm Tue-Sun; closed Mon. **Map** p403 R3.

But is it art?

Now Britain's most prestigious art award, the **Turner Prize** was established in 1984. The impetus had come from the Tate Gallery's Patrons for New Art, who came up with the idea of promoting contemporary British art by rewarding 'the person who has made the greatest contribution to art in Britain in the previous 12 months' with £10,000. However, the prize was a low-key affair until 1991, when Channel 4 took over sponsorship and not only doubled the prize money but dedicated several hours of programming, including a live broadcast of the ceremony itself, to the Turner.

With greater coverage has come greater controversy. Since the early '90s two major groups have emerged, one firmly backing what it sees as a prize that rewards bold, innovative art, and another, larger, group who dismiss it as a meaningless payday for egomaniacal chancers and use it as a stick with which to beat modern art in general. Particularly scathing criticism has been reserved for '90s winners, which have included Damien Hirst's pickled animals (1995) and, in 1998, shit paintings – quite literally, given that he uses elephant dung as materials – by Chris Ofili.

In 1993, irreverent music/art show-offs the K Foundation mockingly offered a £40,000 prize to the year's worst artist. The 'winner' was Rachel Whiteread for her concrete casts of the interior of a house; Whiteread, of course, also won the Turner Prize. In essence, the arguments break down to whether you see 1999 nominee Tracey Emin's *Bed* as a cathartic examination of human emotion and interaction and, by extension, a comment on the ultimate futility of our transient existence, or just a bed with a load of crap on it.

Of course, such controversy is actually productive, and while the prize may be annually ridiculed in the tabloid press and equivalent TV shows, its increased coverage has at least got the British public talking about modern art, no mean feat on this reactionary island. It has made household names of artists such as Emin and Hirst, and launched the global phenomenon of BritArt.

At the very least, the debate is healthy. And it's a debate that kicks off each June, when the nominations are announced. A show featuring the work of the four nominees opens at the Tate Britain in mid- to late October, with the prize awarded about a month later.

Arts & Entertainment

Part of the Lux Centre (*see p292*), so it's not surprising that this gallery has a bias towards video work. Last year's highlights included Peter Land's 'Introduction to My Work'.

Matt's Gallery
42-4 Copperfield Road, Mile End, E3 (8983 1771). Mile End tube. **Open** noon-6pm Wed-Sun; also by appointment. **No credit cards.**

Artists invited to show at this wonderful site are given free rein to do what they will with the space. In the past, artists such as Richard Wilson have taken the opportunity to dig through the concrete floor of the gallery. The year 2001 will see installations from Matthew Tickle and Elisabeth Ballet.

The Showroom
44 Bonner Road, Bethnal Green, E2 (8983 4115/ www.theshowroom.org). Bethnal Green tube. **Open** 1-6pm Wed-Sun; closed Mon, Tue. **No credit cards.**

The peculiar, broken triangle space here often dictates the kind of exhibits: artists have made work specifically for the space. The Showroom provides four major exhibitions of newly commissioned work each year, featuring established and emerging artists.

Victoria Miro
16 Wharf Road, Islington, N1 (7336 8109/ www.victoria-miro.com). Angel tube/Old Street tube/rail. **Open** 10am-6pm Tue-Sat; closed Mon, Sun. **Credit** AmEx. **Map** p402 P3.

Miro's move from Cork Street reflects the dispersion of contemporary art from Mayfair. The gallery continues to show a mixed clutch of artists, representing the likes of Peter Doig and Chris Ofili.

Wapping Project
Wapping Hydraulic Power Station, Wapping Wall, Wapping, E1 (7680 2080/www.wapping-wpt.com). Wapping tube. **Open** noon-11pm Tue-Sat; noon-6pm Sun; closed Mon. **Credit** AmEx, DC, MC, V.

This former hydraulic power station was converted into a large and singular exhibition space and opened in October 2000. Its remit is new work from artists, designers and those working in electronic media, and the venue is certainly one on which to keep an eye.

White Cube²
48 Hoxton Square, Hoxton, N1 (7930 5373/ www.whitecube.com). Old Street tube/rail. **Open** 10am-6pm Tue-Sat; closed Mon, Sun. **Credit** AmEx, MC, V. **Map** p403 R3.

Unlike his Duke Street HQ, Jay Jopling's immaculate new space can properly accommodate exhibitions of more than one work at a time. Expect appearances from the likes of the Chapmans and Mona Hatoum.

South

Delfina Project Space
51 Southwark Street, Bankside, SE1 (7357 6600/ www.delfina.org.uk). London Bridge tube/rail. **Open** 11am-6pm Wed-Sun; closed Mon, Tue. **No credit cards. Map** p404 P8.

Delfina combines studios, a nice restaurant and a large exhibition space. Last year saw a a couple of major painting shows: London-based abstract artists such as DJ Simpson were gathered together, while autumn's 'Salon' included Glenn Brown, Franz Ackermann, Karen Kilimnik and Sean Landers.

Hales Gallery
70 Deptford High Street, Deptford, SE8 (86941194/ halesgallery@btinternet.com). New Cross tube/ Deptford rail/Deptford Bridge DLR. **Open** 9am-5pm Mon-Sat; closed Sun. **Credit** AmEx, MC, V.

Hales has been around since 1992, serving tea and sandwiches upstairs and spotlighting new artists downstairs. Some of its artists have been garnering a fair degree of attention of late, not least Turner Prize nominee Tomoko Takahashi. While you're in the area, the **Museum of Installation** (MOI), also on the High Street (no.175; 8692 8778), is worth a look.

Jerwood Gallery
171 Union Street, Bankside, SE1 (020 7654 0171/www.jerwoodspace.co.uk). Borough or Southwark tube. **Open** 10am-6pm Tue-Sat; noon-6pm Sun; closed Mon. **Map** p404 O8.

Opened in September 1998 in a former Victorian school building, the Jerwood concentrates on young British artists. It has attracted attention with a good line-up of shows and is well established in the London art world. Contenders for the Jerwood Painting Prize are given wall space each autumn.

Milch
2-10 Tinworth Street, Vauxhall, SE11 (7735 7334/ www.milch.co.uk). Vauxhall tube/rail. **Open** times vary. **No credit cards.**

Down by railway arches to the south of the river is this gallery, headed by Lisa Panting. The gallery's *raison d'être* is to commission and showcase new work, with a focus on first-time UK presentations, performance-/event-based projects and publishing.

Percy Miller Gallery
39 Snowsfields, Bankside, SE1 (7207 4578/ www.percymillergallery.com). London Bridge tube/rail. **Open** 11am-6pm Tue-Fri; 11am-3pm Sat; closed Sun, Mon. **No credit cards. Map** p405 Q9.

This gallery opened in the autumn of 1999, and presents a diverse array of work of mid-career artists and newcomers from the UK and abroad. In its first year of operation, it played host to the work of Hadrian Pigott, Emily Jo Sargent and Andrew Miller.

South London Gallery
65 Peckham Road, Camberwell, SE5 (7703 9799/ www.southlondongallery.org). Oval tube, then 36 bus/ Elephant & Castle tube/rail, then 12, 171 bus. **Open** 11am-6pm Tue, Wed, Fri; 11am-7pm Thur; 2-6pm Sat, Sun; closed Mon. **No credit cards.**

The large SLG has hosted an eclectic mix of shows in recent years, bringing in new talent and re-checking older heavyweights such as Julian Schnabel. 2001 will see Barbara Kruger return to Britain, and a new show from sculptor Bill Woodrow.

The best Galleries

Lisson
A winning gallery out in Marylebone (see p294).

Matt's Gallery
Unique space, unique installations (see p296).

White Cube²
Hirst, Emin, Taylor-Wood and more (see p296).

Matt's Gallery. See p296.

Other spaces

Further spaces listed in the Sightseeing chapter, include the **Design Museum** (see p80), the **Geffrye Museum** (see p155), the **Museum of London** (see p91) and the **V&A** (see p140).

Architectural Association
36 Bedford Square, Fitzrovia, WC1 (7887 4000/ www.arch-assoc.org.uk). Tottenham Court Road tube. **Open** 10am-7pm Mon-Fri; 10am-3pm Sat; closed Sun. **No credit cards. Map** p399 K5.
The Architecture Association often holds thought-provoking exhibitions that tend to look at architecture in its broadest context. In addition to shows, the association also hosts talks and discussions.

British Cartoon Centre
7 Brunswick Centre, Bernard Street, Bloomsbury, WC1 (7278 7172/www.cartooncentre.com). Russell Square tube. **Open** noon-6pm Mon-Fri; times vary Sat, Sun. **Credit** MC, V. **Map** p402 N5.
The Cartoon Art Trust charity organises and co-ordinates exhibitions and workshops for adults and children on cartoons, caricature, comics and animation. Shows planned for 2001 include manga cartoons, *The Simpsons* and Ronald Searle.

Crafts Council
44A Pentonville Road, Islington, N1 (7278 7700/ www.craftscouncil.org.uk). Angel tube. **Open** 11am-6pm Tue-Sat; 2-6pm Sun; closed Mon. **Credit** AmEx, MC, V. **Map** p402 N2.

The Council showcases the nation's craft output in a range of fields. Shows often take a theme and demonstrate work in that area. The finalists of the Jerwood Applied Art Prize: Jewellery are shown in autumn.

Royal Institute of British Architects
66 Portland Place, Marylebone, W1 (7580 5533/ www.architecture.com). Oxford Circus or Regent's Park tube. **Open** 10am-6pm Mon, Wed-Fri; 10am-9pm Tue; 10am-5pm Sat; closed Sun. **Credit** MC, V. **Map** p398 H5.
RIBA is based in a monumental edifice built by Grey Wornham in 1934. The gallery celebrates the profession's great and good while checking out emerging architecture from around the world. RIBA also hosts a programme of discussions, which last year brought Frank Gehry and Charles Jencks to Portland Place.

Photography

Photofusion
17A Electric Lane, Brixton, SW9 (7738 5774/ www.photofusion.org). Brixton tube/rail. **Open** 10am-6pm Tue, Thur, Fri; 10am-8pm Wed; 11am-5pm Sat; closed Mon, Sun. **Credit** MC, V.
Aided by council and commercial grants, this co-operative has kept to its community roots and holds an impressive library of social documentary photos. One of the highlights of last year was Flip Schulke's photographs charting the rise of Muhammad Ali.

Photographers' Gallery
5-8 Great Newport Street, Covent Garden, WC2 (7831 1772/www.photonet.org.uk). Leicester Square tube. **Open** 11am-6pm Mon-Sat; noon-6pm Sun. **Membership** £25/yr; £15/yr concessions. **Credit** AmEx, DC, MC, V. **Map** p401 K6.
Since 1971, the Photographers' Gallery has been promoting contemporary photography and has been instrumental in encouraging national galleries to hold photographic shows while still mounting 24 of its own each year.

Special Photographers Company
21 Kensington Park Road, Notting Hill, W11 (7221 3489/www.specialphotographers.com). Ladbroke Grove or Notting Hill Gate tube. **Open** 10am-6pm Mon-Thur; 10am-5.30pm Fri; 11am-5pm Sat; closed Sun. **Credit** AmEx, MC, V. **Map** p394 A6.
The Special Photographers Company gallery aims to represent serious snappers by exhibiting a wide range of work. The gallery holds a large collection of prints from landscape to abstract.

Zelda Cheatle Gallery
99 Mount Street, Mayfair, W1 (7408 4448/ photo@zcgall.demon.co.uk). Bond Street or Green Park tube. **Open** 10am-6pm Tue-Fri; 11am-4pm Sat; closed Mon, Sun. **Credit** AmEx, MC, V. **Map** p400 G7.
Specialising in the exhibition and sale of vintage and contemporary fine art photography, Zelda Cheatle holds a wide range of British, European, American, South American and Eastern European work.

Gay & Lesbian

Come out, come out, wherever you are…

London's gay scene continues to thrive. A combination of economic prosperity and ever improving attitudes has enabled homosexuality to parade itself to the British masses like never before. Gay cabinet ministers and pop stars? *Soooo* 20th century. For Chrissakes, 2000 witnessed sequels to gay TV dramas, a Gay Day at the Dome, and even a gay lifestyle show at the mammoth Olympia.

The Manchester-based Manto group opened a branch on Soho's Old Compton Street – London's gay ground zero – in spring 2000, the biggest gay bar in town. Its Soho rivals then all seemed to undergo refurbishment carried out by the same design team, and you'll have to look elsewhere if you don't like clean lines and neutral colours. For a less generic experience, seek out other clusters of gay life: among them, Vauxhall in the south and dyke heaven Stoke Newington (*see p304* **Where the girls are**) in the north.

Behind the headline-grabbers and the generic gay temples of **Old Compton Street** London's gay scene is flourishing in more varied and interesting ways. Last year alone, there was a two-week arts festival to accompany Mardi Gras, two competing National Lesbian Beauty

Contests, Mr Black UK awards and a South Asian arts festival. Women, too, have more choice than ever and, since the **Candy Bar** moved to bigger premises, a flagship venue worthy of the name. And club-wise, there's something for everyone, excellent gay salsa and gay bhangra nights among the options. You'd be hard pushed to find this kind of variety anywhere else in the world.

Predictably, conflicts remain. Resentment continues to simmer that London's Pride event, usually held on the first Saturday in July, has been split in two. The post-march festival is now a highly commercial event that will cost you at least a tenner in advance, while Pride veterans comment that the non-gay presence is growing, a trend of which some, mistakenly, are critical. Worse still, the alternative gay festival **Summer Rites**, usually held in Brockwell Park on the first Saturday in August, was cancelled in 2000 amid claims that previous bills hadn't been paid. Other more secure events to look out for in the gay calendar include the London Lesbian & Gay Film Festival, held predominantly at the **National Film Theatre** (7928 3232) during the first two weeks of April.

Arts & Entertainment

A night out with the boys at **G.A.Y**. *See p299.*

For up-to-the-minute information on what's going on, you're best off armed with the current week's copy of *Time Out*, as well as either *Boyz* or *QX*, freesheets available in most gay bars. Gay life is also appearing on the magazine racks as never before: joining *Gay Times*, the fashion-conscious *Attitude* and lesbian bible *Diva* is *Fluid*, aimed at a young, up-for-it crowd, while the politically motivated *Pink Paper* will now set you back £1.80 at newsagents. The UK's largest gay website is www.rainbownetwork.com, while www.gingerbeer.co.uk provides a nice overview of the lesbian scene in London.

Clubs

Be warned: club nights come and go with remarkable speed, so always call ahead. And clubbing in London is not a cheap thrill, you can expect to pay around £10 admission at the trendiest places. What's more, while most pubs and bars are usually free – many holding excellent club nights – drinks are almost always expensive: you'll pay £2.50 for a bottle of beer if you're lucky.

Central London is served by a network of night buses (bus numbers are prefixed with an N); only those for venues outside central London are listed. Women only means lesbians.

Atelier

The End, 18 West Central Street, St Giles's, WC1 (7419 9199). Holborn or Tottenham Court Road tube. **Open** *Club* 9pm-3.30am Thur. **Admission** £5; free w/flyer before 11pm. **No credit cards.** **Map** p399 L6.
A trendy night from the team behind Coco Latte, with groovy laid back house on the main floor.

Club Kali

The Dome, 1 Dartmouth Park Hill, Tufnell Park, N19 (7272 8153). Tufnell Park tube/N20, N134 bus. **Open** *Club* 10pm-3am 1st and 3rd Fri of mth. **Admission** £6, £4 concessions. *Before 11pm* £5, £3 concessions. **No credit cards.**
A fortnightly Asian lesbian and gay club with authentic eastern aromas of bhangra, hindi and arabic and a friendly atmosphere. Recommended.

Club Travestie Extraordinaire

Stepney's, 373 Commercial Road (entrance in Aylward Street), Stepney, E1 (7790 1763). Whitechapel tube. **Open** *Club* 9pm-2am Sat. **Admission** £5. **No credit cards.**
A TV/drag club that's been going for 20 years. Cross-dressers and their friends make up the clientele.

Crash

Arch 66, Goding Street, Vauxhall, SE11 (7820 1500/www.crashlondon.co.uk). Vauxhall tube/rail. **Open** *Club* 10.30pm-6am Sat. **Admission** £10. **Credit** AmEx, DC, MC, V (admission only).

The Muscle Marys' club of choice, with four bars, two dancefloors and two chill-out areas. Resident DJs include Tom Stephan, Antoine and Alan X.

DTPM

Fabric, 77A Charterhouse Street, Clerkenwell, EC1 (7439 9009/www.dtpm.net). Barbican tube/ Farringdon tube/rail. **Open** *Club* 10pm-late Sun. **Admission** £12; £8 concessions, members. **Credit** MC, V (bar only). **Map** p402 O5.
This popular night caters for a 'polysexual' crowd. The party pumps to soul, jazz, R&B, hip hop, disco, Latino house and progressive to hard house.

Exilio Latino

Houghton Street, Holborn, WC2 (07956 983230 mobile/07931 374391 mobile/www.exilio.co.uk). Holborn tube. **Open** *Club* 10pm-3am Sat. **Admission** £6. **No credit cards.** **Map** p399 M6.
This popular, relaxed gay salsa night draws a happy crowd, with a good mix of sexes and ages.

Factor 25

The Rock, Hungerford House, Victoria Embankment, WC2 (07901 943108 mobile/www.factor25.com). Embankment tube. **Open** *Club* 7pm-late Sun. **Admission** £8; £5 non-members before 8pm, members all night. **No credit cards.** **Map** p401 L8.
A weekly dance and cruise session down by the river.

Fiction

The Cross, King's Cross Goods Yard, off York Way, King's Cross, N1 (7439 9009/www.dtpm.net). King's Cross tube/rail. **Open** *Club* 11pm-late Fri. **Admission** £12; £8 before 11.30pm. **Credit** MC, V. **Map** p399 L2.
The DTPM crew draw a 'polysexual' crowd in this swanky venue. The three floors offer progressive house and mellow moods. Quality clubbing, if pricey.

G.A.Y.

Astoria & LA2, 157 Charing Cross Road, Soho, WC2 (7734 6963/0906 100 0160 premium rate/www.g-a-y.co.uk). Tottenham Court Road tube. **Open** *Club* 10.30pm-4am Mon, Thur; 11pm-4am Fri; 10.30pm-4.30am Sat. **Map** p399 K6.
Jeremy Joseph hosts London's biggest gay trash bash, attracting a young, unpretentious crowd. Monday's and Thursday's G.A.Y. Pink Pounder at LA2 have cheap drinks and entry (free with flyer), and Friday's G.A.Y. Camp Attack ('70s/'80s music) at the Astoria with big-name PAs strutting their stuff on Saturdays (£1 or £2 with flyer).

Heaven

The Arches, Villiers Street, Charing Cross, WC2 (7930 2020/www.heaven-london.com). Embankment tube/Charing Cross tube/rail. **Open** 10.30pm-3am Mon, Wed; 10.30pm-5am Fri; 10pm-5am Sat; closed Tue, Thur, Sun. **Admission** £1-£10. **No credit cards.** **Map** p401 L7.
Heaven celebrated its 21st birthday in 2000 and keeps packing in the punters. Monday's Popcorn offers commercial house on the main floor, funky house in the Dakota Bar and indie tunes in the Star Bar. Fruit Machine on Wednesdays sees handbag on

Arts & Entertainment

the main floor, funk in the Urban FM room and harder stuff in the Powder Room. Friday night is There: dance in the Star Bar and alternative dance in the Dakota Bar. Saturday is one big gay party: fierce house on the main floor, underground house garage in the Star Bar and soul and swing in the Dakota Bar.

LTD: Limelight Tea Dance
Limelight, 132 Shaftesbury Avenue, Soho, W1 (7437 4303/www.ku-bar.co.uk). Leicester Square tube. **Open** *Club* 6pm-midnight Sun. **Admission** £6; £4.50 w/flyer; £2 w/flyer before 7pm. **Credit** AmEx, MC, V. **Map** p399 K6.
Hi-NRG pop for a crowd shaking their worries away, with regular PAs. Unsophisticated fun.

Loose
Sunset Strip, 30 Dean Street, Soho, W1 (7437 7229). Tottenham Court Road tube. **Open** *Club* 8pm-1am Tue. **Map** p399 K6.
At this girly strip night, a diverse crowd of lesbians knock back the tequila and plant those notes on professional pole dancers. A sexy women-only occasion.

Popstarz: The Remix
Scala, 275 Pentonville Road, King's Cross, N1 (7833 2022/www.popstarznightclub.com). King's Cross tube/rail. **Open** *Club* 10pm-5am Fri. **Admission** £8; £7 w/flyer; £5 members, students. Free for all before 11pm. **Credit** MC, V. **Map** p399 L3.
The original and biggest London indie night is now in the super Scala. Indie, trash, funk and disco help to make it a top party night.

Royal Vauxhall Tavern
Kennington Lane, Vauxhall, SE11 (7582 8212). Vauxhall tube/rail/N2, N36, N44 bus. **Open** 9pm-2am Mon-Sat; noon-midnight Sun. **Admission** free on weekdays; £4 Sat; £3 Sun. **No credit cards.**
On Saturday, Duckie (7737 4043, www.duckie.co.uk) brings your 'low brow homo hurdy gurdy' for lesbians, gay men and friends. There are also lots of special events here: check *Time Out* for weekly details.

More Science Less Arts
Upstairs at the Garage, 20-22 Highbury Corner, Islington, N5 (7607 1818/07957 340803 mobile). Highbury & Islington tube/rail/N43 bus. **Open** *Club* 9pm-3am every 4th Sat. **Admission** £5; £4 concessions. **No credit cards.**

This new indie night from the Club V crowd features Asian breakbeats, big beat, drum 'n' bass and hip hop. On alternate Saturdays, the same team bring you Evol, featuring indie, rock and retro.

Substation Soundshaft
behind Heaven, Hungerford Lane, off Craven Street, Charing Cross, WC2 (7820 1500). Embankment tube/Charing Cross tube/rail. **Open** *Club* 10.30pm-5am Fri. **Admission** £5. **No credit cards**. **Map** p401 L7.
Men's cruisey late-night venue.

Substation South
9 Brighton Terrace, Brixton, SW9 (7737 2095). Brixton tube/rail/N2, N3, N37, N109 bus. **Open** 10pm-3am Mon; 10.30pm-2am Tue; 10.30pm-3am Wed; 10.30pm-late Thur; 10.30pm-5am Fri; 10.30pm-6am Sat; 10pm-late Sun. **Admission** £3-£10. **No credit cards**.
This popular south London cruise venue offers a succession of steamy nights. Y-Front (Mon), a grope 'n' grind fest; Massive (Tue), 'for larger men and their admirers'; and Blackout (Thur) are men-only cruise nights. Boot Camp (Wed) is for male fetish fans (uniforms, leather, jocks, boots). Weekends start with a mainly male, cruisey crowd at Dirty Dishes (Fri), followed by Saturday's NY style house/garage of Queer Nation (mixed gay). On Sundays, indie kids flock in for the fun-packed, mixed-gay Marvellous.

Trade
Turnmills, 63B Clerkenwell Road, Clerkenwell, EC1 (7700 5352/www.tradeuk.net). Farringdon tube/rail. **Open** *Club* 4.30am-late Sun. **Admission** £15; £12 w/flyer; £10 members. **No credit cards**. **Map** p402 N4.
The prince of clubs is now in its tenth year and still draws a muscular crowd dancing to hard sounds in a cavernous maze of rooms. DJs Alan Thompson, Malcolm Duffy et al spin in the main room, and, in the Lite Lounge, DJs are joined by live vocals.

Tube
5-6 Falconberg Court, Soho, W1 (7287 3726/www.tube-club.co.uk). Tottenham Court Road tube. **Open** 10.30pm-3am Tue, Wed; 10.30pm-6am Fri; 10.30pm-5am Sat; 10.30pm-4am Sun; closed Mon, Thur. **Admission** £1-£7. **No credit cards**. **Map** p399 K6.

The best Gay nights out

For ogling beautiful men
Fiction (*see p299*).

For ogling beautiful women
Loose (*see above*).

For outrageous cabaret
Duckie (*see above*).

For sleaze
Substation Soundshaft (*see above*).

For out-and-out camp
West Central (*see p305*).

For fabulous food
First Out (*see p302*).

Hello Duckie. *See p300.*

Babe on Tuesdays and Fridays (happy house and pop), Cheap Thrills on Wednesdays (Motown and disco), and Wig Out on Saturdays ('70s, '80s and '90s).

Up
Rhythm Factory, 16-18 Whitechapel Road, Whitechapel, E1 (7375 3774/http://come.to/up-club). Aldgate East or Whitechapel tube. **Open** *Club* 10pm-late Sat. **Admission** £8. **No credit cards. Map** p405 S6.
Fortnightly club playing deep and progressive house for a good-looking crowd. Catch it as it takes off.

XXL
London Bridge Arches, 53 Southwark Street, London Bridge, SE1 (no phone/www.fatsandsmalls.com). London Bridge tube/rail. **Open** *Club* 10pm-3am Sat. **Admission** £8; £6 concessions, members. **No credit cards. Map** p404 P8.
A new club aimed at big, proud, hairy hunks.

Pubs & bars

Most of the places below are open to gay men and lesbians unless otherwise specified; we've tried to make clear which venues have less to offer female customers.

Admiral Duncan
54 Old Compton Street, Soho, W1 (7437 5300). Leicester Square tube. **Open** noon-11pm Mon-Sat; noon-10.30pm Sun. **Credit** AmEx, MC, V. **Map** p399 K6.
A traditional gay pub in the heart of Soho frequented by by a down-to-earth, mainly male crowd.

Barcode
3-4 Archer Street, Soho, W1 (7734 3342). Piccadilly Circus tube. **Open** 1pm-1am Mon-Sat; 1-10.30pm Sun. **Credit** MC, V. **Map** p401 K7.

This recently refurbished, relaxed two-floor bar is cheaper than many Soho hangouts. The cruisier basement is open 8pm-1am Wed-Sat.

Black Cap
171 Camden High Street, Camden, NW1 (7428 2721). Camden Town tube. **Open** 1pm-2am Mon-Thur; 1pm-3am Fri, noon-3am Sat; noon-midnight Sun. **Credit** MC, V.
A popular north London pub with a beer garden, famous mostly for its drag shows.

BJ's White Swan
556 Commercial Road, Limehouse, E14 (7780 9870). Limehouse DLR. **Open** 9pm-1am Mon; 9pm-2am Tue-Thur; 9pm-3am Fri, Sat; 5.30pm-midnight Sun. **Credit** MC, V.
BJ's offers discos and cabaret every Tuesday and Thursday, strip shows every Monday and Wednesday and a tea dance evening every Sunday.

The Box
32-34 Monmouth Street, Covent Garden, WC2 (7240 5828). Leicester Square tube. **Open** *Café* 11am-5pm Mon-Sat; noon-6pm Sun. *Bar* 5-11pm Mon-Sat; 6-10.30pm Sun. **Credit** AmEx, DC, MC, V. **Map** p399 L6.
Light, bright and buzzing, the Box boyz serve drinks, coffee and food to a mixed crowd.

Brompton's
294 Old Brompton Road, Earl's Court, SW5 (7370 1344/www.bromptons-club.com). Earl's Court tube. **Open** 8pm-2am Mon-Sat; 6pm-midnight Sun. **Credit** MC, V. **Map** p396 B11.
A popular men's venue with two bars and a cabaret stage. The bar, with a separate club (there's regular cabaret), caters to gays and lesbians every night of the week except Tuesday, when it's men only. Sunday's Privates on Parade offers male strippers.

Arts & Entertainment

The Box. *See p301.*

Candy Bar

23-24 Bateman Street, Soho, W1 (7494 4041/ www.candybar.easynet.co.uk). Tottenham Court Road tube. **Open** 5pm-1am Mon, Tue; 5pm-3am Wed, Thur, Fri, 4pm-3am Sat; 5pm-midnight Sun. **Admission** £5 after 9pm Fri, Sat. **No credit cards.** **Map** p399 K6.

London's flagship lesbian bar is now in a bigger and brighter venue, and benefits from later opening hours. Men are welcome as guests.

Central Station

37 Wharfdale Road, King's Cross, N1 (7278 3294/ www.centralstation.co.uk). King's Cross tube/rail. **Open** 5pm-2am Mon-Wed; 5pm-3am Thur; 5pm-4am Fri; 1pm-4am Sat; 1pm-midnight Sun. **Credit** MC, V. **Map** p399 L2.

This 'community pub' has a bar on the ground floor, the UK's only gay sports bar on the first floor, a meeting place upstairs, and an underground club too. Bulk (Wed) is a serious men-only night, with cruise nights Blacksmiths (boots only) on Mondays and Glory Hole on Thursdays, and cabaret nights on Fridays and Saturdays, filling out the calendar.

Compton's of Soho

53-55 Old Compton Street, Soho, W1 (7479 7961/ www.comptons-of-soho.co.uk). Piccadilly Circus tube. **Open** noon-11pm Mon-Sat; noon-10.30pm Sun. **Credit** MC, V. **Map** p399 K6.

Shaved heads and bomber jackets are to the fore in this Soho staple men's bar spread over two floors.

Drill Hall

16 Chenies Street, Fitzrovia, WC1 (7631 1353). Tottenham Court Road tube. **Open** 6-11pm theatre nights. **Map** p399 K5.

The bar at this lesbian and gay theatre is women only on Monday nights, and boasts a vegan café.

The Edge

11 Soho Square, Soho, W1 (7439 1313/ www.edgesoho.co.uk). Tottenham Court Road tube. **Open** noon-1am Mon-Sat; 1-10.30pm Sun. **Credit** AmEx, MC, V. **Map** p399 K6.

A Soho standard, this mixed bar is usually jammed.

Escape

8-10 Brewer Street, Soho, W1 (7734 2626/ www.kudosgroup.com). Leicester Square tube. **Open** 4pm-3am Mon-Sat; 4-10.30pm Sun. **Credit** AmEx, MC, V. **Map** p401 K7.

This popular gay bar, which features video screens and occasional club nights, is a good pre-club venue.

First Out

52 St Giles High Street, St Giles's, WC2 (7240 8042). Tottenham Court Road tube. **Open** 10am-11pm Mon-Sat; 11am-10.30pm Sun. **No credit cards.** **Map** p399 K6.

The first lesbian and gay veggie eaterie in London. On Fridays, there's a pre-club night, Girl Friday (8-11pm; for women and male guests).

Freedom Café-Bar

60-66 Wardour Street, Soho, W1 (7734 0071). Leicester Square or Tottenham Court Road tube. **Open** 11am-3am Mon-Sat; noon-midnight Sun. **Admission** £3 after 11pm Mon-Thur, Sun; £5 after 10pm, £6 after 10.30pm Fri, Sat. **Credit** MC, V. **Map** p399 K6.

An invariably busy joint that serves both booze and food to a hip mixed crowd.

Glass Bar

West Lodge, Euston Square Gardens, 190 Euston Road, Bloomsbury, NW1 (7387 6184). Euston tube/rail. **Open** 7pm-late Mon; 5pm-late Tue-Fri; 6pm-late Sat; closed Sun. **Admission** £1 Mon-Fri; £2 Sat. **No credit cards.** **Map** p398 J4.

London's largest women-only members' bar has drinks at pub prices on two floors. It's cosy and welcoming, though knock loudly and bear in mind that during the week there's no admission after 11.30pm.

The Hoist

Railway Arch, 47C South Lambeth Road, Vauxhall Cross, Vauxhall, SW8 (7735 9972). Vauxhall tube/rail. **Open** 10pm-3am Fri, Sat; 9pm-1am Sun; closed Mon-Thur. **No credit cards.**

Men's cruise bar. Leather, rubber and uniform.

King Edward VI

25 Bromfield Street, Angel, N1 (7704 0745/ www.eddyvi.freeserve.co.uk). Angel tube. **Open** noon-midnight daily. **Credit** MC, V. **Map** p402 N2.

A busy, mixed gay pub with a café-bar upstairs, a beer garden and a friendly, welcoming, local crowd.

King William IV

77 Hampstead High Street, Hampstead, NW3 (7435 5747). Hampstead tube. **Open** noon-11pm Mon-Sat; noon-10.30pm Sun. **Credit** AmEx, DC, MC, V.

A warm, friendly pub in the heart of Hampstead with good food and a nice beer garden.

Ku Bar

75 Charing Cross Road, Soho, WC2 (7437 4303/www.ku-bar.co.uk). Leicester Square tube. **Open** noon-11pm Mon-Sat; 1-10.30pm Sun. **No credit cards.** **Map** p401 K7.

Ku-Bar attracts a with a young, scene-friendly crowd.

Sex and the city

These might, relatively speaking, be enlightened times. But, believe it or not, it's still technically illegal for two men to kiss or hold hands in public in the UK. It's also illegal for a man to importune another man for sex, or for more than two persons to be present in consensual homosexual acts. Provisions against sex in public places apply to gay men, but not their heterosexual counterparts, and not women, gay or straight.

Which is not to say you'll be locked up for puckering up: that's unlikely, especially in London. Prosecutions are still made under this arcane law, though. Only last year, a gay man from Yorkshire won his appeal at the European Court of Human Rights after being convicted of gross indecency for taking part in a gay orgy at his home.

Last summer, the Home Office produced a consultation document to instigate a new code of sex offences more in line with what you'd expect of a liberal 21st-century democracy. Most controversially, it accepted the legitimacy of well-known cruising grounds – such as Hampstead Heath and Clapham Common – indicating that an offence would only be committed in situations where the perpetrator knew or

should have known that their actions were likely to be observed by others who would not ordinarily wish to see them.

The document raised a few hackles, to say the least. Gay men allowed to have it away in public? Whatever next?! Bolder queer activists stood their ground, though, protesting over plans by Camden Council and owners the Marquess and Marchioness of Tavistock to gate and close Russell Square at night in a bid to stop gay cruising. Love will find a way, however, and now, most of the action takes place a block away in the more intimate surroundings of Bloomsbury Square.

During the consultation period and beyond, commentators will no doubt fulminate. But boys will be boys, and cruising will always be a part of the colourful tapestry of London. Once night falls, skip down the steps from the car park of Jack Straw's Castle pub in Hampstead and follow the path right. You'll find the walkway dotted with motionless figures, like statues in an Italian garden. As you continue, these creatures become ever more exotic. And when you get to the picturesque vantage point before Golders Hill Park, you'll hear a nocturnal bird-call that is, in fact, the slap of hand on buttock.

Where the girls are

Accessible from central London via the 73 bus, Stoke Newington is as close to a lesbian district as London has. That said, it's still typically understated; like everywhere else, clubs and bars come and go quickly, and the transience makes it hard to pin down. Time will tell if the lesbian scene in Stokey will develop it into more of a women's district, or whether the lesbians will be priced out completely. Already, lots of women are opting to live in less pricey South Tottenham: a bit further up the road, but N16 is still within easy reach for a night out.

The area's atmosphere is a curious mix of trashy and villagey. Its multiculturalism is demonstrated fantastically by its restaurants: French-style pavement cafés rub shoulders with South Indian, Thai, Turkish and even Welsh eating places.

The main stops include **Due South** (35 Stoke Newington High Street, N16, 7249 7543), a friendly lesbian and gay pub with relaxingly scruffy leather sofas, a pool table, a beer garden and a restaurant. It's lesbian owned and run, with themed nights (salsa, drama classes), a women-only night on Thursdays and great roast potatoes with the Sunday lunches.

Elsewhere, the **Oak Bar** (79 Green Lanes, N16, 7354 2791) also has themed club nights, which change regularly and are as original in name as they are eclectic in musical selection. There are also strip competitions, women with large dogs, and friendly and not-so-friendly regulars. Blush (8 Cazenove Road, N16, 7923 9202), meanwhile, is a lesbian and gay café bar, just round the corner from the train station. Small but stylish, with regular happy hours, a pool table and affable gay male staff, the place is still trying to decide what it is.

Occasional club nights at other venues also brighten the calendar a little. Among them are those at **Cheeky B's** (162B Stoke Newington High Street, N16, 7394 7083) on the third Saturday of the month; the **Harem and Oriental Dance Show** (basement of 129 Stoke Newington High Street, N16, 7249 0213) on the second and last Saturdays of the month from 10.30pm-4am; and Shark, held at **The Point** (79 Stoke Newington High Street, N16), on the last Saturday of every month from 10pm-3am.

Too, the area's other bars, bookshops, shops, and restaurants are decidedly lesbian-friendly. The **Thai Café** (Northwold Road, N16), for example, is a favourite spot for lesbians, old and young: don't be put off by the exterior: the food here is amazing and cheap. And almost opposite Due South is **Sylvia's Piano Bar** (Stoke Newington High Street, N16), where the atmosphere is laid back, the food is lovely and the piano playing takes you to 1920s Paris. It's a venue that should be rivalling the popular **Vortex** (Stoke Newington Church Street, N16, 7254 6516). Instead, it inexplicably spends most of its time with its shutters down: opening hours vary wildly, so call ahead to check before you make the trip.

Kudos

10 Adelaide Street, Covent Garden, WC2 (7379 4573/www.kudosgroup.com). Charing Cross tube/rail. **Open** 11am-11pm Mon-Sat; noon-10.30pm Sun. **Credit** AmEx, MC, V. **Map** p401 L7.
This recently refurbished boys' bar caters for a smarter crowd than some of its Soho comrades.

Manto

30 Old Compton Street, Soho, W1 (7494 2756/www.mantogroup.com). Leicester Square or Piccadilly Circus tube. **Open** 11am-midnight Mon-Sat; 11am-10.30pm Sun. **Credit** AmEx, MC, V. **Map** p399 K6.
A gigantic busy boys' bar over three levels on Old Compton Street. Food is served on the first floor, though it's usually mellowest in the basement.

Popstarz Liquid Lounge

257 Pentonville Road, King's Cross, N1 (www.popstarz.org). King's Cross tube/rail.
Open 5.30pm-2am Thur; 5.30pm-1am Fri; 8pm-3am Sat. **Admission** free-£5. **No credit cards. Map** p399 M3.
This friendly late-night bar – which may be changing its name (to Sahara), but not its line-up, during 2001 – has DJs, drinks at reasonable prices and nightly fixtures, such as the famous Pre-Popstarz Piss-Up on Fridays and Saturday's Miss-Shapes indie night, now geared more towards women.

Retro Bar

2 George Court, off Strand, Charing Cross, WC2 (7321 2811). Charing Cross tube/rail.
Open noon-11pm Mon-Sat; noon-10.30pm Sun. **Credit** MC, V. **Map** p401 L7.
A mixed gay indie/retro bar whose music is of '70s, '80s, new romantic, goth and alternative varieties. Look out, too, for theme nights, karaoke, quizzes, tribute nights and DIY DJ clubs (an audition is compulsory, by the way).

The **Vespa Lounge**.

Rupert Street

*50 Rupert Street, Soho, W1 (7292 7141). Leicester
Square or Piccadilly Circus tube.* **Open** *noon-11pm
Mon-Sat; noon-10.30pm Sun.* **Credit** *MC, V.*
Map *p401 K7.*
This large, trendy and busy glass-fronted bar is
right by the Prowler emporium. The upmarket
crowd don't mind paying upmarket prices.

Two Brewers

*114 Clapham High Street, Clapham, SW4 (7498
4971). Clapham Common tube.* **Open** *4pm-2am
Mon-Thur; 4pm-3am Fri, Sat; noon-midnight Sun.*
Admission *£5; £2 before 11pm; free Sun.*
Credit *MC, V.*
A recently refurbished local gay men's cabaret bar
and club; one of the best venues in south London.

Vespa Lounge

*Upstairs at The Conservatory, St Giles High Street,
St Giles's, WC2 (7836 8956). Tottenham Court
Road tube.* **Open** *6-11pm Mon-Sat; 6-10.30pm Sun.*
No credit cards. Map *p399 K6.*
Laughing Cows, a comedy night held on the last
Sunday of every month, is one of the highlights at
this new-ish women-only bar behind Centre Point.

West Central

*29-30 Lisle Street, Soho, WC2 (7479 7981).
Leicester Square tube.* **Open** *noon-11pm Mon-Sat;
noon-10.30pm Sun.* **Basement bar** *10.30pm-2am Wed,
Thur; 10.30pm-3am Fri, Sat; closed Mon, Tue, Sun.*
Credit *MC, V.* **Map** *p401 K7.*
This three-floor bar has a camp, fun atmosphere.
Among the club nights is Fairylea, which offers
trashy disco to an up-for-it crowd every Saturday.

The Yard

*57 Rupert Street, Soho, W1 (7437 2652). Piccadilly
Circus tube.* **Open** *2-11pm Mon-Sat; closed Sun.*
Credit *AmEx, DC, MC, V.* **Map** *p401 K7.*
The Yard is unique among Soho bars for its court-
yard, which really comes into its own in summer.

Dining clubs

A relatively recent phenomenon, dining clubs
put together (for a price) civilised nights out in
restaurants for those who are tired of the gay
scene. The Champagne Dining Club (8525 5656,
champs@diningclub.freeserve.co.uk) organises
lesbian-only evenings, while the Out and Out
Dining Club (8998 5674, www.outandout.co.uk)
and Gusto (www.geocities.com/gusto_dining)
are strictly for the boys.

Sport

Sauna Bar

*29 Endell Street, Covent Garden, WC2 (7836 2236/
www.thesaunabar.com). Covent Garden tube.*
Open *noon-midnight daily.* **Admission** *Before
4pm Mon-Fri £10. Other times £12; £10 concessions.*
Credit *MC, V.* **Map** *p399 L6.*
Recently revamped, the former Covent Garden Health
Spa is now primarily a sauna. It's also men only.

Soho Athletic Club

*10-14 Macklin Street, Covent Garden, WC2
(7242 1290). Covent Garden or Holborn tube.*
Open *6.30am-10pm Mon-Fri; 10am-10pm Sat;
noon-6pm Sun.* **Membership** *£325-£440/yr;
£18-£22/wk; £6-£8/day.* **Map** *p399 L6.*
A huge, friendly gym, open to both men and women,
with cardiovascular and resistance machines and
plenty of free weights. There's also normal aerobics,
a therapy room, a café and a beauty therapist on site.

Accommodation

For more accommodation, *see p43.*

Accommodation Outlet

*32 Old Compton Street, Soho, W1 (7287 4244/fax
7734 2249/www.outlet.co.uk). Leicester Square tube.*
Open *10am-7pm Mon-Fri; noon-5pm Sat; closed Sun.*
Map *p399 K6.*
A service for lesbian and gay flat-seekers, landlords
and those looking for short-term holiday accommodation. It can find rooms in the West End from £45
as part of its holiday accommodation service.

Number Seven

*7 Josephine Avenue, Brixton, SW2 (8674 1880/
www.no7.com). Brixton tube/rail.* **Rooms** *8 (all en
suite).* **Rates** *£39-£69 single; £59-£109 double; £99-
£129 triple; £109-£139 quad.* **Credit** *AmEx, MC, V.*
A Victorian townhouse in a quiet tree-lined street in
buzzing Brixton. Run by friendly John and Paul (and
their dog Dougal), this small (though not cheap)
B&B is clean and comfortable. Clubbers take note:
it's handy for Brixton venues such as Substation
South (*see p300*).
Hotel services *Fax. Garden. Laundry. Parking.
Safe.* **Room services** *Air-conditioning. Hairdryer.
Radio. Refrigerator. Satellite TV. Tea/coffee.*

Philbeach Hotel

*30-31 Philbeach Gardens, Earl's Court, SW5
(7373 1244/www.philbeachhotel.freeserve.co.uk).
Earl's Court tube.* **Rooms** *40 (14 en suite).* **Rates**
(incl breakfast) £35-£60 single; £65-£90 double.
Credit *AmEx, DC, MC, £TC, V.* **Map** *p396 A11.*
A well-established gay hotel, particularly favoured
by transvestites (there's a cross-dressing party every
Monday). There is at least a late-opening bar and
restaurant, Wilde About Oscar.
Hotel services *Bar. Fax. Garden. Laundry.
Multilingual staff. Restaurant. Safe. TV & Internet.*
Room services *Room service (24hrs). Telephone. TV.*

Arts & Entertainment

Music

Strike up the band for one of the most impressive music scenes in the world.

Classical & Opera

Precious few world-class classical composers have ever hailed from London. However, whether by accident or design, the city evolved several centuries ago into a focal point for musicians and composers and in the year 2001, though other cities in Europe and the US have caught up, when it comes to classical music, London is still near the top of the global tree.

After all, what other city can boast four orchestras on a par with the London Symphony Orchestra (resident at the **Barbican Centre**), the Philharmonia, the London Philharmonic Orchestra (both based at the **South Bank Centre**; see p307) and the roving Royal Philharmonic Orchestra, along with two opera companies of the calibre of **ENO** and the **Royal Opera** (see p307)? And then there are the smaller ensembles, from the modernist London

Sinfonietta to the old-fashioned Gabrieli Consort; the plethora of terrific musicians, whether groups or soloists, that visit the city for much-heralded concerts; or the smaller venues, such as the churches in the City (see p310) and the three London colleges, that ice the cake to melodious effect. And if you're still not convinced, then remember that there's no music festival anywhere in the world that, in terms of both size and quality, can touch the **Proms** (see p309). In other words, book your tickets now.

Major venues

Barbican Centre
Silk Street, The City, EC2 (7638 4141/7638 8891/ www.barbican.org.uk). Barbican tube/Moorgate tube/ rail. **Box office** 9am-8pm daily. **Tickets** £6-£35. **Credit** AmEx, MC, V. **Map** p402 P5.
What the Barbican lacks in architectural beauty and accessibility, it *really* lacks in architectural beauty and accessibility. However, despite the confusing layout – which powers-that-be have tried and failed to alleviate several times over the years – the Barbican redeems itself with its cultural activities. Aside from the cinemas (see p289), galleries (see p95) and theatres (see p330), there's a music programme in the the Barbican Hall led by the London Symphony Orchestra, the centre's resident orchestra and one of the best in the world. The City of London Sinfonia, the BBC Symphony Orchestra and the English Chamber Orchestra also perform regularly, with the long-running 'Great Orchestras of the World' series offering a chance to catch some of the, um, great orchestras of the world. Add in a vastly improved selection of contemporary music and the free foyer music, and, assuming you avoid the hysterically naff Raymond Gubbay-promoted concerts that clog up the calendar, you have a fine enterprise.

London Coliseum
St Martin's Lane, Covent Garden WC2 (box office 7632 8300/fax credit card bookings 7379 1264/ minicom 7836 7666/www.eno.org). Leicester Square tube/Charing Cross tube/rail. **Box office** By phone 24hrs daily. **Tickets** £3-£58. *Day tickets* to personal callers after 10am Mon-Sat and by phone from 2.30pm Mon-Sat. **Credit** AmEx, DC, MC, V. **Map** p401 L7.
Though its thunder has been stolen in the last year or two by the arguments over the rebuilding and reopening of the Royal Opera House (see p307), the English National Opera, which makes its home at the Coliseum, should not be overlooked. ENO, which hands over the Coliseum to ballet during Christmas

The best Live music

For *NME* cover stars
The **Brixton Academy** (see p312).

For Next Big Things
The **Monarch** (see p315).

For storytellers & troubadours
The **12 Bar Club** (see p316).

For fat ladies singing
The **Royal Opera House** (see p307).

For fat ladies singing in English
English National Opera at the **London Coliseum** (see p307).

For jazz the old-fashioned way
Ronnie Scott's (see p319).

For low-budget musical travel
Mwalimu Express at the **Bread & Roses** (see p315).

For more or less anything
The **BBC Sir Henry Wood Promenade Concerts** (see p309).

and summer, likes to think of itself as an approachable, populist but still artistically worthy company. To a large extent, it's right: tickets are cheaper than at the ROH, all the works are sung in English, and you're more likely to see an adventurous production here than in Covent Garden. Indeed, thanks to Peter Sellars' awesome 2000 take on John Adams' *Nixon in China*, the company's reputation is as high as it's been for a decade or so.

Royal Albert Hall

Kensington Gore, South Kensington, SW7 (information 7589 3203/box office 7589 8212/ www.royalalberthall.com). South Kensington tube/ 9, 10, 52 bus. **Box office** 9am-9pm daily. **Tickets** £3-£100. **Credit** AmEx, MC, V. **Map** p397 D9.

Completed in 1871, named for Queen Victoria's husband (who had died ten years earlier and had been the original proponent of a hall on this site) and financed largely by the sale of over a thousand 999-year leaseholds on seats in the auditorium, the Albert Hall is today best known for hosting the Proms (*see p309*). Other classical events held at this mammoth venue tend to be grandiose affairs, frequently operatic in bent and of minimal artistic worth.

Royal Opera House

Covent Garden, WC2 (7304 4000/ www.royaloperahouse.org). Covent Garden tube. **Box office** 10am-8pm Mon-Sat; closed Sun. **Tickets** £6-£150. **Credit** AmEx, DC, MC, V. **Map** p399 L6.

They took their time, but was it worth it? The jury's out. After a hugely expensive renovation project, the ROH opened again at the turn of the new century. And a stunning building it is, too: the Vilar Floral Hall makes for a suitably grand entrance, while the bars and restaurants are vast improvements. The music programme remains largely the same – mostly classical productions of classic operas, with the occasional big star in the lead role – while tickets remain prohibitively expensive and technical difficulties still beset the place. But at least the music now has a setting it deserves. *See also p311* **Burn, baby, burn**.

St James's Church Piccadilly

197 Piccadilly, St James's, W1 (7734 4511). Piccadilly Circus tube. **Open** 8am-6.30pm daily. **Admission** free-£17; tickets available at the door 1hr before start of performance. **No credit cards**. **Map** p400 J7.

An odd yet delightful Wren church. Events here are varied: aside from the lunchtime recitals (Mon, Wed, Fri) there's also a series of talks and lectures each month. There's no set day/date plan for evening concerts, but the music is often delicious. *See p116.*

St John's, Smith Square

Smith Square, Westminster, SW1 (7222 1061/ www.sjss.org.uk). St James's Park or Westminster tube. **Box office** 10am-5pm Mon-Fri, or until start of performance on concert nights; from 1hr before start of performance Sat, Sun. **Tickets** £5-£30. **Credit** MC, V. **Map** p401 K10.

Situated in the heart of political London, St John's church has been a concert venue for almost 40 of its 270-plus years. It now hosts regular concerts of varying degrees of quality. Though the acoustics aren't great for larger ensembles and it's not especially comfortable, it's boosted by its crypt, which holds a lovely, secluded bar and restaurant.

St Martin-in-the-Fields

Trafalgar Square, Covent Garden, WC2 (church 7766 1100/concert information 7839 8362/ www.stmartin-in-the-fields.org). Charing Cross tube/ rail. **Box office** 10am-6pm Mon-Sat, or until start of that evening's performance. **Admission** *Lunchtime concerts* donations requested. *Evening concerts* £6-£16. **Credit** MC, V. **Map** p401 L7.

St Martin-in-the-Fields is not, as its name suggests, set in an idyllic, pastoral location. Rather, it's right on Trafalgar Square overlooking one of the capital's liveliest traffic hotspots. Once inside, though, the peace and quiet makes it easy to forget where you are. The lunchtime recitals (1.05pm Mon, Tue, Fri) largely feature student musicians, and are supplemented by evening concerts (Thur, Fri, Sat and some Tues), usually including baroque repertoire. The **Café-in-the-Crypt** is a lovely place for lunch, too.

South Bank Centre

Belvedere Road, South Bank, SE1 (7960 4242/ www.sbc.org.uk). Embankment tube/Waterloo tube/rail. **Box office** 9am-9pm Mon-Sat; 9.30am-9pm Sun. **Tickets** £5-£60. **Credit** AmEx, DC, MC, V. **Map** p401 M8.

Its design has divided both architectural gurus and locals since it was built – glorious modernist statement or stolid concrete carbuncle? Take your pick – but the concerts at the SBC are usually interesting enough to put such arguments in the background. The Centre encompasses three spaces: the **Royal Festival Hall**, which stages mainly symphony concerts and events at the more popular end of the spectrum (including rock events), although the acoustics arguably don't suit amplified music; the **Queen Elizabeth Hall**, a third of the size of the RFH, and home to chamber groups, semi-staged operas and the occasional idiosyncratic theatrical event; and the cosy **Purcell Room**, where you'll find small chamber groups, recitals and general esoterica. In addition, there's a bookshop, foyer music, a pricey record store, a poetry library, several cafés, bars and restaurants, including the **People's Palace** (*see p208*), and some stunning views over the river. It will be interesting to see how the centre absorbs the loss of David Sefton, the SBC's former Head of Contemporary Culture who left in 2000 to take up a similar post at UCLA.

Wigmore Hall

36 Wigmore Street, Marylebone, W1 (7935 2141). Bond Street tube. **Box office** *In person Apr-Oct* 10am-8.30pm Mon-Sat; 10.30am-8pm Sun. *Nov-Mar* 10am-8.30pm Mon-Sat; 10.30am-5pm Sun. *By phone Apr-Oct* 10am-7pm Mon-Sat; 1-6.30pm Sun. *Nov-Mar* 10am-7pm Mon-Sat; 1-4pm Sun. **Tickets** £5-£35. **Credit** AmEx, DC, MC, V. **Map** p398 G6.

#1 for best availability and best prices for London Theatre

Before you book direct or through your travel agent, check the prices on **LondonTown.com/theatre**

Lowest Price Policy

LondonTown.com is London's most popular tourism website and, as such, has significant buying power to deliver low prices and wide availability on the complete range of London's theatre.

Built in 1901 for pianomaker Friedrich Bechstein and seized as enemy property during World War I, the building at 36 Wigmore Street finally opened as the Wigmore Hall in 1917. The intimate auditorium is attractively decorated – the cupola over the stage, depicting the Soul of Music, is a wonder – and maintains a delightfully old-fashioned atmosphere. Long may it continue to do so, if it means the concerts and recitals – including the bargain Monday lunchtime series recorded for transmission on BBC Radio 3 – continue to set such a superlative standard. The staff are friendly, the ticket prices manageable and the acoustics impeccable. In short, it's a must-visit.

Festivals

The **Proms** would probably be enough for most cities. However, London has a great many other classical music festivals well worthy of investigation. We've limited ourselves to listing the annual events, though the **Barbican** (*see p306*), the **Royal Festival Hall** (*see p307*) and, occasionally, the **Wigmore Hall** (*see p307*) all offer themed events and seasons throughout the year.

BBC Sir Henry Wood Promenade Concerts

Royal Albert Hall, Kensington Gore, South Kensington, SW7 (information 7765 5575/ box office 7589 8212/www.bbc.co.uk/proms). South Kensington tube/9, 10, 52 bus. **Date** 20 July-15 Sep 2001. **Tickets** £3-£35. **Credit** AmEx, MC, V. **Map** p397 D9.

Better known, of course, as the Proms, this three-month jamboree at the Royal Albert Hall is one of the best music festivals in the world. The annual series, held from 20 July until 15 September 2001, encompasses everything you might expect (noted orchestras, classic works, the jingoistic Last Night) and many events you might not (jazz gigs, late-night early music recitals, world music). Tickets for the seatless 'Proms' area in front of the stage cannot be bought in advance but are incredibly cheap, and viewing a concert from here is as quintessential a London cultural experience as you'll find.

City of London Festival

Venues in and around The City (information 7377 0540/box office 7638 8891/www.colf.org.). **Date** 26 June-19 July 2001. **Tickets** free-£40. **Credit** AmEx, MC, V.

Three weeks of wildly disparate events at venues including the Barbican and St Paul's, along with some City churches, livery halls and outdoor venues.

Covent Garden Festival

Venues in Covent Garden, WC2 (7379 0870/ www.cgf.co.uk). **Date** 14 May-2 June 2001. **Tickets** free-£50. **Credit** AmEx, MC, V. **Map** p399 L6.

An excellent festival packed with consistently interesting artists and inspired performer-venue juxtapositions. Many events are held in St Paul's Church

Wigmore Hall: face the music. *See p307.*

(*see p124*; nothing at all to do with the cathedral) on Covent Garden Piazza, the nearby Freemasons' Hall (*see p125*) and the Peacock Theatre.

Hampton Court Palace Festival

Hampton Court, East Molesey, Surrey (Ticketmaster 7344 4444). Hampton Court rail/riverboat from Westminster or Richmond to Hampton Court Pier (Apr-Oct). **Date** 7-17 June 2001. **Tickets** £15-£85 (approx). **Credit** AmEx, MC, V.

Less cutting-edge cultural event and more tourist attraction with bells on, the Hampton Court Palace Festival is a nice enough place to kill an evening with some so-so classical repertoire.

Holland Park Theatre

Holland Park, Kensington High Street, Kensington, W8 (7602 7856). High Street Kensington or Holland Park tube. **Date** June, Aug 2001. **Tickets** £10-£25. **Credit** AmEx, MC, V. **Map** p394 A8.

One of London's poshest parks hosts music, opera, dance and drama in its open-air theatre every year. If the weather holds, it's a treat. *See also p335.*

Kenwood Lakeside Concerts

Kenwood House, Hampstead Lane, Highgate, NW3 (information 8233 7435/box office 7413 1443). Archway, Golders Green or Highgate tube/210 bus/East Finchley tube, then courtesy bus on concert nights. **Date** July, Aug 2001. **Tickets** £16.50-£30 (approx). **Credit** AmEx, MC, V.

All the usual classical and baroque suspects are wheeled out every year at this Saturday night series of outdoor musical events. Bring a picnic, and try and go on a fireworks night.

Marble Hill Concerts

Marble Hill Park, Richmond Road, Twickenham, Middx (information 8233 7435/box office 7413 1443). St Margaret's rail or Richmond tube/rail, then 33, 90, 290, H22, R70 bus. **Date** July, Aug 2001. **Tickets** £12.50-£15. **Credit** AmEx, MC, V.

Almost identical to the Kenwood series (*see p309*), the open-air Marble Hill festival, held on Saturdays in summer, offers undemanding repertoire in a pleasant location.

Spitalfields Festival

Christ Church, Commercial Street, Spitalfields, E1 (7377 1362). Aldgate East tube/Liverpool Street tube/rail. **Date** 4-22 June 2001, 13-21 Dec 2001. **Tickets** free-£25. **Credit** MC, V. **Map** p403 S5.
A loveable variety of twice-yearly musical treats take place in E1. Many of the concerts are held in Hawksmoor's Christ Church Spitalfields.

City lunchtime concerts

The daytime concerts in the plethora of historic old churches scattered in and around the City are a wonderful way to while away a lunchtime. Many of the churches in the Square Mile have historic musical associations – the **Church of the Holy Sepulchre Without Newgate** on Giltspur Street even has a Musicians' Chapel – and maintain them, in a small way, with regular lunchtime concerts by local musicians, many of them students. The acoustics are marvellous, the settings unique and the musicians generally excellent. Concerts are normally either free or with an 'admission by donation' policy. The **City Information Centre** (7332 1456), by St Paul's Cathedral, can provide further details.

In addition to the venues below, regular lunchtime organ concerts are held at several churches outside the City, including **Temple Church**, off Fleet Street, EC4 (7353 8559), **Grosvenor Chapel**, South Audley Street, W1 (7499 1684) and **St James's**, Clerkenwell Close, EC1 (7251 1190); phone for details.

St Anne & St Agnes *Gresham Street, The City, EC2 (7606 4986). St Paul's tube.* **Performances** 1.10pm Mon, Fri. **Map** p404 P6.
St Bride's *Fleet Street, The City, EC4 (7427 0133). Blackfriars tube/rail.* **Performances** 1.15pm Tue, Wed, Fri (except Aug, Advent, Lent). **Map** p404 N6.
St Lawrence Jewry *Guildhall, The City, EC2 (7600 9478). Mansion House, Bank or St Paul's tube.* **Performances** 1pm Mon, Tue. **Map** p404 P6.
St Margaret Lothbury *Lothbury, The City, EC2 (7606 8330). Bank tube.* **Performances** 1.10pm Thur (except Aug and between Christmas & New Year). **Map** p405 Q6.
St Martin within Ludgate *Ludgate Hill, The City, EC4 (7248 6054). St Paul's tube/Blackfriars tube/rail.* **Performances** 1.15pm Wed. **Map** p404 O6.
St Mary-le-Bow *Cheapside, The City, EC2 (7248 5139). Bank or St Paul's tube.* **Performances** 1.05pm Thur. **Map** p404 P6.
St Michael Cornhill *Cornhill, The City, EC3 (7626 8841). Bank or Monument tube.* **Performances** 1pm Mon. **Map** p405 Q6.
St Olave Hart Street *Hart Street, The City, EC3 (7488 4318). Tower Hill tube/Fenchurch Street rail.* **Performances** 1.05pm Wed, Thur. **Map** p405 R7.

St Stephen Walbrook *39 Walbrook, The City, EC4 (7283 4444). Bank tube/Cannon Street tube/rail.* **Performances** 12.30pm Fri (except Good Friday and Friday nearest Christmas). **Map** p404 P7.

Other venues

Blackheath Halls

23 Lee Road, Blackheath, SE3 (8463 0100/ www.blackheathhalls.com). Blackheath rail/54, 89, 108, 202, N53 bus. **Box office** 10am-7pm Mon-Sat; closed Sun. **Tickets** £2.50-£15. **Credit** AmEx, MC, V.
A pleasant, leafy location and a diverse music programme, encompassing anything from pop and rap to regular classical or world music.

Royal College of Music

Prince Consort Road, Knightsbridge, SW7 (7589 3643/www.rcm.ac.uk). South Kensington tube. **Map** p397 D9.
London's leading music college stages chamber concerts every weekday during termtime (at 1.05pm), with the occasional larger event in the evening. Most concerts are free and open to the public, and here, as at the other two big London music colleges, you get the chance to catch tomorrow's stars today.

If the concerts here don't satiate your need to hear young musicians, though, then rest assured. Both of London's other two major music colleges, the **Guildhall School of Music & Drama** (Silk Street, The City, EC2, 7589 3643, www.gsmd.ac.uk) and **Trinity College of Music** (11-13 Mandeville Place, Marylebone, W1, 7935 5773, www.tcm.ac.uk), operate a programme or regular concerts, featuring soloists and ensembles from the colleges in question working their ways through a vast and eclectic variety of music.

Resources

British Music Information Centre

10 Stratford Place, Marylebone, W1 (7499 8567/ www.bmic.co.uk). Bond Street tube. **Open** noon-5pm Mon-Fri; closed Sat, Sun. **Recitals** 7.30pm Tue, Thur (except Aug). **Tickets** £3-£5. **No credit cards. Map** p398 H6.
If you want to find out anything about any British composer, this is where to head. The library holds books, scores, recordings (both audio and video) and there are occasional lectures. There are also twice-weekly recitals of modern British music.

National Sound Archive

British Library, 96 Euston Road, Somers Town, NW1 (7412 7440/www.bl.uk/collections/ sound-archive). Euston or King's Cross tube/rail. **Open** 10am-8pm Mon; 9.30am-8pm Tue-Thur; 9.30am-5pm Fri, Sat; closed Sun. **Map** p399 K3.
If you've ever made a record – or, perhaps, done a vox-pop for radio – then you'll be in here somewhere. Listening is free, but it's advisable to call ahead with your request.

Arts & Entertainment

Burn, baby, burn

Tradition stretches over almost every facet of English life, whether encouraged or disavowed. But take one look at the spectacular, avowedly modern façade of the **Royal Opera House** in Covent Garden (*see p307*) and it's hard to see where the history kicks in. However, London's main opera house, recently and controversially the subject of a multi-million-pound facelift, is merely the latest in a long line of theatres to have stood on or near its Covent Garden site. To find the first, we have to return to the era of Handel, back the best part of 270 years.

A theatre has stood in Covent Garden since 1732, when Edward Shepherd built the Theatre Royal, then easily London's most luxurious theatre, for pantomimist John Rich. This first theatre staged a number of crucial productions in its 76 years of existence, both theatrical – the premieres of *She Stoops To Conquer* and *The Rivals* – and musical. Handel wrote for Covent Garden between 1735 and 1752, premiering works such as *Solomon*, *Samson*, *Judas Macabbaeus*, *Belshazzar* and *Alexander's Feast* here, as well as staging the first London performance of *Messiah* a year after its 1742 Dublin premiere; Haydn also premiered *Creation* here in 1800.

But in a precursor of the sort of strife that would befall the venue in later years, the house burned to the ground in 1808. A new theatre was quickly erected to Robert Smirke's designs – pictured above, in an 1828 drawing by Thomas H Shepherd – and proved similarly popular. It also proved similarly important: the first performances in

English of Mozart's operas *Don Giovanni* and *The Marriage Of Figaro* were held here in 1817 and 1819 respectively, while in 1853 and 1855, Verdi's *Rigoletto* and *Il Trovatore* received their English premieres. However, again the theatre burned down in 1856, and again it was rebuilt.

The new building, which opened in May 1858, turned out to be still more important than the previous brace, though it only really became popular after its nearest rival, Her Majesty's Theatre, burned down in 1867. Wagner's *Lohengrin* received its first English outing here, as did *Aida, Tosca, Madame Butterfly, Salome, Der Rosenkavalier* and *Elektra*. In 1932, the Covent Garden Opera Company took a new lease on the building and appointed Sir Thomas Beecham the principal conductor, a move that boosted the company's popularity and led to the renaming of the building as the Royal Opera House in 1939.

By 1946, the Sadler's Wells Ballet Company – who, ten years later, would become the Royal Ballet – had moved in; in 1968, the Covent Garden Opera Company were granted the Royal seal of approval and became the Royal Opera. Its post-war years have seen any number of important performances, not least from British composers such as Britten and Vaughan Williams, and visits from the cream of the world's opera community. And with its dramatic refurb, it looks like it will continue to do so for some time to come. Fire permitting, of course.

Rock, Roots & Jazz

Say what you like about Britpop – and most people don't say very nice things at all – but the mid-1990s rock movement did at least manage to put London back on the rock music map after over a decade of decay. As a result, the live music scene is as good as it's been in ages, with roots and jazz more than holding their own in a disparate array of venues across town.

Tickets

Prices for gigs vary greatly and can go as high as £50 for the stellar names. However, average ticket prices for a well-known band at most of the biggish venues is between £9 and £15, while lesser-known indie, jazz and folk groups can be seen for around a fiver at the pubs and bars detailed below. While tickets for the latter are usually available only on the door, it's advisable to buy tickets in advance for most other gigs: many sell out in double-quick time.

Try to buy direct from the venue as it'll save on cheeky top-up fees levied on most bookings. If the venue has sold out, you'll have to go to an agent, of which the biggest are **Ticketmaster** (7344 4444, www.ticketmaster.co.uk), **Stargreen** (7734 8932, www.stargreen.co.uk) and **Ticketweb** (7771 2000, www.ticketweb.co.uk). All take credit cards. Try to avoid buying from the fast-talking chancers with violent tendencies – otherwise known as touts – who hang around outside the bigger venues: you'll pay a fortune for what may be a forged ticket.

Rock venues

If it's new acts you're after, try the pubs around Camden Town and Kentish Town, such as the **Monarch** and the **Dublin Castle** (for both, *see p315*). Bigger bands tend to play one of two venue chains, the most ubiquitous of which is that owned and operated by the Mean Fiddler group, whose autonomy on the London scene has reached scary proportions with their acquisition of the **Astoria** (*see below*) and the LA2, which they've now renamed the **Mean Fiddler** (*see p314*). And for the superstars? Well, grit your teeth, bite the bullet and put up and shut up at one of the three arena venues, none of which make more than cursory concessions towards atmosphere and comfort.

Major venues

In addition to the venues listed below, the **South Bank Centre**, the **Royal Albert Hall** (for both, *see p307*) and, increasingly, the **Barbican Centre** (*see p306*) all host rock and pop gigs along with the occasional jazz bash, as does the **Hackney Empire**.

Astoria

157 Charing Cross Road, Soho, WC2 (box office 7344 0044/www.meanfiddler.com). Tottenham Court Road tube. **Box office** *In person* 11am-7pm Mon-Sat; closed Sun. *By phone* 24hrs daily. **Tickets** £8-£15. **Credit** AmEx, MC, V. **Map** p399 K6.

A generic if central rock venue, host to everything from run-of-the-mill indie to chart pop (the latter at its popular G.A.Y. night). Decent views represent the main plus, with an ugly stairwell mural and over-zealous security staff two of the minuses. However, all may change: the Astoria was acquired in mid-2000 by the all-powerful Mean Fiddler group.

Brixton Academy

211 Stockwell Road, Brixton, SW9 (7771 2000/ www.brixton-academy.co.uk). Brixton tube/rail. **Box office** *In person* 1-3pm Mon-Fri; noon-3pm Sat; closed Sun. *By phone* 9am-7pm Mon-Sat; closed Sun. **Tickets** £10-£20. **Credit** MC, V.

One of the best places to see bands in London, due largely to the fact that the sloping floor does allow you to actually *see* them without having to stand on tippy-toes. It's intimate for a venue its size (it holds over 4,000), though when the hall is at anywhere less than two-thirds full, the cavernous interior means the sound quality is muddied by echo. Conveniently, there are bars at almost every corner of the hall.

Earl's Court Exhibition Centre

Warwick Road, Earl's Court, SW5 (7385 1200). Earl's Court tube. **Box office** 9am-6pm Mon-Fri; 9am-2pm Sat; closed Sun. **Tickets** £5-£50. **Credit** MC, V. **Map** p396 A11.

The clue is in the name: it's an exhibition centre, and so was not designed to host live music. To cynics, that's putting it mildly: horrendous acoustics, over-priced concessions and less atmosphere than the moon make this one you might want to avoid.

Forum

9-17 Highgate Road, Kentish Town, NW5 (information 7284 1001/box office 7344 0044/ www.meanfiddler.com). Kentish Town tube/rail/ N2 bus. **Box office** *In person* 10am-6pm Mon-Sat; closed Sun. *By phone* 24hrs daily. **Tickets** £5-£15. **Credit** AmEx, MC, V.

The Forum, owned and operated by the Mean Fiddler, is the capital's leading mid-sized venue. Decent sound and views help, of course, but the atmosphere's the thing: the Forum seems to draw out the best in its crowds, many of whom have been lubricating themselves before the show at the **Bull & Gate** (*see p314*) a few doors down.

Hammersmith Apollo

Queen Caroline Street, Hammersmith, W6 (7416 6080). Hammersmith tube. **Box office** *In person* 10am-6pm Mon-Sat; closed Sun. *By phone* 24hrs daily. **Admission** £10-£40. **Credit** AmEx, MC, V.

A gargantuan theatre that's recently started hosting more and more gigs after a period when it was dominated by *Riverdance*-type events. It's all-seated, but don't let that put you off: acoustics and sightlines are both generally excellent.

London Arena

Limeharbour, Isle of Dogs, E14 (7538 1212/ www.londonarena.co.uk). Crossharbour & London Arena DLR. **Box office** *In person* 9am-7pm Mon-Fri; 10am-3pm Sat; closed Sun. *By phone* 9am-8pm Mon-Fri; 10am-3pm Sat; closed Sun. **Tickets** £5-£50. **Credit** MC, V.

A mammoth aircraft hangar with no qualifications for hosting gigs: the acoustics are shocking, the concessions are even more overpriced than normal, and it's two blocks east of The Middle Of Nowhere.

Ocean

270 Mare Street, Hackney, E8 (switchboard 8986 5336/box office 8533 0111/24hr bookings 7314 2800/www.ocean.org.uk). Hackney Central or Hackney Downs rail. **Box office** *In person* 10am-6pm daily; later on performance nights. *By phone* 24hrs daily. **Tickets** £1-£30. **Credit** AmEx, MC, V.

A major new £17-million venue set to open in the heart of Hackney in March 2001, Ocean will offer three separate, flexible spaces with capacities of up to 2,100, up to 300 and 100. As befits a place with such varied facilities, the music programming will be eclectic, run on something of an anything-goes basis, and there'll be club nights on Fridays and Saturdays. A training centre, rehearsal rooms and a separate café-bar are also planned for what looks set to be the major London venue opening of 2001.

Shepherd's Bush Empire

Shepherd's Bush Green, Shepherd's Bush, W12 (7771 2000/www.shepherds-bush-empire.co.uk). Shepherd's Bush tube. **Box office** *In person* noon-6pm Mon-Sat; closed Sun. *By phone* 9am-7pm Mon-Fri; noon-6pm Sat; closed Sun. **Tickets** £5-£20. **Credit** MC, V.

A missed opportunity, yet still an above-average venue. Though the sound quality is arguably the best in London and the building itself (once a BBC TV theatre) is a delight, only basketball players and those prescient enough to turn up on stilts will be able to see anything from the standing-only stalls area, while fire regulations mean the two balconies are both no-smoking areas (this is a rock venue, for Chrissakes). Expect to see – or not, if you're downstairs – anyone from Iggy Pop to Nitin Sawhney.

Wembley Arena

Empire Way, Wembley, Middx (8902 0902). Wembley Park tube/Wembley Central tube/rail. **Box office** *By phone* 24hrs daily. **Tickets** £5-£100. **Credit** AmEx, DC, MC, V.

The closure of the stadium has left the 12,500-capacity Arena – and, a lot less often, the 7,500-capacity Conference Centre – as Wembley's music venues. For reasons of acoustics, transport, price and atmosphere, you might want to pass on both.

Head out east for the delights of the **Spitz**. *See p314.*

Club venues

100 Club
100 Oxford Street, Fitzrovia, W1 (7636 0933/ www.the100club.co.uk). Oxford Circus or Tottenham Court Road tube. **Open** *Gigs* 7.30pm-midnight Mon-Thur; noon-3pm, 8.30pm-2am Fri; 7.30pm-1am Sat; 7.30-11.30pm Sun. **Admission** £5-£12. **No credit cards. Map** p399 K6.
Notorious for having hosted what many think was the first great punk gig in 1976, as well as for '60s shows by the Stones and the Kinks, the impossibly central 100 Club splits its time between trad jazz and cultish indie. Try not to get stuck behind a pillar.

Borderline
Orange Yard, Manette Street, Soho, W1 (7734 2095/www.borderline.co.uk). Tottenham Court Road tube. **Open** *Gigs* 7-11pm Mon-Fri, some Sats. *Clubs* 11.30pm-3am Mon-Thur; 11.30pm-4am Sat, Sun. **Admission** *Gigs* £5-£10. *Clubs* £3-£8. **Credit** MC, V. **Map** p399 K6.
After a fallow few years, the Borderline is, happily, again hosting gigs by bands that anyone other than their friends and close relations might want to listen to, many of an alternative country bent. A great little basement space in a handily central location.

Dingwalls
Middle Yard, Camden Lock, Chalk Farm Road, Camden, NW1 (information 7267 1577/box office 7428 5929). Camden Town or Chalk Farm tube. **Box office** 11pm-11pm Mon-Sat; 11am-10.30pm Sun. **Open** *Gigs* 7.30pm-midnight, nights vary. **Admission** £5-£12. **Credit** AmEx, MC, V.
Dingwalls' Friday and Saturday nights are block-booked by Jongleurs comedy club (*see p283*), though midweek nights often see a gig or two, including some showcases. The multiple levels mean the venue is best suited to sit-down, table-top affairs.

Garage
20-22 Highbury Corner, Highbury, N5 (information 8963 0940/box office 7344 0044/ www.meanfiddler.com). Highbury & Islington tube/rail. **Box office** *In person* 4-7pm on show nights. *By phone* 24hrs daily. **Open** *Gigs* 8pm-midnight Mon-Thur, some Suns; 8pm-3am Fri, Sat. **Admission** £4-£10. **Credit** MC, V.
The line-ups are often good here (US and UK indie, on the whole), but the acoustics are lousy, the air-conditioning is worse and the door staff are to be avoided. Smaller acts play Upstairs At The Garage.

Mean Fiddler
157 Charing Cross Road, Soho, WC2 (7344 0044/ www.meanfiddler.com). Tottenham Court Road tube. **Box office** *In person* 11am-7pm Mon-Sat; closed Sun. *By phone* 24hrs daily. **Tickets** £8-£15. **Credit** AmEx, MC, V. **Map** p399 K6.
The views are not uniformly great for gigs at The Venue Formerly Known As The LA2, but the sound usually is, and the place's multi-roomed layout makes it suited to the clubs that often take place.

Rock Garden
The Piazza, Covent Garden, WC2 (7240 3961/ www.rockgarden.co.uk). Covent Garden tube. **Open** 5pm-3am Mon-Thur; 5pm-4am Fri, Sat; 7pm-midnight Sun. *Gigs* 8pm daily. **Admission** £4-£12. **Credit** AmEx, DC, MC, V. **Map** p401 L6.
If its Covent Garden location hasn't already scared you off, the music here probably will: bands here are of the clueless up-and-coming variety, while the punters could be similarly pigeonholed. It's hard to believe that this was a prime venue in the late 1970s.

Spitz
Old Spitalfields Market, 109 Commercial Street, Spitalfields, E1 (7392 9032/www.spitz.co.uk). Aldgate East tube/Liverpool Street tube/rail. **Open** 11am-11pm Mon-Sat; 11am-10.30pm Sun. *Gigs* 8-11pm Mon-Sat. **Admission** £4-£10. **Credit** MC, V. **Map** p403 R5.
As close to an anything-goes venue as you'll find in London, the Spitz – named for its proximity to Spitalfields Market – is a bar, a restaurant, a café, an art gallery, a club and a music venue. Expect, as they say, the unexpected, though odd-ish jazz does tend to play a large part in proceedings.

Underworld
174 Camden High Street, Camden, NW1 (7482 1932). Camden Town tube. **Open** *Gigs* 7pm-3am, nights vary. **Admission** £3-£12. **No credit cards.**
A cut above the Camden pub venues on size alone: the labyrinthine corridors at Underworld lead to a strange-shaped basement room spoilt mainly by the obtrusive pillars that prop up the World's End pub above it. Indie stuff dominates.

University of London Union (ULU)
Manning Hall, Malet Street, Bloomsbury, WC1 (7664 2030/www.ulu.lon.ac.uk). Goodge Street tube. **Open** *Gigs* 8-11pm, nights vary. **Admission** £5-£10. **Credit** MC, V. **Map** p399 K4.
ULU's a student venue, and so the acts who play here are invariably indie acts big on the collegiate circuit. The hall itself is characterless, though the subsidised beer means you probably won't notice.

WKD
18 Kentish Town Road, Camden, NW1 (7267 1869). Camden Town tube. **Open** noon-2am Mon-Wed; noon-2.30am Thur; noon-3am Fri, Sat; noon-1am Sun. *Gigs* 8pm, nights vary. **Credit** MC, V. **Admission** free-£7.
Café, bar, club, gallery… imagine a funkier **Spitz** (*see above*) and you won't be far out. Reggae, soul and world music mix with more traditionally clubby stuff at this nice little spot.

Pubs & bars

Bull & Gate
389 Kentish Town Road, Kentish Town, NW5 (7485 5358). Kentish Town tube/rail. **Open** 11am-11pm Mon-Sat; noon-10.30pm Sun. *Gigs* 8.30pm daily. **Admission** £3-£5. **No credit cards.**

The quintessential Camden venue, despite the fact it isn't even in Camden. The dingy backroom hosts three-bands-a-night extravaganzas featuring ensembles you're unlikely to hear from ever again.

Dublin Castle
94 Parkway, Camden, NW1 (7485 1773). Camden Town tube. **Open** 11am-midnight daily. *Gigs* 9pm Mon-Sat; 8.30pm Sun. **Admission** £3.50-£5. **No credit cards.**
Everything a Camden indie venue should be, especially since it was cleaned up a little. The back room – where the bands play – is tiny and, on busy nights, uncomfortable. But hey! The bar's open until midnight.

Hope & Anchor
207 Upper Street, Islington, N1 (7354 1312). Highbury & Islington tube/rail. **Open** noon-1am daily. *Gigs* 9pm daily. **Admission** £3.50-£5. **No credit cards. Map** p402 O1.
Slightly smaller than a matchbox, the Hope & Anchor started holding gigs again a few years back, having made its name in the 1970s with all manner of pub-rock affairs.

Monarch
49 Chalk Farm Road, Camden, NW1 (7691 4244/www.barflyclub.com). Chalk Farm tube. **Open** 7.30am-11pm Mon-Thur; 11am-2am Fri, Sat; 11am-10.30pm Sun. *Gigs* 8.30pm daily. **Admission** £4-£6. **No credit cards.**

Guitars rule at Camden's **Monarch**.

London's leading purveyor of indie music, the Barfly club has settled in at the Monarch, one of the nicer Camden boozers, after leaving the Falcon in 1999. Expect an array of *NME*-sponsored up-and-comers.

Water Rats
328 Gray's Inn Road, Bloomsbury, WC1 (7837 7269/www.plumpromotions.co.uk). King's Cross tube/rail. **Open** *Gigs* 8pm-midnight Mon-Sat. **Admission** £4-£6. **No credit cards. Map** p399 M3.
Since the departure of the Splash Club (now known as the Barfly), the live music at this King's Cross pub has dropped off. Still, you will find the occasional indie-flavoured gem here in among the dross.

Roots venues

Acoustic Café
17 Manette Street, Soho, WC1 (7439 0831). Tottenham Court Road tube. **Open** 7pm-late Mon-Thur; 7pm-3am Fri, Sat; closed Sun. *Gigs* 8.30pm Mon-Sat. **Admission** £3-£4. **No credit cards. Map** p401 L7.
A miniscule hole-in-the-wall type venue that's something of a poor man's 12 Bar Club (*see p316*) but that can throw up interesting newcomers.

Africa Centre
38 King Street, Covent Garden, WC2 (7836 1973/www.africacentre.org.uk). Covent Garden tube. **Open** *Gigs* 11.30pm Fri. *Clubs* 9.30pm-3am Fri, Sat. **Admission** £6-£8. **Credit** MC, V. **Map** p401 L7.
The Africa Centre plays host to top African bands most Friday nights, as well as staging occasional gigs on other nights. There's a specialist bookshop on the first floor and a basement restaurant/café.

Bread & Roses
68 Clapham Manor Street, Clapham, SW4 (7498 1779). Clapham Common or Clapham North tube/37, 88, 133, 137, 345 bus. **Open** 11am-11pm Mon-Sat; noon-10.30pm Sun. *Gigs* 1-5pm Sun. **Admission** free. **No credit cards.**
This pub hosts the Mwalimu Express, one of the city's best world music events, taking in the sounds and food of a different city each week. *See also p225.*

Cecil Sharp House
2 Regent's Park Road, Camden, NW1 (7485 2206/www.efdss.org.com). Camden Town tube. **Open** *Gigs* 7pm, nights vary. **Admission** £3-£6. **No credit cards.**
Folk music heaven. The club on Tuesdays is fun in a hey-nonny-nonny kind of way, but beware of frequent invitations to 'Join in on the refrain'.

Hammersmith & Fulham Irish Centre
Blacks Road, Hammersmith, W6 (8563 8232/www.lbhf.gov.uk/irishcentre). Hammersmith tube. **Open** *Gigs* nights vary. **Admission** £4-£8. **No credit cards.**
This small and friendly craic dealer plays host to all manner of Irish music events from free ceilidhs to biggish-name Irish acts like the Popes.

Arts & Entertainment

The teensy-weensy **12 Bar Club**.

tronica to indie and rock, though beware of the pre-dictably echoey acoustics.

Jazz venues

606 Club
90 Lots Road, Chelsea, SW10 (7352 5953/ www.606club.co.uk). Earl's Court or Fulham Broadway tube/11, 22 bus. **Open** 7.30pm-1.30am Mon-Wed; 8pm-2am Thur-Sat; 8.30-11.30pm Sun. *Gigs* 8pm-1am Mon-Wed; 9.30pm-1.30am Thur; 10pm-2am Fri, Sat; 9.30-11.30pm Sun. **Admission** *Music charge* £5 Mon-Thur, Sun; £6 Fri, Sat. **Credit** MC, V. **Map** p396 C13.
An unusual venue in that it (admirably) hosts main-ly local and young jazz musicians. Instead of an admission fee, there's a music charge added to your bill. On Fridays and Saturdays, visitors must have a meal; Monday to Thursday you can only consume alcohol if you eat. Food is good, if pricey.

Bull's Head
373 Lonsdale Road, Barnes, SW13 (8876 5241). Barnes Bridge rail. **Open** 11am-11pm Mon-Sat; noon-10.30pm Sun. *Gigs* 8.30pm Mon-Sat; 2-4.30pm, 8-10.30pm Sun. **Admission** £3-£10. **Credit** AmEx, DC, MC, V.
This delightful riverside boozer is something of a jazz landmark, and still offers up gigs by musos both from here and the US. There's nary a better place in the capital to while away a sunny summer's day.

Jazz Café
5 Parkway, Camden, NW1 (information 8963 0940/box office 7344 0044/www.jazzcafe.co.uk). Camden Town tube. **Open** 7pm-1am Mon-Thur; 7pm-2am Fri, Sat; 7pm-midnight Sun. *Gigs* 9pm daily. **Admission** £6-£20. **Credit** AmEx, MC, V.
One of the best Mean Fiddler venues. The music is usually good, although the jazz tag is something of a misnomer: sounds will be anything from funk and soul to singer-songwriters. That it manages to cre-ate such a decent atmosphere despite the awful '80s decor and incessant nattering of the industry types on the balcony is only to its credit.

Pizza Express Jazz Club
10 Dean Street, Soho, W1 (restaurant 7437 9595/ Jazz Club 7439 8722/www.pizzaexpress.co.uk). Tottenham Court Road tube. **Open** *Restaurant* 11.30am-midnight daily. *Jazz Club* 7.45pm-midnight daily. *Gigs* 9pm daily. **Admission** £10-£20. **Credit** AmEx, DC, MC, V. **Map** p399 K6.
Excellent contemporary jazz can usually be found in the basement of this branch of Pizza Express, though most of their restaurants offer live music in some shape or form.

Pizza on the Park
11 Knightsbridge, Knightsbridge, SW1 (7235 5273). Hyde Park Corner tube. **Open** 8.30am-midnight Mon-Fri; 9.30am-midnight Sat, Sun. *Gigs* 9.15pm daily. **Admission** £10-£20. **Credit** AmEx, DC, MC, V. **Map** p400 G8.

Swan
215 Clapham Road, Stockwell, SW9 (7978 9778/ www.theswanstockwell.com). Stockwell tube. **Open** 5pm-midnight Mon-Wed; 5pm-2am Thur; 5pm-3am Fri; 7pm-3am Sat; 7pm-2am Sun. *Gigs* 9.30pm daily. **Admission** £1.50-£6 (normally free Mon-Wed and before 11pm Thur and 10pm Sun). **Credit** MC, V.
An Irish pub that specialises in semi-trad music most evenings, with big names and rock acts in the upstairs dancehall at weekends. The atmosphere, like the music, is raucous.

12 Bar Club
22-23 Denmark Place, off Denmark Street, WC2 (information 7916 6989/box office 7209 2248/ www.12barclub.com). Tottenham Court Road tube. **Open** 8pm-1am Mon-Sat; 8pm-midnight Sun. *Gigs* 9pm daily. **Admission** £5-£10. **Credit** MC, V. **Map** p399 K6.
A gloriously postage-stamp-sized backroom just off Denmark Street's Tin Pan Alley, the popular 12 Bar is London's most intimate venue. It's split between two levels, and offers a terrific mix of country, folk, singer-songwriters and occasional rock stuff.

Union Chapel
Compton Terrace, Islington, N1 (7226 1686/ www.unionchapel.org.uk). Highbury & Islington tube/rail/N19, N65, N92 bus. **Open** *Gigs* 8pm, nights vary. **Tickets** £3-£13. **No credit cards.**
A church, basically, albeit one that stages semi-reg-ular gigs. Expect everything from folk and elec-

Arts & Entertainment

Life on the street

As careers go, it's not one for which there are many courses: it's all pretty much on-the-job training. Nor is it particularly glamorous. Still, the job security is pretty good, the hours are fine, and the cash-in-hand nature of payment should allow for a few dubious tax breaks.

Of course, if that was all there was to it, then we'd all be in there having a go. Well, thank your lucky stars we're not, for London's current array of buskers – aka street musicians – already provide more than enough noise pollution for one city. That they manage so to do when busking is illegal almost everywhere is as damning an indictment of the Met police as you'll find.

But if you're going to walk these mean streets, you should be warned exactly what to expect. Buskers are everywhere in central London, particularly around Covent Garden, Leicester Square and Piccadilly Circus, and are positively unavoidable on the Underground. You thought the traffic and the licensing laws were annoying? Believe us: it's nothing compared to hearing the collected works of Lennon and McCartney destroyed on a daily basis.

Most of London's buskers fall into one of three categories, of which the most prevalent is the clueless, have-acoustic-guitar-will-travel type. He bought a Beatles songbook when he was 12, and is bloody well going to get his money's worth. Typically found in every tube station you'll ever use, he'll serenade you with *Get Back*, *Wonderwall*, *Imagine*, *Wonderwall*, *Blowin' In The Wind*, and *Wonderwall*. Oh, and then *Wonderwall* again.

Second up is the out-of-work musician. Usually a little more professional (remember, it's all relative), he often comes with his own amp, and – as with the many jazz instrumentalists honking and squawking their way around town – a backing tape. Expect jazz standards, light classical numbers or AOR

classics from their West End perches, either below ground in a tube station or at street level in Covent Garden or Leicester Square.

And then there's the didgeridoo player (didgeridooist? Didgeridooer? Didgeridoofus? Whatever), the most irritating of all. For no reason, they're all over the tube like a rash, particularly (and inexplicably) on the Northern line. Their repertoire is limited to arrrrrrrrwoo-ah*woo*-ah*woo*-ah*woo*-ah*woooo* (repeat to fade). You have no idea how annoying this gets after, oh, about five seconds.

Though they're not as ubiquitous as the aforementioned, dishonourable mentions in London's Busking Hall of Shame go, in no particular order, to the capital's bagpipists, bongo players and shit accordionists. Many of the latter, irritatingly, perform while walking up and down tube carriages during a journey rather than assuming the standard platform position, making them all but impossible to avoid.

But in among this cavalcade of mediocrity, there are some gems. The Bloke Who Plays Blues Harmonica Outside Waterstone's On Charing Cross Road At Night is usually worth a gander. No trip to Covent Garden is complete without first being irritated by The Quasi-Mexican Pan-Pipe Troupe but then charmed by the classical standards hacked out by The Starving Music Students String Quartet. And then there's The Curly-Haired Guy At Waterloo Station, the exception to the rule that buskers of type no.1 detailed above have to be dreadful; The Medieval Lute Bloke Down By The Clink; and London's Singing Bus Conductor (name of Duke Baysee, works on the no.38 route, donations not accepted, all change at the next stop puh-lease).

But the rest? Thirty seconds in their company and you'll come to the conclusion that music and democracy go together like pizza and peas. Don't give 'em money. It'll only encourage 'em.

A tasteful and rather swanky pizza parlour in Knightsbridge that plays host to jazz artists at the decent end of mainstream. The finger-spot lighting is a treat, as are the pizzas.

Ronnie Scott's
47 Frith Street, Soho, W1 (7439 0747/ www.ronniescotts.co.uk). Leicester Square or Tottenham Court Road tube. **Open** 8.30pm-3am Mon-Sat; 7.30-11pm Sun. *Gigs* 9.30pm Mon-Sat; 8.30pm Sun. **Admission** £4-£20. **Credit** AmEx, DC, MC, V. **Map** p399 K6.
Easily London's best-known jazz club, and one of the most famous in the world. In the absence of Scott, who died in the mid-1990s, Pete King has maintained the ambience of club to perfection. It's not cheap to either get in or drink here, and the chattering of the expense-accounters can get annoying, but the sound is great and the quality of music (acts play two sets a night here for a week at a time, sometimes more) usually outstanding.

Vortex
139-141 Stoke Newington Church Street, Stoke Newington, N16 (7254 6516/www.palay.ndirect.co.uk/ vortex.jazz). Stoke Newington rail/67, 73, 76, 106, 243 bus. **Open** 10am-11.30pm Mon-Thur; 10am-midnight Fri, Sat; 11am-11pm Sun. *Gigs* 9pm daily. **Admission** free-£10. **Credit** MC, V.
A supremely relaxed venue that's a favourite of London's jazz community for the friendliness of the vibe, the cosiness of the room and the excellence of the mainly veggie food.

Best of the rest

While large-scale, big-name events such as **Glastonbury**, the **Reading Festival** (for both, *see p320*) and the **Notting Hill Carnival** (*see p263*) dominate Britain's summer festival season, London offers plenty of smaller events. Most of the capital's fields and open spaces will stage some sort of bash during the year: keep an eye on *Time Out* for details of festival line-ups. Phone nearer the time to check dates and prices.

Jazz is pretty much sewn up by the year's two big productions: the autumn **Soho Jazz Festival** (ten days in September/October; 7437 6437, www.sohojazzfestival.co.uk) and the **Oris London Jazz Festival** (phone 7405 5974 for dates). In addition, the **Coin Street Festival** (June to September; 7928 0960, www.coinstreetfestival.org) offers a wide array of performances, and includes the **Latin American Gran Gran Fiesta**. The festival usually ends with Thameside fireworks.

Charles Wells Cambridge Folk Festival
Cherry Hinton Hall Grounds, Cambridge (01223 357851/www.cam-folkfest.co.uk). **Date** 27-29 July 2001. **Tickets** £18-£50 (approx). **Credit** AmEx, MC, V.

Pizza Express Jazz Club: saxy. *See p316*.

Don't worry if folk – along with cajun, blues and gospel – are not your bag. If your mind is even slightly open to hearing things outside your normal sphere of listening, and you like the idea of hanging around in the grounds of a lovely country house with a bunch of like-minded individuals, then book your tickets (which go on sale in May) quickly.

Essential
Stanmer Park, Brighton, East Sussex (information 01273 888787/box office 01273 709709/ www.essentialfestival.com). **Date** 14-15 July 2001. **Tickets** £30 (approx). **Credit** AmEx, MC, V.
This relative newcomer evolved from an annual college barn dance. Although it's no longer a student event, the audience is generally youngish and laid-back. The weekend usually consists of a dance day and a roots day, and tickets are sold on a daily basis.

Fleadh
Finsbury Park, N4 (information 8961 5490/bookings 7344 0044/www.fleadhfestival.com). Finsbury Park tube/rail. **Date** June/July (phone to check). **Tickets** £30 (approx). **Credit** AmEx, MC, V.
Pronounced 'flar' – it's Gaelic for 'party' – the Mean Fiddler's annual day out in Finsbury Park is now about as Irish as Jack Charlton. Still, the line-ups are usually solid if generally unsurprising, and if nothing else, it's a grand excuse to get fall-down drunk.

Jazz, you like it, nightly at Stoke Newington's terrific **Vortex** club. *See p319.*

Glastonbury Festival

Worthy Farm, Pilton, Somerset (www.glastonburyfestivals.co.uk). **Date** late June, but no event in 2001.

Glasto was founded by farmer Michael Eavis in the 1960s, and has spiralled into a megalithic stoner-fest loved by generations of wasters. The atmosphere draws as many as does the music, though whether acres of muddy fields, appalling toilet facilities and every juggler in the western world is really all that some see it as is a moot point. However, expect about a zillion acts spread over about a million stages, from rock and folk to jazz and dance to world and cabaret.

Due to safety concerns brought on by the amount of gatecrashers at 2000's event, there'll be no festival in 2001. However, expect the event to return the following year; a box office number will be advertised in *Time Out* magazine from around March.

Guildford Festival

Stoke Park, Guildford, Surrey (01483 536270/ www.guildford-live.co.uk). **Tickets** £30 per day (approx). **Credit** AmEx, MC, V.

It's the least cutting-edge festival of them all, but Guildford is fun, not least because its capacity is smaller than all other festivals of its ilk. The line-ups usually offer a couple of genuine headline acts and some less appealing filler, but the event as a whole is very pleasant and pleasingly un-music biz.

Meltdown

Royal Festival Hall, South Bank, SE1 (7960 4242/ www.sbc.org.uk). **Date** 24 June-8 July 2001. **Tickets** vary. **Credit** AmEx, DC, MC, V.

A fantastic idea, this, albeit one that isn't always brought to ideal fruition. Each year, the RFH gets a notable figure to programme a series of events: previous curators have included Laurie Anderson, Elvis Costello, and, in 2000, Scott Walker. The choices range from the inspired to the insipid, but there'll usually be something worth investigating.

Reading Festival

Richfield Avenue, Reading, Berks (information 8963 0940/box office 7344 0044). **Date** 24-26 Aug 2001. **Tickets** £35 per day (approx); £85 weekend (approx). **Credit** AmEx, MC, V.

Held over the August Bank Holiday weekend and ostensibly marking the end of the English summer (such as there is one), this three-day, big-budget Mean Fiddler-organised fandango within a short train ride of London usually provides an excellent line-up spread over several stages, with the biggest of the big matching wits with the up-and-comers and flavours-of-the-month. The whole thing is exhausting, but that's kind of the point.

V2001

Hylands Park, Chelmsford, Essex (0870 165 5555). **Date** 18-19 Aug 2001 (unconfirmed). **Tickets** phone for details. **Credit** AmEx, MC, V.

With so many festivals on the calendar, some find it surprising that V2001 (formerly V2000, V99, V98, etc, and held 45 miles out of London) has managed to survive. However, given that it's backed by Virgin (hence the 'V'), which treats it as a weekend-long ad, it's not that astonishing at all. Expect an array of biggish indie bands, lots of Virgin branding and not a great deal of excitement.

Sport & Fitness

Put some vim and vigour into your visit.

See the Sport section of *Time Out* for the pick of the action, as well as contacts and 'things to do' in everything from archery to wrestling. Fitness, complementary therapy and alternative living are covered in the Body & Mind section. Alternatively, phone **Sportsline** (7222 8000) – though you'll probably find the line perpetually busy – or contact your nearest leisure centre.

Athletics

These venues are open to casual users, but are also home to athletics clubs, which can offer a more structured and competitive approach to track and field.

Barnet Copthall Stadium *Great North Way, Barnet, NW4 (8457 9915). Mill Hill East tube.* **Cost** £2/day; £73 season ticket.
Crystal Palace National Sports Centre *Ledrington Road, Crystal Palace, SE19 (8778 0131/www.crystalpalace.co.uk). Crystal Palace rail.* **Cost** £2.25/day.
Millennium Arena *Battersea Park, East Carriage Drive, Battersea, SW11 (8871 7537). Battersea Park rail.* **Cost** £1.70/day.
Parliament Hill Track *Highgate Road, Hampstead Heath, NW5 (7435 8998). Gospel Oak rail.* **Cost** £1.70/day; £27 season ticket.

Baseball & softball

Contact BaseballSoftball UK for details of playing opportunities. To find out your nearest team, visit their website or send a stamped, self-addressed envelope to the above address.

BaseballSoftball UK *Ariel House, 74A Charlotte Street, Fitzrovia, London W1P 1LR (7453 7055/ www.baseballsoftballuk.com).*

Cycling

Herne Hill is the oldest cycle stadium in the UK and London's only velodrome, while Lee Valley caters for BMX, road racing, time-trialling, cyclo-cross and mountain biking on various purpose-built tracks and stages a variety of events on weekends and summer weekdays. For bike hire, *see p361*.

Herne Hill Velodrome *Burbage Road, Herne Hill, SE24 (7737 4647). Herne Hill rail.* **Open** *Summer* 10am-12pm, 6-8.30pm Tue, Thur; 6-8.30pm Fri;

9am-1.30pm Sat; closed Mon, Wed, Sun. *Winter* 9am-1.30pm Sat; closed Mon-Fri, Sun. **Cost** £4.15; from £1.30 under-16s.
Lee Valley Cycle Circuit *Quartermile Lane, Stratford, E15 (8534 6085). Leyton tube.* **Open** *Summer* 8am-8pm daily, but check availability. *Winter* 8am-3.30pm Mon-Fri; closed Sat, Sun. **Cost** *With bike hire* £4.30; £3.30 under-16s. *With own bike* £2.20; £1.10 under-16s.

Golf

Contact the English Golf Union (01526 354500, www.englishgolfunion.org) for more on courses in the capital. Membership is not essential at the 18-hole public courses listed below. There's no course at Regent's Park, but there is a range and lessons can be booked by appointment.

Airlinks Golf Course *Southall Lane, Hounslow, Middx (8561 1418). Hayes & Harlington rail, then 195 bus.* **Fees per round** £11 Mon-Fri; £17 Sat, Sun.
Brent Valley Golf Course *Church Road, Hanwell, W7 (8567 1287). Ealing Broadway tube/rail.* **Fees per round** £7.50 Mon; £10 Tue-Fri; £14.50 before noon Sat, Sun; £12 after noon Sat, Sun.
Chingford Golf Course *Bury Road, Chingford, E4 (8529 5708). Chingford rail.* **Fees per round** £10.70 Mon-Fri; £14.80 Sat, Sun; £5.35 under-18s, OAPs after 10am Mon-Fri. (Note: golfers must wear a red shirt as the course is on a public thoroughfare.)
Lee Valley Golf Course *Picketts Lock Lane, Edmonton, N9 (8803 3611/ www.leevalleypark.org.uk). Ponders End rail.* **Fees per round** *Members* £9.40 Mon-Fri; £12 Sat, Sun. *Non-members* £11.50 Mon-Fri; £14.20 Sat, Sun.
Regent's Park Golf & Tennis School *Outer Circle, Regent's Park, NW1 (7724 0643). Baker Street tube.* **Open** 8am-9pm daily. **Map** p398 G2.

Hyde Park Stables. *See p322.*

Richmond Park Gold Course *Roehampton Gate, Priory Lane, Richmond, SW15 (8876 3205/ www.gcmgolf.com). Richmond tube/rail.* **Fees per round** £15 Mon-Fri; £18 Sat, Sun (cost reduces the later in the day you play).

Stockley Park Golf Course *off Stockley Road (A408), Uxbridge, Middx (8813 5700). Heathrow Terminals 1, 2 & 3 tube, then U5 bus.* **Fees per round** *Hillingdon residents* £21 Mon-Fri; £29 Sat, Sun. *Non-residents* £24 Mon-Fri; £34 Sat, Sun.

Horse riding

Hyde Park Stables offers pleasant treks through the park, but only if you book ahead. Wimbledon Village offer classes and horses to suit riders of all ages (from three up) and abilities, with rides on Wimbledon Common, Putney Heath and Richmond Park.

Hyde Park Stables *63 Bathurst Mews, Paddington, W2 (7723 2813/www.hydeparkstables.com). Lancaster Gate tube.* **Open** *Summer* 10am-5pm Tue-Fri; 8.30am-5pm Sat, Sun; closed Mon. *Winter* 10am-sunset Tue-Fri; 8.30am-sunset Sat, Sun; closed Mon. **Fees** *Group lessons* £32/hr; £30/hr children. *Individual lessons* £55/hr. *Ride around Hyde Park* £30. **Map** p395 D6.
Branch: *Kensington Stables* 11 Elvaston Mews, South Kensington, SW7 (7589 2299).

Wimbledon Village Stables *24 High Street, Wimbledon, SW19 (8946 8579/www.wvstables.com). Wimbledon tube/rail.* **Open** 8am-5pm Tue-Sun; closed Mon. **Fees** £25-£30/hr.

Ice skating

Ice rinks need regular refreezing and sweeping, so session times vary from day to day and from season to season. Generally, sessions last two hours, and rinks are open from approximately 10am to 10pm; phone for more specific details. Broadgate is one of London's only permanent outdoor rink (open late Oct-Apr); another opens for a few weeks over Christmas in the courtyard of Somerset House (*see p98*). Streatham has recently had a big refurb; and both Lee Valley and Leisurebox have popular disco nights.

Broadgate Ice Rink *Broadgate Circus, Eldon Street, The City, EC2 (7505 4068). Liverpool Street tube/rail.* **Admission** £5; £3 under-16s, concessions. **Skate hire** £1. **Map** p403 Q5.

Lee Valley Ice Centre *Lea Bridge Road, Lea Bridge, E10 (8533 3154/www.leevalleypark.org.uk). Blackhorse Road tube, then 158 bus/Walthamstow Central tube, then 158 bus.* **Admission** £4.50; £3.50 children. **Skate hire** £1.

Leisurebox *17 Queensway, Bayswater, W2 (7229 0172). Bayswater or Queensway tube.* **Admission** £5. **Skate hire** £1. **Map** p394 C6.

Streatham Ice Arena *386 Streatham High Road, Streatham, SW16 (8769 7771/ www.streathamicearena.co.uk). Streatham rail.* **Admission** £5; £4 under-12s. **Skate hire** £1.50.

Strike! **Rowans Bowl.** *See p324.*

Karting

All the tracks below have bookable daytime and evening sessions; phone for details of available times and, also, prices.

Daytona Raceway *Atlas Road, Acton, NW10 (8961 3616/www.daytona.co.uk). North Acton tube.*
Playscape Pro Racing *Streatham Kart Raceway, 390 Streatham High Road, Streatham, SW16 (8677 8677/www.playscape.co.uk/karting). Streatham rail.*
Raceway *Central Warehouse, North London Freight Terminal, York Way, King's Cross, N1 (7833 1000/www.theraceway.net). King's Cross tube/rail.*

Sport & leisure centres

Badminton, squash, swimming, exercise classes, gym and various indoor sports are on offer at public sports centres. Members usually receive discounts. You should phone well in advance if you're hoping to book a court or hall. For further centres, look in the *Yellow Pages* under 'Leisure Centres', or call **Sportsline** (7222 8000).

Admission prices for the following centres vary depending on the activity and time of day. Ask about membership rates if you're planning to use the facilities over a long period of time.

Chelsea Sports Centre

Chelsea Manor Street, Chelsea, SW3 (7352 6985). Sloane Square tube. **Open** 7am-10pm Mon-Fri; 8am-6.30pm Sat; 8am-10pm Sun. **Map** p397 E12. A 25-m swimming pool plus a teaching pool, weights, badminton, yoga and exercise classes.

Jubilee Hall Leisure Centre

30 The Piazza, Covent Garden, WC2 (7836 4835/ www.jubileehallclubs.co.uk). Covent Garden tube. **Open** 7am-10pm Mon-Fri; 10am-5pm Sat, Sun. **Map** p401 L7. A well-equipped but busy gym, with plenty of free weights as one of its main attractions. Martial arts, exercise classes and complementary therapies are also on offer. Last entry is 45 minutes before closing.

Arts & Entertainment

Michael Sobell Leisure Centre

Hornsey Road, Holloway, N7 (7609 2166/ www.aquaterra.org). Holloway Road tube/Finsbury Park tube/rail. **Open** 9am-11pm Mon-Fri; 9am-6pm Sat; 9am-9.30pm Sun.

The facilities at this north London centre are excellent, if showing signs of wear and tear, and include squash, trampolining, exercise classes, skating and a wide range of sports in the massive main arena.

Mornington Sports & Leisure Centre

142-50 Arlington Road, Camden, NW1 (7267 3600/ www.holmesplace-camden.co.uk). Camden Town tube. **Open** 7am-9pm Mon-Fri; 10am-5pm Sat, Sun. **Map** p398 J2.

The usual range of team sports – volleyball, basketball and football – are offered at this small centre, as are a gym and plenty of exercise classes.

Porchester Centre

Queensway, Bayswater, W2 (enquiries 7792 2919/ spa 7792 3980/www.courtneys.co.uk). Bayswater, Queensway or Royal Oak tube. **Open** 7am-10pm Mon-Fri; 8am-8pm Sat, Sun. **Map** p394 C6.

Swimming, gym, exercise classes and squash are on the programme. The Porchester Spa includes art-deco-style relaxation areas, Turkish hot rooms, Russian steam rooms, sauna, plunge pool and a range of complementary therapies.

Queen Mother Sports Centre

223 Vauxhall Bridge Road, Victoria, SW1 (7630 5522/www.courtneys.co.uk). Victoria tube/rail. **Open** 6.30am-10pm Mon-Fri; 8am-8pm Sat, Sun. **Map** p400 J10.

Just refurbished, this centre boasts a well-equipped gym, two exercise studios, badminton, swimming and diving, martial arts and beauty treatments.

Seymour Leisure Centre

Seymour Place, Marylebone, W1 (7723 8019/ www.courtneys.co.uk). Edgware Road or Marble Arch tube. **Open** 7am-10pm Mon-Fri; 7am-8pm Sat; 8am-8pm Sun. **Map** p395 F5.

This '30s-style centre has a swimming pool, sports hall, fitness room, steam and sauna suite, plus a Courtney's gym with separate tariffs. The 'Move It' programme of exercise classes is justly renowned.

Swiss Cottage Sports Centre

Winchester Road, Swiss Cottage, NW3 (7413 6490/ www.holmesplaces-camden.co.uk). Swiss Cottage tube. **Open** 7am-9.30pm Mon-Fri; 8am-7.30pm Sat, Sun.

As well as a gym and two fine indoor swimming pools, there are facilities for squash, badminton and five-a-side football.

Swimming

To find your nearest swimming pool, try the *Yellow Pages* or **Sportsline** (7222 8000). A few of the better-known ones follow (*see also p322* **Sport & leisure centres**). For pools particularly suited to children, *see p271*.

Indoor pools

Highbury Pool *Highbury Crescent, Highbury, N5 (7704 2312/www.aquaterra.org). Highbury & Islington tube/rail.* **Open** 6.30am-9pm Mon-Fri; 7.30am-7pm Sat; 7.30am-9pm Sun. *Women only* 7-9pm Tue. **Admission** £2.80; £1.20 under-16s; free under-4s.

Ironmonger Row Baths *Ironmonger Row, Finsbury, EC1 (7253 4011/www.aquaterra.org). Old Street tube/rail.* **Open** 6.30am-9pm Mon; 6.30am-8pm Tue-Thur; 6.30am-7pm Fri; 9am-6pm Sat; noon-6pm Sun. **Admission** £2.80; £1.20 under-16s; free under-3s. **Map** p402 P4.

Oasis Sports Centre *32 Endell Street, Covent Garden, WC2 (7831 1804).Holborn tube.* **Open** *Indoor pool* 6.30am-6.30pm Mon-Fri; 9.30am-5pm Sat, Sun. *Outdoor pool* 7.30am-9pm Mon-Fri; 9.30am-5pm Sat, Sun. **Admission** £2.90; £1.10 under-16s; free under-5s. **Map** p399 L6.

Outdoor pools

Brockwell Lido *Dulwich Road, Herne Hill, SE24 (7274 3088/www.thelido.co.uk). Herne Hill rail.* **Open** *May-Sept* 6.45-10am, noon-7pm Mon-Fri; 11am-7pm Sat, Sun. *Oct-Apr* closed. **Admission** £2-£4; £1.50-£2.50 children.

Hampstead Heath Ponds *Hampstead Heath, NW3 (7485 4491). Hampstead tube/Gospel Oak or Hampstead Heath rail/C2, C11, 214 bus.* **Open** 7am-dusk daily. **Admission** free.

Oasis Sports Centre *See above.*

Parliament Hill Lido *Hampstead Heath, Gordon House Road, NW5 (7485 3873). Gospel Oak rail/ C11 bus.* **Open** *May-Sept* 7-9.30am, 10am-6pm daily. *Oct-Apr* 7-9.30am daily. **Admission** £1.50-£3.70; free 7-9.30am.

Richmond Pools on the Park *Old Deer Park, Twickenham Road, Richmond, Surrey (8940 0561/ www.springhealth.co.uk). Richmond tube/rail.* **Open** *Mar-Sept* 6.30am-7.45pm Mon; 6.30am-9pm Tue-Fri; 7am-6pm Sat, Sun; *Oct-Feb* call for details. **Admission** £2.50-£3.60.

Serpentine Lido *Hyde Park, W2 (7298 2100). Knightsbridge or South Kensington tube.* **Open** usually for two months over summer; phone for times and admission prices. **Map** p395 E8.

Tooting Bec Lido *Tooting Bec Road, Tooting Bec Common, Tooting, SW17 (8871 7198). Tooting Bec tube/Streatham rail.* **Open** *Jun-Sept* 10am-8pm daily. *Oct-May* closed except for club members. **Admission** £2.60-£3.10; £2.10-£2.25 children.

Tennis

Many of London's parks have tennis courts, which usually cost little or nothing to hire. Private facilities and coaching – among them the two outdoor courts and six indoor courts at the Islington Tennis Centre – are more pricey, but **Sportsline** (7222 8000) may be able to help. If you want to test your shots on grass, then phone or write (with a stamped self-addressed envelope) to the Information Department at the

Lawn Tennis Association, Queen's Club, Palliser Road, London W14 9EG (7381 7000, www.lta.org.uk) who publish leaflets on where you can play. They're published on a county-by-county basis: Middlesex includes central London, while Essex, Surrey and Hertfordshire cover outlying areas.

Islington Tennis Centre *Market Road, Barnsbury, N7 (7700 1370/www.aquaterra.org). Caledonian Road tube.* **Open** 7am-10pm Mon-Fri; 8am-10pm Sat, Sun. **Fees** *Outdoor* £5-£6/hr. *Indoor* £13.50-£15/hr.

Tenpin bowling

Tenpin bowling is popular as both a competitive sport and for a fun night out. Listed here are a few of the capital's best bowling centres; for other choices you can call the British Tenpin Bowling Association (8478 1745). Prices vary from place to place and depend on the time of day, but the average is somewhere around £5 per game, including the hire of shoes. *See also p322* **Leisurebox**.

Rowans Bowl *10 Stroud Green Road, Finsbury Park, N4 (8800 1950/www.rowans.co.uk). Finsbury Park tube/rail.* **Open** 10.30am-1am Mon-Thur; 10.30am-3.30am Fri, Sat; 10.30am-1.30am Sun. **Lanes** 24.

Streatham Mega Bowl *142 Streatham Hill, Streatham, SW2 (8671 5021/www.megabowl.co.uk). Streatham Hill rail.* **Open** 10am-midnight daily. **Lanes** 36.

XS Superbowl *15-17 Alpine Way, Beckton, E6 (7511 4440/www.xsleisure.co.uk). East Ham tube then 101 bus/Beckton DLR.* **Open** noon-midnight daily. **Lanes** 22.

Netting a Wimbledon ticket

Gaining admission to **Wimbledon**, aka the-one-they-all-want-to-win, is among life's more troublesome tasks. Seats on Centre and Number One courts are allocated by ballot: you must write (enclosing an SAE) for an application form between 1 September and 31 December, which rules out getting posh seats for this year's tournament, held 25 June to 8 July 2001.

For most people, the outside courts are a cheaper but still enjoyable proposition. You'll need hours to spare for the inevitable queueing, but once you're in, the freedom to wander from court to court means you're never far from the action. Later in the day, you can buy returned show-court tickets for a fraction of their face value, with proceeds going to charity.

All England Lawn Tennis Club (Wimbledon)

PO Box 98, Church Road, Wimbledon, SW19 (8944 1066/information 8946 2244/ www.wimbledon.org). Southfields tube.

Watersports

Capital specialises in rowing; the DS&WC offers dragonboat racing, sailing, rowing and canoeing; the DWC has jet-skiing; and Lee Valley has windsurfing, sailing, water-skiing and canoeing. Phone for details of exact times and prices.

Capital Rowing Centre *Polytechnic Boathouse, Ibis Lane, Chiswick, W4 (07973 314199 mobile/ www.capitalrowing.com). Chiswick rail.* **Open** times vary, daily.
Docklands Sailing & Watersports Centre *Millwall Dock, Westferry Road, Docklands, E14 (7537 2626/www.docklandswatersports.co.uk). Crossharbour DLR.* **Open** *Summer* 9.30am-11pm Mon-Fri; 9.30am-5pm Sat, Sun. *Winter* times vary; phone for details.
Docklands Watersports Club *Tereza Joanne, Gate 14, King George V Dock, Woolwich Manor Way, Woolwich, E16 (7511 7000/www.tereza-joanne.com). Gallions Reach DLR/North Woolwich rail.* **Open** *Summer* 10am-dusk Wed-Sun; closed Mon, Tue. *Winter* 10am-dusk Thur-Sun; closed Mon-Wed.
Lee Valley Watersports Centre *Banbury Reservoir, Harbet Road, Chingford, E4 (8531 1129/www.leevalleypark.org.uk). Angel Road rail.* **Open** times vary Mon-Fri; 10am-dusk Sat, Sun.

Yoga

The following places are open daily, though it's always best to phone to check what's on offer in the way of classes and treatments. The Iyengar Institute specialises in Iyengar, a focused and precise style of yoga; Triyoga offers classes, therapies and Pilates in its 6,000 square feet of space; Yogahome offers classes in almost every style from £6; and the Yoga Therapy Centre offers treatment for asthma, hypertension, arthritis, diabetes, ME, menstrual problems and stress-related illness as well as more general classes. *See also p322* **Chelsea Sports Centre**.

Iyengar Institute *223A Randolph Avenue, Maida Vale, W9 (7624 3080/www.iyi.org.uk). Maida Vale tube.*
Triyoga *6 Erskine Road, Primrose Hill, NW3 (7586 5939/www.triyoga.uk). Primrose Hill rail.*
Yogahome *11 Allen Road, Stoke Newington, N16 (7249 2425/www.yogahome.com). Bus 73.*
Yoga Therapy Centre *Homeopathic Hospital, 60 Great Ormond Street, Bloomsbury, WC1 (7419 7195/www.yogatherapy.org). Russell Square tube.* **Map** p399 L4.

Spectator sports

Basketball

This fast-expanding sport has a number of teams in the capital. The London Towers play in the elite Dairylea Dunkers Championship and

two European competitions. For details, phone the English Basketball Association (0113 236 1166, www.basketballengland.org.uk). The season runs from September to May.

London Towers *Crystal Palace National Sports Centre, Ledrington Road, Crystal Palace, SE19 (8776 7755/www.london-towers.co.uk). Crystal Palace rail.* **Admission** £8; £6 concessions.

Boxing

Boxing is a sport under fire. A December 2000 ruling confirming that the British Boxing Board of Control were liable for compensation to boxer Michael Watson, injured in a fight in 1991, set a dangerous, potentially costly precedent for the sport. However, serious calls for a ban are still relatively rare and fans of the sport can still see major fights around London. Seats can cost from £20 to £200, more for a big world-title bout. Most promotions take place at York Hall on Old Ford Road, E2 (8980 2243), though major championship fights are staged at bigger venues like Earl's Court, Wembley Arena or the London Arena (*see p328*). For information, phone the BBBC (7403 5879, www.bbbofc.com).

Cricket

County Championship matches are staged over four days, so if you haven't got much time, it's advisable to catch one of the one-day matches in the NatWest Trophy or Norwich Union National League. For regular county games (everything except the semi-finals and finals of knockout competitions), tickets cost £10 or less; tickets for internationals are far harder to come by.

Middlesex play at Lord's, the spiritual and administrative home of the game and host to Test matches and all major cup finals. The Oval is home to Surrey and is rather more populist (look out for the occasional day-night game); it traditionally hosts the final test of the summer. The season runs April to September.

Lord's *St John's Wood Road, St John's Wood, NW8 (MCC information 7289 1611/tickets 7432 1066/ www.lords.org). St John's Wood tube.*
Foster's Oval *Kennington Oval, Kennington, SE11 (7582 7764/www.surreyccc.co.uk). Oval tube.*

Football

Tickets for FA Carling Premiership matches are now scarce for casual spectators. Every league game at Arsenal, Charlton Athletic or Chelsea is a sell-out; similarly, it would be unwise to turn up at Tottenham or West Ham on the off-chance of gaining admission. However, London clubs also feature in all three divisions of the Nationwide League: at this lower level tickets

Arts & Entertainment

are cheaper and more readily available. The prices quoted below are for adult non-members buying on a match-by-match basis.

Clubs

Arsenal *Arsenal Stadium, Avenell Road, Highbury, N5 (7413 3366/www.arsenal.com). Arsenal tube.* **Tickets** £16.50-£32. FA Carling Premiership.
Barnet *Underhill Stadium, Barnet Lane, Barnet, Hertfordshire (8449 6325). High Barnet tube.* **Tickets** £8-£10 standing; £12-£15 seated. Nationwide League Division 3.
✐ **Brentford** *Griffin Park, Braemar Road, Brentford, Middlesex (8847 2511/www.brentfordfc.co.uk). South Ealing tube/Brentford rail.* **Tickets** £10 standing; £10-£16 seated. Nationwide League Division 2.
Charlton Athletic *The Valley, Floyd Road, Charlton, SE7 (8333 4010/www.cafc.co.uk). Charlton rail.* **Tickets** only available to season-ticket holders. FA Carling Premiership.
Chelsea *Stamford Bridge, Fulham Road, Chelsea, SW6 (7386 7799/www.chelseafc.co.uk). Fulham Broadway tube.* **Tickets** £25-£33. FA Carling Premiership. **Map** p396 B13.
Crystal Palace *Selhurst Park, Whitehorse Lane, Selhurst, SE25 (8771 8841/www.cpfc.co.uk). Selhurst rail.* **Tickets** £7-£25. Nationwide League Division 1.
Fulham *Craven Cottage, Stevenage Road, Fulham, SW6 (7893 8383/www.fulhamfc.co.uk). Putney Bridge tube.* **Tickets** £13 standing; £17 seated. Nationwide League Division 1.
Leyton Orient *Matchroom Stadium, Brisbane Road, Leyton, E10 (8926 1111/www.leytonorient.com). Leyton tube.* **Tickets** £11 standing; £13-£15 seated. Nationwide League Division 3.
Millwall *The Den, Zampa Road, Bermondsey, SE16 (7231 9999/www.millwallfc.co.uk). South Bermondsey rail.* **Tickets** £13-£18. Nationwide League Division 2.
✐ **Queens Park Rangers** *Loftus Road Stadium, South Africa Road, Shepherd's Bush, W12 (8740 2575/www.qpr.co.uk). White City tube.* **Tickets** £14-£20. Nationwide League Division 1.
Tottenham Hotspur *White Hart Lane, Bill Nicholson Way, High Road, Tottenham, N17 (08700 112222/www.spurs.co.uk). White Hart Lane rail.* **Tickets** £24-£48. FA Carling Premiership.
Watford *Vicarage Road, Watford, Herts (01923 496010/www.watfordfc.co.uk). Watford High Street rail.* **Tickets** £16-£25. Nationwide League Division 1.
West Ham United *Boleyn Ground, Green Street, West Ham, E13 (8548 2700/ www.westhamunited.co.uk). Upton Park tube.* **Tickets** £25-£45. FA Carling Premiership.
Wimbledon *Selhurst Park, Whitehorse Lane, Selhurst, SE25 (8771 8841/www.wimbledon-fc.co.uk). Selhurst rail.* **Tickets** £15-£25. Nationwide League Division 1.

Golf

Two of the UK's most famous courses lie within easy reach of London, with Wentworth the venue for the World Matchplay tournament every October. Phone for details.

A win for **England's cricketers**. *See p325.*

Sunningdale *Ridgemount Road, Sunningdale, nr Ascot, Berks (01344 621681). Sunningdale rail.*
Wentworth *Wentworth Drive, Virginia Water, Surrey (01344 842201/www.wentworthclub.com). Virginia Water rail.*

Greyhound racing

Greyhounds chase a dummy hare around the track, and punters place bets on likely-looking dogs. Britain's second most popular spectator sport (after football) is great fun for an evening out, and very user-friendly for the uninitiated. All tracks have several bars and restaurants, and more information on the sport and all these venues can be gleaned from www.thedogs.co.uk.

Catford Stadium *Adenmore Road, Catford, SE6 (8690 8000). Catford or Catford Bridge rail.* **Races** 7.30pm Mon; 7.20pm Thur, Sat. **Admission** £4.
Romford Stadium *London Road, Romford, Essex (01708 762345). Romford rail.* **Races** 7.35pm Mon, Wed, Fri, Sat. **Admission** £1.50-£5.
Walthamstow Stadium *Chingford Road, Walthamstow, E4 (8531 4255/ www.wsgreyhound.co.uk). Walthamstow Central tube.* **Races** 7.30pm Tue, Thur, Sat. **Admission** free-£5.
Wimbledon Stadium *Plough Lane, Wimbledon, SW17 (8946 8000/www.wimbledondogs.co.uk). Tooting Broadway tube/Wimbledon tube/rail/ Earlsfield or Haydons Road rail.* **Races** 7.30pm Tue, Fri, Sat. **Admission** £3-£5.

Horse racing

The horse racing season is roughly divided into flat racing (Apr-Sept) and National Hunt (aka jumps racing; Oct-Apr). Evening meetings are held in summer. These days courses cater for everyone from dedicated punters to day-tripping families, with plenty of places to eat and drink. There's no compulsion to bet, but it does add to the fun.

Ascot

High Street, Ascot, Berks (01344 622211/ www.ascot.co.uk). Ascot rail. **Admission** £5-£20.
Big hats invade Britain's premier flat racing course in June for a highlight on the society calendar: the Royal Meeting, when the Queen drops in for a flutter and admission prices rocket. In 2001, the Royal Meeting will be held from 19-21 June (Ladies' Day is on 21 June), and booking is essential. *See also p262.*

Epsom

Epsom Downs, Epsom, Surrey (01372 726311/ www.epsomderby.co.uk). Epsom, Epsom Downs or Tattenham Corner rail. **Admission** £5-£16.
The Oaks and the Derby are both run at Epsom (8 and 9 June 2001 respectively). In contrast to the exclusive Royal Meeting at Ascot, 'Derby Day' is a traditional Londoners' day out, with pearly kings, jellied eels, palm readers and a funfair all adding to the bustling atmosphere. *See also p262.*

Kempton Park

Staines Road East, Sunbury-on-Thames, Middx (01932 782292/www.kempton.co.uk). Kempton Park rail. **Admission** £6-£17.
This popular course holds meetings throughout the year. An annual highlight is the King George VI Stakes, run on Boxing Day (26 Dec).

Sandown Park

Portsmouth Road, Esher, Surrey (01372 463072/ www.sandown.co.uk). Esher rail. **Admission** £5-£17.
Generally considered the best equipped of the southeast tracks and a regular award-winner to prove it, Sandown's major occasions include the Whitbread Gold Cup (28 Apr 2001) and the Coral Eclipse Stakes (7 July 2001).

Windsor

Maidenhead Road, Windsor, Berks (01753 865234/www.windsorracing.co.uk). Windsor & Eton Riverside rail. **Admission** £4-£16.

Windsor takes advantage of its picturesque riverside setting with a shuttle boat service operating to and from the town before and after meetings. The figure-of-eight course, with a head-on view of the last five furlongs, can make it difficult to work out which horse is winning, though in the balmy ambience of the popular evening meetings, you may not care.

Ice hockey

The London Knights were created in 1998 as part of British ice hockey's expansion, and play (with some success) in the Sekonda Superleague. Slough play in the lower-grade British National League. The season runs from September to March, with games most weekends.

London Knights *London Arena, Limeharbour, Docklands, E14 (7538 1212/www.knightice.co.uk). Crossharbour & London Arena DLR.* **Admission** £12-£18; £7 concessions; £1 discount for advance bookings.

Slough Jets *Ice Arena, Montem Lane, Slough, Berks (information 01753 822658/tickets 01753 821555/www.sloughjets.co.uk). Slough rail.* **Admission** £8; £4.50 children.

Motor sport

Bangers, hot rods and stock cars provide family-oriented motorised mayhem on Sunday evenings. The season takes a summer break in June and July.

Wimbledon Stadium *Plough Lane, Wimbledon, SW17 (8946 8000). Tooting Broadway tube/ Wimbledon tube/rail/Earlsfield or Haydons Road rail.* **Admission** £9; £4 under-15s, OAPs.

Rugby league

Owned by Richard Branson's Virgin, the Broncos are the only professional rugby league team outside the game's traditional northern heartland and work hard to dispel local indifference to the 13-a-side code. The Super League season runs March to September.

London Broncos *The Valley, Floyd Road, Charlton, SE7 (8853 8001/www.londonbroncos.co.uk). Charlton rail.* **Admission** £10-£15; £3-£5 children.

Rugby union

The oval-ball revolution has brought professional status and an increase in standards, but clubs find it hard sustaining necessarily large squads on gates of around 3-5,000. Many leading internationals play their club rugby here, notably with Harlequins, London Wasps and Saracens. The Zurich Premiership and lower-grade National League seasons run from August to May, and most games are played on Saturday and Sunday afternoons.

Sunday football. *See p325.*

Arts & Entertainment

Spectator sports

A London football derby
Passions run high when local rivals meet, with Tottenham–Arsenal the biggest of all (*see p325*).

The first day of a Lord's Test
Pray for sunshine (*see p325*).

Derby Day
Horses for courses (*see p327*).

The London Marathon
Let the runners lead you through the streets of London (*see p261*).

Wimbledon
Game, set and match, if you can get in (*see p324*).

Greyhound racing
Dogs, beer and a bet: top fun (*see p326*).

Twickenham is the home of English rugby, and has been magnificently rebuilt in recent years: crowds of over 60,000 can now watch internationals and major cup finals. Tickets for matches in the Six Nations Championship (Jan-Mar) are distributed via affiliated clubs and are almost impossible for casual spectators to obtain. Those for cup finals and other matches are easier to come by; phone for details.

Twickenham *Whitton Road, Twickenham, Middx (information 8892 2000/tickets 8831 6666/www.rfu.com). Twickenham rail.*

Clubs

Esher *369 Molesey Road, Hersham, Surrey (01932 220295). Hersham rail.* **Admission** £5. National League Division 2.

Harlequins *Stoop Memorial Ground, Langhorn Drive, Twickenham, Middx (0870 887 0230). Twickenham rail.* **Admission** £12-£20. Zurich Premiership.

London Wasps *Loftus Road Stadium, South Africa Road, Shepherd's Bush, W12 (8743 0262/www.wasps.co.uk). White City tube.* **Admission** £11-£17. Zurich Premiership.

London Welsh *Old Deer Park, Kew Road, Richmond, Surrey (8940 2368/www.london-welsh.co.uk). Richmond tube/rail.* **Admission** £8 standing; £11 seated; £4 concessions. National League Division 1.

Rosslyn Park *Priory Lane, Upper Richmond Road, Roehampton, SW15 (8876 6044). Barnes rail.* **Admission** £8. National League Division 2.

Saracens *Vicarage Road Stadium, Watford, Herts (01923 496200/www.saracens.com). Watford High Street rail.* **Admission** £10-£30. Zurich Premiership.

Tennis

Wimbledon (for which, *see p324* **Netting a Wimbledon ticket**) is preceded by the Stella Artois, where stars from the men's circuit warm up for Wimbledon. It's very popular with both spectators and corporate hospitality companies. The 2001 event will be held from 11 to 17 June.

Queen's Club *Palliser Road, Hammersmith, W14 (7385 3421/www.queensclub.co.uk). Barons Court tube.*

Major venues

Crystal Palace National Sports Centre
Ledrington Road, Crystal Palace, SE19 (8778 0131/ www.crystalpalace.co.uk). Crystal Palace rail.
London's only major athletics stadium needs a complete overhaul, but it still stages a Grand Prix track and field meeting every summer. The sports centre hosts a huge variety of activities and competitions, including basketball, netball, martial arts, hockey and weightlifting. Following repeated threats of closure, Crystal Palace was reprieved in late 1997 and has since been made a Grade II listed building.

London Arena
Limeharbour, Docklands, E14 (7538 1212/ www.londonarena.co.uk). Crossharbour & London Arena DLR/D8, D9 bus.
In the shadow of Canary Wharf, the Arena provides an impressively modern and comfortable setting for major indoor sports. Londoners know it best as the home of ice hockey's Knights (*see p327*). Big boxing promotions are often staged here.

Wembley Arena/Conference Centre
Empire Way, Wembley, Middx (8902 0902/ www.wembley.co.uk). Wembley Park tube/Wembley Stadium rail. **Open** *Box office* 8am-9pm Mon-Sat; 9am-8pm Sun.
By early 2001, the proposed rebuilding of Wembley Stadium was in limbo. Demolition work, which was to have started in late 2000, had yet to begin, and it looked unlikely that the stadium would be rebuilt in time for its scheduled completion date of 2004, if at all. In the meantime, major football matches and rugby league's Challenge Cup final will be played elsewhere, with Old Trafford in Manchester and the Millennium Arena in Cardiff the most likely venues. Wembley Arena remains, however, staging the likes of show jumping and basketball; nearby Wembley Conference Centre hosts boxing and snooker.

Arts & Entertainment

Theatre

From modern musicals to ancient classics, London's theatre is as you like it.

The Beautiful Game. *See p331.*

See p331.

Arts & Entertainment

First things first: there is more to London theatre than the showy musicals and starry dramas that have made the West End's name. Although Theatreland boasts an array of such shows, there's an unmissable world of fringe and low-key performances to match that of any great city. It's worth the effort to hunt out less obvious plays in smaller, more intimate venues for a real taste of what London theatre can offer the punter. On a good night, a great show in a grotty pub can outshine ten Lloyd Webbers.

In this chapter, as in *Time Out* magazine's comprehensive theatre listings, productions and theatres are split into three categories: West End, Off-West End and Fringe. West End refers to the part of central London lying to the west of the City, where most of the big musicals and major dramas can be found, but it also refers to the cultural status of its leading theatres; the **Royal National Theatre** (*see p330*), for example, is classified as West End, even though it is located south of the river).

The most reliable of West End venues, with repertory rather than fixed, long-running programmes, are the building-based companies such as the aforementioned Royal National

Theatre (three stages in the South Bank Centre), the **Royal Shakespeare Company** (*see p330*; during the winter months, two theatres in the Barbican and one at the Young Vic) and **Shakespeare's Globe** (*see p330*) more than just a heritage gimmick). The Royal Court (*see p330*), meanwhile, is the country's most dynamic new writing theatre, now re-installed in its Sloane Square home.

Off-West End refers to the next rung down in terms of financial means, and generally offers the best mix of quality and originality. These theatres are usually heavily subsidised, paying minimum wages or, in some cases, no wages at all. Top writers, directors and actors are lured, instead, by the prospect of artistic liberty. But even these places have their own pecking order: wealthier theatres such as the **Young Vic** (*see p336*) and the **Almeida** (*see p333*) lead the pack, with the likes of the **Gate** and the **King's Head** (for both, *see p335*) often dependent on fresh-out-of-drama-college hopefuls prepared to work for nothing to make their names.

The Fringe, meanwhile, is scattered all over London, a theatrical underclass where standards are much more variable. There is, of course, a lot of good work to be found, and many of the biggest names in British theatre started their careers in these more humble venues. But finding such shows is, in practice, like winning the lottery. Among the most reliable are the **Finborough**, the **New End** and the **Grace** (for all, *see p336*), struggling in adverse financial circumstances to develop bold artistic policies.

Tickets & information

Tickets for big musicals are pricey and can be hard to obtain. **Ticketmaster** (7344 4444, www.ticketmaster.co.uk) and **First Call** (7420 0000, www.firstcall.co.uk) offer advance tickets, but watch out for those big bad booking fees, which can bump up the price by at least ten per cent. The cheapest option is to buy your tickets in person with cash direct from the theatre. Bear in mind that many theatres offer 24-hour phone sales by rolling over to a big ticket merchant – such as the two mentioned above – when the box office closes, which means that tickets are subject to booking fees; to avoid extra fees, call during office hours. For more on tkts, a half-price ticket booth in Leicester Square, *see p331* **tkts, please**.

Many West End theatres also offer reduced-price tickets for performances that have not sold out. These seats, available only on the night, are known as 'standby' tickets, and sell for about half what a top-priced ticket would cost. We've listed standby prices in this section, but be sure to call to check both availability and conditions (some standby tickets are limited to students, and it varies from theatre to theatre as to when standbys are put on sale).

West End

Building-based repertory companies

Royal Court
Sloane Square, Chelsea, SW1 (7565 5000/ www.royalcourttheatre.com). Sloane Square tube. **Box office** 10am-6pm Mon-Sat; closed Sun. **Tickets** 10p-£24.50; all tickets £5 Mon. **Credit** AmEx, MC, V. **Map** p400 G11.
The Royal Court is the undisputed epicentre of new writing in Britain. Having been in exile in the West End, in 2000 it settled back into its long-time Sloane Square home after a £25-million refurbishment. It boasts two spanking new performing spaces – the imaginatively titled 'Upstairs' (small studio theatre) and 'Downstairs' (proscenium arch main stage) – as well as a snazzy restaurant and bar.

Royal National Theatre
South Bank, SE1 (information 7452 3400/box office 7452 3000/www.nt-online.org). Waterloo tube/rail.

The reconstructed **Shakespeare's Globe**.

Box office 10am-8pm Mon-Sat; closed Sun. **Tickets** *Olivier & Lyttelton* £10-£30. *Cottesloe* £12-£22. *Standby* £8, £16. **Credit** AmEx, DC, MC, V. **Map** p401 M7.
Under the captaincy of populist ex-RSC and West End musical maestro Trevor Nunn, Britain's leading theatre has established a core rep company to perform its catch-all diet of musicals, classics and contemporary drama. Set in the concrete mausoleum of the South Bank Centre, the RNT contains three theatres: the Olivier's large, open platform for the big shows, the Lyttelton's traditional proscenium arch for mid-sized productions, and the recently refitted Cottesloe's flexible studio space accommodating smaller, more cutting-edge productions. A new exterior performance space, Theatre Square, and refurbishment of the theatre's front-of-house were completed in 2000 and redevelopment of the sound, scenery, staging and lighting is underway.

Royal Shakespeare Company
Barbican Centre, Silk Street, The City, EC2 (7638 8891/www.rsc.org.uk). Barbican tube/Moorgate tube/rail. **Box office** 9am-8pm daily. **Tickets** £5-£35. *Standby* £12, £7. **Credit** AmEx, MC, V. **Map** p402 P5.
The RSC is the principal custodian of Shakespeare's legacy in Britain, but it also stages works by new and classical writers of relevance to the Bard, as well as doing a sideline in money-spinning musicals such as *Les Misérables*. Aside from national tours, it divides its time between its main home in Stratford-upon-Avon at the Royal Shakespeare Theatre, the Swan and The Other Place in Stratford, and, between October and May, the Barbican Centre (the huge Barbican Theatre and the more intimate space of The Pit) and now also the Young Vic in Waterloo (*see p336*). In 2001, productions are planned of *The Duchess of Malfi*, *The Tempest*, *As You Like It*, *Romeo and Juliet*, *Richard II*, *Henry IV* and a new play entitled *Back to Methuselah*.

Shakespeare's Globe

*New Globe Walk, Bankside, SE1 (7401 9919/
www.shakespeares-globe.org). Blackfriars or Mansion
House tube.* **Box office** 10am-5pm Mon-Fri; closed
Sat, Sun. **Tickets** £5-£27. **Credit** AmEx, MC, V.
Map p404 O7.

Under Mark Rylance, the Globe has established itself
as a serious theatre, staging plays from May to
September in the open-air theatre that replicates the
original Globe. With the background noise of modern life and the transient interest of coach parties, the
theatre is no great friend of artistic nuance. However,
it offers interesting insights into how Will dealt with
mob dynamics, and the productions are rarely less
than fun. The Inigo Jones Theatre, a replica Jacobean
indoor playhouse, will be used to stage plays in winter when it's completed in 2002. See also *p75*.

Long-runners & musicals

Most theatres have evening shows Monday to
Saturday (starting 7.30-8pm) and matinees on
one weekday (usually Wednesday) and
Saturday. Check *Time Out* magazine for details.

An Inspector Calls

*Garrick Theatre, 2 Charing Cross Road, Covent
Garden, WC2 (7494 5085/www.rutheatres.com).
Leicester Square tube.* **Box office** *In person* 10am-
8pm Mon-Sat. *By phone* 24hrs daily. **Tickets** £12-£30.
Standby £15. **Credit** AmEx, MC, V. **Map** p401 K7.

Stephen Daldry's production of JB Priestley's repertory warhorse is an expressionist psychological and
social parable, set in a sort of giant doll's house on
stilts in the middle of an Edwardian slum.

Art

*Wyndhams Theatre, Charing Cross Road, Covent
Garden, WC2 (7369 1736). Leicester Square tube.*
Box office *In person* 10am-6pm Mon; 10am-8pm
Tue-Sat; 10am-6pm Sun. *By phone* 9am-9pm
Mon-Sat; 10am-6pm Sun. *Ticketmaster* 24hrs daily.
Tickets £9.50-£29.50. **Credit** AmEx, MC, V.
Map p401 K7.

Yasmina Reza's lightweight satire of three men
whose friendship is blown apart when one buys an
overpriced painting. The oft-changing cast usually
features at least one big name.

The Beautiful Game

*Cambridge Theatre, Earlham Street, Covent
Garden, WC2 (7494 5080/www.rutheatres.com).
Covent Garden tube.* **Box office** *In person* 10am-
7.45pm daily. *By phone* 24hrs daily. **Tickets**
£10-£37. **Credit** AmEx, MC, V. **Map** p399 L6.

Ben Elton and Andrew Lloyd Webber's rather
peculiar collaboration is unlikely to be a winner on
a par with some of its composer's predecessors, but
it's a satisfactory alternative to *Starlight Express* for
football fans.

Blood Brothers

*Phoenix Theatre, Charing Cross Road, St Giles's,
WC2 (7369 1733). Tottenham Court Road tube.*
Box office *In person* 10am-7.45pm Mon-Sat; closed
Sun. *By phone* 9am-9pm Mon-Sat; 10am-6pm Sun.
Ticketmaster 24hrs daily. **Tickets** £12-£35. *Standby*
£15. **Credit** AmEx, MC, V. **Map** p399 K6.

Willy Russell's likeable, long-running melodrama
about two brothers separated at birth and exiled to
separate ends of the social ladder is filled with
Scouse sentiment and toe-tapping songs.

tkts, please

It looks unassuming enough, but the small
Clock Tower building on the south side of
Leicester Square has been supplying an
invaluable service to theatregoers for years.
As suggested by its former name – the Half-
Price Ticket Booth – the booth sold cut-price
tickets for shows across the West End. In
February 2001, it changed its handle to **tkts**,
a name familiar to anyone who's enjoyed
theatre in New York. Thankfully, the new
moniker did not herald any great change in
the range of services provided.

Tickets for West End shows are sold here
on a first-come, first-served basis on the day
of the performance only, with each ticket
subject to a service charge of £2.50 and a
maximum of four per customer. However, the
discounts on offer are often spectacular:
tickets for almost every West End show can
be snapped up, often with as much as 50 per

cent off face value. The great prices more
than make up for the strict conditions and a
bit of queueing.

Of course, the opportunity to buy cut-price
tickets is not that rare in London. But what
sets tkts apart is the fact that it's run by the
Society of London Theatre, a non-profit-making
organisation. On the other hand, most of
the gaudy booths advertising cheap theatre
seats around the rest of Leicester Square are
entirely unofficial and, often, more than a little
dodgy. Avoid them at all costs.

tkts is one of the few outlets in town where
you can be sure of a genuine, cheap ticket
and a hassle-free purchase. For the thrifty or
those travelling on a budget, it's a godsend.

tkts

*Leicester Square, WC2. Leicester Square
tube.* **Open** 10am-7pm Mon-Sat; noon-3.30pm
Sun. **Credit** AmEx, DC, MC, V. **Map** p401 K7.

Buddy

Strand Theatre, Aldwych, Holborn, WC2 (7930 8800/www.trh.co.uk). Covent Garden tube/ Charing Cross tube/rail. **Box office** *In person* 10am-6pm Mon; 10am-8pm Tue-Sat; 12.30-4pm Sun. *By phone* 10am-8pm Mon-Sat; 12.30-4pm Sun. **Tickets** £13.50-£35. **Credit** MC, V. **Map** p399 M6.
A singalong, nostalgic review of the rise and nose-dive of Buddy Holly. Expect dancing in the aisles before the curtain goes down.

Cats

New London Theatre, Drury Lane, Covent Garden, WC2 (7405 0072/www.catsthemusical.com). Covent Garden or Holborn tube. **Box office** *In person* 10am-7.45pm Mon-Sat; closed Sun. *By phone* 10am-8pm Mon-Sat; closed Sun. *Ticketmaster* 24hrs daily. **Tickets** £10.50-£37.50. *Standby* £15. **Credit** AmEx, DC, MC, V. **Map** p399 L6.
Based on TS Eliot's *Old Possum's Book of Practical Cats*, Lloyd Webber's awful patchwork pussyfest is London's longest-running musical.

Chicago

Adelphi Theatre, Strand, Covent Garden, WC2 (Ticketmaster 7344 0055). Charing Cross tube/rail. **Box office** *In person* 10am-8pm Mon-Sat; closed Sun. *By phone* 24hrs daily. **Tickets** £16-£36. **Credit** AmEx, MC, V. **Map** p401 L7.
Kander and Ebb's tale of two murderous broads who connive a route from Death Row to Easy Street is fast becoming a West End staple.

Les Miserables

Palace Theatre, Shaftesbury Avenue, Soho, W1 (7434 0909/www.lesmis.com). Leicester Square tube. **Box office** 10am-8pm Mon-Sat; closed Sun. *Ticketmaster* 24hrs daily. **Tickets** £7-£37.50. *Standby* £17.50. **Credit** AmEx, DC, MC, V. **Map** p399 K6.
Boubil and Schonberg's 15-year-old money-spinner idealises the struggle between paupers and villains in Victor Hugo's revolutionary Paris.

The Lion King

Lyceum Theatre, Wellington Street, WC2 (0870 243 9000). Covent Garden tube/Charing Cross tube/rail. **Box office** *In person* 10am-8pm Tue-Sat; closed Mon. *By phone* 8.30am-10pm Mon-Fri; 8.30am-9.30pm Sat; 10am-8pm Sun. *Tickets Direct* 24hrs daily. **Tickets** £15-£37.50. **Credit** AmEx, MC, V. **Map** p401 L7.
A wildly acclaimed Disney extravaganza about a lion cub struggling to grow up. The 'animals' are represented in a remarkable number of ways and compensate for the elements of Hollywood flash.

Mamma Mia!

Prince Edward Theatre, Old Compton Street, Soho, W1 (7447 5400/www.mamma-mia.com). Leicester Square tube. **Box office** *In person* 10am-7pm Mon-Sat; closed Sun. *By phone* 24hrs daily. **Tickets** £15-£35. **Credit** AmEx, MC, V. **Map** p399 K6.
This hugely popular '70s musical was designed to link Abba's greatest hits into a continuous if entirely spurious story. Perpetually sold out.

The Mousetrap

St Martin's Theatre, West Street, Covent Garden, WC2 (7836 1443). Leicester Square tube. **Box office** 10am-8.15pm Mon-Sat; closed Sun. **Tickets** £11-£28. **Credit** AmEx, MC, V. **Map** p399 K6.
An absurdly long-running mystery from the mistress of suspense, Agatha Christie, *The Mousetrap* has been in the West End for 49 years.

Notre Dame de Paris

Dominion Theatre, Tottenham Court Road, Fitzrovia, W1 (0870 607 7460 local rate/ www.ticketsdirect.co.uk). Tottenham Court Road tube. **Box office** *In person* 10am-8pm Mon-Sat; closed Sun. *By phone* 24hrs daily. **Tickets** £10-£37.50. *Standby* £15. **Credit** AmEx, MC, V. **Map** p399 K5.
A modern-day take on the noted Victor Hugo novel, which, despite athletic choreography and a not altogether unpleasant soft rock score, is not worth the considerable effort it takes to follow.

Phantom of the Opera

Her Majesty's Theatre, Haymarket, St James's, SW1 (7494 5400/www.thephantomoftheopera.com). Piccadilly Circus tube. **Box office** *In person* 10am-6pm Mon-Sat; closed Sun. *By phone* 24hrs daily. **Tickets** £10-£37.50. **Credit** AmEx, MC, V. **Map** p401 K7.
Lloyd Webber's long-running musical about a deformed theatre-goer who becomes obsessed with a beautiful opera singer is his best to date.

Cameron Mackintosh's latest smash, **The Witches of Eastwick**. *See p333.*

Starlight Express

Apollo Victoria Theatre, Wilton Road, Pimlico, SW1 (0870 400 0800 local rate/www.starlight-express.co.uk). Victoria tube/rail. **Box office** *In person* 9am-8pm Mon-Sat; closed Sun. *By phone* 24hrs daily. **Tickets** £12.50-£30. *Standby* £13.50. **Credit** AmEx, MC, V. **Map** p400 H10.

A Lloyd Webber musical that depends less on the music and more on the spectacle of the cast flying round on rollerblades impersonating trains. It's dated worse than year-old milk.

The Witches of Eastwick

Prince of Wales Theatre, Coventry Street, W1 (7839 5972/www.witchesofeastwick.com). Leicester Square tube. **Box office** *In person* 10am-7pm Mon-Wed, Fri; 10am-2pm, 3-7pm Thur, Sat; closed Sun. *By phone* 24hrs daily. **Tickets** £12.50-£37.50. **Credit** AmEx, MC, V. **Map** p399 L6.

Based on the film, which in turn was based on the John Irving book, this musical has lust, betrayal, revenge and a tuneful if unmemorable score.

The Woman in Black

Fortune Theatre, Russell Street, WC2 (7836 2238). Covent Garden tube. **Box office** 10am-8pm Mon-Sat; closed Sun. **Tickets** £10-£28.50. *Standby* £10. **Credit** AmEx, DC, MC, V. **Map** p399 L6.

Susan Hill's ghostly two-hander has become a persistently popular West End spine-chiller.

Off-West End

Almeida

Omega Place, off Caledonian Road, King's Cross, N1 (7359 4404/www.almeida.co.uk). King's Cross tube/rail. **Box office** *In person* 5.30-7pm Mon-Fri; 1-7pm Sat; closed Sun. *By phone* 24hrs daily. **Tickets** £5-£27.50. **Credit** AmEx, MC, V. **Map** p399 L2.

For over a decade, actor-directors Ian McDiarmid and Jonathan Kent have maintained a steady flow of lively, highbrow drama at the Almeida. While the Islington theatre is refurbished (it's scheduled to reopen in spring 2001), plays will be staged in this specially converted King's Cross space.

BAC (Battersea Arts Centre)

Lavender Hill, Battersea, SW11 (7223 2223/ www.bac.org.uk). Clapham Junction rail/77, 77A, 345 bus. **Box office** *In person* 10.30am-6pm Mon; 10.30am-9pm Tue-Sat; 4-7pm Sun. *By phone* 10.30am-6pm Mon; 10.30am-7pm Tue-Sat; 4-7pm Sun. **Tickets** £4-£12.50; 'pay what you can' Tue. **Credit** MC, V.

With three theatres (a main house and two studios) that carry much of the capital's best fringe work, the BAC lives up to its self-appointed status as the 'National Theatre of the Fringe'.

The Bush

Shepherd's Bush Green, Shepherd's Bush, W12 (8743 3388/www.bushtheatre.co.uk). Goldhawk Road or Shepherd's Bush tube. **Box office** *In person* 6.30-8pm Mon-Fri; 7-8pm Sat; closed Sun. *By phone* 10am-8pm Mon-Sat; closed Sun. **Tickets** £7-£13. **Credit** AmEx, MC, V.

West End shows

An Inspector Calls

Stephen Daldry does JB Priestley to perfection (*see p331*).

Art

An oft-changing, all-star cast continues to wow in Yasmin Reza's hit play (*see p331*).

Chicago

Showy, sassy and the best song-and-dance show in town (pictured; *see p332*).

Les Misérables

A cut above any Lloyd Webber production, *Les Mis* is the pick of the big blockbuster musicals (*see p332*).

One of the most important venues for new writing in London, the recently refurbished Bush is a springboard for young writers into the bigger theatres (such as Conor McPherson, author of *The Weir*).

Donmar Warehouse

41 Earlham Street, Covent Garden, WC2 (7369 1732/www.donmar-warehouse.com). Covent Garden tube. **Box office** *In person* 10am-8pm Mon-Sat; closed Sun. *By phone* 9am-9pm Mon-Sat; 10am-6pm Sun. *Ticketmaster* 24hrs daily. **Tickets** £14-£24. *Standby* £12. **Credit** AmEx, MC, V. **Map** p399 L6.

Under the direction of Sam Mendes, the Donmar has continued to produce a variety of old and new plays, visiting and in-house shows to a very high standard with casts that are often peppered with big names.

Drill Hall

16 Chenies Street, Fitzrovia, WC1 (7637 8270). Goodge Street tube. **Box office** *In person* 10am-7.30pm Mon-Fri; 11am-7.30pm Sat; closed Sun. *By phone* 11am-7pm Mon-Sat; 11am-6pm Sun. **Tickets** £6-£12. **Credit** AmEx, MC, V. **Map** p399 K5.

London's biggest gay and lesbian theatre stages its own work and shows from all over the world. Mondays are women-only from 6pm and Thursday is non-smoking, but this is not a separatist venue.

Arts & Entertainment

GREAT NIGHTS OUT

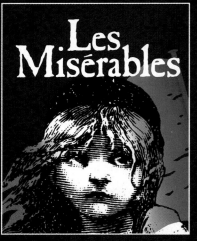

PALACE THEATRE
020 7434 0909
www.lesmis.com

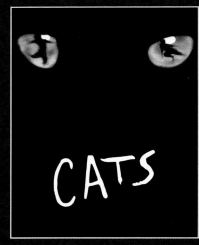

NEW LONDON THEATRE
020 7405 0072
www.catsthemusical.co.uk

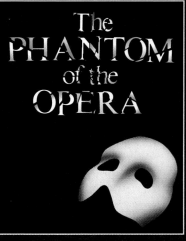

HER MAJESTY'S THEATRE
020 7494 5400

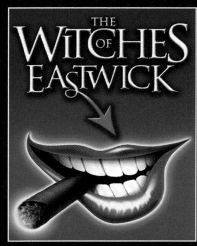

PRINCE OF WALES THEATRE
020 7839 5987

The Gate

*The Prince Albert, 11 Pembridge Road, Notting Hill,
W11 (7229 0706). Notting Hill Gate tube.* **Box
office** 10am-6pm Mon-Fri; closed Sat, Sun. **Tickets**
£6-£12; 'pay what you can' Mon. **Credit** MC, V.
Map p394 A7.

Located above a pub, the Gate is known for its high-
quality, low-budget drama and radical set design.

Hampstead Theatre

*Avenue Road, Swiss Cottage, NW3 (7722 9301/
www.hampstead-theatre.co.uk). Swiss Cottage tube.*
Box office 10am-7.30pm Mon-Sat; closed Sun.
Tickets £7-£17. **Credit** MC, V.

Under the direction of Jenny Topper, the Hampstead
is widely respected for its contemporary drama.

Holland Park Theatre

*Holland Park, off Kensington High Street,
Kensington, W8 (7602 7856/www.operalondon.com).
High Street Kensington tube.* **Box office** May-Aug 18
10am-6pm, 10am-8pm (performance nights) Mon-Sat;
closed Sun. **Tickets** £26; £20.50 concessions. **Credit**
AmEx, MC, V. **Map** p394 A8.

Set against the backdrop of Holland House, this outdoor theatre seats 720. The season of opera and ballet runs for ten weeks during the summer.

King's Head

*115 Upper Street, Islington, N1 (7226 1916). Angel
tube/Highbury & Islington tube/rail.* **Box office**
10am-8pm Mon-Sat; 10am-4pm Sun. **Tickets** £4-
£14. **Credit** MC, V. **Map** p402 O1.

Islington's **King's Head** theatre sits at
the back of a charming old pub.

London's oldest pub theatre stages a variable diet of
small-scale musicals, plays and revues. The bar's
midnight licence and musical evenings make it a
busy all-round winner, though it is currently under
threat due to the local council withdrawing funding.

Lyric Hammersmith

*King Street, Hammersmith, W6 (8741 2311/
www.lyric.co.uk). Hammersmith tube.* **Box office** *In
person* 10am-8pm Mon-Sat; closed Sun. *By phone*
10am-7pm Mon-Sat; closed Sun. **Tickets** £5-£19.
Credit AmEx, DC, MC, V.

Fine facilities and a good reputation for alternative
mainstream work. There are two theatres; a proscenium main stage and a smaller-scale studio space.

Open Air Theatre

*Regent's Park, NW1 (7486 2431/www.open-air-
theatre.org.uk). Baker Street tube.* **Repertory
season** May-Sept, phone for details. **Tickets** £9-
£23. *Standby* £9 (approx). **Credit** AmEx, DC, MC, V.
Map p398 G3.

A delightful venue in which to watch outdoor
productions during summer. Count on a couple of
alfresco Shakespeares, a musical and a family show.
Keep your fingers crossed for favourable weather.

Orange Tree

*1 Clarence Street, Richmond, Surrey (8940 3633/
www.orangetreetheatre.co.uk). Richmond tube/rail.*
Box office 10am-7pm Mon-Sat; closed Sun.
Tickets £5-£15. **Credit** MC, V.

This small, smart bear pit of a venue has been flourishing under the directorship of Sam Walters and his
prescribed diet of wholesome, closely directed (often)
costume drama in the round, with little or no set.

Riverside Studios

*Crisp Road, Hammersmith, W6 (8237 1111/
www.riversidestudios.co.uk). Hammersmith tube.*
Box office *In person* noon-9pm daily. *By phone*
24hrs daily. **Tickets** £10-£25. **Credit** MC, V.

One of London's most imaginative and lively arts
centres, the Riverside comprises three studio spaces,
a rep cinema, a café and a bar, and hosts a varied
programme of theatre, comedy, visual art, dance, TV
shows and commercial events.

Theatre Royal Stratford East

*Gerry Raffles Square, Stratford, E15 (8534 0310).
Stratford tube/rail.* **Box office** 10am-6pm Mon-Sat;
closed Sun. **Tickets** £5-£15. **Credit** AmEx, MC, V.

This consistent powerhouse of popular community-
oriented drama, musicals and revue has been
responsible for launching West End hits like *East is
East*. After a major redevelopment it's due to reopen
in spring 2001 in an extremely well-equipped centre
with five performing arts spaces.

Tricycle

*269 Kilburn High Road, Kilburn, NW6 (7328 1000).
Kilburn tube.* **Box office** 10am-9pm Mon-Sat; 2-9pm
Sun. **Tickets** £8.50-£15. **Credit** MC, V.

The Tricycle specialises in high-quality black and
Irish shows aimed at its local population. In 2000, its

Arts & Entertainment

play *Colour of Justice* won best touring production in the Barclays Theatre Awards. The centre also incorporates its own art gallery and super-comfy cinema, as well as one of Kilburn's more agreeable bars.

Young Vic

66 The Cut, Waterloo, SE1 (7928 6363/ www.youngvic.org). Southwark tube/Waterloo tube/ rail. **Box office** 10am-7pm Mon-Sat; closed Sun. **Tickets** £7-£21. **Credit** MC, V. **Map** p404 N8.
The Young Vic is equipped with a well-proportioned studio space and large main house that regularly plays host to touring companies as big as the Royal Shakespeare Company – which stages a season here from March to May 2001 – and names as bankable as Jude Law.

Fringe

The Bridewell

Bride Lane, off Fleet Street, Blackfriars, EC4 (7936 3456/www.bridewelltheatre.co.uk). Blackfriars tube/ rail. **Box office** noon-6pm Tue-Sat; closed Mon, Sun. **Tickets** £4-£16.50. **Credit** DC, MC, V. **Map** p404 N6.
A good-sized theatre with a decent mixture of musicals and new works, often produced by national theatre companies, as well as an irregular programme of lunchtime productions.

Chelsea Centre

World's End Place, King's Road, Chelsea, SW10 (7352 1967/www.btinternet.com/~chelseacentre/). Sloane Square tube then 11, 22, 211 bus/Earl's Court tube then 328 bus. **Box office** *In person* 7-9pm Mon-Sat; closed Sun. *By phone* 10am-9pm Mon-Sat; closed Sun. **Tickets** £5-£9. **Credit** MC, V. **Map** p396 C13.
This small King's Road venue premieres the work of both emerging and established playwrights.

Etcetera Theatre

Oxford Arms, 265 Camden High Street, Camden Town, NW1 (7482 4857). Camden Town tube. **Box office** 10am-8pm Tue-Sun; closed Mon. **Tickets** £5.50-£8. **No credit cards.**
A classic tiny pub theatre in Camden Town with a perennially lively programme of works by ambitious young theatre folk. There are usually two different shows a night.

Finborough Theatre

Finborough Arms, 118 Finborough Road, Earl's Court, SW10 (7373 3842/ http://finboroughtheatre.itgo.com). Earl's Court tube. **Box office** 4-8.30pm daily. **Tickets** £6-£8. **No credit cards.** **Map** p396 B12.
This pub venue nurtures new writing, some of which has gone on to the West End and Broadway.

Grace Theatre

Latchmere Pub, 503 Battersea Park Road, Clapham Junction, SW11 (box office 7794 0022/pub 7223 3549). Clapham Junction rail. **Box office** 9am-6pm daily. **Tickets** £7-£9. **Credit** MC, V.

A burgeoning, ambitious venue deep in the heart of Clapham whose increasingly exciting programme is helping to raise its profile.

Jermyn Street Theatre

16B Jermyn Street, St James's, W1 (7287 2875/ www.jermynstreet.co.uk). Piccadilly Circus tube. **Box office** 11am-7pm Mon-Fri; 1-7pm Sat; closed Sun. **Tickets** £8-£12. **Credit** MC, V. **Map** p400 J7.
A small studio theatre in the heart of the West End that mixes its own ambitious cocktails of musicals, revues and classics.

New End Theatre

New End, Hampstead, NW3 (7794 0022/ www.newend.co.uk). Hampstead tube. **Box office** 10am-8pm Mon-Fri; 1-8pm Sat, Sun. **Tickets** £10-£15. **Credit** MC, V.
A small, Hampstead theatre that stages adventurous work at ever-improving standards.

Oval House

52-4 Kennington Oval, Oval, SE11 (7582 7680/ www.ovalhouse.dircon.co.uk). Oval tube. **Box office** 3-9pm Tue-Sat; closed Mon, Sun. **Tickets** £5-£8. **Credit** MC, V.
London's second gay and lesbian venue after the Drill Hall (*see p333*) has two theatres hosting work, often by respected, subsidised companies.

Pleasance Theatre

Carpenters Mews, North Road, N7 (7609 1800/ 8753). Caledonian Road tube. **Box office** 10am-6pm daily. **Credit** MC, V.
This offshoot of one of the Edinburgh Fringe's most successful venues is a large, commercially ambitious fringe theatre with generally sound productions.

Southwark Playhouse

62 Southwark Bridge Road, Bankside, SE1 (7620 3494/www.southwark-playhouse.co.uk). Borough or Southwark tube/London Bridge tube/rail. **Box office** 11am-7.30pm Mon-Sat; closed Sun. **Tickets** £5-£9. **No credit cards.** **Map** p404 P8.
This small theatre aims high with a daring programme of writing and music, with mixed results.

Warehouse Theatre

Dingwall Road, Croydon, Surrey (8680 4060/ www.warehousetheatre.co.uk). East Croydon rail. **Box office** 10am-5pm Mon; 10am-8.30pm Tue; 10am-10pm Wed-Sat; 3-7pm Sun. **Tickets** £5.50-£11. **Credit** AmEx, DC, MC, V.
An alternative, suburban theatre (a little more suburban than alternative) funded for its mix of conventional and unconventional new plays.

White Bear

138 Kennington Park Road, Kennington, SE11 (7793 9193). Kennington tube. **Box office** 10am-6pm Mon-Sat; noon-6pm Sun. **Tickets** £6-£8. **No credit cards.**
Occupying the back room of a seedy bar, this can be fringe theatre at its most depressing, but it can also rise to admirable and original heights.

Trips Out
of Town

Trips Out of Town   **338**

Feature boxes

Trips Out of Town

London: been there, done that. Now it's time to get out.

The thrills of the big city are all very well, but there comes a time when most of us need to escape the traffic, the noise, the pollution and the crush. Many visitors (and most Londoners) are unaware of the attractions lurking outside the M25 – and how easily accessible they are. Most of the places we list in this chapter are within an hour and a half's rail journey of London (although some will then require a further bus or taxi ride).

PLANNING A TRIP

The best place to start is at the new **Britain Visitor Centre** (*see below*). Here you can get guidebooks, free leaflets and advice on any destination in the UK and Ireland; you can also book rail, bus, air or car travel, reserve tours, theatre tickets and accommodation; there's even a bureau de change, a branch of Thomas Cook, a ticket agency and a bookshop. Alternatively, a host of information and advice on destinations across the country is available at www.visitbritain.com, the website of the **British Tourist Authority**. Visitors are also advised to visit the tourist information centre in the town they visit as soon as they arrive, which will provide leaflets, further information about accommodation and where to eat, and details of local attractions.

Britain Visitor Centre

1 Regent Street (south of Piccadilly Circus), SW1 (no phone/www.visitbritain.com). Piccadilly Circus tube. **Open** *Jan-July, Oct-Dec* 9am-6.30pm Mon-Fri; 10am-4pm Sat, Sun. *Aug & Sept* 9am-6.30pm Mon-Fri; 9am-5pm Sat; 10am-4pm Sun. **Credit** AmEx, MC, V. **Map** p401 K7.
Personal callers only.

Opening times & prices

For main entries below we include full details of opening times, admission and transport details, but be aware that these can change without notice. If you are planning a trip around one particular sight, **always phone first to check that it is open**. Many attractions close down during the winter (typically between November and March inclusive), although major sights are open year round. In the 'Where to stay' sections, the accommodation prices listed are the range for a double room. **Note that in main listings credit cards are only accepted where specified**.

By train

To find out train times and ticket prices, call **0345 484950**. (If you want to reserve your tickets in advance by credit card, ask for the appropriate number.) Always make sure you ask about the cheapest ticket for the journey you are planning and be aware that for longer journeys, the earlier you book, the cheaper the ticket. The **rail travel centres** in all of London's mainline stations (as well as in Heathrow and Gatwick airports and the British Travel Centre, for which *see above*) will also be able to help with timetable information and ticket booking. The train journey times we give are the fastest available.

If you want timetable information over the web, go to www.virgintrains.co.uk. Tickets for any train operator in the UK can be bought on the Net at www.thetrainline.com.

London mainline rail stations

Charing Cross *Strand, WC2.* **Map** p401 L7.
For trains to and from south-east England (including Dover, Folkestone and Ramsgate).

Euston *Euston Road, Euston, NW1.* **Map** p399 K3.
For trains to and from the north and north-west of England and Scotland, and a suburban line north to Watford.

King's Cross *Euston Road, King's Cross, N1.* **Map** p399 L2.
For trains to and from the north and north-east of England and Scotland, and suburban lines to north London and Hertfordshire.

Liverpool Street *Liverpool Street, The City, EC2.* **Map** p403 R5.
For trains to and from the east coast (including Harwich) and Stansted Airport; also trains to East Anglia and suburban services to east and north-east London.

Paddington *Praed Street, Paddington, W2.* **Map** p395 D5.
For trains to and from the south-west, west, and south Wales and the Midlands.

Victoria *Terminus Place, Victoria, SW1.* **Map** p400 H10.
For fast trains to and from the Channel ports (Folkestone, Dover, Newhaven); also trains to and from Gatwick Airport, plus suburban services to south and south-east London.

Waterloo *York Road, Waterloo, SE1.* **Map** p401 M8.
For fast trains to and from the south and south-west of England (Portsmouth, Southampton, Dorset, Devon), plus suburban services to south-west London.

By coach

Coach and bus travel is almost always cheaper than rail travel, but almost always slower. **National Express** (0870 580 8080) runs routes to most parts of the country; its coaches depart from Victoria Coach Station on Buckingham Palace Road, five minutes' walk from Victoria rail and tube stations. **Green Line** buses (0870 608 7261, www.greenline.co.uk) operate within an approximate 30-mile (48-kilometre) radius of London. Their main departure point is Eccleston Bridge, SW1 (Colonnades Coach Station, behind Victoria station).

Victoria Coach Station

164 Buckingham Palace Road, Victoria, SW1 (7730 3466). Victoria tube/rail. **Map** p400 H11. Britain's most comprehensive coach company **National Express** – which runs services to destinations all over England, Scotland and Wales – and **Eurolines** (01582 404511, www.eurolines.co.uk) – which travels to the Continent – are based at Victoria Coach Station. There are many other companies operating to and from London (some departing from Marble Arch).

By car

If you are in a group of three or four people, it may be cheaper (and more flexible) to hire a car (*see p361*). And if you plan to take in several sights within an area, then this is probably the only realistic way of getting around. The road directions given in the listings below should be used in conjunction with a map. (Note that, for example, 'J13 off M11' means 'come off the M11 motorway at junction 13'.)

Town & city breaks

Bath

Flanked by two Areas of Outstanding Natural Beauty in the Cotswolds (*see p354*) and the Mendips, Bath is a sleek, immaculately groomed supermodel of a city. Comprised of slender Georgian streets, tanned stone and

Further reading

For a more in-depth look at getaways within easy reach of London, refer to the *Time Out Book of Weekend Breaks* (Penguin, £12.99). The *Time Out Book of Country Walks* (Penguin, £9.99) details 52 walks in the countryside around London.

beautifully proportioned curves, it's the only city in the UK to have been awarded the distinction of being a World Heritage Site.

The area surrounding Bath's natural hot springs was home to a Celtic settlement even before the Romans founded Aquae Sulis almost 2000 years ago. However, it's with the baths that the Romans built over the spring that the city is most closely associated (to the extent that it is named after them) and today the **Roman Baths Museum** (01225 477785, www.romanbaths.co.uk) is the city's most famous attraction. Offering an excellent acoustiguide tour of what are the most impressive non-military Roman remains in Britain, the museum is made all the more evocative by the fact that the waters still bubble up from the earth here (250,000 gallons a day at 46.5°C), just as they did in Roman times. There are plans afoot to restore the baths as a spa; meanwhile you can taste the waters in the adjoining **Pump Room** (which was immortalised by Jane Austen), but a pot of Earl Grey might go down better.

Overlooking the baths is **Bath Abbey** (01225 422462, wwwbathabbey.org), a 15th-century rebuilding of an earlier Norman structure, itself built on the site of the Saxon church where Edgar, the first king of a united England, was crowned in 973. It's a beautifully light, harmonious building, boasting some fine fan vaulting and stained glass.

Bath has close on 20 museums, most of them excellent. These include **The Building of Bath Museum** on Lansdown Road (01225 333895, www.bath-preservation-trust.org.uk), the highlight of which is a spectacular model of the city, and, in Bennett Street, the **Museum of East Asian Art** (01225 464640, www.east-asian-art.co.uk), which contains a fine collection of Chinese jade carvings. Opposite, in the grand **Assembly Rooms** (once the social focus of Georgian high society in Bath), there's the renowned **Museum of Costume** (01225 477789, www.museumofcostume.co.uk), illustrating posh togs dating back to the late 16th century. The **Victoria Art Gallery** on Bridge Street (01225 477233, www.victoriagal. org.uk) houses the region's permanant collection of British and European art from the 15th century to the present day and the **American Museum** (01225 460503, www.americanmuseum.org) at Claverton Manor offers a fascinating and effectively presented series of reconstructed 17th- to 19th-century American domestic interiors. A recent addition to the city's attractions is the **Jane Austen Centre**, which charts the five-year period that the author spent in Bath between 1801 and 1805.

Brighton's bunion-inducing beach.

But Bath's greatest attraction is simply its streets, the grandest of which is the much-photographed **Royal Crescent**, a breathtaking sweep of 30 houses designed by John Wood the Younger (1767-75). **No.1 Royal Crescent** (01225 428126, www.bath-preservation-trust.org.uk) is furnished in authentic period style with a fully restored Georgian garden and is open to the public. Nearby is the magnificent **Circus**, which was designed by the elder John Wood and completed by his like-named son in 1767, composed of three crescents forming a circle. With its three tiers of columns, it's been described as 'the Colosseum turned outside in', and is, in many ways an even finer creation than Royal Crescent. Stand in the middle and try out the powerful echo.

Not all of Bath's streets are so imposing – there are also plenty of narrow alleyways, particularly in the area to the north of **Abbey Churchyard**, an open space popular with street entertainers. There is plenty of good shopping too, centred largely around Milsom, Union and Stall streets and Southgate.

The **River Avon** adds greatly to the appeal of the city and is spanned by **Pulteney Bridge**, an Italianate masterpiece by Robert Adam, which is lined with shops and supported by three elegant arches. There are walks beside the river and the adjacent Kennet and Avon Canal. Boats may be hired in summer from the Boating Station on Forester Road.

Further information

Getting there: *By train* from Paddington (1 hour 15mins). *By coach* National Express (3 hours 20mins). *By car* J18 off M4 then A46, use park 'n' rides to get into the centre.

Where to stay: Haydon House (9 Bloomfield Park; 01225 444919, www.haydonhouse.co.uk; £75-

£95) offers superior B&B and splendid breakfasts, five minutes' drive from the centre. **Holly Lodge** (8 Upper Oldfield Park; 01225 424042, www.hollylodge.co.uk; £79-£97) is another classy B&B. Regency elegance in the centre of town is provided at the **Queensberry Hotel** (Russell Street; 01225 447928, www.bathqueensberry.com; £120-£210). A more affordable central option is **Harington's Hotel** (8-10 Queen Street; 01225 461728, www.haringtonshotel.co.uk; £88-£108).

Where to eat & drink: Sally Lunn's **Refreshment House & Museum** (01225 461634, www.sallylunns.co.uk) in North Parade Passage is the oldest house in Bath; here you can sample the famous buns made fashionable by Sally Lunn in the 1680s. The best of Bath's many restaurants are top-rank curry house **Jamuna** at 9-10 High Street (01225 464631), Michelin two-star **Lettonie** at 35 Kelston Road (01225 446676), the **Moon & Sixpence** wine bar/bistro at 6A Broad Street (01225 460962), the fine French **Clos du Roy**, next to the Theatre Royal (01225 444450), the classy, cosy **Moody Goose** (01225 466688) on Kingsmead Square and the excellent low-priced **Hullaballoos** at 36 Broad Street (01225 443323). Popular pubs include the **Coeur de Lion** in Northumberland Place, the **Boater** on Argyle Street (by the river) and the **Saracen's Head** on Broad Street.

Tourist information centre: Abbey Chambers, Abbey Churchyard (01225 477101, www.visitbath.co.uk). **Open** *May-Sept* 9.30am-6pm Mon-Sat; 10am-4pm Sun. *Oct-Apr* 9.30am-5pm Mon-Sat; 10am-4pm Sun.

Brighton

From the elegant splendour of its Regency squares and the old-fashioned propriety of **Hannington's** department store to the seedy glamour of Kemptown and reckless hedonism West Street, Brighton is a town of contradictions. (Or, more accurately, a city, recently upgraded to that status in tandem with its neighbour Hove.) It is appropriate indeed that its best-known landmark is the outrageous **Royal Pavilion** (01273 290900, www.royalpavilion.brighton.co.uk). Built by John Nash in 1823 for the Prince Regent (later George IV), the Pavilion (none too subtly) blends elements of Indian, Chinese and Islamic architecture, and nowhere in Brighton better reflects the town's diversity, extravagance and exuberance. The adjacent **Brighton Museum & Art Gallery** (01273 290900, www.royalpavilion.brighton.co.uk), home to a good crop of 20th-century and ethnic art and artefacts, is also well worth a visit. It's currently closed for a refurb but opens again in autumn 2001. The nearby **Brighton Dome** (01273 709709) regularly plays host to comedy and rock concerts.

Brighton has much else to offer the visitor. The English Channel for a start: it may be freezing cold most of the year and the beach steep and pebbly rather than sandy, but it's still the sea. The gaudy **Palace Pier** is packed with archetypal seaside attractions – slot machines, funfair, fish and chips. On a clear day you can gaze west from the top of the helter skelter to the Isle of Wight, or along the shore to the derelict, skeletal West Pier (currently undergoing restoration) and genteel Hove.

Between the piers, beachfront arches house cafés, bars and clubs – notably the **Zap** (01273 821588, www.zapproductions.co.uk) and **Honey** (01273 202807, www.thehoneyclub.co.uk) clubs and the lively **Fortune of War** pub. Contrast these with the neighbouring **Brighton Fishing Museum** (01273 723064) and crafts shops or the **Sea Life Centre** (01273 604234, www.sealife.co.uk), housed in a beautiful 19th-century aquarium.

When the sea loses its fascination, duck into **The Lanes**, a warren of old fisherman's cottages that currently house a variety of antiques and specialist shops punctuated by pubs and cafés, between West Street and the Old Steine. If these prove too expensive, cross North Street and explore the vibrant **North Laine** area for vintage clothing, street fashion, records, kitsch and cafés of every kind, or visit the **Duke of York's** (01273 626261) at Preston Circus, quite possibly the cosiest independent cinema in the UK.

However, there's more to Brighton than sea, sights and shops. More and more people come (and return) here for the atmosphere – an eclectic cocktail of traditional seaside resort and liberal lifestyles. Brighton will embrace anyone – as the town's large gay community, anarchists, artists, eccentrics and celebs will testify – and enchant all.

Further information

Getting there: *By train* from Victoria (from 50mins), or from King's Cross (1 hour 10mins). *By coach* National Express (1 hour 50mins). *By car* M23 then A23.

Where to stay: The **Adelaide** (51 Regency Square; 01273 205286; double £65-£86) is old, four-star and mid-priced; the **Twenty One** (21 Charlotte Street; 01273 686450, www.s-h-systems.co.uk/hotels/21; double £60-£95) offers a friendly welcome and a tasty breakfast; the poshest place in town remains **The Grand** (King's Road; 01273 224300, www.grandbrighton.co.uk; double £210-£300); the other end of the scale is **Brighton Backpackers** (75-76 Middle Street; 01273 777717, www.brightonbackpackers.com; from £10 per person).

Where to eat & drink: For food, try the enticing Anglo-Asian dishes at the unpromisingly sited **Black Chapati** (12 Circus Parade, New England Road; 01273 699011), north of the rail station, the inspired vegetarian café **Terre à Terre** at 71 East Street (01273 729051) or the first-rate French food at **La Fourchette** at 101 Western Road (01273 722556). Drink in **The Cricketers**, 15 Black Lion Street, the **Great Eastern** at 103 Trafalgar Street or the **Bath Arms**, nestling in the heart of the Lanes at 3-4 Meeting House Lane.

Events: Second in the UK only to Edinburgh, the **Brighton Festival** (01273 700747, www.brighton-festival.org.uk) fills the first three weeks of May with theatre, comedy, art, music and literature. On Sundays throughout the year Madeira Drive on the seafront hosts diverse events – notably the **London to Brighton Bike Ride** in June and the **London to Brighton Veteran Car Run** in November. Monthly listings guides *Impact* and *The List* are available from newsagents, or find out what's going down by tuning in to the what's on run-down on Surf 107FM (6.30-7pm Mon-Fri). For gay listings, see the monthly *G Scene* or visit Scene 22 (129 St James Street; 01273 626682).

Tourist information centres: *10 Bartholomew Square* (0906 7112255, www.visitbrighton.com). Open *Jan-June, Sept-Dec* 9am-5pm Mon-Fri; 10am-5pm Sat; 10am-4pm Sun. *July & Aug* 9am-6.15pm Mon-Fri; 10am-6pm Sat; 10am-4pm Sun. *Hove Town Hall, Church Road, Hove* (0906 7112255). Open *Jan-Jun, Sept-Dec* 9am-5pm Mon-Fri. *July & Aug* 11am-5pm Mon-Fri; closed Sat & Sun.

Cambridge

There is a casual air to Cambridge that lingers in the stonework of the old centre, drifts in the breeze above the waters of the River Cam and permeates the grassy glades that edge the town to the south and west and encroach upon parts of a centre that should, by rights, be built up with houses, roads and multi-storey car parks.

The **university** has dominated life in Cambridge since the 14th century. The oldest of the colleges is **Peterhouse** on Trumpington

Street, endowed in 1284. The original hall still survives, though most of the present buildings are 19th century. Just up the road is **Corpus Christi**, founded in 1352. Its Old Court dates from that time and is linked by a gallery to the 11th-century **St Bene't's Church**, the oldest building in town. Just across the road is 15th-century **Queens'**. Most of the original buildings, including the beautiful timbered president's lodge, survive and the inner courts are wonderfully picturesque.

Next to Queens' is, logically enough, **King's**, founded by Henry VI in 1441, and renowned for its **chapel** (1446-1515; 01223 331155). Considered one of the greatest Gothic buildings in Europe, the interior, containing its original stained glass, is breathtaking. Famous King's alumni include EM Forster, Rupert Brooke and John Maynard Keynes. To the north is **Trinity**, founded in 1336 by Edward III and refounded by Henry VIII in 1546. We're reliably informed that the college can count more Nobel laureates among its alumni than the whole of France. A fine collection of Tudor buildings surrounds the Great Court where, legend has it, Lord Byron used to bathe naked in the fountain with his pet bear. Wittgenstein studied and taught at Trinity; the library where he occasionally worked, designed by Wren, is open to visitors for two hours after lunch each day. Further on, at the corner of Bridge and St John's Streets, is the **Round Church** (the oldest of the four remaining round churches in England), home to the **Cambridge Brass Rubbing Centre**.

Behind the main group of colleges is **The Backs**, a series of beautiful meadows, some still grazed by cows, bordering the willow-shaded **River Cam**, which is spanned by several fine footbridges. It's a perfect spot for summer strolling, or you can hire a punt and drift lazily along the river.

The city also has its non-collegiate attractions: visit the **Fitzwilliam Museum** on Trumpington Street (01223 332900, www.fitzmuseum.cam.ac.uk) for its outstanding collections of antiquities and Old Masters or **Kettle's Yard** for its fascinating permanent and temporary exhibitions of 20th-century art; climb the tower of **Great St Mary's Church** on King's Parade for far-reaching views; take a short walk to the **Scott Polar Research Institute** (01223 336540, www.spri.cam.ac.uk) in Lensfield Road; admire the **Botanic Gardens** (01223 336265) in Bateman Street; or simply wander along the charming streets. Unsurprisingly, Cambridge is an excellent place to buy books – new, second-hand and antiquarian – and the daily market in Market Square is always a pleasure to browse.

Further information

Getting there: *By train* from King's Cross (50mins). *By coach* National Express (1 hour 50mins). *By car* J11 or J12 off M11.

Where to stay: Cambridge is short on characterful accommodation. Two decent options are **Arundel House** (01223 367701, www.arundelhousehotels. co.uk; double £68-£96) at 53 Chesterton Road, a fine early Victorian terrace overlooking the Cam, and **De Freville House** (01223 354993; double £55-£60) at 166 Chesterton Road.

Where to eat & drink: For posh nosh, try the quality French cooking at **Midsummer House** (01223 369299) on Midsummer Common, the global cuisine at **22 Chesterton Road** (01223 351880) or the bargain-priced oriental goodies at **Dojo** in Miller's Yard, Mill Lane (01223 363471). Sup a jar in the comfy, well-worn **Eagle** on St Bene't Street, the rowing-mad (no-smoking) **Free Press** on Prospect Row, which also offers decent lunchtime food, or the **Pickerel Inn** on Magdalene Street, the oldest pub in Cambridge.

Events: The city hosts the **Cambridge Shakespeare Festival** during July and August. Performances are held mainly outside, and remain as true to the text as possible.

Tourist information centre: The Old Library, Wheeler Street (01223 322640, www.tourismcambridge.com). *Open Apr-Oct* 10am-6.30pm Mon-Fri; 10am-5pm Sat; closed Sun. *Nov-Mar* 10am-5.30pm Mon-Fri; 10am-5pm Sat; closed Sun.

Canterbury

When St Augustine converted King Ethelbert to Christianity in 597, Canterbury became the cradle of English Christianity: long stretches of its medieval walls still stand and the magnificent **cathedral** (01227 762862, www.canterburycathedral.org), with its superb stained glass, stone vaulting and vast Norman crypt, is now the mother church of Anglicans worldwide. A plaque near the altar marks the spot where Archbishop Thomas à Becket was

Canterbury cathedral gate.

Oxford's **Radcliffe Camera**. *See p345.*

Further information

Getting there: *By train* from Victoria to Canterbury East (1 hour 20mins), or from Charing Cross to Canterbury West (1 hour 30mins). *By coach* National Express (1 hour 50mins). *By car* A2 then M2 and A2.

Where to stay: Try the 600-year-old **Falstaff** (01227 462138, www.corushotels.com; double £95-£105) at 8-10 St Dunstan's Street or the flower-strewn B&B **Magnolia House** (01227 765121, www.freespace.virgin.net/magnolia.canterbury; double £78-£110) at 36 St Dunstan's Terrace.

Where to eat & drink: If you fancy Italian, go to **Tue e Mio** at 16 The Borough (01227 761471); for oriental, try **Bistro Vietnam** at 72 Castle Street (01227 760022);. for Mexican, sample **Café des Amis du Mexique** at 95 St Dunstan's Street (01227 464390); for classy French cooking, head for **La Bonne Cuisine** (01227 450552) in the Canterbury Hotel at 71 New Dover Road. Drink in the young and lively **Three Tuns** in Castle Street, the **Bell & Crown** in Palace Street or the **Bishop's Finger** on St Dunstan's Street. Canterbury is stuffed with tearooms and coffee shops.

Tourist information centre: 34 St Margaret's Street (01227 766567, www.canterbury.co.uk). **Open** *Jan-Easter* 9.30am-5pm Mon-Sat; closed Sun. *Easter-October* 9.30am-5.30pm Mon-Sat; 10-4pm Sun. *Nov & Dec* 9.30am-5pm Mon-Sat; 10-4pm Sun.

Oxford

Founded by the Saxons, Oxford began its development in the early 8th century around a priory established by St Frideswide on the site where Christ Church now stands. Its slow but steady growth in importance and influence received the royal seal of approval when Henry I built his Palace of Beaumont there in the early 12th century, at much the same time as the first students were beginning to gather. Their numbers were boosted in 1167 when Paris University was closed to the English, and by the end of the century Oxford was firmly established as England's first university town. Today, the university comprises a federation of 41 independent colleges and halls, many in architecturally spectacular buildings.

Most are usually open to the public, and a short-list of the finest includes **Christ Church**, with its famous Tom Tower and a chapel so grand that it serves as Oxford's cathedral. Nearby **Merton**, founded in 1264, boasts a marvellous medieval library and garden, but **University College** was Oxford's first college, endowed in 1249. **Magdalen** (pronounced, for no apparent reason, 'mord-lin') is often said to be the loveliest college. Its grounds include a deer park and a meadow where the rare snakeshead fritillary still blooms every April.

Other centres of academia in Oxford include the **Bodleian Library** (01865 277000, www.bodley.ox.ac.uk) off Broad Street,

murdered on 29 December 1170 by four overzealous knights who had overheard King Henry II moaning, 'Will no one rid me of this turbulent priest?' and decided to do the troubled king a favour. Becket's tomb has been a site of pilgrimage ever since. **Trinity Chapel** contains the site of the original shrine plus the tombs of Henry IV and the Black Prince.

The small city centre can become overcrowded in summer but still retains its charm. **Eastbridge (St Thomas's) Hospital** (01227 471688), on the High Street, dates from the 12th century and contains a medieval mural, sundry antique treasures and a crypt; there are the remains of a Roman townhouse and mosaic floor at the **Roman Museum** on Butchery Lane (01227 785575, www.canterbury.co.uk/museums/roman); and the **Royal Museum & Art Gallery** (01227 452747, www.canterbury.co.uk/museums) on the High Street covers the history of the area. **King's School** is where Elizabethan playwright Christopher Marlowe, author of *Dr Faustus*, was educated. Meanwhile, a more recent addition to the town's attractions is the **Canterbury Tales Visitor Centre** (01227 479227), which aims to recreate the experience of Chaucer's 14th-century pilgrims.

begun in 1598; the dinky, elegant **Radcliffe Camera**, England's earliest example of a round reading room (1737); and **The Oxford Story** (01865 728822) on Broad Street, where a popular animatronic 'dark-ride' gives an entertaining, one-hour introduction to the university's history.

But Oxford is as much town as gown, and its attractions do not begin and end with the colleges. The **Ashmolean Museum** (01865 278000, www.ashmol.ox.ac.uk) is the country's oldest public museum and houses extensive collections of antiquities from Egypt, Greece, Rome and the Near East as well as a wide variety of art, sculpture, ceramics, glass and silverware from around the world. **Carfax Tower** (01865 792653) is the only surviving part of the 14th-century church of St Martin. Notable for its two 'quarter-boy' clocks (that chime every quarter-hour), it also provides great views of the town if you have the puff to climb the 99 steps to the top. The **Museum of Modern Art** (01865 722733, www.moma. org.uk) in Pembroke Street has established an international reputation for its pioneering exhibitions of contemporary and 20th-century work. At the other extreme, the **Pitt Rivers Museum of Archaeology & Anthropology** (01865 270927, www.prm.ox.ac.uk) on Parks Road is an atmospheric galleried Victorian building housing a world-famous collection of ancient ethnic artefacts.

If all this sounds exhausting, a browse around the town's boutiques provides a gentler pastime. Little Clarendon Street and the recent development at Gloucester Green offer some interesting specialist shops; the classy **Covered Market**, linking High Street and Market Street, opened in 1774, is a foodie's delight; or, if you're shopping for antiques, investigate Park End Street between the bus and railway stations.

The countryside pushes green fingers into the heart of the town, with the **Oxford Canal**, the **River Thames** (sometimes called the Isis, from the Latin 'Tamesis') and the **Cherwell** (pronounced 'Char-well') providing opportunities for strolling and punting. For the classic view of Matthew Arnold's 'dreaming spires' you must climb Boar's Hill three miles (two kilometres) to the south-west.

Further information

Getting there: *By train* from Paddington (1 hour), then use your rail ticket for a free ride into the centre on one of Oxford's pioneering electric buses (every 10mins). *By coach* frequent, cheap, fast services from several London departure points; details from National Express (1 hour 40mins), Stage Coach (01865 727000) and Oxford Bus Company (01865 785400). *By car* J8 off M40 then A40; use the park 'n' rides.

Where to stay: The upmarket 17th-century **Old Parsonage** (01865 310210, www.oxford-hotels-restaurants.co.uk; £165-£200) at 1 Banbury Road, one-time home to the undergraduate Oscar Wilde, is perennially popular, with a good bar and food. The city's classiest new accommodation is the sleekly luxurious **Old Bank Hotel** (01865 799599, www.oxford-hotels-restaurants.co.uk; £155-£300) at 92-94 High Street.

Where to eat & drink: There's upmarket fare in basic surrounds at the **Cherwell Boathouse** (01865 552746, www.cherwellboathouse.co.uk) off Bardwell Road; classy Italian cooking at **Il Cortile** at the Bath Place Hotel (01865 791812, www.bathplace.co.uk) off Holywell Street; and Raymond Blanc's swish, metropolitan brasserie **Le Petit Blanc** (01865 510999, www.petit-blanc.com) at 71-72 Walton Street. Oxford is well supplied with taverns – the busy 16th-century **King's Arms** at 40 Holywell Street can be overwhelmed by students but has good beer and decent pub grub; there's good food and real ale at the low-beamed, 16th-century **Turf Tavern** off Bath Place; or try the **Eagle & Child**, favoured watering hole of CS Lewis and JRR Tolkien.

Tourist information centre: The Old School, Gloucester Green (01865 726871, www.visitoxford.org). **Open** *Easter-Oct* 9.30am-5pm Mon-Sat; 10am-3.30pm Sun. *Nov-Easter* 9.30am-5pm Mon-Sat; closed Sun.

Stratford-upon-Avon

Where there's a Will… there's a thriving tourist industry and, these days, some of Stratford borders on the tasteless in its exploitation of the Shakespeare connection. The gaudy souvenirs and Shakespearian-themed cafés can get a little overpowering but there are still a good many genuinely interesting attractions. Top of the list are the Shakespeare properties, five picturesque Tudor houses that function as museums and are worth visiting in their own right. (All are on 01789 204016.) There are three in the town centre: **Shakespeare's Birthplace** on Henley Street (which underwent major restoration in 2000, adding period room-settings to the hall, parlour, kitchen and bedchambers); **Hall's Croft** on Old Town, named after Dr John Hall, who married the Bard's daughter Susanna; and **Nash's House**, on Chapel Street, which belonged to the first husband of his granddaughter, Elizabeth. In its garden are the foundations of **New Place**, Shakespeare's last home, which was demolished in 1759.

A mile and a half away at Shottery, and accessible from Stratford by public footpath, is **Anne Hathaway's Cottage**, where Shakespeare's wife lived before she married. The girlhood home of his mother, **Mary Arden's House** (01789 204016), is at Wilmcote, a pleasant four-mile (6.5-kilometre) stroll along the Stratford Canal. Both may also be reached by bus; there are trains to Wilmcote.

Shakespeare was educated at **Stratford Grammar School**, which you can see on Church Street, and buried in **Holy Trinity Church**, which has a fine riverside setting and supposedly the playwright's tomb (although the whereabouts of his body are disputed). The dramatist's most meaningful memorials are his plays, and the **Royal Shakespeare Theatre** is the place to see them (tickets sell out fast though). The adjoining **Swan Theatre** stages a variety of classics, while **The Other Place** is for modern and experimental work. For bookings call 01789 403403. If you can't get a ticket, make do with a backstage tour or a visit to the **RSC Collection**, a museum of props and costumes (tours 01789 403405).

Relief from all things Shakespearian is easily achieved. Stratford has been a market town since 1169 and, in a way, that's still what it does best. See it on a Friday, when the awnings go up over the stalls at the top of Wood Street and locals flock in from the outlying villages. And wander round the town centre, which still maintains its medieval grid pattern. Many fine old buildings survive, among them **Harvard House** (01789 204016) on the High Street, dating from 1596. It was the home of Katharine Rogers, the mother of John Harvard, founder of Harvard University Today it contains a nationally important collection of pewter dating from Roman times to the 19th century.

The town's charms are enhanced by the presence of the **River Avon** and the **Stratford Canal**. The canal basin is usually crammed with narrowboats and there are walks beside both waterways. Blending heritage and hospitality with its local history exhibitions, craft shop and bar/restaurant, **Cox's Yard** (01789 404600, www.coxsyard.co.uk), a new development on the banks of the Avon, is a pleasant destination for your journey's end.

Further information

Getting there: *By train* from Paddington (2 hours 10mins). *By coach* National Express (2 hours 45mins) or Guide Friday (01789 294466, www.guidefriday. com) from Euston. *By car* J15 off M40 then A46.

Where to stay: The pick of the many B&Bs is **Caterham House** (01789 267309; £76-£80) at 58 Rother Street, close to the Royal Shakespeare Theatre. Another good choice is **Victoria Spa Lodge** (01789 267985; £60) on Bishopton Lane.

Where to eat & drink: Among the many eating options is the excellent bistro **The Opposition** (01789 269980) on Sheep Street, the imaginative, highly rated **Russon's** (01789 268822) at 8 Church Street and the popular modern cooking at **Desport's** at 13-14 Meer Street (01789 269304). Drink with the thespians at the **Dirty Duck** (aka the **Black Swan**) on Waterside, or the low-beamed **Queen's Head** on Ely Street, renowned for its real ales.

Tourist information centre: Bridgefoot (01789 293127, www.shakespeare-country.co.uk). **Open** *Easter-Oct* 9am-6pm Mon-Sat; 11am-5pm Sun. *Nov-Easter* 9am-5pm Mon-Sat; closed Sun.

Castles

Arundel

West Sussex (01903 882173/www.arundelcastle.org). **Getting there** *By train* from Victoria (1 hour 30mins). *By car* A24 then A280 and A27. **Open** *Apr-26 Oct* noon-5pm Mon-Fri, Sun (last entry 4pm); closed Sat. Closed 27 Oct-Mar. **Admission** £7.50; £4.50-£6.50 concessions; £20 family.

The beautiful, imposing Arundel Castle has its origins in the 11th century, although the original building was badly damaged during the Civil War and owes its current appearence to extensive remodelling in the 18th and 19th centuries. There's plenty to see inside, including a fine collection of 16th-century furniture and paintings by Van Dyck, Gainsborough, Reynolds and Mytens among others. Don't miss the 14th-century Fitzalan Chapel, home to the tombs of the Dukes of Norfolk past, and mercifully showing no signs of the time when Cromwell used it as a stable.

Arundel also has its own neo-Gothic 19th-century **cathedral**, more impressive outside than in, plus some agreeable shopping and a handful of decent alehouses – try the busy Eagle on Tarrant Street.

Hever

Hever, nr Edenbridge, Kent (01732 865224, www.hevercastle.co.uk). **Getting there** *By train* Victoria to Edenbridge (1 hour), then 5-min taxi journey, or Victoria to Hever (1 hour), then 1-mile walk. *By car* J5 off M25 then B2042 and B269 or J6 off M25 then A22, A25 and B269. **Open** *Castle Mar-Nov* noon-dusk daily. *Gardens* 11am-dusk daily. **Admission** £8; £4.40-£6.80 concessions; £20.40 family. *Garden only* £6.30; £4.20 -£5.40 concessions; £16.80 family. **Credit** MC, V.

Hever Castle was the childhood home of Anne Boleyn; Henry VIII is said to have courted the ill-fated queen in the magnificent gardens of this enchanting, double-moated, 13th-century castle. Most of the furniture, paintings and objects inside are the legacy of the American millionaire William Waldorf Astor, who bought the estate in 1903 and spent a huge amount of time, money and effort in restoring it. The grounds now boast award-winning Italianate gardens with loggia, classical sculpture and a colonnaded piazza, as well as a large lake and rose garden. One of Hever's most popular attractions, a water maze (open Apr-Oct), invites bravehearts to reach a folly in the middle of a large pond by means of stepping-stone paths while avoiding water obstacles made by jets of water. There's also a more conventional yew maze and the Guthrie Miniature Model Houses Collection, which depicts country-house living from medieval to Victorian times. Special events, including jousts and medieval tournaments, are staged during the summer months.

Windsor Castle.

Leeds Castle

Broomfield, nr Maidstone, Kent (01622 765400, www.leeds-castle.co.uk). **Getting there** *By train* Victoria to Bearsted (1 hour), then 10-min bus transfer. *By car* J8 off M20. **Open** *Mar-Oct* 10am-7pm daily (last entry 5pm). *Nov-Feb* 10am-5pm daily (last entry 3pm).
Admission *Castle* £10; £6.50-£8.50 concessions; £29 family. *Park only* £8.50; £5.20-£7 concessions; £24 family. **Credit** MC, V.

Though the name may suggest a more northerly location, Leeds Castle is actually to be found in Broomfield, five miles (8km) east of Maidstone, where its stunning location on two small islands in the middle of a lake have earned it a reputation as the loveliest castle in the world. The original castle was built by the Normans nearly 900 years ago and was converted into a royal palace in the 16th century by Henry VIII. It now contains a mish-mash of medieval furnishings, paintings, tapestries and, bizarrely, the world's finest collection of antique dog collars.

The castle's greatest attractions, however, are external. Apart from the flower-filled gardens, there's the Culpeper Garden (an outsize cottage garden), an aviary containing over 100 rare bird species and, best of the lot, a maze, which centres on a spectacular underground grotto adorned with stone mythical beasts and shell mosaics. Facilities for disabled visitors are good (a leaflet is available in advance). Special events are held throughout the year (phone for details). The combined train journey, transfer and entrance ticket (book in advance at Victoria station) is the best deal going at £18.50 (£9.25 children).

Windsor

High Street, Windsor (01753 831118/www.royal residences.com). **Getting there** *By train* Paddington to Slough, then change for Windsor Central (45mins); Waterloo to Windsor Riverside (1 hour). *By car* J6 off M4. **Open** *Mar-Oct* 9.45am-5.15pm daily (last entry 4pm). *Nov-Feb* 9.45am-4.15pm daily (last entry 3pm). **Admission** Mon-Sat £11; £5.50-£9 concessions; £27.50 family. **Credit** AmEx, MC, V.

There has been a castle in Windsor since 1070, when William the Conqueror built the first fortifications to protect the western approaches to London. However, the structure has since been strengthened and extended by successive monarchs so that the modern edifice of what is now the largest castle in England is a hotchpotch of architectural fancies from the last nine centuries. Highlights include Queen Mary's Dolls' House, designed by Edward Lutyens and built over three years by 1,500 craftsmen, to such detail that even the toilets flush; the State Apartments, now fully restored following the 1992 fire; and the Perpendicular Gothic St George's Chapel (closed to the public on Sundays), where Henry VIII is buried. Try to coincide your visit with the Changing of the Guard, which takes place outside the Guardroom in the Lower Ward on alternate days at 11am.

Country houses

Althorp, the Spencer family home and the burial place of Diana, Princess of Wales, is a 90-minute drive from London in Northamptonshire. For more information phone 01604 592020 or visit the website at www.althorp.com. Note that the house is open only during July and August.

In an English country garden

Boy, do the English love their gardens. And the south-east of the country, by virtue of its long-term affluence and relatively tameable landscapes, contains a fair few open-to-the public examples that make the average gardener go green-fingered with envy.

Groombridge Place Gardens

Groombridge, Kent (01892 863999).
Getting there *By rail* Charing Cross to Tunbridge Wells (53mins) then 10-min taxi ride. *By car* J5 off M25 then A21, A26 and B2176. **Open** *Mar-Oct* 9am-6pm/dusk daily. **Admission** £6.50; £5.50 3s-12s, OAPs; £20 family. **Credit** AmEx, MC, V.

It comes as little surprise that this medieval site has inspired artists and writers over the centuries (including filmmaker Peter Greenaway and Sir Arthur Conan Doyle for *The Valley of Fear*). Though the current house, which dates from the 17th century, is closed to the public, visitors can explore the surrounding parkland. With a listed walled garden set against a 17th-century moated mansion and walks through the award-winning 'Enchanted Forest', spring-fed pools and waterfalls giving way to dramatic views over the Weald, the possibilities for waxing lyrical are endless. A great place for kids.

Audley End

Saffron Walden, Essex (01799 522842).
Getting there *By train* Liverpool Street to Audley End (1 hour) then 1-mile walk or 2-min taxi ride. *By car* J8 off M11 then B1383.
Open *Apr-Sept* noon-5pm Wed-Sun; closed Mon & Tue. *Oct* 11am-4pm Wed-Sun; closed Mon & Tue. **Admission** £6.75; £3.40-£5.10 concessions; £16.90 family. **Credit** MC, V.

The magnificent Jacobean mansion of **Audley End** was the largest house in the country when it was built for Thomas Howard, First Earl of Suffolk, in 1614. It was later owned by Charles II, but given back to the Howards in the 18th century, who demolished two-thirds of it to make it more manageable. More than 30 rooms are open to the public today, many of which have been restored to Robert Adam's 1760s designs. 'Capability' Brown landscaped the grounds. Phone to book a guided tour.

Saffron Walden (1 mile/1.5km from Audley End) is an appealing market town containing many timber-framed houses with decorative plastering (known as 'pargeting'). Eight miles (13km) south-west is the village of **Thaxted**, where Gustav Holst wrote much of *The Planets* and site of a superb three-tiered, half-timbered Guildhall, dating

Nymans

Handcross, West Sussex (01444 400321/ www.nationaltrust.org.uk/southern).
Getting there *By train* Victoria to Three Bridges (45mins) then 15-min taxi ride. *By car* M23 then A23 and B2114.
Open *Mar-Oct* 11am-6pm/dusk Wed-Sun; closed Mon & Tue. *Nov-Mar* 11am-4pm Sat, Sun; closed Mon-Fri. **Admission** £6; £3 5s-18s; £15 family ticket. **Credit** MC, V.

Four miles (6km) south of Crawley is one of the finest of all English gardens. Set high on the edge of the Sussex Weald, Nymans is a showpiece of rare shrubs and trees. Highlights include the walled garden, the hidden sunken garden and some wonderful woodland walks. Parts of the house are now open to the public.

Sheffield Park

nr Uckfield, East Sussex (01825 790231).
Getting there *By train* Victoria to Hayward's Heath (45mins) then 15-min taxi ride. *By car* J10 off M23 then A264, A22 and A275.
Open *Jan, Feb* 10.30am-4pm Sat, Sun. *Mar-Oct* 10.30am-6pm/dusk Tue-Sun. *Nov, Dec* 10.30am-4pm Tue-Sun. **Admission** £4.20; £2.10 5s-17s; £10.50 family.

from the 15th century (01371 831339). There are many other fine villages and much great walking in the area.

Blenheim Palace

Woodstock, Oxfordshire (01993 811325, www.blenheimpalace.com). **Getting there** *By train* Paddington to Oxford (1 hour) then 30-40-min bus ride. *By car* J9 off M40 then A34 and A44.
Open *Palace & gardens Mid Mar-Oct* 10.30am-5.30pm daily (last entry 4.45pm). *Park* 9am-4.45pm daily. **Admission** £9.50; £4.80-£7.30 concessions; £25 family. *Park only* £6 per car (incl occupants), £2 adult; £1 concessions. **Credit** AmEx, DC, MC, V.

As a prize for beating the French at the Battle of Blenheim, John Churchill, Duke of Marlborough, was promised the money to build this immense, extravagant baroque fantasy. Its construction was acrimonious, as Parliament refused to stump up all the necessary cash and Churchill's wife quarrelled with the architect, Sir John Vanbrugh (she had wanted Wren for the job). Baroque masterpiece it may be, but the scale of the building means that it overwhelms rather than charms, and the speedy tours of the plush, antique-packed interior don't leave much time for reflection. The gardens, land-

Trips Out of Town

The major draw of the sleepy heart of Sussex is its array of splendid gardens. The most majestic of these is Sheffield Park, located ten miles (16km) north of Lewes. Yet another 18th-century 'Capability' Brown creation, the gardens were modified in the early 20th century but retain a grand landscape feel. There are five lakes connected with cascades and waterfalls in the early spring, fine specimens of azalea and rhododendron in early summer and autumn hues from rare trees.

Sissinghurst

Sissinghurst, Cranbrook, Kent (01580 712850). **Getting there** *By train* Charing Cross to Staplehurst (53mins) then 10-min taxi ride. *By car* J5 off M25 then A21 and A262. **Open** *Apr-mid-Oct* 1-6.30pm Tue-Fri; 10am-5.30pm Sat, Sun. **Admission** phone for details. **Credit** AmEx, MC, V.

Sissinghurst is the greatest of the Kent gardens. Here Vita Sackville-West and her husband Harold Nicolson transformed a ruined 16th-century mansion (closed to the public) and grounds into a paradise of colour and fragrance. Alas, the edenic lure of Sissinghurst is so powerful that coachloads of trippers frequently swamp the place and timed tickets are the norm.

Stowe

Buckinghamshire (gardens 01280 822850/house 01280 818282/ www.nationaltrust.org.uk). **Getting there** *By train* Euston to Milton Keynes (40mins) then bus to Buckingham (30mins) then 5-min taxi ride. *By car* J10 off M40 then A43 and A422 or J14 off M1 then A5 and A422. **Open** Seasonal hours; phone for details. **Admission** *Gardens* £4.60; £2.30 concessions; £11.50 family. *House* £3; £1.50 concessions.
No credit cards.

Three miles (5km) north-west of Buckingham, Stowe is quite possibly the most important and spectacular 18th-century landscaped garden in the country. Its 132 hectares (325 acres) were first laid out in 1680, but were transformed over the following 100 years by a mix of tree-plantings, (six) lake-makings and (32) temple-buildings. To 'Capability' Brown's naturalistic landscape-shaping were added monuments by almost every big-name architect of the time, including James Gibbs, John Vanbrugh and William Kent. The overall effect is beautiful, idyllic and, above all, quintessentially English. Little of the house can be seen because it is occupied by Stowe School.

scaped by the ubiquitous 'Capability' Brown, are splendid (and contain a butterfly house, adventure play area, maze, putting greens and mini-train). Winston Churchill was born here in 1874 (five rooms are dedicated to the wartime PM) and is buried with his wife and parents in the nearby church at **Bladon**.

The handsome, well-scrubbed Oxfordshire town of **Woodstock** has a long history of royal connections but now chiefly services visitors to Blenheim and the Cotswolds (*see p354*). It's an agreeable refreshment stop. If you want to avoid the worst of the crowds, try the Black Prince pub on Oxford Street.

Hatfield House

Hatfield, Hertfordshire (01707 262823). **Getting there** *By train* from King's Cross to Hatfield (25mins). *By car* J4 off A1(M). **Open** *House Late Mar-Sept* noon-4pm Tue-Thur; 1-4pm Sat, Sun; closed Mon. *Gardens Late Mar-Sept* 11am-6pm Tue-Sun; closed Mon. **Admission** £6.60; £3.30 concessions. *Gardens only* (East & West) Fri £6; (West only) Tue-Sun £4. **Credit** MC, V.

Hatfield House is one of the largest and most impressive Jacobean mansions in the country. Built in 1607-11 for Sir Robert Cecil (and remaining in the hands of his family today), it stands on the site of Tudor Hatfield Palace, where Elizabeth I spent much of her childhood. Cecil demolished most of the 16th-century building, although one wing survives. The grand interior contains some fine furniture and wonderful Tudor and Jacobean portraits. Outside, the 17th-century formal gardens were laid out by John Tradescant. The entrance is opposite the station.

Polesden Lacey

Dorking Road, Surrey (01372 458203, www.nationaltrust.org.uk/regions/southern). **Getting there** *By train* Waterloo to Westhumble or Dorking (40mins) then 10-min taxi ride. *By car* A3 then A246 and A24. **Open** *House Apr-Oct* 1-5pm Wed-Sun, bank holiday Mondays; closed Mon & Tue. *Grounds* 11am-6pm/dusk daily. **Admission** £7; £3.50 concessions; £17.50 family. *Grounds only* £4; £2 concessions; £10 family. **Credit** MC, V.

Three miles (5km) west of Box Hill (*see p354*) is the Regency villa of Polesden Lacey. This was the honeymooning ground for the Queen Mother and the late George VI more than 70 years ago. Tucked into the folds of the Surrey North Downs, the house and gardens give way to splendid views over woodland and commons. Within the grounds, tree-lined walks,

Trips Out of Town

'The Time Out Guides still lead the pack' **The Times**

The **Time Out City Guides** spectrum

Available from all good booksellers

Take the plunge at **Thorpe Park**. See p352.

See p352.

walled rose gardens and a charming thatched bridge over a typical Surrey sunken lane all make for a right royal day out.

Waddesdon Manor

Waddesdon, nr Aylesbury, Buckinghamshire (01296 653203/www.waddesdon.org.uk). **Getting there** *By train* Marylebone to Aylesbury (53mins) then bus. *By car* J9 off M40 then A41. **Open** *House Apr-June, Sept, Oct* 11am-4pm Wed-Sun, bank holiday Mondays; closed Mon & Tue. *Grounds Mar-Christmas* 10am-5pm Wed-Sun, bank holiday Mondays; closed Mon & Tue. **Admission** £10; £7.50 5s-16s. *Grounds only* £3; £1.50 5s-16s. **Credit** MC, V.

Five miles (8km) north-west of Aylesbury, château-like Waddesdon Manor looks fantastically out of place in the English countryside. Built by the obscenely wealthy Rothschild family between 1874 and 1889, the house contains a magnificent collection of 17th- and 18th-century decorative arts. Panelling from 19th-century Parisian houses lines the walls, Savonnerie and Aubusson carpets cover the floors, and fine gold boxes, rare books and majolica are among the exhibits. The star attraction is one of the world's finest selections of Sèvres porcelain. The splendid rococo aviary in the grounds is also worth a look, as are the Rothschild wine-packed cellars (where tastings are on offer).

Woburn Abbey

Woburn, Bedfordshire (01525 290666, www.woburnabbey.co.uk). **Getting there** *By train* Euston to Leighton Buzzard (45mins) then 15-min taxi ride; King's Cross to Flitwick (45mins) then 10-min taxi ride. *By car* J13 off M1 then A4012. **Open** *1 Jan-Mar* 11am-4pm Sat, Sun; closed Mon-Fri. *Apr-Oct* 11am-4pm Mon-Sat; 11am-5pm Sun. *Oct* 11am-4pm Sat; 11am-5pm Sun; closed Mon-Fri. **Admission** £7.50; £3-£6.50 concessions; under-12s free; £19-£24 family ticket. **Credit** MC, V.

Home of the Dukes of Bedford for more than 350 years, 18th-century Woburn Abbey is hugely popular with daytrippers, due in large part to its **Safari Park** (half-price admission with a ticket for the abbey), winner of the English Tourism Council's Visitor Attraction of the Year award in 2000. The abbey itself – so called because it was built on the foundations of a 12th-century Cistercian monastery – is a grand old house, containing some superb Tudor portraits.

Trips Out of Town

Family attractions

Many of the other destinations in this chapter are great for families – particularly the castles and seaside towns. Woburn Abbey (see p351) has a fine safari park.

Chessington World of Adventures

Leatherhead Road (A243), Chessington, Surrey (0870 444 7777/www.chessington.com). **Getting there** *By train* Waterloo to Chessington South (30mins). *By coach* Flightline 777 bus from Victoria Coach Station (1 hour). *By car* J9 off M25 or A3. **Open** phone for details. **Admission** £19.95; £16 4s-13s; £12 concessions; free under-4s; £63 family. **Credit** AmEx, MC, V.

A member of the Tussauds Group, this frenetic 26-hectare (65-acre) theme park and zoo is certainly fun (if a little tacky), but prepare to pay through the nose for the pleasure. If you take the train to get here, hang on to your tickets as there's usually reduced-price admission for rail passengers. Attractions include Rameses' Revenge, the Vampire (a suspended rollercoaster), the Safari Skyway Monorail and the Power of the Samurai, a ride that requires 'all your physical, mental and philosophical strength' to conquer. Best of luck. Advance tickets bought by phone or on-line are often cheaper.

Legoland Windsor

Winkfield Road, Berkshire (0870 504 0404, www.legoland.co.uk). **Getting there** *By train* Paddington to Windsor Central, change at Slough (30mins), or to Windsor & Eton Riverside (49mins) then shuttle service (small charge). *By car* J6 off M4, J3 off M3 or J13 off M25, then follow signs. *By coach* Green Line runs a daily service from Victoria (08706 087 261). **Open** *10 Mar-3 Nov* 10am-6pm daily (10am-8pm during summer school hols). **Admission** £18.50; £15.50 3s-15s; £12.50 OAPs. **Credit** AmEx, MC, V.

Modelled on the Danish original, this award-winning theme park is a bright, clean, family affair that's sure to be a hit with most two- to 12-year-olds. The huge site is split into various activity zones. Miniland is packed with slick reconstructions of famous European buildings, from Tower Bridge to Mont St Michel. Duplo Gardens has a water-play area and cascades of chunky plastic, while the Castleland adventure area has the Dragon Knight's rollercoaster ride. Kids can get their Legoland licence in the Driving School, before heading on to Wild Woods to pan for gold and ride the Pirate Falls. Phone for details of special events and an info sheet on facilities and access for guests with disabilities.

Thorpe Park

Staines Road, Chertsey, Surrey (0870 444 4466, www.thorpepark.com). **Getting there** *By train* Victoria to Staines, change at Clapham Junction (45 mins), or Hatton Cross tube, then link bus. *By car* J11 or J13 off M25. **Open** phone to check. **Admission** £19; £15 4s-13s; £12 OAPs. **Credit** AmEx, MC, V.

Top five

Picture postcards

Pint-sized panorama

Big Ben! The Loch Ness Monster! Mont St Michel! Shoot all the world's greatest sights, each rendered in teensy plastic bricks, at **Legoland Windsor**. See p352.

Chocolate box kitsch

The stone villages of the **Cotswolds**, enfolded in gentle hills, are almost too cutesy to be true. But they are true. See p354.

Castles in the air

Leeds Castle, rising from a pair of islands in a lake, is officially the loveliest castle in the world. See p347.

Kiss me quick

Brighton has the archetypal seaside tack on its funfair-filled Palace Pier. Go on, kiss me quick. See p340.

Kiss me Kate

Stratford-upon-Avon contains every Shakespeare cliché in the anthology, plus some must-see historic landmarks for the Bard core. See p345.

Like Chessington, this attractively landscaped 202-hectare (500-acre) theme park is a member of the Tussauds Group. Entertaining around one million visitors a year, Thorpe Park provides all the usual attractions, including stunt shows, a working farm, 'fungle jungle' adventures, ghost rides, oversized and overfriendly cartoon characters, No Way Out, a backwards ride in the dark, and the newly opened Tidal Wave, Europe's highest water ride. Tickets are cheaper in advance by phone or on-line.

Whipsnade Wild Animal Park

nr Dunstable, Bedfordshire (0870 520 0123, www.whipsnade.co.uk). **Getting there** *By train* King's Cross to Luton (33mins) or Euston to Hemel Hempstead (25mins) then bus or 20-min taxi ride. *By car* J9 off M1 then A5 and B4540. **Open** *Apr-Oct* 10am-6pm Mon-Sat; 10am-7pm Sun. *Nov-Mar* 10am-4pm daily. **Admission** £9.90; £7-£7.50 concessions. **Credit** AmEx, MC, V.

Set in 243 hectares (600 acres) of beautiful parkland, Whipsnade is one of Europe's largest conservation centres. It is home to over 2,500 animals, many of which are endangered in wild. There's a host of family favourites, including elephants, bears, giraffes, tigers and rhinos, as well as a variety of less familiar species. Kids will especially love the

Trips Out of Town

Runwild Play Area, Children's Farm, the Great Whipsnade Railway and the penguin feeding, but there are several attractions that adults can enjoy too, including the Birds of the World demonstration, Squirrel Monkey Island and Tiger Falls.

Out in the country

Despite appearances, London's sprawl does not go on forever. There's wonderful walking country within easy reach of the city, particularly in the North Downs, south of London; the Chilterns to the north-west; and the Cotswolds to the west. You could also walk a stretch of the **Thames Path**, which follows a 180-mile (288-km) stretch of river from its source near Kemble in Gloucestershire via the Cotswolds, Oxford, the Chilterns, Windsor and through London to the Thames Barrier at Woolwich. Leaflets are available from tourist information centres.

Country Lanes *9 Shaftesbury Street, Fordingbridge, Hampshire SP6 1JF (01425 655022/www.countrylanes.co.uk).*
Take the train from London and be met at your destination by representatives from Country Lanes, who will then lead you on cycling or walking tours of the New Forest and the Cotswolds. There are day trips, short breaks and six-day tours. Visit the website or phone for a brochure.

The Chilterns

Getting there: *By train* from Paddington to Henley (55mins); Paddington to Bourne End then change for Marlow (1hr 5mins). *By car* Henley/Marlow J8 off M4 then A404(M) and A4130 or J4 off M40 then A404 and A4155. *Wendover* J20 off M25 then A41 and A4011 or A40 and A413.

Stretching in a broad arc around the north-west of London, the Chilterns rarely receive more than a cursory glance out of the window from the coachloads of tourists powering through to Oxford and Stratford. Yet this gently hilly region has some great walking and excellent pubs (if also some charmless towns) and is easily and quickly accessible from the capital.

At the place where Oxfordshire, Berkshire and Buckinghamshire meet is cocky little **Henley** (tourist office: 01491 578034, www.oxfordshire.co.uk/centres). This wealthy commuter burg becomes the centre of braying-toff life for five days at the end of June when the Henley **Royal Regatta** hits town (*see p263*), but is otherwise most useful as a base from which to explore the wonderful villages and countryside to the north. Some of the best walking in the Chilterns can be found around **Frieth** and **Nettlebed**, and the Prince Albert pub in the former and Carpenters Arms in Crocker End near the latter are good spots to hole up with a pint or two after a hike. There's also fine walking further north around **Wendover**.

The old stocks at **Stow-on-the-Wold** in the **Cotswolds**.

Chipping Camden's market hall.

Another good (if very popular) place from which to explore the southern Chilterns and the Thames Valley, **Marlow** is a relaxed little town with some good Georgian architecture and a fine pub – the Two Brewers on St Peter's Street – where Jerome K Jerome wrote part of *Three Men in a Boat*. Other notable literary residents of Marlow have included Percy and Mary Shelley and TS Eliot.

The cutesy village of **Cookham**, four miles (7km) east of Marlow, is famed as the home of one of Britain's greatest and most idiosyncratic 20th-century painters, **Stanley Spencer**. Several of his deceptively naïve, sex-and-God-obsessed works are displayed in the **Stanley Spencer Gallery** (01628 471885, www.cookham.com) on the High Street.

The Cotswolds

Getting there *By train* Paddington to Moreton-in-Marsh (1 hour 20mins). *By car* M40 then A40 and A44.

Nowhere in England is there such a harmonious relationship between buildings and landscape as in the Cotswolds. The enchanting stone villages and incomparable 'wool churches' that characterise the area were built by the medieval merchants who grew rich from the profits of the local wool trade. Routinely described as 'honey-coloured', the stone is actually extremely variable, yet its ubiquitous use helps to unify a region that sprawls generously over six counties.

Parts of the Cotswolds suffer horrible congestion on summer weekends, but it's always localised. While crowds buzz around **Bourton** and **Bibury**, equally charming villages such as **Stanton** and **Stanway** slumber gently on, almost undisturbed. The small Cotswold towns are often even more memorable than the villages. Places such as **Stow-on-the-Wold**, whose elegant 17th-century houses look down on the square (the tourist information centre is found here; 01451 831082, www.cotswold.gov.uk); **Winchcombe**, with its gargoyle-encrusted church and its wonderful setting; **Broadway**, where cottage gardens of wisteria, clematis and old roses spill out on to the High Street; and, best of all, **Chipping Campden**, with its 600-year-old houses and glorious wool church.

Chipping Campden is also the starting point of the **Cotswold Way** long-distance path. Fortunately,

Cotswold footpaths are as suitable for Sunday strollers as hardened hikers. Well-maintained and waymarked, they converge on every town and village. The ancient Eight Bells Inn in Chipping Campden (01386 840371), the Old White Lion in Winchcombe (01242 603300) and the pricier Grapevine Hotel in Stow-on-the-Wold (01451 830344) are all recommended bases. For **Stratford-upon-Avon**, *see p345*.

Epping Forest

Information Centre, High Beech, Loughton, Essex (020 8508 0028/www.eppingforest.org.uk). **Getting there** *By train* Loughton then 2-mile walk or 5-min taxi ride. *By car* J26 off M25. **Open** *Apr-Oct* 10am-5pm Mon-Sat; 11am-5pm Sun. *Nov-Mar* 11am-3pm Mon-Fri; 10am-dusk Sat; 11am-dusk Sun.

The 2,430 hectares (6,000 acres) left of this once massive ancient forest are still mighty impressive, and perfect for walking, cycling, horse riding, picnicking, blackberrying and mushrooming. Wander down wheelchair- (and pushchair-) friendly paths, among ancient oaks adjacent to the visitors' centre and around Connaught Water. The friendly staff can offer suggestions for walks or supply leaflets and a detailed map to help with explorations. Be warned that the visitors' centre is a two-mile (3km) uphill walk from Loughton tube station. You're best off buying a map of the forest beforehand (try Edward Stanford; *see p231*), having a coffee in Loughton town when you get off the tube and then walking to the information centre through the forest rather than along the main roads. Alternatively, continue on the tube for a couple of stops to Theydon Bois, a pretty, largely unspoiled village with a green and duck pond, and wander into the forest from there.

The North Downs

Getting there *By train* Waterloo to Boxhill & Westhumble or Dorking (40-50 mins) then 10-min taxi ride. *By car* A3 then A243 and A24.

The bones of the landscape of England south of London are the Downs – North and South – long chalk ridges facing each other across the Weald. The South Downs are more spectacular, but the North Downs are far closer to the capital; so close that you can enjoy some of the South-east's best views little more than 20 miles (32km) from the heart of London.

A long-distance footpath, the **North Downs Way**, runs for 140 miles (224km) from Farnham in Surrey to the White Cliffs of Dover. Opportunities for shorter walks are plentiful, and the ancient market town of **Dorking** is a good centre. There's easy access from here to **Box Hill**, which has been a popular picnic spot since the days of Charles II – avoid weekends if you can. The William IV pub in nearby Mickleham is a popular place for liquid and solid refreshment. Not far away is **Polesden Lacey** (*see p349*) and **Ranmore Common**, which offers good walks on the south slopes of the Downs. Another good spot for walking, six miles (9km) south-west of Dorking, is **Leith Hill**, the highest point in south-east England.

Directory

Feature boxes

Directory

Getting Around

For details of London's domestic rail and coach stations, *see p338*.

By air

Gatwick Airport

01293 535353/www.baa.co.uk/ gatwick. About 30 miles (50km) south of central London, off the M23.
Three rail services link Gatwick to London. The quickest is the **Gatwick Express** (0990 301530, www.gatwickexpress.co.uk) to Victoria station, which takes about 30-35 minutes and runs 24 hours daily: every 15 minutes between 5.50am and midnight, then hourly between 12.35am and 5.20am. Tickets cost £10.20 for a single, £11.70 for a day return (after 9.30am) and £20.40 for a period return (valid for 30 days). Under-15s get half-price tickets, while under-5s travel for free. British Airways and American Airlines offer check-in services at Victoria.

Connex South Central (08457 484950, www.connex.co.uk) also runs a rail service between Gatwick and Victoria, with trains running approximately every 15 minutes during the day and every hour from 1am to 4am. It takes between three and eight minutes longer than the Gatwick Express but, on the plus side, tickets are cheaper, costing £8.20 for a single, £8.30 for a day return (after 9.30am) and £16.40 for a period return (valid for one month). Again, under-15s get half-price tickets, and under-5s go for free.

If you are staying in the Bloomsbury area or want to connect with trains at King's Cross or Euston, the **Thameslink** (08457 484950, www.thameslink.co.uk) service might prove more convenient. It runs via Blackfriars, City Thameslink, London Bridge Farringdon and King's Cross, and frequency and journey times vary with the time of day. Tickets (to King's Cross) cost £9.80 (single) and £19.60 (return).

The **Airbus A5** (08705 747777) to Victoria Coach Station (*see p388*) is the cheapest option for travelling into London, but it's also the most time-consuming with a journey time of about 90 minutes. Buses run 4.15am to 9.15pm daily, every hour. Tickets

cost £8 for a single or £10 for a return (valid for three months). Under-15s get half-price tickets; under-5s ride for free.

But if you really want your hand held from airport to hotel and don't mind paying £20 each way, try **Hotelink** (01293 532244, fax 01293 531131, www.hotelink.co.uk). You can book in advance by fax or online with a credit card, giving them your flight details, and someone will meet your plane and shuttle you in to your hotel in central London.

Unless you have more money than sense and/or an expense account to die for, forget **taxis**. You'll end up paying £90 for the torporous, hour-plus journey into central London.

Heathrow Airport

0870 000 0123/www.baa.co.uk/ heathrow. About 15 miles (24km) west of central London, off the M4.
The **Heathrow Express** (0845 600 1515, www.heathrowexpress.co.uk), which runs from the airport to Paddington station every 15 minutes between 5am and midnight daily, takes 15-20 minutes and is the quickest and most efficient way of travelling between Heathrow and central London. The train can be boarded at one of the airport's two underground stations (Terminals 1, 2 and 3, or Terminal 4). Tickets cost £12 each way or £22 return (£11 or £20 return if booked over the Internet); under-16s travel free (up to four children per paying adult). Many airlines, including British Airways, American Airlines and United Airlines, now have check-in desks at Paddington for both hand and hold luggage.

A longer but far cheaper journey is by tube on the **Piccadilly line**. Tickets for the 50- to 60-minute ride into central London cost £3.60 one way (£1.50 under-16s). Trains run every few minutes from about 5am to 11.45pm every day except Sunday, when they run 6am to 11pm. There's a tube station at Terminal 4 and another serving Terminals 1, 2 and 3.

Between 4am and 8pm, the **Airbus A2** (08705 808080) runs two buses an hour from all four terminals at Heathrow to 16 points within central London. These double-deckers have ample room for luggage and are accessible to wheelchair users, though be warned: they're not quick, with journey time to King's

Cross around one hour 45 minutes. Tickets cost £7 single or £10 for a return. Under-16s pay £3.50 for a single and £5 for a return.

As at Gatwick, **Hotelink** (01293 532244, fax 01293 531131, www.hotelink.co.uk) offers a hand-holding service for £14 each way.

Taxi fares to central London are high (around £45) and the journey time is about 45-60 minutes, often far longer during the rush hour.

London City Airport

7646 0000/www.londoncityairport. com. 9 miles (14km) east of central London, Docklands.
Silvertown & City Airport rail station, on the Silverlink Line (*see p359*), is a couple of minutes' walk from the London City Airport terminal, and offers a service that runs approximately every 20 minutes via Stratford, where you can pick up a Central line tube.

Most people, though, head into London on the blue and white **Shuttlebus** (7646 0088), whose 30-minute ride to Liverpool Street station goes via Canary Wharf. The shuttle bus leaves every 10 minutes from 6.50am to 9.10pm during the week, and from 6.50am to 10pm on Saturdays and 11am to 10pm on Sundays. Tickets to Liverpool Street station cost £5 one-way, with the fare to Canary Wharf a mere £2.

The journey by **taxi** to the City takes about 30 to 40 minutes and will cost around £20.

Luton Airport

01582 405100/www.london-luton.co.uk. About 30 miles (50km) north of central London, off the M1 at junction 10.
The newly opened **Luton Airport Parkway** station is close to the airport, but not in it: there's still a short shuttle-bus ride. The Thameslink service (08457 484950) calls at a number of central London stations including King's Cross and has a journey time of 30 to 40 minutes. Trains leave every five to ten minutes and cost £9.50 single, £19 for a return, or £10 for a cheap day return (available only after 9.30am Monday to Friday).

For a cheaper but longer journey, take the **Green Line 757** coach service (0870 6087261, www.greenline.co.uk), which runs from Luton to Victoria Station about three times an hour. The journey takes 90 minutes, and costs £7.50 for a single or £12 for a return (valid for three months). Under-15s get half-price tickets; under-5s go free.

A **taxi** from the airport into central London will take an hour at the very least, and will set you back a not inconsiderable £65 or so.

Stansted Airport

0870 000 0303/www.baa.co.uk/ stansted. About 35 miles (60km) north-east of central London, J8 off the M11.
The quickest way to get to London from Stansted is on the **Stansted Express** train (08457 484950) to Liverpool Street station; the journey time is 40-45 minutes. Trains leave every 15 to 30 minutes depending on the time of day, and tickets cost £12 for a single and £22 for a return; under-15s get all tickets at half-price.

Airbus coaches (0870 574 7777), meanwhile, run to Victoria Coach Station every half-hour at peak times, hourly at other times. The journey takes about one hour 30 minutes, with stops at Hendon Central and Finchley Road tube stations and at Marble Arch. A single ticket costs £7, with a return (valid for six months) clocking in at £10; under-16s travel half-price.

The hour-plus **taxi** ride to central London will cost around £80.

By rail

Eurostar

Waterloo International Terminal, SE1 (08705 186186/ www.eurostar.com). Waterloo tube/rail. **Map** p401 M8.
Probably the most fun way to reach (and escape from) London is via the Channel Tunnel and Eurostar. The company now operates five routes from London: Paris, Disneyland Paris, Brussels, Lille, and the ski train, which goes to Bourg St Maurice and Moutiers during the season (Saturdays only).

Standard class fares to Brussels and Paris range from £70 for a weekend day return (£110 for first class) to £500. If you book at least 14 days in advance and stay two nights or over a Saturday, then the Leisure Apex 14 return fare is a bargain at £70. Look out for other special offers nearer the time.

The journey time to Paris is three hours, and just two hours 40 minutes to Brussels (the tunnel section takes a measly 22 minutes). Services are frequent: there are currently between 16 and 20 trains a day to Paris from Monday to Saturday, and either ten or 11 to Brussels. On Sundays, ten to 12 trains run to Paris, with seven or eight heading to Brussels.

Public transport

Information

All the information below can be accessed online at www.londontransport.co.uk and www.thetube.com, or by phoning 7222 1234. Transport for London (formerly London Transport) also run Travel Information Centres provide maps and information about the tube, buses and Docklands Light Railway (DLR). You can find them in the stations listed below. For lost property information, see *p370*.

Travel Information Centres

Euston 7.15am-6pm Mon-Sat; 8.30am-5pm Sun. **Map** p399 K3.
Hammersmith Bus Station 7.15am-6pm Mon-Fri; 8.15am-6pm Sat; closed Sun.
Heathrow Airport *Terminals 1, 2 & 3 tube station* 6.30am-7pm Mon-Sat; 7.15am-7pm Sun. *Terminal 1* 7.15am-10pm Mon-Sat; 8.15am-10pm Sun. *Terminal 2* 7.15am-5pm Mon-Sat; 8.15am-5pm Sun. *Terminal 4* 6am-3pm Mon-Sat; 7.15am-3pm Sun.
King's Cross 8am-6pm Mon-Sat; 8.30am-5pm Sun. **Map** p399 L2.
Liverpool Street 8am-6pm Mon-Fri; 8.45am-5.30pm Sat, Sun. **Map** p403 R5.
Oxford Circus 8.45am-6pm Mon-Sat; closed Sun. **Map** p398 J6.
Piccadilly Circus 8.45am-6pm daily. **Map** p401 K7.
St James's Park 8.15am-5.30pm Mon-Fri; closed Sat, Sun. **Map** p401 K9.
Victoria 7.45am-7pm Mon-Sat; 8.45am-7pm Sun. **Map** p400 H10.

Fares & tickets

Bus and tube fares are based on a zone system. There are six zones stretching 12 miles (20 kilometres) out from the centre of London. For most visitors to London, the Travelcard (*see below*) is by far the cheapest way of getting around. Beware of on-the-spot £10 penalty fares – fines by any other name – for anyone caught travelling without a valid ticket. Staff are not known for accepting excuses, so buy your ticket before you travel.

Adult fares

The single underground fare for adults within Zone 1 is £1.50, or £1.90 for Zones 1 and 2, rising to £3.60 for an all-zones single fare. Single bus fares are 70p for a journey outside Zone 1 and £1 for a journey within Zone 1 or which crosses the Zone 1 boundary.

Buying individual tickets is the most expensive way to travel. If you are likely to make three or more journeys in one day, or if you are staying in London for more than a day, it's always better value to buy a Travelcard (*see below*).

Child fares

On all buses, tubes and local trains, under-16s are classified as children; under-5s travel free. Under-16s pay a child's fare until 10pm; after 10pm (buses only) they pay an adult fare. Fourteen- and 15-year-olds must carry Child Rate Photocards, available from any post office: take a passport-size photo and proof of age (passport or birth certificate) with you. The single underground fare for children in Zone 1 is 60p, or 80p covering Zones 1 and 2; rising to £1.50 for an all-zone ticket. Single child bus fares cost 40p to anywhere in London.

One-Day LT Cards

One-Day LT Cards will only be of interest if you intend to travel during peak times (ie before 9.30am on weekdays) and make several journeys during the day. They are valid on buses (including night buses), underground services (except those running to and from Bakerloo line stations north of Queen's Park; this section of track is not run by Transport for London) and Docklands Light Railway (DLR) services, but not on overland rail services or airbuses. The cards cost £5.10 for Zones 1 and 2; £6.20 for Zones 1-4 and £7.70 for Zones 1-6 (child £2.50 Zones 1 and 2; £3 Zones 1-4; £3.30 Zones 1-6).

Travelcards

The most economical way to get around London is with a Travelcard. These can be used on the tube system, buses, rail services, Docklands Light Railway and some Green Line buses, and can be bought at all tube and rail stations as well as at appointed newsagents. The most convenient cards for short-term visitors are the One-Day or One-Week Travelcards, though monthly and yearly tickets are also available.

One-Day Travelcards can be used after 9.30am on weekdays and all day at weekends. You can make unlimited journeys within the zones you select. They cost £4 for Zones 1

Directory

and 2, £4.30 for Zones 1-4 or £4.90 Zones 1-6 (£2 for a child all-zone ticket). One-Day Travelcards are now valid until 4.30am and can be used on N-prefixed night buses.

Family Travelcards are available for families and groups of one or two adults travelling with between one and four children. Like regular One-Day Travelcards, they are valid after 9.30am Monday to Friday and all day on weekends and public holidays, and can be used until 4.30am; they cost £2.60 for Zones 1 and 2, £2.80 Zones 1-4 or £3.20 Zones 1-6 (child 80p Zones 1-6).

If you'll be travelling on consecutive weekend days, it's probably worth getting a Weekend Travelcard, which allow travel on consecutive weekend days or public holidays, and not on N-prefixed night buses. They cost £6 for Zones 1 and 2, £6.40 Zones 1-4 and £7.30 Zones 1-6 (child £3 Zones 1-6).

One-Week Travelcards offer unlimited journeys throughout the selected zones for seven days, including use of N-prefixed night buses, and are valid around the clock. Weekly Travelcards cost £15.90 for Zone 1; £18.90 for Zones 1 and 2; £22.40 for Zones 1-3; £27.60 for Zones 1-4; £33.30 for Zones 1-5; £36.40 for all zones (child £6.60 Zone 1; £7.70 Zones 1 and 2; £10.30 Zones 1-3; £12.80 Zones 1-4; £14.10 Zones 1-5; £15.40 Zones 1-6).

Carnet

If you're planning on making a lot of short-hop journeys within Zone 1 over a period of several days, it makes sense to buy a carnet of ten tickets for £11.50 (£5 for children). This brings down the cost of each journey to £1.15 rather than the standard £1.50. Note that if you exit a station outside of Zone 1 and are caught with only a carnet ticket, you are liable to a £10 penalty fare.

Photocards

Photocards are required for all bus passes and Travelcards except the One-Day and Weekend versions. Child-rate photocards are required for five- to 15-year-olds using child-rate Travelcards and bus passes. Fourteen and 15-year-olds need a child-rate photocard in order to buy any ticket at the discounted rate.

London Underground

Although short distances are best covered on foot, travelling on the capital's underground rail system – known as the tube – is the quickest way to get around London. That said,

lines frequently suffer from delays, escalators are sometimes out of action and, occasionally, there are station and line closures (typically at weekends because of engineering work). Crime is not a major problem on the tube, although you would be wise to avoid getting into an empty carriage on your own, but beware of pickpockets. Smoking is illegal anywhere on the underground system.

Using the system

Tickets can be purchased from a station ticket office or self-service machines. Unfortunately, staff in ticket offices rarely speak foreign languages and can be remarkably gruff and unhelpful. You can buy most tickets, including carnets and One-Day LT Cards (see p357), from self-service machines, but for anything covering a longer period, you'll need to show a valid photocard to a ticket officer. Note that, because of staff shortages, ticket offices in some of the less busy stations often close early (around 7.30pm). In any case, try and keep a little change with you at all times: the queues at ticket offices can be time-consuming, and using a ticket machine is usually far quicker. Ticket machines are supposed to give change, but often run out – and they don't accept cards.

To enter the tube, put your ticket through the automatic checking gates with the black magnetic strip facing down, and pull it out of the top to open the gates. Exiting the system at your destination is done in much the same way, though if you have a single journey ticket, it will be retained by the gate as you leave.

There are 12 underground lines, colour-coded on the tube map, of which the newest is the much-delayed £1.9-billion Jubilee Line extension. It finally opened in late 1999 and now links Green Park in the West End to Stratford in east London via Waterloo, Bermondsey, North Greenwich and Canary Wharf.

Underground timetable

Tube trains run daily, starting at around 5.30am every day except Sunday, when they start an hour to two hours later depending on the line. The only exception is Christmas Day, when there is no service. Generally you won't have to wait more than ten minutes for a train, and during peak times the service should run every two or three minutes. Times of last trains vary, though they're usually around 11.30pm-1am every day

except Sunday, when they finish 30 minutes to an hour earlier. The only all-night public transport is by night bus (see p359). If you want to avoid the worst of the rush-hour crush, don't travel between about 8am and 9.30am and 4.30pm and 6.30pm.

Docklands Light Railway (DLR)

7363 9700/www.dlr.co.uk.

The DLR is administered as part of the tube system. Its driverless trains run on a raised track from Bank (Central or Waterloo & City lines) or Tower Gateway, close to Tower Hill tube (Circle and District lines), to Stratford, Beckton and down the Isle of Dogs to Island Gardens. During 1999 this latter branch was extended south across (or, rather, under) the Thames to Greenwich and on to Lewisham. Trains run from 5.30am to around 12.30am Monday to Friday, 6am-12.30am Saturday and 7.30am-11.30pm Sunday.

The DLR is keen to promote itself as much as a tourist attraction as a transport system. To this end it offers 'Sail and Rail' tickets that combine unlimited travel on the DLR with a riverboat trip between Greenwich and Westminster Piers (boats departing from 10.30am to 6.30pm; see p359) plus discounts on selected museums and sights. Starting at Tower Gateway, special trains leave on the hour (from 10am) with a DLR guide giving passengers the low-down on the area as the train glides along. Tickets cost around £8.50 for adults, £4.50 for kids.

Buses

Travelling on London's extensive bus network is one of the most pleasurable and enlightening ways of getting to know the city. However, allow plenty of time: progress through the invariably dreadful traffic can be very slow during the morning and evening rush hours, and even outside these times, the buses are hardly about to break any land speed records.

Certain routes still use the venerable red Routemaster buses – the ones you can hop on and off at the back – but modern buses are taking over. The latter are cheaper to run as they are operated by a single driver/conductor, but this also makes them slower.

Night buses

Night buses are the only form of public transport that runs through the night. They operate from around 11pm to 6am, about once an hour on most routes (more frequently on Fridays and Saturdays). All pass through central London and the majority stop at Trafalgar Square, so head there if you're unsure which bus to get. Night buses have the letter 'N' before their number, and are now free to holders of One-Day Travelcards, Weekend Travelcards, Family Travelcards and One-Day LT cards. Pick up a free map and timetable from one of the LT Travel Information Centres (*see p357*). Night bus fares from central London are £1.50; there are no child fares.

Green Line buses

Green Line buses (0870 608 7261, www.greenline.co.uk) serve the suburbs and towns within a 40-mile (64km) radius of London. Their main departure point is Eccleston Bridge, SW1 (Colonnades Coach Station, behind Victoria).

Stationlink buses

The red and yellow Stationlink buses (7222 1234) are convenient for the disabled, the elderly, people laden with luggage or those with small children. The service connects all the main London rail termini (except Charing Cross) on a circular trip. Buses run every hour from about 9am to 7pm (phone for details). The fare is £1 for adults, 50p for fives to 15s.

Rail services

Independently owned commuter services run out of all the city's main line rail stations (*see p338*). Travelcards are valid on these services within the relevant zones. **Silverlink** (01923 207258, www.silverlinktrains.com; or National Rail Enquiries on 08457 484950) is a useful and underused overground service that carves a huge arc through the north of the city, running from Richmond (in the south-west) to North Woolwich (in the east), via London City Airport. The line connects with the tube network at several stations. Trains run about every 20 minutes every day except Sunday, when they run every half-hour, and offer a refreshing alternative to the

tube with great views of London's back gardens.

For more information about train travel, *see p338*, and for property left on trains, *see p370*.

Water transport

Often overlooked, the river makes a speedy way of getting about, and is less congested than other modes of transport. The times of services vary, but, as a rule, most operate every 20 minutes to one hour between about 10.30am and 5pm. Services may be more frequent and run later in summer. Call the individual operators below for details of schedules and fares. The names in bold below are the names of piers: the central ones are on the maps at the back of this Guide.

Westminster–Greenwich (50mins)
Westminster Passenger Services 7930 4097.

Westminster–Tower (30mins)
City Cruises 7930 9033.

Westminster–Festival (5mins)–
London Bridge City (20mins)–
St Katharine's (5mins)
Crown River Cruises 7936 2033.

Westminster–(Thames) Barrier Gardens (1hr 10mins)
Thames Cruises 7930 3373.

Westminster–Kew (1hr 30mins)–
Richmond (30mins)–**Hampton Court** (1hr 30mins)
Westminster Passenger Service Association 7930 2062.

Embankment–Tower (30mins)–
St Katharine's (5mins)–
Greenwich (25mins)
Catamaran Cruises 7987 1185.

Greenland Dock–Canary Wharf (2mins)–**St Katherine's** (5mins)–
London Bridge City (3mins)–
Blackfriars (4mins)–
Savoy (2mins)
Collins River Enterprises 7237 9538.

Savoy–Cadogan (18mins)–
Chelsea (2mins)
Riverside Launches 0831 574774.

Waterloo/Westminster–Tower (30mins)
City Cruises 7030 9033.

Greenwich–(Thames) Barrier Gardens (25mins)
Campion Launches 8305 0300.

Lunch & dinner cruises
Lunch cruises daily from Embankment (1hr-1hr 15mins):

Woods River Cruises 7480 7770/ Bateaux London 7925 2215. Dinner cruises (2 days a week to daily) from Westminster, Embankment and Savoy (2hrs 30mins-4hrs): City Cruises 7237 5134/Bateaux London 7925 2215/ Silver Sturgeon (Woods River Cruises 7480 7770).

Taxis

Black cabs

Licensed London taxis are commonly known as black cabs – even though they now come in a variety of colours thanks to the advent of on-cab advertising – and are a quintessential feature of London life. They all have a yellow 'For Hire' sign and a white licence plate on the back of the vehicle. Drivers of black cabs must pass a test called 'The Knowledge' to prove they know the name of every street in central London, where it is and the shortest route to it.

When a taxi's 'For Hire' sign is switched on, it can be hailed in the street (though, annoyingly, some cabbies switch off the sign even if free, picking up fares as and when they please). If a taxi stops, it is then the cabbie's responsibility to take you to your destination, provided it is within seven miles. In reality, though, some – albeit a minority – turn their noses up at south London, or, indeed, anywhere they don't fancy going. **Radio Taxis** (7272 0272) and **Dial-a-Cab** (7253 5000) both run 24-hour services for black cabs (with a pick-up charge).

Any enquiries or, indeed, complaints about black cabs should be made to the Public Carriage Office (7230 1631, 9am-4pm Mon-Fri, closed Sat, Sun). Remember to note the badge number of the offending cab, which should be clearly displayed in the rear of the cab and also on its back bumper. For lost property, *see p370*.

Minicabs

Minicabs (saloon cars) are generally cheaper than black cabs, especially at night and weekends. However, the drivers are usually unlicensed, often untrained, sometimes uninsured, frequently unreliable and, occasionally, dangerous. In some places – Victoria station, or in and around Soho late at night, to name but two – drivers tout for business on the street. Avoid them at all costs: aside from the fact that minicabs can't legally be hailed in the street, the drivers are often imbecilic ruffians who barely know their own way home, let alone to your front door, and will charge you the earth in order to get you there.

Having said that, there are plenty of trustworthy and licensed minicab firms; ask for a recommendation. **Addison Lee** (7387 8888) is one of the bigger companies, and claims to do pick-ups from all areas. Women travelling alone may prefer to use **Lady Cabs** (7254 3501), which employs only women drivers. Whoever you use, ask the price when you book and confirm it with the driver when the car arrives.

Driving

If you've heard that driving in central London is tough, just wait until you try to find somewhere to park. If you park illegally, you'll probably get a £60-£80 parking ticket (which will be reduced by 50 per cent if you pay within 14 days). Worse still, you may find your car has been immobilised by a yellow triangular wheel clamp, or even towed away and impounded. The retrieval procedure, to put it mildly, is no easy ride (*see p361*). If you can possibly avoid driving in central London, then do so, especially since there are so many public transport options.

Breakdown services

If you are a member of a motoring organisation in another country, check to see if it has a reciprocal agreement with a British organisation.

AA (Automobile Association)

Information 0990 500600/ breakdown 0800 887766/ new members 0800 444999/ www.theaa.co.uk. **Open** 24hrs daily. **Credit** MC, V.
You can call the AA if you break down. Membership prices start at £43 a year for standard roadside assistance, going up to £137 a year. They only offer annual membership for the UK, but you can get temporary breakdown cover from the AA for Europe.

ETA (Environmental Transport Association)

Freepost KT4021, Weybridge, Surrey KT13 8RS (01932 828882/ www.eta.co.uk). **Open** *Office* 8am-6pm Mon-Fri; 9am-4pm Sat; closed Sun. *Breakdown service* 24hrs daily. **Credit** MC, V.
The green alternative, if you don't want part of your membership fees used for lobbying the government into building more roads, as happens with the AA and RAC. Basic membership is £20 a year for individuals and £25 for families.

RAC (Royal Automobile Association)

RAC House, 1 Forest Road, Feltham, Middx TW13 7RR (emergency breakdown 0800 828282/office & membership 0990 722722/ www.rac.co.uk). **Open** *Office* 8am-9pm Mon-Fri; 9am-5pm Sat; 10am-4pm Sun. *Breakdown service* 24hrs daily. **Credit** AmEx, DC, MC, V.
Ring the enquiries number and ask for the Rescue Service. Membership costs from £39 for basic cover to £140 for the most comprehensive, plus £75 for European cover.

Parking

Central London is scattered with parking meters. However, finding a free meter could take several hours. And even if you do locate one, it'll cost you up to £1 for every 15 minutes to park there, and you'll be limited to two hours on the meter. Parking on a single

yellow line, a double yellow line or a red line (designating a red route) at any time during the day is illegal, and will likely wind up with you being fined, clamped or even towed.

However, in the evening (from 6pm or 7pm in much of central London) and at various times at weekends, parking on single yellow lines becomes both legal and free. If you find a clear spot on a single yellow line during the evening, check a nearby sign before you leave your car: this sign should tell you at which times parking is legal on this particular yellow line, as times vary from council to council and even from street to street. It's a similar story with meters, which become free after a certain time in the evening and at various times on weekends: check before paying, as it could save you several quid. Parking on double yellow lines and red routes is, by and large, illegal at all times.

NCP (7499 7050) has a number of phenomenally expensive 24-hour car parks in and around central London. Prices vary with location, but expect to pay £6-£10 for two hours up to £30-£50 for 24 hours. Among its central car parks are those at Arlington House, Arlington Street, St James's, W1; 21 Bryanston Street, Marylebone, W1; and 2 Lexington Street, Soho, W1.

A word of warning, though. The vast majority of public car parks in central London are underground, and despite the best efforts of the owners, a few are frequented by drug users after a quiet place in which to smoke, snort or inject. In other words, take care when leaving and returning to your car, and take your valuables with you.

Clamping

The immobilising of illegally parked vehicles by attaching a clamp to one wheel is commonplace in London. There will be a label attached to the car telling you which payment centre to phone or visit. Some boroughs let you pay over the phone with a credit card, while others insist you go in person. Either way, you'll have to stump up a £45 clamp release fee and pay a parking fine of £40-£80 (there's a 50% discount on the fine if you pay within two weeks).

Staff at the payment centre will promise to de-clamp your car some time within the next four hours but can't tell you exactly when. You are also warned that if you don't remove your car immediately, they could clamp it again. This means you may have to spend quite some time waiting by your car.

If you feel you have been clamped unfairly, the appeals procedure and contact number will be printed on the back of your ticket. If your appeal is turned down and you would like to take it further, call the Clamping and Vehicle Section (7747 4700), an independent governing body.

Vehicle removal

If your car has mysteriously disappeared, chances are that, if it was legally parked, it's been nicked; if not, it's probably been hoisted on to the back of a truck and taken to a car pound, and you're facing a stiff penalty: a fee of £125 is levied for removal, plus £15 per day from the first midnight after removal. To add insult to injury, you'll probably get a parking ticket of £40-£80 when you collect the car (there's a 50% discount if you pay within 14 days). To find out where your car has been taken and how to retrieve it, call the Trace service hotline (7747 4747).

Vehicle hire

To hire a car, you must have at least one year's driving experience with a full current driving licence; in addition, many car hire firms refuse to rent to people under the age of 23. If you are an overseas visitor, your current driving licence is valid in Britain for a year. Prices for car hire vary considerably; always ring several competitors for a quote (see the Yellow Pages). As well as the companies listed below – call or check the web to find out the location of your nearest office – Easycar's online-only service, at www.easycar.co.uk, offers extremely competitive rates, so long as you don't mind driving a heavily branded car around town.

Avis *0990 900500/www.avis.co.uk.* Open 24hrs daily. Credit AmEx, DC, MC, V.
Budget *0800 181181/ www.gobudget.com).* Open 8am-10pm daily. Credit AmEx, DC, MC, V.
Europcar *7255 2339/ www.eurocar.com.* Open 8am-6pm Mon-Fri; 8am-1pm Sat; closed Sun. Credit AmEx, DC, MC, V.
Hertz *0870 599 6699/ www.hertz.com.* Open 24hrs daily. Credit AmEx, DC, MC, V.

Motorbike hire

Scootabout *1-3 Leeke Street, King's Cross, WC1 (7833 4607/ www.hgbmotorcycles.co.uk). King's Cross tube/rail.* Open 9am-6pm Mon-Fri; closed Sat, Sun. Credit MC, V. Map p399 M3.
Any British driving licence or foreign motorbike licence qualifies you to drive a 50cc moped, the hire charge for which starts at £15.50 per day or £91.50 per week. Hiring an ST1100 Pan European costs £71.50 per day or £365 per week. All rental prices include 250 miles per day, with excess mileage at 10p a mile, AA cover, insurance and VAT. Helmet hire costs £2 per day or £12 per week. Bikes can only be hired with a credit card and after a £350 deposit has been made.

Cycling

Despite the efforts of some local councils, central London remains, on the whole, an unfriendly place for cyclists. The traffic is overwhelming and unsympathetic, fumes can be appalling in summer and potholes proliferate. A safety helmet, filter-mask and determined attitude are advisable. However, cyclists shouldn't forget that they have as much responsibility as motorists for driving safely. So no jumping those red lights.

London Cycling Campaign

Unit 228, Great Guildford Business Square, 30 Great Guildford Street, SE1 0HS (7928 7220/www.lcc.org.uk). Open Phone enquiries 2-5pm Mon-Fri; closed Sat, Sun.
Get the definitive guide to pedalling around London, *On Your Bike,* and the *Cyclists' Route Map* (£4.95 for both), from the LCC. It includes tips on maintenance, security and the law. LCC members enjoy a host of other benefits (membership from £5.50).

Cycle hire & storage

Bikepark

11 Macklin Street, Covent Garden, WC2 (7430 0083/ www.bikepark.co.uk). Covent Garden or Holborn tube. Open 8.30am-7pm Mon-Fri; 10am-6pm Sat; closed Sun. Hire £12 first day; £6 second day; £4 per day thereafter. Deposit £200. Credit MC, V. Map p399 L6.
Leave your bike in secure parking (50p per hour; £2 for 24 hours; £20 a month), and make use of the changing facilities at this branch (there are showers at the Chelsea branch at 67 New King's Road, SW3, 7731 7012). There's also a repair service and you can hire a hybrid or mountain bike and accessories for commuting or touring.

London Bicycle Tour Company

1A Gabriel's Wharf, 56 Upper Ground, South Bank, SE1 (7928 6838/www.londonbicycle.com). Southwark tube or Blackfriars or Waterloo tube/rail. Open Easter-Oct 10am-6pm daily. Nov-Easter by appointment. Hire £2.50 per hour; £12 first day; £6 per day thereafter. Deposit £100 (unless paying by credit card). Credit AmEx, DC, MC, V. Map p404 N7.
In addition to bike hire and the ever-more popular rollerblade hire (£2.50 per hour), this company, as the name implies, conducts daily bicycle tours (approx three hours). Its West End tour on Sundays costs £11.95, and it also offers weekend breaks in the countryside around London.

Walking

As with any great city, the best way to see London is on foot. However, unlike many other great cities, the layout of London's streets is extremely complicated, so much so that even locals carry maps around with them most, if not all, of the time. Prepare to get lost on at least a semi-regular basis.

We have included a selection of street maps covering central London in the back of this book (starting on page 390). However, we recommend that you also buy a separate map of the city: both the standard Geographers' *A–Z* and Collins' *London Street Atlas* versions come in a variety of sizes and are very easy to use.

NEVER CLOSE!

Cheap, fast
Internet access
Could not be simpler!

We are open 24 hours a day @ 5 central London locations

Send emails, plan your day's activity or even use our webcams to send a picture home to friends and family!

Internet access all day, everyday from just **£1**

easyEverything
the world's largest Internet cafés

Resources A-Z

Addresses

London addresses invariably come with a postcode attached. This helps determine where the street is found, but also helps differentiate between streets with the same name in different parts of London (there are 20 Park Roads in the city, for example).

A London postcode written in its most basic form takes a points of the compass – N, E, SE, SW, W and NW, plus EC (East Central) and WC (West Central) – and then a number; for example, N1, WC2, SE24, etc. With the exception of those numbered 1, which denote the area nearest the centre of London, the numbers are ordered alphabetically by area. For example, in east London, Whitechapel takes E1 as it's closest to central London, but then E2 is Bethnal Green, E3 is Bow, E4 is Chingford, E5 is Clapton, and so on. For a complete list of London areas and their postcodes, *see p366* **London postcodes**.

Age restrictions

You must be 17 or over to drive in the United Kingdom, and 18 in order to be able to buy cigarettes or be served alcohol (to be safe, carry photo ID if you're under 22, or look as if you might be). The age of consent for both heterosexuals and homosexuals is 16.

Business

The proudly pink *Financial Times* (daily) is the most authoritative newspaper for facts and figures in the City and all over the world. If you are after in-depth analysis, and some considered domestic and international news, try *The Economist* magazine (weekly).

Conventions & conferences

London Tourist Board & Convention Bureaux

7932 2000/www.londontown.com. The LTB runs a venue enquiry service for conventions and exhibitions. Request (by phone or e-mail) an information pack, which lists hotels and centres that host events, together with their facilities.

Queen Elizabeth II Conference Centre

Broad Sanctuary, Westminster, SW1 (7222 5000/www.qeiicc.co.uk). St James's Park tube. **Open** 8am-6pm Mon-Fri; closed Sat, Sun. *Conference facilities* 24hrs daily. **Map** p401 K9. This unattractive, purpose-built centre close to the Houses of Parliament has some of the best conference facilities in the capital. There are rooms with capacities from 30 to 1,100, and communications equipment is available (including a broadcast-spec TV studio).

Couriers & shippers

DHL and FedEx offer local and international courier services; Excess Baggage is the UK's largest shipper of baggage.

DHL *181 Strand, Covent Garden, WC2 (08701 100 300/www.dhl.co.uk). Charing Cross tube/rail.* **Open** 10am-8.45pm Mon-Fri; 10am-5.45pm Sat; closed Sun. **Credit** AmEx, DC, MC, V. **Map** p401 L7.
Excess Baggage Company *168 Earl's Court Road, Earl's Court, SW5 (0800 783 1085/www.excess-baggage.com). Earl's Court tube.* **Open** 8am-6pm Mon-Fri; 9am-2pm Sat; closed Sun. **Credit** AmEx, MC, V. **Map** p396 B10.
Federal Express *0800 123800/www.fedex.com/gb.* **Open** 24hrs daily. **Credit** AmEx, DC, MC, V.

Office hire & business centres

ABC Business Machines

59 Chiltern Street, Marylebone, W1 (7486 5634/www.abcbusiness.co.uk). Baker Street tube. **Open** 9am-5.30pm Mon-Fri; 9.30am-12.30pm Sat; closed Sun. **Credit** MC, V. **Map** p398 G5.

Faxes, answerphones, computers, photocopiers and audio equipment are among the items on hire at ABC.

British Monomarks

Monomarks House, 27 Old Gloucester Street, Bloomsbury, WC1 (7419 5000/7404 5011/bm@monomark.co.uk). Holborn tube. **Open** 9.30am-5.30pm Mon-Fri; closed Sat, Sun. **Credit** AmEx, MC, V. **Map** p399 L5. Services including mail forwarding, email, fax and 24-hour telephone answering.

Secretarial services

Reed Employment, Staff Agency

143 Victoria Street, Westminster, SW1 (7834 1801/www.reed.co.uk). Victoria tube/rail. **Open** 8am-6pm Mon-Fri; closed Sat, Sun. **Map** p400 J10. Reed supplies secretarial, computing, accountancy and technical services to registered companies. This branch specialises in secretarial and admin.

Typing Overload

67 Chancery Lane, Holborn, WC2 (7404 5464/www.typingoverload.com). Chancery Lane tube. **Open** 9.30am-5.30pm Mon-Fri; closed Sat, Sun. **Credit** AmEx, DC, MC, V. **Map** p399 M5. Come here for a speedy and pro-fessional typing service.
Branch: 35 Brompton Road, Brompton, SW3 (7823 9955).

Translators & interpreters

Central Translations

21 Woodstock Street, Mayfair, W1 (7493 5111/www.central translations.co.uk). Bond Street tube. **Open** 9am-5pm Mon-Fri; closed Sat, Sun. **Map** p398 H6. Be it typesetting, proofreading, translation or the use of an interpreter, Central can work with almost every language under the sun.

1st Translation Company

24 Holborn Viaduct, The City, EC1 (7329 0032/www.1st-translation-co.com). Chancery Lane tube. **Open** 9.30am-6pm Mon-Fri; closed Sat Sun. **Map** p404 N5. More than 50 languages can be translated. Interpreters from £220.

Directory

Consumer

Most shops will happily offer a full refund for faulty or defective goods. However, should you experience any difficulty in obtaining a refund, contact the Trading Standards department of your local council, which can provide help and legal advice.

Customs

When entering the UK, non-European Union citizens and anyone buying duty-free goods should be aware of the following import limits:

- 200 cigarettes or 100 cigarillos or 50 cigars or 250 grams (8.82 ounces) tobacco;
- 2 litres still table wine plus either 1 litre spirits or strong liqueurs (over 22 per cent alcohol by volume) or 2 litres fortified wine (under 22 per cent abv), sparkling wine or other liqueurs;
- 60cc/ml perfume;
- 250cc/ml toilet water;
- other goods to the value of £145 for non-commercial use;
- the import of meat, meat products, fruit, plants, flowers and protected animals is restricted or forbidden.

Since the Single European Market agreement came into force at the beginning of 1993, people over the age of 17 arriving from an EU country have been able to import large quantities of goods for their own personal use. But Customs officials may need convincing that you do not intend to sell any of the goods.

Disabled

Compared to some European cities, London is relatively friendly to the mobility-impaired. But it's also relative. While many of the capital's sights make provision for wheelchair users, the great headache for those who have problems getting around is transport. For information on provisions for the disabled on the tube, check out the *Access to the Underground* booklet,

available free from ticket offices or from LT's Unit for Disabled Passengers (172 Buckingham Palace Road, SW1 9TN, 7918 3312, lt.udp@ltbuses.co.uk) and at LT Travel Information Centres (*see p357*). The unit also provides details on buses and Braille maps. All DLR stations have wheelchair access.

We thoroughly recommend *Access in London* by Gordon Couch, William Forrester and Justin Irwin (Quiller Press, 1996), which includes detailed maps of step-free routes and accessible tube stations alongside a guide to adapted toilets, and sections on shopping, accommodation and entertainment. The guide is available at some bookshops, for £7.95, or free of charge (a donation is appreciated) from Access Project, 39 Bradley Gardens, W13 8HE, or by calling 7250 3222.

The organisations below offer help to disabled visitors to London. For the National Bureau for Students with Disabilities, *see p376*.

Artsline
54 Chalton Street, Somers Town, NW1 (tel/minicom 7388 2227/ www.artsline.org.uk). Euston tube/rail. **Open** 9.30am-5.30pm Mon-Fri; closed Sat, Sun. **Map** p399 K3.
Information on disabled access to arts and entertainment events in London and on adapted facilities in cinemas, art galleries, theatres, etc.

Can Be Done
7-11 Kensington High Street, Kensington, W8 5NP (8907 2400/ www.canbedone.co.uk). High Street Kensington tube. **Open** *Phone enquiries* 9am-5.30pm Mon-Fri; noon-1pm Sat; closed Sun. **Map** p396 A9.
This small tour operator can tailor holidays and tours in London to the needs of disabled people.

DAIL (Disability Arts in London)
Diorama Arts Centre, 34 Osnaburgh Street, Fitzrovia, NW1 (7916 6351/ minicom 7691 4201/www.dail. dircon.co.uk). Great Portland Street tube. **Open** 10.30am-6.30pm Mon-Fri; closed Sat, Sun. **Map** p398 H4.
DAIL produces a monthly magazine containing listings, reviews and

articles on the arts and the disabled (voluntary subscription of £10 per year). DAIL is part of LDAF (London Disability Arts Forum; 7916 5484), which organises events for disabled people in London.

DIAL (National Association of Disablement Information & Advice Lines)
01302 310123. **Open** 9am-5pm Mon-Thur; 9am-4pm Fri; closed Sat, Sun.
Details of local groups in the UK that can offer free information and advice on all aspects of disability.

William Forrester
1 Belvedere Close, Guildford, Surrey, GU2 6NP (01483 575401).
William Forrester is a London Registered Guide and, as he's a wheelchair user himself, has extensive experience in leading tours in the capital for disabled individuals and groups. Book early.

Greater London Action on Disability (GLAD)
336 Brixton Road, Brixton, SW9 (7346 5800/information line 7346 5808/minicom 7346 5811). Brixton tube/rail.
Open *Phone enquiries* 9am-5pm Mon-Fri; closed Sat, Sun. *Information line* 1.30-4.30pm Mon, Wed, Fri; closed Tue, Thur, Sat, Sun.
GLAD is a voluntary organisation providing, via local associations, valuable information for disabled visitors and residents. Its publications include the fortnightly *Update*, containing extracts from articles in the national newspapers and magazines that relate to the disabled, and the monthly *London Disability News*.

Holiday Care Service
For listings, see p43.
An advisory service specialising in holiday accommodation for disabled visitors.

Royal Association for Disability & Rehabilitation (RADAR)
12 City Forum, 250 City Road, Islington, EC1 (7250 3222/ www.radar.org.uk). Old Street tube/rail. **Open** 8am-4pm Mon-Fri; closed Sat, Sun. **Map** p402 P3.
The central organisation for disabled voluntary groups. Through RADAR you can get advice on almost any aspect of life. The Association publishes Bulletin, a monthly newsletter, which has articles on news-oriented subjects such as housing and education.

Directory

Tripscope

Alexandra House, Albany Road, Brentford, Middx TW8 (tel/minicom 8580 7021/ www.justmobility.co.uk/tripscope).
Open *Phone enquiries* 9am-4.45pm Mon-Fri; closed Sat, Sun.
Jim Bennett and Adrian Drew's information/advice service for the elderly and disabled can help with all aspects of getting around London, the UK and overseas. It's chiefly an enquiry line, but you can write in or e-mail them via the website if you have difficulty with the telephone.

Wheelchair Travel & Access Mini Buses

1 Johnston Green, Guildford, Surrey GU2 6XS (01483 233640/ www.wheelchair-travel.co.uk).
An excellent source of converted vehicles for hire, including adapted minibuses (with or without driver), plus cars with hand controls and 'Chairman' cars.

Electricity

As in the rest of Europe, the United Kingdom uses a standard 220-240V, 50-cycle AC voltage. British plugs use a cumbersome three pins rather than the two-pin variety found in most of Europe, so travellers with appliances from mainland Europe will need to bring an adaptor, as will travellers planning on using US appliances, which run off 110-120V, 60-cycle.

Embassies & consulates

For other embassies, consulates and high commissions check the telephone directory and *Yellow Pages* under 'Embassies'.

American Embassy *24 Grosvenor Square, Mayfair, W1 (7499 9000/ www.usembassy.org.uk). Bond Street or Marble Arch tube.* **Open** 8.30am-5.30pm Mon-Fri; closed Sat, Sun. **Map** p400 G7.
Australian High Commission *Australia House, Strand, Holborn, WC2 (7379 4334/ www.australia.org.uk). Holborn or Temple tube.* **Open** 9.30am-3.30pm Mon-Fri; closed Sat, Sun. **Map** p401 M6.

Canadian High Commission *38 Grosvenor Street, Mayfair, W1 (7258 6600/www.canada.org.uk). Bond Street tube.* **Open** 8-11am Mon-Fri; closed Sat, Sun. **Map** p400 H7.
Irish Embassy *17 Grosvenor Place, Belgravia, SW1 (7235 2171). Hyde Park Corner tube.* **Open** 9am-1pm, 2.30-5pm Mon-Fri; closed Sat, Sun. **Map** p400 G9.
New Zealand High Commission *80 Haymarket, St James's, SW1 (7930 8422/ www.newzealandhc.org.uk). Piccadilly Circus tube.* **Open** 9am-5pm Mon-Fri; closed Sat, Sun. **Map** p401 K7.
South African High Commission *South Africa House, Trafalgar Square, St James's, WC2 (7451 7299/www.southafricahouse.com). Charing Cross tube/rail.* **Open** 8.45am-12.45pm Mon-Fri; closed Sat, Sun. **Map** p401 K7.

Emergencies

In the event of a serious accident, fire or incident, call **999** – free from any phone, including payphones – and specify whether you require ambulance, fire service or police. For addresses of London hospitals, *see p367*; for helplines, *see p368*; and for details of police stations in the city, *see p373*.

Gay & lesbian

Help & information

Big Up

Unit 41, Eurolink Business Centre, 49 Effra Road, London SW2 1BZ (7501 9315/www.bigup.co.uk).
Open *Phone enquiries only* 9.30am-6pm Mon-Fri; closed Sat, Sun.
An organisation run by and for gay African and Afro-Caribbean men, providing support and health information. Postal enquiries should be directed to the address above.

Black Lesbian & Gay Helpline

7620 3885. **Open** times vary.
The operating times of this advice line vary with volunteer availability.

Jewish AIDS Trust

1331 High Road, Whetstone, N20 9HR (8446 8228/www.jat-uk.org).
Open 9.30am-5.30pm Mon-Thur; 9.30am-1.30pm Fri; closed Sat, Sun.
Provides information, counselling, financial, practical and social support and education.

London Friend

7837 3337. **Open** 7.30-10pm daily.
A lesbian and gay helpline offering confidential information and support.

London Lesbian & Gay Switchboard

7837 7324. **Open** 24hrs daily.
Everything you want to know about queer life in the capital, but prepare for a long wait to get through.

Naz Project

8741 1879. **Open** 9.30am-5.30pm Mon-Fri; closed Sat, Sun.
The Naz Project serves the (gay and straight) Asian community, with counselling and information on HIV, AIDS and sexual health in South Asian, Middle Eastern, South American, Horn of African and North African languages.

Health

Free emergency medical treatment under the National Health Service (NHS) is available to:

● European Union nationals, plus those of Iceland, Norway and Liechtenstein. People from these countries are also entitled to specific treatment for a non-emergency condition on production of form E112.
● Nationals (on production of a passport) of Bulgaria, Czech and Slovak Republics, Gibraltar, Hungary, Malta, New Zealand, Russia, former Soviet Union states (except Latvia, Lithuania and Estonia) and the former Yugoslavia.
● Residents, irrespective of nationality, of Anguilla, Australia, Barbados, British Virgin Islands, Channel Islands, Falkland Islands, Iceland, Isle of Man, Montserrat, Poland, Romania, St Helena, Sweden, Turks & Caicos Islands.
● Anyone who at the time of receiving treatment has been in the UK for the previous 12 months.
● Anyone who has come to the UK to take up permanent residence.
● Students and trainees whose course requires them to spend more than 12 weeks in employment during their first year. Students and others living in the UK for a settled purpose for more than six months may be accepted as ordinarily resident and not liable to charges.
● Refugees and others who have sought refuge in the UK.
● Anyone formally detained by the immigration authorities.

Directory

London's postcodes

E1	Whitechapel, Stepney, Mile End	**N21**	Winchmore Hill	**SE27**	West Norwood, Tulse Hill
E2	Bethnal Green, Shoreditch	**N22**	Wood Green	**SE28**	Thamesmead
E3	Bow, Bromley-by-Bow	**NW1**	Camden, Regent's Park, North Marylebone	**SW1**	Westminster, Belgravia, Pimlico
E4	Chingford, Highams Park	**NW2**	Cricklewood, Dollis Hill, Neasden	**SW2**	Brixton
E5	Clapton	**NW3**	Hampstead, Belsize Park, Swiss Cottage	**SW3**	Chelsea, Brompton
E6	East Ham, Beckton	**NW4**	Hendon, Brent Cross	**SW4**	Clapham
E7	Forest Gate, Upton Park	**NW5**	Kentish Town	**SW5**	Earl's Court
E8	Hackney, Dalston	**NW6**	Kilburn, Queens Park, West Hampstead	**SW6**	Fulham, Parsons Green
E9	Homerton	**NW7**	Mill Hill	**SW7**	South Kensington
E10	Leyton	**NW8**	St John's Wood	**SW8**	South Lambeth, Vauxhall
E11	Leytonstone, Wanstead	**NW9**	The Hyde, Kingsbury, Colindale	**SW9**	Stockwell, North Brixton
E12	Manor Park	**NW10**	Willesden, Harlesden, Kensal Green	**SW10**	World's End, West Brompton
E13	Plaistow	**NW11**	Golders Green	**SW11**	Battersea, Clapham Junction
E14	Poplar, Isle of Dogs, Millwall			**SW12**	Balham
E15	Stratford, West Ham	**SE1**	Waterloo, Southwark, Bermondsey	**SW13**	Barnes, Castelnau
E16	Victoria Docks & North Woolwich	**SE2**	Abbey Wood	**SW14**	Mortlake
E17	Walthamstow	**SE3**	Blackheath, Westcombe Park	**SW15**	Putney, Roehampton
E18	Woodford	**SE4**	Brockley, Crofton Park, Honor Oak Park	**SW16**	Streatham, Norbury
		SE5	Camberwell	**SW17**	Tooting
EC1	Clerkenwell, Barbican	**SE6**	Catford, Hither Green	**SW18**	Wandsworth, Earlsfield
EC2	The City (north-east)	**SE7**	Charlton	**SW19**	Wimbledon, Merton, Collier's Wood
EC3	The City (south-east)	**SE8**	Deptford	**SW20**	Wimbledon West, Wimbledon South
EC4	The City (west)	**SE9**	Eltham, Mottingham		
		SE10	Greenwich	**W1**	Mayfair, Soho, Marylebone, Fitzrovia
N1	Islington	**SE11**	Lambeth, Kennington	**W2**	Bayswater, Paddington
N2	East Finchley	**SE12**	Lee, Grove Park	**W3**	Acton
N3	Finchley Central	**SE13**	Lewisham, Hither Green	**W4**	Chiswick
N4	Finsbury Park, Manor House	**SE14**	New Cross	**W5**	Ealing
N5	Highbury	**SE15**	Peckham, Nunhead	**W6**	Hammersmith
N6	Highgate	**SE16**	Rotherhithe, South Bermondsey, Surrey Docks	**W7**	Hanwell
N7	Holloway	**SE17**	Walworth	**W8**	Kensington
N8	Hornsey, Crouch End	**SE18**	Woolwich, Plumstead	**W9**	Maida Vale, Warwick Avenue
N9	Lower Edmonton	**SE19**	Crystal Palace, Norwood	**W10**	North Kensington, Ladbroke Grove
N10	Muswell Hill	**SE20**	Anerley, Penge	**W11**	Notting Hill, Holland Park
N11	New Southgate	**SE21**	Dulwich	**W12**	Shepherd's Bush
N12	North Finchley	**SE22**	East Dulwich	**W13**	West Ealing
N13	Palmers Green	**SE23**	Forest Hill	**W14**	West Kensington
N14	Southgate	**SE24**	Herne Hill		
N15	South Tottenham, Seven Sisters	**SE25**	South Norwood	**WC1**	Bloomsbury
N16	Stoke Newington, Stamford Hill	**SE26**	Sydenham	**WC2**	Holborn, Covent Garden
N17	Tottenham				
N18	Upper Edmonton				
N19	Upper Holloway, Archway, Tufnell Park				
N20	Whetstone, Totteridge				

● People with HIV/AIDS at a special clinic for the treatment of sexually transmitted diseases. The treatment covered is limited to a diagnostic test and counselling associated with that test.

There are no NHS charges for the following:

● Treatment in Accident & Emergency departments.
● Certain district nursing, midwifery or health visiting.
● Emergency ambulance transport.
● Diagnosis and treatment of certain communicable diseases including STDs.
● Family planning services.
● Compulsory psychiatric treatment.

Any further advice should be obtained from the Patient Services Manager at the hospital where treatment is to be sought.

Accident & emergency

Below are listed most London hospitals that have 24-hour accident and emergency departments. Those located within central London are marked on the maps at the back of this Guide by a white cross on a red square.

Charing Cross Hospital *Fulham Palace Road, Hammersmith, W6 (8846 1234). Barons Court or Hammersmith tube.*
Chelsea & Westminster Hospital *369 Fulham Road, Chelsea, SW10 (8746 8000). Bus 14, 73, 211.* **Map** p396 C12.
Guy's Hospital *St Thomas Street (entrance Snowsfields, off Weston Street), Bankside, SE1 (7955 5000). London Bridge tube/rail.* **Map** p404 P8.
Homerton Hospital *Homerton Row, Homerton, E9 (8510 5555). Homerton rail/22B bus.*
Royal Free Hospital *Pond Street, Hampstead, NW3 (7794 0500). Belsize Park tube/Hampstead Heath rail.*
Royal London Hospital *Whitechapel Road, Whitechapel, E1 (7377 7000). Whitechapel tube.*
St George's Hospital *Blackshaw Road, Tooting, SW17 (01708 465000). Tooting Broadway tube.*
St Mary's Hospital *Praed Street, Paddington, W2 (7886 6666). Paddington tube/rail.* **Map** p395 D5.
St Thomas's Hospital *Lambeth Palace Road, Lambeth, SE1 (7928 9292). Westminster tube/Waterloo tube/rail.* **Map** p401 M9.

University College Hospital *Grafton Way, Fitzrovia, WC1 (7387 9300). Euston Square or Warren Street tube.* **Map** p398 J4.
Whittington Hospital *St Mary's Wing, Highgate Hill, Archway, N19 (7272 3070). Archway tube.*

Complementary medicine

British Homeopathic Association

15 Clerkenwell Close, Clerkenwell, EC1R OAA (7566 7800/ www.trusthomeopathy.org).
Open *Phone enquiries only* 9am-5pm Mon-Fri; closed Sat, Sun.
The BHA will give you the address of your nearest homeopathic chemist and doctor.

Contraception & abortion

Family planning advice, contraceptive supplies and abortions are free to British citizens on the National Health Service. This also applies to EU residents and foreign nationals living, working and studying in Britain. If you decide to go private, contact one of the organisations listed below. You can also phone 7837 4044 for your nearest branch of the **Family Planning Association**.
From 2001, the 'morning after' contraceptive pill, effective for up to 72 hours after intercourse, will be available over the counter at chemists.

British Pregnancy Advisory Service

0845 304030/www.bpas.org. **Map** p400 H10.
Contraception advice, contraceptives and the morning-after pill are available. The service carries out pregnancy tests and makes referrals to BPAS nursing homes for private abortions. Call the above number to find your nearest branch and book an appointment.

Brook Advisory Centre

233 Tottenham Court Road, Fitzrovia, W1 (enquiries 7323 1522/ helpline 0800 018 5023). Goodge Street or Tottenham Court Road tube. **Open** *Phone enquiries* 9.30am-7.30pm Mon-Thur; 9.30am-3pm Fri;

noon-2pm Sat; closed Sun. *Walk-in clinic* noon-6.30pm Mon-Thur; noon-2.30pm Fri; noon-2pm Sat; closed Sun. **Map** p399 K5.
There are 13 Brook Advisory family planning clinics in central London: call for your nearest. Advice and referrals are given on sexual health, contraception and abortion. Brook is primarily aimed at young people and will not see people who are over 30 years old (it's free for under-21s).

Marie Stopes House

Family Planning Clinic/Well Woman Centre *108 Whitfield Street, Fitzrovia, W1 (family planning 7388 0662/termination 0845 300 8090/www.mariestopes.org.uk). Warren Street tube.* **Open** 9am-5pm Mon-Sat; closed Sun. **Map** p398 J5.
Contraceptives, treatment and advice for gynaecological complaints, counselling for sexual problems and referral for abortion; fees vary.

Dentists

Dental care is free under the NHS to the following British residents:

● Under-18s.
● Under-19s in full-time education.
● Pregnant women and those with a baby under the age of one when treatment begins.
● People receiving Income Support, Jobseeker's Allowance, Family Credit or Disability Working Allowance.

All other patients, NHS or private, must pay. NHS charges start from around £4 for a check-up or a filling. To find an NHS dentist, get in touch with the local Health Authority or a Citizens' Advice Bureau (*see p369*). Private dentists can charge whatever they like. We list emergency services below.

Dental Emergency Care Service

7955 2186. **Open** 8.45am-3.30pm Mon-Fri; closed Sat, Sun.
DECS refers callers to a surgery open for treatment (private or NHS).

Guy's Hospital Dental School

Guy's Tower, St Thomas Street, Bankside, SE1 (7955 4317). London Bridge tube/rail.
Open 8.45am-3pm Mon-Fri; closed Sat, Sun. **Map** p405 Q8.
A free walk-in dental emergency service for all-comers.

Directory

Doctors

If you are a British citizen or working in the UK, you can go to any general practitioner (GP). If you are not visiting your usual GP, you will be asked for details of the doctor with whom you are registered, so your records can be updated. People who are ordinarily resident in the UK, including overseas students, are also permitted to register with an NHS doctor.

Great Chapel Street Medical Centre

13 Great Chapel Street, Soho, W1 (7437 9360/gcs.medical@virgin.net). Tottenham Court Road tube. **Open** 11am-12.30pm, 2-4pm Mon, Tue, Thur; 2-4pm Wed, Fri; closed Sat, Sun. **Map** p399 K6.
Walk-in NHS surgery for anyone without a doctor.

Hospitals

For a list of hospitals with A&E departments, *see p367*; for other hospitals, see the *Yellow Pages*; and for details on what to do in an emergency, *see p365*.

Opticians

For details of opticians in London, *see p248*.

Pharmacies

Most pharmacies keep regular shop hours, usually around 9am to 6pm every day except Sunday, when most are closed. However, there are a handful of late-opening pharmacies in London, for which *see p257*.

Prescriptions

Though some drugs can be bought over the counter in the UK, many more are only available on prescription. A pharmacist will dispense medicines on receipt of a prescription from a GP. An NHS prescription costs £5.90 at present (some people, such

as children under the age of 16 and people over 60, are exempt, and contraception is free for all). If you're not eligible to see an NHS doctor, you will be charged cost price for medicines prescribed by a private doctor.

Pharmacists must be qualified and can advise on the appropriate treatments for minor ailments from behind the counter.

STDs, HIV & AIDS

NHS Genito-Urinary Clinics (such as the Centre for Sexual Health; *see below*) are affiliated to major hospitals. They provide free, confidential treatment of sexually transmitted diseases (STDs) and other problems such as thrush and cystitis, offer information and counselling about HIV and other STDs, and can conduct a confidential blood test to determine HIV status. For other helplines, *see below*, and for details on abortion and contraception services, *see p367*.

AIDS Helpline

0800 567123/minicom 0800 521361. **Open** 24hrs daily.
A free and confidential information service. Another helpline (0800 917227) caters for various languages at 6-10pm on specific days: Bengali (Mon), Urdu (Tue), Arabic (Wed), Gujerati (Thur), Hindi (Fri), Punjabi (Sat) and Cantonese (Sun).

Audrey Lorde Clinic

Ambrose King Centre, Royal London Hospital, Turner Street, Whitechapel, E1 (7377 7312). Whitechapel tube. **Open** 9.30am-5pm Fri (appointments only).
A weekly lesbian health clinic, offering smears, HIV testing, information and counselling.

Axis

Mortimer Market Centre, Mortimer Market, off Capper Street, Bloomsbury, W1 (7530 5050). Warren Street tube. **Open** 7-9pm Thur. **Map** p398 J4.
A sexual health clinic for gay and bisexual men and women under 26. An appointment is recommended but not essential. Axis also offers drugs information for gay men.

Centre for Sexual Health

Genito-Urinary Clinic, Jefferiss Wing, St Mary's Hospital, Praed Street, Paddington, W2 (7886 1697). Paddington tube/ rail. **Open** *Walk-in clinic* 8.45am-5pm Mon; 8.45am-6pm Tue, Fri; 11.45am-6pm Wed; 8am-1pm Thur; closed Sat, Sun. *Appointments* 5-7pm Mon; 10am-noon Sat. **Map** p395 D5.
A free and confidential walk-in clinic. New patients must arrive 30 minutes before closing.

Terrence Higgins Trust Lighthouse

52-54 Gray's Inn Road, WC1 (admin 7831 0330/helpline 7242 1010/www.tht.org.uk). **Open** *Helpline* noon-10pm daily.
This charity, formed from a merger of the UK's two largest HIV charities in October 2000, advises and counsels those with HIV/AIDS, their relatives, lovers and friends. Free leaflets about AIDS are available. The Trust also gives advice about safer sex.

Helplines

See also above **STDs, HIV & AIDS***. For gay and lesbian helplines, see p365.*

Alcoholics Anonymous

7833 0022/www.alcoholics-anonymous.org.uk. **Open** *Helpline* 10am-10pm daily.
Operators put you in touch with a member in your area who can act as an escort to your first meeting.

Childline

Freepost 1111, London N1 OBR (0800 1111/7239 1000/www.childline.org.uk). **Open** *Phone lines* 24hrs daily.
Free helpline for children and young people in trouble or danger.

Citizens' Advice Bureaux

CABs are run by local councils and offer free advice on legal, financial and personal matters. Check the phone book for your nearest branch.

Contact Capital

7484 4000. **Open** *Helpline* 9am-9pm Mon-Fri; closed Sat, Sun.
This helpline tackles queries about anything. If the staff can't answer your query themselves, they'll put you in touch with someone who can. It's always busy, so keep trying.

Just Ask

50 Crispin Street, Whitechapel, E1 (7247 0180). Aldgate East tube/Liverpool Street tube/rail.

Open *Counselling* 10am-9pm Mon-Thur; 10am-5pm Fri; closed Sat, Sun. *Helpline* 10am-6pm Mon-Thur; answerphone after-hours. *Closed Aug.* **Map** p405 R6.
Counselling is targeted at people aged 35 and under who are homeless, unemployed or on a low income, but advice will be given to anyone with a personal problem.

London Rape Crisis Centre
7837 1600. **Open** times vary.
Free, confidential rape counselling. Due to cuts in funding, there are no set opening times for this phone line.

NHS Direct
0845 4647. **Open** 24hrs daily.
A first-stop service for medical advice on all subjects from trained health professionals.

MIND
Granta House, 15-19 Broadway, Stratford, E15 (8519 2122/ information line 8522 1728/0845 766 0163/www.mind.org.uk).
Open *Information line* 9.15am-5.15pm Mon-Fri; closed Sat, Sun.
Callers to this mental health charity will be referred to one of 34 London groups. MIND's legal service advises on maltreatment, wrongful detention and sectioning.

Narcotics Anonymous
7730 0009/www.ukna.org.
Open 10am-10pm daily.
Run by members of the fellowship, this helpline offers advice and informs callers of their nearest meeting.

Rape & Sexual Abuse Centre
8239 1122. **Open** noon-2.30pm, 7-9.30pm Mon-Fri; 2.30-5pm Sat, Sun.
Support and information for those who have experienced rape or sexual abuse.

Refuge Helpline
0990 995443. **Open** 24hrs daily.
Refuge referral for women suffering domestic violence. When phones are not manned, an answerphone will give alternative numbers for immediate help.

Rights of Women
7251 6577. **Open** *Helpline* times vary.
Legal advice for women.

Samaritans
7734 2800/www.samaritans.org.uk.
Open 24hrs daily.
The Samaritans will listen to anyone with emotional problems. It's a popular service, so do persevere when phoning.

Victim Support
National Office, Cranmer House, 39 Brixton Road, Kennington, SW9 (0845 303 0900). Oval tube.
Open *Support line* 9am-9pm Mon-Fri; 9am-7pm Sat, Sun.
Victims of crime are put in touch with a volunteer who provides emotional and practical support, including information on legal procedures and advice on compensation. Interpreters can be arranged.

Insurance

Insuring personal belongings is highly advisable, and difficult to arrange once you have arrived in London, so organise it before you travel.

Medical insurance is often included in travel insurance packages, and it's important to have it unless your country has a reciprocal medical treatment arrangement with Britain. EU citizens (and those from Iceland, Norway and Liechtenstein) are entitled to free emergency healthcare in hospitals under the NHS. Those wanting specific treatment under the NHS will need form E112, while citizens of these countries studying in the UK for less than six months are entitled to full NHS treatment if they have form E128.

Internet

London is a very net-friendly, both for the casual visitor and the resident. A great many hotel rooms have modem points, and some of those that don't offer surfing capabilities in a bar or café. There are also a huge number of cybercafés around town (*see below*), of which the biggest are those in the **easyEverything** chain.

If you want to get set up online over here, you're also in luck. Massive competition in the ISP sector has meant that prices have plummeted, and there are now a great many ISPs that do not charge a subscription fee, only billing

for calls. We suggest that you check one of the UK's many internet publications for details on current deals at the time you arrive; the best is *Internet* magazine.

For the best London websites, *see p381*.

Internet access
Café Internet *22-24 Buckingham Palace Road, Belgravia, SW1 (7233 5786/www.e-comstore.net). Victoria tube/rail.* **Open** 8am-10pm Mon-Fri; 10am-8pm Sat; 10am-6pm Sun.
Net access £2/hr. **Terminals** 30. **Map** p400 H10.
Cyberia Cyber Café *39 Whitfield Street, Fitzrovia, W1 (7681 4200/ www.cyberiacafe.net). Goodge Street tube.* **Open** 9am-9pm Mon-Fri; 11am-7pm Sat; 11am-6pm Sun.
Net access no charge (must buy a drink). **Terminals** 19. **Credit** MC, V. **Map** p399 K5.
easyEverything *9-13 Wilton Road, Belgravia, SW1 (7233 8456/ www.easyeverything.com). Victoria tube/rail.* **Open** 24hrs daily.
Net access £1/30mins-2hrs (varies depending on number of other users). **Terminals** over 400. **Map** p400 H10. **Branches** are numerous; check the phone book.
Global Café *15 Golden Square, W1 (7287 2242/www.globalcafe.net). Oxford Circus or Piccadilly Circus tube.* **Open** 9am-11pm Mon-Sat; noon-10.30pm Sun. **Net access** 50p/5mins; £5/hr. **Terminals** 10. **Map** p400 J7.
Intercafé *25 Great Portland Street, Marylebone, W1 (7631 0063/ www.intercafe.co.uk). Oxford Circus tube.* **Open** 7.30am-7pm Mon-Fri; 9.30am-5pm Sat; closed Sun. **Net access** £3/half-hr; £5/hr. **Terminals** 9. **Credit** MC, V. **Map** p398 J5.
Note that Intercafé is licensed to serve alcohol and therefore admits over-18s only.
Webshack *15 Dean Street, Soho, W1 (7439 8000/www.webshack-cafe.com). Tottenham Court Road tube.* **Open** 10am-11pm Mon-Sat; 1-9pm Sun. **Net access** £3/half-hr; £5/hr. **Terminals** 20. **Credit** DC, MC, V. **Map** p399 K6.

Left luggage

Airports
Call the following numbers for details on left luggage.
Gatwick Airport *South Terminal 01293 502014/North Terminal 01293 502013.*

Heathrow Airport *Terminal 1 8745 5301/Terminal 2/3 8759 3344/Terminal 4 8745 7460.*
London City Airport *7646 0000.*
Luton Airport *01582 394063.*
Stansted Airport *01279 663213.*

Rail & bus stations

Post-terrorism, London stations tend to have left-luggage desks rather than lockers. In order to find out if a train station offers this facility, call 7928 5151.

Legal help

If you get into legal difficulties, visit a Citizens' Advice Bureau or contact one of the groups listed below. For an explanation of the legal aid system, contact the Legal Aid Board.

Community Legal Services Directory

0845 608 1122/www.justask.org.uk. **Open** 8am-11pm daily.
This free telephone service guides those with legal problems to government agencies and law firms that may be able to help.

Joint Council for the Welfare of Immigrants (JCWI)

115 Old Street, Hoxton, EC1 (7251 8706). Old Street tube/rail. **Open** *Phone enquiries* 2-5pm Tue-Thur; closed Mon, Fri-Sun.
This telephone-only advice line for immigrants with legal troubles offers guidance and referrals.

Law Centres Federation

Duchess House, 18-19 Warren Street, Fitzrovia, W1 (7387 8570). Warren Street tube/rail. **Open** *Phone enquiries* 10am-6pm Mon-Fri; closed Sat, Sun.
Law Centres offer free legal help to people who cannot afford to pay a lawyer. This central office provides referrals only, and will connect you with your nearest centre. Bear in mind that law centres can only offer advice to people living or working in the immediate area.

Release

388 Old Street, Hoxton, EC1 (7729 9904/after-hours 7603 8654). Old Street tube/rail. **Open** 24hrs daily.
This group offers free addiction counselling and legal advice to those with drug problems, or whose drug

dependency has left them in legal trouble. It also provides referrals to addiction counsellors, law firms and governmental organisations.

Libraries

Unless you are a resident of the city, it's unlikely you'll be able to join a lending library. However, the following are all central, and open for reference, copying and browsing.

British Library

96 Euston Road, Somers Town, NW1 (7412 7000). King's Cross tube/rail. **Open** 10am-8pm Mon; 9.30am-8pm Tue-Thur; 9.30am-5pm Fri, Sat; closed Sun. **Map** p399 K3.

Holborn Library

32-8 Theobald's Road, Bloomsbury, WC1 (7974 6345). Chancery Lane tube. **Open** 10am-7pm Mon, Thur; 10am-6pm Tue, Fri; 10am-5pm Sat; closed Wed, Sun. **Map** p399 M5.

Kensington & Chelsea Central Library

Philimore Walk, Kensington, W8 (7937 2542). High Street Kensington tube. **Open** 9.30am-8pm Mon, Tue, Thur, Fri; 9.30am-1pm Wed; 9.30am-5pm Sat; closed Sun. **Map** p396 A9.

Victoria Library

160 Buckingham Palace Road, Belgravia, SW1 (7641 4287). Victoria tube/rail. **Open** 9.30am-7pm Mon, Tue, Thur, Fri; 10am-7p Wed; 9.30am-5pm Sat; closed Sun. *Music library* 11am-7pm Mon-Fri; 10am-5pm Sat. **Map** p400 H10.

Westminster Reference Library

35 St Martin's Street, Westminster, WC2 (7641 4636). Leicester Square tube. **Open** 10am-8pm Mon-Fri; 10am-5pm Sat. **Map** p401 K7.

Lost property

Always inform the police if you lose anything, if only to validate insurance claims. *See p373* or the *Yellow Pages* for your nearest police station. Only dial the emergency number (999) if violence has occurred. Lost passports should be reported both to the police (*see p373*) and to your embassy (*see p365*).

Airports

The following lost property offices deal only with items lost in the airports concerned. For property lost on the plane contact the airline or handling agents dealing with the flight.

Gatwick Airport *01293 503162.*
Heathrow Airport *8745 7727.*
London City Airport *7646 0000.*
Luton Airport *01582 395 219.*
Stansted Airport *01279 663293.*

Public transport

If you have lost property in an overground station or on a train, call 7928 5151; an operator will connect you to the appropriate station. For property lost on a tube or bus, *see below*.

Transport For London

Lost Property Office, 200 Baker Street, Marylebone, NW1 (recorded information 7486 2496). Baker Street tube. **Open** 9.30am-2pm Mon-Fri; closed Sat, Sun. **Map** p398 G4.
Allow three days from the time of loss. If you lose something on a bus, call 7222 1234 and ask for the phone numbers of the depots at either end of the route. Pick up a lost property form from any tube station.

Taxis

Taxi Lost Property

200 Baker Street, Marylebone, NW1 (7833 0996). Baker Street tube. **Map** p402 N2.
This office deals only with property that has been found in registered black cabs. For items lost in a minicab, you will have to contact the office from which you hired the cab.

Media

Magazines

There are more than 6,500 magazines available in the UK. The women's market is the most profitable (and saturated), with *Marie Claire* and *Cosmopolitan* leading where others can only follow, often in pale imitation.
The men's market continues to expand, with *FHM* still doing particularly well at

the moment. Style magazines, such as *i-D* and *Dazed and Confused*, have established themselves in a profitable niche. Weekly TV listings magazines are also big winners: *Time Out* also includes London-related features and interviews, while glossy *Heat* is heavy on celebrity gossip and film and TV features.

If you're looking for something more serious and hard-hitting, there's not much to choose from. *The Spectator*, the *New Statesman* and *Prospect* are about as good as it gets. *Private Eye* offers a fortnightly satirical look at politics and news. *The Big Issue*, sold on the street by homeless people, is also worth a look. *The Economist* covers political and business issues, and you'll find international editions of *Time* and *Newsweek* at most newsagents.

Newspapers

National newspapers fall broadly into three categories. At the lofty, serious end of the scale are the broadsheets: the right-wing *Daily Telegraph* and *The Times* (best for sport) are balanced by the (increasingly unindependent) *Independent* and the *Guardian* (best for arts coverage). All have bulging Sunday equivalents bar the *Guardian* (though it does have a sister Sunday paper, the *Observer*).

The right-wing middle-market leader has long been the truly odious *Daily Mail* (and *Mail on Sunday*). Its rival, the *Daily Express* (and *Sunday Express*) has struggled for some time, and was recently bought out by the man behind a whole array of top-shelf publications.

Finally, at the bottom of the pile are the most popular papers of them all: the tabloids. Still the undisputed leader of the rat pack is the *Sun* (and the

Sunday *News of the World*), which sells around three and a half million copies daily, more than half the daily total of all newspapers sold. The *Daily Star* and the *Mirror* are the other main lowbrow contenders, with the *People* and the *Sunday Mirror* providing sleaze on Sunday.

London's main daily paper, which comes out in several editions through the day (Monday to Friday only), is the right-wing *Evening Standard*, a sort of *Mail* for London. London's free morning paper *Metro*, is distributed at tube stations and contains just enough news and features to occupy the average journey.

Radio

BBC Radio 1 *98.8 FM.* Youth-oriented music station, dealing mostly in pop, rock and dance.
BBC Radio 2 *89.1 FM.* Bland and middle-of-the-road during the day, but increasingly adventurous and worthwhile (if still retro) at night.
BBC Radio 3 *91.3 FM.* The BBC's classical music station.
BBC Radio 4 *93.5 FM, 720 MW, 198 LW.* Speech-only station, loved for its *Today* morning news show and for its soap, *The Archers*.
BBC Radio 5 Live *693, 909 MW.* News and sport, 24 hours a day. Live coverage of major sporting events.
BBC London Live *94.9 FM.* Not a patch on GLR, the station it replaced, but Robert Elms (9am-noon Mon-Fri) and Gideon Coe (7-9pm Mon-Fri, 1-6pm Sat) are still must-listens.
BBC World Service *648 MW.* Transmitted worldwide but available in the UK for a distillation of the best of all the other BBC stations.
Capital FM *95.8 FM.* Inexplicably popular commercial station, complete with irritating DJs and didn't-I-hear-this-about-five-minutes-ago playlist.
Capital Gold *1548 MW.* Retro 'classics' from the '60s to the '80s.
Choice FM *96.9 FM.* Pioneering black-music orientated channel.
Classic FM *100.9 FM.* Lowbrow classical station.
Country *1035 MW.* Yee haw.
Heart *106.2 FM.* Where less is most definitely MOR.
Jazz FM *102.2 FM.* Anodyne, often narcolepsy-inducing smooth jazz dominates, more's the pity.
Kiss *100.0 FM.* London's dance station. Not for the feint of heart.

Liberty *963, 972 MW.* Faux kitschy, largely retro music station.
LBC *1152 MW.* Non-stop phone-ins and chat. The cabbies' favourite.
News Direct *97.3 FM.* News, weather, travel and business.
Spectrum *558 MW.* Researched, produced and presented by various ethnic communities.
Talk Radio *1053, 1089 MW.* Exactly what you'd expect.
Virgin *105.8 FM.* Tiring mix of music, chat and Chris Evans.
XFM *104.9 FM, 1215 MW.* Self-described indie station.

Television

The next generation of television in the UK will be digital. Sky Digital, ONdigital and various digital cable TV companies currently offer services that reproduce and expand on the established analogue offerings listed here.

Network channels

BBC1 The Corporation's mass-market station. There's a smattering of soaps and game shows, and the odd quality programme. Daytime programming, however, stinks. As with all BBC radio and TV stations, there are no commercials.
BBC2 In general, BBC2 is also free of crass programmes. That doesn't mean the output is riveting, just not insulting. It offers a cultural cross-section and plenty of documentaries; recently it has also been competing with Channel 4 in the Friday-night comedy stakes.
ITV Carlton, who provide the weekday programming for ITV, cram their schedules with mass-appeal shows and frequent ad breaks. Any successful formula is repeated ad infinitum, with little of merit to break up the monotony. LWT (London Weekend Television) takes over from Carlton at the weekend to offer more of the same.
Channel 4 C4's output includes some pretty mainstream fare, especially its extremely successful US imports (*Friends, ER, The Sopranos* etc), but it still comes up with some gems, particularly films.
Channel 5 Britain's newest terrestrial channel offers a mix of sex, US TV movies, sex, rubbish comedy, sex, more sex and American sport. Oh, and sex.

Satellite, digital & cable channels

The non-network sector is now crammed to bursting with stations on a variety of formats (satellite, cable and fast-expanding digital, though most are not worth bothering with at all. Listed below are the pick of the pack.

BBC News 24 The Beeb's rolling news network.
Bravo B-movies and cult TV.
CNN News and current affairs.
Discovery Channel Science and nature documentaries.
FilmFour Channel 4's movie outlet, with 12 hours of programming daily.
History Channel Self-explanatory.
MTV Rock/pop channel that borrows from its US counterpart.
Paramount US and Brit sitcoms.
Performance Dance, theatre and opera, plus interviews.
Sky Moviemax Blockbusters.
Sky Movies Gold Classic movies.
Sky News Rolling news.
Sky One Sky's version of ITV.
Sky Sports Sports. There are also Sky Sports 2 and Sky Sports 3.
TNT Cartoons and classic repeats.
UK Arena Classical concerts and all things arts-related.
UK Gold Reruns of yesteryear's BBC and ITV successes.
UK Horizon Science documentaries.
VH-1 MTV for grown-ups.

Money

The nation's currency remains the pound sterling (£). One pound equals 100 pence (p). 1p and 2p coins are copper; 5p, 10p, 20p and the seven-sided 50p coins are silver; the £1 coin is yellow-gold; the £2 coin is silver in the centre with a circle of yellow-gold around the edge. Paper notes are as follows: blue £5, orange £10, purple £20 and red £50. You will probably find an increasing number of places pre-empting the Government and accepting euros (€), but don't rely on it.

You can exchange foreign currency at banks and bureaux de change (*see below*). If you're here for a long stay, you may need to open a bank or building society account. To do this, you'll probably need to present a reference from your bank at home, and certainly a passport as identification.

Western Union

0800 833833/www.westernunion.com. The old standby for bailing cash-challenged travellers out of trouble, but it's pricey.

ATMs

Aside from inside and outside banks themselves, cash machines are also found in some supermarkets, selected other shops (such as the Virgin Megastore, for which *see p256*), and in tube and rail stations. The vast majority accept withdrawals on major credit cards, and most also allow withdrawals using the Maestro/Cirrus debit system.

Banks

Minimum banking hours are 9.30am to 3.30pm Monday to Friday, but most branches close at 4.30pm and a few even stay open until 5pm.

Exchange and commission rates on currency vary hugely, and it pays to shop around. Commission is sometimes charged for cashing travellers' cheques in foreign currencies, but not for sterling travellers' cheques, provided you cash the cheques at a bank affiliated to the issuing bank (get a list when you buy your cheques); it's also charged if you change cash into another currency. You always need ID, such as a passport, when exchanging travellers' cheques.

Bureaux de change

You will be charged for cashing travellers' cheques or buying and selling foreign currency at a bureau de change. Commission rates, which should be clearly displayed, vary. **Chequepoint** (13 London branches), **Lenlyn** (26 London branches) and **Thomas Cook** (149 London branches, many within branches of the HSBC bank) are reputable bureaux. Major rail and tube stations in central London have bureaux de change, and there are many in tourist areas. Most are open 8am-10pm, but those listed below are open 24 hours daily.

Chequepoint
548 Oxford Street, Marylebone, W1 (7723 1005). Marble Arch tube. **Map** p398 G6.
222 Earl's Court Road, Earl's Court, SW5 (7370 3238). Earl's Court tube. **Map** p396 B10.
2 Queensway, Bayswater, W2 (7229 0093). Queensway tube. **Map** p394 C6.

Credit cards

Most shops, restaurants, ticket agents, garages, box offices and the like, as well as selected bars and museums, will accept credit cards. Visa and Mastercard are the most widely accepted, with American Express and Diners Club taken in noticeably fewer establishments.

Lost/stolen credit cards

Report lost or stolen credit cards immediately to both the police and the 24-hour services listed below. Inform your bank by phone and in writing.

American Express *01273 696933.*
Diners Club *01252 513500/ 0800 460800.*
JCB *7499 3000.*
MasterCard/Eurocard *0800 964767.*
Switch *0113 277 8899.*
Visa/Connect *0800 895082.*

Tax

With the exception of a few choice items (food, books, newspapers, children's clothing, etc), purchases in the UK are subject to VAT – value-added tax, aka sales tax – of 17.5 per cent. However, unlike in the US, this tax is always included in prices quoted in shops, in that a price tag of £10 means you pay £10, not £11.75.

Beware, though, hotels, which often naughtily quote room rates exclusive of VAT: always be sure to ask whether or not the rate you have been quoted includes tax.

Opening hours

Listed below are some general guidelines on opening hours in London. However, the key word is 'guidelines': hours can vary in all cases. If you're after the opening hours of a specific establishment, see the listing in the chapter in question.

Banks 9am-4.30pm (some close at 3.30pm) Mon-Fri.
Bars 11am-11pm Mon-Sat; noon-10.30pm Sun.
Businesses 9am-5pm Mon-Fri (except media/internet, which generally operate later hours).
Post offices 9am-5.30pm Mon-Fri; 9am-noon Sat.
Shops 10am-6pm Mon-Sat.

Police stations

The police are a good source of information about the locality and are used to helping visitors find their way. We have listed a handful of central London police stations in this section of the guide (*see below*). If you have been robbed, assaulted or involved in an infringement of the law, go to your nearest police station (if it's not listed here, either look under 'Police' in the phone book or call Directory Enquiries on 192).

If you have a complaint to make about the police, there are several things you can do. Ensure that you take the offending police officer's identifying number, which should be displayed on his or her epaulette. You can then register a complaint with the **Police Complaints Authority**, 10 Great George Street, SW1P 3AE (7273 6450). Alternatively, contact any police station or visit a solicitor or a Law Centre.

Police stations
Belgravia Police Station
202-206 Buckingham Palace Road, Pimlico, SW1 (7730 1212). Victoria tube/rail. Map p400 H10.
Charing Cross Police Station
Agar Street, Covent Garden, WC2 (7240 1212). Charing Cross tube/rail. Map pp401 L7.

Chelsea Police Station
2 Lucan Place, Chelsea, SW3 (7589 1212). Sloane Square tube. Map p397 E10.
Islington Police Station
2 Tolpuddle Street, Islington, N1 (7704 1212). Angel tube. Map p402 N2.
Kensington Police Station
72 Earl's Court Road, Kensington, W8 (7376 1212). High Street Kensington tube. Map p396 B11.
King's Cross Police Station
76 King's Cross Road, King's Cross, WC1 (7704 1212). King's Cross tube/rail. Map p399 M3.
Marylebone Police Station
51-9 Seymour Street, Marylebone, W1 (7486 1212). Baker Street tube/Marylebone tube/rail. Map p395 F6.
Paddington Green Police Station 4 Harrow Road, Paddington, W2 (7402 1212). Edgware Road tube. Map p394 C5.
West End Central Police Station 27 Savile Row, W1 (7437 1212). Piccadilly Circus tube. Map p400 J7.

Postal services

You can buy stamps at all post offices and also at many newsagents. Current prices are 19p for second-class and 27p for first-class letters and letters to EU countries. Postcards cost 36p to send within Europe and 45p to countries outside Europe. Rates for other letters and parcels vary according to weight and destination.

Post offices

Post offices are usually open 9am-5.30pm Monday to Friday and 9am-noon Saturday, with the exception of **Trafalgar Square Post Office** (24-28 William IV Street, WC2; 7484 9304; Charing Cross tube/rail), which is open 8am to 8pm Monday to Thursday, 8.30am to 8pm Friday and 9am to 8pm Saturday. The busiest time of day is usually 1-2pm.

Listed below are the other main central London offices. For general post office enquiries, call the central information line on 0345 223344 or consult www.postoffice-counters.co.uk.

43-44 Albemarle Street Mayfair, W1 (7493 5620). Green Park tube. Map p400 J7.
111 Baker Street Marylebone, W1 (7935 3701). Baker Street tube. Map p398 G5.
202 Great Portland Street Marylebone, W1 (7636 9935). Great Portland Street tube. Map p398 H4.
32A Grosvenor Street Mayfair, W1 (7629 2480). Bond Street tube. Map p400 H7.
3-9 Heddon Street Mayfair, W1 (7734 5556). Piccadilly Circus tube. Map p400 J7.
19 Newman Street Fitzrovia, W1 (7636 9995). Tottenham Court Road tube. Map p398 J5.
43 Seymour Street Marylebone, W1 (7723 0867). Marble Arch tube. Map p395 F6.

Poste restante

If you intend to travel around Britain, friends from home can write to you care of a post office, where mail will be kept at the enquiry desk for up to one month. Your name and 'Poste Restante' must be clearly marked on the letter above the following address: Post Office, 24-28 William IV Street, London WC2N 4DL. Bring ID when you come to collect your mail.

Religion

Anglican
St Paul's Cathedral For listings details, see p84. **Services** 7.30am, 8am, 12.30pm, 5pm Mon-Fri; 8am, 8.30am, 12.30pm, 5pm Sat; 8am, 10.15am, 11.30am, 3.15pm, 6pm Sun. Map p404 O6.
Times vary due to special events; phone to check.
Westminster Abbey For listings details, see p134. **Services** 7.30am, 8am, 12.30pm, 5pm Mon-Fri; 8am, 9.20am, 3pm Sat; 8am, 10am, 11.15am, 3pm, 5.45pm Sun. Map p401 K9.

Baptist
Bloomsbury Central Baptist Church 235 Shaftesbury Avenue, Covent Garden, WC2 (7240 0544/ www.bloomsbury.org.uk). Tottenham Court Road tube.
Open 10am-4pm Mon-Fri; 10am-8.30pm Sun; closed Sat. Friendship Centre noon-2.30pm Tue; 10.30am-8.30pm Sun; closed during services, Aug. **Services** 5.30pm Tue; 7.30pm Wed; 11am, 6.30pm Sun. Map p399 L6.

Buddhist

Buddhapadipa Temple
*14 Calonne Road, Wimbledon,
SW19 (8946 1357/www.buddha
padipa.org). Wimbledon tube then 93
bus.* **Open** *Temple* 1-6pm Sat, Sun.
Meditation retreat 7-9pm Tue, Thur;
4-6pm Sat, Sun.

Catholic

London Oratory *For listings
details, see p93.* **Services** 7am, 8am
(Latin mass), 10am, 12.30am, 6pm
Mon-Fri; 7am, 8am, 10am, 6pm, Sat;
7am, 8.30am, 10am (tridentine), 11am
(sung Latin), 12.30pm, 3.30pm
4.30pm 7pm Sun. **Map** p397 E10.
Westminster Cathedral *For
listings details, see p91.* **Services**
eight daily masses Mon-Fri; seven
daily masses Sat; 7am, 8am, 9am,
10.30am, noon, 5.30pm, 7pm Sun.
Map p400 J10.

Hindu

Swaminarayan Hindu Mission
*105-119 Brentfield Road, church
End, NW10 (enquiries Amrish Patel
8961 5031). Neasden tube/Harlesden
tube/rail.* **Open** 9am-6.30pm daily.
Services 11.45am, 7pm daily.
In addition to a large prayer hall,
this huge complex contains a
conference hall, a marriage suite,
sports facilities, a library and a
health clinic.

Islamic

London Central Mosque
*146 Park Road, St John's Wood,
NW8 (7724 3363). Baker Street
tube/bus 74.* **Open** dawn-dusk daily.
Services phone for details.
East London Mosque *82-92
Whitechapel Road, E1 (7247 1357/
www.eastlondon-mosque.org.uk).
Aldgate East or Whitechapel tube.*
Open phone for details. **Services**
Friday prayer 1.30pm (1pm in
winter). **Map** p405 S6.

Jewish

Liberal Jewish Synagogue *28 St
John's Wood Road, St John's Wood,
NW8 (7286 5181/www.ljs.org).
St John's Wood tube.* **Open** *Enquiries*
9am-5pm Mon-Thur; 9am-1pm Fri.
Services 6.45pm Fri; 11am Sat.
**West Central Liberal
Synagogue** *109 Whitfield Street,
Fitzrovia, W1 (7636 7627). Warren
Street tube.* **Services** 3pm Sat.
Map p398 J4.

Methodist

Methodist Central Hall
*Westminster Central Hall, Storey's
Gate, Westminster, SW1 (7222
8010/www.wch.co.uk). St James's
Park tube.* **Open** *Chapel* 9am-5pm
Mon-Fri. **Services** 12.45pm
Wed; 10am, 11am, 6.30pm Sun.
Map p401 K9.

Quaker

**Religious Society of Friends
(Quakers)** *Friends House, 173-177
Euston Road, Bloomsbury, NW1
(7387 3601/www.quaker.org.uk).
Euston tube/rail.* **Open** 8.30am-9pm
Mon-Fri. **Meetings** 11am Sun.
Map p399 K3.

Safety & security

Violent crime is relatively rare
in London, but, as in any major
city, it is unwise to take any
risks. Pickpockets and thieves
specifically target unwary
tourists. Use common sense
and follow these basic rules:

● **Keep** your wallet and purse out
of sight. Don't wear a wrist watch
(they are easily snatched). Keep
your handbag securely closed.
● **Don't** leave a handbag, briefcase,
bag or coat unattended, especially
in pubs, cinemas or fast-food
restaurants, on public transport,
or in crowds.
● **Don't** leave your bag or coat
beside, under or on the back of
your chair.
● **Don't** put your bag on the floor
near the door of a public toilet.
● **Don't** wear expensive jewellery
or watches that can be easily
snatched.
● **Don't** keep your passport, money,
credit cards, etc, together. If you
lose one, you'll lose all.
● **Don't** put your purse down on the
table in a restaurant or on a shop
counter while you check the bill.
● **Don't** carry a wallet in your back
pocket, and don't flash your
money or credit cards around.

Smoking

Smoking is permitted in almost
all pubs and bars – though an
increasing number now have
non-smoking areas – and in
most restaurants, though try
and specify when you book
that you'd like a table in the
smoking section. Smoking,
though, is forbidden in shops
and on public transport.

Study

Being a student in London will
be an exciting if depressingly
expensive affair. Whether you
are here to study or just
visiting, *Time Out's* annual
Student Guide, available

from many bookshops and
newsagents from October each
year, provides the lowdown
on what London has to offer
students and how to survive
in the big city.

Throughout this Guide,
entry prices for students at
museums, art galleries, sights,
sports venues and other places
are usually designated
'concessions'). You'll have to
show ID (an NUS or ISIC card)
to get these rates. Students,
whether EU citizens or not,
wanting or needing to find
work in the UK as a way of
boosting their funds, should
turn to *p379*.

Language classes

All the places listed below
offer a variety of language
courses; call for full details.

**Aspect Covent Garden
Language Centre**
*3-4 Southampton Place, WC1
(7404 3080/www.aspectworld.com).
Holborn tube.* **Map** p399 L5.
Central School of English
*1 Tottenham Court Road, W1
(7580 2863/www.centralschool.co.uk).
Tottenham Court Road tube.*
Map p399 K5.
Frances King School of English
*77 Gloucester Road, SW7 (070
0011 2233/www.francesking.co.uk).
Gloucester Road tube.* **Map** p395 F9.
London Study Centre
*Munster House, 676 Fulham Road,
SW6 (7731 3549/www.londonstudy
centre.com). Parsons Green tube.*
Sels College *64-65 Long Acre,
WC2 (7240 2581/www.sels.co.uk).
Covent Garden tube.* **Map** p399 L6.
Shane English School
*59 South Molton Street, W1
(7499 8533/www.saxoncourt.com).
Bond Street tube.* **Map** p398 H6.

Students' unions

Many students' unions will
only let in students with the
relevant ID, so be sure to carry
your NUS or ISIC card with
you at all times to ensure
entry. Below, taken from the
Time Out Student Guide, are
those with the five best student
bars in the capital, which offer
a good night out at student-
friendly prices.

Directory

Imperial College *Beit Quad,
Prince Consort Road, SW7 (7589
5111). South Kensington tube.*
Open *noon-2pm, 5-11pm Mon, Tue,
Thur; noon-2pm, 5pm-midnight Wed;
noon-2pm, 5pm-1am Fri; 12.30-11pm
Sat; 12.30-10.30pm Sun (times vary
out of termtime).* **Map** p397 D9.
International Students House
*229 Great Portland Street, W1
(7631 8300 ext 744). Great Portland
Street tube.* **Open** *noon-2pm, 5-11pm
Mon-Thur; noon-2pm, 5pm-2am Fri;
5.30-midnight Sat; 7-10.30pm Sun.*
Map p398 H4.
King's College *Macadam Building,
Surrey Street, WC2 (7836 7132).
Temple tube.* **Open** *Waterfront noon-
11pm Mon-Fri; 8-11pm Sat; closed
Sun. Tutu's 9pm-2am Fri; 10.30pm-
3am Sat; closed Sun.* **Map** p401 M7.
**University of London Union
(ULU)** *Malet Street, WC1 (7664
2000). Goodge Street or Russell
Square tube.* **Open** *11am-11pm
Mon-Fri; 11am-1am Fri, Sat; noon-
10.30pm Sun.* **Map** p399 K4.
University of North London
*166-220 Holloway Road, N7 (7607
2789 ext 2291). Holloway Road tube.*
Open *11am-11pm Mon, Tue, Thur;
11am-2am Wed; 11am-late Fri;
11am-6am Sat.*

Universities

Brunel University *Clevedon
Road, Uxbridge, Middlesex (01895
274000/students' union 01895
462200). Uxbridge tube.*
City University *Northampton
Square, EC1 (7477 8000/students'
union 7505 5600). Angel tube.*
Map p402 O3.
Guildhall University *Calcutta
House, Old Castle Street, E1 (7320
1000/students' union 7320 2233).
Aldgate East tube.* **Map** p405 S6.
South Bank University *Borough
Road, SE1 (7928 8989/students'
union 7815 6060). Elephant & Castle
tube/rail.* **Map** p404 O9.
**University of East London
(Stratford Campus)** *Romford
Road, E15 (8590 7722/students'
union ext 4210). Stratford tube/rail.*
University of Greenwich
*Wellington Street, SE18 (8331
8000/students' union 8331 8268).
Woolwich Arsenal rail.*
University of Kingston *Penrhyn
Road, Kingston, Surrey (8547
2000/students' union 8547 8868).
Kingston rail.*
University of London *see below.*
University of Middlesex *Trent
Park, Bramley Road, N14 (8362
5000/students' union 8362 6450).
Cockfosters or Oakwood tube.*
University of North London
*166-220 Holloway Road, N7 (7607
2789/students' union 7753 3367).
Holloway Road tube.*

University of Westminster
*309 Regent Street, W1 (7911
5000/students' union 7915 5454).
Oxford Circus tube.* **Map** p398 H4.
University of London
Many students in London attend one
of the 34 colleges, spread across the
city, that make up the huge
University of London; only the six
largest are listed below. All London
universities (with the exception of
Imperial College) are affiliated to the
National Union of Students (NUS).

NUS London Regional Office
(7272 8900/www.nus.org.uk). **Open**
9.30am-5pm Mon-Fri.
Goldsmiths' College *Lewisham
Way, SE14 (7919 7171/students'
union 8692 1406). New Cross/New
Cross Gate tube/rail.*
Imperial College *Exhibition
Road, SW7 (7589 5111/students'
union 7594 8060). South Kensington
tube.* **Map** p397 D9.
King's College *Strand, WC2
(7836 5454/students' union 7836
7132). Temple tube.* **Map** p401 M7.
**London School of Economics
(LSE)** *Houghton Street, WC2 (7405
7686/students' union 7955 7158).
Holborn tube.* **Map** p399 K4.
**Queen Mary & Westfield
College (QMW)** *Mile End Road,
E1 (7975 5555/students' union
7975 5390). Mile End or Stepney
Green tube.*
**University College London
(UCL)** *Gower Street, WC1 (7679
2000/students' union 7387 3611).
Goodge Street or Warren Street
tube/Euston tube/rail.* **Map** p399 K4.

Useful organisations

For BUNAC and the Council on
International Educational Exchange, *see p379.*

**National Bureau for Students
with Disabilities** *Chapter House,
18-20 Crucifix Lane, SE1 (0800 328
5050/www.skill.org.uk/minicom 0800
068 2422).* **Open** *Phone enquiries
1.30-4.30pm Mon-Fri; closed Sat, Sun.*
Information and advice.

Telephones

Dialling & codes

The codes for London changed
in 2000. The old 0171 and
0181 codes – not long in
operation themselves – were
replaced by a single new code,
020, with a **7** or **8** added to the
original seven-digit number to
create a new 11-digit number.

For example, 0171 813 3000
became 020 7813 3000.
Throughout this book, London
numbers have been listed
without their code.

Making a call

If you want to call a London
number from within London,
you omit the code (020) and
dial the last eight digits. If you
are calling from outside the
UK, dial the international
access code from the country
from which you're calling, then
the UK code 44, then the full
London number, omitting for
the first 0 from the code. For
example, to make a call to
020 7813 3000 from the US,
dial 011 44 20 7813 3000.

To dial abroad from the UK,
first dial 00 (the international
access code), then the country
code (see below for a list),
followed by your number.

International codes

Australia 61; **Austria** 43; **Belgium**
32; **Brazil** 55; **Canada** 1; **Czech
Republic** 420; **Denmark** 45;
France 33; **Germany** 49; **Greece**
30; **Hong Kong** 852; **India** 91;
Iceland 354; **Ireland** 353;
Israel 972; **Italy** 390; **Japan** 81;
Netherlands 31; **New Zealand** 64;
Norway 47; **Portugal** 3512; **South
Africa** 27; **Spain** 34; **Sweden** 46;
Switzerland 41; **USA** 1.

Public phones

Public payphones take coins,
credit cards or prepaid phonecards (sometimes all three).
The minimum cost is 20p
(which will buy you a 110-
second local phone call), but
some payphones, such as
counter-top ones found in
many pubs, require more.

British Telecom
phonecards
*Available from post offices and
many newsagents.* **Cost** *20p per unit;
cards in denominations of £2, £5,
£10 and £20.*
Call boxes with the green Phonecard
symbol take prepaid cards. A notice
tells you where to find the nearest
stockist. A digital display shows the
units remaining on your card.

Operator services

Operator

Call **100** for the operator in the following circumstances: when you have difficulty in dialling; for an early-morning alarm call; to make a credit card call; for information about the cost of a call; and for help with international person-to-person calls.

Dial **155** if you need to reverse the charges (call collect) or if you can't dial direct, but be warned that this service is very expensive.

Directory enquiries

Dial **192** for any number in Britain, or **153** for international numbers. Phoning directory enquiries from a private phone is expensive, and only two enquiries are allowed per call. However, if you phone from a public call box, calls are free.

Talking Pages

This 24-hour free service lists the numbers of thousands of businesses in the UK. Dial **0800 600900** and say what type of business you require, and in what area of London.

Telephone directories

There are three phone directories for London: two for private numbers and one for companies. These are available at post offices and libraries. Hotels have them too and they are issued free to all residents, as is the *Yellow Pages* directory, which lists businesses and services. A searchable Yellow Pages is available at www.yell.com.

Mobile phones

Mobile phones in the UK work on either the 900 or 1800 GSM system used throughout much of Europe. If you are travelling to the UK from Europe, check whether your service provider has a reciprocal arrangement with a UK-based service provider before travelling.

The situation is more complex for US travellers. If your service provider in the US uses the GSM system, it will probably run on the 1900 band; this being the case, you will need a tri-band phone,

and your provider needs to have a reciprocal arrangement with a UK provider.

The simplest option, though, may be to buy a 'pay as you go' phone (about £30-£70). Calls are more expensive than with a subscription package, but there's no monthly fee and calls are charged not by billing but by buying (widely available) cards that slot into your phone in denominations of £10 and up. Check before you buy whether the phone is capable of making and receiving international calls.

Telegrams

There is no longer a domestic telegram service, but you can still send telegrams abroad: call 0800 190190. This is also the number to call if to send an international telemessage: phone in your message and it will be delivered by post the next day (£8.99 for up to 50 words, an extra £1 for a card).

Time

London operates on Greenwich Mean Time, which is five hours ahead of the US's Eastern Standard time. In spring (25 March 2001; 31 March 2002) the UK puts its clocks forward by one hour to British Summer Time (BST). In autumn (28 Oct 2001; 27 Oct 2002) the clocks go back to GMT again.

Tipping

In Britain it's accepted that you tip in taxis, minicabs, restaurants (some waiting staff rely heavily on gratuities), hairdressers, hotels and some bars (not pubs). Ten per cent is normal, with some restaurants adding up to 15 per cent. Always check if service has been included in your bill: some restaurants include service and then leave the space for a gratuity on your credit card slip blank.

Toilets

Public toilets are few and far between in London, a situation exacerbated by the fact that pubs and restaurants reserve their toilets for customers only. However, all main-line rail stations and a very few tube stations – Piccadilly Circus, for one – have public toilets (you may be charged a small fee), while it's usually possible to sneak into a large department store such as John Lewis.

Tourist information

The **London Tourist Board** (LTB; 7932 2000) runs the information centres listed below, all of which can supply a free map of central London. For more details, check online at www.londontown.com.

The opening times given are for winter; hours are usually longer for the rest of the year.

Heathrow Terminals 1, 2, 3 *Tube station concourse, Heathrow Airport.* **Open** 8am-6pm daily.
Liverpool Street Station *Tube station concourse, The City, EC2.* **Open** 8am-6pm Mon-Fri; 8.45am-5.30pm Sat, Sun. **Map** p403 R5.
Victoria Station *Victoria Station forecourt, Belgravia, SW1.* **Open** 8am-7pm Mon-Sat; 8am-6pm Sun. **Map** p400 H10.
Waterloo International Terminal *Arrivals Hall, South Bank, SE1.* **Open** 8.30am-10.30pm daily. **Map** p401 M8.

For information on travel in the rest of Britain, *see p338.*

There are also tourist information offices in Greenwich, next to St Paul's (**Map** p404 O6) and on the south side of London Bridge (**Map** p405 Q8).

Visas & immigration

Citizens of EU countries do not require a visa to visit the UK; citizens of other countries, including the USA, Canada

Weather report

Average daytime temperatures, rainfall and hours of sunshine in London

	Temp (°C/°F)	Rainfall (cm/in)	Sunshine (hrs/dy)
Jan	6/43	45/1.8	1.9
Feb	6/43	30/1.2	2.5
Mar	8/46	43/1.7	3.3
Apr	10/50	37/1.5	5.3
May	13/55	47/1.9	6.3
June	16/61	44/1.8	6.2
July	19/66	46/1.8	6.7
Aug	19/66	42/1.7	6.6
Sept	16/61	39/1.6	5.0
Oct	13/55	56/2.2	3.5
Nov	9/48	46/1.8	2.3
Dec	7/45	49/2.0	1.5

and New Zealand, require a valid passport for a visit of up to six months in duration.

To apply for a visa, and to check your visa status **before you travel**, contact the British Embassy, High Commission or Consulate in your own country. The visa allows you entry for a maximum of six months. For information about work permits, *see p379*.

The immigration department of the Home Office deals with queries about immigration, visas and work permits from Commonwealth countries.

Home Office *Immigration & Nationality Directorate, Block C, Whitgift Centre, Wellesley Road, Croydon CR9 1AT (0870 606 7766/ application forms 0870 241 0645/ www.homeoffice.gov.uk/ind/hpg.htm).* **Open** *Phone enquiries 8.45am-4.45pm Mon-Thur; 8.45am-4.30pm Fri; closed Sat, Sun.*

Weights & measures

The United Kingdom is gradually moving towards full metrication. Distances continue to be measured in miles but recent legislation means that all goods are now officially sold in metric quantities, with no legal requirement for the imperial equivalent to be given.

Conversions

1 centimetre (cm) = 0.39 inches (in)
1 inch (in) = 2.54 centimetres (cm)
1 yard (yd) = 0.91 metres (m)
1 metre (m) = 1.094 yards (yd)
1 mile = 1.6 kilometres (km)
1 kilometre (km) = 0.62 miles
1 ounce (oz) = 28.35 grammes (g)
1 gramme (g) = 0.035 ounces (oz)
1 pound (lb) = 0.45 kilogrammes (kg)
1 kilogramme = 2.2 pounds (lb)
1 pint (US) = 0.8 pints (UK)
1 pint (UK) = 0.55 litres (l)
1 litre (l) = 1.75 pints (UK).

When to go

Climate

Prepare yourself for the unpredictability of the British climate. For some guidance try **Weathercall** on 0891 500401 (50p per minute at all times).

Spring extends approximately from March to May, though winter often seems to stretch well beyond February. March winds and April showers may turn up either a month early or a month late. May is generally very pleasant.
Summer – June, July and August – can be unpredictable, with searing heat one day followed by sultry greyness and thunderstorms the next. The combination of high temperatures, humidity and pollution can create problems for anyone with hayfever or breathing difficulties.

Autumn starts in September, although the weather can still have a mild, summery feel. Real autumn comes with October when the leaves start to fall. Then the cold sets in and November hits with a reminder that London is situated on a fairly northerly latitude.
Winter may contain the odd mild day, but don't bank on it. December, January and February are generally pretty chilly in London, although snow is rare. A crisp, sunny winter's day in the capital is hard to beat.

Public holidays

On public holidays (known as bank holidays), many shops remain open, but public transport services are less frequent, generally running to a Sunday timetable. The exception is Christmas Day, when almost everything shuts.

New Year's Day Mon 1 Jan 2001; Tue 1 Jan 2002.
Good Friday Fri 13 Apr 2001; Fri 29 Mar 2002.
Easter Monday Mon 16 Apr 2001; Mon 1 Apr 2002.
May Day Holiday Mon 7 May 2001; Mon 6 May 2002; .
Spring Bank Holiday Mon 28 May 2001; Mon 27 May 2002.
Summer Bank Holiday Mon 27 Aug 2001; Mon 26 Aug 2002.
Christmas Day Tue 25 Dec 2001; Wed 25 Dec 2002.
Boxing Day Wed 26 Dec 2001; Thur 26 Dec 2002.

Women

The women's movement may currently keep a low profile, but London is home to dozens of women's groups and networks, from day centres to rights campaigners, as a browse through websites such as www.gn.apc.org/ womeninlondon or www.wrc.uninet.co.uk will reveal.

SAFETY/HARASSMENT

Visiting women are unlikely to be harassed, beyond a friendly 'love' now and again. Bar the very occasional sexually motivated attack, the streets of London are no more dangerous to women than they are to men, if you follow the usual precautions (*see p375*).

Directory

National Library of Women

London Guildhall University, Calcutta House, Old Castle Street, Whitechapel (7320 1189/www. lgu.ac.uk/fawcett). Aldgate or Aldgate East tube. **Open** *Term time* 10.15am-8.30pm Mon, Wed-Fri; closed Tue, Sat, Sun. *Vacations* 9am-5pm Mon, Wed-Fri; closed Sat, Sun. **Map** p405 S6.
Europe's largest women's studies archive makes a £4 million move in spring 2001 to larger premises, also on Old Castle Street, with exhibition space presenting subjects such as the suffragette movement. Staff are usually happy to help with general woman-related queries.

Working in London

Finding temporary work in London can be a full-time job in itself. But providing you can speak decent English, are an EU citizen or have a work permit, you should be able to find something in catering, labouring, bar/pub or shop work. Graduates with an English or foreign-language degree could try teaching. If your English isn't great, there's always the mind-numbing distributing of free magazines. You can also try for seasonal work in tourist spots. Ideas can be found in *Summer Jobs in Britain*, published by Vacation Work, 9 Park End Street, Oxford OX1 1HJ (£9.99 plus £1.50 p&p). The **Central Bureau for Educational Visits & Exchanges** (*see below*) has other useful publications.

To find work, look in the *Evening Standard*, local and national papers and newsagents' windows. Employers advertise vacancies on Jobcentre noticeboards; there is often temporary and unskilled work available. Most districts of London have a Jobcentre; look in *Yellow Pages* under 'Employment Agencies'.

For relatively lucrative office work, sign on with temp agencies if you have good typing (40 words per minute upwards) or word processing skills and can dress the part.

Work permits

With few exceptions, citizens of non-European Economic Area (EEA) countries need a work permit before they are legally able to work in the UK, which they must obtain before making the journey here.

Employers who have vacancies that they are unable to fill with a resident or EEA national must apply for a permit to the Department for Education & Employment (*see below*). Permits are issued only for jobs that carry a high level of skill and experience.

Au pairs

The option of au pairing is only open to citizens of the countries listed below aged between 17 and 27. Try contacting an agency in your own country or look in the *Yellow Pages* under 'Employment Agencies'. Such work usually provides free accommodation, but wages tend to be low. The following countries are in the **Au Pair Scheme**: Andorra, Bosnia-Herzegovina, Croatia, Cyprus, Czech Republic, Faroe Islands, Greenland, Hungary, Macedonia, Malta, Monaco, San Marino, Slovak Republic, Slovenia, Switzerland and Turkey.

Sandwich students

Approval for course-compulsory sandwich placements at recognised UK colleges must be obtained by the college from the DfEE's **Overseas Labour Service** (*see below* **Dept for Education & Employment**).

Students

Visiting students from the US, Canada, Australia or Jamaica can get a blue BUNAC card enabling them to work in the UK for up to six months. BUNAC cards are not difficult to obtain, but they must be acquired in advance. Contact the Work in Britain Department of the **Council on International Educational Exchange** or call **BUNAC** (*see below*). BUNAC students should obtain an application form OSS1 (BUNAC) from BUNAC. This should be submitted to the nearest Jobcentre to obtain permission to work.

Working holidaymakers

Citizens of Commonwealth countries aged 17-27 may apply to come to the UK as a working holidaymaker. This allows them to take part-time work without a DfEE permit. They must contact their nearest British Diplomatic Post in advance.

Useful addresses

BUNAC

16 Bowling Green Lane, Clerkenwell, EC1 (7251 3472/www.bunac.org.uk). Farringdon tube/rail. **Open** 9.30am-5.30pm Mon, Tue Thur; 9.30am-7pm Wed; 9.30am-5pm Fri; closed Sat, Sun. **Map** p402 N4.

Central Bureau for Educational Visits & Exchanges

British Council, 10 Spring Gardens, St James's, SW1 (7930 8466/www. britishcouncil.org). Charing Cross tube/rail. **Open** 9am-5.30pm Mon-Fri; closed Sat, Sun. **Map** p401 K8.
This office deals with the organisation of visits outside the UK, but otherwise you can obtain copies of its useful publications.

Council on International Educational Exchange

Work in Britain Department, 633 3rd Avenue, New York, NY 10017, USA (00 1 212 822 2600). **Open** 9am-5pm Mon-Fri; closed Sat, Sun.

Department for Education & Employment

Overseas Labour Service, Level 5, Moorfoot, Sheffield S1 4PQ (0114 259 4074/www.dfee.gov.uk/ols). **Open** *Phone enquiries* 9am-5pm Mon-Fri; closed Sat, Sun.
Enquiry line. Employers seeking work permit application forms should phone 0990 210224 or visit the website.

Home Office

Immigration & Nationality Directorate, Block C, Whitgift Centre, Wellesley Road, Croydon CR0 1AT (0870 606 7766/www.homeoffice. gov.uk/ind/hpg.htm). **Open** *Phone enquiries* 8.45am-4.45pm Mon-Thur; 8.45am-4.30pm Fri; closed Sat, Sun.
Advice on whether or not a work permit is required.

Overseas Visitors Records Office

180 Borough High Street, Borough, SE1 (7230 1208). Borough tube/Elephant & Castle or London Bridge tube/rail. **Open** 9am-4.30pm Mon-Fri; closed Sat, Sun. **Map** p404 P9.
Formerly the Aliens Registration Office run by the Metropolitan Police, the Overseas Visitors Records Office charges £34 to register a person if they have a work permit.

Directory

Further Reference

Books

Fiction

Peter Ackroyd
Hawksmoor; The House of Doctor Dee; Dan Leno & the Limehouse Golem; Great Fire of London
Intricate studies of arcane London.
Martin Amis *London Fields*
Darts and drinking way out east.
Jonathan Coe
The Dwarves of Death
Mystery, music, mirth, malevolence.
Norman Collins
London Belongs to Me
A witty saga of goings-on in Kennington in the 1930s.
Wilkie Collins
The Woman in White
A midnight encounter has dire consequences.
Joseph Conrad *The Secret Agent*
Anarchism in seedy Soho.
Charles Dickens
Oliver Twist; David Copperfield; Bleak House; Our Mutual Friend
Four of the master's most London-centric novels.
Sir Arthur Conan Doyle
The Complete Sherlock Holmes
Reassuring sleuthing shenanigans.
Christopher Fowler *Soho Black*
Walking dead in Soho.
Graham Greene
The End of the Affair
Adultery, Catholicism and Clapham Common.
Patrick Hamilton *20,000 Streets Under the Sky; Hangover Square*
A yearning romantic trilogy set among Soho sleaze; love and death in darkest Earl's Court.
Alan Hollinghurst
The Swimming Pool Library
An evocation of gay life around Russell Square.
Stewart Home
Come Before Christ and Murder Love
Paranoia, food sex and tour-guide psycho-rap.
Maria Lexton (vol 1)/ Nicholas Royle (vol 2) (eds)
Time Out Book of London Short Stories Volumes 1 & 2
London-based writers pay homage to their city.
Colin MacInnes
City of Spades; Absolute Beginners
Coffee and jazz, Soho and Notting Hill.
Derek Marlowe *A Dandy in Aspic*
A capital-set Cold War classic.
Michael Moorcock
Mother London
A love-letter to London.
Iris Murdoch *Under the Net*
The adventures of a talented but wastrel writer.

Courttia Newland *The Scholar*
Life is full of choices for a kid on a West London estate.
Kim Newman *The Quorum*
Intrigue surrounds a Docklands-based media magnate.
George Orwell
Keep the Aspidistra Flying
A saga of struggling writer and reluctant bookshop assistant.
Derek Raymond
I Was Dora Suarez
The blackest London noir.
Nicholas Royle *The Director's Cut*
London's seedy underbelly exposed.
Geoff Ryman *253*
The lives of tube travellers.
William Sansom
Selected Short Stories
Lyrical tales of Londoners at large.
Will Self *Grey Area*
Short stories.
Iain Sinclair
Downriver; Radon Daughters; White Chappell, Scarlet Tracings
The Thames's own *Heart of Darkness* by London's laureate; William Hope Hodgson via the London Hospital; Ripper murders and book dealers.
Muriel Spark
The Ballad of Peckham Rye
The devil incarnate spreads mayhem in Peckham.
Barbara Vine
King Solomon's Carpet
Going Underground.
Evelyn Waugh *Vile Bodies*
A satire on the too-shamemaking antics in 1920s Mayfair.
Angus Wilson
The Old Men at the Zoo
London faces down oblivion.
Virginia Woolf *Mrs Dalloway*
Joyce's *Ulysses* transplanted to London, this time with a female lead.

Non-fiction

Peter Ackroyd
London: The Biography
A fascinating, wilfully obscurantist history of the city.
Felix Barker & Ralph Hyde
London as it Might Have Been
Schemes that never made it past the drawing board.
Daniel Farson *Soho in the Fifties*
An affectionate portrait of the many pubs and characters of Soho.
Derek Hammond *London, England*
A witty, enthusiastic celebration of the capital.
Stephen Inwood
A History of London
A recent, readable history.
Jack London
The People of the Abyss
Extreme poverty in the East End.

Nick Merriman (ed)
The Peopling of London
A fascinating account of 2,000 years of settlement.
George Orwell
Down and Out in Paris and London
An autobiographical account of waitering and starving.
Samuel Pepys *Diaries*
Fires, plagues, bordellos and more.
Roy Porter *London: A Social History*
An ambitious, all-encompassing history of London.
Iain Sinclair
Lights Out for the Territory
The time-warp visionary walks across London.
Richard Trench
London Under London
An entertaining investigation of the subterranean city.
Ben Weinreb & Christopher Hibbert (eds)
The London Encyclopaedia
Fascinating, thorough, indispensable.

Films

Alfie *dir. Lewis Gilbert* (1966)
What's it all about, Michael?
Beautiful Thing
dir. Hettie MacDonald (1996)
A tender, amusing coming-of-age flick set in south-east London.
A Clockwork Orange
dir. Stanley Kubrick (1971)
Over-stylised and over-hyped, but Kubrick's vision still shocks.
Blow-Up
dir. Michelangelo Antonioni (1966)
Swingin' London captured in unintentionally hysterical fashion.
Croupier *dir. Mike Hodges* (1997)
Gambling and drinking dominate Hodges's terrific flick.
Death Line *dir. Gary Sherman* (1972)
Cannibalism on the tube. Yikes.
Jubilee *dir. Derek Jarman* (1978)
A horribly dated but still interesting romp through the punk era.
The Krays *dir. Peter Medak* (1990)
The Kemp brothers excel as the notorious East End gangsters.
Life is Sweet; Naked; Secrets & Lies; Career Girls
dir. Mike Leigh (1990; 1993; 1996; 1997)
A mocking but affectionate look at Metroland; a bleak but compelling character study; familial tensions in 1990s Britain; the past and present lives of old friends.
Lock, Stock & Two Smoking Barrels; Snatch
dir. Guy Ritchie (1998; 2000)
Mr Madonna's pair of East End faux-gangster flicks.
London *dir. Patrick Keiller* (1994)
Halfway between fiction and documentary; excellent, too.

The Long Good Friday
dir. John MacKenzie (1989)
Bob Hoskins stars in the classic
London gangster flick.
Mona Lisa; The Crying Game
dir. Neil Jordan (1986; 1992)
Prostitution, terrorism and – the
twist – transvestism come under
Jordan's camera.
Mrs Dalloway
dir. Marleen Goris (1997)
Vanessa Redgrave stars in this
adaptation of the Woolf novel.
Nil by Mouth
dir. Gary Oldman (1997)
A violent, uncompromising but truly
compelling tale of working-class life.
Notting Hill
dir. Roger Michell (1999)
Hugh Grant and Julia Roberts get it
on in west London.
Peeping Tom
dir. Michael Powell (1960)
Powell's creepy murder flick still
shocks 40 years after release.
Performance *dir. Nicolas
Roeg, Donald Cammell* (1970)
The cult movie to end all cult movies
made west London cool for life.
Wonderland
dir. Michael Winterbottom (1999)
A gritty, verité London classic of
love, loss and deprivation.

Music

Albums

Alabama 3
Exile on Coldharbour Lane (1997)
Brixtonian reprobates fuse gospel
and rap in entertaining fashion.
Animals That Swim *I Was The
King, I Really Was The King* (1996)
An overlooked slice of London genius
from Stoke Newington's finest.
Blur *Modern Life is Rubbish*
(1993); *Park Life* (1994)
A pair of modern classics from the
Essex exiles.
The Clash *London Calling* (1979)
Epoch-making, if often amusingly
naïve, punk classic.
MJ Cole *Sincere* (2000)
The best UK garage long-player yet.
As they say, it's a London thing.
Ian Dury & The Blockheads
New Boots & Panties (1977)
The late, lamented Dury's
seminal masterpiece.
Handel *Water Music; Music For the
Royal Fireworks* (1717; 1749)
Relive the glory days of the 18th
century. Or something like that.
The Jam
This is the Modern World (1977)
Paul Weller at his splenetic,
energetic, pre-Dadrock finest.
Madness *Rise & Fall* (1982)
The nutty boys wax lyrical about
their beloved home, although any one
of their several best-ofs makes for a
more consistently entertaining listen.

Morrissey *Vauxhall & I* (1994)
The former Smiths frontman's
finest solo album sees him leave
Manchester behind once and for all.
Anthony Newley
The Very Best of... (1997)
Swingin' retrospective of everyone's
favourite Cockney scallywag.
The Rolling Stones *December's
Children (and Everybody's)* (1965)
An early Stones record that exudes a
moody cool. Not so much about
London as evocative of the city.
The Sex Pistols
Never Mind The Bollocks (1977)
The best punk album, and a
definitively London record.
Simon Warner
Waiting Rooms (1997)
Rarely has contemporary decadence
been captured so entertainingly.

Songs

assorted *A Foggy Day (in London
Town); A Nightingale Sang in
Berkeley Square; I Live in Trafalgar
Square; Let's All Go Down the Strand;
London Bridge is Falling Down;
Maybe It's Because I'm a Londoner*
Big Audio Dynamite
London Bridge
David Bowie *London Boys*
Lloyd Cole *Charlotte Street*
Elvis Costello & The Attractions
(I Don't Want to Go to) Chelsea
Ray Davies *London Song*
Donovan *Sunny Goodge Street*
Nick Drake *Mayfair*
Fairport Convention
Breakfast in Mayfair
Tim Finn *Suicide on Downing Street*
The Goons *Dalston*
Eddy Grant *Electric Avenue*
Bert Jansch *Soho*
Billy Jenkins *Exodus from Bromley*
Jethro Tull
Jeffrey Goes to Leicester Square
The Kinks *Denmark Street;
Muswell Hillbillies; Waterloo Sunset*
Alexis Korner *East Street*
Phil Lynott *Solo in Soho*
Ralph McTell *Streets of London*
The Members *Blackfriars Bridge;
Chelsea Nightclub*
Pet Shop Boys
King's Cross; West End Girls
The Pogues *A Rainy Night in Soho;
Misty Morning, Albert Bridge*
The Pretty Things
13 Chester Street
Eddi Reader *Kiteflyer's Hill*
Diana Ross *Big Ben*
Roxy Music *Do the Strand*
St Etienne *London Belongs to Me*
Sham 69 *Hersham Boys*
Simple Minds *Chelsea Girl*
Al Stewart *Soho (Needless to Say)*
Sugar Minott *Riot Inna Brixton*
Richard Thompson
Chelsea Embankment
XTC *Towers of London*
Warren Zevon
Werewolves of London

Websites

BBC London Live
www.bbc.co.uk/londonlive
The successor to the much-loved
GLR offers online news, travel,
weather, entertainment and sport,
as well as details of London's radio
and TV schedules.
Bog Standard
*http://zeus.slais.ucl.ac.uk/
toilets/index.htm*
How useful: a searchable database of
public toilets in central London. It
could, though, do with updating.
Book2Eat *www.book2eat.com*
Make your reservations for London's
restaurants through this website.
Greater London Authority
www.london.gov.uk
See what Ken and co are up to at the
London Assembly.
The Guide *www.theguide.net*
The Guide claims to take locals and
visitors beyond the West End to
explore the city's fringe arts and
entertainment scene.
intoitnow.com *www.intoitnow.com*.
A Londoners' guide to life after work,
with details of evening classes, clubs
and special events.
London Active Map
*www.uktravel.com/london/
londonmap.html*.
Click on a tube station and find out
which attractions are nearby.
London Life *www.londonlife.com*
An entertainment and lifestyle site.
LondonTown *www.londontown.com*
The official tourist board website is
stuffed full of information and offers.
London Underground Online
www.thetube.com
A website devoted to the capital's
beleaguered underground network.
Pubs.com *www.pubs.com*
London's traditional boozers.
The River Thames Guide
www.riverthames.co.uk
The river has recently regained its
position at the centre of the capital's
consciousness. This website provides
useful information on the places and
events along its banks.
This is London
www.thisislondon.co.uk
The online version of the London
Evening Standard.
Time Out *www.timeout.com*
The *Time Out* site is an essential
source of information, with an online
guide, updated London-based
features, and access to a massive
database of shops and services.
Transport for London
www.londontransport.co.uk
The official website for buses, DLR,
river services and other forms of
transport in the capital, with real-
time travel information and journey
planning resources. For information
on the underground, *see above*
London Underground Online.

Directory

Index

Figures in **bold** indicate sections
containing key information. *Italics*
indicate illustrations.

Advertisers' Index

Please refer to the relevant sections
for addresses and telephone numbers.

Places of interest or entertainment	
Railway stations	
Underground stations	
Parks	
Hospitals	
Casualty units	
Churches	
Districts	MAYFAIR

0   500 m

© Copyright Time Out Group 2001   1/4 mile

Maps

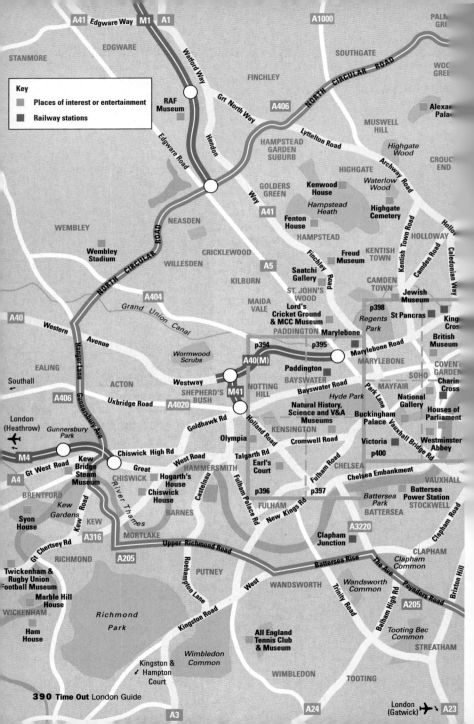

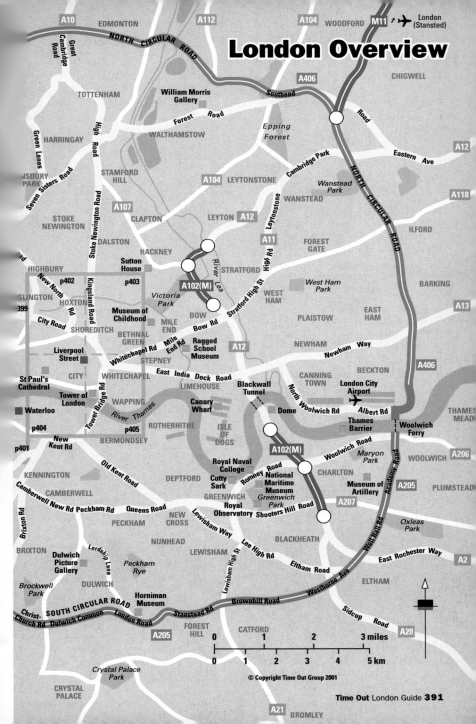

London Overview

© Copyright Time Out Group 2001

Central London by Area

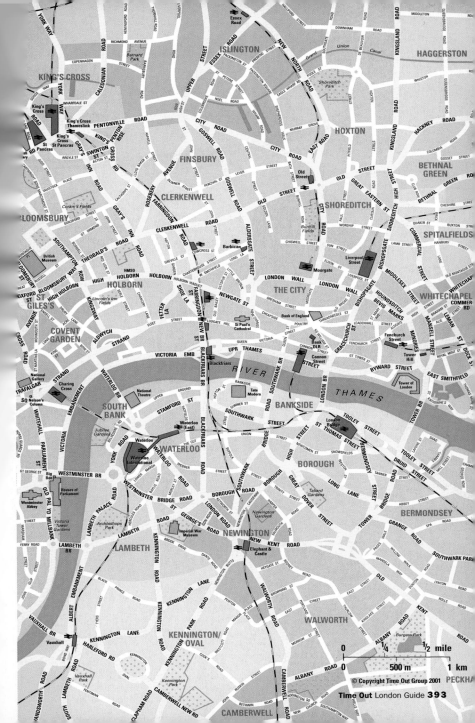

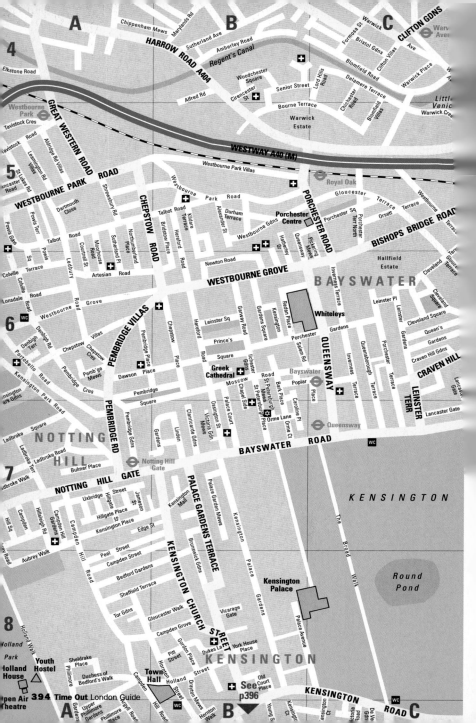

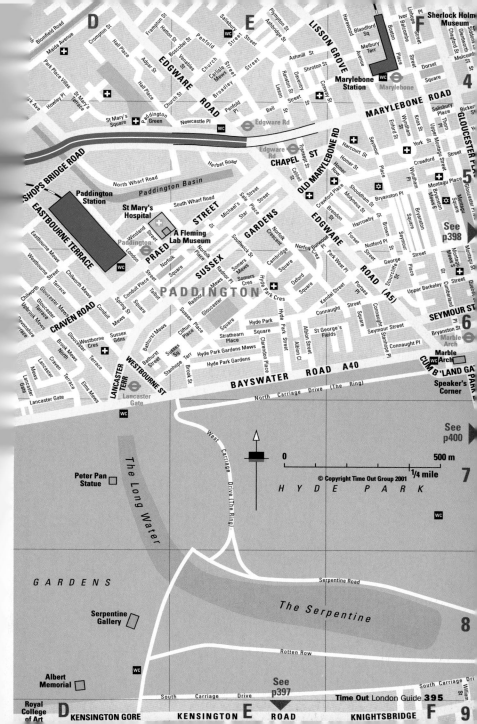

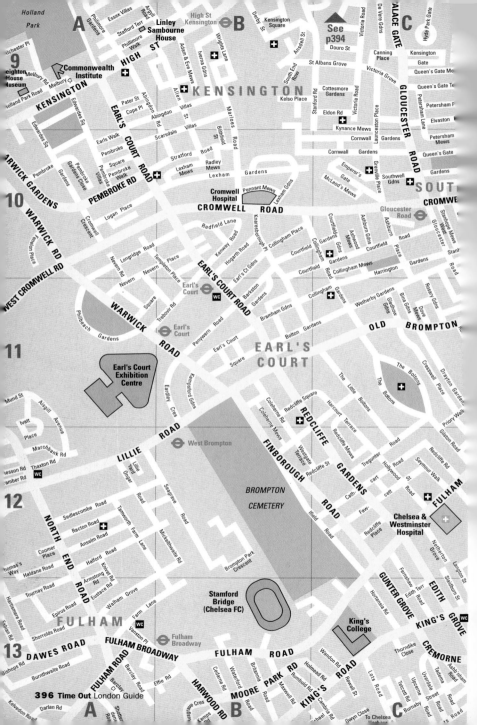

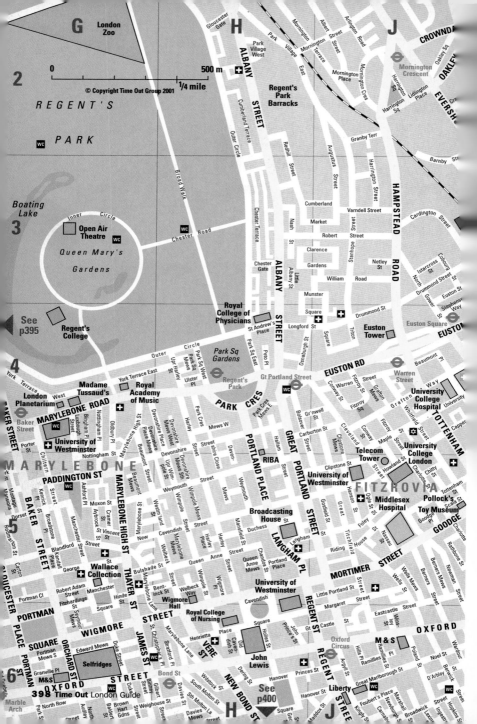

London
Zoo

2

0   500 m

© Copyright Time Out Group 2001   ¼ mile

CROWNDA

H   **J**

OAKLF

Mornington
Crescent

EVERSH

Park
Village
West

ALBANY

Gloucester
Gate

Park Village East

Albert Street

Arlington Road

Mornington Terrace

Mornington Street

Mornington Place

Mornington Cres

Harrington Sq

Lidlington
Place

Granby Terr

Cardington Street

Barnby

REGENT'S

STREET

Regent's
Park
Barracks

Cumberland Terrace

Outer Circle

Redhill Street

Augustus Street

Harrington Street

HAMPSTEAD

ROAD

Colnbrook St

Istarcross St

Drummond Street

North Gower St

Euston St

Stephenson
Way

Euston

wc

PARK

Boating
Lake

3

Chester Terrace

Nash Street

Cumberland
Market

Varndell Street

Robert   Street

Clarence
Gardens

Stanhope Street

Netley
Street

Inner   Circle

Open Air
Theatre

Queen Mary's

Gardens

wc

Broad   Walk

Chester   Road

Chester Gate

ALBANY

STREET

Little Albany St

Munster

Square

William   Road

Longford St

Euston Square

Euston
Tower

EUSTON

See
p395

Regent's
College

Royal
College of
Physicians

St Andrew's
Place

Drummond St

Triton Square

Warren
Street

Beaumont Pl

EUSTON RD

University
College
Hospital

University

4

York   Terrace

Outer   Circle

York Terrace East

Upr Harley St

Ulster
Pl

Park Sq West

Park Square East

Peto Pl

Park Sq
Gardens

Regent's
Park

Gt Portland Street

wc

Bolsover St

Conway St

Warren St

Fitzroy St

Grafton
Mews

Warren
Mews

Conway St

Grafton
Way

Whitfield   St

Gower St

University
College
London

PORTLAND

TOTTENHAM

Madame
Tussaud's

Royal
Academy
of Music

PARK   CRES

Park Cres Mews W

MARYLEBONE   ROAD

London
Planetarium

Baker
Street

Nottingham Place

Nottingham St

York Terrace East

Devonshire
Mews West

Devonshire
Mews South

Devonshire
Place

Weymouth   Street

Harley   Street

Mansfield St

Carburton St

Clipstone St

Clipstone
Mews

Cleveland   Street

Maple   St

Howland   St

Telecom
Tower

Charlotte   St

University
College
London

University of
Westminster

Chitty St

Tottenham

FITZROVIA

Pollock's
Toy Museum

GOODGE

Porter St

MARYLEBONE

University of
Westminster

wc

PADDINGTON ST

BAKER

STREET

Chiltern   St

Montagu
Mansions

Dorset St

Kenrick Pl

Broadstone Pl

Blandford St

Kendall
Place

George Street

Manchester Street

Ashford St

Cramer St
St Vincent
St

Aybrook St

Moxon St

New

Marylebone
Lane

Cavendish
Mews

Harley

Wimpole

Mansfield Mews

Duchess   St

Langham

Foley

Riding   House   St

Ogle St

Berners St

Middlesex
Hospital

Wells Mews

Nassau   St

Newman

Rathbone Pl

MARYLEBONE HIGH ST

Beaumont
St

Devonshire Close

Hallam

Great

PORTLAND PLACE

GREAT   PORTLAND

Gosfield St

Great
Titchfield   St

Hanson   St

STREET

Foley

Cleveland   St

Eastcastle St

Rathbone
Mews

RIBA

Broadcasting
House

LANGHAM PL

Little Portland St

MORTIMER   STREET

5

Wallace
Collection

THAYER   ST

Bulstrode St

Bentinck St

Welbeck
Way

Wigmore
Hall

Marylebone Lane

Queen Anne
Mews

Chandos St

Portland Mews

Queen Anne St

JAMES ST

VERE

Henrietta   Place

Old
Cavendish St

John
Prince's St

Great Castle St

Margaret
Street

John Adam
St

REGENT ST

Little Portland St

Ramillies St

Poland   St

Noel St

D'Arblay

Beak

Wardour

Broadwick

Kingly St

Foubert's Place

Marshall

St

Hopkins St

Bridle

Newburgh St

GOODGE

Royal College
of Nursing

University of
Westminster

Henrietta   Place

Wigmore   Street

Cavendish

Square

Holles St

REGENT ST

OXFORD

Oxford
Circus

M & S

Liberty

wc

Great Marlborough St

WIGMORE   STREET

Selfridges

Edward Mews

Duke Mews

Granville Pl

Portman
Mews S

wc

OXFORD

STREET

Stratford Place

John
Lewis

Hanover

NEW   BOND   ST

Princes St

Hanover Sq

See
p400

Gilbert St

Binney St

Weighouse St

South Molton La

Davies Mews

Duke St

PORTMAN

PLACE

PORTMAN

SQUARE

Portman Cl

Robert Adam
Street

Fitzhardinge St

Seymour   St

Manchester
Square

Hinde   St

George Street

Nth Audley

Brown
Hart Gdns

Mount
Row

WIGMORE

Blandford St

Dorset St

GLOUCESTER

Baker

Montagu
Mansions

Carton St

York   Terrace

Chiltern St

398 Time Out London Guide

Marble
Arch

M & S

Park St

North Row

Carlos
Place

Mount
Row

Davies
Mews

Stratton
Street

Grosvenor St

Maddox   St

Conduit St

H   **J**   **STREET**

6

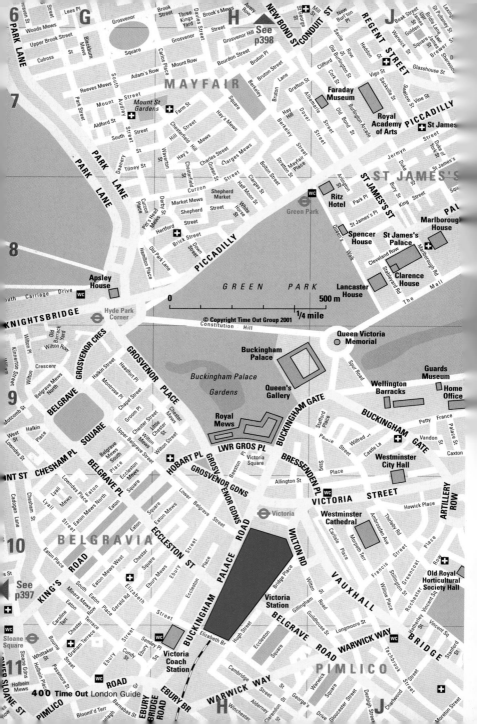

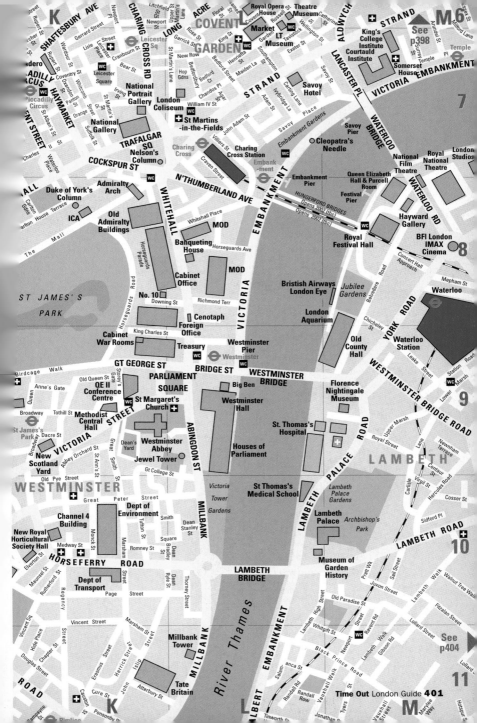

N

Lofting Road
Barnsbury Street
Ripplevale Grove
Richmond Cres
Richmond
Avenue
Thornhill Road
Lonsdale
Square
Cloudesley
Square
Cloudesley St
Barnsbury Road
Copenhagen St
Dewey Rd
Ritchie St
Tolpuddle Street
Chapel Market
Penton Street
Donegal St
Baron St
White Lion Street
Cloudesley Rd

Town Hall
O
Braes St
Canonbury Villas
Essex Road rail station
P
Eccleshourne Rd
Rotherfield

Seabon St
Waterloo Terr
Florence St
Hawes St
Halton Road
UPPER STREET
Milner
Square
Milner Place
Gibson
Liverpool Road
Pentrid St
Almeida St
Cross Street
Dagmar Terr
Theberton Street
Gaskin St

Greenman Road
Popham Road
Popham Rd
Basire Street
Greenman St
Dibden St
ESSEX ROAD
Britannia Row
Packington Street
Prebend St
St Paul Fields
Coleman Street
Linton Street
Arlington Aven
NEW NORTH RO

Business Design Centre
Barford St
ISLINGTON GREEN
Charlton Place
I S L I N G T O N
Camden Passage

Cruden St
Raleigh Rd
St Peters Street
Chantry St
Rheidol Terrace
Packington Square

UPPER STREET
Islington High St
Duncan Street
Colebrooke Row
Gerrard Road
Noel Road
Devonia Road
Grantbridge St
Danbury St
Burgh St
Frome St
Baldwin Terr
Regent's Canal
Eagle Wharf R
Napier R

Pentonville Road
Angel
ANGEL

0   500 m
© Copyright Time Out Group 2001
1/4 mile

See p399
Great Percy Street
Claremont Square
Claremont Cl
Myddelton Square
Chadwell Street
Way
Friend St
GOSWELL STREET
Watkey St
CITY ROAD
Vincent Terrace
Ella Street
Graham Street
Nelson Terr
City Garden Row
Coombs St
City Road Basin
Wharf Road
Wenlock Road
Sturt St
Micawber St
Wenlock Stre
Shaftesbu
Taplow Street
Shepherdess Walk
Bletchley
Windsor Terr
Under-

Lloyd Sq
Lloyd Baker Street
Margery St
Yardley St
Inglebert St
Amwell Street
River St
Merlin St
Wilmington Square
ROSEBERY AVENUE
Hardwick St
Myddelton St
Gloucester Way
Arlington Way
ST JOHN STREET
Friend St
Rawstone Street
Spencer Street
Northampton Square
Ashby St
Sebastian St
Wyclif St
Whiskin St
King Sq
Central Street
Macclesfield St
Dingley Road
LEVER STREET
Mora St
Galway St
Radnor St
BATH STREET
BUNHILL

Mount Pleasant Sorting Office
ROSEBERY AVENUE
FARRINGDON
Exmouth Market
Northampton Road
Bowling Green La
Pear Tree Court
Crawford Passage
Warner Street
Back Hill
Herbal Hill
CLERKENWELL RD
Corporation Row
Woodbridge Street
House of Detention
Sans Walk
Clerkenwell Close
Aylesbury Rd
St John's Lane
SKINNER ST
PERCIVAL ST
Agdon St
Cyrus St
Compton Street
Dallington St
Northburgh Street
Great Sutton St
GOSWELL ROAD
Seward Street
Pear Tree St
Bastwick Street
Gee Street
OLD STREET
Mitchell St
Helmet Row
Garrett St
Banner Street
Bartholomew Sq
Ironmonger Row
Whitecross
Golden Lane
Chequer St
Dufferin St
Fortune St
Errol Street
WC
Lamb's Passage

C L E R K E N W E L L
Clerkenwell Grn
CLERKENWELL ROAD
Museum of the Order of St John
ST JOHN STREET
Britton Street
Turnmill Street
St John's Lane
Eagle Ct
WC
Charterhouse Square
Charterhouse
St Barts Medical College
Barbican
BEECH STREET
Arts Centre
CHISWELL
Silk Street
Guildhall School of Music & Drama

Portpool Lane
Leather Lane
HATTON GARDEN
Hatton Wall
Cross Street
Saffron Hill
Kirby St
Bleeding Heart Yd
Greville Street
Baldwin's Gdns
Brooke St
FARRINGDON ROAD
CLERKENWELL RD
Farringdon
Cowcross Street
CHARTERHOUSE STREET
LONG LANE
WC
See p404
Barbican Centre
St Giles
Museum of London
Fore Street
P
St Alphage Gard

Chancery Lane
HOLBORN
N
402 Time Out London Guide
O
WEST SMITHFIELD
Smithfield Market
Cloth Fair
Little Britain
St Bartholomew the Great
Hosier Lane
Moor

N
1
2
3
4
5

DALSTON

Moreton Rd
Almorah Rd
Cleveland Street
Northchurch Road
Lawford Road
De Beauvoir
Square
Mortimer Rd
Mapledene Rd
Lavender Gr
Holly St

1

Southgate Gr
Southgate
Road
Downham
Road
Road
Hertford
De Beauvoir Crescent
KINGSLAND ROAD
Haggerston Road
Albion
Square
Albion
Livermore Rd
Scriven St
Queensbridge Drive
Shrubland Road
Brownlow Rd

Sherbourne St
Wilton
Square
Baring Street
Balmes Road
Lee Street
Acton Mews
Swan St
Clarissa St
Dunston Rd
Dunston Rd
Pownall Row

Penn St
Poole St
Bridport Place
Hyde Rd
Whitmore Road
Orsman Road
Halcomb
Mill Row
Phillipp Street
Regent's Canal
Whiston Road
Laburnum Road
Whiston Road

Shoreditch Park

Wimbourne St
Cropley Street
Mintern Street
Hemsworth Street
Nuttall St
Hows Street
Thurtle Rd
Kent St
HAGGERSTON
Haggerston Park

2

Wenlock Street
Murray Grove
Buckland St
Purcell St
Cherbury St
Crondall Street
Regan Way
Stanway Street
Geffrye Museum
Shenfield St
Geffrye Street
Pearson Street
Ormsby Street
Appleby Street
Dunloe
Weymouth Ter
Queensbridge Road
Street
Ropley St

New North Road
Provost Street
Nile Street
Falkirk Street
Cremer Street
Nazral St
Long St
Union Wk
HACKNEY
ROAD
Ravenscroft Street
Horchio St
Shipton Street
Columbia Road
Quilter St

HOXTON

Bevenden St
Haberdasher St
Vestry St
Fanshaw
EAST ROAD
KINGSLAND ROAD
Waterson St
Union St
Wellington Row
GOSSET ST

3

Moorfields Eye Hospital
Peerless Street
Chart St
Buttesland St
Chart St
Corsham St
Beeches St
Charles Square
Pitfield Street
Boot St
Hoxton
Square
Hoxton Street
Drysdale St
COLUMBIA ROAD
Austin St
Virginia Rd
Chambord St
Turin Street
Satchwell St
Granby St
St Matthew's Row

Old Street
Cranwood St
Brunswick Place
Mallow St
Cowper St
Leonard Street
Willow Street
OLD STREET
Rivington Street
Charlotte Road
Bateman's Row
Calvert Ave
Arnold
Circus
Club Row
Padbury Ct
Chilton St
Bacon Street
4

Featherstone St
ROW
CITY ROAD
John Wesley's House
Bunhill Fields Burial Grounds
Tabernacle Street
Paul Street
Luke Street
Epworth St
Scrutton St
Phipp St
GREAT EASTERN STREET
CURTAIN RD
New Inn Yard
Holywell Lane
Old Nichol Street
Redchurch Street
SHOREDITCH
Boundary Street
GREEN ROAD
BETHNAL
SLATER ST
CHESHIRE ST
Shoreditch
Pedley St

Bunhill Fields
Bonhill St
Worship Street
Finsbury
Worship Street
Holywell Row
Curtain Road
Hearn St
Plough Yard
SHOREDITCH HIGH STREET
Fleur de Lis St
Wheeler St
Quaker Street
Calvin St
Grey Eagle St
BRICK LANE
Code St
Buxton Street
Hunton St
Spital St
Woodseer St
Deal St
5

Ropemaker Street
MOORGATE
Finsbury Pavement
South Place
Eldon St
Christopher St
Dysart St
Sun Street
Earl Street
Clifton St
Pindar St
Snowden St
Appold Street
Sun Street
Primrose St
Spital Sq
Folgate Street
Elder St
Blossom St
Lamb St
COMMERCIAL ST
Hanbury Street
Princelet Street
Wilkes St
Fournier St
Princelet Street
Heneage St

Broadgate Centre
Liverpool Street Station
See p405
Spitalfields Market
Christ Church
Brushfield Street
Artillery Lane
Steward Street

Street Index

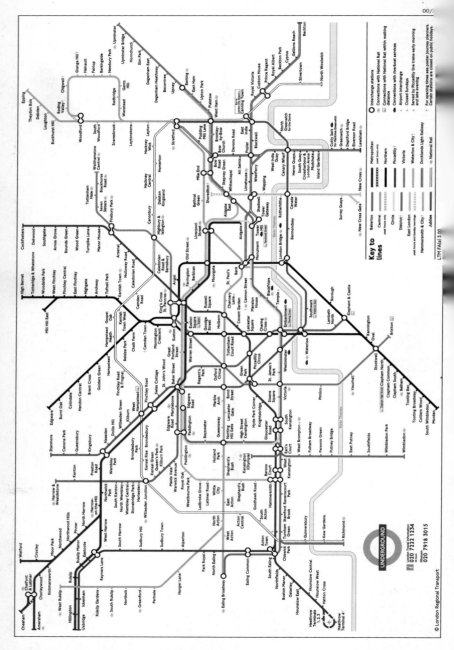

Visit Time Out's website at **www.timeout.com**
or email your comments to **guides@timeout.com**
(NINTH EDITION)

TimeOut London Please let us know what you think

About this guide...

1. How useful did you find the following sections?

	Very	Fairly	Not very
In Context	☐	☐	☐
Accommodation	☐	☐	☐
Sightseeing	☐	☐	☐
Eat, Drink, Shop	☐	☐	☐
Arts & Entertainment	☐	☐	☐
Trips Out of Town	☐	☐	☐
Directory	☐	☐	☐
Maps	☐	☐	☐

2. Did you travel to London...?

Alone ☐	With children ☐
As part of a group ☐	On vacation ☐
On business ☐	To study ☐
With a partner ☐	I live here ☐

3. How long was your trip to London? (write in)

_____ days

4. Where did you book your trip?

Time Out Classifieds ☐
On the Internet ☐
With a travel agent ☐
Other (write in) ☐

_____
_____
_____

5. Where did you first hear about this guide?

Advertising in *Time Out* magazine ☐
On the Internet ☐
From a travel agent ☐
Other (write in) ☐

6. Is there anything you'd like us to cover in greater depth?

_____
_____
_____
_____

7. Are there any places that should/ should not* be included in the guide? (*delete as necessary)

_____
_____
_____
_____
_____
_____

8. How many other people have used this guide?

none ☐   1 ☐   2 ☐   3 ☐   4 ☐   5+ ☐

9. What city or country would you like to visit next? (write in)

_____
_____

About other Time Out publications...

10. Have you ever bought/used any other *Time Out* magazine?

Yes ☐   No ☐

11. Have you ever bought/used any other Time Out City Guides?

Yes ☐   No ☐

If yes, which ones?
_____

12. Have you ever bought/used other Time Out publications?

Yes ☐   No ☐

If yes, which ones?
_____

About you...

13. Title (Mr, Ms etc): _____

First name: _____

Surname: _____

Address: _____
_____
_____

Postcode: _____

Email: _____

Nationality: _____

14. Date of birth: ☐☐/☐☐/☐☐

15. Sex: male ☐   female ☐

16. Are you...?

Single ☐☐
Married/Living with partner ☐

17. What is your occupation? ☐☐

_____

18. At the moment do you earn...?

under £15,000	☐
over £15,000 and up to £19,999	☐
over £20,000 and up to £24,999	☐
over £25,000 and up to £39,999	☐
over £40,000 and up to £49,999	☐
over £50,000	☐

☐ Please tick here if you do not want to hear about offers and discounts from Time Out and relevant companies.

Time Out Guides

FREEPOST 20 (WC3187)
LONDON
W1E 0DQ